Lecture Notes in Computer Science   10676

Commenced Publication in 1973
Founding and Former Series Editors:
Gerhard Goos, Juris Hartmanis, and Jan van Leeuwen

More information about this series at http://www.springer.com/series/7409

Tien-Chi Huang · Rynson Lau
Yueh-Min Huang · Marc Spaniol
Chun-Hung Yuen (Eds.)

Emerging Technologies for Education

Second International Symposium, SETE 2017
Held in Conjunction with ICWL 2017
Cape Town, South Africa, September 20–22, 2017
Revised Selected Papers

 Springer

Editors
Tien-Chi Huang
National Taichung University of Science
  and Technology
Taichung City
Taiwan

Rynson Lau
City University of Hong Kong
Kowloon
Hong Kong

Yueh-Min Huang
Department of Engineering Science
National Cheng Kung University
Tainan
Taiwan

Marc Spaniol
University of Caen Normandie
Caen
France

Chun-Hung Yuen
City University of Hong Kong
Kowloon
Hong Kong

ISSN 0302-9743   ISSN 1611-3349   (electronic)
Lecture Notes in Computer Science
ISBN 978-3-319-71083-9   ISBN 978-3-319-71084-6   (eBook)
https://doi.org/10.1007/978-3-319-71084-6

Library of Congress Control Number: 2017959625

LNCS Sublibrary: SL3 – Information Systems and Applications, incl. Internet/Web, and HCI

Printed on acid-free paper

This Springer imprint is published by Springer Nature
The registered company is Springer International Publishing AG
The registered company address is: Gewerbestrasse 11, 6330 Cham, Switzerland

Preface

SETE 2017, the Second Annual International Symposium on Emerging Technologies for Education, was held in conjunction with ICWL 2017 organized by the Hong Kong Web Society. SETE was open to the public for organizing a workshop or track to achieve diversity in the symposium. Fueled by ICT technologies, the e-learning environment in the education sector has become more innovative than ever before. Diversified emerging technologies containing various software and hardware components provide the underlying infrastructure needed to create enormous potential educational applications incorporated by proper learning strategies. Moreover, these prevalent technologies might also lead to changes in the educational environment and thus in learning performance. Moreover, new paradigms are also emerging with the purpose of bringing these innovations to a certain level where they are widely accepted and sustainable. Therefore, this symposium aims at serving as a meeting point for researchers, educationalists and practitioners to discuss state-of-the-art and in-progress research, exchange ideas, and share experiences about emerging technologies for education. This symposium provides opportunities for the cross-fertilization of knowledge and ideas from researchers in diverse fields that make up this interdisciplinary research area. We hope that the implications of the findings of each work presented at this symposium can be used to improve the development of educational environments.

This year's conference was located in the Cape Town, the second-most populous urban area in South Africa and one of the most multicultural cities in the world.

This year we received 123 submissions from 13 countries worldwide. After a rigorous double-blind review process, 65 papers were selected as full papers, yielding an acceptance rate of 58%. These contributions cover the latest findings in areas such as: emerging technologies of design, model and framework of learning systems, emerging technologies support for intelligent tutoring, emerging technologies support for game-based and joyful learning, emerging technologies enhanced language learning, emerging technologies supported collaborative learning, and emerging technologies in pedagogical issues.

Moreover, SETE 2017 featured keynote presentations and four workshops, covering active ageing and digital inclusion, smart learning by emerging educational paradigm, social and personal computing for Web-supported learning communities, application and design of innovative learning software.

We would like to thank the Organizing Committee and especially the organization co-chairs, Yueh-Min Huang and Rynson Lau, for their efforts and time spent to ensure the success of the conference. We would also like to express our gratitude to the Program Committee members for their timely and helpful reviews. And last but not least, we would like to thank all the authors for their contribution in maintaining a high-quality conference – we count on your continued support in playing a significant role in the Web-based learning community in the future.

September 2017

Yueh-Min Huang
Rynson Lau
Tien-Chi Huang
Chun-Hung Yuen
Marc Spaniol

Organization

Conference Co-chairs

Yueh-Min Huang   National Cheng-Kung University, Taiwan
Rynson Lau   City University of Hong Kong, Hong Kong, SAR China

Program Co-chairs

Tien-Chi Huang   National Taichung University of Science and Technology, Taiwan
Chun-Hung Yuen   City University of Hong Kong, Hong Kong, SAR China
Marc Spaniol   Université de Caen Normandie, France

Program Committee

Andreja Istenic Starcic   University of Ljubljana, Slovenia
Chengjiu Yin   Kobe University, Japan
Chi-Cheng Chang   National Taiwan Normal University, Taiwan
Chia-Chen Chen   National Chung Hsing University, Taiwan
Di Zou   The Hong Kong Polytechnic University, Hong Kong, SAR China
Dimitra Anastasiou   Luxembourg Institute of Science and Technology, Luxembourg
Gabriella Dodero   Free University of Bozen-Bolzano, Italy
Hsiu-Mc Huang   National Taichung University of Science and Technology, Taiwan
Jong Hyuk Park   Seoul National University of Science and Technology, Korea
Kinshuk   University of North Texas, USA
Matej Zajc   University of Ljubljana, Slovenia
Miltiadis D. Lytras   American College of Greece, Greece
Ming-Chi Liu   National Cheng Kung University, Taiwan
Mu-Yen Chen   National Taichung University of Science and Technology, Taiwan
Neil Yen   University of Aizu, Japan
Pedro Peris-Lopez   University Carlos III of Madrid, Spain
Pei-Ling Chien   Osaka University, Japan
Tak-Lam Wong   The Hong Kong Institute of Education, Hong Kong, SAR China
Ting-Ting Wu   National Yunlin University of Science and Technology, Taiwan
Vera Yu Shu   National Changhua University of Education, Taiwan

Wadee Alhalabi   King Abdulaziz University, Saudi Arabia
Yao-Ting Sung   National Taiwan Normal University, Taiwan
Yong-Ming Huang   Chia Nan University of Pharmacy and Science, Taiwan
Yu-Lin Jeng   Southern Taiwan University of Science and Technology,
                          Taiwan
Zhenguo Yang   City University of Hong Kong, Hong Kong, SAR China

Main Organizer

Co-organizers

Contents

Emerging Technologies of Design, Model and Framework of Learning Systems

Effect of Using Digital Pen Teaching System Behaviors on Learning Achievements in a Mathematics Course 3
  Yu-Sheng Su, Ting-Jou Ding, Po-Han Wu, and Chiu-Nan Su

Satisfaction Analysis for Agricultural Worker Digital Course Learning Platform 9
  Jui-Hung Chang, Ren-Hung Hwang, and Hung-Hsi Chiang

Emerging Technologies Supported in ICT Education 19
  Leila Goosen and Toppie N. Mukasa-Lwanga

System of Information Systems as Support for Learning Ecosystem 29
  Saleh Majd and Abel Marie-Hélène

A User Study About the Usage of a Learning Management System in a South African University 38
  Liezel Cilliers, Siyanda Ntlabathi, and Palesa Makhetha

Emerging Technologies Support for Intelligent Tutoring

Efficacies of 3D Immersive Virtual World Classrooms 45
  Judy F. Chen, Clyde A. Warden, and Hsiu Ju Lin

Using the Gartner Hype Cycle to Evaluate the Adoption of Emerging Technology Trends in Higher Education – 2013 to 2016 49
  Tania Prinsloo and J.P. Van Deventer

An Analysis of 3D-Printing Familiarity Among Students in a Technical University 58
  Kuen-Ming Shu, Chi-Cheng Chang, and Yih-Her Yan

Lecturers Perceptions on Blackboard: An Investigation of Blackboard Usage in a Nursing Department at a Traditional University 64
  Liezel Cilliers and Elzette van Niekerk

Emerging Technologies Support for Game-Based and Joyful Learning

The Use of a Learning Management System to Facilitate Student-Driven Content Design: An Experiment 75
  Riana Steyn, Solly Millard, and Joyce Jordaan

A Curriculum Approach to Improving Cyber Safety
in South African Schools   95
    E. Kritzinger

Towards Understanding How Game Based Learning Can Enhance
Flipped Learning.   106
    M.J. Hattingh and S. Eybers

Can Video (Created with PowerPoint and TTSAPP) Replace
"Normal" Lectures?.   116
    Robert Huberts

Effectiveness of Learning with the Support of a Virtual Environment
(Experiment in University Teaching)   125
    Hana Mohelska and Marcela Sokolova

Emerging Technologies of Pedagogical Issues

The Design of a STEM-Oriented Project-Based Course for the Higher
Grades of Elementary Schools   137
    Yi-wen Lin and Tzone-I Wang

Scorecard Approach for Cyber-Security Awareness   144
    Tsosane Shabe, Elmarie Kritzinger, and Marianne Loock

Using AHP to Project-Based Learning Develop in Machinery
Manufacturing of Technology Universities Students   154
    Dyi-Cheng Chen, Ci-Syong You, and Ying-Chia Huang

Introducing the Maker Movement to Information Systems Students   161
    Machdel Matthee, Marita Turpin, and Dennis Kriel

LeSigLa_EC: Learning Sign Language of Ecuador   170
    D. Rivas, M. Alvarez, W. Tamayo, V. Morales, R. Granizo, G. Vayas,
    V. Andaluz, M. Huerta, and G. Clotet

Pre-exit Survey of Final Year Students to Assess the Mechanical
Engineering Curriculum   180
    Emmanuel Glakpe and Esther Akinlabi

Innovative Project-Based Learning   189
    Ren-Hung Hwang, Pao-Ann Hsiung, Yau-Jane Chen,
    and Chin-Feng Lai

Selected Factors Supporting the Learning Organization   195
    Vaclav Zubr and Hana Mohelska

Factors Influencing Social Media Adoption and Continued Use
in Academia: A Case Study at a Traditional University   203
  Liezel Cilliers and Obrain Murire

Emerging Technologies Supported Personalized and Adaptive Learning

Generalization of Tooltips: An Assistive Technology Extension   213
  Saira-Banu Adams, William D. Tucker, and Isabella M. Venter

An Accurate Brainwave-Based Emotion Clustering for Learning Evaluation . . .   223
  *Ting-Mei Li, Hsin-Hung Cho, Han-Chieh Chao, Timothy K. Shih,
  and Chin-Feng Lai*

System of Evaluation for Reading Based on Eye Tracking   234
  *D. Rivas-Lalaleo, V. Luna, M. Álvarez, V. Andaluz, W. Quevedo,
  A. Santana, G. Vayas, M. Navas, and M. Huerta*

Emerging Technology and Engineering Education

Teaching of IA-32 Assembly Language Programming
Using Intel® Galileo   245
  *Tan Chee Phang, Shaiful Jahari b. Hashim,
  Nurul Adilah bt. Abdul Latiff, and Fakhrul Zaman Rokhani*

Identifying Drivers of Remanufacturing in Nigeria   252
  Ifije Ohiomah, Clinton Aigbavboa, and Jan-Harm Pretorius

Factors Affecting the Evolution of Welding and Fabrication Education
from the Perspective of Engineering Technology Graduates in Nigeria.   260
  Eghosa Eguabor, Clinton Aigbavboa, and Jan-Harm Pretorius

Industry Expectation from Graduates of Welding and Fabrication
from the Perspective of Engineering Technology Graduates in Nigeria.   269
  Eghosa Eguabor, Clinton Aigbavboa, and Jan-Harm Pretorius

Benefits of Minimised Wastage in Construction Sites: A Gauteng
Province Case Study   278
  Godfey Shai Thaphelo, Clinton Aigbavboa, and Ohiomah Ifije

Introduction of Construction Experience to the Classroom:
What Approaches Should Be Adopted   284
  Aliu John and Aigbavboa Clinton

SpeL (International Workshop on Social and Personal Computing for Web-Supported Learning Communities)

A Platform for Developing and Maintaining Competences
in PBL Supervision   297
   Dorina Gnaur and Hans Hüttel

Website Analysis in the Context of Practicing Geography:
From First Impression to Recommendation – Case Study   304
   Miloslava Cerna

Adaptive Practising Using Mobile Touch Devices   314
   Libor Klubal, Katerina Kostolanyova, and Vojtech Gybas

Using Social Media to Enhance Student Engagement   320
   Audrey J.W. Mbogho

Evaluation of the Blended Learning Approach in the Course
of Business English – A Case Study   326
   Blanka Klimova

Modeling a Peer Assessment Framework by Means of a Lazy
Learning Approach   336
   *Maria De Marsico, Andrea Sterbini, Filippo Sciarrone,
   and Marco Temperini*

ADOILS (Application and Design of Innovative Learning Software)

A Framework Design for On-line Human Library   349
   Tien-Wen Sung, Ting-Ting Wu, and Yi-Chen Lu

Design and Evaluation of Mobile Cuisine Guiding System
for English Learning Applications   355
   C.-H. Hunag, J.-F. Fang, H.-R. Chen, P.-H. Tseng, and J.-J. Chang

The Development of an Affective Tutoring System for Japanese
Language Learners   363
   Yu Chun Ma and Hao-Chiang-Koong Lin

A Study on the Behavioral Patterns Formed by Subjects with Different
Cognitive Styles in Playing Augmented Reality Interaction Games   372
   Meng-Chun Tsai and Hao-Chiang-Koong Lin

Exploration of Learning Effectiveness, Cognitive Load and Attitude
on Mobile E-book Introduced in Nursing Education   382
   Lei Chang, Ting-Ting Wu, Chih Wei Chao, and Jim-Min Lin

The Ideal and Reality of Implementing Technology into English
Language Teaching: A Case Study of Using a Peer Review System   391
   Wei-Wei Shen, Ming-Hsiu Michelle Tsai, and Jim-Min Lin

Digital Storytelling and Mobile Learning: Potentials
for Internationalization of Higher Education Curriculum.   400
   Andreja Istenic Starcic, Po-Sen Huang, Roza Alexeyevna Valeeva,
   Liliia Agzamovna Latypova, and Yueh-Min Huang

**SLEEP (International Workshop on Smart Learning by Emerging
Educational Paradigm)**

Using Educational Robotics to Support Elementary School Students'
Electrical Engineering Knowledge: A Preliminary Analysis   409
   Pan-Nan Chou and Yen-Ning Su

Understanding Students' Continuance Intention to Use Virtual
Desktop Service   413
   Yong-Ming Huang and Chien-Hung Liu

Exploring the Development and Evaluation of Integrating Emerging
Technology into a STEAM Project   420
   Yu-Kai Chen and Chi-Cheng Chang

Inference of Learning Creative Characteristics by Analysis
of EEG Signal   425
   Shih-Yeh Chen, Chin-Feng Lai, Ren-Hung Hwang, Chu-Sing Yang,
   and Ming-Shi Wang

Developing a Curriculum of Maker Education in Taiwan
Higher Education   433
   Tien-Chi Huang, Shu-Hsuan Chang, Vera Yu Shu, Preben Hansen,
   and Sung-Lin Lee

A Real-Time Assessment of Programming Through Debugging
Log Analytic   438
   Yu-Lin Jeng, Qing Tan, Yu Shu, and Sheng-Bo Huang

Using Facial Expression to Detect Emotion in E-learning System:
A Deep Learning Method.   446
   Ai Sun, Ying-Jian Li, Yueh-Min Huang, and Qiong Li

Maker Movement Influence on Students' Learning Motivation
and Learning Achievement – A Learning Style Perspective   456
   Jan-Pan Hwang

Synchronous Collaboration in English for Tourism Classes   463
   YiChun Liu

The Jacobian Matrix-Based Learning Machine in Student.   469
   Yi-Zeng Hsieh, Mu-Chun Su, and Yu-Lin Jeng

UMLL (International Symposium on User Modeling and Language Learning)

Lexical Bundle Investigation for Automated Scoring of Business
English Writing   477
   Shili Ge, Xue Yu, and Xiaoxiao Chen

Designing Interactive Exercises for Corpus-Based English Learning
with Hot Potatoes Software   485
   Xiaowen Wang and Tianyong Hao

An Explicit Learner Profiling Model for Personalized Word Learning
Recommendation   495
   Di Zou, Haoran Xie, Tak-Lam Wong, Fu Lee Wang, Reggie Kwan,
   and Wai Hong Chan

Mobile-Assisted Language Learning: Using WeChat in an English
Reading Class.   500
   Nana Jin

Discovering the Recent Research in Natural Language Processing
Field Based on a Statistical Approach   507
   Xieling Chen, Boyu Chen, Chunxia Zhang, and Tianyong Hao

A CRFs-Based Approach Empowered with Word Representation
Features to Learning Biomedical Named Entities from Medical Text   518
   Wenxiu Xie, Sihui Fu, Shengyi Jiang, and Tianyong Hao

Computer-Assisted Content Analysis in Risk Identification
of Public-Private Partnership Projects.   528
   Yingying Qu

Pedagogical Principle Based E-learning Exploration: A Case
of Construction Mediation Training   539
   Yingying Qu, Zhiwen Yu, Hao Cong, and Tianyong Hao

An Approach to Constructing Sentiment Collocation Dictionary
for Chinese Short Text Based on Word2Vec   548
   Jianfeng Zhou, Boyu Chen, and Yangqing Lin

A Construction Method for the Semantic Relation Corpus
of Traditional Chinese Medicine   557
    Jing Chen, Haitao Wang, Liangliang Liu, Xiaoru Zhang, Jing Zhao,
    Fan Zhang, and Xinyu Cao

Author Index   565

Emerging Technologies of Design, Model and Framework of Learning Systems

Effect of Using Digital Pen Teaching System Behaviors on Learning Achievements in a Mathematics Course

Yu-Sheng Su[1(✉)], Ting-Jou Ding[2], Po-Han Wu[3], and Chiu-Nan Su[4]

[1] Research Center for Advanced Science and Technology,
Department of Computer Science and Information Engineering,
National Central University, Taoyuan, Taiwan
addison@csie.ncu.edu.tw
[2] Department of Materials and Energy Engineering,
Ming Dao University, Pitou, Taiwan
tjding@mdu.edu.tw
[3] Department of Mathematics and Information Education,
National Taipei University of Education, Taipei, Taiwan
pohanwu.academic@gmail.com
[4] Department of Information Management,
Nan-Jeon University of Science and Technology, Tainan, Taiwan
cnsu@mail.njtc.edu.tw

Abstract. The emerging technologies and digital materials have gradually been popular in primary school campus. In this paper, we develop a digital pen teaching system, which is based on the teaching ideas of primary school teachers. By mathematics teaching approach, with combined with the digital pen system, it could provide plentiful application service to trigger elementary students' interesting, and thus, teachers are able to obtain students' learning conditions conveniently, and also, timely feedbacks could be given to every student. The experiment results show that students on the quantity of the digital pen teaching system used is positively correlated with students' learning achievements.

Keywords: Digital pen teaching system · Mathematics · System logs · Learning analytics

1 Introduction

The emerging technologies and digital materials have gradually been popular in primary school campus. The paper and pen are primary tools for knowledge learning and knowledge building. Sellen and Harper [15] indicate that students use pens and paper to write notes, work out the mathematical exercises, and do their homework during the class. Compared to typing on a computer, the use of pens and paper is simpler and more intuitive, also, it allows students to write and read more lucidly [10]. Steimle et al. [11] conduct a real experiment of their study on college students who use pens and paper for taking notes. The experiment results show that 77% of the 408 students used

© Springer International Publishing AG 2017
T.-C. Huang et al. (Eds.): SETE 2017, LNCS 10676, pp. 3–8, 2017.
https://doi.org/10.1007/978-3-319-71084-6_1

pens and paper to make annotations and that only 8% used a laptop computer to take notes. This indicates that pens and paper still play an importance role in note-taking [3].

Currently, elementary schools in Taiwan still use the method of giving lectures to teach mathematics. Elementary school teachers usually pass knowledge onto students by giving lectures, and the teacher is the center of this type of teaching. Students would listen to the lectures and learn their lessons independently. Long lectures tend to become tedious, and it is very difficult for students to remain focused in long lectures [6, 7]. In a conventional mathematical learning approach, the key point is often focused on the process and skill of doing mathematical exercises. The lack of effective learning tools is the main reason for low learning effectiveness [1, 2, 4, 6, 16]. Therefore, researchers suggest that using good learning tools in mathematics courses would improve the situation [9].

In this paper, we develop a digital pen teaching system (DPTS), which is based on the teaching ideas of primary school teachers [5, 13, 14]. In order to conduct our experiment activity, the DPTS is assimilated into the mathematics course in elementary schools. Teachers adapt the DPTS for designing the mathematical exercises while students use the digital pen for completing the mathematical exercise assignment, and on the other hand, the learning procedure of using the digital pen and paper is digitalized while the traditional intuitionistic handwritten paper is retained for reference at the same time. The DPTS could provide plentiful application service to trigger elementary students' interesting, and thus, teachers are able to obtain students' learning conditions conveniently and timely feedbacks could be given to every student. A quasi-experimental design was adopted to set up the experiment activity from an elementary school located in northern Taiwan, which involved 30 third-grade students and the whole project lasts for four weeks. In the experiment, we conducted a real mathematics course in a primary school so as to explore whether there is any influence on the digital pen teaching system log and learning outcomes would be made. Moreover, we analyzed system logs recorded by the DPTS in which the mathematics courses the students participate. The results are discussed, and several suggestions for teachers and students are proposed.

2 Research Design

2.1 Participants

The subjects of this study are third-grade students of an elementary school in northern Taiwan. Thirty students from one class participated in the experiment while a teacher teaches the class. The class is able to use the digital pen teaching system in a mathematics course, where students in the group were divided into small units of five people. A group leader was assigned by the teacher to maintain learning status of the unit.

The teaching materials used in the experiment is a section in the third-grade mathematics textbook for the second semester. The titled of the section was "Two-Step Multiplication and Division." The mathematical exercises and assignments used in the experiment was designed by one elementary school mathematics teacher who have the teaching experience for no less than 5 years.

2.2   Procedure

In the experimental procedure, each of the learning sessions lasted 120 min and was conducted once a week for four weeks. The procedure has four phases, as follows.

Phase 1: Before the learning activity began, the teacher briefly explains how to use the digital pen and the dot paper, and students should pay attention to the announcement. The teacher also printed out a mathematical exercise assignment in order to help out students' discussion on a piece of dot paper for students to practice in the classroom.

Phase 2: In the beginning of the activity, the teacher conducts roll-calling by using the DPTS, and students responded by checking on a roll-calling slip on the table. This approach has significantly reduces the time of roll-calling in the classroom. After the roll-calling is completed, the teacher would give each of the students a mathematical exercise assignment and explain the mathematical questions on the assignment to make sure that all of the students understand them.

Phase 3: Students would answer questions independently. They can answer the questions according to their science knowledge and also by using mathematical formulas, texts, and illustrations. After answering the questions, they may check on the "send" box on the paper to upload the answers to the DPTS.

Phase 4: The teacher would select answers from the group that are suitable for group discussion and further conduct a follow-up session. The teacher selects a group member to tell the group the results of students' discussion. The teacher would then use the DPTS handwriting function to let other groups see how they solved the mathematical exercise. This function not only can clearly demonstrate the process of mathematical calculation solutions but also can reduce unnecessary time for copying down the process.

After the learning activity ended, a post-test on learning effectiveness is conducted. Moreover, we analyzed system logs recorded by using the DPTS in which students the mathematics course participate.

2.3   Instruments and Data Analysis

There are two kinds of collected data, namely the DPTS system logs and the students' post-tests. To compare the students' participation behaviors and learning performances, the data is then analyzed using the IBM SPSS software. Before data analysis, the dependent variables are checked for normal distribution and homogeneity of variance. The system logs provide statistical information for each student on the quantity of DPTS used, the time spent of DPTS used, and the time spent of the mathematical exercise assignment completed. The quantity of DPTS used is defined that the number of times that a student uses the DPTS in the experiment activity. The time spent of DPTS used is defined that the number of time spent that a student uses the DPTS in the experiment activity. The time spent of the mathematical exercise assignment completed is defined that the number of time spent that a student uses the DPTS to complete the mathematical exercise assignment in the experiment activity. The statistical information helps us to understand the DPTS usage data contributions of each student.

At the end of the semester, a post-test is conducted to obtain students' learning performance. The post-test used in this research is designed by the mathematics teacher. The post-test included 5 free-response questions. The students have to use mathematical formulas or illustrations to demonstrate their calculation process. A perfect score would be 100. The Kuder-Richardson Formula 20 (KR-20) reliability test is used to estimate the post-test data [8]. The Cronbach's α value is 0.82, indicating high reliability.

3 Results

In the experiment, we want to explore how students' behaviors of DPTS using in an elementary mathematics course affect their learning performance.

3.1 Descriptive Statistics

During the four-week experiment, all students participated in the mathematics course, which applies DPTS as a tool, are from an elementary school. After class, the DPTS logs is stored in the DPTS database. The system logs includes three behavioral variables, namely the quantity of DPTS used, the time spent of DPTS used, and the time spent of the mathematical exercise assignment completed. Table 1 shows that the means and standard deviations of the variables are related to students' behaviors of using the DPTS and learning achievements.

Table 1. Descriptive statistics of using DPTS behaviors and learning performance.

Variables	Mean	S.D.
Learning performance	76.82	12.27
The quantity of DPTS used	18.28	6.50
The time spent of DPTS used	141815.30	214147.00
The time spent of the mathematical exercise assignment completed	42436.12	16796.72

As the statistics indicated in Table 1, the mean value of the time spent of DPTS used variable is higher than the mean value of the time spent of the mathematical exercise assignment completed variable. The finding indicates that the standard deviation (S.D.) value of the time spent in using the DPTS and completing the mathematical exercise assignment is too large. From students' interview, we think that while some students spent more time in using the DPTS and doing the mathematical exercise assignment, the other students tend to spend less time in using the DPTS and completing the mathematical exercise assignment.

3.2 Correlation Analysis of Using DPTS Behaviors and Learning Achievements

In the experiment, the Pearson's correlation analysis was used to measure the relationships between using DPTS behaviors and learning achievements. The experiment result is shown in Table 2 and some findings are discussed below.

Table 2. Correlation statistics of using DPTS behaviors and learning outcomes.

No.	Variables	1	2	3	4
1	Learning performance	1	0.48*	−0.13	0.48*
2	The quantity of DPTS used		1	0.51*	0.82**
3	The time spent of DPTS used			1	0.33
4	The time spent of the mathematical exercise assignment completed				1

$p < 0.05$*, $p < 0.01$**

Table 2 shows correlation statistics of using DPTS behaviors and learning achievements. The quantity of DPTS used variable is positively correlated with achievements learning performances, implying that the better the students are, the more time is spent on doing the mathematical exercise assignment.

4 Conclusions and Future Works

This research is built upon a digital pen teaching system (DPTS) to support the teachers in carrying out a feasibility study on DPTS-enabled mathematics courses. We explore the effect of using the DPTS behaviors on students' learning performance. The system logs can be analyzed to generate useful information for teachers to improve their instructional design.

The experiment results show that students on the quantity of the DPTS used is positively correlated with learning achievements. Moreover, we found that a positive correlation exists between the quantity of DPTS used and the time spent of the mathematical exercise assignment completed. However, the negative correlation is found between students on the time spent of the mathematical exercise assignment completed and students' learning outcomes. Therefore, understanding how students' behaviors in applying the DPTS affect their learning performance may give teachers useful information to improve their instructional design and provide insights for content and instructional designers to develop personalized learning supports.

In future studies, we suggest that the design of learning activities can be expanded to more disciplines and also situational application related technologies, such as collaborative learning [12] and blended learning [13, 14].

Acknowledgements. This study is supported in part by the National Science Council of the Republic of China. (MOST 106-2622-S-008 -002 -CC3 and MOST 106-2511-S-008-006)

References

1. Sellen, A.J., Harper, R.H.R.: The Myth of the Paperless Office. MIT Press, Cambridge (2003)
2. Alvarez, C., Salavati, S., Nussbaum, M., Milrad, M.: Collboard: fostering new media literacies in the classroom through collaborative problem solving supported by digital pens and interactive whiteboards. Comput. Educ. **63**, 368–379 (2013)
3. Cole, E., Pisano, E.D., Clary, G.J., Zeng, D., Koomen, M., Kuzmiak, C.M., Seo, B.K., Lee, Y., Pavic, D.: A comparative study of mobile electronic data entry systems for clinical trials data collection. Int. J. Med. Inform. **75**(10), 722–729 (2006)
4. Huang, S.J., Yang, J.H., Chiang, H.C., Su, Y.S.: Effects of situated mobile learning approach on learning motivation and performance of EFL students. J. Educ. Technol. Soc. **19**(1), 263–276 (2016)
5. Huang, S.J., Su, Y.S., Yang, J.H., Liou, H.H.: A collaborative digital pen learning approach to improving students' learning achievement and motivation in mathematics courses. Comput. Educ. **107**, 31–44 (2017)
6. Weinstein, C.E., Mayer, R.E.: The teaching of learning strategies. In: Handbook of Research on Teaching, vol. 3, pp. 315–327 (1986)
7. Llamas-Nistal, M., Fernández-Iglesias, M.J., González-Tato, J., Mikic-Fonte, F.A.: Blended e-assessment: migrating classical exams to the digital world. Comput. Educ. **62**, 72–87 (2013)
8. Landis, J.R., Koch, G.G.: The measurement of observer agreement for categorical data. Biometrics **33**(1), 159–174 (1977)
9. Nussbaum, M., Alvarez, C., McFarlane, A., Gomez, F., Claro, S., Radovic, D.: Technology as small group face-to-face collaborative scaffolding. Comput. Educ. **52**(1), 147–153 (2009)
10. O'Hara, K., Sellen, A.: A comparison of reading paper and on-line documents. In: Proceedings of the ACM SIGCHI Conference on Human Factors in Computing Systems, pp. 335–342 (1997)
11. Steimle, J., Gurevych, I., Mühlhäuser, M.: Notetaking in university courses and its implications for elearning systems. In: DeLFI, vol. 5, pp. 45–56 (2007)
12. Su, Y.S., Huang, S.J., Ding, T.-J.: Examining the effects of MOOCs learners' social searching results on learning behaviors and learning outcomes. Eurasia J. Math. Sci. Technol. Educ. **12**(9), 2517–2529 (2016)
13. Su, Y.S., Huang, S.J., Yang, J.H.: Effects of annotations and homework on learning achievement: an empirical study of scratch programming pedagogy. J. Educ. Technol. Soc. **18**(4), 331–343 (2015)
14. Su, Y.S., Yang, J.H., Hwang, W.Y., Huang, C.S.J., Tern, M.Y.: Investigating the role of computer-supported annotation in problem solving based teaching: an empirical study of a scratch programming pedagogy. Br. J. Educ. Technol. **45**(4), 647–665 (2014)
15. Sellen, A.J., Harper, R.H.: The Myth of the Paperless Office. MIT Press, Cambridge (2002)
16. Rogoff, B.: Apprenticeship in Thinking: Cognitive Development in Social Context. Oxford University Press, Oxford (1990)

Satisfaction Analysis for Agricultural Worker Digital Course Learning Platform

Jui-Hung Chang[1,2(✉)], Ren-Hung Hwang[3], and Hung-Hsi Chiang[2]

[1] Computer and Network Center, National Cheng Kung University,
Tainan City 701, Taiwan
changrh@mail.ncku.edu.tw
[2] Department of Computer Science and Information Engineering,
National Cheng Kung University, Tainan City 701, Taiwan
P76051331@mail.ncku.edu.tw
[3] Department of Computer Science and Information Engineering,
National Chung Cheng University, Minxiong, Taiwan
rhhwang@cs.ccu.edu.tw

Abstract. In the era of knowledge economy, learning has become increasingly important, it is more and more convenient to acquire the information in a fast way and E-learning has become increasingly popular. Under this trend, the traditional teaching method in the classroom will not be the only choice any longer and the application of E-learning system will be the important trend in the future. In recent years, related governmental departments also vigorously promote the E-learning system. Some special courses enable learners to firstly possess the prior knowledge of agriculture and then the relevant agricultural knowledge is digitalized; lastly, the professional teachers will be equipped for teaching and a system platform for high-efficient learning will be provided through E-learning. The learning effectiveness desired by this research through the establishment of an agricultural E-learning platform is shown as below: (1) apply E-learning platform to increase learning variety, further enhance learners' knowledge-ability and learning willingness, break through the territory restriction in learning and facilitate the learning; (2) apply satisfaction survey and assessment mechanism to understand the learning effectiveness of E-learning platform. This research established the agricultural E-learning platform and used students' satisfaction with information contents and course contents for E-learning system obtained through the satisfaction survey to present the positive affirmation. Therefore, it can be known that E-learning is greatly helpful to improve agricultural workers' learning.

Keywords: Agricultural E-learning platform · Satisfaction survey · Learning process · E-learning

1 Introduction

Information and Communications Technology (ICT) has improved the learning and teaching procedure and its resources also exceed the traditional teaching resources. As a result, the generation of E-learning system has a deep effect on education and has

© Springer International Publishing AG 2017
T.-C. Huang et al. (Eds.): SETE 2017, LNCS 10676, pp. 9–18, 2017.
https://doi.org/10.1007/978-3-319-71084-6_2

changed the teacher-student relationship in traditional teaching. ICT has improved the learning and teaching procedure and its resources also exceed the traditional teaching resources. Talebian et al. (2014) took the students in agricultural higher education in Iran as the research subjects to research and observe the advantages & disadvantages, convenience and restriction when ICT and E-learning are applied together.

As a kind of future education, E-learning can replace traditional learning and overcome the limitation in space and time. Due to its importance in public sectors, learning field has been increasing rapidly in recent years. Dreheeb et al. (2016) proposed the system quality of E-learning. The success of E-learning system depends on system quality and sustained use. According to user's opinion, it is found that the attributes and functions of usability, reliability and efficiency have the effect on the E-learning system used. Therefore, the research target of Dreheeb et al. is to develop the suitable model for E-learning to meet user's demand from the perspective of using E-learning system.

In recent years, ICT has been extended to agriculture and enterprises related to agriculture. The research of Manoj and Chimoy Kumar (2013) aims to conduct the 2-year E-learning plan in Kerala. Their research applied E-learning strategy, established virtual learning environment and adopted the tools used in communications technology to explain the diversity of tools applied in E-learning technology and their convenience, so as to greatly facilitate the establishment of E-learning system.

Governmental agencies attach increasing importance to enhancement of human qualities, the pursuit of excellence and talent cultivation to meet the demand of a modern country. The main purpose of talent cultivation is overall development and improvement of organizational capability, inheritance of experience and the maintenance of core competence. Conducting agricultural survey is a heavy work. How to complete the agriculture survey work successfully and smoothly is of great importance to the cultivation of agricultural workers, so as to increase work efficiency and enhance the data application value. In terms of the existing method, the training, learning and work conferences are usually held on a regular basis to develop agricultural workers' appropriate capabilities, offer on-the-job training and improve agricultural professional prior knowledge-ability, but agricultural work is heavy and if personnel reshuffle occurs frequently and they often need to make use of business trips to go to fixed places to learn, the huge cost for manpower training will be caused.

In conclusion, in addition to the design of an agricultural E-learning platform, this research also provided the adaptive online agricultural digital textbooks and designed questionnaires to understand the satisfaction with E-learning system and improve system functions. Only in this way can we enhance the investigated students' learning motivation and increase the learning effectiveness. Meanwhile, this research made an analysis to know whether the results have the positive effect on the use of system. If learners can increase learning efficiency through the use of E-learning system, their usage intention can also be enhanced, which is the goal this research intends to achieve.

The contributions of this research are as follows:

- Establish agricultural E-learning platform and offer agricultural investigators this platform to conduct course learning in place of face-to-face teaching, so as to facilitate personnel's learning and reduce expenditure.

- Make use of satisfaction survey to understand learners' acceptance of and satisfaction with E-learning system.

The remainder of this paper is organized as follows: Sect. 2 is the literature review; Sect. 3 describes the architecture of agricultural E-learning platform; Sect. 4 is the detailed description for the assessment and research methods of system satisfaction; Sect. 5 summarized conclusion and future works.

2 Related Work

E-learning has become a trend recently. For the adults, they can continue to learn by giving consideration to both work and family. Such culture of active learning has deeply affected learner's motivation because this learning mechanism is not bound by time and space.

The booming development of ICT has changed the learning and teaching process. People can apply the E-learning where the teaching resources far exceed the traditional learning resources. Sogol Talebian et al. investigated the agricultural students in Iran who had applied ICT to education to understand the advantages and disadvantages, convenience and restriction, etc. brought by E-learning.

With the adoption of actually participatory action method, Camilius Sanga et al. developed a discussion channel to spread the knowledge related to agriculture and agriculture science and technology information and such information comes from agents or Agricultural University and so on. 19 villages in Tanzania were selected in the experiment to develop this system by m-learning and e-learning. The experimental result proves that this system can provide the agricultural suggestions and information which can be gained through mobile phone and network for these 380 small tenant farmers.

Šárka Hošková-Mayerová and Zdena Rosická presented the E-learning experience and method from 3 universities and also mentioned how the E-learning will improve the learning efficiency.

Valentina Arkorful and Nelly Abaidoo researched many researchers' literature and academic researches on E-learning as well as the teaching status by combining E-learning in higher educational institution. These researches are mostly based on the investigation.

2.1 Satisfaction Scale

It is very important to assess the satisfaction with the development of E-learning technology (Bekele 2010; Ho and Dzeng 2010). In order to understand the E-learning learners' usage satisfaction, it is of great significance for the research scholars to assess the satisfaction and lots of scholars also universally apply the satisfaction scale for assessment. (Bekele 2010; Ho and Dzeng 2010; Ong et al. 2009) put forward that satisfaction assessment can help to understand that it is important to understand the major factors of system and those factors affecting user's intention for system. At the same time, more suggestions can be offered for the future analysis and design of system, so that user's usage of system can be more specific and user can better accept it. The assessment of satisfaction scale can be used to analyze whether the system meets the user's demand to further understand the benefits achieved by the system (Ong et al. 2009). As for satisfaction scale, Ong et al. (2009) summarized much relevant information about research achievements previously, among which Information Systems Success Model (D&M IS Success Model) proposed by Delone and McLean (1992) and satisfaction assessment model proposed by Huang et al. (2012) can be used to assess learners' satisfaction.

3   Architecture of Agricultural E-learning Platform

This research describes and plans the several module units of the agricultural E-learning platform. The proposed system architecture is shown in Fig. 1 and it will be described below.

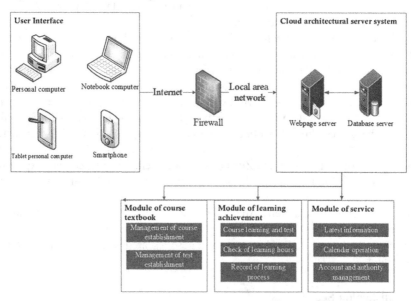

Fig. 1. Architecture diagram of agricultural E-learning system

The description for the architecture diagram of cloud mobile E-learning system is shown below:

It is mainly divided into the modules of service, learning achievement, course textbooks, etc. and personnel role is divided into general learner and course administrator.

The database for agricultural mobile E-learning system is mainly MySQL in charge of the data storage and acquisition, webpage server is mainly Apache and program language is mainly PHP. The course activities and contents are complex, so Xml with highly expandability and structuralization as well as better data organization ability is applied to achieve flexible data processing and application.

In user interface, the device used by user can be assessed in the server management and maintenance system through the Internet to obtain the operation module related to system management and operation.

The server management and maintenance system is mainly constructed in the currently most popular cloud computing environment. The cloud virtual machine will be established on this system. The cost for the establishment of server and maintenance human power can be avoided in cloud computing environment, the storage space and system resource can be added whenever possible according to its needs (like CPU, Memory), and meanwhile information safety is protected, which is of great help to proceed with the research.

The main modules of service, learning achievement and course textbook are described as below:

[Module of Service]

- It mainly contains the following sub-operations: latest announcement, calendar operation, account and authority management

Latest announcement: learners can acquire the relevant information related to latest system and course activities. Any latest online course can be established through this operation.

Calendar operation: the course learning in the certain scheduling can be planned and the activity data can be set in advance.

Account and authority management: managers will do the setting about whether the account is used and what kind of roles (teacher or student) it includes.

[Module of Learning Achievement]

Figure 2 is the **main system interface of the module of learning achievement**

- **Course learning, check of learning hours and record of learning process**

Course learning: users learn through the related course textbooks established on the system and they can also combine the sharing and discussion function to share and discuss the contents related to course with each other.

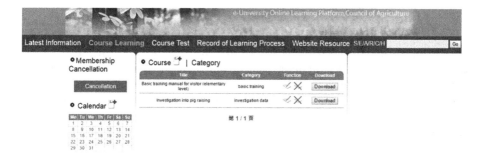

Fig. 2. Interface of learning achievement

Testlet test: it refers to the test for the learners' learning achievement, so that learners can test their relevant learning effectiveness through the course learning after learning.

Record of learning process: if learners pass the test, the relevant learning process will be recorded.

[Module of Textbook Learning]

- **Management of course establishment and test establishment**

Management of course establishment: the relevant course textbooks will be up-loaded for management and maintenance.

Management of test establishment: relevant question bank for testing can be established according to the relevant course textbooks. After learners learn this course, they can use the relevant question bank for testing established by this operation for learning assessment.

4 Research into System Satisfaction Assessment

In addition to the establishment of an E-learning system and adaptive teaching materials, this research also surveyed learners' satisfaction with this E-learning system. The relevant description is shown below. This experiment conducted the questionnaire analysis against learners who had used agricultural E-learning system to understand the satisfaction assessment for the use of this set of system and course.

4.1 Design of Satisfaction Scale of E-learning System

The main contents of this scale adopted Likert 5-point scale for scoring and assessment, with a total of 11 items. The answering options include: 1. Extremely satisfactory, 2. Dissatisfactory, 3. General, 4. Satisfactory. 5. Extremely satisfactory. If you choose Option 1, "Extremely", you get 1 score; if you choose Option 5. "Extremely satisfactory", you get 5 scores. Testees' higher scores mean higher satisfaction. Conversely, the Testees' lower scores mean lower satisfaction.

The pre-test was done against the questionnaire items, so as to understand whether the designed items can conform to the results expected by us and analyze the questionnaire reliability.

4.2 Pre-test

Prior to formal test, a pre-test was done against a small sample size. The samples were collected through Google form questionnaire, with totally 16 questionnaires retrieved. All the testees have filled in the questionnaire completely and there are 16 valid questionnaires. SPSS statistics software was used to conduct fundamental statistics and reliability analysis. The pre-test is applied to understand whether the satisfaction scale conforms to consistency (Table 1).

Table 1. List of questionnaire items

Item	Item code
1. I feel satisfied with the stability of online learning system of agricultural statistics	Q1
2. The information contents provided by online learning system of agricultural statistics are correct	Q2
3. The information contents provided by online learning system of agricultural statistics can meet my demands	Q3
4. I feel satisfied with the contents of "survey course on face-to-face interview"	Q4
5. I feel satisfied with the contents of "survey course on live-stock and agriculture"	Q5
6. I feel satisfied with the contents of "survey course on major farmer"	Q6
7. I feel satisfied with "the introduction course of statistical information and system operation"	Q7
8. I feel satisfied with "the course for the collection of survey experience of agricultural statistics"	Q8
9. I am joyful to use online learning system of agricultural statistics	Q9
10. I feel satisfied with the information learned from online learning system of agricultural statistics	Q10
11. On the whole, my interaction with online learning system of agricultural statistics is satisfactory	Q11

1. Reliability Analysis:

Cronbach's α coefficient is used as the reliability of questionnaire pre-test and it means that a value lying between 0 and 1 is measured to represent the consistency of questionnaires. Larger Cronbach's α value means higher reliability and more stable scale. General speaking, Cronbach's α value above .70 is optimal.

Under the circumstance that no item is deleted in this scale, Cronbach's α is 0.945 (high reliability); it can be known from the Field "α Coefficient after the deletion of single item" in Table 2 that Cronbach's α will not increase after the deletion of any item. Therefore, it is concluded that no item is deleted.

2. Conclusion:

It can be known from the reliability analysis that the consistency of this scale is higher, signifying it is stable. Therefore, the scale without deleting any item is used as the satisfaction scale for E-learning system in the formal test.

4.3   Formal Questionnaire Survey and Satisfaction Assessment

Google form questionnaire was used to collect samples with totally 50 questionnaires retrieved. All the testees have filled in the questionnaire completely and there are 50 valid questionnaires. SPSS statistics software was used to conduct statistical analysis to understand testees' satisfaction with E-learning system.

Table 2. Reliability analysis result of "satisfaction scale for E-learning system"

Item code	α coefficient after the deletion of single item
Q1	0.945
Q2	0.937
Q3	0.939
Q4	0.941
Q5	0.938
Q6	0.938
Q7	0.936
Q8	0.939
Q9	0.945
Q10	0.945
Q11	0.940

1. Single sample t-test ($\alpha = 0.05$)

$H\_0{:}\mu\_i < 3$; $H\_1{:}\mu\_i \geq 3$; i = 1, 2, 3, ..., 11. When significance (p-vlaue) ≥ 0.05, H_0 is not rejected. So, there is no enough evidence to prove that the average satisfaction score ≥ 3; when significance (p-vlaue) < 0.05, H_0 is rejected. So, there is enough evidence to prove that the average satisfaction score ≥ 3, signifying the average satisfaction of this item is greater than "general" and testees have the good affirmation for this item.

It can be known from Table 3 that each item's p-value < 0.001, so H_0 is rejected. However, there is enough evidence to prove that each item's average satisfaction is greater than "general", signifying users using the system have the good affirmation for E-learning system through the questionnaire filled.

Table 3. Items of satisfaction scale for E-learning system (Average mean, Standard deviation, and p-value)

Item code	Mean	Standard deviation	p-value
Q1	3.76	0.309	<0.001
Q2	3.80	0.408	<0.001
Q3	3.80	0.490	<0.001
Q4	3.84	0.504	<0.001
Q5	3.90	0.418	<0.001
Q6	3.82	0.477	<0.001
Q7	3.88	0.393	<0.001
Q8	3.86	0.490	<0.001
Q9	3.84	0.464	<0.001
Q10	3.88	0.475	<0.001
Q11	3.84	0.382	<0.001

2. Summary:

According to the analysis results of satisfaction scale for E-learning system, learners show positive affirmation both for the information contents and course contents of E-learning system.

5   Conclusion and Future Works

The satisfaction scale is used to understand that agricultural E-learning system is helpful to learner's learning. It can rapidly improve the prior knowledge related to agriculture, the learning becomes flexible without the limitation in time and space, training cost can be reduced and the training process can be understood quickly to reduce the employment of teachers and increase learning time. Resources can be recycled to fully reduce cost. Learners can record the learning process and fully understand their own status through system learning for review and modification. In this way, learners can achieve the optimal condition, which is also the goal of establishing agricultural E-learning system.

This research only conducts the survey on satisfaction with system and course contents. More dimensions can be assessed and analyzed in the future, such as education background, age, information ability, effect on acceptance of E-learning system, etc. All the topics above are interesting and deserve to be further discussed.

References

Bekele, T.A.: Motivation and satisfaction in internet-supported learning environments: a review. Educ. Technol. Soc. **13**(2), 116–127 (2010)

Sanga, C., Mlozi, M., Haug, R., Tumbo, S.: Mobile learning bridging the gap in agricultural extension service delivery: experiences from Sokoine university of agriculture, Tanzania. Int. J. Educ. Dev. Inf. Commun. Technol. (IJEDICT) **12**(3), 108–127 (2016)

DeLone, W.H., McLean, E.R.: Information systems success: the quest for the dependent variable. Inf. Syst. Res. **3**(1), 60–95 (1992)

Dreheeb, A.E., Basir, N., Fabil, N.: Impact of system quality on users' satisfaction in continuation of the use of e-learning system. Int. J. e-Education e-Business, e-Management e-Learning **6**(1), 13–20 (2016)

Ho, C.L., Dzeng, R.J.: Construction safety training via e-Learning: learning effectiveness and user satisfaction. Comput. Educ. **55**(2), 858–867 (2010)

Huang, Y.M., Liu, C.H., Lee, C.Y., Huang, Y.M.: Designing a personalized guide recommendation system to mitigate information overload in museum learning. Educ. Technol. Soc. **15**(4), 150–166 (2012)

Manoj, R., Chimoy Kumar, G.: The benefits of the e-learning agricultural project kissankerala to digital immigrants and digital natives. Turkish Online J. Distance Educ. **13**(2), 152–153 (2013)

Ong, C.S., Day, M.Y., Hsu, W.L.: The measurement of user satisfaction with question answering systems. Inf. Manag. **46**(7), 397–403 (2009)

Hošková-Mayerová, Š., Rosická, Z.: E-learning pros and cons: active learning culture? Procedia – Soc. Behav. Sci. **191**(2), 958–962 (2015)

Talebian, S., Mohammadi, H.M., Rezvanfar, A.: Information and communication technology (ICT) in higher education: advantages, disadvantages, conveniences and limitations of applying e-learning to agricultural students in Iran. Procedia – Soc. Behav. Sci. **152**(7), 300–305 (2014)

Arkorful, V., Abaidoo, N.: The role of e-learning, advantages and disadvantages of its adoption in higher education. Int. J. Instruct. Technol. Distance Learn. **12**(1), 29–42

Emerging Technologies Supported in ICT Education

Leila Goosen[1]([⊠]) [iD] and Toppie N. Mukasa-Lwanga[2] [iD]

[1] University of South Africa, Pretoria 0003, Gauteng, South Africa
GooseL@unisa.ac.za
[2] School of Computing, Johannesburg 1710, South Africa
MukasTN@UNISA.ac.za

Abstract. The authors introduce research, which provides a qualitative perspective on academics' use of emerging technologies on the institutional learning management system, to address the challenges of teaching Information and Communication Technology modules in an open and distance e-learning context. The paper proceeds to a literature review on research into how academics use emerging technologies to increase throughput rates, in some cases in open and/or distance e-learning contexts. Arguments presented center on formulating concepts within a theoretical and conceptual framework. The paper mainly discusses findings aimed at providing a qualitative perspective on academics' use of emerging technologies to address the challenges of teaching Information and Communication Technology modules in an open and distance e-learning context. Conclusions are presented, including a summary of the most important findings. The findings make an original contribution regarding emerging trends in, and promote the development of knowledge in fields related to, academics' use of emerging technologies.

Keywords: Emerging technologies · Information and Communication Technology · Open and distance e-learning

1 Introduction

1.1 Purpose and Objectives of the Study

The study reported on in this paper represents a single site study of the School of Computing (SoC), in the College of Science, Engineering and Technology (CSET) at the University of South Africa (UNISA). This institution of tertiary education offers open and distance e-learning, and draws its student population from all over the world. The institutional Learning Management System (LMS) offers a range of technologies aimed at maximizing the collaboration between academics and students.

The authors introduce research with the **aim** of providing a qualitative perspective on academics' use of emerging technologies for effective teaching to address the challenges of Information and Communication Technology (ICT) modules in an open and distance e-learning context. Although Mukasa-Lwanga and Goosen [1] investigated the use of such technologies towards effective and meaningful teaching in an open distance learning Computing context, their paper provided a quantitative perspective.

© Springer International Publishing AG 2017
T.-C. Huang et al. (Eds.): SETE 2017, LNCS 10676, pp. 19–28, 2017.
https://doi.org/10.1007/978-3-319-71084-6_3

The cost of lack of throughput is very high, not only for higher education institutions, which offer Open and Distance e-Learning (ODeL), but also for their students. In order to work towards achieving the aim as stated, the **objective**, which will be used as focus for the research reported on in this paper, is to indicate how academics used various emerging technologies for selected School of Computing modules. Qualitative data, relating to how academics are using various emerging technologies for renewing their ICT teaching practices by building on the past to create new energies, and specifically for renewing their students' learning experiences and assessment, will mainly be provided.

1.2   Research Questions

The research reported here focuses on the following primary research question: How are academics using emerging technologies for effective teaching to address the challenges of ICT modules in an open and distance e-learning context? The secondary question to assist in delving into the primary research question is: What are academics' perceptions about the use of emerging technologies?

1.3   In the Remainder of This Paper

The paper proceeds to a review of the literature on research into how academics use emerging technologies for effective teaching, in order to thus increase throughput rates, in some cases in open and/or distance e-learning contexts. Main arguments presented center on formulating and situating significant concepts within an appropriate theoretical and conceptual framework.

Although some perspectives on quantitative findings are provided, the paper mainly discusses findings aimed at providing a qualitative perspective on academics' use of emerging technologies for effective teaching to address the challenges of ICT modules in an open and distance e-learning context.

Conclusions are presented, including a summary of the most important findings. The authors show how the findings of this research could make a significant and original contribution regarding emerging trends in, and the promotion and development of knowledge in fields related to, academics' use of emerging technologies for effective teaching in an open and distance e-learning context. By analyzing these findings, together with ideas for best practice provided in applicable literature, suggestions can be formulated to improve the instruction of ICT modules presented in an open and distance e-learning context.

2   Theoretical and Conceptual Frameworks

Koohang et al. [2] investigated learning objects from the perspective of constructivist theory through to application, and Frankola [3] interrogated why students drop out, while Swanepoel and Mays [4] worked towards a framework to support transformation through quality assurance at the University of South Africa.

2.1 Open and Distance E-learning Contexts

According to Van Schoor [5, p. 41], considerable research on student "retention and throughput has been done at residential" institutions of tertiary education. The University of South Africa definition of open distance education details it as "a multi-dimensional concept aimed at bridging" distances between students and their institution of tertiary education, academics, courseware and peers regarding time, geography, economics and communication [5, p. 40]. Open and distance e-learning "focuses on removing barriers to access" e-learning, flexibility of e-learning provision, student centeredness, supporting students and constructing e-learning programs with the expectation that students can succeed. Neuman and Blodgett [6] state that distance education offers the opportunity to increase students' enrolment and promote diversity. According to these same authors, distance students in remote locations often indicate tremendous satisfaction, to reflect their appreciation for bringing the program to them.

Ng [7] stated that because of the major reasons of personal development, career advancement and socializing considerations, interest is a common purpose among such adult students. A student's characteristics, however, influence training outcomes, because the individual's ability and motivation affect performance [8].

The virtual nature of ODeL, however, together with the anonymity of students, present some challenges to the education system. In support of this statement, Block [9] asserts that open and distance students need to learn how to prioritize their lives and educational endeavors. In addition to this, Block [10] stated that distance requires students to consistently regulate their learning process. This is due to the multiple goals, which may be exhibited among open and distance students, and some goals may take precedence over others. Self-regulated learning is controlling one's own conduct in order to achieve a goal. This is one personality trait that is considered important for students' progress in an ODeL context. As Tuckman [11] puts it, many students treat the opportunity for self-pacing as an invitation to procrastinate. This is because the absence of an on-site lecturer makes this behavior difficult to control. Students need to make decisions about, and to exercise control over, their learning activities in terms of pace, depth and coverage of content, type of media accessed and time spent on studying [12]. A point noted by Taylor [13] is that for open and distance e-learning, students' early engagement is more elusive than for on-campus students, and often only commences when an assessment task is due.

3 Literature Review

3.1 Learning Management Systems

Various studies, such as those by Frankola [3], Swanepoel and Mays [4] and Van Schoor [5], reiterated the importance of student support, specifically at institutions of tertiary education offering open and distance e-learning, to enhance overall student performance. Related literature, which presented opportunities for further investigation, included Davis and Venter [14] - although they looked at performance and success in an open and distance e-learning context, their students were postgraduate ones in a business module - and whereas Chen and Tsai [15] considered students' attitudes towards e-learning at Taiwan University, this paper will study academics' views from an African perspective.

Van Schoor [5] pointed out that the assessment of students' academic preparedness for studying in an open and distance e-learning context is one of the numerous factors, which contribute to success. Nel and Ndeya-Ndereya [16] pointed to the lack of face-to-face contact between open and distance e-learning students and their lecturers as one of the foremost reasons why e-learning contexts are often experienced as being impersonal, lonely and lacking social presence.

Because of their physical separation from their open and distance e-learning lecturers, some students could only use email and the discussion forums available on the learning management system to communicate - a student quoted in an article by Davis and Venter [14] really appreciated this. Picciano [17] shares the same view on the importance of interaction for a successful module, but advises that the nature and extent of the interaction have to be considered to equate the learning outcome. This is in line with the constructivist view of learning and the zone of proximal development, suggested by Vygotsky [18], which proposes that a student's cognitive development is highly dependent on social interaction and collaboration with more capable and knowledgeable others.

The development of a learning management system, myUNISA, "has seen the establishment of" e-learning support for all of the modules offered [4, p. 7]. There is, however, a need to develop an understanding that the overall student experience is affected by "a wide range of different stakeholder contributions and" interdependent activities [4, p. 9] as a result of "the cumulative effect of many subsystems that need to work in harmony." Such a context requires active student "engagement with the learning process and multiple opportunities for interaction between" both students and other students, as well as students and their lecturers [4, p. 17].

4   Research Methodology

Aspects relating to the data collection instrument, population, sampling technique and sample, validity and reliability of the instrument and data analysis were also discussed in an earlier paper [x].

4.1   Research Design

Mixed-method research was used to ensure that the evidence obtained would be enable the researchers to answer the research questions as unambiguously as possible [19]. Such a mixed-method research strategy is useful when only the qualitative or quantitative approach is inadequate to best understand a research problem [20].

When using a qualitative mode of inquiry, most data take the form of words, as opposed to figures, and generally, researchers search through and explore these until they develop a deeper understanding. A case study research design investigates a restricted system (the so-called 'case'), which employs numerous sources of data located in the situation. In the project discussed in this paper, the focus will be on several entities (modules) [21], with each case represented by a particular module, selected for use as an example of a particular instance.

As an example of a research design that had been implemented in a previous investigation, Liu [22] used a phenomenological study as part of a qualitative, interactive design in order to investigate student interaction experiences in an open and distance e-learning context [23]. The study reported on in this paper also uses aspects of a phenomenological study, which attempt to describe participants' perceptions, perspectives and understandings.

4.2 Validity and Reliability

In terms of qualitative data collection, Maree and Van der Westhuizen [23] raised the argument that the intensely personal participation and comprehensive replies from participants capture adequate levels in terms of validity and reliability. The use of a variety of strategies to enhance validity is required in especially qualitative research, since the validity of such designs include the extent to which perceptions and interpretations made had shared meaning between participants and the researchers. Several resources ought to be employed for comparing findings with each other, for ensuring the internal validity of qualitative research [23]. As suggested by McMillan and Schumacher [21], decisions were therefore made on how to ensure that the data collected is valid. Reliability with regard to qualitative studies can be regarded as findings being consistent with data collected [23]. Dimensions towards reliability are therefore also being ensured in the more qualitative parts of the study.

McMillan and Schumacher [21] agreed that validity in quantitative research can also include issues of reliability. The use of multi-method strategies could produce diverse insights regarding topics of interest and augment how credible, transferable, dependable and confirmable such data and resultant findings, as well as the analysis thereof, are [21]. These strategies also allow for the inclusion of quantitative research, enabling McMillan and Schumacher [21] to indicate triangulation as being critical for the facilitation of interpretive validity. Such validity relates to data, interpretations and/or the conclusions arrived at by using a particular research method in a specific context for a certain reason [23].

4.3 Data Analysis

In agreement with suggestions by McMillan and Schumacher [21], the less experienced researcher (the second author) had especially qualitative data analyzed independently by another more experienced researcher (the first author), who had not been involved in obtaining the data. Findings could be analyzed to obtain a representation of the applicable participants and their contexts. Data analysis was done by coding, organizing and combining related information into themes and categories [24]. Two themes were identified, that is, how each classified event was used for ODeL and how it was used to increase pass rates.

5 Discussion of Findings

Aspects relating to numbers and rankings for the gross survival rates of selected modules across various years, including 2010, the averages for each of these modules, as well as for Learning Management System (LMS) use, were discussed in an earlier paper [x]. Table 1 shows that correlations between various of these aspects are all negative.

Table 1. Correlations for 2010 and averages compared to use of emerging technologies.

Elements being compared	Correlations for numbers	Correlations for rankings
2010 vs. LMS use (excluding no LMS use)	−0.308	−0.409
Average vs. LMS use (excluding no LMS use)	−0.371	−0.341

Please note that whereas Goosen and Mukasa-Lwanga [25] reported details relating to a sub-set of seven academics, this paper shows these for the full complement of thirteen. Just less than two-thirds (8; 62%) of the academics, who ended up participating in the interviews, were female, while the largest bracket of them are relatively young (see Table 2).

Table 2. Ages of participants.

Elements	Numbers	Percentages
36–40 years	6	46%
41–45 years	1	8%
46–50 years	3	23%
Older than 50 years	3	23%

Eight of the interviewees each had a Master's degree as highest academic qualification, together with two Bachelor degrees and three Honors degrees. Four of the interviewees also had a Higher Education Diploma as formal educational qualification, while none of the others had any such educational qualifications.

Almost half each of participants had between five and ten, and between eleven and twenty years' experience of teaching in an open and distance (e-learning) context, while only a single participant had more than thirty years (see Table 3). The majority of them also had more than 5 years' experience of using the institutional learning management system (see Table 4).

It is important to note that the number of responses for the modules in Table 5 exceeds the number of academics interviewed, as most of them were interviewed in relation to more than one module that they had been involved with. The majority of the

Table 3. Experience of teaching in an open and distance e-learning context.

Elements	Numbers	Percentages
5–10 years	6	46%
11–20 years	6	46%
More than 30 years	1	8%

Table 4. Years' experience of using the institutional learning management system.

Elements	Numbers	Percentages
5 years	4	30%
More than 5 years	9	70%

Table 5. Average number of students on module.

Elements	Numbers	Percentages
100–250	6	30%
251–500	5	25%
501–750	3	15%
751–1000	2	10%
More than 1000	4	20%

applicable modules that were discussed with the academics during their interviews had an average of between 100 and 250 students usually taking these modules per semester/year. The fact that four of the modules discussed during the interviews have an average of more than a thousand registered students each, however, casts a whole new light on what these academics have to say …

Table 6 shows that only one of these academics had three years' experience of teaching a particular module, two more on them had four years' experience, while the majority (ten) of the academics had more than that in terms of all of the other applicable modules.

Table 6. Years' experience of teaching a particular module.

Elements	Numbers	Percentages
3 years	1	8%
4 years	2	15%
More than 4 years	10	77%

As an example of what was discussed in the interviews, the primary academic of three modules chose to be interviewed on only one of these, because her use of technology was the same for the three modules. Based on the concept of ODeL, academic D would augment the module content using additional resources. She would use announcements to inform students of any new happenings on the module. She referred to announcements as a means of bridging the communication gap between the academic and students. Students would also be made aware of where to access or buy the prescribed books. On these modules, academic D envisaged the use of discussion forums as an important means of promoting interaction among students.

6 Conclusion

The following conclusion section will review the main points of the paper, including a summary of the most important findings, elaborate on the importance of the work and suggest applications and extensions.

One way to explain the correlations found in Table 1, with regard to 2010 and averages compared to use of learning management system technologies, would be that for modules with relative high rates, less effort would be expected with regard to learning management system technologies, and the other way around. This explanation specifically held with regard to two of the modules that one of the academics were interviewed on: while these modules have rankings in terms of both 2010 and averages placing them firmly in the lowest third, these same modules both have rankings regarding myUNISA use in the top 10.

There are barriers/challenges to using emerging technologies in ODeL. So and Bush [26] talk about physical separation, which refers to the space between a student and academic, or between student and student. Although, as stated by academic D, the use of technology by academics and students bridges this gap, there is lack of social interaction [27], as well as feelings of isolation on the part of students, as pointed out by Andersson [28], and more effort is expected from ODeL students than students at residential universities [29].

The academics' responses during the interviews confirmed the effectiveness of using emerging technologies on the pass rates of modules, consequently leading to enhanced throughput rate. Wang et al. [30] **recommend** such initiatives, which help to improve pass rates.

These findings suggest that more dedication is still required from the students to control their learning, and through proper time management, they could contribute immensely to improving their performance. This finding also supports earlier research by Koohang et al. [2] and Schunk and Zimmerman [31].

References

1. Mukasa-Lwanga, T.N., Goosen, L.: Using technology towards effective teaching and meaningful learning in an open and distance learning computing context. In: Proceedings of the ISTE International Conference on Mathematics, Science and Technology Education, Mopani Camp in Kruger National Park, Limpopo, South Africa (2014)
2. Koohang, A., Riley, L., Smith, T., Schreurs, J.: E-learning and constructivism: from theory to application. Interdisc. J. E-Learning Learn. Objects 5(1), 91–109 (2009)
3. Frankola, K.: Why online learners drop out. Workforce 80(1), 53–60 (2001)

4. Swanepoel, L., Mays, T.: Quality assurance at Unisa: towards a framework to support transformation. Progressio **32**(2), 6–20 (2010)
5. Van Schoor, W.A.: The assessment of academic preparedness in an ODL institution. Progressio **32**(2), 40–51 (2010)
6. Neuman, K.M., Blodgett, B.P.: Success and failure in undergraduate distance education: the experiences of two social work programs. In: Baccalaureate Program Directors National Conference, Detroit (2009)
7. Ng, C.-H.: Motivation among older adults in learning computing technologies: a gounded model. Educ. Gerontol. **34**(1), 1–14 (2007)
8. Burke, L.A., Hutchins, H.M.: Training transfer: an integrative literature review. Hum. Resource Dev. Rev. **6**(3), 263–296 (2007)
9. Block, J.: Library anxiety and distance learning graduate student: a case study of Eastern Michigan university. Michigan Libr. Assoc. (MLA) Forum **5**(3), Article 5 (2007)
10. Block, J.: Distance education and the digital divide: an academic perspective. Online J. Distance Learn. Adm. **13**(1) (2010). http://www.westga.edu/ ∼ distance/ojdla/spring131/block131.html
11. Tuckman, B.W.: The effect of motivational scaffolding on procrastinatinators' distance learning outcomes. Comput. Educ. **49**(2), 414–422 (2007)
12. Hung, M., Chour, C., Chen, C., Own, Z.: Learner readiness for online learning: scale development and student perceptions. Comput. Educ. **55**(3), 1080–1090 (2010)
13. Taylor, J.A.: Assessment in first year university: a model to manage transition. J. Univ. Teach. Learn. Practice **5**(1), 19–33 (2008)
14. Davis, A., Venter, P.: The long walk to success: drivers of student performance in a postgraduate ODL business course. In: Proceedings of the 5th International Conference on e-learning, Universiti Sains Malaysia, Penang, Malaysia (2010)
15. Chen, R., Tsai, C.: Gender differences in Taiwan university students' attitudes toward web-based learning. Cyber Psychol. Behav. **10**(5), 645–654 (2007)
16. Nel, L., Ndeya-Ndereya, C.N.: Enhancing online social presence: the role of communication. Progressio **33**(1), 116–137 (2011)
17. Picciano, A.G.: Beyond student perceptions: issues of interaction presence, and performance in an online course. J. Asynchron. Learn. Netw. **6**(1), 21–39 (2002)
18. Vygotsky, L.S.: Mind in Society: Development of Higher Psychological Process. Harvard University Press, Cambridge (1978)
19. De Vaus, D.A., De Vaus, D.: Research Design in Social Research. SAGE, London (2001)
20. Creswell, J.W.: Research Design: Qualitative, Quantitative and Mixed Methods Approaches. SAGE Publications Inc., London (2014)
21. McMillan, J.H., Schumacher, S.: Research in Education: Evidence-Based Inquiry, 7th edn. Pearson, Boston (2010)
22. Liu, S.L.: Student interaction experiences in distance learning courses: a phenomenological study. Online J. Distance Learn. Adm. **11**(1) (2008)
23. Maree, K., Van der Westhuizen, C.: Planning a research proposal. In: Maree, J.G. (ed.) First steps in research, pp. 24–45. Van Schaik, Pretoria (2007)
24. Brazeley, P.: Analysing qualitative data: more than just 'identifying themes'. Malaysian J. Qual. Res. **2**, 6–22 (2009)
25. Goosen, L., Mukasa-Lwanga, T.: Educational technologies in distance education: beyond the horizon with qualitative perspectives. In: Proceedings of the South Africa International Conference on Educational Technologies, Pretoria (2017)
26. So, H., Brush, T.A.: Student perceptions of collaborative learning, social presence and satisfaction in a blended learning environment: relationships and critical factors. Comput. Educ. **51**(1), 318–336 (2008)

27. Dennen, V.D., Wieland, K.: From interaction to intersubjectivity: facilitating online group discourse processes. Distance Educ. **28**(3), 281–297 (2007)

28. Andersson, A.: Letters from the field: e-learning students change of learning behaviour in Sri Lanka and Bangladesh. In: Proceedings of the 7th European Conference on e-Learning (ECEL), Agia Napa, Cyprus (2008)

29. Pretorius, A.M., Prinsloo, P., Uys, M.D.: Student performance in introductory microeconomics at an African open distance learning institution. Africa Educ. Rev. **6**(1), 140–158 (2009)

30. Wang, Y., Peng, H., Huang, R., Hou, Y., Wang, J.: Characteristics of distance learners: research on relationships of learning motivation, learning strategy, self- efficacy, attribution and learning results. Open Learn. **23**(1), 17–28 (2008)

31. Schunk, D.H., Zimmerman, B.J.: Influencing children's self-efficacy and self-regulation of reading and writing through modeling. Reading Writing Q. **23**(1), 7–25 (2007)

System of Information Systems as Support for Learning Ecosystem

Saleh Majd and Abel Marie-Hélène[(✉)]

Sorbonne Universités, Université de Technologie de Compiègne,
CNRS HEUDIASYC, UMR 7253, CS 60319, 60203 Compiègne cedex, France
{majd.saleh,marie-helene.abel}@utc.com

Abstract. Today's learners advance in an environment of fast evolving Information and Communications Technologies (ICT). These learners cannot be supported effectively by the learning strategies of the past. Knowledge is important for the progress of learners, but it is getting harder to obtain with the overwhelming amount resources produced by many Information Systems in the learning ecosystem. In order to manage the knowledge for learners we are following the approach of System of Information Systems (SoIS) as support for learning ecosystem. The SoIS gives the learning ecosystem the opportunity to explore how individual and organizational learning can be enhanced through a combination of different Information Systems in the learning ecosystem. In this context, we look into the orchestration of the SoIS that can provide the ability to index, share, and annotate important resources in the learning ecosystem. In that sense, this paper addresses the approach of System of Information Systems (SoIS) as support of learning ecosystem.

Keywords: Learning ecosystem · System of information systems · Collaboration platform

1 Introduction

1.1 Social Context

Recently, there has been unprecedented growth in learners' reliance on Information and Communication Technologies (ICT), especially web-based ICTs. Today, nearly most of the viral tasks are carried out by web-based Information Systems. This is made possible as a consequence of the recent growth of communication technologies and Information Systems. As a result, learners depend on many Information Systems to produce, work with, and manage resources. In the process of working at this manner, numerous amounts of digital resources are produced. In overall view, learners deal with huge amount of resources distributed over different Information Systems. In order to reduce this overhead, it would be useful to offer assistance to learners so that they can access the resources in an easy, time saving and organized manner. One of the possible ways in this direction concerns the sharing of information. It is therefore interesting to consider the association of different means within the framework of a learning ecosystem in order to produce knowledge from available resources. The goal is to

© Springer International Publishing AG 2017
T.-C. Huang et al. (Eds.): SETE 2017, LNCS 10676, pp. 29–37, 2017.
https://doi.org/10.1007/978-3-319-71084-6_4

allow learners manage the resources produced by different Information Systems and collaborate with each other over these resources.

1.2 Scientific Context

ICT is making many incremental changes to learning ecosystems as information and collaboration systems are introduced to learners on regular basis. This dependency on increasing numbers of Information Systems will require pooling the resources from these different systems to allow for more collaboration [6]. That will create the challenge of managing the huge amount of resources produced in the context of learning ecosystem. In the literature, this challenge is addressed using collaboration tools, recent technologies such as web 2.0 and cloud computing, and knowledge management methodologies. As an attempt to study the relation between learners and the collaboration tools available as web 2.0 technologies, [7] conducted a survey to examine learners' satisfaction and the effectiveness of collaboration systems on the learning experience. It is evident from the results that learners benefit from collaboration systems to access resources anytime and anywhere. The benefit is more when the collaboration system allows for group collaboration and supports digital conversations and discussions.

Regarding the infrastructure, [2] focuses on the advances of cloud computing to the infrastructure of learning ecosystem and the way to store its resources. Opposed to the traditional learning ecosystem, the one empowered by a cloud computing infrastructure allows for more flexible resources management. The key factor is in resources, flexibly, being distributed in many machines and Information Systems connected over a network.

Many Information Systems are being used in the environment of learning ecosystem. According to [5], learners use these systems to generate and share ideas, explore their thinking, and acquire knowledge from other learners. However, due to the failure of indexing methods, learners often fail to reach their desired resources. By using a proper indexing mechanism, learners can plan and select the appropriate resources, based on their own needs and preferences.

We can describe the current situation for learning ecosystems as a group of Information Systems that do not take into account the context of collaboration and the possibility of sharing resources [4]. So, we believe it is necessary to consider:

– The willingness to share resources with a community to achieve a common goal,
– The fact that the shared resources can come from different Information Systems.

In order to meet these needs, we propose to consider a learning ecosystem as a System of Information Systems (SoIS) developed using a collaborative model and introduce new functionalities such as sharing, indexing, annotating and voting for resources.

1.3 Plan

This paper is organized as follows: Sect. 2 presents our approach for managing heterogeneous resources in a learning ecosystem. In Sect. 3, the model of the SoIS is presented. Section 4 contains the prototype of the SoIS (It is called MEMORAeSoIS). Section 5 presents a discussion about the experiment of MEMORAeSoIS prototype with the students at the University of Technology of Compiegne. Finally, this paper is concluded with the prospective ideas and features of the SoIS in Sect. 6.

2 Our Approach

In order to find a solution for the problem of overwhelming amount of resources produced within the learning ecosystem, we aim on having a centralized access point where a learner can find, share, and index the resources. Learners can then work and collaborate with these resources. This will save time for the learner and facilitate capitalizing knowledge from different projects and sources. We use the approach of System of Information Systems (SoIS) to implement this central access point as support for the learning ecosystem. The resources accessed by the SoIS can be indexed based on a shared terminology. The learner will have the ability to index resources deemed relevant by the learner who wishes to share them. Learners can then specify why they are relevant through voting and commenting on them. The learner also can share the resources within different sharing spaces containing different members of the learning ecosystem. Other members can easily find the resources indexed and shared with them in their sharing space. All indexed and shared resources presented to the learner by the SoIS may be annotated, commented, and their usefulness can be rated. This enables community driven discussions, for example about the validity of certain resource.

Furthermore, if all the resources can be accessed from centralized platform, added value can be achieved by including a voting functionality.

As mentioned in [8], there are different approaches concerning the coordination of systems in a distributed environment such as SoIS. We choose primarily to focus on the approach of Leader/Follower. In the Leader/Follower approach, a System is designated as the leader of the orchestration of the SoIS while the other systems are designated as followers that can link to the SoIS by following the leader. According to [3], the leader system should provide an added value to the digital ecosystem in which it is operating, by allowing for more communication among the different systems participating in the SoIS. Within the context of our research, the leader system should emphasize on these points:

- Support sharing of resources.
- Support communication of different Information Systems.
- The references for shared resources should be stored and retrieved easily.

Based on these points we can view the leader system as the organizer of the SoIS. It can be considered to contain a knowledge base that holds all the necessary information of the SoIS (learners' accounts, activities log, references of shared resources, etc.). It should also control the communication line linking all member Information Systems in the SoIS. In addition, it should allow the sharing, indexing, and accessing the resources in the SoIS. Ultimately, the leader system is responsible for providing all the services for the learners in the SoIS to facilitate collaboration and learning process.

Within the environment of the SoIS, overwhelming amount of resources is shared by learners on different Information Systems. The main problem addressed by this paper is how to support the learning ecosystem of learners with the approach of SoIS, and to provide the means to index, share, annotate and vote for resources.

3   Model

As mentioned before, the model of SoIS is based on a collaborative model called MEMORAe-core2 model. The MEMORAe-core2 collaborative model was developed as part of the MEMORAe project [1]. This project aims to manage heterogeneous resources within organizations and to facilitate organizational learning. Collaboration is considered from the point of view of sharing and exchange heterogeneous resources between collaborators.

Users are modeled in MEMORAe-core2 by considering an organization as a set of interacting users. Each user can provide support to organizational learning. Each user and group of users is associated with a sharing space where the resources are visible/accessible.

Resources are modeled as "information vectors". Each resource is indexed by one or more indexing keys. A resource can be viewed based on its sharing space and index key.

When examining the model of SoIS it is useful to take into account the representation of resources in MEMORAe-core2 model and build upon it the representation of resources in SoIS. The model is presented in (Fig. 1). The model highlights the position of an agent, either as an Information System or as a user. The model also shows how resources are created by users and contained in the member systems of the SoIS, while the leader system is only showing those resources through a reference key. Each resource has a reference which functions as a link between the resource and the leader system. This key can be an HTML tag, a Database Identifier, or social bookmark as a Hash tag. The leader allows the indexing of references of resources by the index key and sharing it within different sharing spaces.

We also deployed the function of voting so that users evaluate a resource by relevance to its index and sharing space where the resource is visible. As shown in (Fig. 1), vote is a resource in the model of the SoIS. It is related with IndexKey by the relation hasTarget as shown in (Fig. 1).

The SoIS allows the users to interact with various heterogeneous resources coming from different Information Systems in many ways. The user can view the referenced resources, index the important ones, share them within different sharing spaces, annotate, comment and vote on them. An added value can be achieved by tracing the users' activities in the SoIS. The importance of these traces comes from their role in the reasoning process of the recommender system proposed by [10].

In the model of SoIS we can view the leader system as a knowledge base that handles storing, organizing, and sharing of resources from different Information Systems. MEMORAe-core2 model aims, by its design, to facilitate knowledge sharing and capitalization within those different systems (Fig. 2).

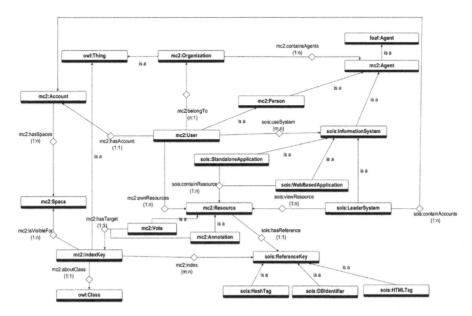

Fig. 1. Model of the SoIS.

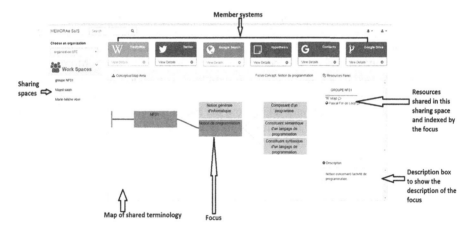

Fig. 2. SoIS prototype main screen

4   MEMORAeSoIS

The member systems of the SoIS are autonomous and work separately of each other. Each of which has its own services and databases. While some systems are openly providing an API for requesting their services, other systems are closed and operate as a black box. Information can be represented in different ways within different systems, thus, the SoIS might face some difficulties accessing resources, unless the services of that system are available through an API. More detailed illustration about the SoIS architecture can be found in [9]. The added value of the SoIS is found in the ability to index resources using a map of shared terminology among collaborators and share resources within different sharing spaces. That will give the users of the SoIS the ability to collaborate over resources and rate them. These features are not available when the Information Systems were working separately. In the premise of the SoIS the learners can share resources from different external systems and vote on them with simplicity and ease.

Other than the leader system the prototype links various Information Systems that are different in their purpose and goals, hence they produce different types of resources. These systems are: TiddlyWiki (wiki pages content management), Twitter (search for tweets by hashtag), Google Search (search the web using google search engine), Hypothesis (web page annotation tool), Google Contacts (your google contact), Google Drive (file upload and storage).

The purpose of the prototype is to provide hands-on experience for our solution to the problem of managing resources in learning ecosystem, sharing, voting for, and annotating these resources with the help of a map of shared terminology. After login, the learner can choose an organization that he/she belongs to. The learner might have one or more organizations to choose from. Based on the chosen organization, the SoIS will view a map specific to that organization and can be used to index the heterogeneous resources. The learner will also have access to the sharing spaces. For each learner there is at least two sharing spaces; one global for the whole organization and the other is the personal sharing space. Resources of the member systems are referenced in their respected tabs. The learner can view all the referenced resources for each system and index them by an index key (the index key represents a node in the map of shared terminology), and share the indexed resources in a sharing space. Moreover, on each box that is used to access a member system there is a button with a "plus" sign. This button will allow the user to navigate through all the resources available in the dedicated Information System and select from the list of resources which are going to be indexed by the map and shared in certain sharing spaces. The panel to navigate through resources is shown in (Fig. 3).

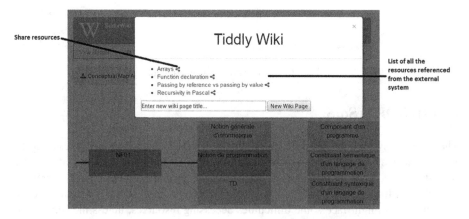

Fig. 3. Panel to access resources available in the TiddlyWiki, or create new ones.

After indexing the important resources, users are able to annotate and vote for those resources. The annotation and votes are themselves considered as resources. They, as well, can be indexed and shared in their own right.

In the platform, you can vote and comment on a resource by clicking the icon next to the indexed resource. Then you can choose a score (1 to 5) from the dropdown list, and click the vote button. You can also add a comment about this resource to justify your vote as seen in (Fig. 4).

Fig. 4. Vote and comment panel.

5 Discussion

For the prototype to be tested we currently collect feedback data from students at the University of Technology of Compiegne (UTC) to evaluate the usefulness of MEM-ORAeSoIS. The students are enrolled in a computer science course focused on the subjects of algorithms and programming. We will use their feedback on MEMOR-AeSoIS based on two aspects; a survey form, and hands-on sessions with the platform. For the setup of this test, each student is provided with an account. This account has access to a map of concepts representing the course in which students are enrolled. Students then can index, share, annotate, and vote on resources related to this course. Also, each student has three sharing spaces in the platform: a personal sharing space, a sharing space for the group in which the student belongs, and a last sharing space with the instructor of the course.

Students at UTC usually have access to an online course management and collaboration platform called Moodle. Moodle benefits the students with a learning environment that supports assignment submission, discussion forum, files download, grading, instant messages, online quizzes, and wiki. The aforementioned features help a student to post queries, search for information, read daily posts and comments, and lastly takeâ€"up an online quiz. In overall view, Moodle provides an encompassing solution for collaboration and course management in a learning ecosystem. What is missing here is a mechanism for sharing and indexing resources in a way that makes it easy for students to find and work with. MEMORAeSoIS provides this mechanism on top of its ability to connect the learner with different Information Systems that can help him/her with the learning process. MEMORAeSoIS introduces the idea of a map of shared terminology that is used to index the resources in the learning ecosystem. Furthermore, resources from Moodle can indexed and shared within MEMORAeSoIS as weblinks as seen in (Fig. 5).

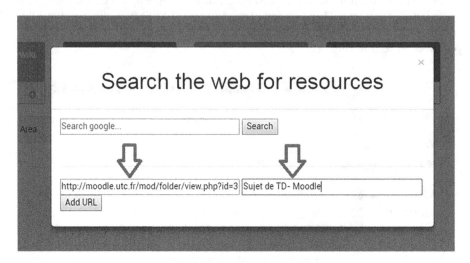

Fig. 5. Add resources from Moodle in MEMORAeSoIS.

The students themselves participate in the construction of the map in MEMOR-AeSoIS. This is also a positive point in favor of MEMORAeSoIS, as the map comes out based on students' needs and requirements. the map represents the notions to be covered in the course. It is a representation of the course content. The map was defined by the instructors. During the course, the students asked to expand the map with a branch intended for tutorials (TDs) in order to be able to index the resources related to the contents of these TDs. They can thus access the resources by the TD or by the topic treated in the TD; for example: The third TD covers the topic of conditional statements in pascal. When the students want to index resources related to this topic they can index them by the node "TD3" and the node "conditional statements".

6 Conclusion and Future Work

The goal of this paper was modeling and developing a System of Information Systems as support for learning ecosystem. The resources are the result of different learners working on different projects, using several Information Systems in the digital environment of a learning ecosystem. The aim was focused towards facilitating resources management in a System of Information Systems (SoIS), and to model and develop MEORAeSoIS. To achieve this goal this paper undertakes an effort to present the social and scientific context of this research and define the state of the art, then move to present our approach that helped in realizing the model of the SoIS composed of various Information Systems with the inspiration of MEMORAe-core2 collaborative model. This paper found potentials in adapting the MEMORAe-core2 to manage the resources produced by different systems in the SoIS. It was also clear that combining resources from various Information Systems and manage them within the leader system will result in an added value to learners not present when those systems were operating separately. The added value that we aim to achieve in MEMORAeSoIS prototype is the ability to index, share, annotate, vote, and comment on resources. Furthermore, the SoIS can upgrade this value by tracking the activities of learners and providing analysis of these activities to determine learners' competence levels at certain subjects. The prototype is being tested by the students at the University of Technology of Compiegne (UTC) to evaluate the usefulness of MEMORAeSoIS.

The next step is to expand our work to implement the learners' trace and introduce new Information Systems to MEMORAeSoIS based on the prototype presented in this paper and learners' needs. MEMORAeSoIS should keep simple interface, with all the resources as far from the user as a single click, to keep the users experience useful and friendly.

Acknowledgement. This project is done under ECOPACK project and funded by ANR-13-ASTR-0026 program.

References

1. Abel, M.H.: Knowledge map-based web platform to facilitate organizational learning return of experiences. Comput. Hum. Behav. **51**, 960–966 (2015)
2. Dong, B., Zheng, Q., Yang, J., Li, H., Qiao, M.: An e-learning ecosystem based on cloud computing infrastructure. In: Ninth IEEE International Conference on Advanced Learning Technologies, pp. 125–127. IEEE (2009)
3. Dong, H., Hussain, F.K.: Digital ecosystem ontology. In: IEEE International Symposium on Industrial Electronics, pp. 2944–2947. IEEE (2007)
4. García-Peñalvo, F.J., Hernández-García, Á., Conde, M.Á., Fidalgo-Blanco, Á., Sein-Echaluce, M.L., Alier, M., Llorens-Largo, F., Iglesias-Pradas, S.: Learning services-based technological ecosystems. In: Proceedings of the 3rd International Conference on Technological Ecosystems for Enhancing Multiculturality, pp. 467–472. ACM (2015)
5. Lau, A., Tsui, E.: Knowledge management perspective on e-learning effectiveness. Knowl.-Based Syst. **22**(4), 324–325 (2009)
6. Laurillard, D.: E-learning in higher education. In: Changing Higher Education: the Development of Learning and Teaching, pp. 71–84 (2006)
7. Liaw, S.S.: Investigating students perceived satisfaction, behavioral intention, and effectiveness of e-learning: a case study of the blackboard system. Comput. Educ. **51**(2), 864–873 (2008)
8. Lozano, R., Spong, M.W., Guerrero, J.A., Chopra, N.: Controllability and observability of leader-based multi-agent systems. In: 47th IEEE Conference on Decision and Control, pp. 3713–3718. IEEE (2008)
9. Majd, S., Marie-Hélène, A., Véronique, M., Claude, M., David, V.: Integration of brainstorming platform in a system of information systems. In: Proceedings of the 8th International Conference on Management of Digital EcoSystems, pp. 166–173. ACM (2016)
10. Wang, N., Abel, M.H., Barthes, J.P., Negre, E.: Mining user competency from semantic trace. In: IEEE 19th International Conference on Computer Supported Cooperative Work in Design (CSCWD), pp. 48–53. IEEE (2015)

A User Study About the Usage
of a Learning Management System
in a South African University

Liezel Cilliers[1(✉)], Siyanda Ntlabathi[2], and Palesa Makhetha[3]

[1] Information Systems Department, University of Fort Hare, Alice, South Africa
lcilliers@ufh.ac.za
[2] Manager Teaching and Learning, University of Fort Hare, Alice, South Africa
[3] Development Economics, University of Fort Hare, Alice, South Africa

Abstract. South African universities are increasing the number of students that are admitted to their degree programs. This came as a result of massification of higher education which in turn reduces student-lecturer interaction and ability to monitor the progress of the student. Lecturers are suing technologies such as Learning Management Systems (LMS) as the solution to support these large class environments, but seldom make the effort to pedagogically integrate the technology into the teaching and learning environment. This paper investigates to what extent a LMS has been integrated into teaching and learning at a traditional university. This paper will make use of a case study to provide descriptive insight into how a LMS has been integrated into 31 large classes in the past three years dating 2015–2017 at a traditional university. The usage patterns of lecturers making use of the LMS are examined through the user statistics that were collected during this time from course request forms. The results show that the main function of the LMS during the past 3 years was course management. The LMS was used for evaluation and communication purposes, while the collaboration and teaching categories are still underdeveloped. The recommendation is then that lecturers are encouraged to properly integrate a LMS into their teaching pedagogy, and not simply use it as a management tool.

Keywords: Teaching and learning · Traditional university · Massification · Learner management system

1 Introduction

South African universities have a problem with the throughput rate of students. The Council of Higher Education [1] has previously published that 55% of students that enter South African universities will never graduate, while only 5% of the enrolled non-white students is expected to finish their undergraduate degrees in the prescribed time [1, 2]. Fisher and Scott [3] describe higher education in South Africa as a 'low-participation, high attrition system' that is trying to correct the inequalities of the past. In order to address the skewed racial profiles at many universities, South African universities are increasing the number of students that are admitted to their degree

© Springer International Publishing AG 2017
T.-C. Huang et al. (Eds.): SETE 2017, LNCS 10676, pp. 38–42, 2017.
https://doi.org/10.1007/978-3-319-71084-6_5

programs [4]. This has resulted in the massification of higher education which in turn reduces student-lecturer interaction and ability to monitor the progress of the student [2, 5]. To solve these challenges, universities need to make use of technology, such as a Learner Management System (LMS), to improve the teaching and learning environment for their students and lecturers.

A LMS is an information system that can be used to facilitate web-based learning [6]. The LMS enable the processing, storing and dissemination of educational material and support administration and communication associated with teaching and learning [7]. While many universities in South Africa have utilized a LMS, the integration of these systems in the teaching and learning environment remains poorly understood. Many lecturers use the LMS to manage their courses or simplify assessments, but do not move beyond this initial stage to improve the communication and collaboration among students [8, 9]. The purpose of this paper is to investigate to what extent a LMS has been integrated into teaching and learning at a traditional university during the past 3 years.

2 Literature Review

The massification of higher education is a problem in both developed as well as developing countries. Altbach [4] states that there are two stages of massification that universities must address. The first stage of massification is categorised by universities struggling to cope with the increased amount of students, the need for expanded infrastructure and larger classes. The second stage involves the university coming to terms with the implications of the new diverse and often disadvantaged student body. These students need more attention than the lecturer can provide in a large class, while the progress of the student cannot be easily measured. To solve this problem, many universities have invested in LMS to enable lecturer to interact and monitor their students better.

One of the advantages of a LMS is that it can be implemented on a large scale for the entire university, with lecturers using the system to support course management and student learning [10, 11]. Some of the benefits of a LMS in higher education include [6]:

- Increased efficiency of teaching as information is more readily available;
- Cost effective;
- Improves the student's learning experience;
- Satisfy students' expectations of new technology;
- Staying competitive with other institutions; and
- Responding to the massive demand for greater access to higher education.

Blackboard was first released in 1998 and is an interactive eLearning platform that involves both the lecturer and student to create, utilise and share digital contents [12]. Blackboard consists of three sets of eLearning tools: interactive, resources and assessment tools, which El Zawaidy [13] loosely describes as communication and content functions. For a LMS to be used effectively, Wright et al. [14] stated that it was important to take "a pedagogical rather than a technological approach to support students' learning". Very often lecturers see a LMS as an eLearning portal that provide students with access to information or provide a convenient method to conduct tests rather than defining the expected learning outcomes that the LMS should support. Instead of using the LMS to manage a course, the LMS should be incorporated in the pedagogy of the teaching and learning in the classroom to support the learning needs of students [15].

3   Research Methodology

A case study design will be used for this study, describing the usage of an LMS within a teaching and learning environment. The traditional university where this study was conducted is located in the Eastern Cape. The Academic Development Centre of the institution identified Blackboard as an appropriate LMS in 2008. A case study design was seen as the most relevant in describing realities. Purposive sampling was used as all 31 cases were included in the study on the basis of their large class numbers (100 students or more). The Blackboard course request forms that had been submitted by the 31 lecturers responsible these classes for the past three years constituted the cases for the study.

Data was obtained from the Blackboard course request documents which solicit information on the number of student in the module, the rationale for the module and purpose sections for which lecturers specifically want to use Blackboard, for example, Sect. 2: asks for course code and number of students; Sect. 3: what will BB be used for e.g. resource deployment, communication, assessment, interactive student engagement, course management, and Sect. 4: How will you evaluate the intervention. Data from the documents were first analysed quantitatively and then later further analysed qualitatively. Coding was done in accordance with the categories of usage functions given within Blackboard.

4   Results

A sample of 31 large classes was used to investigate the different usages of Blackboard. The Snelbecker model was used to classify the different usages of Blackboard (5, 10). The first category, transmission of the course contents, is regarded as course management. The second and third categories are combined in the evaluation category. During the fourth category the lecturer uses the LMS to encourage class discussions (communication category) while the last category (5) deals with computer based instruction (collaboration).

Table 1 shows popularity of each usage category for Blackboard. From 2015 to 2017, course management was the most popular category followed by the evaluation and communication categories. Lecturers became more aware of the different functions of Blackboard during the 3-year period. Student-centred learning was enabled making use of collaboration functions of Blackboard in about half the large classes. Evaluation also increased by 55% during the 3-year period as more lecturers started using this function to test students. Lecturers increasingly made use of the LMS for teaching

Table 1. Total number of classes making use of blackboard

Years	Teaching	Communication	Collaboration	Course management	Evaluation
2015	5 (16%)	15 (48%)	7 (23%)	30 (97%)	9 (29%)
2016	13 (42%)	20 (65%)	10 (32%)	28 (90%)	20 (65%)
2017	17 (55%)	25 (81%)	16 (51%)	28 (90%)	26 (84%)

purposes, as attested by the 39% increase over the 3-year period. This shows that the lecturers are starting to incorporate the LMS into their teaching pedagogy. Blackboard was used for both teaching and collaboration in just more than half of the classes. While this present a significant increase in the usage of these categories, it also shows that lecturers have not incorporated the LMS into their teaching pedagogies. The university is also not offering blended learning at present.

5   Conclusion and Recommendations

This paper aimed to investigate the extent to which LMS has been integrated into teaching and learning at a traditional university by providing a descriptive insight into the usage areas of modules with large classes in the past three years dating 2015–2017 through a case study research.

The limitation of this study is that it only looked at the large classes, and did not take into consideration the smaller classes that may use Blackboard in a different way. The study also relied on the course request forms and did not interview the lecturers that may have changed their instruction method during the course of the subject. The recommendation of the study is then that the LMS is not being used to its full potential and that efforts must be made to encourage lecturers to incorporate the LMS in their teaching pedagogy. This will enable the traditional university to provide innovative teaching methods, such as blended learning, to their students and continue teaching during periods of unrest.

References

1. Higher Education South Africa: Strategic Framework for HESA. Insight, Cheltenham, pp. 1–15 (2015)
2. Council on Higher Education: A Proposal for Undergraduate Curriculum Reform in South Africa: The Case for a Flexible Curriculum Structure. CHE, Johannesburg (2013)
3. Fisher, G., Scott, I.: The role of higher education in closing the skills gap in South Africa. Background Paper 3 for 'Closing the skills and technology gap in South Africa'. The World Bank, Washington D.C. (2011)
4. Altbach, P.G.: Globalization and forces for change in higher education. The International Imperative in Higher Education. GPHE, pp. 7–10. SensePublishers, Rotterdam (2013). https://doi.org/10.1007/978-94-6209-338-6_2
5. Prosser, M., Trigwell, K.: Qualitative variation in approaches to university T & L in Large first-year classes. High. Educ. **67**(6), 783–795 (2013)

6. Coates, H., James, R., Baldwin, G.: A critical examination of the effects of learning management systems on university teaching and learning. Tert. Educ. Manag. **11**, 19–36 (2005)

7. McGill, T., Klobas, J.: A task-technology fit view of learning management system impact. Comput. Educ. **52**, 496–508 (2009)

8. Murire, O., Cilliers, L.: An evaluation of social media use in teaching and learning: a case study at a historically Black universities. In: The Conference Proceedings of UFH Centenary Conference, 4–5 July 2016. UFH, Alice (2016)

9. Nkonki, V., Ntlabathi, S., Mkonqo, L.: Explaining influences in the adoption of blackboard at an institution of higher learning. In: International Conference on e-Learning, p. 301. Academic Conferences International Limited (2013)

10. Browne, T., Jenkins, M., Walker, R.: A longitudinal perspective regarding the use of VLEs in higher education institutions in the United Kingdom. Interact. Learn. Environ. **14**, 177–182 (2006)

11. Cilliers, L.: Barriers to the implementation of a learner management system in higher education. In: ICERI2014 Conference 2014, Seville, Spain, 18–20 November 2014 (2014)

12. Kim, J., Do, J.: Learning management system: medium for interactive communication. Int. J. Appl. Eng. Res. **11**(2), 1073–1076 (2016)

13. El Zawaidy, H.: Using Blackboard in online learning at Saudi universities: faculty member's perceptions and existing obstacles. Int. Interdisc. J. Educ. **3**(7), 141–150 (2014)

14. Wright, G., Betts, H., Murray, P.: Health Informatics Masters Education, Online Learning and Student Support. IMIA Yearbook of Medical Informatics (2005)

15. Mtebe, J.S., Raisamo, R.: A model for assessing learning management system success in higher education in sub-saharan countries. Electron. J. Inf. Syst. Dev. Ctries. **61**, 1–17 (2014)

16. Cohen, L., Manion, L., Morrison, K.: Research Methods in Education. Routledge/Taylor and Francis, London/New York (2007)

Emerging Technologies Support for Intelligent Tutoring

Efficacies of 3D Immersive Virtual World Classrooms

Judy F. Chen[1]($\boxtimes$), Clyde A. Warden[2], and Hsiu Ju Lin[3]

[1] Food and Beverage Management Department,
Overseas Chinese University, Taichung, Taiwan
jfc@ocu.edu.tw
[2] Marketing Department, National Chung Hsing University, Taichung, Taiwan
warden@dragon.nchu.edu.tw
[3] Department of Applied Foreign Languages,
Chaoyang University of Technology, Taichung, Taiwan
hjlin@cyut.edu.tw

Abstract. Virtual 3D immersive virtual environments are no longer novel, with current college freshmen having grown up with virtual gaming environments. Implementing virtual world classrooms, complete with student and teacher avatars, is increasingly achievable by individual teachers. Virtual world classrooms match the effectiveness of traditional classrooms while brining an up-to-date element into the class and satisfying increasing demands for distance learning. Hotel tourism management is a good example of how virtual worlds can give students opportunities not possible in the physical classroom—allowing students to receive both lectures and perform simulations. The question addressed in this study is what are the personal experiences of mainstream students and teachers when attempting to execute and participate in such a virtual world class? Using an action research approach, we developed a rich description of student and teacher efficacy toward a virtual world 3D immersive classroom. Findings describe four main categories of student reactions: Dialogue, Convenience, Technology, and Motivation. Content analysis describes the positive and negative experiences as well as feelings that make up these categories. The specific benefits and challenges of a virtual world classroom are described, informing teachers considering adopting a virtual world classroom.

Keywords: 3D simulation · Efficacy · English as a foreign language · Hotel and tourism management · Technology training · Virtual world

1 Introduction

Role playing is quite suitable for skill obtainment in applied fields, such as tourism management (difficult to enact in a traditional classroom). Beyond skill obtainment, teachers can better capture student attention and increase motivation by employing tools college age students are quite familiar with. Growing up with massively multi-player online role-playing games (MMORPG) entertainment, today's college student is well experienced with 3D virtual worlds, where social interaction, through abstract representations of self, is quite normal. Implementing such an approach, however,

© Springer International Publishing AG 2017
T.-C. Huang et al. (Eds.): SETE 2017, LNCS 10676, pp. 45–48, 2017.
https://doi.org/10.1007/978-3-319-71084-6_6

within a university teaching environment falls outside of the normal gaming realm students have experienced. How students react to the mixture virtual worlds with class exercises and goals comprises the student-focused track of research addressed in this study.

2   Literature Review

Learning in virtual environments, even simple settings, has been found to result in equivalent learning rates compared to real-world classroom settings. Student academic achievement within a virtual world is on par with students in traditional lecture settings, even for demanding engineering classes (Okutsu et al. 2012). Simply being able to manipulate objects within a basic virtual world helps students improve skills (Pasqualotti and Freitas 2002). Feelings of presence in a virtual world do not lead to better or increased learning, but learning is not significantly worse than in physical classrooms (Persky et al. 2009), while feelings of engagement are increased as participants collaborate in ways constrained by physical school settings. Traditional classrooms make realistic role playing nearly impossible, especially for large class size. Cultural conventions can also make role playing difficult in settings where students feel loss of face or are discouraged from self expression. It is because of this ability to overcome geographic constraints and simulate non-classroom settings that teachers have adopted Second Life for simulations, such as business settings (Jin 2009).

Hospitality/Tourism Management (HTM) curriculums are heterogeneous across universities (Scott et al. 2008; Stergiou et al. 2008). One of the few commonalities, however, is an emphasis on introduction to industry standards through observation and internships. In general, HTM education is preparing students for employment in a field that is itself undergoing rapid and significant disintermediation from technology. Busby and Huang (2011) emphasized the importance of at least assuring students understand the context of these changes, i.e., technology. Virtualization of many aspects of the HTM industry has already occurred. As early as 1995, Williams and Hobson (1995) point out the opportunity for VR in tourism, emphasizing the core value of tourism is the experience, which VR can produce with increasing fidelity. Additionally, virtual augmentation is leading the way in reducing unnecessary travel, improving efficiency, and adding to travel experiences, such as Google, Bing Maps and Google Glass. Even if virtual reality is not replacing tourism, it is increasingly playing a role in consumer search and evaluation, meaning increased experience with virtual tools will improve students' job preparedness for the HTM industry.

3   Methodology

The current research frame focuses on student experience of a virtual world class, through their own voices over a semester. An existing tourism class, in an applied foreign language department, is the setting for this study. The undergraduate elective class focuses on English used in the tourism/management industry, along with concepts of tourism management and key attributes of service, such as hotel room types, customer complaints, and destination attractions. Class enrollment included 89 students (self-selected convenience sample). Valid responses included 74 students: 60 females and 14 males, with an average age of 20.47. The virtual world used for class meetings is Open Wonderland. The NVIVO software package is used for analysis and categorization of the grounded theory approach.

4   Results

Checking on the overall effectiveness of the virtual world and students' participation in it, a survey is administered to measure feelings of presence. For the survey questions concerning the feeling of presence, we employ the 7-item telepresence scale. Respondents indicated agreement with statements along a 1 to 7 scale, with 7 = agree very strongly and 1 = disagree very strongly.

The survey was administered twice in the semester, once after the second virtual world experience and then after the final virtual world meeting. The seven questions exhibited a high reliability (Cronbach's Alpha = 0.88). A t-test between the two survey results shows no statistically significant changes across the semester, with feelings of presence, showing a consistent experience. Table 1 reports the overall mean values of the two surveys, showing students felt a moderate level of presence.

Table 1. Feelings of presence during data collection period

Variable	Mean	Std dev
(A1) During the class, I felt I was in the world the computer created	3.49	1.20
(A2) During the class. I forgot that I was in the middle of a trial	3.80	1.53
(A3) During the class, my body was in the room, but my mind was inside the world created by the computer	3.19	1.17
(A4) The SIM world seemed to me "somewhere I visited" rather than "something I saw"	3.14	1.25
(A5) I felt I was more in the "SIM world" than the "real world" around me when I was doing the exercise in class	3.24	1.37
(A6) I forgot about my immediate surroundings when I was navigating through the SIM location	2.92	1.35

5   Discussion

Students are impressed with the opportunities for dialogue within a virtual world. Combining foreign language learning and professional topics (English for Specific Purposes) works well in cultural locations where self-expression in traditional classrooms is discouraged (Chen et al. 2011). It is not a coincidence that the social aspects of MOORPG are valued by students, since this is a key aspect of online gaming success, with games like World of Warcraft, attracting groups of players, called guilds (Chen et al. 2008). Introducing the social communication aspect of MOORPGs into a class with a communication aspect has clear advantages appreciated by students in this study. Simulating actions, such as hotel management, is simply impossible in the classroom setting, leading students to express excitement over the vividness of the virtual world.

6 Conclusion

Many schools are facing pressures to expand their online educational opportunities. Virtual worlds present an excellent opportunity to retain many of the benefits of classroom interaction, on the job training, and distance learning.

References

Busby, G., Huang, R.: Integration, intermediation and tourism higher education: conceptual understanding in the curriculum. Tour. Manag. **33**, 108–115 (2011)

Chen, C.-H., Sun, C.-T., Hsieh, J.: Player guild dynamics and evolution in massively multiplayer online games. CyberPsychol. Behav. **11**(3), 293–301 (2008)

Chen, J.F., Warden, C.A., Wen-Shung Tai, D., Chen, F.S.: Level of abstraction and feelings of presence in virtual space: business english negotiation in open wonderland. Comput. Educ. **57** (3), 2126–2134 (2011)

Jin, S.-A.A.: Avatars mirroring the actual self versus projecting the ideal self: the effects of self-priming on interactivity and immersion in an exergame, Wii Fit. CyberPsychol. Behav. **12**(6), 761–765 (2009)

Okutsu, M., DeLaurentis, D., Brophy, S., Lambert, J.: Teaching an aerospace engineering design course via virtual worlds: a comparative assessment of learning outcomes. Comput. Educ. **60**, 288–298 (2012)

Pasqualotti, A., Freitas, C.M.D.S.: MAT[sup 3D]: a virtual reality modeling language environment for the teaching and learning of mathematics. CyberPsychol. Behav. **5**(5), 409–422 (2002)

Persky, S., Kaphingst, K.A., McCall, C., Lachance, C., Beall, A.C., Blascovich, J.: Presence relates to distinct outcomes in two virtual environments employing different learning modalities. CyberPsychol. Behav. **12**(3), 263–268 (2009)

Scott, N.M., Puleo, V.A., Crotts, J.C.: An analysis of curriculum requirements among hospitality and tourism management programs in AACSB colleges of business in the United States. J. Teach. Travel Tour. **7**(4), 71–83 (2008)

Stergiou, D., Airey, D., Riley, M.: Making sense of tourism teaching. Ann. Tour. Res. **35**(3), 631–649 (2008)

Wang, Y., Chen, N.S., Levy, M.: The design and implementation of a holistic training model for language teacher education in a cyber face-to-face learning environment. Comput. Educ. **55** (2), 777–788 (2010)

Warden, C.A., Stanworth, J.O., Ren, J.B., Warden, A.R.: Synchronous learning best practices: an action research study. Comput. Educ. **63**, 197–207 (2012)

Williams, P., Hobson, J.: Virtual reality and tourism: fact or fantasy? Tour. Manag. **16**(6), 423–427 (1995)

Using the Gartner Hype Cycle to Evaluate the Adoption of Emerging Technology Trends in Higher Education – 2013 to 2016

Tania Prinsloo[✉] and J.P. Van Deventer

University of Pretoria, Pretoria, South Africa
{tania.prinsloo, phil.vandeventer}@up.ac.za

Abstract. The landscape of higher education is changing, with more techno-savvy students entering these institutions. The aim of this paper is to identify the trends of the Gartner Hype Cycles for Emerging Technologies for 2013 and 2016 and to compare the rate of adoption by higher education institutions worldwide. The research approach is a quantitative meta-analysis. Results indicate that higher education institutions are slow to adopt emerging technologies and rather adopt technologies once they have become common in the everyday lives of people. A possible solution is to find innovative and cheaper ways of incorporating the emerging trends in higher education.

Keywords: Gartner's Hype Cycle · Emerging technologies · Higher education

1 Introduction

Higher education is changing rapidly due to globalization and increasing internationalization [2]. The student entering higher education today is technologically much further advanced than five years ago [4]. Technology is not only embedded in their everyday lives, but also part of their higher education experience [5]. The landscape of higher education is adapting to new technologies and trends, with institutions implementing new technologies to attract students [2]. Technology adoption, however, is different for diverse technologies [1]. The aim of this article is to compare the rate of adoption of emerging technologies by higher education institutions from 2013 to 2016, to the Gartner Hype Cycle for Emerging Technologies, to determine if universities are staying ahead or lagging behind.

2 Background

Roy Amara is quoted as saying "we tend to overestimate the effect of a technology in the short run and underestimate the effect in the long run" [3]. Higher education institutions need to position themselves to remain competitive in the technological domain. One way of measuring the performance of these institutions is by comparing them to Gartner's Hype Cycle for Emerging Technologies.

© Springer International Publishing AG 2017
T.-C. Huang et al. (Eds.): SETE 2017, LNCS 10676, pp. 49–57, 2017.
https://doi.org/10.1007/978-3-319-71084-6_7

2.1   The Gartner Hype Cycle

The Gartner Hype Cycle is a graphical representation of the newest emerging technology trends worldwide and is published annually from 1995 [7]. The hype cycle starts with the overenthusiastic adopters, through five phases, until the new technology finds its use in the market [13]. Figure 1 illustrates the hype curve.

Fig. 1. The gartner hype cycle curve [13]

The five phases of the hype curve are described by Lajoie and Bridges [12].

2.2   Gartner's Hype Cycles for Emerging Technologies: 2013 to 2016

The 2013 and 2016 hype cycles are shown and elaborated on in this section to be able to look forward and backward regarding technology adoption in higher education institutions.

The 2013 Hype Cycle for Emerging Technologies
Figure 2 below describes the Hype Cycle for Emerging Technologies in 2013 [9].

The 2016 Hype Cycle for Emerging Technologies
Figure 3 below describes the Hype Cycle for Emerging Technologies in 2016 [10].

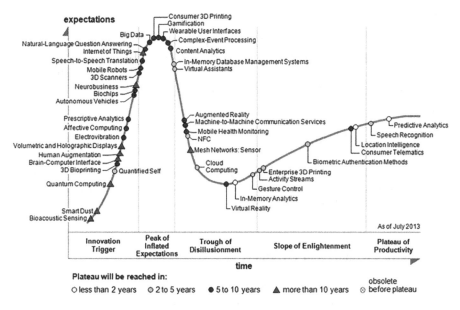

Fig. 2. Hype cycle for emerging technologies, 2013 [9]

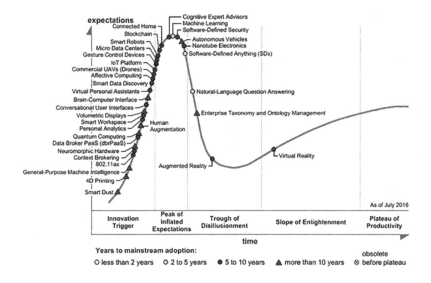

Fig. 3. Hype cycle for emerging technologies, 2016 [10]

3   Research Question

The main research question asked in this paper is: to what extend is higher education incorporating emerging technology trends compared to Gartner's Hype Cycle for Emerging Technologies?

The secondary questions are:

- How many trends identified in the 2013 Hype Cycle for Emerging Technologies have been adopted by higher education institutions from 2013 to 2016?
- How many trends identified in the 2016 Hype Cycle for Emerging Technologies have been adopted by higher education institutions from 2013 to 2016?

4   Research Methodology

The research methodology is a quantitative meta-analysis. Meta-analysis is used to synthesize quantitative information from related studies and produce results that summarize a whole body of research [6]. The selection criteria for the data gathering was:

4.1   Identify the Study and Inclusions

- To perform a specific Google Scholar search that included the words "tertiary institution" or "tertiary institutions" or "higher education" and the "keyword/s" identified in both the 2013 and 2016 Gartner Hype Cycles of Emerging Technologies [8, 10]. The dates were limited to 2013 to 2016. The search criteria had to be very specific, only searching for the term "education", for example, would lead to incorrect results.
- To identify the same keywords from the Hype Cycles in the proceedings of the International Symposium on Emerging Technologies for Education (SETE) of 2016.
- To then give the total score of results from the two sets of data above in the Total column.
- To also perform a general Google Scholar search with only the keywords from the Hype Cycles from 2013 to 2016 to see if the trends identified have been researched at all in scholarly literature and to what extent.

4.2   Exclusions

The keywords had to be present in the results exactly as they are referred to by Gartner, limiting the possible number of search results. This was done because of time- and resource constraints.

4.3   Abstract the Data from the Study

All the data was then summarized in two tables, Tables 1 and 2.

Table 1. Keyword meta-analysis of the gartner hype cycle for emerging technologies of 2013 [8]

Keyword from hype cycle	2013	2014	2015	2016	SETE 2016	Total	Total general google scholar results
On the Rise							
Bioacoustic sensing	0	0	0	0	0	0	20
Smart dust	0	0	0	0	1	1	2 820
Quantum computing	1	0	0	0	0	1	16 300
3D bioprinting	0	0	0	0	0	0	2 200
Brain-computer interface	1	0	0	0	0	1	17 100
Human augmentation	0	1	0	0	1	1	595
Volumetric and holographic display	1	0	1	0	0	2	4
Electrovibration	0	0	0	0	0	0	456
Affective computing	0	0	0	0	0	0	13 400
Prescriptive analytics	0	0	0	0	0	0	1 400
Autonomous vehicles	1	0	0	0	0	0	16 500
Biochip	0	0	0	0	0	0	15 900
Neurobusiness	0	0	0	0	0	0	61
At the Peak							
3D scanners	1	0	0	0	0	1	4 100
Mobile robots	0	0	0	0	0	0	21 000
Speech-to-speech translation	0	0	0	0	0	0	1 400
Internet of things (IoT)	2	0	0	1	0	3	46 900
Natural-language question answering	0	1	0	0	0	1	702
Big data	0	4	3	4	1	11	61 400
Consumer 3D printing	0	0	0	0	0	0	216
Gamification	0	3	2	3	1	6	16 200
Wearable user interfaces	0	0	0	0	0	0	85
Complex-event processing	0	0	0	0	0	0	6 630
Content analytics	0	0	0	0	0	0	1 040
Sliding Into the Trough							
In-memory database management systems	0	0	0	0	0	0	110
Virtual assistants	0	1	0	0	0	1	950
Augmented reality	0	1	2	3	1	7	27 100
Machine-to-machine communication services	0	0	0	0	0	0	35
Mobile health monitoring	0	0	0	0	0	0	1 350
Near-field technology (NFC)	0	0	1	1	0	2	318
Mesh networks: sensor	0	0	0	0	0	0	55
Cloud computing	4	3	8	9	0	24	74 400
Virtual reality	7	6	5	7	0	27	82 500
In-memory analytics	0	0	0	0	0	0	554
Gesture control	0	0	0	0	0	0	4 850
Climbing the Slope							
Active streams	0	0	0	0	0	0	556
Enterprise 3D printing	0	0	0	0	0	0	54
Biometric authentication methods	0	0	0	0	0	0	447
Consumer telematics	0	0	0	0	0	0	96
Location intelligence	0	0	0	0	0	0	654
Entering the Plateau							
Speech recognition	3	1	1	1	1	7	29 400
Predictive analytics	0	1	0	0	0	1	16 500

Table 2. Keyword meta-analysis of the gartner hype cycle for emerging technologies of 2016 [10]

Keyword from hype cycle	2013	2014	2015	2016	SETE 2016	Total	Total general google scholar results
On the Rise - 2016							
Smart dust	0	0	0	0	1	1	2 820
4D printing	0	0	0	0	0	0	559
General-purpose machine intelligence	0	0	0	0	0	0	1
802.11ax - next generation wireless local area networks	0	0	0	0	0	0	1 680
Context brokering	0	0	0	0	0	0	29
Neuromorphic hardware	0	0	0	0	0	0	1 120
Data broker PaaS (dbrPaaS)	0	0	0	0	0	0	1
Quantum computing	1	0	0	0	0	1	16 300
Human augmentation	0	1	0	0	1	1	595
Personal analytics	0	0	0	0	0	0	478
Smart workspace	0	0	0	0	0	0	38
Volumetric displays	0	0	0	0	0	0	732
Conversational user interfaces	0	0	0	0	0	0	41
Brain-computer interface	0	0	0	0	0	0	16 800
Virtual personal assistants	0	0	0	0	0	0	156
Smart data discovery	0	0	0	0	0	0	20
Affective computing	0	0	0	0	0	0	13 500
Commercial UAVs (Drones)	0	0	0	0	0	0	19 800
IoT platform	0	0	0	0	0	0	1 940
At the Peak							
Gesture control devices	0	0	0	0	0	0	34
Micro data centers	0	0	0	0	0	0	151
Smart robots	0	0	0	0	0	0	426
Blockchain	0	0	0	0	0	0	4 700
Connected home	0	0	0	0	0	0	2 260
Cognitive expert advisors	0	0	0	0	0	0	2
Machine learning	0	0	0	0	1	1	262 000
Software-defined security	0	0	0	0	0	0	131
Autonomous vehicles	0	0	0	0	0	0	16 600
Nanotube electronics	0	0	0	0	0	0	1 230
Software-defined anything (SDx)	0	0	0	0	0	0	51
Sliding Into the Trough							
Natural language question answering	0	0	0	0	0	0	702
Enterprise taxonomy and ontology management	0	0	0	0	0	0	1
Augmented reality	0	1	2	3	1	7	27 100
Climbing the Slope							
Virtual reality	7	6	5	7	0	27	82 500
Entering the Plateau							
None identified							

4.4   Analyze the Data Statistically

A graph was plotted to identify the adoption of the trends by higher education institutions for the results of both the Hype Curves of 2013 and 2016.

5   Results

5.1   Main Findings

Gartner's Hype Cycle 2013

The keyword meta-analysis of the Gartner Hype Cycle for Emerging Technologies for 2013 is shown in Table 1 above.

It can be noted that "Cloud Computing" and "Virtual Reality" had the highest scores. Results for "Cloud Computing" at higher education institutions showed an upward trend, while the results for "Virtual Reality" remained mostly the same annually. The only other result worth mentioning was that of "Big Data", with a total score of 11 over the four study year period. Figure 4 below graphically illustrates how the hype curve trends have been adopted by higher education institutions, with the peak at the third phase and not the second, as with the typical Gartner Hype Curve. There was not enough data to do the analysis annually, so the results were totaled.

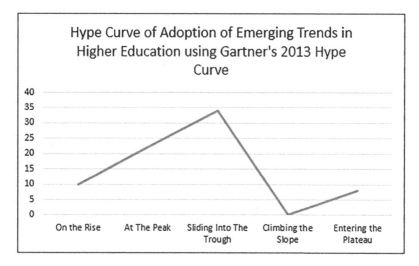

Fig. 4. The hype curve of emerging trends in higher education from 2013 to 2016 based on gartner's hype cycle for emerging technologies of 2013

Gartner's Hype Cycle 2016

The keyword meta-analysis of the Gartner Hype Cycle for Emerging Technologies for 2016 is shown in Table 2 below.

"Virtual Reality" was once again the top scorer, followed by "Augmented Reality". Only four of the other keywords scored once, namely "Smart Dust", "Quantum

Computing", "Human Augmentation" and "Machine Learning". Figure 5 below show the how the hype curve trends have been adopted by higher education institutions based on Gartner's Hype Curve for Emerging Technologies for 2016.

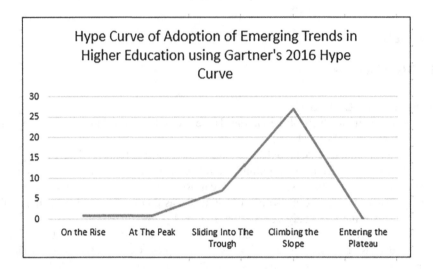

Fig. 5. The hype curve of emerging trends in higher education from 2013 to 2016 based on gartner's hype cycle for emerging technologies of 2013

It can be seen from Fig. 5 the graph looks almost the opposite of the Gartner Hype Curve, with the scores climbing in the third phase and peaking in the fourth phase. Again, the results were grouped and totaled for the four-year period.

5.2 Discussion

It is evident from Figs. 4 and 5 that higher education institutions did not adopt the newest emerging technology trends. The 2013 Hype Curve begins to resemble the Gartner Hype Cycle for Emerging Technologies for 2013, but the peak is only at the third phase and not the second phase. "Virtual Reality" and "Cloud Computing" are most adopted in both the specific Google Scholar search as well as only the keywords themselves. The 2016 Hype Curve scores only on the third and fourth phases of the Gartner Hype Cycle for Emerging Technologies for 2016, with "Machine Learning" popular in the general keyword search, but only mentioned once in the specific keyword search. The results indicate that higher education institutions tend to adopt the technologies only once they reached maturity.

6 Conclusion and Future Research

It is concluded that only a handful of trends from both the 2013 and 2016 Gartner Hype Cycle for Emerging Technologies were adopted by higher education institutions. Possible reasons include budget constraints; taking a more conservative approach to new technologies; and adopting trends after they had proved to have wide acceptance. Bill Gates adapted the quotation of Roy Amara and said "we always overestimate the change that will occur in the next two years and underestimate the change that will occur in the next ten. Don't let yourself be lulled into inaction" [11]. As higher education institutions, it is our role and responsibility to expose students to new technologies, however, time and resources may be limited. We should not lose sight of the trends, but rather focus on innovative and less expensive ways of incorporating the trends into tertiary institutions. Future research could include to update the findings annually based on the new Hype Cycles published and also to include the context of the keywords, not only the exact keywords to obtain a broader picture.

Acknowledgements. The support given by the writing clinic presented by the Department of Research and Innovation at the University of Pretoria is gratefully acknowledged.

References

1. Aldunate, R., Nussbaum, M.: Teacher adoption of technology. Comput. Hum. Behav. **29**(3), 519–524 (2013)
2. Altbach, P.G., Reisberg, L., Rumbley, L.E.: Trends in Global Higher Education: Tracking an Academic Revolution. UNESCO Pub. Sense, Paris (2009)
3. Almara, R.: Amara's Law (n.d.). http://www.pcmag.com/encyclopedia/term/37701/amara-s-law
4. Borokhovski, E., Bernard, R.M., Tamim, R.M., Schmid, R.F., Sokolovskaya, A.: Technology-supported student interaction in post-secondary education: a meta-analysis of designed versus contextual treatments. Comput. Educ. **96**, 15–28 (2016)
5. Dahlstrom, E., Walker, J., Dziuban, C.: ECAR study of undergraduate students and information technology (2013). https://library.educause.edu/ ~ /media/files/library/2014/10/ers1406.pdf
6. Egger, M., Smith, G.D.: Meta-analysis. potentials and promise. BMJ Br. Med. J. **315**(7119), 1371 (1997)
7. Fenn, J., Raskino, M.: Mastering the Hype Cycle: How to Choose the Right Innovation at the Right Time. Harvard Business Press, Brighton (2008)
8. Gartner Inc: Gartner's Hype Cycle Special Report for 2013 (2013a). https://www.gartner.com/doc/2574916?ref=SiteSearch&sthkw=Gartner%27s%20Hype%20Cycle%20Special%20Report%20for%202013&fnl=search&srcId=1-3478922254
9. Gartner Inc: Gartner's 2013 Hype Cycle for Emerging Technologies maps out evolving relationship between humans and machines (2013b). http://www.gartner.com/newsroom/id/2575515
10. Gartner Inc: Gartner's 2016 Hype Cycle for Emerging Technologies Identifies Three Key Trends That Organizations Must Track to Gain Competitive Advantage (2016). http://www.gartner.com/newsroom/id/3412017
11. Gates, B.: Bill Gates Quotes BrainyQuote (n.d.). https://www.brainyquote.com/quotes/quotes/b/billgates404193.html
12. Lajoie, E.W., Bridges, L.: Innovation decisions: using the gartner hype cycle. Libr. Leadersh. Manag. **28**(4), 1–7 (2014)
13. Linden, A., Fenn, J.: Understanding Gartner's Hype Cycles. Strategic Analysis Report No. R-20-1971. Gartner, Inc. (2003)

An Analysis of 3D-Printing Familiarity Among Students in a Technical University

Kuen-Ming Shu[1(✉)], Chi-Cheng Chang[2], and Yih-Her Yan[3]

[1] Department of Mechanical and Computer-Aided Engineering,
National Formosa University, No. 64, Wunhua Rd., Huwei, Yunlin, Taiwan
kmshu@nfu.edu.tw
[2] Department of Technology Application and Human Resource Development,
National Taiwan Normal University,
No. 162, He-Ping East Road Sec1, Taipei, Taiwan
samchang@ntnu.edu.tw
[3] Department of Electrical Engineering, National Formosa University,
No. 64, Wunhua Rd., Huwei, Yunlin, Taiwan

Abstract. Three-dimensional (3D) printing, also known as additive manufacturing, can be any 3D printing processes. Products created by commercially available 3D printing machines are mainly from plastics and macromolecule materials. Since the 3D printing technology is widespread, the application of 3D printers can be seen in all kinds of businesses, such as private enterprises, government offices, laboratories, and educational institutions. If the 3D printing technology can be included in regular curricula, students' learning motivations and achievements can be enhanced. The present study investigated technical university students' cognition about 3D printing, and proposed a low-cost 3D-metal powder printer for instructional purposes in order to improve 3D printing engineering education in Taiwan.

Keywords: 3D-metal powder printing · Instructional materials · Technical university

1 Introduction

Technical innovations resulting from the industrial revolutions have made life more convenient. The first industrial revolution in the 18th century started an era in which manpower was replaced by machines. The second industrial revolution, in the 19th century, was appliance-oriented which accelerated global economic growth. The third industrial revolution was the development of the Internet and basic and applied sciences. Today, 3D printing apparatuses become one of the most important technologies for rapid prototyping that could be useful for industry 4.0.

An object created by a 3D printer is obtained through layer-by-layer printing based on a 3D file [1], as shown in Fig. 1. This starts with the loading of a 3D CAD file, and then converts the file to the Stereo Lithography (STL) format. Afterward, the STL file is processed in horizontal x and y axes, and materials of Stereo Lithography Apparatus (powders or solids) are fed through a material sprayer, with the help of a laser light

© Springer International Publishing AG 2017
T.-C. Huang et al. (Eds.): SETE 2017, LNCS 10676, pp. 58–63, 2017.
https://doi.org/10.1007/978-3-319-71084-6_8

illuminator or an ultraviolet (UV) illuminator. Finally, the platform moves vertically in z-axis so that more material can be layer-by-layer added to the 3D object until the process is completed.

Fig. 1. 3D printing process.

2 Applications and New Research Trend on 3D Printing

To enhance learning efficiency, 3D printers are becoming a popular instructional tool [2, 3]. This not only lowers the hardware cost but also help students to shorten their design and prototyping time. With the advance in control technology and software development, the use of 3D printers in classrooms improves the effectiveness of teaching and learning on science, technology, engineering, and mathematics.

3 Analysis of Technical University Student's Cognition About 3D Printing

Participants were students enrolling in an elective general education course, named Technology and Life Application at National Formosa University, located in middle Taiwan. There was a total of 117 participants. 70% of them were males and 30% were females. 50% of the participants were engineering students, 9% electrical engineering students, 21% management students, and 20% liberal arts students. According to the results from the investigation:

1. Familiarity toward 3D printing: About 99% of the students had heard about 3D printing.
2. Reference for 3D printing: 50% of the students knowing about 3D printing from news media, 24% from newspaper and magazine reports, 26% from family and friends, 65% from academia, and 2% from other sources.
3. Usability of 3D printing: 85% of the students have no experience with 3D printers.

4. Possession of 3D printed products: 25% of the students had 3D printed products.
5. Interests of 3D printing: 89% of the students were interested in 3D printing.
6. Understanding of 3D printing processes and principles: 32% of the students did not understand, 60% slightly understood, and 8% completely understood 3D printing processes and principles.
7. Prospect of popularization of 3D printed products: 99% of the students believed that 3D printed products could be applied to and popularized more in daily life.
8. Understanding of 3D printed materials: 97% of the students believed that plastics could be printed, 60% believed that rubber could be printed, 58% believed that cement could be printed, 40% believed that chocolate could be printed, and 30% believed that cake could be printed.

4 Reasons for Promoting 3D-Metal Powder in Education

The metal 3D printing technology can overcome limitations on product applications, which enhances the practicability of 3D printing products. Although the future application for 3D printing is promising, the domestic 3D-metal-powder printing technology still remains in an initial development phase and the budget for schools is not enough to purchase such expensive equipment for instructional purposes. Therefore, in order to effectively promote engineering education, 3D-metal-powder printing teaching aids and instructional materials should be developed.

5 Principles of 3D-Metal-Powder Printers

Existing commercially available 3D printers are mainly for processing plastics and macromolecules, such as acrylonitrile butadiene styrene (ABS) and polylactic acid (PLA). Due to the low coherence of ABS and PLA, the printed products can only be simple models or parts. Principles for 3D-metal printers are shown in Fig. 2. The most

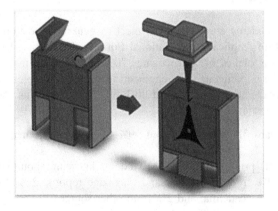

Fig. 2. Principles of 3D-metal-powder printing.

common process is the selective laser melting (SLM), in which materials such as pellets and powders are laid on the platform and melted into the desired position by a high-energy laser. And, the product is created by repeating the process with different heights of the platform.

6 Steps for Designing an Instructional Purpose 3D-Metal-Powder Printer

The steps for designing an instructional purpose 3D-metal-powder printer include

1. Choose an appropriate laser processing device that is available.
2. Use aluminum alloy to create frames and employ a 3D printer to establish a mechanism for delivering metal powder.
3. Design and manufacture a working platform and an overflow collection tank, and install them to the laser position.
4. Develop a lifting and lowering mechanism for the working platform, so that the platform can be positioned to the desired height based on the computer's command.
5. Create a teaching aid by fabricating the laser processing machine, frames, delivery mechanism, printing platform, position mechanism, vacuum pumps, and nitrogen bottle, as shown in Fig. 3.
6. Have the working platform moved to the place specifically for printing and cover with the quartz glass with vacuum pumps extracting air and filling in a protecting gas. Then, test the prototype 3D-metal-powder printer until it is working properly. Fig. 4 shows the 3D-metal-powder printer.

Fig. 3. Instructional equipment of 3D-metal-powder printing.

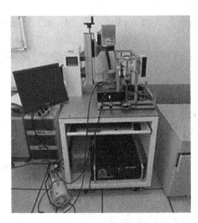

Fig. 4. A 3D-metal-powder printing machine designed by this research.

7 Knowledge and Technology That Students Can Gain

The development of the 3D-metal-powder printing technique may be divided into the following steps:

First, a 3D model can be designed by computer-assisted design software. The graphic file for the design can be cut into 3D graphic sections with the contours based on the conception of computed tomography. The contours of the sections will then be transferred to G-code in order to control the 3D printer. The G-code uses the concept of Numerical Control (NC) to control the machine. In other words, G-code is a communicative language between the operator and the NC machine. The NC code may be generated by manual keying in or by loading a computer program, and the cutting tools can be moved according to the parameter settings.

Most 3D-metal-powder printings are completed by laser sintering. The major components for the laser sintering include a sealed chamber, powder bed (A) in manufacturing area, counter, reverse rotation roller (B), cylinder (C), piston (D) in manufacturing area, powder delivery system (E), and x-y axis scanning system (F). The sealed chamber is filled with nitrogen in order to avoid explosion resulting from large amounts of powders. Furthermore, the temperature indoor is kept lower than the temperature of the melting point, which raises the temperature of laser for sintering the powders and speeds up the printing process.

During the printing, the powder delivery piston moves up about a thickness of a layer, depending on the thickness of the section of the object. The reverse rotation roller (B) spreads the powders evenly on the powder bed (A) in the printing area. The x-y axis scanning system (F) leads lasers to sinter powders in the area of the cross section of the object. The piston (D) in the printing area moves down about a thickness of a layer and repeats the steps abovementioned, and then the 3D object can be completely printed.

With the design and manufacturing process of the metal-power printer, students can learn metal powder options, material delivery design, control of the feeding amount of the metal powders, sinter's appearance design, 3D graphic file conversion, and control of sinter's laser parameters, as well as the calculation for the amount of gas extraction and delivery.

8   Conclusion

Based on the experimental results, the conclusion is presented as follows:

1. According to the investigation, technical university students had a high learning interest in 3D printing.
2. The 3D-metal-powder printing prototype developed in the project is innovative. The development process can be a useful reference to other schools in engineering education. It will not only enhance the quality of instructions but also improves the effectiveness of students' learning.

Acknowledgment. The authors would like to thank for the financial support from National Science Council of the Republic of China under the contract number MOST 105-2622-S-150-001-CC3.

References

1. Cummins, K.: The rise of additive manufacturing. The engineer, 24 May 2010. http://www.theengineer.co.uk/the-rise-of-additive-manufacturing/
2. Schelly, C., Anzalone, G., Wijnen, B., Pearce, J.M.: Open-source 3-D printing technologies for education: bringing additive manufacturing to the classroom. J. Vis. Lang. Comput. **28**, 226–237 (2015)
3. Grujović, N., Radović, M., Kanjevac, V., Borota, J., Grujović, G., Divac, D.: 3D printing technology in education environment. In: Proceeding of 34th International Conference on Production Engineering, pp. 323–326. University of Nii, Faculty of Mechanical Engineering (2011)
4. Irwin, J., Pearce, J.M., Opplinger, D., Anzalone, G.: The reprap 3-D printer revolution in STEM education. Paper Presented at 121st ASEE Annual Conference and Exposition, Indianapolis, IN. Paper ID #8696 (2014)
5. Zhang, C., Anzalone, N.C., Faria, R.P., Pearce, J.M.: Open-source 3D-printable optics equipment. PloS One **8**(3), e59840 (2013)

Lecturers Perceptions on Blackboard: An Investigation of Blackboard Usage in a Nursing Department at a Traditional University

Liezel Cilliers[(✉)] and Elzette van Niekerk

Information Systems Department, University of Fort Hare, Alice, South Africa
lcilliers@ufh.ac.za

Abstract. Online learning environments have become an established presence in higher education, but their effectiveness in the teaching and learning environment must still be evaluated. A learner management system can be used to provide course content, evaluate the students and course, improve collaboration and blended learning environments. These functions are especially important for nursing students that have practical obligations that take them away from the campus. The purpose of this article is then to evaluate the perceptions of nursing lecturers at a traditional university in South Africa after they first started using a LMS. Perceptions of nursing lecturers were assessed making use of focus groups. The research evaluated the perceptions of the staff during a focus group after they participated in 3 workshops that trained them to make use of Blackboard. The results show that staff had a favourable view of the learning management system but needed more assistance than what was anticipated initially. These implications for teacher education staff interested in providing high quality learning environments within an online space are provided.

Keyword: Learner management system · Blackboard · Nursing department · Traditional university

1 Introduction

Learning management systems (LMS), such as Blackboard, are at the forefront of these technological developments as it enables HEI to incorporate technology into traditional lecture based courses, provide resources for distance learners and introduce blended learning [1–3]. Blended learning is especially important in courses such as nursing where students are expected to participate in practical work which is conducted off campus. A LMS allows for technology mediated instruction in these cases as students can access resources off-campus allowing them to continue with their studies [4].

While LMS are popular in Higher Education, it is also very expensive to implement which means that it is important to understand how a LMS can be used to its full potential. The LMS offer an interactive medium of learning which can be customised by each lecturer to meet the need of their particular class [4]. However, the LMS must be incorporated correctly into traditional teaching practices in order to be efficient [2].

© Springer International Publishing AG 2017
T.-C. Huang et al. (Eds.): SETE 2017, LNCS 10676, pp. 64–71, 2017.
https://doi.org/10.1007/978-3-319-71084-6_9

In addition, the LMS must also be managed by the lecturer in order to be effective. Literature suggests that the current state of use tend to focus on administration purposes or delivery of course content rather than improving pedagogical tasks [4–7]. The purpose of this article is then to evaluate the perceptions of nursing lecturers at a traditional university in South Africa after they first started using a LMS. While the LMS has been implemented at the university for almost 10 years, the nursing department only recently started promoting e-learning, and in particular the LMS, to improve teaching and learning. The perceptions of Blackboard from this new user group of lecturers can be used as a baseline to plan future interventions to increase the use of the LMS at the university. The rest of the paper is structured as follow: the literature that discusses LMS systems is next, followed by the discussion of the the-oretical foundation of the paper. The methodology and discussion of results follows after which the paper concludes.

2 Literature

A LMS can be implemented on a large scale at a higher institution in order to support course management and student learning [8]. There are several commercial LMS available, such as Blackboard, NextEd, Sakai and WebCT Vista [9]. It is estimated that in South Africa between 55% and 62% of higher education institutions make use of WebCT or Blackboard. The faculties where a LMS is most popular are the faculties of commerce; education and health as these areas often need to provide mixed-mode or off-campus delivery of course work [5].

Lecturers have reported that they are able to interact with and monitor their students better when they make use of a LMS. Some of the benefits of a LMS in higher education include [10]: increased efficiency of teaching as information is more readily available; cost effective; improves the student's learning experience; satisfy students' expectations of new technology; staying competitive with other institutions; and responding to the massive demand for greater access to higher education.

Blackboard was first released in 1997 and is an interactive eLearning platform that allows both the lecturer and student to create, utilise and share digital contents [11]. Blackboard consists of three sets of eLearning tools: interactive, resources and assessment tools, which El Zawaidy [12] loosely describes as communication and content functions. Interactive, or collaborative learning, is supported by most LMS, but very few lecturers actually make use of this feature. Interactivity can be classified into four types which include learner-content, learner-instructor, learner-learner, and learner-interface [13]. These interactions can occur synchronously or asynchronously and include features such as announcements, discussions, virtual classroom, chat and email [4]. Resource tools are used by lecturers to generate content for their classes; collect informational resources and pass it onto students; and schedule weekly modules or tasks [7]. Assessment tools, such as automated tests, e.g. multiple choice tests, can be marked by the system. This type of test, while it does have a place, also reinforces positivist epistemological assumptions and should not be used as the dominant form of testing and feedback in higher education. The majority of LMS implemented in African countries has not been successful as very few lecturers make use of the system when it is available [14]. Universities in Nigeria, Zimbabwe and Ghana have all reported low usage rates of LMS among lecturers [14–16]. Reasons for the failure of LMS systems in Africa have been identified in Table 1.

2.1 Individual Challenges

For a LMS to be used effectively, Wright et al. [17] stated that it was important to take "a pedagogical rather than a technological approach to support students' learning". Lecturers are often more familiar with transmitting information and assessment using technology than creating computer-based interactions or discussion forums which enforces traditional teaching models [4]. One of the most cited problems associated with a LMS is that despite the availability of the technology to improve teaching and learning, lecturers have not incorporated the LMS in their pedagogical practice in order to take advantage of the functionalities provided by the technology [8]. There has been very little effort in the past to analyze the impact of LMSs on teaching practices and pedagogy in higher education [18]. Rather, the research that has been conducted focused either on the technology itself, or the adoption of the LMS in the institution.

One of the key limitations of a LMS is the difficulty associated with learning how to use the system [4]. There are two phases to this learning process as the lecturers must first learn how to use the new technology and then how to incorporate it into their teaching pedagogies. Many lecturers do not have the motivation or time to become expert users of LMS. This means that the lecturers does not move away from technical issues towards pedagogical concerns and subsequently do not use the LMS in more create ways to improve teaching and learning [19].

Blackboard is viewed as a supplementary teaching tool which is mostly used to search for the material, notify students to write assignments, and used for drill and practice exercises [20]. Lecturers are not using the LMS to promote student-centered learning to improve teaching, but may even fear that online interactions will replace face-to-face interaction between the lecturers and students [19]. This perception is perpetuated by LMS report capabilities that make use of quantitative data in disconnected datasets (e.g. page hits, total postings), and not in learning orientated data visualization methods. This makes it difficult for lecturers to identify and visualise the impact of the LMS activities on student engagement [10].

3 Methodology

The study made use of a case study based designed. The traditional university, situated in the Eastern Cape, implemented Blackboard in 2009, but it was not until recently that the Department of Nursing decided to actively make use of the LMS [21]. The department has not made use of Blackboard as a teaching tool on a consistent basis. In 2016, a facilitator was appointed within the department to champion the use of e-learning. The facilitator has embarked on a variety of activities to teach and support the nursing lecturers to make use of Blackboard. The teaching activities include one on one sessions, group sessions and focus groups where lecturers are encouraged to share their success stories. Support is provided through individual consultations and a learning guide that was developed by the facilitator that can be used by the individual to refresh their Blackboard skills when needed.

The e-learning specialist in the Faculty of Health Sciences did Blackboard training with the lecturers of the Department of Nursing, starting in November 2016. There was 5 one-day training session where all the lecturers from the Nursing Department, ranging from year 1–4, took part in the training. The initial session had 20 attendees. The training started with the introduction to Blackboard and the various functions available. During the training the participants were shown how to personalize their courses and how to add content to the course modules in the form of Power- Point slides, videos, images etc. A manual for the lecturers was developed with step by step instructions on how Blackboard works.

At the beginning of 2017, the training sessions continued with 12 attendees. During the second session the lecturers could load their own content onto Blackboard. The majority of the lecturers loaded study material and study guides for the students. The Announcements feature of Blackboard was used to introduce themselves to the students and to welcome them to the New Year.

The third workshop focused on how to load Assignments and how to grade these after submissions. There were 10 lecturers present during this training session. The lecturers were given assignments and practiced on how to load it onto their courses. The participants were asked to log onto the system as students and pretended to submit the final assessment. It helped them to actually see how the students would access it. For Assessment purposes the Grade Centre of Blackboard was introduced, where the lecturers could see the uploaded Assignment and were shown how to grade the Assignments.

During the last workshop the lecturers were shown how the set tests where the student or course can be evaluated. The advantage of this assessment method is that the LMS will mark the assessment automatically when it closes. Other features of Blackboard that will be taught in future courses include Discussion groups, Wiki's and Journals, etc.

The data collection for this study was conducted making use of a 90-min focus group where 9 lecturers were present. A convenience sampling method was used as all the lecturers that had participated in the workshops were invited to attend the focus group. The facilitator made use of semi-structured interview questions to guide the conversation while the participants were given an opportunity to show the rest of the groups what they have done with the LMS for their courses. A laptop and projector was available to the participants for this purpose. The interview was recoded with the permission of the participants and later transcribed. The transcriptions were analysed making use of thematic content analysis. The themes that were identified from the text are discussed in the next section.

4   Discussion

The purpose of this article is then to evaluate the perceptions of nursing lecturers at a traditional university in South Africa after they first started using a LMS. McLoughlin and Lee (2008) stated that "currently, e-learning pedagogies at universities and colleges appear to be fuelled largely by learning management systems (LMS's) that replicate these traditional paradigms in an online setting. They conform to a "student-as-information consumer" model, thus reinforcing instructor-centred approaches to teaching, learning and knowledge, as opposed to being conducive to constructivist modes of learning that enable a high degree of learner self-direction and personalisation."

The lecturers indicated that they found Blackboard to be a useful tool to improve teaching and learning. The functions that were used most often were to provide information, notes and articles to students; announcements regarding course work; assignment submissions and evaluation of the students. These activities are all in the first (transmission of course content) and second level (student evaluation) of Snelbecker's model which is to be expected since the group has not progressed to the further levels in the workshops yet. Interestingly, the Academic Assessment Centre at the university do encourage lecturers to make use of Blackboard for course evaluations, but none of the lecturers had made use of this option. What also became evident is the while the students were on strike during #Feesmustfall, Blackboard became vital because now the lecturers could load their content for the students while they were not attending classes. In the past the notes were loaded onto the V-drive and the students could only assess it in the library. Students were prevented from accessing the library during the strike and now they could access their notes without any hassles. None of the lecturers considered using Blackboard for a blended approach to learning, but simply wanted to distribute their course content.

Lecturers acknowledged that Blackboard do provide user statistics, such as number of views for each student, but none seem to understand that these statistics could be used for purposes other than to check if students could access Blackboard if they did not submit an assignment on time. Lecturers did not use this information in a punitive way e.g. to check if the student is lying about the reason why they could not access Blackboard, but rather to make sure that their student cohorts could access the information as is illustrated in the next quote by participant A:

'I can track the views of the students to see how many students were able to access assignments.'

This view could be indicative of the lack of confidence that lecturers have in their own ability to load assignments and tests which is understandable as they have only started to use the LMS during the past few months. A few of the participants did indicate that the learner guide that was provided during the workshops were valuable to refresh their skill. Some also indicated that a similar guide for the students would be helpful to improve their skill.

The second theme that was identified during the interviews have to do with the function of Blackboard to set a submission date and time for assignments. The lecturers mostly made use of paper submissions before the LMS was introduced, which allowed the students more flexibility with the hand in procedure. While the lecturers were happy with the different types of tests that were available, Participant B summarised the anxiety of the students when they first started making use of Blackboard with the following comment:

"They (the students) were worried and fighting amongst themselves. Once I told them how the system works, they were relieved and continued to submit for me."

The need to manage the transition from paper based to electronic submission needs to be managed by the lecturer to decrease this anxiety. The help guide can also play an important role in this process.

The third theme is centred around the positive impact that the LMS can make on the ability of the lecturer to track large classes. Many of the lecturers felt that the LMS provided them with enough information to track students' progress and identify those students that need additional assistance. Lecturers further elaborated on this theme with the purpose of self-evaluation where the student can mark themselves making use of a preloaded rubric and then compare this mark to that of the lecturer. Participant had this to say about self-evaluation:

"It makes them (the student) think about what they write. If they give themselves 10/10 and you think they got nought, you have something to discuss."

The fourth theme identified all the problems that the lecturers had with Blackboard. The lecturers felt that there were inconsistencies in the system that meant that not all the students could see the attachments or assessments. Once the facilitator demonstrated these tasks, some of the lecturers did acknowledged that they may not have uploaded the attachments and assessments correctly. However, they did not know how to identify if something was wrong and had to wait for the students to report these problems. A further problem was the lack of experience that the students had regarding Blackboard. The students had not used Blackboard before, and many complained that they did not know how to upload assignments. Lecturers felt that even if they spent time in class demonstrating to student how to do this, there would be students that are absent due to practical commitments and they would fall behind. In general, the group agreed that there was not enough training for students on how to use Blackboard. In response to this problem, many lecturers allowed the students to submit via e-mail as well in case their Blackboard submission failed.

5   Conclusion

In general, the lecturers 'perception of the LMS was very positive. The advantages of the LMS for teaching as reported by the lecturers included efficiency of communication, storage of materials, access to materials, engagement, instant feedback, and out of class interactions. Area of concern reported by the staff included the user-friendliness of the system and navigation problems especially for the students. The use of a help guide for both lecturers and students were provided as a solution to the possible problems experienced by these groups. None of the lecturers made use of the LMS for course evaluation, discussion groups or computer based instruction even though they acknowledge the benefit that these categories would provide to their teaching. In general, while the perceptions of the lecturers where positive, none had incorporated the LMS in their pedagogical practices, but were using the LMS for course management.

References

1. Cele, N., Cilliers, L.: Providing sustainable information technology services in higher education in a developing country. In: Proceedings of the South African Institute of Management Scientists (SAIMS), 30 August–1 September 2015, Cape Town (2015)
2. Coates, H.: A model of online and general campus-based student engagement. Assess. Eval. High. Educ. **32**(2), 121–141 (2007)
3. Malikowski, S.R., Thompson, S.R., Theis, J.G.: A model for research into course management systems: bridging technology and learning theory. J. Educ. Comput. Res. **36**(2), 149–173 (2007)
4. Heirdsfield, A., Walker, S., Tambyah, M., Beutel, D.: Blackboard as an online learning environment: what do teacher education students and staff think? Aust. J. Teach. Educ. **36**(7), 1–16 (2011)
5. Wright, G., Van Niekerk, E., Cilliers, L., Seekoe, P.: The next stage of development of e-learning in South Africa. In: Proceedings of 11th International Conference on e-Learning 2017, Lisbon, Portugal, 1–3 August 2017 (2017)
6. Ottenbreit-Leftwich, A.T., Glazewski, K.D., Newby, T.J., Ertmer, P.A.: Teacher value beliefs associated with using technology: addressing professional and student needs. Comput. Educ. **55**(3), 1321–1335 (2010)
7. Norton, P., Hathaway, D.: Exploring two teacher education online learning designs: a classroom of one or many? J. Res. Technol. Educ. **40**(4), 475–495 (2008)
8. Browne, T., Jenkins, M., Walker, R.: A longitudinal perspective regarding the use of VLEs in higher education institutions in the United Kingdom. Interact. Learn. Environ. **14**, 177–182 (2006)
9. Dawson, S., Heathcote, L., Poole, G.: Harnessing ICT potential: the adoption and analysis of ICT systems for enhancing the student learning experience. Int. J. Educ. Manag. **24**(2), 16–29 (2010)
10. Cilliers, L.: Barriers to the implementation of a learner management system in higher education. In: ICERI2014 Conference 2014, Seville, Spain, 18–20 November 2014 (2014)
11. Kim, J., Do, J.: Learning management system: medium for Interactive communication. Int. J. Appl. Eng. Res. **11**(2), 1073–1076 (2016)
12. El Zawaidy, H.: Using blackboard in online learning at Saudi Universities: faculty member's perceptions and existing obstacles. Int. Interdisc. J. Educ. **3**(7), 141–150 (2014)
13. Ellis, R.A., Ginns, P., Piggott, L.: E-learning in higher education: some key aspects and their relationship to approaches to study. High. Educ. Res. Dev. **28**(3), 303–318 (2009)
14. Ssekakubo, G., Suleman, H., Marsden, G.: Issues of adoption: have e-learning management systems fulfilled their potential in developing countries? In: Proceedings of the South African Institute of Computer Scientists and Information Technologists Conference on Knowledge, Innovation and Leadership in a Diverse, Multidisciplinary Environment, Cape Town, South Africa, pp. 231–238 (2011)
15. Bhalalusesa, R., Lukwaro, E.E., Clemence, M.: Challenges of using e-learning management systems faced by the academic staff in distance based institutions from developing countries: a case study of the Open University of Tanzania. Huria J. OUT **14**, 89–110 (2013)
16. Kotoua, S., Ilkan, M., Kilic, H.: The growing of online education in sub Saharan Africa: case study Ghana. Procedia-Soc. Behav. Sci. **191**, 2406–2411 (2015)
17. Wright, G., Betts, H., Murray, P.: Health informatics masters education, online learning and student support. IMIA Yearb. Med. Inf. (2005)
18. McGill, T., Klobas, J.: A task-technology fit view of learning management system impact. Comput. Educ. **52**, 496–508 (2009)

19. Mohsen, M.A., Shafeeq, C.: EFL teachers' perceptions on blackboard applications. Engl. Lang. Teach. **7**(11), 108–119 (2014)
20. Koc, M.: Student teachers' conceptions of technology: a metaphor analysis. Comput. Educ. **68**, 1–8 (2013)
21. Nkonki, V., Ntlabathi, S., Mkonqo, L.: Explaining influences in the adoption of Blackboard at an institution of higher learning. In: International Conference on e-Learning, p. 301. Academic Conferences International Limited (2013)

Emerging Technologies Support for Game-Based and Joyful Learning

The Use of a Learning Management System to Facilitate Student-Driven Content Design: An Experiment

Riana Steyn[✉], Solly Millard, and Joyce Jordaan

University of Pretoria, Pretoria 0002, South Africa
riana.steyn@up.ac.za

Abstract. Technology is everywhere, we only need to look around and observe the world around us. Teaching any course today cannot be done without some form of technology incorporated, if not the central point of delivering material and content to students.

Everywhere we look, students are sitting on their phones, or with tablets, why not allow students to use these devices to enhance their education, and learn something from the time they spent looking at a screen?

This paper explores this notion of allowing students to use a blackboard learning management system (LMS) as well as any other relevant technology and design their own "textbook chapter" based on a specific theme or topic provided to them. A hybrid approach was adopted as an experiment to see how the lecturers can use an LMS to improve their students' experience of using the LMS in an attempt to improve their own knowledge.

Students felt blackboard assisted them to understand the context and in particular felt that this assignment assisted them to understand the topic "use cases" better. In the end, the main goals were to ensure that students used technology to grasp the content and this was indeed the case.

Keywords: Blackboard · Hybrid learning · Learning management system · Student · Teaching approach

1 Introduction

The approach to teaching has long been based on the model of handing a student a textbook which includes all the content required for the term, semester or even year. But in today's world where one cannot have any discipline free from technology, can this model still be followed? Technology is everywhere, we don't need a reference to state that, we only need to look around and observe the world around us. Going to a coffee shop or restaurant, it is almost scary to see how many people are busy with their phones and not talking to the person sitting opposite them. The same can be said for the classrooms. Everywhere we look, students are sitting on their phones, or with tablets, and even the "uncool" student has a laptop... who uses that any more... On a more serious note, this is reality for us as educators, the reality of the students we work with

© Springer International Publishing AG 2017
T.-C. Huang et al. (Eds.): SETE 2017, LNCS 10676, pp. 75–94, 2017.
https://doi.org/10.1007/978-3-319-71084-6_10

are "always on/never off" as coined by Ashraff [1] and Pullan [2] and these are the students we see every day. Linking onto this, Turpie [3] said that "new technology and digital media engage young people from the day they enter the world" in other words, they are almost born with a phone in the hand. The students referred to here are the millennials which are "the first generation growing up with the internet" [2].

A non-academic reference on Wikipedia calls these students generation Z [4]. This is the "new era" we are living in and it will only get better or "worse" depending on your viewpoint. So why not allow students to use these devices to enhance their education, and learn something from all the time they spent looking at a screen? Puttnam [5] rightfully states that "if we want to win back the trust of young people, we need to engage far more effectively with their world – learn to view technology, and the way in which they relate to it – through their eyes." Why not use the time spent on screens more productively and allow them to create their own learning material, their own e-books, which are increasingly used throughout the world [6].

Many universities in western countries are forced to engage in a blended-learning environment where technology-mediated learning and face-to-face sessions have to merge [7]. Kirkwood and Prince [8] also noted that technology is no longer a field only for the enthusiasts or novel users, all lecturers should engage with technology. Laurillard [9] realised the importance to understand this new context of technology and mention that we should find means to embed our understanding of technology with the existing classroom. As tertiary education institutions we have to find ways of not just asking students to use technology to replicate known content, which seems a bit historic, but allow them to use these technologies in "disruptive" ways [5], even if that means to allow them to create their own content which they would then use to grasp the concepts better. Davidson et al. [10] talks about the notion of getting students to become "active participants in the learning process", and not just having them sit in a classroom, listening to a lecturer and then repeating the theory back to the lecturer. This paper explores this notion of allowing students to use a blackboard learning management system (LMS) as well as any other relevant technology and design their own "textbook chapter" based on a specific theme or topic provided to them. A hybrid approach was adopted as an experiment to see how the lecturers can use an LMS to improve their students' experience of using the LMS in an attempt to improve their own knowledge.

The research question addressed in this paper is: can student learning increase from using a LMS to build their own content?

This paper will firstly discuss literature concerning hybrid learning approaches and collaborative learning after which the LMS used will be introduced. This paper will focus on the tools used in creating the "own" textbook chapter, as a means to gain a better understanding of the student's experience of the project. It will also see whether or not the students felt that there was value in building their own content and if such an approach enhanced their learning experience. The literature section will be followed by the methodology section after which the data analysis will be discussed and then this paper will conclude.

2 Background

2.1 Hybrid Learning Approach

Teaching any course today cannot be done without some form of technology incorporated, if not the central point of delivering material and content to students [11].

Blended learning, hybrid learning, e-learning … which one it is? According to Moodley et al. [11], there are numerous terms which in the end means the same approach. Bonk and Graham [12] defines blended learning as the combination of "face-to-face instructions with computer-mediated instruction". Bender [13] talks about hybrid learning, where a course that has face-to-face classes on campus, has an additional web-component linked to the course. Woods et al. [14] confirms this by talking about web-based augmentation of the traditional classroom setting. This way one can continue with the class even when the class time or contact time has stopped. Bender [13], Rosenberg [15] and Wilson [16] talks of the best of both worlds, this phenomenon of combining physical classroom interactions with some sort of web component.

Some of the benefits which hybrid learning can bring about is noted as an improvement to large classroom efficiency, increase in student-led learning approaches, improvement of the overall student morale and satisfaction, student achievement and skills acquisition is enhanced and it even seem as if withdrawal and absenteeism is reduced [14]. They continue to say that in the future all institutions will engage in what they call a 90-10 rule, thus there will not be 100% face-to-face or 100% online but a mix of these two approaches.

Laurillard [9] says one must focus on the traditional learning theory which basically says "what it takes to learn". Almost forget all the other jargon, and come back to the basics of teaching and learning and ask what it takes to learn. She continues to say that the adaption of technologies for learning should ultimately address this question.

According to Bender [13] there are certain characteristics which one has to take into account when working with students and incorporating a hybrid approach. These characteristics are:

- Independence and responsibility: Insecure students prefer more contact time with a lecturer and receive more authoritative guidance from the lecturer;
- Authoritarianism: An authoritarian student wants to listen to a lecturer who controls their teaching;
- Anxiety: An anxious student prefers highly structured environments and the more anxious, the bigger the desire for structure, support and encouragement. This tends to fluctuate throughout the semester;
- Intelligence: Students are seen as individual learners who bring various diversities into the classroom. Online learning also brings about different learning styles which should foster interactive learning and collaboration. It is seen that "*good teaching should be cognizant of and tailored to the diversity of learners*" [13];
- Motivation: Class room scenarios brings about peer pressure where online learning has a much bigger focus on self-reliance. Pullan [2] also notes that online learners tend to have a higher level of internal motivation. Lam et al. [17] found that

collaboration had a positive influence on motivation to learning. It would be interesting to see what the peer pressure effect was in the online group-assignment, as discussed in this paper;

- Introversion-extroversion: Introverts learn better when "fed" the information where extroverts learn better when working with their peers, typically also extroverts. However, on the flip-side, it seems as if introverts care much more for feedback than extroverts. It will be interesting to see if there is a correlation between introvert/extrovert and motivation as well as learning preferences in this paper;
- Gender: There seems to be a correlation between gender and achievement as it is said that females are more concerned about achievement than their male counterparts. Although this will make for an interesting study, this paper does not focus on gender studies and thus it will not be discussed in detail in this paper;
- Cognitive style: Learning facts tend to result in the need for contact time with the lecturer. It will be interesting to see how these students study and prefer to learn.

Continuing, Pullan [18] also notes the following characteristics for online learners: self-motivation, taking full responsibility and commitment. She continues to say that students today are hybrid learners, who take both campus-based and online courses. Thus one needs to realise that these students want to learn online, and they will do that anyway, the question is how we can include a hybrid learning approach into our "old" teaching approach to help the student better grasp the content.

Riffel and Sibley (2005) as cited in Wilson [16] found that online task-oriented assignments led to the same or in some cases better outcomes than just following the traditional method of lecturing. They continue to say that online students made use of the textbook in more cases, contacted other students for help more and more frequently worked in groups outside the classroom. Hybrid learning is seen as a technique which can be followed when introducing an active learning strategy [19] which in essence is allowing students to do certain activities and reflect on what they are doing. It is noted that teachers facilitate learning, but the students have to take responsibility for the actual learning. Although they defined active learning in the end as an in classroom activity, they also noted that it might continue outside of the classroom. This paper focuses on the notion of continuing the "in class teaching" with a combination of online notes and using features of Blackboard such as blogs and wikis, to facilitate further or continues learning.

This paper will focus on the following student characteristics to determine if these are relevant to the students:

- Responsibility/independence;
- Authoritarianism;
- Anxiety;
- Motivation;
- Introvert/extrovert;
- Cognitive style.

There is however a flip-side to this approach, a blended learning or hybrid approach allows students to control their own time and place for learning [11], providing a proper infrastructure is the reason for successful blended learning approaches. This paper will further investigate the infrastructure used by the students to complete the assignment as this cannot be ignored especially in the South African context.

This paper will from now on talk about a hybrid-approach to eliminate any confusion.

2.2 Learning Management System

Using a new technology can be a daunting task, this could even hinder the learning process or experience of using the system. However, over time and as one becomes more familiar with the technology, one can start to focus more on the content than on figuring out how the system works [13].

That being said, as mentioned earlier, the type of student we engage with today is very different from the student type of ten, even five years back. In 2009, Selwyn [20] notices that the 21st century student learns in ways far removed from a formal setting such as a school or library. The processing skills which these student poses or have developed are essentially different from the "older" generation IT users. Already in 2001 Prensky [21] acknowledged that students think and process information on a totally different level, and that was nearly 17 years ago. Ashraf [1] mentions techno-savvy and digitally-literate students, and linking them back to lecturers, "students demand excellent, inspired, interactive teaching" [1]. Students born between 1980 and 2000, called the Millennial generation [22], are the students sitting in our classrooms today. Pacansky-Brock [22] listed some interesting facts based on the American student of today: 94% of them are internet users, 94% have cell phones, and 83% are active users of social networking. Junco and Mastrodicasa (2007) as cited in Pullan [2] did a study amongst 7 705 students which resulted in the following interesting statistics: 97% of students have computers, 76% use instant messaging, 34% of the students use websites as their primary source of news and thus emphasising the fact that "these student live online" [2].

This proof that students are engaged online most of the day, they are connected the whole time. It is for this reason that the researcher wanted to explore ways to use technology to grow the students' learning experience and knowledge as they are already connected.

An urban university in South Africa used Blackboard as their Learning management system (LMS). Blackboard was founded in 1997 [23] with their vision being "a user-friendly means by which college professors could put course information, including syllabi, reference sites and study guides on the web". It is estimated that in North America, Blackboard controls up to 80% of the academic course management system market.

There are numerous benefits of using Blackboard as the learning management system, as mentioned by Bradford [23] which are:

- Increased availability;
- Access to the internet anytime and anywhere;
- Quick feedback;
- Improved communication;
- Tracking;
- Skills building.

Although Blackboard is the LMS used at the tertiary institution in focus, it is important to understand where Blackboard fits into the learning process when viewed from a pedagogical point of view. According to Laurillard [9] the learning process is characterised as:

- "instructionism": influenced technology being used for presentations and testing;
- "constructionism": learning by constructing a model or object, thus using some kind of modelling tool programming language;
- "socio-cultural learning": using communities as a form of learning through discussion;
- "collaborative learning": combining constructionism and socio-cultural learning, using the technologies that support both.

She continues to say that if you apply all these approaches, you are following "the conversational framework" [9] which takes all the complexities of these pedagogies and shows the complexity of the learning process in one view. However, this paper will focus on the four learning processes as discussed above and indicate why certain aspects of the assignment were asked and why students had to complete the tasks in a specific way.

Blackboard is the LMS used by the urban University where this study was conducted and is often referred to as ClickUp. Blackboard offers a vast number of functions, although the ones explored in this paper were wikis, blogs and group collaboration which have not been used actively yet in the course. The research approach follows.

3 Research Approach

As part of a second year course called "Systems analysis and design" which is being presented at an urban University, one of the key concepts which students have to grasp and struggle with is "Use cases diagrams and narratives". Due to the fact that the lecturing staff realised that there is a shortage of well-structured textbook for their degree, the idea of creating a student-led textbook emerged. The students had to complete an assignment focusing specifically on Use cases. Some of the key objectives of the course are:

- Describe the benefits of use-case modelling;
- Define actors and use cases and be able to identify them from context diagrams and other sources;
- Describe the relationships that can appear on a use-case model diagram;
- Describe the steps for preparing a use-case model;
- Describe how to construct a use-case model diagram;
- Describe the various sections of a use-case narrative and be able to prepare one;
- Apply all the above study objectives to a case study and/or problem statement and/or real-life business problem.

To be able to address these objectives the students had to complete an assignment where they had to base their answer on "Use cases". This was an experiment to see how Blackboard can be used to assist in own content creation, if at all, and how students perceive the use of Blackboard in general. Using this course as a case study shed some light on how the LMS can be used to facilitate learning. A total number of 142 students were registered for this course and these students had to work in groups consisting of not more than 5 students, in the end there were 26 groups. Students selected their own group members although the one or two odd students who did not have groups were placed with groups of three students.

3.1 Assignment Background

As part of the first deliverable of the assignment, students had to define use case diagrams by answering questions and writing a wiki on Blackboard. This used "collaborative learning" as they had to work as a group and write the Wiki collaboratively [9].

They also had to submit 10 Powerpoint slides which included their theory from their wiki to show how they would teach use case diagrams. Focusing on the "instructionism" [9].

They were asked to select a real-life business case which they investigated and analysed and "write-up" the case on not more than two pages. As part of this write up, they had to identify a business problem and typical requirements which could be used to develop a system for this business. They also had to make a 5 min video introducing the business. This part of the assignment was done on Blackboard where each group had their own blog only they could see. This part mostly focused on "collaborative learning" [9], social interaction not just amongst group members but also with a business owner using various technologies to complete the assignment.

The second deliverable of the project involved them having to take their case and explain how one will draw a use case diagram based on the theory which they had to submit in deliverable 1. They had to make a small video drawing use cases and explain how they went about to draw it, as if they are teaching the use case theory based on their case. This part mostly focused on a combination of "instructionism" from the student's side and "constructionism" [9] which allowed them to take the role of instructor and also allowed them to make a video and upload that to YouTube.

Lastly, they also had to do one narrative of one of the use cases which had to be a business critical use case, thus no CRUD (create, read, update or delete) use cases were allowed.

All the assignments were marked based on a rubric.

4   Research Methodology

The students were asked to complete an online questionnaire based on their experience of the assignment after completing the assignment. This paper followed a positivist approach as it analysed the data obtained from the survey using statistical analysis techniques. The data was analysed using simple statistical techniques due to the low responses (only 59 responses), however this will allow patterns to emerge which will then be evaluated based on the literature and the rest of the findings [24].

After the assignments were completed, the students had to complete an online survey. In the end, 59 out of a possible 142 students completed a self-administered questionnaire which was analysed using quantitative methods. The data obtained from the questionnaire were exported into a CSV file, and send to the statistician, who assisted in analysing the responses using IBM SPSS Statistics version 23. The statistician and researcher were in continuous discussions during this process to ensure that the results reflected the actual responses to the questionnaires. All responses were analysed, based on the questions as well as the literature discussed earlier, in the following section.

5 Data Analysis and Findings

Of the total of 59 responses, 41 were male and 18 were females.

85% of the students were between 19 and 22 years old, however, considering that all students born between 1980 and 2000 are millennials as discussed earlier [22], all of the respondents were millennials.

The students had to provide the name of the degree which they are studying: almost all of the students that completed the survey study some of the technology degree with the majority of the respondents studying B.Com Informatics, 64%, and 20% studying BIT Information Technology.

The majority of the students were enrolled for the module for their first time, 79%.

Twenty five students considered themselves to be extroverts and 34 said they are introverts.

Turpie's [3] statement says that students today are engaged in new technology and prefer digital media. Firstly, to better understand whether infrastructure would have played a role in completing the assignment as well as the general connectivity level of these students, they were asked to give an indication of the nature of their connectivity. Table 1 shows that most students have access to the internet either through Wi-Fi access or their own data. It was interesting to see that most of the students, 84.5% used Wi-Fi on campus and thus the value of providing Wi-Fi to these students were crucial. It does not seem as if connectivity was a problem in completing this assignment (Table 1).

Table 1. Student connectivity

Connectivity	At home (n = 58) (%)	On Campus (n = 58) (%)
WIFI only	55.2	84.5
3G/own data	31.0	13.8
No connectivity	13.8	1.7

They were then asked how connectivity played a role specifically in completing this assignment. This was asked according to the various aspects of the assignment. Thus the focus was on Blogs, wikis and group collaboration although youtube uploading was also a critical part of the assignment. One student did not answer the question. Although some students struggled on and off, it does not seem as if connectivity was a problem to complete the assignment (Table 2).

Table 2. Connectivity to Blackboard

	Blogs (%)	Wiki (%)	Uploading YouTube (%)	Group collaboration (%)
No issues, thus connectivity was amazing	58.6	60.3	50.0	51.7
Struggled on and off	34.5	36.2	36.2	41.4
Could not connect during peak-periods (between 8:00 and 19:00 daily)	6.9	3.4	10.3	5.2
Could not connect at all	0	0	3.4	1.7

Next they were asked when last they read a printed newspaper versus on their mobile device. This should show whether Turpie [3] was correct when he said young people are engaged with online media from the day that they are born (Table 3).

Table 3. Frequency reading news paper

Frequency	Printed news paper (%)	Newspaper on mobile device (%)
Today	5.1	37.3
In the last week	22.0	33.9
During the last month	59.3	16.9
I have never read a newspaper	13.6	11.9

According to Table 3 it is clear that most students read the newspaper using a mobile device to get news on current affairs, however, it was interesting to see that 59.3% of the students indicated that they have read a printed newspaper in the last month.

Students were asked if they watch TV, and if so, how, streaming, on a TV set or both options. Seventy three per cent of the students indicated that they do watch TV. Of the 73% or 43 respondents, 20 respondents said they watch TV on a TV set, five said they only watch TV through streaming and 18 said they watch TV both on a TV box and streaming.

Although the use of streaming was expected to be higher, it seems as if there is no clear preference as to how these students prefer watching TV.

To further understand the student profile, these students were asked if they love reading and if they prefer to read any printed format material such as books, textbooks etc. The majority of the students said they do not love reading, (56% of the respondents). Although this number was quite high 71% of all the students indicated that they do read using printed format. The reason why is not clear.

About 80% of the students indicated that they have the prescribed textbook for the specific module which is only in available in printed format. Asking them if they used the textbook for the specific assignment their responses are visible in Table 4. It is important to note that 12 students did not answer this question (Table 4).

Table 4. Textbook frequency

Frequency	Response (%)
I never use it	12.8
Almost never	38.3
Sometimes	42.6
Almost every day	4.3
Always	2.1

What is alarming is that just over 50% of the students never or almost never used the textbook, and almost 43% said they sometimes used it. This then raise the question, what did they use to get the information? They were then asked to what extent they used alternative resources, such as other printed textbooks, Google, Youtube or any other resources.

Focusing specifically on Blackboard and the assignment at hand, the students were asked to what extent they used the following resources for this assignment. The most significant finding is the fact that Google was the most used resource, (64%) which in fact is not a surprise, this is what we all do when we struggle with something, we "Google it". Under other, some students did mention that they used the lecture notes provided (6 respondents).

Other resources which the students listed included the lecture slides as well although only six students referred to these. It is clear from Table 5 that electronic resources, such as Google, Youtube or Wikipedia were used to better understand the specific topic.

Table 5. Other resources used

Frequency	Other Printed textbook (n = 57) (%)	Google (n = 58) (%)	Wikipedia (n = 58) (%)	Youtube (n = 58) (%)
I never use it	31.6	1.7	31.0	6.9
Almost never	29.8	1.7	20.7	19.0
Sometimes	33.3	32.8	30.0	35.5
Almost every day	3.5	25.9	6.9	20.7
Always	1.8	37.9	10.3	19.0

The students then had to rank who they go to first for assistance. The results in Table 6 clearly show that they approach group members first. What was interesting was that students will rather go to Youtube before asking the lecturers, proving their reliance on technology. This could also be due to accessibility which is easier to YouTube than to the lecturer (Table 6).

Table 6. Who are approached for help?

Who/where the go to for help	Position ranked
My group members	1
Assistant lecturers	2
Fellow class mates	2
YouTube	3
Lecturer	4
Textbook	5
Library	6

When asking the students how they felt to approach a business in the real-world, and cross referencing this to introverts/extroverts, there was a significant association between introvert/extrovert and emotions experienced when they have to talk to someone in a real business ($\chi2$ (1) = 0.021). This showed that more extroverts were excited and enthusiastic, to talk to a real life business, than was expected under the assumption of no association.

Asking the students how they prefer to learn, Table 7 gives a clear overview of how students prefer to learn. All the students answered the question. Grouping agree and strongly agree together, 88% said they prefer practicing the diagrams by actually drawing it, similarly, 88% said tutor sessions helped them a lot where the tutors also drew the diagrams with them. Almost 82% said collaborating with friends, while 80% of the students prefer going to Youtube to understand difficult concepts and are also using Clickup (Blackboard) extensively. The percentages of students who indicated that they learn through Attending classes, Reading the textbook and working through the theory only were far below 80% (71%, 66% and 53% respectively). The interesting part of these results were that using technology was not the first choice, but tutor session and collaboration (Table 7).

These results were similar to the findings in Table 7. The tutor sessions are presented by the assistant lecturers, thus explaining why tutor sessions and assistant lecturers featured similarly in "who I asked for help" as well as "how I prefer to learn". It is interesting that authoritarianism, where students prefer to sit in a class room and have their teaching controlled by a lecturer does not seem to be applicable for a lecturer but rather for a tutor or assistant lecturer.

Students were asked how they experienced the assignment of being able to design their own textbook. 64% said they felt the assignment helped them to understand the topic of use cases better, 63% said they were able to apply the theory to their practical drawing of the use cases and only 54% said that this assignment helped them to better

Table 7. I prefer learning through:

I learn easier through:	Strongly disagree (%)	Disagree (%)	Agree (%)	Strongly agree (%)
Attending classes	1.7	27.1	55.9	15.3
Reading the textbook	3.4	30.5	50.8	15.3
Working through the theory only	3.4	44.1	47.5	5.1
Youtube difficult concepts to understand them better, thus I watch videos	6.8	13.6	40.7	39.0
Practicing drawing the diagrams myself, thus working through numerous case studies	1.7	10.2	44.1	44.1
Using Clickup Extensively	1.7	18.6	49.2	30.5
Collaborating with my fellow students and discussing the work	6.8	11.9	40.7	40.7
Tutor sessions	1.7	10.2	37.3	50.8

analyse a business. The main focus of this paper, being Blackboard was evaluated by asking the students how they felt about using the different parts of blackboard for the assignment (n = 57) (Table 8).

From Table 8 above it seems as if the majority of the students (76% or more) found working on Blackboard easy or had a neutral feeling towards it. There were, however, students who did not like it at all, (25% for wikis; 25% for blogs; only 1 student said he/she did not like Clickup itself). 74% of the students said overall that Clickup (Blackboard) itself was easy to use, which in the end, means that using Clickup (Blackboard) for this assignment was a good idea.

The researchers then wanted to see if there was a correlation between these experiences and their understanding of the topic uses cases. There was a moderate evidence of an association between uploading their videos onto Youtube and how students viewed doing the assignment as an auxiliary tool to understand the topic better (Fisher exact test = 0.081). The same was true for Making business case video (Fisher

Table 8. Experience using Clickup (blackboard)

Your experience using the following Clickup tools	Easy to use (%)	Neutral feeling towards technology (%)	Did not like it at all (%)
Wikis	50.9	24.6	24.6
Blogs	43.9	31.6	24.6
Uploading video to Youtube (adding link)	66.7	24.6	8.8
Working as a group on the same blog	40.4	38.6	21.1
Making business case video	54.4	31.6	14.0
Video to illustrate drawing use cases	56.1	28.1	15.8
The use of Clickup itself	73.7	24.6	1.8

exact test = 0.079) and making the video to illustrate drawing use cases (Fisher exact test = 0.070). Thus it seems as if the video part of the assignment did have an effect on whether the students believed that it to improve their understanding of use cases. The reason why is not clear however this might make for an interesting future study.

The students had to say what emotions they felt when receiving and doing this assignment, which is essentially designing your own content. Of the 57 students who completed the question 25% said they were excited, 37% said they felt responsible to ensure that the content was accurate, 18% said they were more motivated to do well, 10% said they felt anxious and 10% said they were not interested at all. Thus the majority of the students did seem to enjoy doing the assignment and take responsibility for doing well. Linking back to the characteristics of the students, it is interesting to see that a large percentage of the students felt responsible to ensure the content was accurate. It is also interesting to see that the options "motivation" and "anxious" were also selected by some students.

In the end, the students were asked three questions to see the overall picture. The first question was: if they were given practical examples in an electronic format, what would they rather prefer. 50% said they would prefer the electronic version, 28% said they still prefer the classroom interaction with the lecturer, 7% only used ClickUp for subject information and 15% said they still prefer a printed textbook.

The second focus question was if they thought using Clickup (Blackboard) assisted them in creating their own content for the theme "use cases". 76.7% of the 56 respondents who answered the question said "yes". The last question asked if they thought doing this assignment helped them to understand the topic use cases better, and in the end, 92% of the 56 students said "yes".

6   Discussion

A large number of research endeavours are currently focusing on technology and the classroom or hybrid learning, and this paper is no exception. This paper set out to see if Blackboard as an LMS can be used to assist students to learn through own content creation and thus the research questions addressed in this paper is: can students benefit from using a LMS to build their own content?

Initiated as an experiment as part of a hybrid teaching approach the reserachers wanted to see if the students can take responsibility and ownership of their content and design a textbook based on their own knowledge. Focusing on the characteristics of a student as determined in the literature review, it seemed as if the following charac- teristics were indeed the determining factors for these students.

- Responsibility/independence – Students felt responsible to ensure the content was correct;
- Authoritarianism – not necessarily from lecturers but students did want tutor or assistant lecturer's help more as part of their learning approach;
- Anxiety – some students did say they felt anxious both for approaching the business world, which was more the introverts and anxious to do an assignment in a com- pletely different way;

- Motivation – the students were motivated which goes hand in hand with taking responsibility;
- Introvert/extrovert - the extroverts were excited and enthusiastic, to talk to a real life business.
- Cognitive style – This might be the biggest determining factor as one had to determine how these students prefer to lean and in the end, this is their cognitive style of learning:
  - Practicing the diagrams by actually drawing it;
  - Attending tutor sessions;
  - Collaborating with friends;
  - Going to Youtube to understand difficult concepts;
  - Using Clickup (Blackboard) extensively;
  - Google if you don't know.

Seeing if the assignment helped them to learn better, they felt that the assignment did help them understand the topic of use cases better and that they were able to apply the theory to their practical drawing of the use cases although a smaller percentage mentioned that the assignment helped them to better analyse a business.

In the end the aim was to see if student can benefit from such an approach, and the answer was an overwhelming yes. Students felt Blackboard assisted them to understand the context and in particular students felt that this assignment assisted them to understand the topic "use cases" better. In the end, the main goals were to ensure that students used technology and actually grasped the content better.

7 Conclusion

As educators, we have no choice but to adapt our learning approaches to engage more with the students. This assignment was an experiment and in the end it seems as if the students did benefit and actually enjoyed using technology to complete the assignment. The students sitting in front of us today don't necessarily want a manual to teach them how to do something, they want to try and figure it out themselves which is exactly what this assignment was. Can we do it again, definitely; did we learn lessons, for sure; but in the end this was a first step to embrace a hybrid learning approach to see if it can facilitate own content creation by students. Try something new, make mistakes, learn lessons but at least show the students that you are trying and wiling to engage with their world!

Annexure A

Questionnaire layout -Blackboard paper

Respondent number

Personal Information

I hereby give consent that I am willingly completing this questionnaire and I was not forced to complete this

a) Yes	1
b) No	2

1. Gender

Female	1	Male	2

2. How old are you? ……………………………..   years

3. Degree

BCom Informatics	1
BEd - FET: General	2
BIS - Information Science	3
BIT - Information Technology	4
BSc – Geoinformatics	5
BSc Information Technology - Information and Knowledge Systems	6
Other (specify)	7

4. Number of Years enrolled for degree

5. I consider myself to be an:

Introvert "*a person who tends to turn inward mentally. Introverts sometimes avoid large groups of people, feeling more energized by time alone*"	1
Extrovert "*a person concerned more with practical realities than with inner thoughts and feelings; being concerned with the social and physical environment*"	2

6. I Learn easier through:

	Strongly disagree	Disagree	Agree	Strongly agree
a) Attending classes only	1	2	3	4
b) Reading the textbook	1	2	3	4
c) Working through the theory only	1	2	3	4
d) Youtube difficult concepts to understand them better, thus I watch videos explaining how diagrams are being drawn	1	2	3	4
e) Practicing drawing the diagrams myself, thus working through numerous case studies	1	2	3	4
f) Using Clickup extensively	1	2	3	4
g) Collaborating with my fellow students and discuss the work	1	2	3	4
h) Tutor sessions	1	2	3	4

7. Rank the following in terms of who/where you go to first if you struggle with a difficult concept in this subject (thus 1 is who/where you go to first, 2 second etc.)

a) My Fellow classmates	1	2	3	4	5	6	7	8
b) My group members	1	2	3	4	5	6	7	8
c) YouTube	1	2	3	4	5	6	7	8
d) Library	1	2	3	4	5	6	7	8
e) Assistant lecturers	1	2	3	4	5	6	7	8
f) Lecturer	1	2	3	4	5	6	7	8
g) Textbook	1	2	3	4	5	6	7	8
h) Other (Please Specify)	1	2	3	4	5	6	7	8

8. During the assignment, to what extend did you require support from the:

	No Support	A Little support	A lot of support	Extensive support
a) Lecturers	1	2	3	4
b) Assistant Lecturers	1	2	3	4
c) Tutors	1	2	3	4
d) Other (Please Specify)	1	2	3	4

Technology

9 When last have you read a newspaper in printed format?

a) Today	1
b) In the last week	2
c) During the last month	3
d) I have never read a newspaper	4

10 When last have you read a newspaper on your cell phone or tablet?

a) Today	1
b) In the last week	2
c) During the last month	3
d) I have never read a newspaper	4

11 Do you watch TV?

a) Yes	1
b) No	2

12 If Yes to nr. 11, how do you watch TV:

a) On the TV Device	1
b) Streaming on my mobile device	2
c) Both of the above	3
d) Other (Please specify)	4

13 Do you love reading?

a) Yes	1
b) No	2

14 Do you read any printed format articles (books, textbooks etc)

a) Yes	1
b) No	2

15 Do you have the prescribed textbook for this module?

a) Yes	1
b) No	2

16 If yes to 15, When last did you open it up

a) Today / a day ago	1
b) A week ago	2
c) Two weeks ago	3
d) a Month ago	4
e) I have never opened the textbook	5

17 If yes to 15, To what extend did you use the textbook for this assignment?

a) I never used it	1
b) Almost never	2
c) Sometimes	3
d) Almost every day	4
e) Always	5

18 To what extend did you use the following resources for this assignment?

	I never used it	Almost never	Sometimes	Almost every day	Always
a) Other printed books	1	2	3	4	5
b) Google	1	2	3	4	5
c) Wikipedia	1	2	3	4	5
d) YouTube	1	2	3	4	5
e) Other (Please specify)	1	2	3	4	5

19 Being able to "design" a textbook for use cases allowed me to (select all relevant options)

a) Understand the theory behind use cases better	1
b) Being able to apply the theory to the practical drawing of use cases	2
c) Understand how to analyse a business better	3
d) Know which questions to ask a business owner when trying to identify requirements	4
e) Understand the importance of systems in the business environment	5

20 Did the notion of having to talk to someone in a "real" business setting make you feel

a) Stressed	1
b) Anxious	2
c) Intimidated	3
d) Rather avoided it	4
e) Excited	5
f) Enthusiastic, could not wait to start	6

21 If I were given practical examples in an electronic format, I would rather study using the

a) Electronic version	1
b) Still prefer a prescribed printed textbook	2
c) Still prefer classroom interaction with the lecturer	3
d) Only use Clickup for subject information	4

22 How do you connect to the internet at home?

a) Wifi Only	1
b) 3G / own data	2
c) No connectivity	3

23 How do you connect to the internet on campus?

a) Wifi Only	1
b) 3G / own data	2
c) No connectivity	3

24 Have you ever used Tshwane free wifi for your studies?

a) Yes	1
b) No	2

25 How did connectivity play a role in uploading your assignment for the following activities?	No issues, connectivity was amazing	Struggled on and off	Could not connect during peak-periods (between 8:00 - 19:00 daily)	Could not connect at all
a) Blogs	1	2	3	4
b) Wiki	1	2	3	4
c) Uploading YouTube	1	2	3	4
d) Collaborating as a group	1	2	3	4

26 What did you use to record your group's video?
  a) Cellphone
  b) Tablet
  c) Video camera
  d) Other (Please specify)

27 If you used your cellphone for the recording, which cellphone do you have?
  a) Iphone
  b) Samsung
  c) Hauwei
  d) Blackberry
  e) Other (Please Specify)

28 Which software did you use to make your use case videos?

29 What was your experience with using the following tools on Clickup or Technology	Easy to use	Neutral feeling towards technology	Did not like it at all
a) Wikis	1	2	3
b) Blogs	1	2	3
c) Uploading your video to youtube	1	2	3
d) Working as a group on the same blog	1	2	3
e) Making the business case video	1	2	3
f) Making the video to illustrate drawing use cases	1	2	3
g) The use of Clickup itself	1	2	3

GROUPWORK

30 Who was your client (Name of the business you analysed)?

31 How did you identify the business

32 How many group members were you

33 How did you meet your group members?

   a) We were friends before we started

   b) During the INF 271 class

   c) We were placed together as a group by the lecturers

   d) Other (Please specify)

34 How did you as a group communicate (thus talked to each other) (select all relevant options)

   a) WhatsApp group only   `1`

   b) Face-to-face meetings   `2`

   c) Library workspace   `3`

   d) Online meetings such as Skype   `4`

   e) We never communicated face-to-face, we each just used Clickup by
seeing what each group member did   `5`

35 How did you as a group collaborate (work jointly on an activity or project) (select all relevant options)

   a) WhatsApp group only

   b) Face-to-face meetings

   c) Library workspace

   d) Online meetings such as Skype

   e) We never communicated face-to-face, we each just used Clickup by
seeing what each group member did

36 Did you as a group experience any group issues?

   a) Yes

   b) No

37 If yes to 36, how did you as a group resolve the group issues?

   a) Meetings

   b) Group split up

   c) Responsibility was only on one or two individuals and therefore these individuals completed the assignment

   d) Other (Please explain)

38 Being able to develop our own content for a textbook made me feel:

   a. Excited

   b. Responsible to ensure the content is accurate

   c. Anxious

   d. More motivated to do well

   e. Not interested at all

39 Do you think using Clickup assisted you in creating your own content for the theme "use cases" for this subject?

   a) Yes

   b) No

40 Do you think doing this assignment helped you to understand the topic "Use cases" better?

   a) Yes

   b) No

References

1. Ashraf, B.: Teaching the Google-eyed YouTube generation. Educ. Train. **51**(5/6), 343–352 (2009)
2. Pullan, M.C.: Student support services for millennial undergraduates. J. Educ. Technol. Syst. **38**(2), 235–253 (2009)

3. Turpie, J.: Creative engineers. In: Holden, J., Wright, S., Kieffer, J., Newbigin, J. (eds.) CreativityMoneyLove: Learning for the 21st Century (2012)
4. Generation Z-Wikipedia, 9 Feb 2017. https://en.m.wikipedia.org/wiki/generation_Z
5. Puttnam, L.: Creative learning through technology. In: Holden, J., Wright, S., Kieffer, J., Newbigin, J. (eds.) CreativityMoneyLove: Learning for the 21st Century (2012)
6. Guedet, G., et al.: Collective design of an e-textbook: teachers' collective documentation. J. Math. Teach. Educ. **19**(2), 187–203 (2016)
7. Kirkwood, A., Price, L.: Learners and learning in the twenty-first century: what do we know about students' attitudes towards and experiences of information and communication technologies that will help us design courses? Stud. High. Educ. **30**(3), 257–274 (2005)
8. Kirkwood, A., Prince, L.: Technology-enhanced learning and teaching in higher education: what is 'enhanced' and how do we know? A critical literature review. Learn. Media Technol. **39**(2), 6–36 (2014)
9. Laurillard, D.: The Pedagogical challenges to collaborative technologies. Comput. Support. Collab. Learn. **4**, 5–20 (2009)
10. Davidson, N., Major, C.H., Michaelsen, L.K.: Small-Group learning in higher education - cooperative, collaborative, problem-based and team-based learning: an introduction by Guest editors. J. Excel. Coll. Teach. **25**(3&4), 1–6 (2014)
11. Moodley, P., Singh, R.J., Cloete, J.: Exploring student perceptions of using the learning management system and social media for blended learning at a rural University. Progressio **37**(1), 68–82 (2015)
12. Bonk, C.J., Graham, C.R.: The Handbook of Blended Learning: Global Perspectives, Local Designs. Pfeiffer, San Francisco (2006)
13. Bender, T.: Discussion-Based Online Teaching to Enhance Student Learning: Theory, Practice, and Assessment, 2nd edn. Stylus Publishing, LLC, Sterling (2012). 256 p.
14. Woods, R., Baker, J.D., Hopper, D.: Hybrid structures: faculty use and perception of web-based courseware as a supplement to face-to-face instruction. Internet High. Educ. **7**, 281–297 (2004)
15. Rosenberg, M.J.: Knowledge management and learning: Perfect togeher. In: Reiser, R.A., Dempsey, J.V. (eds.) Trends and Issues in Instructional Design and Technology. Pearson, Boston (2012)
16. Wilson, R.W.: In-class-online hybrid methods of teaching planning theory: Assessing impacts on discussion and learning. J. Plan. Educ. Res. **28**, 237–246 (2008)
17. Lam, L., Lau, N., Ngan, L.C.W: An investigation of the factors influencing student learning motivation with the facilitation of cloud computing in higher education context of Hong Kong. In: Hybrid learning: Theory, application and practice, Toronto, Canada (2013)
18. Pullan, M.C.: Student support services for millennial undregraduates. J. Educ. Technol. Syst. **38**(2), 235–251 (2010)
19. Mitchell, A., Petter, S., Harris, A.L.: Learning by doing: twenty successful active learning exercises for information systems courses. J. Inf. Technol. Educ.: Innov. Pract. **16**, 21–26 (2017)
20. Selwyn, N.: The digital native – myth and reality. Aslib Proc. New Inf. Perspect. **61**(4), 364–379 (2009)
21. Prensky, M.: Digital natives, digital immigrants. Part 1. On Horiz. **9**(5), 1–6 (2001)
22. Pacansky-Brock, M.: Best Practices for Teaching with Emerging Technologies. Routledge, New York (2013). 161 p.
23. Bradford, P., et al.: The blackboard learning system: the be all and end all in educational instruction. J. Educ. Technol. Syst. **35**(3), 301–314 (2007)
24. Oates, B.J.: Researching Information Systems and Computing. SAGE Publications Ltd., London (2006). 341 p.

A Curriculum Approach to Improving Cyber Safety in South African Schools

E. Kritzinger[(✉)]

University of South Africa, Pretoria, South Africa
kritze@unisa.ac.za

Abstract. Information and communication technology (ICT) has become part of the daily life of school learners. School learners have access to ICT devices and the internet to improve education, to socialise and for entertainment. Using ICT devices connected to the internet has a vast number of advantages to school learners. However, the negative side of using these devices (e.g. cyber risks and threats) can unfortunately have long-lasting emotional and physical effects on growing school learners. Cyber risks and treats include cyber bullying, access to inappropriate material and identity theft. School learners can become cyber victims if they are not educated in the dangers of cyber risks and threats and in the correct way of protecting themselves and their information. Currently, the South African school system provides for limited to no teaching of cyber safety awareness. This research proposes that cyber safety awareness programmes be integrated into the school system through the life orientation education stream. The research created and tested a proposed educator's guide on cyber safety awareness based on the Curriculum and Assessment Policy Statement (CAPS) approach to grade 4 and grade 6 learners in South African schools. The research included a pre- and post-test to investigate whether cyber safety awareness increased through the teaching of cyber safety within a classroom setup.

Keywords: Actions · Awareness · Schools · Curriculum

1 Introduction

With the growing dependency on technology in the daily lives of people, users of technology are connecting to information and communication technology (ICT) devices to improve education, engage in social networking, improve the working environment, create entertainment and gather information. Users of ICTs and ICT devices can be compartmentalised into different technology user groups (Kritzinger and Von Solms 2010). These user groups range from industry/organisational users and home users to school learners (children). Each of the user groups has different expectations, outcomes and interactions while they are being connected to the internet/cyber space. Internet access offers school learners vast advantages and support the underlying principles of education and global consecutiveness. However, the advantages of internet access are overshadowed by looming internet (cyber) risks and threats. Cyber space has also become an environment in which online criminals (predators) are attempting to control

© Springer International Publishing AG 2017
T.-C. Huang et al. (Eds.): SETE 2017, LNCS 10676, pp. 95–105, 2017.
https://doi.org/10.1007/978-3-319-71084-6_11

and exploit unexpected and ill-informed online users (Chandrashekhar et al. 2016; UNICEF 2012). Unfortunately, in many instances, the compromised cyber users are school learners (Brown et al. 2014; Department of Education & Prevention Centre for Justice and Crime 2012; Govender and Skea 2015; Smit 2015). School learners are seen as "soft targets" in cyber space and they are vulnerable to cyber risks (Srivastava 2017). According to Wall (2001), cyber risks can be grouped into four categories, namely deception/theft, pornography, violence and cyber trespass. Cyber risks and threats include cyber bullying (stalking), identity theft and access to inappropriate material. Most of the time, school learners share their personal details online without realising the effect and the possible consequences of their actions (Furnell 2010). The social and emotional effect of cyber bullying via social media presents an even greater cyber threat (Van Royen et al. 2017). Cyber victimisation can happen continuously and in most cases it is seen as hidden acts of crime against learners (Badenhorst 2011).

Access to ICT devices, internet capabilities and social media dependency have increased rapidly in the past few years due to growing broadband access and decreased cost of ICT devices. More school learners have internet access; they use their cellphones as the primary ICT device (Ahad and Anshari 2017; Livingstone et al. 2014). School learners perceive that having cellphones and access to the internet will improve information sharing, social interaction and school tasks (Ahad and Anshari 2017). This constant access and use of technology can lead to cyber risks and threats, however. It is therefore vital that school learners be educated in and made aware of cyber risks and threats as well as that they gain knowledge of protecting themselves and their information. Schools are identified as the best place to incorporate cyber safety awareness (Livingstone et al. 2014). Several countries, including the UK, USA and Australia, support education on cyber safety and have already implemented initiatives to incorporate the teaching of cyber safety into the school curriculum. Currently, South Africa is ill-prepared to create and grow a cyber safety awareness culture among school learners (Kritzinger et al. 2017). The South African education system has not planned to integrate cyber safety awareness initiatives into the current school environment (Kritzinger et al. 2017). No active legislation exists that prescribes improving cyber safety among internet users or school learners in particular. Some movements have been started to deal with cyber safety issues like cyber bullying and sexting, but only on an informative basis (South African Department of Basic Education 2015). Nationally, cyber safety research has been on the rise, but schools are still not taking sufficient action to prevent or minimise cyber-attacks (including cyber bullying) among school learners (Rigby 2017).

This research will therefore focus primarily on school learners and the learning pedagogy of improving cyber safety awareness among them. The research originated from the lack of current cyber safety awareness programmes in South African schools. The objective of the research was to create an educator's guide on cyber safety that is based on the Curriculum and Assessment Policy Statement (CAPS) to improve cyber safety knowledge and skills among school learners. This research was tested by means of a quantitative approach, using a three-stage data gathering method that includes a pre- and post-test with a teaching section in between the testing phases. The research also created an educator's guide to deal with cyber bullying among grade 4 and grade 6 school learners. The scope of the research includes cyber bullying as only one of a wide range of cyber threats (risks). The process of this research can be duplicated to create additional documentation that will include additional cyber risks. The primary focus of the research was to investigate if cyber safety education and awareness can be incorporated into the school curriculum to improve school learners' knowledge, perceptions and actions regarding cyber safety.

2   Cyber Safety Among School Learners

Schools are adapting to technology and are starting to move to a more technological approach to teaching and learning. The teaching and learning pedagogy are evolving to ensure that school learners are exposed to technology to prepare them for the future. The future will be technology driven, especially in the working environment that school learners will enter in a few years' time. It is therefore essential that schools incorporate technology to some extent to ensure the readiness of school learners for the future (De Lange and Von Solms 2012). However, with this integration of technology comes the responsibility to educate school learners in how to use technology properly and how to protect themselves while using ICT devices – especially in cyber space (Kritzinger and Padayachee 2013; Smit 2015).

2.1   Advantages

The advantages of technology for educational purposes are widely known and accepted (Alsied and Pathan 2013; Plowman et al. 2012; Shanmugam et al. 2014). If technology is correctly used in education, it can improve social interaction and collaborative learning, among other things, and provide access to lifelong learning (Heflin et al. 2017). The use of ICT can also increase empathy and acceptance of diversity by means of modelling the prosocial behaviours of others (HUDA et al. 2017). If ICT is correctly and responsibly incorporated and used, the advantages of ICT-integrated learning can benefit school learners as a holistic approach to education.

2.2   Disadvantages

Overshadowing the advantages of technology are the possible cyber risks and treats to which school learners can (and will be) exposed. This exposure can affect learners' emotional and social wellbeing negatively. Different cyber risks for school learners can be divided into the following three main categories (Stone 2013) (Table 1):

Learners are exposed to all these cyber risks while being connected to the internet; these risks cannot be avoided. However, learners should be educated on identifying cyber risks, minimising exposure to cyber risks and mitigating exposure if a risk does occur. Educating learners on the awareness of cyber risks is the responsibility of schools, teachers and parents alike. This research will focus primarily on cyber education and awareness in the school environment.

Table 1. Three categories of cyber risks (Stone 2013)

Individuals' intention to harm learners	Learners' exposure to harmful online interactions	Learners placing themselves in a harmful or potentially harmful situation through the following actions
• Cyber bullying • Cyber grooming • Impersonation • Blackmail • Cyber snooping • Identity theft • Social engineering • Online predators	• Inappropriate content/material • Digital reputational ruin • Social platforms and chatrooms • Viruses, malware, • Cookies	• Illegal file sharing • Plagiarism and free downloads • Inappropriate online postings • Copyright infringements • Non-ethical postings of others' • Sexting

2.3   School Curriculum

Including cyber safety awareness programmes in the school environment has been done at international level in countries such as the USA, UK and Australia. In South Africa, these programmes have been initiated to a lesser extent. The countries mentioned above have started the process of including compulsory cyber safety education in the school environment. Some initiatives that schools can implement to improve cyber safety include the following (Kritzinger et al. 2017):

- incorporating cyber security into the school curriculum
- providing cyber security workbooks that are age appropriate
- training teachers to assist with and guide the education of school learners
- lending support at school in terms of incident handling and disciplinary measures
- supplying material (posters, brochures, pamphlets, etc.) for increasing cyber security awareness
- involving parents
- providing once-off initiatives
- launching national initiatives (e.g. cyber security awareness week)
- creating and implementing ICT policies and procedures in schools

The research proposes that cyber safety awareness be incorporated into the school environment using a curriculum-based approach (Kritzinger 2016; Von Solms and Von Solms 2014). In terms of the South African Constitution, schools are ultimately responsible for the safe keeping of school learners. This includes safe keeping within the ICT domain. This can be achieved by including a cyber safety section in the school curriculum.

3   Proposed Cyber Safety Awareness School Approach

Currently in South Africa, no official curriculum document is dealing specifically with cyber safety awareness for any grade. This means that school learners do not receive any cyber safety awareness teaching that has been prescribed in the current CAPS. This research proposes that cyber safety awareness programmes be incorporated into the CAPS. The researcher developed an educator's workbook to provide lesson plans that support the life orientation topic of recognising and dealing with cyber bullying for grade 4 and grade 6 learners. The workbook includes learner activities that are based on CAPS and are grade specific. The educator's guide directs the teacher through individual lesson plans based on the workbook activities. The guide is CAPS aligned and it includes aspects of cyber bullying for grade 4 and grade 6 learners. Topics for grade 4 learners include aspects such as (1) emotions, (2) conflict between friends and peers, (3) cyber bullying uncapped, (4) how to respond to cyber bullying and (5) protecting yourself against cyber bullying. Topics for grade 6 learners include aspects such as (1) peer pressure, (2) dealing with conflict, (3) cyber bullying, (4) taking a closer look at the bully and breaking the bullying habit, and (5) dealing with cyber bullying. This scope of this research focused on cyber bullying only as one of many cyber risks and it was directed specifically at grade 4 and grade 6 learners. However, the research can be expanded to include all cyber-related risks for all grades. Figure 1 depsicts learner activities and Fig. 2 depicts the section of the educator's guide.

The documents depicted in Figs. 1 and 2 were used as part of a quantitative research approach to test the effect of cyber safety awareness in the school environment and formed part the lessons the teacher presented to the participants.

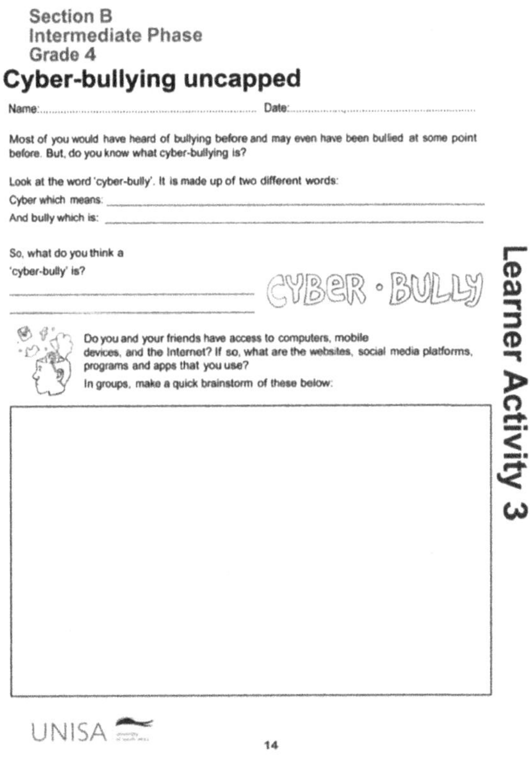
Section B
Intermediate Phase
Grade 4

Cyber-bullying uncapped

Name:........................ Date:........................

Most of you would have heard of bullying before and may even have been bullied at some point before. But, do you know what cyber-bullying is?

Look at the word 'cyber-bully'. It is made up of two different words:

Cyber which means: ____________________

And bully which is: ____________________

So, what do you think a 'cyber-bully' is?

CYBER • BULLY

Do you and your friends have access to computers, mobile devices, and the Internet? If so, what are the websites, social media platforms, programs and apps that you use?

In groups, make a quick brainstorm of these below:

Learner Activity 3

UNISA

14

Fig. 1. Learner activity

Section B
Intermediate Phase
Grade 4

Lesson 3 – Cyber-bullying Uncapped	Time: 3 hour
Learning Area: Life Skills (Grade 4, Term 2)	

Curriculum Standards (CAPS)
Development of the self
Bullying: how to protect self from acts of bullying
- Examples of acts of bullying
- Appropriate responses to bullying: where to find help
- Weekly reading by learners: reading for enjoyment
- Reading about appropriate responses to bullying

Lesson Objectives

This lesson aims to introduce and explain the pros and cons as well as the dangers of the internet and technology. It also aims to unpack the concept of cyber-bullying and to give tips on how to deal with it.

Content	Skills	Values
Learners to write a definition of cyber-bullying.	Summarising and critical thinking.	To gain an understanding of what cyber-bullying is.
Learners to brainstorm their personal uses of the Internet and technology in groups.	Thinking and reasoning skills; group work skills; social skills; reporting skills. Thinking and reasoning.	To personally assess which parts of the Internet they use and therefore decide where they may be at risk.
Learners to write up the pros and cons of technology.	Thinking and reasoning; public speaking; social skills.	Technology has many positive uses but, it also presents many dangers.
Class to discuss different cyber-bullying scenarios.	Group work; leadership skills; role-play skills.	
Learners to spend time in groups creating a role play on 'cyber-bullying'.	Thinking and reasoning; conflict resolution; social skills.	Cyber-bullying is common and takes many forms.
Class to discuss and read over tips on how to deal with cyber-bullying.		Anyone can be affected. It is important to imagine yourself in a cyber-bullying scenario.
		Learning how to correctly deal with

Resources needed

Photocopies of the Learner Activity worksheet; stationery. Optional: example role-play scripts (educator to create) and role play props or outfits; extension activities in the Resource Section.

Educator preparation before starting

Look through the notes provided and decide how you would like to conduct the lesson beforehand. Make sure that the worksheets are pre-copied so that you can use the maximum amount of teaching time with your class. You might want to tell the learners beforehand that they will be performing a role-play so that they can bring props along. Alternatively, you may wish to get the learners to write and practice their role-plays before this lesson and then perform them in this lesson.

Learner Activities and how to teach them

This lesson should involve plenty of class discussion. Try to foster a non-judgemental and open atmosphere in your class by accepting everyone's perspectives. Give a reasonable amount of time for learners to fill in their answers before moving on to the next activity. Three hours have been allocated for this lesson to allow time for the written exercises and most importantly the role play. Remember to leave a good amount of time for learners to plan and practice their role plays. You will also be able to use these role plays as an assessment opportunity!

Assessment					
Formal Assessment – Use the below rubric to mark each learner in the role play exercise.					
	1	2	3	4	5
Inventiveness					
Insight					
Speaking Skills					
Group Work					
				Total	/20

Answers

The answers for the given activities rely heavily on the learners' personal opinions. Most of the written answers should be arrived through the class discussion. For an exact definition of cyber-bullying, consult the articles in the educator's section.

Educator Guide

Fig. 2. Educator's guide

4   Methodology

The research was based on a quantitative approach that included three stages, namely, stage 1: pre-test; stage 2: teaching by educator on proposed cyber safety awareness; and stage 3: post-test. The research was conducted over a period of four months from May (quarter 2) to August (quarter 3). The research study was conducted in four schools in Gauteng in South Africa, and full ethical clearance was obtained to conduct the study among school learners.

4.1   Stage 1: Pre-test

The pre-test was conducted among 199 grade 6 learners from South Africa in the second quarter of the year. The average age of the learners who participated in the study was 11 years. The gender split included 40% male learners and 60% female learners. The racial split comprised 88% black learners, 7% coloured learners, 4% Indian leaners, and 1% white learners. The pre-test included the topics (1) peer pressure, (2) conflict resolutions and (3) cyber bullying. Learners received no teaching on any of the topics before the pre-test. The pre-test was written in the second quarter of the school year, as teaching on physical bullying is already part of the existing school curriculum for grades 4 and 6.

4.2   Stage 2: Educator's Workbook

This stage consisted of the teaching of the proposed cyber safety awareness curriculum as discussed in Sect. 3 (Figs. 1 and 2). The teachers were provided with an educator's cyber safety workbook that discusses cyber safety issues and the proposed cyber safety awareness curriculum. This stage was done in the second and third quarters after the pre-test.

4.3   Stage 3: Post-test

The post-test was conducted among the same learners used for the pre-test. However, only 188 learners participated in the post-test since 11 learners were absent. The post-test was conducted in August, in the third quarter of the school year. The gender split of learners in the post-test was similar to that of the pre-test.

5   Findings of Research and Discussion

From the research, it was clear that learners are exposed to the cyber space, as 52.1% of the learners were using online resources to conduct research for school projects and 26.6% were using cyber space to find other information that is not school related. This result validates that school learners are connecting to cyber space for educational as well as non-educational purposes. The research also identified the following social media platforms that learners use (1) WhatsApp: 92.6%, (2) Instagram: 26%, (3) Facebook: 21.8%, (4) Snapchat: 9.6% and (5) Other: 6.9%.

An interesting fact is that, according to the rules and policies of all social media platforms, including WhatsApp, Instagram, Facebook and Snapchat, the minimum allowed age of a user of this social software is 13 years. This indicates that learners of all ages are using social media and neither they nor their parents/teachers are adhering to the rules and policies required by these social media tools. This is the first indication of a lack of knowledge and skills when learners connect to cyber space.

The rest of this section is structured according to the data analysis from the pre-test and the post-test after the teachers had an extensive discussion on (1) peer pressure, (2) conflict resolution and (3) cyber bullying with learners.

5.1   Peer Pressure

This section investigated the concept of peer pressure. All the questions on peer pressure were set according to the Likert scale that includes (1) Not likely at all, (2) Not likely, (3) Maybe, (4) Likely, and (5) Very likely.

The first question probed the discussion that learners may have with their parents or teacher about their peer pressure experiences. In the pre-test, the result indicated an average of 3.66 for talking to parents and 3.35 to teachers. After stage 2, the result for the same question increased to 3.73 for talking to parents and 3.51 to teachers. This indicated that some learners would be more open or willing to talk to parents and teachers if cyber peer pressure occurred.

The second question focused on saying no to peer pressure within cyber space. The pre-test result was 4.13 increased to 4.35 in the post-test. This links to the question that asked if the learners would avoid situations where they were pressurised, increasing from 4.13 in the pre-test to 4.35 in the post-test. The last question inquired if learners would avoid other learners that pressurised them. The result show that in the pre-test, 4.10 indicated they would, which increased to 4.24 in the post-test.

5.2   Cyber Bullying

This section focuses on cyber bullying. Close-ended questions were used to measure answers on a percentage scale. The learners were asked if they knew about other learners who had been cyber bullied; according to the result, 21.8% replied "yes". In the post-test, the result increased to 23.4%. This is supported in the finding that 59% of learners identified a cyber incident correctly in the pre-test, the result increased to 76% in the post-test.

In the pre-test, the learners were given three definitions of cyber bullying and 61.6% of the learners identified the correct answer. In the post-test, the result increased to almost 80%. This indicates that the knowledge of learners has increased after stage two. The next section that was tested is conflict resolution. Conflict resolution is the next step after a peer pressure or a cyber-related incident has occurred.

5.3   Conflict Resolution

Conflict resolution is a vital aspect in cyber-related incidents (peer pressure, cyber bullying, and sexting). This section of the research was based on a percentage for the answers obtained. The result of the statement made to learners, "Avoid gossiping about the conflict", indicated 81.2% before stage 2, which increased to 86.7% after stage 2. The result of the second statement, "Take responsibility for your feelings and actions", increased from 94.9% to 96.3% after stage 2. The result of the third statement, "Try to speak to the other person decently when you are angry", increased from 73.6% to 80.3% after the stage 2 awareness session.

5.4   Discussion

The findings of this research indicate that learners' knowledge, perceptions and actions changed after cyber safety awareness had been presented to them. The data analysed identified the following eight findings of which cognisance should be taken:

- Finding 1: School learners are connected to the internet for school as well as personal activities.
- Finding 2: School learners conduct cyber-related activities even if it is against rules and regulations.
- Finding 3: Through cyber safety awareness, school learners will be more open to talk to teachers and parents about cyber-related incidents.
- Finding 4: Learners' awareness will increase through cyber safety education.
- Finding 5: Learners' actions will be directed at protecting themselves in a cyber-related event.
- Finding 6: Learners' knowledge and skills will increase through cyber safety education.
- Finding 7: Learners will deal more effectively with cyber-related incidents.

The research indicates that cyber safety awareness and education will benefit learners, as it will improve their cyber safety skills, knowledge and actions. The research showed successfully that cyber safety awareness education could be incorporated into the school curriculum to ensure the growth of a cyber safety culture in schools. Ultimately, education on cyber safety will provide learners with the knowledge of protecting themselves, which should lead to them becoming responsible cyber users and being safe in cyber space.

6   Conclusion

This research paper proposed increasing cyber safety awareness in South African by means of incorporating cyber safety into the curriculum. The proposed approach was based on CAPS and the research included drafting an educator's guide (workbook), assessment plan and learner activities. The proposed approach was tested among grade 6 learners in South African schools. The quantitative data analysis focuses on peer pressure, cyber bullying and conflict resolution.

From the data analysis, it is evident that in the post-test, learners gained a deeper understanding of what peer pressure entails and of how to deal with peer pressure correctly. There was an increased understanding of what cyber bullying was in the post-test, as well as an overall increase in knowing how to avoid cyber bullying. In view of the above, it can be concluded that the cyber safety workbook was effective in increasing cyber safety knowledge and awareness among grade 6 learners. This research proposes that this curriculum-based approached be adopted for all grades and all cyber-related risks and threats.

References

Ahad, A.D., Anshari, M.: Smartphone habits among youth. Int. J. Cyber Behav. Psychol. Learn. 7(1), 65–75 (2017)

Alsied, S.M., Pathan, M.M.: The use of computer technology in EFL classroom: advantages and implications. Int. J. Engl. Lang. Transl. Stud. 1(1), 61–71 (2013)

Badenhorst, C.: Legal responses to cyber bullying and sexting in South Africa. In: Centre for Justice and Crime Prevention (2011). Available at: http://www.lse.ac.uk/media@lse/research/Research-Projects/Researching-Childrens-Rights/pdf/Issue-Paper-10—Legal-reponses-to-cyberbullying-and-sexting-in-SA.pdf. Accessed 27 March 2016

Brown, C.F., Demaray, M.K., Secord, S.M.: Cyber victimization in middle school and relations to social emotional outcomes. Comput. Hum. Behav. 35, 12–21 (2014)

Chandrashekhar, A.M., Muktha, G.S., Anjana, D.K.: Cyberstalking and cyberbullying?: effects and prevention measures. Imperial J. Interdisc. Res. 2(3), 95–102 (2016)

Furnell, S.: Jumping security hurdles. Comput. Fraud Secur. 2010(6), 10–14 (2010)

Govender, I., Skea, B.: Teachers' understanding of e-safety: an exploratory case in KZN South Africa. Electron. J. Inf. Syst. Developing Countries. 70(5), 1–17 (2015)

Heflin, H., Shewmaker, J., Nguyen, J.: Impact of mobile technology on student attitudes, engagement, and learning. Comput. Educ. 107, 91–99 (2017). https://doi.org/10.1016/j.compedu.2017.01.006

Huda, M., Jasmi, K.A., Hehsan, A., Mustari, M.I., Shahrill, M., Basiron, B., Gassama, S.K.: Empowering children with adaptive technology skills: careful engagement in the digital information age. Int. Electron. J. Elem. Educ. 9(3), 693–708 (2017)

Kritzinger, E.: Short-term initiatives for enhancing cyber-safety within South African schools email. SACJ 28(1) (2016). http://doi.org/10.18489/sacj.v28i1.369

Kritzinger, E., Von Solms, S.H.: Cyber security for home users: a new way of protection through awareness enforcement. Comput. Secur. 29(8), 840–847 (2010)

Kritzinger, E., Bada, M., Nurse, J.R.C.: A study into the cybersecurity awareness initiatives for school learners in South Africa and the UK. In: Bishop, M., Futcher, L., Miloslavskaya, N., Theocharidou, M. (eds.) WISE 2017. IAICT, vol. 503, pp. 110–120. Springer, Cham (2017). https://doi.org/10.1007/978-3-319-58553-6_10

Kritzinger, E., Padayachee, K.: Engendering an e-safety awareness culture within the South African context. In: IEEE AFRICON Conference (2013). 10.1109/AFRCON.2013.6757708

De Lange, M., Von Solms, R.: An e-safety educational framework in South Africa. In: Proceedings of the Southern Africa Telecommunication Networks and Applications Conference (SATNAC) (2012)

Livingstone, S., Kirwil, L., Ponte, C., Staksrud, E.: In their own words: what bothers children online? Eur. J. Commun. 29(3), 271–288 (2014)

Plowman, L., Stevenson, O., Stephen, C., McPake, J.: Preschool children's learning with technology at home. Comput. Educ. 59(1), 30–37 (2012). https://doi.org/10.1016/j.compedu.2011.11.014. Elsevier Ltd.

Rigby, K.: School perspectives on bullying and preventative strategies: an exploratory study. Aust. J. Educ. 61(1), 1–16 (2017)

Van Royen, K., Poels, K., Vandebosch, H., Adam, P.: Thinking before posting? Reducing cyber harassment on social networking sites through a reflective message. Comput. Hum. Behav. **66**, 345–352 (2017)

Shanmugam, K.R., Srinivas, K., Sathyavelu Reddy, K.: Information and communication technology (ICT) in education: advantages, disadvantages, conveniences and limitations. In: Proceedings of NAAC Sponsored National Seminar (2014)

Smit, D.: Cyberbullying in South African and American schools: a legal comparative study. S. Afr. J. Educ. **35**(2), 1–11 (2015)

Von Solms, S., Von Solms, R.: Towards cyber safety education in primary schools in Africa. In: Proceedings of the Eighth International Symposium on Human Aspects of Information Security & Assurance, HAISA 2014, pp. 185–197 (2014)

Srivastava, J.S.: Cyber crime?: kids as soft targets. Int. J. Innovative Comput. Sci. Eng. **4**(1), 31–36 (2017)

Stone, K.: Keeping children and young people safe online: balancing risk and opportunity key messages (2013). http://goo.gl/toJIXq

UNICEF: Your people's navigation of online risks (2012). http://goo.gl/hqaXJ9. Accessed 10 Mar 2014

Wall, D.: Cybercrimes and the internet. In: Wall, D.S. (ed.) Crime and the Internet, pp. 1–17. Routledge, New York (2001)

Towards Understanding How Game Based Learning Can Enhance Flipped Learning

M.J. Hattingh$^{(\boxtimes)}$ (ID) and S. Eybers$^{(\boxtimes)}$ (ID)

University of Pretoria, Private Bag X20, Hatfield 0028, South Africa
{marie.hattingh, sunet.eybers}@up.ac.za

Abstract. The increase in the request for competent, skilled data scientists has prompted higher education institutions to adapt learning strategies. A number of educators have implemented the flipped classroom approach with relative success. However, one challenge highlighted with this approach is how to match the in-class activities with "out-of-class lectures" in order to effectively engage learners during class contact sessions. This paper reports on one initiative to address this challenge through game based learning. A customized "Data Science Pursuit" board game was developed based on the well-known Trivial Pursuit board game. The questions of the customized board game was structured according to Bloom's Taxonomy, where different colour cards tested different competencies. The customized board game was used in conjunction with a flipped classroom approach. Following the implementation of the board game, a questionnaire based on the flipped learning criteria were distributed to the class. The results indicated that the customized board game had relative success in achieving and extending flipped learning. Despite the subjective feedback from leaners final module assessment results indicated a 100% pass rate which has never been achieved before. However, due to the scope of the work covered and the time constraint introduced by limiting the "playing time", not all content, which covered the important concepts of the learning unit, were sufficiently covered. Future explorative studies will be conducted to improve on the limited scope challenge that have emerged from the data.

Keywords: Flipped learning · Game based learning · Hybrid learning · Data science learners

1 Introduction

Upon graduating, graduates need to make a positive contribution to the world filled with dynamic problems and opportunities [1]. The dynamic problems and opportunities are partly created by ubiquitous computing where there is a predominant increase in large data sets. In order to harvest the "intelligence" of these large data sets, there has been an increase in aptly trained data scientists, which has created increased pressure on tertiary institutions to deliver data science learners that are "ready" to operate in the real-world. One approach to achieve this is by means of flipped learning. Flipped learning refers to a teaching strategy where the educators expose learners to content before formal class time and, as a result, obtain deeper learning through various

© Springer International Publishing AG 2017
T.-C. Huang et al. (Eds.): SETE 2017, LNCS 10676, pp. 106–115, 2017.
https://doi.org/10.1007/978-3-319-71084-6_12

activities during formal class time [2]. In [2] it was reported that one of the challenges associated with the flipped learning is how to match the in-class activities with "out-of-class lectures" in order to effectively engage learner centered learning during class contact sessions. The approach chosen to address these challenges, which is reported on in this paper, is game based learning (GBL).

GBL is defined as *"a type of game played with defined learning outcomes"* [3]. Boyle [4] explain that GBL allows for learners to retain important points in teaching appeals to different learning styles, engage learners, induce creative and divergent thinking amongst learners, encourage collaborative problem solving, is an easy means to incorporate peer learning, aids with dips in concentration levels and is a creative ice breaker.

Against this background, the formal research question, of this paper is: *to what extend does game based learning extend the flipped learning experience?*

A brief literature review will be provided on the four pillars of flipped learning, flipped classroom for data warehouse learners and game based learning in Sect. 2. Section 3 will introduce the game based approach used in this study namely "Data Science Pursuit". Section 4 will give a brief overview of the research method whereas a discussion of the results will follow in Sect. 5. The paper concludes with a summary of the results, limitations of the study and suggestions for future research.

2 Literature Review

The following sections will elaborate on the core concepts addressed in this research: firstly, it will clarify and position the concept of flipped learning by explaining the four pillars of FLIP; secondly, it will report on the success of using a flipped classroom environment in the instruction of data science learners and finally it will report on the concept of game based learning and position it within the context of flipped learning.

2.1 The Four Pillars of F-L-I-P

Further to the brief definition of flipped learning provided above, the four pillars of F-L-I-P is one of many pedagogical models developed to support educators to transition from a traditional classroom environment to a flipped classroom environment.

The four pillars of F-L-I-P, developed by Flipped Learning Network (FLN) [5] distinguishes between having a FLIP classroom and learners experiencing FLIP learning. The FLN reason that when educators employ a FLIP classroom approach, it cannot be automatically assumed that learning transpires. The FLN defines FLIP learning as "a pedagogical approach in which direct instruction moves from the group learning space to the individual learning space, and the resulting group space is transformed into a dynamic, interactive learning environment where the educator guides learners as they apply concepts and engage creatively in the subject matter" [5, p. 2]. The FLN proposes key criteria for each of the four pillars of F-L-I-P that need to be met in order to achieve flipped learning. Each of these pillars will be briefly discussed below. The criteria for each pillar was used in the questionnaire detailed in Table 2 (see Sect. 5).

Flexible Environment

The "flexible environment" pillar refers to the various learning spaces available to the learners. The learning spaces must be of such a nature that it allows for individual and group interactions. With the use of Web 2.0 technologies, a flexible learning space can easily be achieved [6]. Institutions often refer to this as hybrid learning or blended learning [7].

Learning Culture

Kirby and Hulan [6] reported on the way in which learning has changed due to the introduction of technology. Traditionally, learning took place within the socio cultural setting as advocated by Vygotsky [8]. However, over the last ten years learners were exposed to learner-centered learning, often requiring them to prepare content prior to class (sometimes in isolation). Therefore, in the context of flipped learning, learning culture refers to the transition from educator-centered approach to a learner-centered approach. This will allow in-class contact time to be used to discuss topics in detail and thereby creating a richer learning opportunity.

Intentional Content

Intentional content refers to the manner in which learning material is presented to learners in order to further their conceptual understanding of work covered. Educators should take care when deciding which work learners should prepare prior to class time, and how class time should then be structured to maximize the learning experience. FLN [5] further propose that educators should ensure that content should be presented scaffolded in order to complement the build up of key concepts.

Professional Educator

In flipped learning, learner centered approach is followed facilitated by the educator. However, this does not imply that the educator is absent. In a flipped learning environment the educator should be available to give continuous feedback to the learner in order to maximize the learning experience. Furthermore, the educator must be able to adjust content and the way it is being presented based on the dynamics of the in-classroom activities [5].

2.2   Flipped Classroom for Data Warehouse Learners

As mentioned above, there is an increasing need for real-world data scientists. As part of the data science curriculum the subject of data warehousing was included to expose and prepare learners to data storage related challenges and opportunities of Big Data (BD). In Eybers and Hattingh [9] it was argued that the "People" category of the proposed Critical Success Factors for BD should include individuals with the required statistical and analytical skills to work on BD projects [10]. The "required skills" aspect has been addressed by a few academics regarding the content of data science curriculums (for example [11, 12]). Turek et al. [13] have extended the learning experience by focusing on how the curriculum should be thought. They advocated three aspects to be included in a data science curriculum: Firstly, "real-world projects" should be used in order to present learners with accessible data and in a real world context. The requirement for real-world projects were supported by [12] who indicated only 10 of the 30 programmes reviewed in the USA had a practical component. Secondly, the ability to work as part of a BD project team is crucial. Thirdly, the early introduction of technical tools is recommended in order to ensure effective team dynamics and team competency. Based on these three aspects, Turek et al. [13] proposed a multi-disciplinary approach to data science education in order to account for both the technical and team related competencies required.

Conversely, Brunner and Kim [14] adopted an online approach whereby learners had access to a variety of resources (videos, notes, virtual environments). These resources were used by learners to acquire knowledge about certain subjects followed by a short online quiz to test their knowledge. A formal online assessment was conducted on a weekly basis. The authors indicated that this approach worked well and only highlighted technology related challenges during the course delivery.

2.3 Game Based Learning

Game based learning (GBL) is making more frequent appearances in the class room as it leaves the stigma of "games in classrooms" behind [15, p. 20]. Plass et al. [3] summarized four arguments in favour of GBL: (1) motivation which refers to a game's ability to keep players engaged during the game such as "stars, points, leaderboards, badges, and trophies". (2) Multi-layered player engagement on a cognitive level, engagement on an affective level, engagement on a behavioral level and finally engagement on a sociocultural level. (3) Adaptivity of the game to account for the learner's specific situation such as his/her level of knowledge. (4) Graceful failure speaks to the ability of learners to "save face" upon failure, it encourage learners to take risks and explore different opportunities. Groff et al. [15] distinguishes between different types of games as summarised in Table 1 below.

For the purposes of this study, a targeted game was developed. Even though it is classified to have a low open-endedness, it appeals to the flipped learning class

Table 1. Different genres of games [15]

Genre	Time to completion	Timescale	Open-endedness	Modes of creative expression	Examples	
					Commercial	Educational
Targeted games (puzzle, mini-games)	1–4 h	Weeks	Low	Style of completion: level creation	Angry Birds	Supercharged!
Linear games	20–40 h	Month	Low	Style of completion: machinema	Viewtiful Joe, Ninja Gaiden	DragonBox
Open-ended sandbox games	100–200 h played over multiple months	2–24 months	High	Style of completion: multiple solution paths, modding	Civilization, SimCity, Minecraft	SimCityEdu, MinecraftEdu, Making History
Persistent Worlds	500 + h	6–48 months	High	Modding; social engineering; game play	World of Warcraft, Everquest	Quest Atlantis

environment to be highly structured [2]. The customized board game employed in the study will be discussed in the following section.

3 "Data Science Pursuit"

The game employed in this study is based on the popular game "Trivial Pursuit". However, rather than different categories of general knowledge questions, "Data Science Pursuit" had different categories based on Bloom's Taxonomy: red and orange cards cover knowledge and comprehension questions, yellow and green cards cover application and analysis questions and purple and blue cards cover synthesis and evaluation type questions. A seventh color, white, was introduced to allow the class to ask a question to the Team that rolled the dice. Figure 1 below illustrates the laminated game board, whilst Figs. 2 illustrates examples of each category of question.

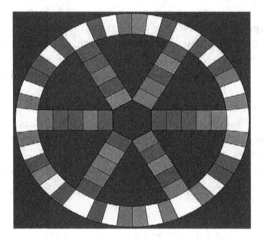

Fig. 1. Board game design (Color figure online)

Red / Orange Knowledge & Comprehension	Yellow / Green Application & Analysis	Purple / Blue Synthesis & Evaluation	Purple / Blue Synthesis & Evaluation
What is the difference between architecture and infrastructure?	Identify the physical components of the physical infrastructure in a DW. Pg 166	What is wrong with the following statement: Select the DW tools first then decide on the architecture. Pg 186	Identify the beneficiary of business metadata and explain why they benefit from it. Pg 209

Fig. 2. Question cards per level (Color figure online)

The class was divided into teams of up to six learners. Each team could choose a color sticker to represent their team, which was placed on the laminated board. Each Team got a turn to throw the dice, and the facilitator allowed one member of the Team to choose a card from the stack corresponding to the color the dice landed on. The questions that formed part of the game, was based on preparatory work that was made available to the learners before the class. The learners had to work through the content and complete an online quiz in preparation for the "game" during class time.

The game was played during the first 30 min of the lecture. Each Team got 30 s to answer the question, upon which they forfeited their points. The points were allocated based on the output from the dice and the Team's ability to answer the question. For example, if the Team throws the dice and it lands on 3, they will be awarded three marks if they answer correctly, if they don't answer correctly they will be awarded zero marks. The winning team was rewarded with chocolates.

4   Research Method

The study aimed to establish to what extent game based learning can contribute to a flipped learning experience. For this reason, the study followed an interpretive, qualitative approach as the researchers wished to obtain an understanding from the learners on their perception of game based learning. At the beginning of the semester, the ground rules for a flipped classroom was established, as advocated by [16] which ensured that all the learners knew what was expected of them in advance. As mentioned in Sect. 3, learners were instructed to prepare a section of work prior to each lecture. During the lecture, the game questions will cover that specific section of work. The class consisted of 38 fourth year learners. Each lecture is one and a half hour long. The customized board game is played during the first 30 min of the lecture. This paper reports on the first of many games played at the beginning of each lecture.

The questionnaire was structured according to the criteria of flipped learning, incorporating aspects of the customized board game. The questionnaire consisted of five parts: Enjoyment and Experience (G), Flexible Learning Environment (F), Learning Culture (L), Intentional Content (I) and Professional Educator (P) on a Likert scale from 1 = Strongly Disagree to 5 = Strongly Agree. Table 2 below illustrates the questionnaire items.

5   Results

All the learners that attended the lecture (34 of a class of 38), took part in the game and completed the questionnaire. Table 2 below illustrate the scores obtained from the questionnaire.

Table 2. Questionnaire items and scores

Index	Item	Min	Max	Avg
G.1	I enjoyed playing the "Data Science Pursuit" game	1.00	5.00	3.79
G.2	The game contributed to a positive learning experience	2.00	5.00	4.00
G.3	After playing the game, I had a better understanding of some of the theoretical concepts	2.00	5.00	3.82
G.4	After playing the game, I had a better understanding of some of the practical concepts	2.00	5.00	3.62
G.5	I would like to play the game again based on questions from the next learning unit	1.00	5.00	3.74
F.1 (a)	The game allowed me to positively interact with lecturers and fellow learners	2.00	5.00	3.91
F.1 (b)	The game allowed me to reflect on the concepts covered during the game	2.00	5.00	3.85
F.2	I was able to make adjustments to my own understanding of concepts based on the feedback/answers given by my peers	2.00	5.00	3.88
F.3 (a)	The game allowed me to learn the theoretical and practical concepts in a different way	2.00	5.00	3.85
F.3 (b)	The game gave me an indication of the extent to which I mastered the concepts (both theoretical and practical)	1.00	5.00	3.85
L.1	The game logically build on concepts covered during other activities (such as preparatory assignments) in the course	2.00	5.00	3.94
L.2	The way content was made available through the game was adequately covered and therefore assisted in my understanding of concepts	2.00	5.00	3.56
I.1	The most important aspect of the learning unit was included in the game	1.00	5.00	3.67
I.2	The game presented contextual examples of the theoretical components covered as part of the learning unit	2.00	5.00	3.41
I.3	The game made content available and accessible to me	2.00	5.00	3.53
P.1	The course facilitators were available and accessible during the game to provide real time feedback on concepts covered in the game	3.00	5.00	4.50

6   Discussion

The data obtained from the questionnaire is discussed using the questionnaire structure, which was based on the different pillars of F-L-I-P learning approach (as discussed in Sect. 2.1).

6.1   Enjoyment and Learning Experience

The results indicated that 76% of the learners enjoyed playing the game. whilst 80% felt that it contributed to a positive learning experience. 76% felt they had a better understanding of theoretical concepts although only 72% felt they had a better understanding of practical concepts. The discrepancy between the theoretical and practical understanding is not unexpected, as the practical concepts will be better explained by real-life projects. In this course learners will complete a real-life project.

74% of the learners agreed that the game based approach should be followed in the next learning unit. Although a benefit of GBL is that it appeals to learners with different learning styles [15] it might not appeal to everyone. Respondent 28 indicated that *"Generally I think I'm just a more formal learner. I'm sure it works for some people, I* don't think I'm one of them". A number of factors can contribute to learners' dislike of the game, namely the type of game chosen, the way it was facilitated or the flipped learning aspects. According to Herreid and Schiller [17] learners that are new to the flipped learning approach is often resistant as it entails a change in the way learning takes place and often requires more preparation effort.

6.2   Flexible Learning Environment

According to FLN [5] a flexible environment is achieved by meeting three objectives: (1) Establish spaces and time frames that permit learners to interact and reflect on their learning as needed. (2) Continually observe and monitor learners to make adjustments where appropriate. (3) Provide learners with different ways to learn content and demonstrate mastery.

The GBL approach has achieved all three objectives. In meeting objective one the flexible learning environment incorporates aspects of blended learning with the game based approach. During the in-class session 78% of learners agreed that the approach allowed them to positively interact with their peers and educators and it allowed them to reflect on the concepts covered during the game.

In meeting the second objective 78% of the learners were able to adjust their own understanding of concepts based on the class discussions. The peer learning aspect is one of the benefits of GBL [4]. Furthermore, the focused discussions around the most important aspects of the learning unit is the benefit of flipped learning [5]. As a consequence learners are "actively involved in knowledge construction as they participate in and evaluate their learning in a manner that is personally meaningful" [5, p. 2].

In meeting the third objective 77% of the learners reported that the GBL approach allowed them to learn theoretical and practical concepts in an alternative way, as well as measuring their mastery of the concepts.

6.3   Learning Culture

According the FLN [5] a learning culture is achieved by achieving the following two objectives: (1) Provide learners with the opportunity to engage in meaningful learning opportunities without the educator being central. (2) Scaffolding these activities and make then accessible to learners through differentiation and feedback. The GBL approach has achieved both these objectives.

In meeting the first objective, class discussions were based on the preparation assignment that had to be done beforehand, as required in the flipped learning approach. 78% of the learners indicated that the combination of preparatory work tested through the board game allowed for positive interaction during class. 92% of the cohort completed the preparatory assignment with an average mark of 62%.

In meeting the second objective only 71% of the learners agreed that the content was adequately covered. An explanation for this relatively low mark is that there was a time limit on the board game. Groff et al. [15] proposed that 1–4 h need to be allocated for a targeted game. Therefore, the 30 min timeslot might not have been sufficient.

6.4 Intentional Content

According the FLN [5] intentional content is developed by meeting the following three objectives: (1) Prioritize concepts used in direct instruction for learners to access on their own. (2) Create and/or curate relevant content (typically videos) for learners. (3) Differentiate to make content accessible and relevant to all learners. The GBL approach met all three objectives related to intentional content.

In meeting this objective 73% of the learners agreed that the most important aspects of the learning unit was included in the game. In meeting the second objective 68% of the learners agreed that the game presented contextual examples of the theoretical components associated with the learning unit. In meeting the third objective 71% of the learners agreed that the game made the content available to them. However, all three objectives' scores are relatively low. Although the educators have prepared a variety of questions based on the different levels of Bloom's Taxonomy, the time constraint encroached on the ability to "play all the cards".

6.5 Professional Educator

According the FLN [5] being a professional educator is achieved by meeting the following three objectives: (1) Make myself available to all learners for individual, small group, and class feedback in real time as needed. (2) Conduct ongoing formative assessments during class time through observation and by recording data to inform future instruction. (3) Collaborate and reflect with other educators and take responsibility for transforming practice.

Only the first objective has been measured with this board game. The role of the educators in facilitating the board game was the most successful aspect of the board game application. 90% of the learners agreed that the educators were available and accessible to provide real time feedback on the concepts covered by the board game.

7 Conclusion

GBL is an appropriate solution to extend the flipped learning experience. The game design elements appealed to the learners and provided an alternative way in which to engage with the content. The facilitation of the game session by the educators allowed for the learners to obtain a deeper understanding of the theoretical aspects of the course. The preparatory work required by the flipped learning approach allowed for interactive engagement of students during class time.

The GBL approach was therefore successful in extending the flipped learning experience. This finding was supported by the final assessment results indicating a 100% module pass rate.

The limitation of this exploratory study is related to the type of game chosen. Within the allocated timeslot, the structure of the game did not allow the learners to get the full benefit of the "complete game".

Future research should therefore be focused on strategies to cover more content in the given time, or alternative game methods should be considered.

References

1. Saulnier, B.M.: Towards a 21st century information systems education: high impact practices and essential learning outcomes. Issues Inf. Syst. **17**(1), 168–177 (2016)
2. "Flipped Classroom Field Guide" (2015). http://tlc.uic.edu/files/2016/02/Flipped-Classroom-Field-Guide.pdf. Accessed 01 June 2017
3. Plass, J.L., Homer, B.D., Kinzer, C.K.: Foundations of game-based learning. Educ. Psychol. **50**(4), 258–283 (2015)
4. Surgenor, P.W.G.: Teaching toolkit. UCD Teach. Learn. **5**, 254–257 (2010)
5. Flipped Learning Network: What is flipped learning? The four pillars of F-L-I-P. Flip. Learn. Netw. **501**(c), 2 (2014)
6. Kirby, E.G., Hulan, N.: Student perceptions of self and community within an online environment: the use of VoiceThread to foster community. J. Teach. Learn. Technol. **5**(1), 87–99 (2016)
7. Erturk, E.: A critical inquiry: teaching systems analysis and design beyond. In: Proceedings of the Computing and Information Technology Research and Education New Zealand 2014 Conference, Auckland, New Zealand, pp. 61–66 (2014)
8. Baker, R.: Examples of scaffolding and chunking in online and blended learning environments. Soc. Sci. Res. Netw. (2010). http://papers.ssrn.com/sol3/papers.cfm?abstract_id=1608133
9. Eybers, S., Hattingh, M.J.: Critical success factor categories for big data: a preliminary analysis of the current academic landscape, pp. 1–11 (2017)
10. Gómez, L.F., Heeks, R.: Measuring the barriers to big data for development: design-reality gap analysis in Colombia's public sector. In: Development Informatics, vol. 62. University of Manchester (2016)
11. Song, I.Y., Zhu, Y.: Big data and data science: what should we teach? Expert Syst. **33**(4), 364–373 (2015)
12. Tang, R., Sae-Lim, W.: Data science programs in US higher education: an interview with the authors. J. eSci. Librariansh. **6**(1), e1105 (2017). https://doi.org/10.7191/jeslib.2017.1105
13. Turek, D., Suen, A., Clark, D.: Pushing data science education into the real world (2015)
14. Brunner, R.J., Kim, E.J.: Teaching data science. Procedia Comput. Sci. **80**, 1947–1956 (2016)
15. Groff, J., McCall, J., Darvasi, P., Gilbert, Z.: Learning, Education and Games, vol. 2. Carnegie Mellon University, Pittsburgh (2016)
16. Demski, J.: 6 Expert Tips for Flipping the Classroom. Tech Enabled Learning (2013). http://campustechnology.com/Articles/2013/01/23/6-Expert-Tips-for-Flipping-the-Classroom.aspx?p=1
17. Herreid, C.F., Schiller, N.A.: Case studies and the flipped classroom (2012)

Can Video (Created with PowerPoint and TTSAPP) Replace "Normal" Lectures?

Robert Huberts[(⊠)] [iD]

University of Johannesburg, Johannesburg, South Africa
roberth@uj.ac.za

Abstract. PowerPoint, a ubiquitous tool used by lecturers and customizable with animation and now with video producing possibilities, and Microsoft Text to Speech Application (SAP15 TTSAPP), now including the more naturally sounding voices of Zira and David, have facilitated the setting up of a video lecture on boiling and condensation, which was presented to a class of 45 fourth year chemical engineering students in a computer laboratory. The original PowerPoint lecture on boiling and condensation was used in this study, and augmented with additional animation and audio to simulate normal lecture practice. The audio was produced by typing the spoken words into the notes section of the PowerPoint slides, and processing these with the TTSAPP. The resulting audio wav files were then included in the sequence on the animation pane, and the presentation saved (also) as a MP4 file video. Students rated the video lecture relative to a normal lecture and supplied additional, mostly positive, comments, and these results are discussed and compared to their performance in the following test. Hence it was concluded that there are initial indications that the learning of students is not adversely affected by having lectures online. This can now be tested for a whole subject, after which one may start thinking of collaboration with other universities to ultimately aim for increased teaching efficiency.

Keywords: PowerPoint · Online lecture · TTSAPP

1 Introduction

Globally, there is a trend of reduced government spending for education and an increase in student numbers [1], and more pressure on lecturers to perform in research rather than in teaching and learning [2]. Authors on online engineering education have indicated that to be broadly accepted and utilized, the quality of online courses must be comparable to or better than the traditional classroom [3]. They state that two of the pillars to judge for quality online learning is student satisfaction and learning effectiveness. The author of a comprehensive book on online teaching often gets asked whether online or on-campus teaching is better, but feels that they are so different that no comparison is possible [4]. Creating visual and auditory learning objects can be challenging, involving learning of new software tools [5].

This work focusses on a lecture of a (one) semester subject, Heat and Mass Transfer, which is presented to fourth year chemical engineering students at seven

© Springer International Publishing AG 2017
T.-C. Huang et al. (Eds.): SETE 2017, LNCS 10676, pp. 116–124, 2017.
https://doi.org/10.1007/978-3-319-71084-6_13

tertiary institutions around South Africa. For the current lecture, the knowledge content has hardly changed over the last 14 years, and recently passed the 5-year cycle scrutiny of the accreditation body (Engineering Council of South Africa). Hence there is considerable duplication of the lecturing effort, not only across the country, but also from one year to the next. (Note that the author is not suggesting that a static knowledge content is ideal; however, in defense of this, one argument could be that the principles of heat and mass transfer are fairly well established and relevant for a long period of time.) The author and many of the author's colleagues' lectures are based on Power-Point presentations in lecture halls, with the lecturer talking to the slides. And writing on a board is unlikely to disappear from an engineering lecture soon either [3]. The author suggests that the talking and additional writing can be included in a standard PowerPoint presentation, eliminating the need to learn new software tools as in [5]. The video of this PowerPoint presentation can be posted online, and the hypothesis of this work is that this simulates an on-campus lecture more closely than the online teaching of [4]. This is then compared to an on-campus lecture by interrogating student satisfaction and learning effectiveness, two of the quality pillars as discussed in the literature [3].

Some lecturers, including the author, are not keen to have their voice and/or persona recorded on a typical video of a lecture as in [6]. In addition, if it is required to modify what was said at a later stage, the author feels it would be inconvenient to set up the equipment, record the modified speech, cut the old audio out of the video and splice in the new. The voice may have changed, or not be available, and the whole lecture may have to be recorded again. Hence the author thought of the idea of rather using a text to speech application (TTSAPP) to produce audio, as has been done before [7]. If audio needs to change, the text can be modified and run through the app again to produce new audio. This will prove to be useful changes to the lecture are proposed over the years.

Recent development has made it possible to save a PowerPoint presentation as a video file. PowerPoint also has an animation facility, which amongst other capabilities can be used to simulate the movement of a laser pointer as the lecturer would use it during a lecture. It can also be used to show an explanatory note on the slide, and then remove it again if required. In addition, audio files can also be included in the animation sequence. It was found that the free software, Microsoft SAP15 TTSAP, was improved with the additions of the more natural sounding voices of David and Zira for Windows 10. The importance of good voices will be revealed in this work. The author feels that the available voices' quality will be improved further in future, adding to the attractiveness of using the technology.

It is the author's contention that, as PowerPoint is universally used in tertiary education, and using the animation and TTSAPP is not beyond most academics' grasp, it is possible for most lecturers to set up their own online lectures without additional cost (except for their time). In order to get an indication if it would be possible to replace traditional lectures in this way, an online lecture was set up and presented in a computer lab in this work. Students were asked for their feedback, and their performance in an assessment was evaluated, to determine whether the simulation was indeed equivalent to the original lecture.

2 Method

2.1 About the Students

59 students were registered for the Heat and Mass Transfer course. The author estimates that more than 90% of the students do not have English as a home language, although most have been in contact with English as a second language at school. Of the registered students, 45 attended the online lecture in the computer lab. The participation in the survey following the lecture was voluntary, and not all students partook. None of the students that had missed the lecture participated in the feedback.

2.2 About the Lecture

The lecture is the fifth one of six offered to the students for the Heat and Mass Transfer course. By the time the fifth lecture was reached, the students already had dealt with the basics of heat transfer, and had gone into detail in the conduction mode of heat transfer as well as internal and external convection.

The first half of the fifth lecture concerned heat transfer during the boiling of liquids. This included the boiling curve and the use of heat transfer correlations for the various boiling regimes.

The second half dealt with heat transfer during condensation. This focused on film condensation and various heat transfer correlations based on Nusselt's analysis.

2.3 Producing the Online Video

The PowerPoint file, used to lecture for the last 14 years by the author as lecturer, was used as the starting point. For a given slide, the author visualized what he would normally do (actions) and say (spoken words) during a lecture.

The normal actions could include moving a laser pointer to a certain position of the slide. In such cases, additional animation was added, in the form of an arrow which moved over the slide, for example. Normal action could also include the appearance of explanatory text or objects on the slide, in which case the animation probably already was present. The additional animation would then have to be timed as required and inserted in the sequence of existing animation.

The spoken words were typed into the notes section underneath the slides. The words for each concept explained were typically listed in separate paragraphs, each of which were allocated an identifying number. Each paragraph was then separately entered in the Microsoft SAP15 TTSAPP. The speak button was pressed to listen to the audio. Words were changed if required, with the speak button being pressed again to listen to the effect of this. Several iterations were often required, which resulted in clear, succinct audio. Once the author was satisfied with the spoken words, these were saved to a correspondingly numbered wav file. The wav audio files were then inserted as media onto the PowerPoint slide. The loudspeaker icon of a given audio file was then moved to the appropriate position on the slide close to the area on the slide relevant to the concept explained. Microsoft Zira, a lady's voice, was used for the boiling section of the lecture, while Microsoft David, a gentleman's voice, was used for the condensation section.

The iterative process described in the paragraph above meant that more preparation went into the delivery of the lecture, and the author wishes to believe that this increases the likelihood of learning by the students. Another effect was the reduction of time as compared to a normal lecture, with the two-hour lecture being reduced to half an hour of online lecture. The author imagines that the spoken part of a normally presented lecture is much less compact and to the point than that in the online lecture of this work.

If a student is has just opened a PowerPoint presentation at a given slide, the loudspeaker audio icon can be clicked to hear the audio applicable to the concept represented in that area of the slide. This can be used if the student is interested in hearing the audio for a specific concept without having to run the whole video or without playing the whole slide from the beginning.

Having the spoken words typed in the notes section of the PowerPoint slides has the beneficial effect of providing a record which can be modified in future if the need arises. In addition, students also have access to the PowerPoint slides, and therefore can read the words if they have problems in understanding the spoken words, or if they just want to learn by reading instead of listening, or if they happen not to have sound on the device used to access the PowerPoint files or videos. One French-speaking post-graduate student told the author it would have helped him a lot to see the words as he struggled to understand English during lectures back when he was busy with his undergraduate studies.

After including all the additional animation and all the audio into the PowerPoint file, it was saved as a normal PowerPoint file and as a video file. The video may be viewed on You Tube [8].

2.4   Presenting the Online Lecture and Collecting Data on Student Perceptions and Performance

The students were notified that the lecture would be presented in a computer lab, and 45 of the 59 students turned up for the lecture (representing about the average attendance of designated lecture periods). They were asked to bring their earphones. Some students were sharing earphones. Two peer tutors were in attendance. After half an hour, the requests for feedback were displayed to students as shown below.

First feedback question. The students were asked to rate the video lecture relative to a normal lecture as follows:

"Please score the lecture relative to one of my other lectures;

"10" means that the online lecture, as it happened in the lab with the tutor, and as it will remain available, is as good (or as bad) as one of my normal lectures with only the normal power point slides being available.

i.e. no better and no worse than a normal lecture.

"0" means it had no value to you.

"20" means it is twice as good as a normal lecture.

Note that consultation, tutorials, tests, formative and corrective assessments would remain as they are.

Choose one of the following numbers that best reflects your judgement:" The students could then select one of 0, 1, 2, etcetera, up to 20.

Second feedback question. The students were also asked to share more thoughts as follows:

"Any other thoughts you would like to share?"

Test 3. Following the online lecture (number 5), another traditional lecture (number 6) was presented to the students regarding radiation and heat/mass transfer analogy. An online test was then written by the students. In the test, a question on boiling regimes from a previous year was repeated, to see if the online lecture had an effect on the transfer of knowledge to the students. In the online video, and arrow was used to indicate the position of the boiling regime, and audio named and described the regime. In addition, a question was asked which the students would have been able to answer had they listened carefully to another audio clip included in the online lecture.

3   Results and Discussion

3.1   Student Rating of Online Lecture

Another lecture (lecture number 6) followed the online lecture, and a test was written based on these two lectures (Test 3 on lectures 5 and 6). The score as a percentage obtained by the students was plotted against the rating of the online lecture between 0 and 20 (10 being just as good/bad as a normal lecture). The results are shown in Fig. 1.

Firstly, it can be seen that 80% of the students rated the online lecture as good as or better than a normal lecture (20 of the 25 data points are on or to the right of 10 on the x-axis). This is in accordance with another study that found that nearly all students found (shorter) online lectures "entertaining enough" or "very entertaining" [9]. A linear trendline was fitted to the data, and although there is a lot of scatter (R^2 is 0.25, whereas 1 indicates a perfect fit), it can be seen that students that struggled in the test were more likely to have given a higher score to the online lecture. This seems to indicate that students that struggle academically see more value in online lectures.

3.2   Student Performance for a Repeated Question

In the third test, a question was posed as follows: "Consider the boiling curve for water and identify the boiling regimes". Online Blackboard software was used to set up this test (see Fig. 2).

This question was also asked a couple of years back, with an average mark of 3.7 being obtained out of 4, and last year, with an average mark of 3.71. The online lecture was also used last year, but with Microsoft Anna as the female voice. (Old question papers with model answers are available to students. However, the model answer to this question only listed the boiling regimes, not disclosing the actual question setup on Blackboard). In the test following the current online lecture, a very similar average

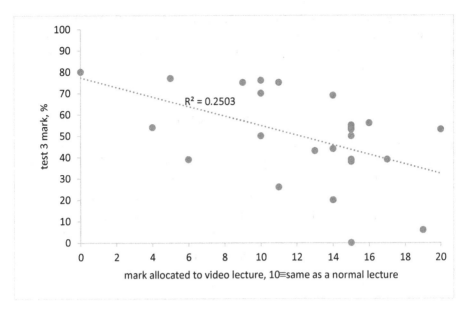

Fig. 1. Mark obtained in test following online lecture (plus another normal lecture) as a function of student allocated mark to online video.

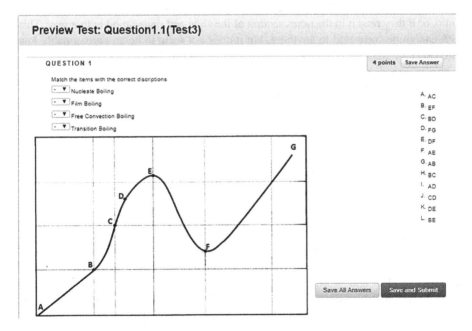

Fig. 2. Question in test 3 regarding boiling regimes.

mark of 3.75 was obtained by the students. This seems to be an indication that having a lecture online has no measurable effect on the learning of students, a result which has been found to be the case generally for online education [3, 10]. This result could possibly have been expected in this work as it was strived to emulate an on-campus lecture.

3.3   Student Performance for a Question Based on an Audio File

In the third test, another question was posed as follows: "Type about two sentences to describe the average heat transfer coefficient due to radiation on Blackboard". The audio file was obtained using the following text and the TTSAPP:

"WARC513b You will need to calculate the average radiation heat traaansfer coefficient, h, bar, rad. Note that, if the formula for heat traaansfer coefficient due to radiation is plugged into Newton's law of cooling, it becomes the Stephen Boltzmann law."

WARC513b is the identifying number of the audio file. The triple a spelling in "traaansfer" results in the word "transfer" sounding more South African.

The formula which was displayed on Blackboard was:

$$\bar{h}_{rad} = \frac{\varepsilon\sigma\left(T_S^4 - T_{sat}^4\right)}{T_S - T_{sat}} \tag{1}$$

13% of the students recalled that the Stephen Boltzmann's law would result. It is presumed that most would have recalled this had they listened to and understood the audio, or if they read it in the notes section of the slide and understood in that way. This 13% cannot be compared to anything, but it does not seem to be an unreasonably low percentage of students remembering a relatively obscure fact.

3.4   Thoughts of the Students Regarding the Online Lecture

21 students chose to give this feedback. Some feedback was that the online lecture was good, with many finding the rewinding aspect appealing and applauding the clarity of the slides:

"if we can have more of such lectures since one is able to pause and play back for better understanding."

"I thought the online lecture highlighted important points very well"

The fact that students appreciated the rewinding aspect of online lectures was also found in the literature [9]. The author is pleased that many students found that the slides were clear; this is not surprising as an iterative process was followed to get the audio sentences as clear and succinct as possible.

One comment was that online lectures would be useful if a lecture could not be attended and the student was absent due to unforeseen circumstances. Five students just expressed a positive response to the lecture, but did not specify why, for example:

"we should have these kind(s) of sessions often."

Sometimes students expressed more than one opinion, which could be positive and negative:

"Overall the video is good but I didn't find the background voice interesting."

In fact, many students complained about the mechanical quality of the voice, and hopefully newer versions will be developed in the future by Microsoft. Two comments were about the effort required (concentration and time rewinding for note-taking). The author was in two minds whether the increased effort was a bad or a good thing! One student made a valid point that the lecturer was not there to answer questions. However, this function could have been performed by the attending peer tutors. Alternatively, there is e-mail or consulting hours.

7 comments were received that students would have liked to see examples of calculations. This is a valid issue; however, the examples were not present in the traditional lecture either and so this was not presumed to reflect negatively on the online lecture. In future, it may make sense to break the lecture up into smaller sections, and have the students do problems in between, perhaps after dealing with an example. One student also suggested that both traditional and online lectures could be presented. The summary of student comments is given in Fig. 3, where it can be seen that about 2/3 of the comments were positive.

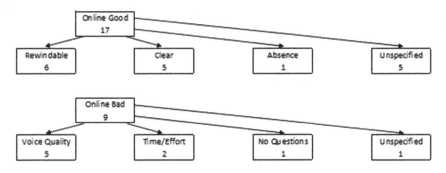

Fig. 3. Student feedback for online lecture.

4 Conclusions

It has been demonstrated that online videos can be set up using PowerPoint and a TTSAPP. Keeping a record of the text in the notes section of the PowerPoint slides, facilitates the making of changes to the text, so that the audio can be redone using the TTSAPP. This avoids having to record a whole lecture again as could well be the case for a simple recording of a lecturer's voice. These notes can also be read by students to aid the learning process. Students can click on the loudspeaker icons to play the audio for a concept in that area of a slide.

Overall, students were positive about the prospect of having online lectures for the subject on offer. 80% of participating students rated the online lecture as good as or better than a traditional lecture, and 2/3 of the comments collected were positive. The rewindability and clarity of the online lecture featured high on the list, but it remains crucial to improve the voice quality of the TTSAPP. There is an indication that struggling students may benefit more from an online lecture due to the support this provides them. There is an initial indication that the learning of students for the subject is not negatively affected by presenting it online; however more extensive testing, perhaps by putting all the lectures of a subject online, will be required to allow assessment of the whole subject and comparison with previous years.

Perhaps after that could one start thinking of rolling out of the online lectures across the country. This could also open the window for collaboration on the content of the lectures while lowering of cost for higher quality online offerings, as suggested in the literature [3], and also the reduction of individual academics' lecturing workload.

References

1. Brew, A.: VII The paradoxical university and the public good. In: Higher Education as a Public Good. Peter Lang, New York (2015)
2. Espinoza, J.: http://www.telegraph.co.uk/education/educationnews/11851642/University lecturers-more-worried-about-research-than-teaching-minister-warns.html. Accessed 28 Apr 2017
3. Bourne, J., Harris, D., Mayadas, F.: Online engineering education: learning anywhere, anytime. J. Eng. Educ. **94**(1), 131–146 (2005). http://digitalcommons.olin.edu/engconpub/1
4. Rutgers University Research Spot Light. https://www.youtube.com/watch?v=ZeEICo6 hU28. Accessed 29 July 2017
5. Becker, M.R., Winn, P., Erwin, S.L.: Student-centered, e-learning design in a University classroom. In: Isaías, P., Spector, J.M., Ifenthaler, D., Sampson, D.G. (eds.) E-Learning Systems, Environments and Approaches, pp. 229–246. Springer, Cham (2015). https://doi. org/10.1007/978-3-319-05825-2_16
6. Lauffenburger, D.: Bioengineering [video] (2006). https://ocw.mit.edu/courses/biological-engineering/20-010j-introduction-to-bioengineering-be-010j-spring-2006/videos/Lecture-1-bioengineering/
7. Salvor: How to put text-to-speech voice in your videos! Make your Youtube videos better! [Video] (2016). https://youtu.be/JcrO0QowGYI
8. Channel: Robert Huberts. https://youtu.be/fvfBHHVPbA4. Accessed 29 July 2017
9. Waldorf, D.J., Schlemer, L.: The inside-out classroom: a win-win strategy for teaching with technology. In: 118th ASEE Annual Conference & Exposition Proceedings: Vancouver, BC (2011)
10. Yousef, A.M.F., Chatti, M.A., Schroeder, U.: Video-based learning: a critical analysis of the research published in 2003–2013 and future visions. In: eLmL 2014, The Sixth International Conference on Mobile, Hybrid, and On-line Learning, pp. 112-119 (2014)

Effectiveness of Learning with the Support of a Virtual Environment (Experiment in University Teaching)

Hana Mohelska$^{(\boxtimes)}$ⓘ and Marcela Sokolovaⓘ

Faculty of Informatics and Management, The University of Hradec Kralove,
Hradec Kralove, Czech Republic
hana.mohelska@uhk.cz

Abstract. Virtual worlds are very universal environments that can also be used as a didactic means that allows for the application of a wide range of activities, as well as various teaching forms and methods. The introductory section of the article presents a definition of virtual worlds on the conceptual and content levels, and also provides a description of their technological concept. The didactic-technological aspects that accelerate most of the opportunities to use virtual worlds within the education process have been determined using available knowledge. The main aim of the research was to clarify whether the appropriate use of virtual environment in the instruction leads to a corresponding student performance in cognitive learning. The partial aim of the research was a mutual comparison of two leaning virtual environments i.e. Second Life and Minecraft, selection of which was intentional as these have currently been the most widely used virtual environments. Application themes of the action research were focused mainly on the phenomena associated with the implementation of virtual collaborative environment. The assessment was realised by means of didactic and managerial criteria.

Keywords: Student performance · Virtual environment · Experiment · Second Life · Minecraft

1 Introduction

The subject of the paper is examining the phenomenon of virtual worlds in the context of didactics, i.e. didactics of information and technical education in terms of their educational function, didactic specifics and possibilities of virtual worlds in teaching. The authors deal with the issue of virtual worlds such as innovative didactic resource, which is useful in the practice of the university. Within the issue, there is a rating system formulated for suitability of virtual worlds for deployment in the educational process and the use is empirically investigated through experiment.

1.1 Definition of Virtual Worlds and Their Didactic Specifics

Given the above formulated objective, the following part of the paper deals with virtual worlds in terms of terminology definition, technology specifics and in terms of

© Springer International Publishing AG 2017
T.-C. Huang et al. (Eds.): SETE 2017, LNCS 10676, pp. 125–133, 2017.
https://doi.org/10.1007/978-3-319-71084-6_14

didactics. This section will define a common theoretical basis, within which we can view virtual worlds as a potential means of education and allowing subsequent classification and categorisation of such environments on the basis of technological-functional and didactic-organisational aspects.

1.2   Initial Concepts for the Field of Virtual Worlds

Virtual worlds are ranked among the virtual environment. The concept of a virtual environment, which falls within the area of virtual reality, is so broad and has undergone significant development so it can indicate fundamentally different objects, in some properties lying at opposite ends of the distinctive range. Therefore, it is crucial to define in detail the concept for the purposes of the paper and further define the extent and place the researched virtual worlds occupy within the virtual environment concept.

1.3   Virtuality - Virtual Reality

According to Jeřábek [1], the concept of virtual, i.e. virtuality, can be examined in terms of philosophy as well as from the point of view of later-established perspective of information technology and ICT. In both concepts this concept has undergone a long evolution during which its meaning has essentially changed. In terms of philosophy we currently perceive the word of virtual in the meaning of "almost the same", "like", "almost real". In normal communication the word virtual is understood as "the opposite of real while the real represents a material fact", 8 although from a detailed examination of the genesis and shifts in the perception of virtual within the philosophical areas it shows that there it is not a semantic opposite to real, as it is a complex conceptual architecture in which, according to Heim [2], "virtual cannot exist without the reality elements on which it is based, and real contains layers of virtuality that precedes reality." Virtual reality is an event or object which is real in its effect but it is not real.

In terms of ICT the term has several meanings. In addition to labelling software systems temporarily replacing or extending hardware features (such as virtual servers, virtual disks, virtual memory, etc.), according to Lévy [3] we could think of virtual reality in the context of an artificial communication environment. In this context, virtual reality may be represented by a theatre stage as well as various chat rooms, forums and websites on the internet, i.e. imaginary places and spaces within communication networks. [4]

On the completely opposite side, the virtual environment in the ICT is considered a simulating environment - virtual reality, computer-generated three-dimensional environment into which a human completely immerses in and experiences immersive interactive experience. [5] In this concept, virtual reality is considered as immersive from all sides but it can't be modified. According to the sense level of immersion, the virtual reality systems are divided into Non-immersive, Semi-immersive and Fully immersive. [2] Interactive virtual reality is active with the possibility of modifications. Similarly, in the issue of virtual reality Heim [2] identifies the concept of passive and active participation of a user, i.e. tension of virtual reality, leading the user from passivity to activity due to the fact that the navigation and orientation in the environment requires creative decisions. The concept of handling and perception that corresponds to Austakalnis' concept of interactions is even further. Environment interacts with the user while it provides sensory sensations evoking emotions to the user. [6]

Means of virtual reality in general are among the so-called new media. Lister [7] in his work in New Media: A critical introduction dealt extensively with the identification of typical and definition characteristics of new media. He formulated six key characteristics of new media - virtuality, immersion, interaction, digitality, dispersion and hypertextuality. Heim [2] identified seven aspects of virtual reality - simulation, interaction, artificiality, immersion, telepresence (active action at a distance), full body immersion and network communication.

1.4   Virtual Environment

The concept of reality involves a complex of objects, relationships and dependencies that surround us. In contrast, the concept of environment within the broad concept of virtual reality implies local embeddedness, which is a common thing for virtual reality, and therefore, this concept is more suitable for the description of virtual worlds.

Also the concept of a virtual environment is used in a relatively wide range of meanings. If the concept of virtual reality is in the context of an artificial communication environment based on a virtual environment, a web page, communication (e.g. a mail or chat) program or applet if it is used within networked community, are then suitable for the definition. The virtual environment in this context is also currently often spoken about in connection with the phenomenon of Web 2.039. Cyberspace is a common synonym for virtual environment. The term cyberspace refers to an artificially created environment with the help of information technology, in which we can find digital objects as well as virtual representation of users. Some authors suggest that cyberspace is an environment of collective intelligence, "the new communications environment that emerges from the global inter-connection of computers. This concept refers not only to the infrastructure of digital communication but also to the huge ocean of information which it contains as well as the human beings who sail in it and supply it." [8]

Říha [9], however, also defines cyberspace in the context of a simulated environment and explains the concept of cyberspace - specifically Avatar Cyberspace (AC) – as a gradual convergence of technology of WWW, MUD42 and virtual reality. He notes that the first virtual world could not occur earlier than after the introduction of the standard of Virtual Reality Modelling Language (VRML) for 3D modelling on the Internet in 1995.

Other frequently used term denoting virtual environment is Multi-User Virtual Environment (MUVE). Previously it was also used as a term that includes games such as Multi User Dungeon (MUD), Object Oriented (MOO), Massive Multi-player Online Role-Playing Game (MMORPG) from which, as previously mentioned, the virtual worlds have emerged by convergence with social networks. Today it is used either as a synonym for virtual world (VW) and also to mark the MMORPG which are not entirely game-focused, i.e. those with a relatively free scenario. A key MUVE feature is the aspect of a story, a quest which does not have to be here at all or can be in the background, for educational use it is important to preserve the relative freedom of movement and non-linearity of the story. [10] Jílková et al. [11] also lists this property as a vital and divides MUVE into virtual worlds oriented in games that usually have predefined "virtual cultures" and on the other side the worlds with an open culture.

Smith-Robbins [12] defines a virtual environment (and prefers the term "virtual worlds") on the basis of four main features:

1. This is the persistence or permanence of the world which continues to exist even after the user disconnects.
2. The possibility of connecting multiple users.
3. Representations of users through avatars.
4. Broad availability through the network.

This group of virtual worlds (which according to the above characteristics does not include for example, CAVE simulator types, etc.) is in the literature often called a desktop virtual environment. Unlike virtual reality systems, the desktop virtual environment does not require special hardware (although the use of special peripherals is not entirely impossible) and is more focused on the user's social communication than on exact simulation and imitation of reality. Virtual reality systems typically do not work well with an avatar, the first person view is used instead of the avatar display and most of these systems are single user.

Although the quality of environment simulation is not too high in virtual worlds compared to special CAVE systems and therefore the level of immersing feeling of the user into the virtual world is relatively low, the important aspect is that the user can move freely in the environment (including flying or teleporting) in 3D virtual space. Another important aspect is the possibility of sharing space and objects between users/players, the possibility of communication and collaboration of the users. Virtual worlds show signs of a collaborative virtual environment and some authors [13–15] emphasise this aspect. According to [16], collaborative virtual environment can include productivity software, such as military simulators, engineering software, software for distributed rendering and distributed simulations (e.g. meteorological forecast models) as well as interactive communication tools (including video-conferencing) and network games.

Some authors have high hopes regarding the future use of the desktop virtual environment, Kapp and O'Driscoll [17] even considers a virtual environment as the internet application of version 3.0. While in the first generation of the Internet the users were connected to the internet formed by mostly static presentations, by which one author appeals to the general public, a shift to the so-called Web 2.0 meant a major change when the pages are dynamically created by the users themselves who mutually interlink "through" the internet. The above-mentioned authors expect a further qualitative Internet shift towards a 3D environment (3D Internet - 3Di) with users "inside" the Internet. Other authors [18, 19] consider the so-called semantic Web (Web 3.0) as the principle of distribution of data processed on the basis of their importance) [18] as the mouth of development of the Internet. The two concepts are not in conflict and their simultaneous use is also possible, or future internet could integrate elements of both concepts.

2   Methodology

2.1   Objective of the Research

The main aim of the research was to clarify whether the appropriate use of virtual environment in the instruction leads to a corresponding student performance in cognitive learning. The partial aim of the research was a mutual comparison of two leaning virtual environments i.e. Second Life and Minecraft, selection of which was intentional as these have currently been the most widely used virtual environments. Application themes of the action research were focused mainly on the phenomena associated with the implementation of virtual collaborative environment. The assessment was realised by means of didactic and managerial criteria.

2.2   Methods Used

The research used the following methods: pedagogical experiment, didactic tests – checking of the input and output knowledge. A suitable method for comparing the effectiveness of two different education systems is a pedagogical experiment. The experimental method uses a special word to describe experimental changes - an independent variable. In our research, the independent variable was the use of virtual environment in training where we have two experimental groups - the first using SecondLife and the other using Minecraft. The third - control group consisted of students where virtual environment is not be used in training.

From the qualitative research methods used in the action research, the analysis of the teacher's record and their subjective evaluation during education was used. A form of structured interviews with students was used to obtain their evaluation during education. Conclusions and recommendations were formulated on the basis of synthesis of lessons learned.

2.3   Research Group

One of the important conditions for the organization of the experiment is that the test and control groups are the most equivalent possible. The empirical research is based on a model of action research conducted by a researcher in the university practice where a total random selection for experimental research is usually impossible. For the selection of the research group the available selection was used. The research group consisted of college students (University of Hradec Králové, Faculty of Informatics and Management) who participated on the Management Methods course in the academic year of 2015/2016. The research was conducted in three selected groups of students of the 1st year of Master's degree, there was 20 students in every gender-balanced group. The research was conducted within one academic year, i.e. 2015/2016.

3 Results and Discussion

3.1 Evaluation of the Effectiveness of Education

At first, it was examined whether learning in a virtual environment is generally as effective as education not using virtual environment.

The aim of this test was to verify the following hypothesis:

There is statistically no significant difference between the performances that are reached by students in the pre-test (input diagnostic test) and post-test (output diagnostic test) included in the control group and the students included in the experimental groups.

At the beginning of the experiments the pre-test was used to verify the initial knowledge of all three groups. Analysis of the results showed that the initial knowledge is similar in all groups, which is a prerequisite to be able to run the experiment.

At the end of the experiment the participants passed the test of output knowledge – post-test – it was created in order to determine the output level of knowledge after experimental exposure. The analysis of the results showed that there is statistically no significant difference between the performance of the control and experimental groups.

Certain differences have already appeared in student evaluation of training. Within the embodiment of feedback, the experimental group students evaluated the research more positively, although the results in the area of cognitive learning were not significantly affected.

3.2 Comparison of Education in Virtual Environment of SecondLife and Minecraft According to the Selected Criteria

Mojžíšek [20] considers effective and efficient attainment of the education and training objectives as the main function of teaching methods. In order to allow the teaching methods to perform this function, they must have some essential qualities. According to [20] a method is didactically effective if it has the following properties:

1. It transmits information and skills which is not distorted in its content.
2. It is formatively effective, i.e. it develops cognitive processes.
3. It is rationally and emotionally compelling, i.e. it attracts the student to experience learning and cognition.
4. It follows the system of science and knowledge.
5. It is educational, i.e. develops moral, social, labour and aesthetic profile of a pupil.
6. It is natural in its course and consequences.
7. It is useful at work, in real life, it brings school closer to life.
8. It is adequate to pupils.
9. It is adequate to teachers.
10. It is didactically economical.
11. It is hygienic.

Table 1 shows the evaluation of didactic efficiency according to the criteria, i.e. properties according to Mojžíšek [20] (see above criteria K1-K11). Evaluation performed by an experienced teacher on a scale of 1 to 5 where 5 is the highest rating.

Table 1. The evaluation of didactic efficiency according to the criteria

Virtual environment	K1	K2	K3	K4	K5	K6
SecondLife	4	5	4	5	4	4
Minecraft	4	5	5	5	5	5
Virtual environment	K7	K8	K9	K10	K11	Average
SecondLife	3	3	3	1	5	3.73
Minecraft	3	5	3	5	5	4.55

Source: custom processing.

The above evaluation of both virtual environments of Second Life and Minecraft shows that the Minecraft virtual environment - average value of criteria is 4.55 points, is didactically more effective than the SecondLife virtual environment (average 3.73 points).

3.3 Creating Scenarios

For virtual environments with an integrated scenario it is only possible to implement training within limits that are provided by this scenario. In this case the scenario significantly influences decisions on selecting which virtual environment. Although there are environments with an integrated scenario developed primarily for educational needs but there are not many of them. Originally pure gaming environments are more often used for certain narrowly defined learning activities (e.g. strategy games to simulate economy, fantasy role-playing games, etc.).

The virtual environments which do not include the scenario are more universal or it is possible to suppress the scenario (e.g. in Minecraft by changing the game mode from Survival to Creative) or it is possible not to use the scenario and ignore it (e.g. focus of SecondLife on integrated economy). [21, 22]

The environments that are open while supporting scripting, are the most versatile. There is sometimes possible to use external specialised tools for creating and editing scenarios (e.g. Pivote tool in SecondLife)

4 Conclusions and Recommendations

Open or partially-open types of virtual environments usually contain integrated tools for creating objects. For some of them, creation of objects is part of the scenario (e.g. in Minecraft the objects are created from raw materials through a kiln and workshop table), in some of them the creation is completely free (e.g. in SecondLife and OpenSim it is possible to create any objects by deriving from basic shapes, so-called prims, in the built-in editor). For a teacher, the import of objects is an interesting option. If the virtual world supports this feature, it is possible to use external tools that can be more efficient in creating of objects in terms of speed as well as in terms of size and sophistication of the objects. E.g. creating a giant spaceship in the Minecraft environment can take hundreds to thousands of hours but it is also possible to create an appropriate model in an external CAD/CAM program and then just import them after the necessary adjustments.

The possibility of scripting is another added value that can only be provided by some environments, which allow the creation of dynamic, interactive or hypermedia objects from static objects. Scriptable environment also facilitates the creation of learning objects as part of the learning scenario.

Full use of learning objects is assumed by an environment that has an integrated concept of avatar inventory and allows sharing or at least changing the ownership of objects. This is important in terms of the distribution of learning objects, submission of student products and to use the objects as motivational and evaluation elements (e.g. remuneration of students with new avatar attributes).

The ability to track and control communication is important for teachers in a virtual classroom as well as in a real classroom. Tools to control communication include:

- Text communication display
- Mute function - disabling communication of a specific avatar
- The possibility of excluding an avatar from the environment (i.e. ban)
- Recording and archiving communication (text as well as voice communication)

The communication as a social aspect is also related to a self-presentation of the user against other users. In comparison of both virtual environment in terms of teaching efficiency, Minecraft appeared to be more efficient. Minecraft offers two main game modes - survival and creative. In the survival mode, the player is placed randomly into generated world without supplies or tools, and the goal is survival and exploration. In the creative mode, the player has unlimited access to all game blocks, unlimited life and the ability to fly. Therefore the player can be fully devoted to the development of different models and structures. The game also supports multi-player mode via local network or the Internet.

Acknowledgments. The paper was written with the support of the specific project 6/2017 grant "Determinants affecting job satisfaction" granted by the University of Hradec Králové, Czech Republic and thanks to help students Kateřina Kožnarová.

References

1. Jeřábek, T.: Využití prostředků rozšířené reality v oblasti vzdělávání. Karlova univerzita, Pedagogická fakulta (2016)
2. Heim, M.: The Metaphysics of Virtual Reality. Oxford University Press, New York (1993)
3. Lévy, P.: Kyberkultura: zpráva pro Radu Evropy v rámci projektu 'Nové technologie: kulturní spolupráce a komunikace'. Karolinum, V Praze (2000)
4. Antonacci, D., DiBartolo, S., Edwards, N., Fritch, K., McMullen, B., Murch-Shafer, R.: The power of virtual worlds in education: a second life primer and resource for exploring the potential of virtual worlds to impact teaching and learning. ANGEL Learn. 1–2 (2008)
5. Brdička, B.: Role internetu ve vzdělávání: studijní materiál pro učitele snažící se uplatnit moderní technologie ve výuce. AISIS, Kladno (2003)
6. Aukstakalnis, S., Lanier, J., Venzara, J., Vokáč, P., Blatner, D., Klimeš, J.: Reálně o virtuální realitě: umění a věda virtuální reality. Jota, Brno (1994)

7. Lister, M. (ed.): New Media: A Critical Introduction, 2nd edn. Routledge, Abingdon (2009)
8. Boellstorff, T.: Coming of Age in Second Life: An Anthropologist Explores the Virtually Human. Princeton University Press, Princeton (2010)
9. Říha, D.: Avatar cyberspace - matrix v embryonálním stadiu? (2011)
10. Barfield, W. (ed.): Fundamentals of Wearable Computers and Augmented Reality, 2nd edn. Taylor & Francis, Boca Raton (2015)
11. Jílková, D., Juhaňák, L., Kantorová, K., Holubcová, E., Ilková, M., Rychtová, V.: Aplikace vzdělávacích a kolaborativních nástrojů ve virtuálním světě Second Life – projekt VIAKISK. Inflow Inf. J. **3**(1), 3–4 (2010)
12. Smith-Robbins, S.: Incommensurate Wor(L)ds: Epistemic Rhetoric and Faceted Classification Of Communication Mechanics in Virtual Worlds. Ball State University, Muncie (2011)
13. Brock, D.C., Moore, G.E. (eds.): Understanding Moore's Law: Four Decades of Innovation. Chemical Heritage Foundation, Philadelphia (2006)
14. Dalgarno, B., Lee, M.J.W.: What are the learning affordances of 3-D virtual environments? Br. J. Educ. Technol. **41**(1), 10–32 (2010)
15. Elliot, M.: Stigmergic collaboration: the evolution of group work. Mc J. **9**(2), 5 (2006)
16. Pečiva, J.: Active transactions in collaborative virtual environments. Ph.D. thesis. Faculty of Information Technology, Brno University of Technology, Brno (2007)
17. Kapp, K.M., O'Driscoll, T.: Learning in 3d: Adding a New Dimension to Enterprise Learning and Collaboration. Pfeiffer, San Francisco (2010)
18. Dede, C., Ketelhut, D., Ruess, K.: Motivation, usability, and learning outcomes in a prototype museum-based multi-user virtual environment. In: Keeping Learning Complex. Mahwah, NJ (2002)
19. Randák, M.: Využití virtuálních světů v edukačním procesu. Karlova univerzita, Pedagogická fakulta, Praha (2016)
20. Mojžíšek, L.: Didaktika: Teorie vzdělání a vyučování. SPN, Praha (1988)
21. Mohelska, H., Sokolova, M.: The creation of the qualitative scenarios in the virtual three-dimensional environment second life. Procedia Comput. Sci. **3**, 312–315 (2011)
22. Mohelska, H., Sokolova, M.: Effectiveness of using e-learning for business disciplines: the case of introductory management course. EM Ekon. Manag. **17**(1), March 2014

Emerging Technologies of Pedagogical Issues

The Design of a STEM-Oriented Project-Based Course for the Higher Grades of Elementary Schools

Yi-wen Lin and Tzone-I Wang$^{(\boxtimes)}$

Department of Engineering Science, National Cheng Kung University,
Tainan, Taiwan
wti535@mail.ncku.edu.tw

Abstract. This study designs a STEM-oriented project-based learning course with hand-on projects for the higher grades of elementary schools to develop their interest in explorative learning by laying the foundations of Science, Technology, Engineering, and Mathematics (STEM). Students are grouped for the course projects to promote their collaborating capability. To investigate the feasibility of such course, this research uses a combination of qualitative research and quantitative research methods to conduct a triangulation on STEM scholastic achievements, teacher's survey, and participant observations. The results indicate, for the higher grades students of elementary schools, the STEM-oriented project-based course has positive and significant improvements on students' STEM scholastic achievements. By participant observations, experts find that students are willing to take the hands-on approach of learning by doing, which makes them find solutions to problems by themselves or with the help of group members. The teacher's survey also shows positive results. This research also observes a performance improvement on students' creativity, collaboration, and communication (3C) capability, but the overall improvement does not reach a significant level.

Keywords: Pre-engineering education · STEM · Project-based learning · Elementary school

1 Introduction

Today, Taiwan's national competitiveness, especially the economy, depends mainly on high-technology industry developments. Talented and well educated engineers are most needed in the coming decades and in a decade, students graduate today from primary schools will become influential on the engineering design and technology development in Taiwan. Developed countries have begun to promote engineering technology education in primary and secondary schools, as pre-engineering courses. Douglas et al. indicated that pre-engineering education often begins with technology

This study is supported by the National Science Council (now Ministry Of Science and Technology) of Taiwan under the project contract No.: MOST 104-2511-S-006-009.

T.-C. Huang et al. (Eds.): SETE 2017, LNCS 10676, pp. 137–143, 2017.
https://doi.org/10.1007/978-3-319-71084-6_15

education in primary and secondary schools and continues at college or university [1–3]. In United States, pre-engineering education courses for primary and secondary schools, based on science, technology, engineering, and mathematics (STEM), have been implanted. Davies and Gilbert indicated that science and technology courses in lots of advanced countries have particularly emphasized on students' hands-on activities in their learning process [4, 5]. It is not difficult to find that most of the pre-engineering education plans are for cultivating students to have the ability of integrating knowledge of technologies, and for teaching them engineering thinking of system philosophy, creativity, collaboration, communication, and ethic, as well as inspiring their interest in engineering [6–8].

2 Methodology and Materials

This study designs a STEM-oriented project-based pre-engineering learning course for higher grade students of elementary schools, which is to promote students' STEM capability and enhance students' creativity, collaboration, and communication (3C) capabilities by hand-on projects. An e-learning platforms is built for programming, accommodating learning material. The course is carefully designed for targeted pupils and is narrated as stories, which guide student to explore the problem, find the solutions to it. An e-learning platform is built for running the course.

2.1 The Course

The course includes hand-on engineering projects, which consist of activities of building a Webduino robot car and controlling it by writing block programs for teamed

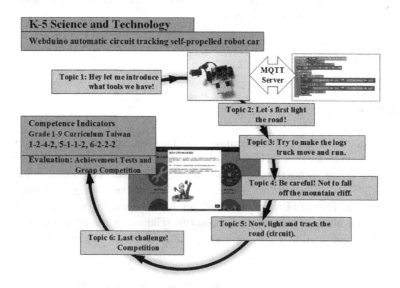

Fig. 1. The course structure

groups of students. A final competition on an oval circuit racing by robot cars is to add gamming elements to the course for further motivating students' interest in learning [9–11]. The course is tied together by the story of a carpenter whose logs truck has problems for the students to solve. Part of the course structure is shown in Fig. 1.

2.2 The e-Learning Platform

The platform built in this study has an online course module to access the course designed in this study, although the hand-on activities can take place in the classroom only. In the classroom, or the computer room, students use Block Programming Module to write program codes, which are sent via a MQTT server to control the Webduino robot car via wireless network. The Student Portfolio Module keeps all the records of students' activities, course reading, code programming, and hand-on competitions.

3   Experiments and Results

To evaluate the performances on students' STEM capability and 3C capability after taking the course, this research uses a combination of qualitative research method and quantitative research method by conducting a triangulation on achievement tests for STEM, teacher's survey, and participant observations. The participants are students in the fifth grade in an elementary school in Tainan, Taiwan. Two classes, 55 students in total, joined the experimental course. Students were grouped into 19 teams of 3(or 2) students by S-distribution according to their grades in science and technology.

3.1 Experimental Process and Evaluations

The STEM achievement tests are evaluated on students' STEM capability by a pre-test and a post-test, while the creativity, collaboration, and communication (3C) abilities are evaluated by two surveys, one before and one after the course respectively. The pre-test for STEM ability contains questions on electricity, implementation, computational thinking, and mathematics. The survey for 3C contains 5-scale self-evaluation questions, 16 for creativity, 9 for collaboration and 15 communication, on students' 3C capabilities. During 6 weeks time, there are six project-oriented lessons, each 40-min, covering topics on basic STEM concepts, a Webduino robot car assembly, blocks programming for driving the robot car, missions to test the assembled robot car, and finally a car circuit-tracking race competition. After the course, the post-test on STEM and the second survey on 3C are held. The other two sources for triangulation, teachers' survey on students' performance and the participant observations are also collected form the classes' teacher and the recruited experts.

3.2 Results and Discussion

Triangulations are on students' STEM capability and 3C ability respectively from collected students' scholastic tests, teacher's survey, and participant observations.

- The STEM Capability

The result of the paired-samples t-test on the pretest and posttest in STEM achievement tests is shown in Table 1. The Cronbach's α is 0.857, which shows a good reliability of the tests. The result of the test shows significant difference (P < 0.05) in electricity, computational thinking, and implementation, but not in mathematics.

Table 1. Results of the paired-samples t-test on STEM capability

	Paired differences					t	df	Sig.
	Mean	Std. deviation	Std. error mean	95% confidence interval of the difference				
				Lower	Upper			
Electricity	−.980	1.750	.250	−1.482	−.477	−3.919	48	.000
Mathematics	−.122	.949	.136	−.395	.150	−.903	48	.371
Computational thinking	−.653	1.508	.215	−1.086	−.220	−3.032	48	.004
Implementation	−3.000	1.926	.275	−3.553	−2.447	−10.905	48	.000
Overall score	−4.755	3.051	.4358	−5.631	−3.878	−10.907	48	.000

The teacher's survey in this research uses a Likert 5-scale questionnaire that has 10 questions on the effectiveness of the project-oriented STEM course. The final score is 47 out of 50. The last source of the triangulation for STEM capability is the participant observations. Some of the observations by the experts are shown in Table 2.

Table 2. Some of the participant observations

- Part of students were distracted when the teacher were illustrating the concept of electricity. They became extremely concentrated on the instructions for the building the robot cars
- Students prefer manipulating blocks programming rather than reading computer materials
- Students were overjoyed at the first time when the robot car they assembled started to move accordingly to their compiled programs

The result of triangulation indicates teachers recognize the course has positive influence on students, which can be confirmed by the paired-samples t-test result in achievement tests. The course is helpful to students' sense of the relations among science, technology, engineering, and mathematics. After taking such STEM course, students learn to find solutions based on science knowledge, and, from integrated projects. On the other hand, the result of paired-sample t-test on STEM capability shows that students' performance on mathematics is less ideal than other subjects. Reviewing the test paper to find it contains only 3 questions for mathematics, as a result, students' minor mistakes can easily affect their grades.

- The 3C Capability

The scores of 3C scales of pretest and posttest are paired for t-test and the result is shown in Table 3. The Cronbach's α is 0.761, which shows a good reliability of the tests. However, the performances in creativity, collaboration, and communication are all not significant (P > 0.05).

Table 3. Results of paired-samples t-test on the 3C capability

	Paired differences					t	df	Sig.
	Mean	Std. deviation	Std. error mean	95% confidence interval of the difference				
				Lower	Upper			
Collaboration	1.061	8.668	1.238	−1.429	3.551	.857	48	.396
Communication	2.122	9.831	1.404	−.701	4.946	1.511	48	.137
Creativity	−.898	9.978	1.425	−3.764	1.968	−.630	48	.532
Overall score	2.285	19.619	2.802	−3.349	7.921	.816	48	.419

In terms of the teacher's survey, this research uses a Likert 5-scale questionnaire that has 3 questions on the effectiveness of the project-oriented 3C capability. The final score is 13 out of 15. The last source for the triangulation for 3C capability is the participant observations. Some of the observations by the experts are shown in Table 4.

Table 4. Results of participant observations

Creativity
- Some teams tried to make robot cars carry some weights to check its mobility
- As a game, some teams make their robot cars push each other head-to-head

Collaboration
- In most of the teams, members are willing to finish the project together, few members are idled or just observing. But disagreements do happen sometimes
- Some teams determine the major operator of the robot car by playing rock–paper–scissors, but most of the teams determine by election

Communication
- There are 3 teams frequently at odds, one of which has serious arguments once. The rest of the teams discuss peacefully. Two teams develop situations that a member tries to do everything alone regardless of others' opinions

For the triangulation, teacher's survey shows positive evaluation on creativity, collaboration, and communication for the project-oriented course. Participant observations show, to a certain degree, students are also doing well in 3C capability. But the results of paired-samples t-test imply students have no significant changes in 3C capability before and after the course. The possible reasons behind this might be:

(1) Work load for the project-based course is high for students; they do not have extra time for themselves to think more deeply. (2) Since upper grades students of elementary schools in Taiwan do not have lot experience on team-works, even though recognizing communication problems, they may have difficulty in finding compromise solutions. (3) In the 3C pretest, most of the students are more subjectively confident in their capability of collaboration and communication with others. But after the course, they may recognize their failures in the reality and give a more objective self-evaluation on these capability. But participant observations do find those teams with faster progress would try to control the robot car with other program blocks. The observation of this study argues that creativity performance can only be promoted by long-term efforts rather than short-term enhancements.

4 Conclusion

This research designs a STEM oriented Project-based Learning course for the pre-engineering education of higher grades of elementary schools. The course contains projects for teamed students to promote their 3C capabilities. By using project-based learning, students have hands-on in real applications which makes them learn by doing and discover solutions to problems by themselves or with the help of group members. Competitions are in the course to promote students' learning motivation. The experimental results indicate that, for the upper grades, the STEM-oriented project-based learning course can significantly improve students' STEM capabilities. Participant observations also shows, by combining theory and hands-on practices, students develop more interest in learning and stronger aspiration than simply listening to lectures. The teacher's survey also confirms the positive evaluations in students' creativity, collaboration, and communication (3C) capabilities, but not to a significantly different level.

References

1. Douglas, J., Iversen, E., Kalyandurg, C.: Engineering in the K-12 Classroom - An Analysis of Current Practices & Guidelines for the Future. A Production of the ASEE Engineering K12 Center (2004)
2. Bull, G., Knezek, G., Gibson, D.: Editorial: a rationale for incorporating engineering education into the teacher education curriculum. Contemp. Issues Technol. Teach. Educ. **9** (3), 222–225 (2009)
3. Gomez, A.G.: Engineering, but how? Technol. Teach. **59**(6), 17–22 (2000)
4. Davies, T., Gilbert, J.: Modelling: promoting creativity whilst forging links between science education and design and technology education. Can. J. Sci. Math. Technol. Educ. **3**(1), 67–82 (2003)
5. Varnado, T.E., Pendleton, L.K.: Technology education/engineering education: a call for collaboration. In: The Proceedings of the International Conference on Engineering Education, Gainesville, FL (2004)

6. Spencer, M., Strong, D.S.: Preliminary investigation of the integration of engineering in to k-12 education. In: The Proceedings of the 55th Annual Meeting of the ISSS, Hull, UK, (2011)
7. Milentijevic, I., Ciric, V., Vojinovic, O.: Version control in project-based learning. Comput. Educ. **50**(4), 1331–1338 (2008)
8. Solomon, G.: Project-based learning: a primer. Technol. Learn. **23**(6), 20–30 (2003)
9. Zichermann, G., Cunningham, C.: Gamification by Design. O'Reilly, Sebastopol (2011)
10. Werbach, K., Hunter, D.: For the Win: How Game Thinking Can Revolutionize Your Business. Wharton Digital Press, Philadelphia (2012)
11. Simões, J., Redondo, R.D., Vilas, A.F.: A Social gamification framework for a K–6 learning platform. Comput. Hum. Behav. **29**(2), 345–353 (2013)

Scorecard Approach for Cyber-Security Awareness

Tsosane Shabe[1](✉), Elmarie Kritzinger[2], and Marianne Loock[2]

[1] School of Computing, University of South Africa, Pretoria 0003, South Africa
Shabetb@hotmail.com
[2] Elmarie Kritzinger, School of Computing,
University of South Africa, Pretoria 0003, South Africa
{Kritze,loockm}@unisa.ac.za

Abstract. This study explores the current state of cyber-security awareness among cell phone users living in South Africa. The study used a scorecard approach to measure the level of cyber-security awareness among cell phone users in Rocklands Township, South Africa. Following a description of the scorecard and its application, a brief discussion of the results obtained is presented. The scorecard suggested that individual respondents (cell phone users) were most likely vulnerable to cyber-security threats due to their lack of adequate cyber-security awareness (and, consequently, in many cases, their behaviour was risky).

Keywords: Cyber-security awareness · Cyber-security threats · Cyber-criminals · Cell phone · Scorecard

1 Introduction

As consumers (cell phone users) embrace the rise of the cell phone (Smartphone) epoch, ways of protecting oneself from cyber attacks has become a global issue [1]. This is substantiated by the flurry of diverse cyber-security awareness initiatives, research and campaigns aimed at providing cell phone users with information about cyber-security threats, as well as preventative measures against such threats. However, although there are measures in place to counter cyber-security threats, it cannot be denied that challenges continue to exist. This might be the case due to cell phone users' lack of understanding/knowledge with regard to the nature of cyber-security threats. In addition, attackers/hackers are also becoming more creative with regard to their methods [2]. Having no formal or informal cyber-security training creates a situation in which many cell phone users are at the mercy of attackers. It is therefore imperative that cell phone users' levels of competence in cyber-space be improved without delay. For the purpose of awareness management, it is necessary to create a baseline of the existing levels of cyber-security awareness.

The rest of this paper is structured as follows: a literature review in Sect. 2, a description of the methodology in Sect. 3, and brief description of the scorecard approach in Sect. 4. Section 5 provides a discussion on the scorecard results, and Sect. 6 offers a conclusion on the study.

© Springer International Publishing AG 2017
T.-C. Huang et al. (Eds.): SETE 2017, LNCS 10676, pp. 144–153, 2017.
https://doi.org/10.1007/978-3-319-71084-6_16

2   Related Work

Technical cyber-security solutions (such as firewalls and antiviruses) have already been developed to address vulnerabilities and cyber-security concerns associated with the use of cell phones. Current cell phones give users the option to enable user authentication, set a firewall and verify the authenticity of downloaded applications. Companies such as Kaspersky, Norton, McAfee, etc. have developed and are selling antivirus software for cell phones. However, if the cell phone user does not understand or is unaware of the cyber-security risks associated with the use of cell phones, technical cyber-security solutions will be a fruitless exercise. Such solutions often fail to prevent all attacks on cell phones [4]. Several studies have highlighted that human beings are often considered to be the weakest link in cyber-security [5–8]. Many people know they need security for their computers, but they are not aware of the need for security in cell phones [9]. This means that cell phone users require the necessary knowledge and skills to identify such threats, as well as the ability to counteract them effectively. The level of alertness needed in order to do so requires constant attention since such threats are continually changing and growing [3].

Currently, there are existing cyber-security awareness and education initiatives in South Africa employed in order to fortify the human link [5, 10]. These initiatives are employed by academic institutions and industry since South Africa has not had cyber-security awareness and education initiatives led by the government [11]. However, the effectiveness of these campaigns has either not been proven or little is known about their effectiveness. The objective of this study was to assess whether South African cell phone users (living in townships) are aware of the cyber-related dangers associated with the use of cell phones. To achieve this, a Scorecard was initiated. The scorecard was used on a trial basis in the case of Rocklands Township in Bloemfontein, Mangaung. The concept of a scorecard and the way in which it was applied to this research scorecard is discussed in Sect. 4. Methodology is discussed next.

3   Methodology

The sample consisted of 138 respondents, 62 of whom were males (45%) and 76 female (55%). The sample was also predominantly comprised of black people. Among the respondents, 40% had a Grade 12 education, 40% possessed a bachelor's degree, 18% had a post-matric qualification. The majority of the respondents (65%) were between the ages of 18 and 25, 22% were between 26 and 30, 7% between 31 and 35, 4% between 36 and 40 years and 2% were between 41 and 46 years and above. With regard to employment. 57% were students, 4% part-time employees, 29% full-time employees, and 4% unemployed (with an income). 7% were unemployed but have no income, and other category was 2%. Lastly, 70% of the work force earned between 0 < R12000, R12 001-R24 000 (10%), R24 001-R36 000 (3%), R36 001-R48 000 (4%), R48 001-R60 000 (1%), R60 001-R120 000 (1%), R120 001-R350 000 (7%), and > R350 000 (3%). Structured questionnaires were given to a sample of cell phone users in this study. The convenience sampling technique was used which is a type of non-probability is sampling. In this type of sampling technique, the sampling units are selected based on the criteria of place and time with regard to the data collection process, and is therefore unrestricted. The convenience sampling method helps in testing and gaining ideas about the subject of interest [14] which, in this case, is the knowledge of cell phone users with regard to cyber-security threats. The respondents were selected on the basis of convenience which means that those who were available and willing to participate in the survey, gave their consent. The anonymity of the respondents was ensured to avoid any ethical dilemmas and to obtain candid responses so as to gain a better and clear understanding of the issue at hand. The survey was conducted and limited to Rockland's, Bloemfontein in South Africa. The target group of the survey was residents of Rockland's aged 35, 36–40, 41–46, 46 and above. The questionnaire contained questions that could be answered as follows: yes, no, and unsure. The responses were given the following weightings: 1 = disagree strongly 2 = disagree 3 = undecided 4 = agree 5 = agree strongly and Yes, No, Unsure and then divided by the number of occurrences, in order to obtain a mean value. The next section discussed the Scorecard approach.

4   Scorecard Approach

This research used a scorecard approach to present the results of the measurements of the level of cyber-security awareness among cell phone users as it existed in Rocklands Township at the time of the study. The term "scorecard" is used cautiously at this point since many might argue that the application here is better referred to as a "dashboard". What is intended here is that the situation vis-à-vis awareness of cyber-security matters (specifically cell phone-related matters) is presented in a summary form (profile) consisting of a number of different attributes. It shows the condition as it existed at the time of the study. In future studies, targets for ideal performance in each category may be determined and the progress towards these "ideal" levels tracked. Generally speaking, scorecards are seen in the context of performance scorecards, which may be used as part of the Balanced Scorecard methodology, but could also be used to monitor the "state of health" and/or progress towards any (organisational) goal. According to 2GC Active Management (2014), the scorecard seen as a balanced scorecard, is an example of a closed-loop controller or cybernetic control applied to the management of the implementation of a strategy. Closed-loop or cybernetic control is where actual performance is measured. The measured value is compared to a reference value and, based on the difference between the two, corrective interventions are made as required. Dashboards, on the other hand, often provide "at-a-glance" views of key performance indicators relevant to a particular objective (or business process).

The results scorecard (shown in the scorecard in this study) is used to assess the cell phone user's behaviour regarding cyber-security risks and threats in order to pinpoint areas of awareness that need improvement. The threats and risks faced by each cell phone user may differ depending on how the cell phone is being used. Respondents reported a wide variety of actions (activities) relative to their use of their cell phones. In light of the literature reviewed, the researcher was able to classify the reported actions according to five categories of risk – actions which would be indicative of the user taking (or being exposed to): (1) very high risk(s), (2) high risks, (3) moderate risks,

(4) low risks, and (5) very low risks. Similarly, the researcher was able to classify responses according to awareness of cyber-security issues based on the literature reviewed. Thus, the responses were categorised by allocating an awareness value. Again, five categories emerged: very low awareness (value = "1"), low awareness (value = "2"), moderate awareness (value = "3"), high awareness (value = "4") and very high awareness (value = "5"). By combining these two variables for each question, it became possible to determine the overall risk rating score (or risk exposure level) of the respondent.

Once the results of the survey had been collected, the scorecard was used to determine the overall risk score or level of the participants. Risk levels are discussed as follows. Very low level of exposure regarding awareness (1): Cell phone users are fully aware of cyber-security threats, and the potential risks and possible consequences of such threats. Low level of exposure in respect of awareness (2): Cell phone users have a good understanding of cyber-security awareness with adequate exposure but they may choose not to comply with good cyber-security principles (high level of awareness/alertness). Moderate level of exposure with reference to awareness (3): Cell phone users are aware of cyber-security threats, as well as potential attacks and risks but they have a gap in their knowledge in terms of identifying or reporting cyber-security events and therefore require training and exposure (moderate level of awareness/alertness). High level of exposure regarding awareness (4): Cell phone users understand cyber-security principles and standards. However, they do not believe that they are truly accountable for the security of their cell phones. They assume that responsibility lies with technology and service providers (low level of awareness/alertness). Very high level of exposure in terms of awareness (5): Cell phone users are not interested in controls and security for reasons known only to them. They exhibit risky behavior that can easily be exploited, thereby making the cell phones more vulnerable to various attacks (very low level of awareness/alertness).

Each question response in the survey has been assigned a cyber-security awareness value (1–5). Based on different weights (disagree, strongly disagree, undecided, agree, strongly agree and also yes, no, unsure), each question response in the survey is multiplied by the number of occurrences divided by the number of survey participants in order to obtain a scorecard rating.

Scorecard rating = awareness rating X number of occurrences/number of survey participants.

To determine the overall rating for each section, all scorecard ratings are added together and divided by the number asked for each section (scorecard rating total/number of questions = Total score for each section). The next section presents the Scorecard results.

5   Scorecard Results and Discussion

The following Sub-sects. (5.1 to 5.9) outlined the findings from the scorecard by discussing the results of each of the questions assessed.

5.1 Security Settings on Cell Phones

The scores of the scorecard were decided by the researcher/interviewer. Based on the questions asked in this section of the study, the researcher used the responses from the survey to assessed the participants' level of awareness with regard to security settings on their cell phones. The results of this assessment are presented in Table 1.

Table 1. Security settings on cell phone

	Level of cyber-security		Scorecard
Is an antivirus installed on your cell phone?	High-risk action	Moderate level	3
Is the antivirus program updated at least once every two weeks?	High-risk action	Moderate level	3
Have you ever tried to change the firewall security settings on your cell phone?	Very high-risk action	Very low level	1
Have you ever tried to change the antivirus software security settings?	Very high-risk action	Very low level	1
Have you ever tried to change the remote access security settings?	Very high-risk action	low level	2
Do you allow script on your cell phone (e.g. Java-script, active-X, Flash)?	High-risk action	Very low level	1
Do you ensure that your device is equipped with the latest antivirus?	High-risk action	Moderate level	3
Total score for this section			14

This section addressed the behaviour of cell phone users with regard to cell phone security settings. Awareness rating for this Section:

= Total cumulative score/number of questions
= [3 + 3+1 + 1+2 + 1+3]/7
= 2

This calculation is applied in the same manner to all other sections. The overall rating of awareness for this section suggested a low level of awareness by participants with issues relating cell phone cyber-security support. This aspect requires urgent attention. Learning interventions covering virus protection, firewall hygiene and scripts are therefore necessary. The next section presents the cell phone systems maintenance part of the questionnaire.

5.2 Cell Phone System Maintenance and Software

The responses obtained from this section of the survey were used to rate the awareness levels of the respondents with regard to cell phone system maintenance and software as depicted in Table 2.

Table 2. Cell phone system maintenance and software

	Level of cyber-security		Scorecard
Do you ever install software from the Internet which can be downloaded for free?	Very high-risk action	Low level	2
Do you use peer-to-peer file sharing software/programs?	Very high-risk action	Very low level	1
Total score for this section			3

This section addressed the participants' behaviour with regard to cell phone system maintenance and software. The evidence of awareness may be inferred based on the actions indicated. These actions/areas were reported as potentially very high risk, and the awareness level may be too low as in the case of the respondents who indicated that they engage in some dangerous practices. The overall awareness rating for this section is 2, suggesting a low level of awareness with issues relating to cell phone security settings. This aspect requires urgent attention, e.g. learning interventions to cover virus protection, firewall hygiene, scripts, and cell phone system maintenance and software.

5.3 Email Access via Cell Phone

This section of the survey assessed the respondents' knowledge with regard to spam and phishing emails as depicted in Table 3.

Table 3. Email access via cell phone

	Level of cyber-security		Scorecard
Does your cell phone have a spam filter?	High-risk actions	Very low level	1
Do you open emails even if you do not know the sender?	Very high-risk actions	Low level awareness	2
Do you open email attachments even if you do not know the sender?	Very high-risk actions	Low level awareness	2
Do you use encryption when sending emails?	High-risk actions	Very low level	1
Do you use web-based email software such as Yahoo, Hotmail, Gmail, etc.?	Potentially high-risk actions	Low level awareness	2
If you use web-based email, do you pay attention to the security settings?	Potentially very high-risk actions	Very low level	1
Total score for this section			9

The overall rating of awareness in this section was 2, indicating a low level of awareness regarding security settings on cell phones. This aspect requires urgent attention, e.g. learning interventions to cover virus protection, malware, etc.

5.4   Cell Phone Cyber-Security Support

In this section, the scorecard sought to establish the support structures that were available to cell phone users, and where they could receive support if necessary (Table 4).

Table 4. Cell phone cyber-security support

	Level of cyber-security		Scorecard
Do you approach a friend if you need support?	High-risk actions	Moderate level	3
Do you approach another party (not listed in statements 1–5) if you need support?	High-risk actions	low level of awareness	2
If the administrator asks you for your password, do you give it to him?	Very high-risk actions	low level of awareness	2
Total score for this section			7

The overall awareness rating for this section is 2, suggesting a low level of awareness with issues relating to cell phone cyber-security support. This aspect requires urgent attention, e.g. learning interventions to cover virus protection, firewall hygiene and scripts.

5.5   Cell Phone Sharing and Social Networking

This section of the scorecard assessed the respondents' knowledge of cyber-security threats related to social networking, and whether they were cautions when participating on social networks using their cell phones.

The overall awareness rating for this section is 2, suggesting a very low level of awareness with regard to issues relating to social networking. This aspect requires urgent attention, e.g. learning interventions to cover virus protection, firewall hygiene, scripts, malware, cell phone system maintenance, awareness, etc.

5.6   Attitudes Towards Cell Phone and Cyber-Security

This section addressed the attitudes, knowledge and awareness of cell phone users regarding cell phone security. This is an extremely high-risk area in Rocklands Township. The overall awareness rating for this section is 3, suggesting a moderate level of awareness with regard to issues relating to cell phone cyber-security support. The answers point to a serious lack of appreciation of the dangers facing cell phone users and a lackadaisical approach to the enforcement of cyber-security standards and adherence to the best practices of cell phone security protocols. The next section addressed participants' experiences with regard to cell phone cyber-security breaches.

5.7   Findings: Scorecard for Cell Phone Security Breaches

The responses gained from this section of the survey were used to rate the awareness level of the respondents as depicted in Table 5.

Table 5. Scorecard for cell phone security breaches

	Level of cyber-security		Scorecard
Have you experienced suspicious activity on your cell phone?	Low-risk actions	Low level of awareness	2
Do you think that you have spyware or adware on your cell phone?	Low-risk actions	Very low level of awareness	3
Have you fallen victim to spyware?	Low-risk actions	Low level of awareness	2
Have you fallen victim to phishing?	Low-risk actions	Low level of awareness	2
Has your identity been "stolen" online?	High-risk actions	Very low level of awareness	2
Have you fallen victim to online scams?	High-risk actions	Very low level of awareness	2
Have financial irregularities been reported on your email banking transactions?	Low-risk actions	Adequate level of awareness	2
Do you know how to determine whether your cell phone has been compromised?	Low-risk actions	Adequate level of awareness	3
Total score for this section			18

Section 1 addressed users' knowledge and experiences with regard to cyber-security breaches. The answers point to a serious lack of knowledge about cyber-security breaches, and show that most of the respondents did not know how to ensure that they were not engaging in any activity that might have led to the loss of their information about bank accounts or cause them to make any false transactions leading to financial loss. This aspect requires urgent, ongoing attention. Learning interventions that cover virus protection, firewall hygiene, scripts, cell phone system, spyware, cyber-security breaches, Web browser security toolbars, anti-phishing filters and honey pots are needed.

5.8   Cyber-Security Training as a Protective Measure

In conclusion, the response to this section is not very encouraging. This may well be another indication of the lack of appreciation of the seriousness of the cyber-security exposure which could be linked to a low level of cyber-security awareness and high levels of ignorance on the part of cell phone users as depicted in Table 6.

The overall rating of awareness in this section was 4, indicating a high level of awareness with regard to cyber-security training as a protective measure. The answers indicate that the attitudes of cell phone users towards cyber-security training were positive. However, most points indicate neutral to negative attitudes towards

Table 6. Cyber-security training as a protective measure

	Level of cyber-security		Scorecard
I would be prepared to provide cyber-security training	Low-risk actions	Adequate level of awareness	3
I would seriously consider cyber-security tips if conveyed to me by educators	Low-risk actions	High level of awareness	5
Total score for this section			8

cyber-security training on the part of the respondents. This is alarming because, if any of these respondents were to face a cyber-security problem, he/she might not be able to handle it efficiently. This aspect requires urgent, ongoing attention, e.g. a learning intervention that covers cyber-security tips.

5.9   Awareness of the Cyber-Security Profile of the Cell Phone

An awareness of the cyber-security profile of the cell phone users of Rocklands resulted from an interpretation of the data obtained from the respondents by means of the questionnaire. The results are summarised in Table 7.

Table 7. Summary scorecard table for rocklands.

Topic	Level of cyber-security	Scorecard
Use of cell phone	Early indications of potentially risky activities	UTR
Options/use regarding security settings options on your cell phone	Probable risky behaviour	2
Options of cell phone system maintenance on your cell phone	Possible risky behaviour	2
Email access via cell phone	Risky behaviour	2
Cell phone support	Awareness low	2
Risk awareness	Awareness dangerously low	1
Taking shortcuts	Awareness dangerously low	3
Experience with cell phone security breaches	Exposures confirmed	2
Attitude to cyber-training as a protective measure	Neutral to negative attitudes towards training in cyber-security	4
Total score for rocklands = 2 (2 + 2 + 2 + 2 + 1 + 3 + 2 + 4/8)		

The overall rating for Rocklands' respondents after the survey was 2. The overall analysis of the survey results indicates negligence/recklessness on the part of the respondents which results in such activities as those shown in Table 7, and which could lead to the loss of secure personal information. At the same time, it underlines the importance of and need for more awareness programmes for cell phone users to provide them with more knowledge about cyber-security threats and countermeasures.

6   Conclusion

This paper discussed a scorecard approach to present the results of the measurements of the level of cyber-security awareness among cell phone users as it existed in Rocklands Township at the time of the study. Scorecards should be used in other areas in South Africa to investigate cyber-security issues. The scorecard could also serve as a guide for planning campaigns to address gaps in the awareness of cyber-security matters in this and other communities in the future. In this research, the scorecard revealed that cell phone users in Rocklands needed assistance as illustrated in Table 7. These cell phone users were seriously exposed to cyber-security risks and threats. As previously reported, many remedies had been identified in the literature review which could be applied in this situation.

References

1. Heidenreich, B., Gray, D.H.: Cyber-security: the threat of the internet. Glob. Secur. Stud. **4** (3), 17–26 (2013)
2. Kumar, P., Joseph, J., Singh, K.: International conference on recent trends in physics 2016 (ICRTP2016). J. Phys.: Conf. Ser. **755**, 011001 (2016)
3. Wright, J., Omar, M.: Cyber security and mobile threats: the need for antivirus applications for smart phones. J. Inf. Syst. Technol. Plan. **5**(14), 40–60 (2012)
4. Sornamageswari, M., Bothma, C.: Phishing detection in websites using neural networks and firefly. Int. J. Eng. Comput. Sci. **5**(9), 18197–18204 (2016)
5. Kortjan, N., Von Solms, R.: A conceptual framework for cyber-security awareness and education in SA. S. Afr. Comput. J. **52**(52), 29–41 (2014)
6. Androulidakis, I., Kandus, G.: Mobile phone security awareness and practices of students in budapest. In: ICDT 2011, The Sixth International, pp. 18–24 (2011). Available from: http://www.thinkmind.org/index.php?view=article&articleid=icdt_2011_1_40_20110. Accessed 8 July 2017
7. Mylonas, A., Kastania, A., Gritzalis, D.: Delegate the smartphone user? Security awareness in smartphone platforms. Comput. Secur. **34**, 47–66 (2013)
8. Dominguez, C.M.F., Ramaswamy, M., Martinez, E.M., Cleal, M.G.: A framework for information security awareness programs. Issues Inf. Syst. **11**(1), 402–409 (2010)
9. Shing, L.P., Shing, L.H., Tech, V., Chiang, M.C., Yang, C.W., Lu, T.: Smartphone security risks: android. Int. J. Electron. Electr. Eng. **4**(4), 346–350 (2016)
10. Kortjan, N.: A cyber security awareness and education framework for South Africa, p. 219 (2013). https://researchspace.csir.co.za/dspace/handle/10204/5941. Accessed 14 May 2017
11. Grobler, M., Dlamini, Z., Ngobeni, S., Labuschagne, A.: Towards a cyber security aware rural community. In: Proceedings of the 2011 Information Security for South Africa (ISSA) Conference, pp. 1–7 (2011). http://goo.gl/680YtV. Accessed 4 May 2017
12. GC Active Management: 2GC Balanced Scorecard Usage Survey. 2GC Active Management (2014). http://2gc.eu/resource_centre/surveys. Accessed 23 Nov 2016
13. Cooper, D.R., Emory, C.W.: Business Research Methods, 5th edn. Irwin, Chicago (1995)
14. Dillon, W.R., Madden, T.J., Firtle, N.H.: Essentials of Marketing Research. Irwin, Illinois (1993)

Using AHP to Project-Based Learning Develop in Machinery Manufacturing of Technology Universities Students

Dyi-Cheng Chen[✉], Ci-Syong You, and Ying-Chia Huang

Department of Industrial Education and Technology,
National Changhua University of Education, Changhua 500, Taiwan
dcchen@cc.ncue.edu.tw

Abstract. While Project-based learning applications have been extensively investigated, the machinery manufacturing for technology universities students is unexplored. First, this study collects the status of machinery manufacturing, the scope of technical knowledge of machinery manufacturing and the relevant literature on Project-based learning performance. Project-based learning has used in the generation of novel ideas for student. In addition, this study involves a quantitative and qualitative content analysis of relevant documents, textbooks and teaching objectives of machinery manufacturing performance, which includes Objectives knowledge, Type of Problems and Projects, Progression, Size and Duration, in 7 hierarchies and 25 indexes. Second, this study assesses these criteria by employing the analytic hierarchy process (AHP) technique to solicit opinions from 10 experts by using questionnaires. Results show that Type of Problems and Projects, Students' Learning, Objectives knowledge, Progression, Size and Duration, Academic Staff and Facilitation, Assessment and Evaluation (0.090), Space and Organization, have weights of 0.215, 0.190, 0.185, 0.131, 0.101, 0.090, 0.088 respectively.

Keywords: Project-based learning · Machinery manufacturing · Analytic hierarchy process (AHP)

1 Introduction

Project-based learning (PBL) provides opportunities for learners to learn new soft skills such as collaboration, communication, negotiation as well as providing opportunities for learners to participate in active learning [1]. Project based learning is often said to promote students' intellectual and social development because the supervisor of the teacher needs to actively participate in the process of acquiring limited knowledge and skills. Therefore, the success of project-based learning is almost entirely dependent on the ability of students with spontaneous initiatives and functions [2]. Jacobo et al. [3] find that working with demonstrator satellites is extremely ambitious for students and shows that they enable wider communication of knowledge. Engineering education is advancing "change" from a curriculum that emphasizes traditional expertise to "multidisciplinary curriculum and interdisciplinary" research towards innovation and entrepreneurial spirit. This trend includes delivery of project-oriented educational

© Springer International Publishing AG 2017
T.-C. Huang et al. (Eds.): SETE 2017, LNCS 10676, pp. 154–160, 2017.
https://doi.org/10.1007/978-3-319-71084-6_17

contents, mechanisms to promote interdisciplinary cooperation in research programs, etc. in a curriculum that leads to the necessity of more frequent review and adjustment [4]. Rasheed et al. [5] applied a project-based self-instruction approach to multimedia production courses. Miner and Link used projects as the vehicle to introduce students to the FEM, as well as a means to enhance the students' enthusiasm for their major [6].

2   Literature Review

2.1   Project-Based Learning (PBL)

Therefore inspiration from Savin-Baden's five models, we have been aligned in a problem and project based curriculum. This approach is much more comprehensive since students on teams collaborate on a common project. We have identified which is important to understand what the projects and teams are organized. We have identified the all these elements are elementary in a curriculum and all the elements of must belongs and object and knowledge, types of problems and projects, progression and size, students' learning, academic staff and facilitation, space and organization and be aligned [7] (Fig. 1).

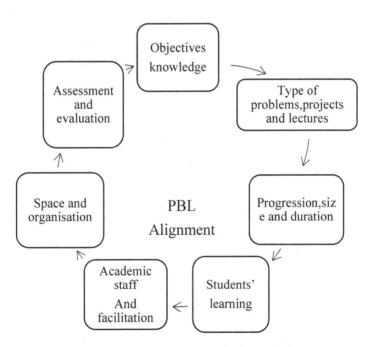

Fig. 1. PBL alignment of elements in the curriculum [7]

When defining the five models, the variation in knowledge are crucial elements [8]. The dimension we chose for this element is more or less the same, but it is expressed differently for disciplinary purposes, knowledge, methodological objectives and interdisciplinary knowledge [9]. **Due to most innovations are based on interdisciplinary and collaborative knowledge.**

There various types of problems and project, for instance, the better defined problems which often with well-defined answers and discipline projects. A project with discipline can be regarded as a research project with a clear theme. The learning goal is for students to learn predefined scientific knowledge [10].

PBL instructors are responsible for constructing learning materials with visible and clear progression. Besides, considering the amount of time that the curriculum gives over to the PBL module is also worthy of noticing.

The attitude, experience and skills of the students are important and it is necessary to establish support courses such as collaboration, teamwork and project management. Normally, students are experiencing individual learning, a more collective and cooperative knowledge process. When students do not know how to accomplish things, natural reactions are to foster a negative attitude or to fight to learn. However, in order to promote the learning process and recognize the importance of these skills, we need to take up the curriculum [12].

The role of academic staffs is also critical in effecting positive outcome of a PBL module. For instance, to provide training that enhance staffs' facilitator role [13] and staff-student interaction ability for the staffs.

de Graaff and Kolmos [14] the organization has to support the curriculum and points out that this space is a problem in promoting the work of the PBL team smoothly. However, spaces and organizations can be organized in various ways. The space can consist of a large lecture room with movable walls and perhaps can be combined with virtual space. Organizations do not have to change completely from traditional systems, but expert knowledge and resource reorganization is an important issue.

The evaluation method chosen to evaluate PBL is the driving force of students' learning among others. Participation in student ownership and democratic curriculum process is important and this will accompany students' participation in curriculum evaluation.

2.2   Machinery Manufacturing

Table 1 shows the major criteria of machinery manufacturing.

The cost of manufacturing the factory has first, the manufacturing costs: the cost of the production process.

1. Material costs: purchased raw materials or hair.
2. Labor costs: directly engaged in production operations of the artificial.
3. Manufacturing costs: in addition to material costs, labor costs, in the production process of all costs incurred, such as insurance, water electricity, depreciation, maintenance fee.

Table 1. Shows the major criteria of machinery manufacturing.

Major criteria	Sub-criteria
Cut into a certain size of the processing method	Turning, boring, grinding, milling, shrinking, broaching, drilling, reaming, sawing, routing
Non-traditional machining	Ultrasonic machining, electrical discharge machining (EDM), electro-arc machining, optical lasers machining, electrochemical processing Electrical chemical machining (ECM),
Change material casting method	Casting, forging, rolling, squeezing, crushing, piercing, swaging, shearing, spinning, stretch forming, roll forming, torch cutting, explosion molding, explosive forming, plastic forming
Electroplating	Mechanical properties, heat treatment, hot working, cold working, shot peening

3 Research Method

3.1 Analytic Hierarchy Process

Analytic Hierarchy Process (AHP) was developed by Saaty [15], a professor at the University of Pittsburgh in 1971, and was mainly used in decision-making issues with uncertainties and with most evaluation criteria. The purpose of the AHP is to systematize the complex problems and to classify the target questions into hierarchical decomposition by dividing the different levels, making the problem easier to assess and understand through the hierarchical approach. The main features of the hierarchical analysis is the use of hierarchical structure of the way, the complex relationship between the factors to establish hierarchical structure At the same time, it is possible to simplify the complex problem by making the two possible pairs of important factors, so that the problem can be more easily evaluated by the quantification, so that the decision maker can make the decision and reduce the risk effectively.

The research assigned a single number drawn from the fundamental 1-9 scale of absolute numbers shown in Table 2 [16]. Pairwise comparison generally refers to any process of comparing entities in pairs to judge, which of each pair is preferred or has a greater amount of some quantitative property.

Table 2. The pairwise comparison scale.

Intensity of Importance	Definition
1	Equal importance
3	Moderate importance
5	Strong importance
7	Very strong or demonstrated importance
9	Extreme importance
2,4,6,8	Intermediate values between two adjacent judgments

4   Results and Discussion

The consistency test was used to screen effective questionnaires and control the reliability of the results. Table 3 shows that the most important seven criteria were as follows: Type of Problems and Projects (0.215), Students' learning (0.190), Objectives knowledge (0.185), Progression, Size and Duration (0.131), Academic Staff and Facilitation (0.101), Assessment and Evaluation (0.090), Space and Organisation (0.088).

Table 3. Weights of 3 major criteria

Major criteria	Weight	Order
Objectives knowledge	0.185	3
Type of problems and projects	0.215	1
Progression, size and duration	0.131	4
Students' learning	0.190	2
Academic staff and facilitation	0.101	5
Space and organisation	0.088	7
Assessment and evaluation	0.090	6

Table 4 shows the relative weight for individual sub-criteria under specific major criteria. Under the evaluation criterion of "Objectives knowledge", the experts suggest that the most important criterion was "Non-traditional machining" (0.264). Under the evaluation criterion of "Type of Problems and Projects", the experts suggest that the most important criterion was "Critical thinking" (0.348). Under the evaluation criterion of "Progression, Size and Duration", the experts suggest that the most important criterion was "Manufacturing costs" (0.367). Under the evaluation criterion of "Students' Learning", the experts suggest that the most important criterion was "Learning Together" (0.263). Under the evaluation criterion of "Academic Staff and Facilitation", the experts suggest that the most important criterion was "Professional competence" (0.310). Under the evaluation criterion of "Space and Organisation", the experts suggest that the most important criterion was "Distance teaching" (0.270). Under the evaluation criterion of "Assessment and Evaluation", the experts suggest that the most important criterion was "Working attitude" (0.354).

Table 4. Weights of 11 sub-criteria

Major criteria	Sub-criteria	Relative weight	Order
Objectives knowledge	Cut into a certain size of the processing method	0.253	2
	Non-traditional machining	0.264	1
	Change material casting method	0.252	3
	Change the physical properties	0.231	4

(*continued*)

Table 4. (*continued*)

Major criteria	Sub-criteria	Relative weight	Order
Type of problems and projects	Critical thinking	0.348	1
	Problem solving ability	0.331	2
	Creativity	0.321	3
Progression, size and duration	Material costs	0.302	3
	Labor costs	0.331	2
	Manufacturing costs	0.367	1
Students' learning	Student teams-achievement divisions	0.233	4
	Teams-games-tournaments	0.243	3
	Team assisted individualization	0.261	2
	Learning together	0.263	1
Academic staff and facilitation	Work ability	0.223	3
	Professional competence	0.310	1
	Competitive advantage	0.261	2
	Research and development capabilities	0.196	4
Space and organisation	Community network	0.254	2
	Distance teaching	0.270	1
	Wisdom sharing	0.231	4
	Internet	0.245	3
Assessment and evaluation	Working attitude	0.354	1
	Workplace ethics	0.320	3
	Etiquette	0.326	2

5   Conclusions

This study determined the industry-oriented most important seven criteria were as follows: Type of Problems and Projects (0.215), Students' Learning (0.190), Objectives knowledge (0.185), Progression, Size and Duration (0.131), Academic Staff and Facilitation (0.101), Assessment and Evaluation (0.090), Space and Organisation (0.088). Based on the results of this survey, it is possible to recognize the importance of PBL, Improve student learning and prepare graduate for professional practice. Both students and teachers support this idea such as teamwork skills, improving student motivation, linking theory and practice, problem solving, etc.

In this study, we applied the AHP approach and found that it is useful for complicated machinery manufacturing project-based learning. Analytical hierarchical processes can be applied to future research on various critical thought curriculum planning problems in education.

References

1. Simon, W.: Investigating the allocation and corroboration of individual grades for project-based learning. Stud. Educ. Eval. **53**, 1–9 (2017)
2. Cameen, K.: Project-based learning and its validity in a thai EFL classroom. Procedia – Soc. Behav. Sci. **192**, 567–573 (2015)
3. Jacobo, R., Ana, L., Juan, M.D.C.: Project based learning experiences in the space engineering education at Technical University of Madrid. Adv. Space Res. **56**, 1319–1330 (2015)
4. Kaveh, P., Vahid M.: Role of project-based learning and entrepreneurship in the evolution of engineering education. In: IACEE 14th World Conference on Continuing Engineering Education Stanford University, 24–27 June (2015)
5. Rasheed, H.A., Nestorovic, S., Elhassan, S.: Designing a self-instructed, project-based multimedia course in engineering education. In: Proceedings of 2000 ASEE Annual Conference and Exposition, St Louis, USA (2000)
6. Miner, S.M., Link, R.E.: A project-based introduction to the finite element method. In: Proceedings of 2000 ASEE Annual Conference and Exposition, St Louis, USA (2000)
7. Xiangyun, D., Erik, D.G., Anette, K.: Research on PBL Practice in Engineering Education. Sense Publishers, Rotterdam/Taipei (2009)
8. Savin, B.M.: Challenging models and perspectives of problem-based learning. In: de Graaff, E., Kolmos, A. (eds.) Management of Change; Implementation of Problem-Based and Project-Based Learning in Engineering, pp. 9–29. Sense Publishers, Rotterdam/Taipei (2007)
9. Christensen, J., Henriksen, L.B., Kolmos, A.: Engineering Science, Skills, and Bildung. Aalborg University Press, Aalborg (2006)
10. Graaff, E.D., Kolmos, A.: Characteristics of problem-based learning. Int. J. Eng. Educ. **19**, 657–662 (2003)
11. Savin-Baden, M., Major, C.: Foundations of Problem-based Learning. Open University Press/SRHE, Maidenhead (2004)
12. Nielsen, J.D., Du, X.Y., Kolmos, A.: A knowledge building approach for learning engineering: a case study of GENSO (student satellite) project. In: Proceedings of SEFI 2008, 36th Annual Conference, European Society for Engineering Education: Conference Theme: Quality Assessment, Employability and Innovation: Celebrating SEFI's 35 years Anniversary. Sense Publishers, Rotterdam/Taipei (2008)
13. Kolmos, A.: Problem-based and project-based learning. In: Skovsmose, O., Christensen, P., Christensen, O.R. (eds.) University Science and Mathematics Education in Transition, pp. 261–282. Springer, London (2008)
14. de Graaff, E., Kolmos, A.: Management of Change; Implementation of Problem-Based and Project-Based Learning in Engineering. Sense Publishers, Rotterdam/Taipei (2007)
15. Saaty, T.L.: An exposition on the AHP in reply to the paper remarks on the analytic hierarchy process. Manag. Sci. **36**, 259–268 (1990)
16. Saaty, T.L.: Relative measurement and its generalization in decision making why pairwise comparisons are central in mathematics for the measurement of intangible factors the analytic hierarchy/network process. Revista de la Real Academia de Ciencias Exactas, Fisicas y Nat. Serie A. Mat. **102**, 251–318 (2008)

Introducing the Maker Movement
to Information Systems Students

Machdel Matthee[1(✉)], Marita Turpin[1], and Dennis Kriel[2]

[1] Department of Informatics, University of Pretoria, Pretoria, South Africa
{machdel.matthee,marita.turpin}@up.ac.za
[2] Department for Education Innovation,
University of Pretoria, Pretoria, South Africa
dennis.kriel@up.ac.za

Abstract. This research reflects on the outcomes of a design thinking assignment given to first year Information Systems students. The assignment entailed the design and making of a corporate gift (or prototype thereof) by making use of the MakerSpace of the University of Pretoria. The assumption was that, by using the technologies provided by the MakerSpace, Information Systems first year students will get a tangible experience of applying design thinking. More importantly though, given the democratizing nature and economic potential of the Maker Movement, we hoped that by using the MakerSpace, students will get an understanding of the Maker Movement philosophy. From the students' feedback, it appears that students characterized the MakerSpace as enjoyable, inspiring, creative and enabling. A number of students noticed the potential for building their own designs and the ease in which rapid prototyping can be done using 3D printing. By using three components comprising the Maker Movement (making, maker spaces and maker as identity) we show that the experience led to a good understanding amongst quite a number of students about what the Maker Movement entails.

Keywords: Maker Movement · Maker space · Information systems · Information systems curriculum · Information systems students · Rapid prototyping · Design thinking

1 Introduction

"I want us all to think about new and creative ways to engage young people in science and engineering, whether it's science festivals, robotics competitions, fairs that encourage young people to create and build and invent – to be makers of things, not just consumers of things."

– President Barack Obama at the Annual Meeting of the National Academies of Sciences (April 27, 2009)

The Maker Movement is gaining traction in South Africa, as in the rest of the world. The Maker Movement is characterized by the "growing number of people who are engaged in the creative production of artifacts in their daily lives and who find physical and digital forums to share their processes and products with others." [1:496]. Hatch [2] refers to the democratizing nature of this movement: design and

© Springer International Publishing AG 2017
T.-C. Huang et al. (Eds.): SETE 2017, LNCS 10676, pp. 161–169, 2017.
https://doi.org/10.1007/978-3-319-71084-6_18

manufacturing are now within the reach of everyday people through powerful computational and fabrication tools. The entrepreneurial and job creation potential of this paradigm is uncontested [3]. At the University of Pretoria (UP), a creative environment, the MakerSpace, was established two years ago. Technologies such as 3D printers, modelling software and Arduino boards are available for students to experiment and tinker with. The facility is staffed by student volunteers and is available to students from all faculties.

The Department of Informatics at UP decided to integrate the use of the MakerSpace in the curriculum of a new prescribed first year module on critical thinking and problem solving. Similar to engineering, problem solving in the information systems field requires not only analytical skills but also the ability to design and create new systems. Traditionally, the teaching of information systems development (ISD) has focused heavily on a linear development process, namely the Systems Development Lifecycle Process (SDLC) [4]. This method still forms the core of ISD teaching at the Informatics Department. However, in practice information systems developers often have to improvise to get working systems implemented under severe time constraints [5], so that a rapid prototyping design process is more appropriate. The Maker Movement's philosophy of creating, tinkering and hacking [6] aligns well with a process of improvisation and rapid prototyping. Furthermore, the Maker Space enables undergraduate students to experience the tangible results of their designs early on in their degree programme, long before they have acquired the ISD skills to have a similar experience from designing and developing software solutions.

In addition, although the MakerSpace can be used by all students, most of them are unaware of the facility and if they are, what the possibilities are of using the technologies. Our assumption was that, by letting students use the MakerSpace in doing their assignment, they will reach some understanding of the potential of the creative environment and the gist of the Maker Movement. The focus of this paper is therefore to reflect on (1) students' opinion on how the MakerSpace influenced their thinking in doing the assignment and (2) the ways in which the exposure to this environment opened their minds to new possibilities.

The next section provides an overview of the first year module and the MakerSpace assignment. This is followed by an analysis of students' opinions regarding the use of the MakerSpace. We conclude with a reflection on the findings.

2   The Problem Solving Module at UP

In this module, students were exposed to problem solving techniques. In addition to analytical techniques, design thinking was introduced as a way of solving problems. We realised that students require more than just analytical skills and the ability to solve textbook type problems, since in real life they are faced with complex and ill-defined problems. Design thinking is suited for dealing with ill-structured, open-ended problems, as opposed to analytical methods that lend themselves better to well-structured problems [7]. Design thinking is further characterised by a problem-solving approach of building or putting together something, in contrast with analytical methods that attempt to solve problems by breaking them down into component parts [8]. This "building" approach of design thinking goes hand in hand with constructionist learning which is student-centred, participative and encourages the making of tangible objects [9].

3   The MakerSpace Assignment

As part of their design thinking module, students received a problem-solving group assignment. They received an open-ended instruction, namely to design and develop a prototype of a corporate gift. In the process, they had to make use of the UP Makerspace in some way. Students were introduced to the Maker Movement during a lecture as well as a guided tour to the UP MakerSpace. At the Makerspace, they were introduced to the facilities and courses offered. Courses on offer included Arduino programming and 3D modelling. The facilities included a colourful "idea space", where students could have their planning meetings and get help from Makerspace assistants. The Makerspace also contained 3D printers and had a range of maker products on display.

Students had to do their assignments by means of a design thinking process. We suggested the Stanford design thinking process, as promoted by Stanford University's Hasso Plattner Institute of Design [10].

This design process consists of five phases: Empathize, Define, Ideate, Prototype and Test. The Empathize phase consists of getting to understand the user – their actions, motivation for the actions, their habits, emotions and world view. This is followed by the Define phase where, through sense making of the user's world, a meaningful problem statement is defined. Once this is done, the designer(s) can give free reign to their imagination and generate as many ideas as possible to solve the problem in the Ideate phase. During the Prototype phase, low resolution prototypes are built and tested at first and later followed by a more refined prototype. Finally, during the Test phase, the user interacts with the prototype(s) to evaluate it after which the prototype is refined. The Test phase provides another opportunity to understand the user through him/her interacting with the prototype meant to solve a specific problem. Although the phases are presented in a linear fashion, the phases are often revisited at any point in the design.

Students were given the opportunity to learn the design thinking process by means of a class exercise. The exercise was an adaptation of the Stanford design thinking crash course [11]. Students had to apply the five step process in pairs. In each pair, Person 1 had to identify a problem related to Person 2's student accommodation situation and design a solution for it, while at the same time, Person 2 designed a solution for Person 1's accommodation situation. Prototypes were made with recycled material in class. Great fun was had as the students designed solutions to better organize their class mates' study areas, designed multi-purpose furniture and addressed issues of privacy and noise, to name a few. The design thinking crash course was experienced as an effective means to get hands-on experience with the design thinking process, as preparation for the student group assignment.

For the group assignment, students also had to identify a potential client for whom they designed the corporate gift, give their product a marketable name and keep within a budget of R200. The Department provided the funds for the production of the prototypes. They also had to document their design thinking processes, rough sketches and 3D models in a blog, which, together with a demonstration of the final prototypes, formed the final mark of the assignment.

We were aware that most of the first year students did not have prior exposure to 3D modelling or the use of 3D printers. While training and facilitation was available at the MakerSpace, the students had to manage their own learning in this regard. They could choose what 3D modelling software to use, and were free to get design ideas from the internet. They were also allowed to get help from family and friends. Our aim was not to develop technological experts, but rather for students to gain exposure to the MakerSpace and maker philosophy in an unconstrained manner.

The prototypes they managed to design and develop were impressive and the class average for the group assignment was high. Section 3.1 below gives more detail about the artefacts that were created.

3.1   Corporate Gift Prototypes

A few examples of the 22 artefacts produced by the students are given below (Table 1). The description of each prototype was taken from the students' blogs.

4   Students' Opinions on the Use of the Maker Space

At the end of the module in June 2016, 81 of the 102 enrolled students completed an online questionnaire, asking students' opinion on several aspects of the module. The focus of this paper is on the answers to the two questions pertaining to the use of the Maker Space in the design and fabrication of the artefact:

Question 1: What influence did the MakerSpace environment have on your assignment?
Question 2: For which kind of problems/projects/products would you consider using the MakerSpace again in the future?

The responses of the students on these two questions were qualitatively analysed and the findings are presented below.

4.1   Influence of the MakerSpace on the Assignment

Students mentioned the role played by services provided by the MakerSpace in the successful completion of their assignment. Services such as 3D printing services, and advice and guidance provided by the staff were highlighted. The maker products in the MakerSpace, served as inspiration to some groups – it sparked ideas on what is doable. Quite a number of students referred to the influence the characteristics of the environment had on their motivation. From their responses the MakerSpace can be considered inspirational, creative, enabling, exciting, and enjoyable. In Table 2 below, we discuss these influences by giving a selection of quotes from the responses to support it, as well as the number of students who referred to it. 69 of the 81 students responded to this question.

Table 1. Prototypes of corporate gifts

Name	Description	Picture
Lamp paperweight	"The decision was made to construct a container which doubles as a paper weight that would contain a flashlight in an internal compartment and would have a variety of external utility features, the features being a multipurpose magnet embedded into the paperweight, a holder for paper clips, three holders for pens and a space to attach a "sticky note" pad."	
Pencil holder – building blocks	"A pencil holder that the users will build themselves."	
Zen Garden	"In the end the Zen garden was the chosen corporate gift as it has much more benefits and uses than any of the other suggestions. Such as, stress relief, a form of healthy escaped, a healthy outlet, etc."	
Mini Candy Machine	"A mini Candy Machine will bring colour into the office as candy is colourful. It will also be unique and make people happy. We would have to make it reusable so that the user will be able to put new candy in."	

4.2 Future Uses of the MakerSpace

In response to Question 2, students pointed out the usefulness of the 3D printers and modeling software provided by the MakerSpace and their intention to use it in future. A number of students foresaw more assignments or projects requiring the use of the

Table 2. Influences identified from responses to Question 1

Influences	Quotes	Number of responses
Services		
3D Printing and modelling	"It was a lot easier and faster to design and 3D print the prototype at the MakerSpace than to find the materials the time to build it ourselves" "The exposure we got to 3D printing as a technology certainly left a huge impression on me and all of my group members" "it helped only with the print of the toy and nothing else" "It helped us in the designing of our prototype" "New skill creating 3D sketches online and gaining knowledge on 3D printing"	20
Advice from staff	"They helped to generate ideas for the assignment" "It helped us in the designing of our prototype"	2
Characteristics of the environment		
Exciting	"Created excitement amongst the group" "It helped us with our ideas and allowed us to be excited to do the assignment" "Gave life to everyone, quite being excited to print something as this was the first time one of us went to print something in 3D in your [sic] lives" "Very exciting and made us more motivated to do well in the assignment, having this opportunity" "MakerSpace was amazing, I loved it, would love to have more assignments such as this"	4
Inspiring	"It was inspiring to explore the existing items already made and use that as inspiration on our item" "It inspired us to think out of the box" "Thank you so much for exposing us to this wonderful place! It gave us knowledge of what the future could hold for us in technology"	3
Creative	"I felt more inclined to think out of the box there, as your surroundings are full of other peoples' creative inventions and designs" "I was completely exposed to a new innovative environment, in which is possibilities are almost endless. It sparked and interest for me in this innovative creative side of informatics" "The MakerSpace made me realise that whatever idea we come up with has to be original, simple, and yet creative"	13
Enabling	"It enabled us to make our product" "They helped us to make a final product for much cheaper" "Made our whole assignment realizable" "It allowed us to use rapid prototyping the first time in our lives" "It made me see my work come to life" "The level of detail and commitment to the design of the prototype and pushing me to constantly iterate until I reach the optimal solution"	4
Challenging	"we took a picture there and realized that people out there are competitive and made sure that we up our game" "It taught us a great deal about compromise since we did not have prior knowledge of CAD or a higher budget, many of our ideals were made obsolete and it taught us that sometimes compromised have to be made in order to succeed"	2

Maker Space during their studies at UP. Most students referred to the exiting possibility of designing something unique or customize existing artefacts and then have it printed. A large number of students considered prototyping as something they would consider using the Maker Space for in future. Table 3 below summarizes the future uses and a selection of quotes supporting the theme. 71 of the 81 respondents, answered this question.

Table 3. Future uses identified from responses to Question 2

Future uses	Quotes	Number of responses
Creating my own unique or customized items	"Projects and problems that involve creating something unique for a client" "designing a cup for someone and personalizing it by using his or her picture" "For my own personal projects to get some advice" "Maybe to print the odd thing or two that I design myself" "Making toys for my future children" "Printing an iPhone charger dock for my phone" "Building electronic gadgets and making robotronics" "Making required or needed parts for a product" "Making a penholder" "When I need an item that is unavailable in South Africa but available online 3D generating sketch site" "Making a gift"	18
Arduino training	"For programming and Arduino courses"	2
Making anything creative	"For projects that require creativity" "Any creative problems that require us to think outside of the box and physically make something to fix it" "Anything with a need for creativity, whether it be making a physical object or not. The assistants help with ideas and practical advice" "Anything that can be made and is a physical item" Any project that a physical object needs to be created, because basically anything can be 3D printed	6
(Rapid) prototyping	"Projects which require a prototype" "MakerSpace is very useful for printing out prototype designs for other projects" "I would use the MakerSpace to build a few of my own concepts that I have in mind and a few ideas that I would like to prototype. This is an excellent place to finally put an idea into an object. I will definitely be pursuing the MakerSpace to build a few of my own projects"	10
Future assignments at UP	"Future assignments in different courses at the TUKS" "any project that requires you to make a physical representation of the goal of the assignment" "also for assignments in business management where we need to create something as future entrepreneurs"	3

5 Discussion

The question now is, did the exposure to the MakerSpace give the students some understanding of the philosophy of the Maker Movement? Halverson and Sheridan [1] identify three components of the Maker Movement: (1) *making* as a set of activities, (2) creative maker environments (*maker spaces*) as communities of practice and (3) *makers* as identities [1:496]. They argue that these three components are interdependent and its existence a necessary condition for any maker culture.

Making refers here to the activities towards the creation of a physical artefact. Hatch [2] considers the construction of physical objects as the one feature which distinguishes the Maker Movement from previous digital revolutions. Students had to follow a structured design approach for the making of the artefact. From students' blogs and responses, it is clear that they understand the MakerSpace as a place which enables one to create physical objects (e.g. "[The MakerSpace can be used for] anything that can be made and is a physical item").

Maker Spaces as communities of practice entail physical places destined for a "group of people to use as a core part of their practice" [1:502]. These spaces are characterized by co-participation and are not regulated. Participants can freely move in and out of the space. Making in these environments involves design thinking, computational thinking and innovation. The idea is to share tools and ideas in order to enable each other as problem solvers [12]. Some students sensed the open and creative character of the MakerSpace at UP. They considered the environment to be creative, inspiring, enabling and enjoyable. Although they did not become part of the community (as far as we know), they were exposed to an example of a maker space.

Maker as identity refers to the identity participants in the Maker Movement take on. They consider themselves *makers* who co-participate within the community to create artefacts. Halverson and Sheridan [1] emphasize that not all participants will take on this identity. From the students responses it is clear that some students will embrace this new identity whereas others not. 18 students saw the opportunity to make their own artefacts in future whereas 3 students clearly said that they will not use the MakerSpace in the future.

From the discussion above, we deduce that for at least some students, the use of the MakerSpace in the assignment let them experience what the Maker Movement is about. The small number of responses for some of the themes shows that we cannot say this for the majority of students, but we believe it is a good beginning. It seems that some students feel more empowered now and might even consider becoming participants in future in the maker culture.

6 Conclusion

This paper argues that by introducing the MakerSpace to a design assignment of Information Systems, the students were not only given the tangible experience of applying design thinking, but were simultaneously exposed to the philosophy of the Maker Movement.

The MakerSpace at UP is only in its second year of existence and some teething problems were experienced in the beginning. Some students complained about the lack of resources and the consequent long printing job queues. We repeated this assignment in 2017 and to deal with bottle neck issues at the MakerSpace, introduced an earlier deliverable to prevent last minute printing jobs. This worked well and no complaints were received in 2017 regarding this issue.

Although we did not collect any demographic data, this is something that should be considered in future research. It would be interesting to understand what type of student takes on the identity of maker. Halverson and Sheridan [1] refer to the male domination in the maker culture. Is this also true for our students? In addition, we believe that some aspects of the Maker Movement philosophy should be applied in the teaching of system design and engineering. For example, how can the learning environment in the computer lab be enhanced such that students experience an open and creative space where they can embrace the identity of information system makers? These and other related questions might be worth the while to investigate.

References

1. Halverson, E.R., Sheridan, K.: The maker movement in education. Harvard Educ. Rev. **84** (4), 495–504 (2014)
2. Hatch, M.: The Maker Movement Manifesto. McGrawHill Education, New York (2014)
3. Seo-Zindy, R., Heeks, R.: Researching the emergence of 3D printing, Makerspaces, Hackerspaces and Fablabs in the Global South: a scoping review and research agenda on digital innovation and fabrication networks. Electron. J. Inf. Syst. Dev. Ctries. **80**(5), 1–24 (2017)
4. Whitten, I.L.D., Bentley, J.L.: Systems Analysis & Design for the Global Enterprise, 7th edn. McGraw-Hill/Irwin, New York (2007)
5. Van der Merwe, C., Turpin, M., Hendriks, S.: The development of a mobile information system to assess the food security of rural communities in South Africa. In: Proceedings of IST-Africa 2017 Conference, Windhoek, Namibia, 31 May–2 June 2017 (2017)
6. Honey, M., Kanter, D.E. (eds.): Design, Make, Play: Growing the Next Generation of STEM Innovators. Routledge, New York (2013)
7. Jonassen, D.H.: Toward a design theory of problem solving. Educ. Tech. Res. Dev. **48**(4), 63–85 (2000)
8. Cross, N.: Designerly ways of knowing. Des. Stud. **3**(4), 221–227 (1982)
9. Alesandrini, K., Larson, L.: Teachers bridge to constructivism. Clearing House **75**(3), 119–121 (2002)
10. Hasso Plattner Institute of Design: An Introduction to Design Thinking Process Guide (2010). http://dschool-old.stanford.edu/sandbox/groups/designresources/wiki/36873/attachments/74b3d/ModeGuideBOOTCAMP2010L.pdf?sessionID=573efa71aea50503341224491c862e32f5edc0a9. Accessed 6 June 2017
11. Hasso Plattner Institute of Design: A Virtual Crash Course in Design Thinking (2017b). http://dschool.stanford.edu/resources-collections/a-virtual-crash-course-in-design-thinking. Accessed 8 June 2017
12. Papavlasopoulou, S., Giannakos, M.N., Jaccheri, L.: Empirical studies on the maker movement, a promising approach to learning: a literature review. Entertain. Comput. **18**, 57–78 (2016)

LeSigLa_EC: Learning Sign Language
of Ecuador

D. Rivas[1]([⊠]), M. Alvarez[1], W. Tamayo[1], V. Morales[1], R. Granizo[1],
G. Vayas[2], V. Andaluz[1], M. Huerta[3], and G. Clotet[4]

[1] Universidad de las Fuerzas Armadas ESPE, Sangolquí, Ecuador
{drrivas,ralvarez,wtamayo,vmorale,rgranizo,
vandaluz}@espe.edu.ec
[2] Pontificia Universidad Católica del Ecuador - Ambato, Ambato, Ecuador
gvayas@pucesa.edu.ec
[3] Universidad Politécnica Salesiana, Cuenca, Ecuador
mhuerta@ieee.org
[4] Universidad Internacional de Valencia, Valencia, Spain
roger.clotet@campusviu.es

Abstract. The Technology in Information and Communication have allowed
the exploration of new techniques in teaching, the development of computerized
tools that improve the user learning experiences. Hearing-impaired people
communicate using sign language, this tool represents the letters of the alphabet
in a gestural way, which is the basis of their communication. In Ecuador, there is
a deficit of teachers in schools for deaf people; for this reason, we propose a
computer program to teach ecuadorian sign language using a gesture sensor as
an input device and output on a monitor, allowing students to improve their
learning experience.

Keywords: Sign language · Leap motion · CSCL

1 Introduction

The use of The Technology in Information and Communication (TIC's) in the world of
teaching has allowed the inclusion of new techniques, such is the case of
Computer-Supported Collaborative Learning (CSCL). At the global level, these techniques have been very supportive for teaching both children and adults at different
levels of education, generating new forms of teaching [1] and strengthen the different
types of collaborative learning [2]. However, in this group are people with special
abilities, that can be isolated in the traditional teaching-learning processes due to their
condition. For this reason the CSCL is considered as an opportunity to develop educational support systems to the addressed to this vulnerable group.

In the work created by [3], they used Support Vector Machines (SVM) as classification techniques. In the proposal made by [4], they did sign recognition with the use
of Kinect. In addition, [5] proposed the use of cameras to minimize errors in classification at the recognition of signs when using both hands. Based on these works it can
be determined that the generation of new techniques for people with disabilities is

© Springer International Publishing AG 2017
T.-C. Huang et al. (Eds.): SETE 2017, LNCS 10676, pp. 170–179, 2017.
https://doi.org/10.1007/978-3-319-71084-6_19

growing. Therefore, this paper proposes a computerized tool that will serve as a better support in the teaching field of ecuadorian sign language for people with hearing impairment. This computerized tool consist in the use of Leap Motion, a sensor for capturing positional finger and hand data, a computerized pattern classification module, and a graphical user interface. With this system is intended to provide an intuitive technological tool and low computational cost. This article is divided into five sections: the Introduction, Section two, Methodology, where the development and the architecture of the tool mainly describes the selected hardware and software elements. Section three, the Analysis of results. Section four, Conclusions are present, and finally the possible future work in Section five is detailed.

2 Methodology

2.1 Current Situation

Most hearing-impaired children come from normal families, wich relatively deprived them with the proper language development and living in a less efficient communicative environment compared to hearing children. According to the Instituto Nacional de Estadística y Censos (INEC) [6] there are 4,926 people with hearing impairments in the province of Cotopaxi, of which 4,636 are older than 13 years old and 290 are under 13 years of age, and there are not enough teachers to teach the language signs in educational centers.

The lack of Linguistic skills shows consequences at the social acceptance. As a solution to the problem can be incorporated into the development of sign language for communication. However, learning can be tedious and present certain difficulties in children. For instance, an interactive and friendly system for children with hearing problems will facilitate the learning of sign language. Since this system serves as support and involves the active participation of the user providing a visual environment, as a result of the learning process, it will be more fun and it will be understand in a better way.

2.2 Identification, Description and Diagnosis of the Problem

Hearing impairment causes both behavioral and performance problems when undetected on time. People with profound deafness need to communicate with others through sign language, similar to the one that is usually used orally.

Acceptance of disabilities has evolved over time, allowing the study to benefit rehabilitation or provide new tools that help to incorporate people hearing impairments into society. This can be done with the help of new technology, creating instruments and devices that overcome the physical and psychological barriers [7].

After the creation of the tactile technology the next step is the recognition of gestures. Currently there are different products in this sense, one of them is the Kinect which gestural system is the best known in the world to be commercialized in a massive way due to its compatibility with other devices like the Xbox. The Xbox is a device used in video games that can be used for other gestural applications [8].

To contextualize the development of the technology, it is important to mention that the Kinect was developed by the Israeli company PrimeSense and Microsoft incorporated it to the console Xbox. This union made it clear that the technology has multiple uses and working together with other companies it`s possible to create new products. In another example, Sony developed technology called Move that has several similarities to the controller of Nintendo's Wii console, pioneer of motion control video game technology. Other companies have also developed gestural control for computers, one of them is Leap Motion, which works especially in the detection of hands and arms, the non-existent delay and its high sensitivity can detect until the movement of the fingers, this device is of small dimensions and Easy manipulation [9].

The most important advantage of gestural interfaces is to send commands or instructions to a machine without the need to be in physical contact with it, so that the commands are transmitted remotely. In addition, this type of interface offers a great possibility of expand the number of signs used for information because of the richness of body language [10].

2.3 System Description

The description of the system consists of three stages Fig. 1, (i) by means of a gestural sensor focused on the recognition of the hands of the user´s hands, captures the signs of

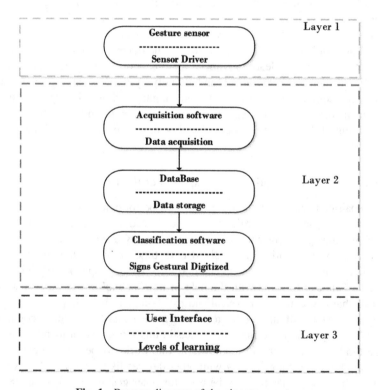

Fig. 1. Process diagram of the signature system

the basic sign language of Ecuador, (ii) To capture the data of the position of the bones of the hand, then to be stored in the database and to form a pattern of each one of the letters of the ecuadorian alphabet in sign language. Finally, in this stage applies techniques of Classification of data with the obtained patterns and is compared with the signals captured by the sensor in real time; (iii) The user interface allows the students to visualize the letters that the student makes and the application determines if they perform correctly, it is also possible to determine the amount of letters that is made in a certain time, so that different degrees of learning can be evaluated.

2.4   Leap Motion

It is a type of gestural sensor based on the technology of Kinect, with the difference that it is oriented only to the recognition of the hands, what makes that device more economic; Its dimensions 8 cm long by 3 cm wide provide greater portability; in spite of this, users can interact in a fluid and precise way with the computer by hand movements without the need to touch the screen, have contact with the mouse or keyboard, it is also compatible with programming languages C++, C#, Java, Python.

Leap Motion has been used successfully in many areas of engineering and 3D design. On the other hand, it is used as a tool for the design of reusable rockets of the company SpaceX.

The main components that make up the Leap Motion sensor: three leds, two monochrome cameras and a microcontroller Fig. 2.

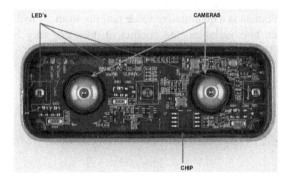

Fig. 2. Leap motion components.

Upon detecting hands reflection of light that reaches the device and impinges on the lenses of the cameras is produced, the data collected by the sensors are stored in a matrix in the microcontroller memory, the data acquired represent a brightness value is quantized to 8 bits, to form an image in grayscale, at this point it is considered that there is a total of 256 possible brightness values, each captured by the image sensor has dimensions of 640 × 120 pixels which can be seen in the displayed Leap Motion [11]

Fig. 3, the speed sensor is that takes data at a rate of up to 200 frames per second and the images are not treated in the device, only collects and sends data to the driver installed in the computer, where the information it becomes accessible for the developer [12].

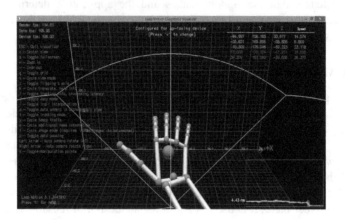

Fig. 3. Leap motion display

2.5   Correlation Statistics

The statistical correlation is a technique that indicates whether two variables are related. The correlation coefficient is a quantitative value ranging from −1 to 1 and indicates the relationship between two variables, the coefficient does not vary by modifying the measuring scale [13] Fig. 4a.

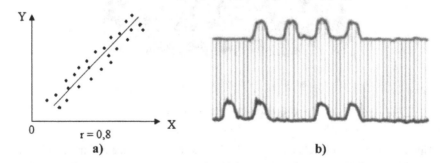

Fig. 4. (a) Positive correlation, (b) Euclidian distance (top) and DTW (lower).

The correlation coefficient can be defined as the covariance between two variables and has the calculation expression (Eq. 1).

$$r = \frac{\sum_{i=1}^{n}(X_i - \bar{X})(Y_i - \bar{Y})(Z_i - \bar{Z})}{\sqrt{\left[\sum_i^n(X_i - \bar{X})^2\right]\left[\sum_i^n(Y_i - \bar{Y})^2\right]\left[\sum_i^n(Z_i - \bar{Z})^2\right]}} \quad (1)$$

2.6 Dynamic Time Warping (DTW)

The DTW algorithm measures the similarity between two trajectories which vary in time or speed, in order to assess the similarity between two trajectories points, the distance between them is calculated. The shorter the distance, the greater the similarity, to calculate Euclidean distance DTW (Eq. 2) is used.

$$d(P, Q) = \sqrt{(p_1 - q_1)^2 + (p_2 - q_2)^2 + \ldots + (p_n - q_n)^2} = \sqrt{\sum_{i=1}^{n}(p_i - q_i)^2} \quad (2)$$

The main function of DTW is to eliminate the difference between the path lengths. The possible lack of temporary alignment paths does not follow a fixed law, but occurs heterogeneously, thus producing variations that increase or decrease the length of the stretch of sequence, then it is necessary to temporarily align paths to make a measure distance between them. To search for an optimal alignment between paths of points, the procedure is to stretch or shrink the time axis iteratively until a minimum global distance in Fig. 4b alignment that produces the Euclidean distance is shown, the ith point first to i-th of the second [14].

2.7 Description of the Graphical User Interface (GUI)

In Fig. 5 shows the window of the menu with the following options:

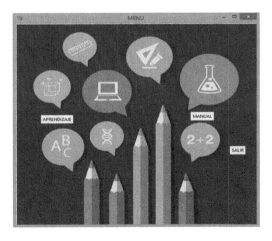

Fig. 5. Menu window.

Learning a window with learning modes ecuadorian sign language. Manual: Get a window with basic instructions to manipulate the learning syste. Exit: Closes the menu window.

In the learning section a menu with the different modes is presented, this window has a pastel green background that motivates learning and relaxation of the person. Set user through gestures (swipe, keytap, screentap) can choose the ways in which to develop their learning Fig. 6; orderly way: Expose sorted letters A → Z; Random mode: Post a certain number of letters in uncertain form; Trial mode: Displays a game mode where the system establishes a score based on the number of letters that the user makes in 30 s.

Fig. 6. Window learning modes.

Once the learning mode the system displays a window that provides visual information letters to the user, if the user performs the configuration specified password correctly the system switches to the next letter, this process is carried on until end mode, there is a gesture that can be used at any time of the program to return to learning mode menu as shown in Fig. 7.

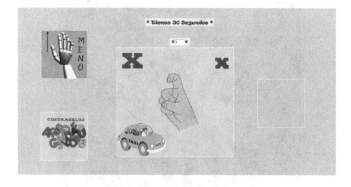

Fig. 7. Learning window sign

2.8 System Usability Scale (SUS) Questionnaire

The purpose of the questionnaire is to provide an easy test to complete, you have a minimum of questions, easy to score and that would measure the usability of software, tools and technical tools. The questionnaire was applied after a user has had the opportunity to use a system, but before any report or discussion takes place, consists of 10 items.

The SUS questionnaire scale is a Likert scale style of 1 to 5, if the user does not feel able to answer a questionnaire item, there will be noted the central value of the scale, to calculate the score of SUS must add contributions of each item. For items 1, 3, 5, 7 and 9, the contribution will be the position of the scale minus 1, to items 2, 4, 6, 8 and 10, the contribution is 5 minus the position on the scale, then multiplies the sum of the results by 2.5 for the overall value. The result will be between 0 and 100 [15].

3 Learning Testing

The tests are performed with a total of 13 users where 46% are children with hearing impairment and 54% are children without hearing impairment. The experimentation of learning takes place in different parts, first the user knows the operation of the system and the interface, then the user must complete the three learning modes that begins with the Sorted Mode, Random Mode and Time Trial Mode.

The number of interactions performed by each of the users is 6 repetitions due to the availability of time of the students and the teacher. All levels of the school are gathered in the same classroom and are directed only by a teacher specializing in sign language.

To improve the user's perception of this result, multiply the value of the same by 100, this way if you made 12 signs in 30 s the interface will show a score of 12000 point, thus encouraging the user to keep trying to achieve a higher score.

The performance and level of learning provided by the system to children with hearing impairment can be seen in Fig. 8a, where it can be seen that the learning curve is exponential and the number of configurations performed increases each time the user

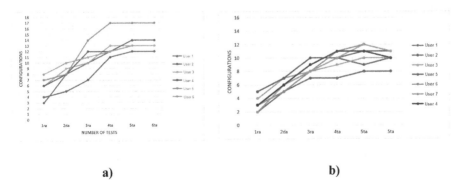

a)   b)

Fig. 8. (a) Curves of learning in deaf users, (b) Curves of learning in listening users

interacts with the system. When performing the test for the fifth and sixth time the curve stabilizes, which means that in an estimated time of 20 min a maximum number of configurations can be made, which can increase while the user continues interacting with the system.

The performance and level of learning provided by the system to children who do not suffer from hearing impairment is reflected in Fig. 8b, where it can be seen that the learning curve is exponential since the number of configurations performed in-creases each time the user interacts with the system.

The average learning curve of Hearing-impaired children in relation to the learning curve of hearing children Fig. 9, it can be observed that the nature of the curves are similar. The two present an exponential growth, regardless of the number of signs performed, due to that, Hearing-impaired children have previous knowledge of sign language their curve has a greater number of configurations performed corresponding to 46.66% unlike Hearing-impaired children that is 33.33%.

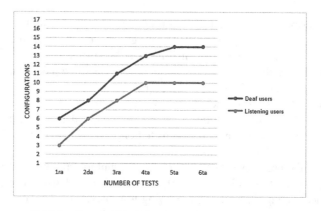

Fig. 9. Curves of learning in deaf vs. listening users

4   Conclusions

The implementation of the ecuadorian basic sign language learning system, based on the dictionary standardized by CONADIS, is a tool that allows learning to children with hearing impairment.

The Leap Motion sensor is optimal for the development of the learning system by providing detailed hand information, such as position and direction of arm vectors, palm and finger bones, lengths, finger thickness, initial and final position vectors, Gestures predefined, ID of each hand and finger, in addition to being economical and small.

In the average learning curves, it is evident that children with hearing impairment exceed 13% of those who do not have this condition, when using the proposed tool.

5   Future Work

The present work will be expanded in the recognition of common phrases that Hearing-impaired people daily uses. In addition, it will include a system of recognition of images and videos in order to expand levels of teaching.

Acknowledgment. The authors thank the ESPE for the support to the execution of the project 2016-PIC-045, "Sistema de soporte a la enseñanza y comprensión de lenguaje de señas básico, aplicando técnicas de clasificación de datos para la interpretación gestual".

References

1. Ludvigsen, S., Arnseth, H.C.: Computer-supported collaborative learning. In: Duval, E., Sharples, M., Sutherland, R. (eds.) Technology Enhanced Learning, pp. 47–58. Springer, Cham (2017). https://doi.org/10.1007/978-3-319-02600-8_5
2. Fischer, F., Kollar, I., Stegmann, K., Wecker, C.: Toward a script theory of guidance in computer-supported collaborative learning. Educ. Psychol. **48**(1), 56–66 (2013)
3. Cervantes, J., García Lamont, F., Santiago, J., Espejel Cabrera, J., Espinosa, A.T.: Clasificación del lenguaje de señas mexicano con SVM generando datos artificiales. Revista Vínculos **10**(1), 328–341 (2013)
4. Chai, X., et al.: Sign language recognition and translation with kinect. Presented at the IEEE Conference on AFGR (2013)
5. Kishore, P., Prasad, M., Prasad, C.R., Rahul, R.: 4-Camera model for sign language recognition using elliptical fourier descriptors and ANN. Presented at the 2015 International Conference on Signal Processing and Communication Engineering Systems (SPACES), pp. 34–38 (2015)
6. INEC - Instituto Nacional de Estadística y Censos: Información Censal
7. Chacón, E., Aguilar, D., Sáenz, F.: Desarrollo de una Interfaz para el Reconocimiento Automático del Lenguaje de Signos. MASKAY Electrónica **4**(1), 14 (2014)
8. Elons, A., Ahmed, M., Shedid, H., Tolba, M.: Arabic sign language recognition using leap motion sensor. Presented at the 2014 9th International Conference on Computer Engineering & Systems (ICCES), pp. 368–373 (2014)
9. Palomar, O.: Leap Motion, un 'superkinect' disponible en mayo, 20 April 2013
10. Bejerano, P.G.: 4 ejemplos de interfaz gestual, 09 November 2013
11. Sosapanta, V., Esteban, P.: Desarrollo e implementación de un sistema de apoyo académico usando instrucciones gestuales para niños mediante el uso del dispositivo Leap Motion Controller (2017)
12. Justinico, O., Cárdenas, P.F., Rodríguez, J.S.: Control gestual de robot de 4 GDL con sensor Leap Motion. Memorias (2015)
13. Vila, A., Sedano, M., López, A., Juan, A.: Correlación lineal y análisis de regresión. Universitat Oberta Catalunya, Barcelona (2004)
14. Alezones-Campos, Z., Baquero-Romero, Y., Borrero-Guerrero, H., Becker, M.: Recognising isolated words for mobile robot navigation control. ORINOQUIA **16**(1), 121–134 (2012)
15. Brooke, J.: SUS-A quick and dirty usability scale. Usability Eval. Ind. **189**(194), 4–7 (1996)

Pre-exit Survey of Final Year Students to Assess the Mechanical Engineering Curriculum

Emmanuel Glakpe[1(✉)] and Esther Akinlabi[2]

[1] Howard University, Washington DC 20059, USA
eglakpe@howard.edu
[2] University of Johannesburg, Auckland Park 2006, South Africa

Abstract. As part of the goals to provide excellent educational opportunities to students, most undergraduate programs in engineering on different continents seek some form of accreditation, be it a part of a national requirement or part of a global initiative. The mechanical engineering program at the University of Johannesburg (UJ) is one such program that prepares many students for engineering practice. As with all such programs, there is always the need to evaluate, assess and institute measures to enhance the effectiveness of teaching and learning methods to better prepare students for the global environment. As part of an initiative of the Carnegie Africa Diaspora Fellowship Program, the mechanical engineering department hosted a Fellow from Howard University, Washington DC to interact with colleagues and students at the UJ to discuss and share best-practice ideas on enhancing teaching and learning. As a start, a survey was prepared and administered to first-semester final year students to assess the learning outcomes of the department and to gather additional information about other factors such as faculty, advising and mentoring, the curriculum, and technology utilization in the curriculum. Overall, the students ranked the learning outcomes and other measures very highly except for the lack of opportunities to enhance managerial and entrepreneurial skills (soft skills) and the to interact with potential employers while matriculating through program. The use of technological tools for engineering applications is highlighted as one of the areas that can be enhanced with minimal investments to improve the learning of engineering subjects.

Keywords: Engineering education · Pre-exit survey · Technology utilization

1 Introduction

1.1 About the University

The University of Johannesburg was established in 2005, out of the merger of three legacy institutions, that is, Technikon Witwatersrand founded in 1921, Rand Afrikaans University founded in 1968 and Vista University founded in 1979, UJ has now transformed into a diverse, inclusive, transformational and collegial institution, with a student population of over 50000, of which 2500 are international students from 52 countries. This makes UJ one of the largest contact universities in South Africa and in

© Springer International Publishing AG 2017
T.-C. Huang et al. (Eds.): SETE 2017, LNCS 10676, pp. 180–188, 2017.
https://doi.org/10.1007/978-3-319-71084-6_20

Africa. The strategic goals of the university include excellence in the following areas of education delivery to its population of students and all stakeholders:

- Global Excellence in Research and Innovation.
- Global Excellence in Teaching and Learning.
- An International Profile Fit for Global Excellence and Stature.
- An Outstanding Student Experience.
- Active Global Reputation Management, and
- An Institution and People Fit for Global Excellence and Stature.

1.2   The Department

In working towards the achievement of the strategic goals, the Department of Mechanical Engineering Science proposed to host a diaspora fellow under the Carnegie Africa Diaspora Fellow Program (CADFP) to work collaboratively with the department in infusing elements of globalization in its core activities of teaching, learning, research and mentoring. The CADFP fellow engaged the faculty in the review and recommend modifications of the curriculum with current best practices in global engineering education. To enhance teaching and learning, the department proposed to explore the use of technology such as Computer Aided and Engineering (CAE) tools in a Problem Based learning environment to better equip students in a dynamic global environment. The CADFP fellow also led seminar discussions on the use of technology in and outside the classroom with the hope of institutionalizing the tools of CAE in the curriculum. The department proposed to begin engineering education research studies to determine the effectiveness of curricula innovations on teaching and learning.

1.3   Purpose of Paper

Engineering education and practice have evolved over the last two decades partly due to the availability of access to data readily for the most part on the web or the use of web resources in sharing information. The internet has revolutionized the way classes are taught, the conduct of research and the communication of results of research discovery. In the effort to continuously improve the curriculum in Mechanical Engineering, there is a need for an external review to assess the existing curriculum, propose changes and additions to content, delivery of lectures, approaches to the enhancement of teaching and learning, and the assessment of learning objectives. Continuous improvement of the curriculum (teaching, learning, and knowledge creation) requires that a mechanism and a process are in place to conduct research in engineering education with the goal of improving critical thinking skills of students in grasping and understanding materials presented in lectures, but most importantly to propose new paradigms that enhance the delivery of the curriculum to students. To meet the needs expressed, the objectives of the collaboration between the CADFP fellow and the host institution were proposed as follows:

- Review the Mechanical Engineering curriculum at UJ
- Propose changes/additions in the enhancement of the curriculum

- Conduct a series of seminars to students and faculty on global engineering education
- Interact with faculty on curriculum assessment and use of results in the enhancement of teaching and learning
- Discuss and initiate joint research projects (engineering education and engineering science research) with faculty and students
- Propose and adopt mentoring strategies that use web resources effectively
- Discuss and implement technology resources (Computer Aided Engineering software and hardware) that enhance teaching and research. Numerous examples on best practices in global engineering education would form the basis for the execution of the proposed objectives.

2   Accreditation and Departmental Learning Outcomes

The mechanical engineering curriculum at the University of Johannesburg is accredited by the Engineering Council of South Africa (ECSA). ECSA is the recognized Engineering body in South Africa to ensure compliance of South Africa as a member of the Washington Accord which is a global accreditation body that regulates engineering practice. Signatories to the Washington Accord are organizations responsible for accrediting engineering programs member states which include Australia, Canada, Chinese Taipei, Hong Kong, Ireland, Japan, Korea, Malaysia, New Zealand, Singapore, South Africa, Turkey, the United Kingdom, and the United States of America. The learning outcomes as stipulated by the department in conformity with ECSA guidelines for the mechanical engineering program at are as follows.

(a) Identify, assess, formulate, interpret, analyze and solve engineering problems creatively and innovatively by applying mathematics, basic science and engineering sciences from first principles.
(b) Plan and manage small engineering projects, demonstrating fundamental knowledge, understanding and insight into the principles, methodologies and concepts that constitute socially responsible (to local and other communities) engineering practice.
(c) Work effectively, individually or with others, as a member of a team, group, organization, community or in multi-disciplinary environments.
(d) Organize and manage him/herself and his/her activities responsibly, effectively, professionally and ethically, accept responsibility within his/her limits of competence, and exercise judgment based on knowledge and expertise.
(e) Plan and conduct limited investigations, research and experiments by applying appropriate theories and methodologies, and perform appropriate data analysis and interpretation.
(f) Communicate effectively, both orally and in writing, with engineering audiences and the community at large, using appropriate structure, style and graphical support.

(g) Use and assess appropriate research methods, skills, tools and information technology effectively and critically in engineering practice, and show an understanding and a willingness to accept responsibility for the impact of engineering activities on society and the environment.

(h) Perform procedural and non-procedural design and synthesis of components, systems, works, products or processes as a set of related systems and assess, where applicable, their social, legal, health, safety and environmental impact and benefits.

(i) Employ various learning strategies and skills to master module outcomes required in fundamental Mathematics, engineering sciences, engineering design research and aspects of management, thereby preparing him/herself to engage in lifelong learning, to keep abreast of knowledge and skills required in the engineering field.

(j) Participate as a responsible citizen in the life of local, national and global communities by acting professionally and ethically.

(k) Demonstrate cultural and aesthetic sensitivity across a range of social context in the execution of engineering activities.

(l) Engineering Management skills.

(m) Explore education and career opportunities.

(n) Organize and develop entrepreneurial opportunities through engineering problem solving, design, technical research and managerial skills.

3 The Curriculum

The mechanical engineering program at the UJ requires students to complete a minimum of 988 credits with a 50% score in each program module or course. The four-year curriculum is presented in Table 1 for each of the eight program semesters. The curriculum is designed to expose students to the basics of Mathematics, Physics/Chemistry, Engineering Sciences, Humanities and Communication, Engineering Design and Practice, and Project Investigation (Research). Including a module in Statistics, students in the program must take mathematics courses that account for over 30% of the total number of credits required for graduation.

The basics of engineering science is covered in many of the "traditional" engineering class modules (including laboratory discover exercises) and account for approximately 30% of the credit requirements for graduation. The applications of engineering sciences, physics and mathematics are realized in many engineering design courses that are offered in each semester of the curriculum. The design modules, including legal and management aspects of engineering practice, account for about 20% of the total credit requirements. In addition to design across the curriculum, students are expected to enroll in a two-semester module on Project Investigation in which they participate in discovery through research on a topic proposed by a faculty member. The modules offered by the program can be grouped into the specialized technical areas of Thermo-Fluids, Materials, Design and Manufacturing.

Table 1. Curriculum of the mechanical engineering science program

Code	Module	Code	Module
First year			
First semester		Second semester	
APM01A1	Applied Mathematics 1A	APM01B1	Applied Mathematics 1B
GKMEEA1	Graphical Communication 1A	GKMEEB1	Graphical Communication 1B
IINEEA1	Introduction to Engineering Design 1A	IINEEB1	Introduction to Engineering Design 1B
MATENA1	Engineering Mathematics 1A	MATENB1	Engineering Mathematics 1B
PHYE0A1	Engineering Physics 1A	PHYE0B1	Engineering Physics 1B
CEM01A1	Chemistry 1A	ETNEEB1	Electrotechnics 1B
Second year			
First semester		Second semester	
APM02A2	Applied Mathematics 2A	APM02B2	Applied Mathematics 2B
MATEAA2	Engineering Mathematics 2A2	MATEAB2	Engineering Mathematics 2B2
MATECA2	Engineering Mathematics 2A1	MATECB2	Engineering Mathematics 2B1
OWMMCA2	Design (Mechanical) 2A	OWMMCB2	Design (Mechanical) 2B
ETNEEA2	Electrotechnics 2A11	MTKMCB2	Science of Materials 2B
STRCIA2	Fluid Mechanics 2A11	SLRBCB2	Strength of Materials 2B
MODEEA2	Modelling 2A	TRDMCB2	Thermodynamics 2B
Third year			
First semester		Second semester	
CPS31A3	Complementary Studies 3A1	INPMCB3	Engineering Practice 3B
CPS32A3	Complementary Studies 3A2	MKEMCB3	Theory of Machines 3B
OWMMCA3	Design (Mechanical) 3A	OWMMCB3	Design (Mechanical) 3B
STAE0A3	Statistics for Engineers 3A01	VVEMCB3	Manufacturing Methods 3B
STRMCA3	Fluid Dynamics 3A	SLRBCB3	Strength of Materials 3B
MLAMCY3	Mechanical Engineering Laboratory 3	COMMCB3	Communication 3B
TMSMCA3	Thermofluids 3A		
MTKMCA3	Science of Materials 3A		
Fourth year			
First semester		Second semester	
OIPMCY4	Design and Engineering Practice 4	OIPMCY4	Design and Engineering Practice 4 (Year module)
PJMMCY4	Project Investigation (Mechanical) 4	PJMMCY4	Project Investigation (Mechanical) 4 (Year module)
WAOMCA4	Heat Transfer 4A	RTICIB4	Legal Applications in Engineering Practice 4B
SLRBCA4	Strength of Materials 4A	EBP3B21	Management Principles and Practice 3B
TRMMCA4	Thermomachines 4A	TMLMCB4	Thermal Systems 4B
MVSMCA4	Advanced Manufacturing Systems 4A	TKNMCB4	Control Systems (Mechanical) 4B

4   Assessment Methodology

In assessing the Mechanical Engineering Science program at the University of Johannesburg, a survey instrument was designed and conducted among the final year students who are only one semester away from graduation. The published literature [1], for example, have documented the use if student exit and other surveys for the assessment of an engineering curriculum. The surveys for this paper were completed by 68 students who took the Advanced Manufacturing Systems final examination in May 2017. The survey respondents were asked to provide feedback anonymously and confidentially on the program curriculum, the faculty, program learning outcomes, facilities and their overall experience at the University. Most of the questions in the survey were designed on the Likert scale ranging from "Strongly Disagree" with a score of 1 to "Strongly Agree" with a score of 5.

5   Results and Discussion

A summary of the results obtained from assessing the departmental learning outcomes (a–n) is shown in Fig. 1. The highest ranked learning outcome (c) with an average score of above 4.3 (86%) shows that the students have developed teamwork skills that are necessary to "work effectively, individually or with others, as a member of a team, group, organization, community or in multi-disciplinary environments". The survey results also reveal a satisfaction among students that the program is satisfying in providing effective instructions in the identification and finding solutions to engineering problems from the application of mathematics, the basic sciences and engineering sciences from first principles.

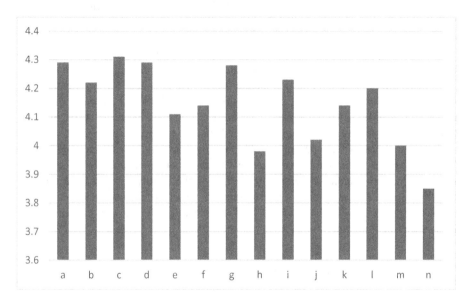

Fig. 1. Assessment of learning outcomes

Most of the learning outcomes were assessed on the average at above 80% except for four (h, j, m and n) that are near or below this threshold. These four outcomes relate mostly to non-engineering aspects of a traditional engineering program in which engineers must take into consideration the legal, social, health, safety and environmental aspects of engineering decision making processes. The survey results also point to the fact that students have not been exposed well to opportunities during their matriculation in the program to explore educational and career options in engineering and to develop entrepreneurial skills through engineering problem solving, design, technical research and the application of managerial skills in the process.

6   Role of Technology Utilization in the Curriculum

The use of technology, in the forms of information technology (IT) and Computer Aided Engineering and Design (CAD and CAE) software, for enhancing the teaching and learning of engineering subjects is required in any progressive mechanical engineering department. The CAD and CAE software allow students to work on assignments efficiently and to enhance their understanding of engineering and scientific principles in problem and project-based learning [2] environments. A department of mechanical engineering department that does not provide the environment for the use of technology efficiently may fall short of achieving its goals as an educational entity.

The learning outcome (g) that addresses the use of appropriate tools and information technology (IT) in engineering practice was ranked highly (4.28/5) by student respondents in the survey. However, the responses to other probing questions on the availability of appropriate tools and the ease of access to such resources seem to be of concern to students. It is apparent that the respondents did distinguish IT resources from technology resources that are meant specifically for engineering design and analyses. Whereas IT resources are widespread on their laptops and mobile phones, the respondents did not respond kindly to the hard-technical resources for the enhancement of teaching and learning. Most of the respondents listed no more than one engineering software, SOLIDWORKS, that they have used during their time in the department. Responses by a few of the students indicated their exposure to other CAE software during the final year when working on individual project work or research assignments. The limited hours of availability of the departmental computer laboratory facility are also mentioned by students as reasons for not using the facility to assist in completing assignments in a timely manner. Other comments about the facility include the inadequate quality of the workstations and low processor speeds and lack of current versions of installed software.

7   Globalization of Curriculum

The strategic goals of the university include goals to enhance its reputation with global recognition in every aspect of university life, including teaching and learning, research and innovation and an outstanding student experience. Although there are a number of research collaborations on a global level in the department, there is no evidence of such collaborations in teaching and learning to enhance engineering education. The department is home to a few students from international institutions who acquire "study abroad certification" at the institution but such a certification is not required of students matriculating the UJ mechanical engineering program. No attempt was made to assess this aspect of engineering education in the survey study reported in this paper.

Within the last decade or more the word "Globalization" has become a buzz word at international conferences on engineering education. Globalization is described as "the development of an increasingly integrated global economy marked especially by free trade, free flow of capital, and the tapping of cheaper foreign labor markets" [3]. Relating the definition of globalization to engineering education would simply imply that a curriculum must prepare its students to take advantage of the globalization of the economies of the world and be able to adapt to various working conditions so that they can be effective as team players in advancing the goals and objectives of their organizations which for the most part are for-profit multinational corporations. A "globalized" engineering curriculum must do more than that to prepare students for the global workforce environment. Some elements [4] of a globalized curriculum are the following:

- Part of graduation requirements could be fulfilled through a period of study abroad.
- Implement faculty and student exchange programs to clarify the global views of the engineering practice.
- Inclusion of extended periods and/or close cooperation with multi-national industry while enrolled in the engineering program.
- Conducting joint projects/research among various departments (multi-disciplinary) and among different universities in different geographical locations and countries.
- Engineering curricula must include languages and cultural studies.
- Engineering programs accreditation must be made global and subject to international quality standards that address industrial expectations.
- Ensure that engineering students are educated in how to develop their critical thinking abilities, innovation and problem solving by offering projects at various stages of their years within the program of engineering and not just at the end of the program.

8 Conclusions and Recommendations

This paper has been produced to describe and assess the mechanical engineering program at the University of Johannesburg, South Africa as part of the CADPF award to link faculty in African Universities with their counterparts in North America in which to share ideas on best practices to enhance global engineering education in this case. In the period of exchange in which the exchange (and one of the authors of the paper) visitor visited the department, a survey was conducted to assess the learning outcomes of the department; discussions were also held with faculty, students and administrators on how best to achieve the teaching and learning goals as formulated by the two institutions involved in the project. The survey was administered to first-semester final year students in which various questions were asked relating to learning outcomes and the overall environment for teaching and learning.

It is refreshing to know that students view the department as successful in achieving the learning outcomes that guide the delivery of educational instruction in the various classes that are required for graduation. There is certainly enough room for instituting changes and/or modifications to enhance teaching and learning. The greatest strength of the department from the survey results is the dedication of the faculty members. Advising and mentoring are the weakest link when asked to rank the level of satisfaction between the faculty, the curriculum, and advising and mentoring. The use of Computer Aided instructional technology (as opposed to Information Technology) tools in enhancing teaching and learning were also featured in the survey on learning outcomes. Although many engineering software tools are available on departmental workstations, most students felt that other than SOLIDWORKS that is taught and used in the early parts of the curriculum delivery, the use of other types of software are not uniformly practiced in the curriculum unless one selects a final year project that requires the use of other engineering software. This conclusion can be drawn among students in the mechanical engineering department at Howard University, the home institution of the CADP fellow. Much can be done in this area at both institutions to enhance the use of current technology and to explore the use of other paradigms on the use of technology to improve teaching and learning.

Although the subject of global engineering education was not a subject of the survey, it is apparent from a review of the curriculum and discussions with students that it is a "traditional" curriculum that is designed for the national community. Students in the program appear to have little or no interactions with the "outside world" until they graduate and enter the workforce with companies that may be multi-national. The university has embarked on several global initiatives at the research and other levels in the academy and this is one area that may need attention in bringing global education into the engineering classrooms at the university.

Acknowledgements. The work reported in this paper would not have been possible without the support of the Carnegie Africa Diaspora Fellowship Program (CADFP). The assistance provided by the Department of Mechanical Engineering Science in making local arrangements and partial support for accommodation expenses and for providing a conducive and satisfying environment for the Fellow is very much appreciated.

References

1. Thigpen, L., Whitworth, H.A.: A successful method to assess student learning outcomes using multiple direct and indirect assessment instruments. In: Proceedings, International Conference on Engineering Education and Research (ICEER), Melbourne, Australia, December 2007
2. Mills, J.E., Treagust, D.F.: Engineering education – is problem based or project-based learning the answer? Australasian J. Eng. Educ. Online Publication 2003–04. http://www.aaee.com.au/journal/2003/mills_treagust03.pdf
3. http://www.merriam-webster.com/dictionary/globalization
4. Mardam-Bey, O., Sarán, S.: Impact of globalization on engineering education in developing countries. ARISER 4(2), 99–102 (2008). http://www.arabrise.org

Innovative Project-Based Learning

Ren-Hung Hwang[1(✉)], Pao-Ann Hsiung[1], Yau-Jane Chen[1],
and Chin-Feng Lai[2]

[1] National Chung Cheng University, Chiayi, Taiwan
rhhwang@cs.ccu.edu.tw
[2] National Cheng Kung University, Tainan, Taiwan

Abstract. The conventional Project-Based Learning (PBL) pedagogy consists of five stages: Preparation, Implementation, Presentation, Evaluation, and Revision. When applied to an application domain, PBL lacks in two features, namely creative thinking and design process. This work tries to bridge the gap by proposing an innovative PBL (iPBL), which integrates two frameworks, namely creative learning and Conceive-Design-Implement-Operate (CDIO). Creative learning helps problem solving to be more innovative, while CDIO associates a proven design process with problem solving so that results are more convergent. iPBL consists of 7 stages including Preparation (P), Conception (C), Design (D), Implementation (I), Operation (O), Evaluation (E), and Revision (R). iPBL has been implemented on an instructional platform for a class of 85 junior students taking the capstone course in our computer science department. There were 46 experiment groups and 39 control groups. For creative thinking, brainstorming and 6-3-5 were applied in the conception phase, SCAMPER in the design phase, and TRIZ in the implementation phase. The application of iPBL to a capstone course demonstrated not only significantly increased creativity, but also a more systematic record and analysis of all creativity tasks.

Keywords: Innovative Project-Based Learning · Innovation · Capstone course

1 Introduction

Capstone course aims to offer students opportunities to solve real-world complex problems, resolve new research issues, gain new perspectives, encourage innovation and creative thinking, and develop written and oral communication skills. In the past, project-based learning (PBL) has been widely adopted as the pedagogy for the Capstone course in many universities worldwide. The traditional approach to conduct PBL usually includes five stages, e.g., the PIPER model [1].

However, from our teaching experiences, we found that PBL is not adequate in meeting the objectives of a typical Capstone course. First, it lacks of pedagogy for encouraging innovation and creative thinking. Thus, in [2], we proposed CPBL model to combine PBL with creative learning. Second, for computer science students the management of software lifecycle is a mandatory requirement which is not covered by PBL. Third, it often does not fit well with the standard Conceive–Design–Implement–Operate (CDIO) framework. CDIO is an innovative educational framework for engineering education [3]. The CDIO Initiative adopted 12 standards to address its

© Springer International Publishing AG 2017
T.-C. Huang et al. (Eds.): SETE 2017, LNCS 10676, pp. 189–194, 2017.
https://doi.org/10.1007/978-3-319-71084-6_21

philosophy. In particular, what is absent in PBL is CDIO's final stage, "Operate, uses the implemented product or process to deliver the intended value, including maintaining, evolving and retiring the system."

Thus, in our reform process of the Capstone course, we proposed a new PBL model which consists of 7 stages to integrate creative learning, software engineering process, and the CDIO framework. As described in Sect. 3, the innovative PBL (iPBL) model presented in this work includes 7 stages, namely Preparation (P), Conception (C), Design (D), Implementation (I), Operation (O), Evaluation (E), and Revision (R). iPBL has been implemented on an instructional platform for a class of 85 junior students taking the capstone course where 46 were in the experiment group and 39 in the control group. Our experimental results show that the application of iPBL to the capstone course not only significantly increased creativity (measured by 2 experts from the industry), but also a more systematic record and analysis of all creativity tasks.

2 Literature Review

2.1 Projected-Based Learning

Project-based learning is a learner-centred pedagogy that involves learners in investigations of real world problems or cases. It provides an opportunity for learners over an extended period of relatively autonomous work; and finally the development of real products or demos [4]. The projects can be complex tasks on the issue or challenging issues, involving learners of design, problem solving, decision making, or investigative activities [5]. Researchers have documented that students become more engaged in learning when they have a chance to dig into complex and challenging problems that closely resemble real life [6]. For students from Computer Science (CS) department, PBL drives them to come up with real products, which is a very unique feature achieved by applying PBL in a Capstone course in the CS department. It is active learning, so more able to maintain motivation effectively [7]. We emphasize on learner-controlled PBL. Learner-controlled PBL helps learners to have a self-monitoring, to clarify the topic, establish goals, planning tasks, information searching and organization, progress control, completing the works, showing new insights and knowledge.

2.2 CDIO

CDIO is an innovative educational framework for next generation engineering education and was designed as open architecture [3]. The overall goals of CDIO are to educate students to master a deep working knowledge of technical fundamentals, lead in the creation and operation of new products and systems, understand the importance and strategic value of their future research work [3]. The four top levels of CDIO's syllabus are to educate students who understand how to conceive – design – implement – operate complex value – added engineering systems in a modern team based engineering environment and are mature and thoughtful individuals [8]. The pedagogical improvements of CDIO include four areas: increase in active and hands-on learning, emphasis on problem formulation and solution, increased emphasis on concept learning, and enhancement of learning feedback mechanisms. Integrating PBL with CDIO fits well for the Capstone course for our Computer Science (CS) department.

3 Innovative Project-Based Learning

The conventional 5-stage PBL pedagogy was modified by including two features, namely creative learning and CDIO. Creative learning was instilled into the main stages of PBL and CDIO was used to elaborate the implementation stage of PBL. The proposed iPBL method consists of 7 stages, including Preparation (P), Conception (C), Design (D), Implementation (I), Operation (O), Evaluation (E), and Revision (R). iPBL can also be applied to other disciplines in the engineering faculty, as long as, creativity and design process are the main concerns of the capstone course of a department.

3.1 Preparation

This is the first step of iPBL in which a group of students start formulating a project by defining the team members including the students and the professor, the project theme, and the project goals. Since this stage is only preparation, creativity is not yet introduced. At the end of this step, the deliverables include a summary of the project, list of team members, project topic, and project goals. Take as running example, a group of 3 students (computer science undergraduates) involved in doing a project on bio-signal analysis and the project goals are an understanding of bio-signal processing and an application in the area of driver fatigue detection.

3.2 Conception

In this step of iPBL, the project execution is initialized by conceptualization of the project through various activities in the form of discussions, target project formulation, determining resource requirements, collecting materials, and accumulating a priori knowledge for conducting the project. Creativity at this stage is introduced by training the students in brainstorming and 6-3-5 brainwriting, which are the two methods that can be applied for developing creative problems. Using these two methods, students collectively arrive at a target problem that is more creative than one that is formulated through conventional discussions. At the end of this step, the deliverables include meeting minutes, brainstorming output, 6-3-5 brainwriting results (1 to 3 ideas), project topic, resource requirements, and a survey of a priori knowledge. Most of the deliverables are constructed or collected collaboratively by the whole group of students using the wiki technique.

In the running example, the target problem is formulated as real-time driver fatigue detection based on heart rate variability (HRV) of electrocardiogram (ECG) signals collected using sensors attached to the ears of the driver. The project resources include ECG sensors, Arduino boards for data collection and processing, database for HRV data retrieving. Materials collected for the project include open source codes and statistical analysis tools. A priori knowledge for the project include background on artificial neural networks (ANN) training and design for HRV related statistics analysis, detection or prediction methods for fatigue level, and error analysis.

3.3   Design

After formulating the target problem and accumulating a priori knowledge, the design phase of iPBL starts solving the problem through a systematic design process similar to software or system engineering design process, where requirements are analyzed and system design analysis performed.

Creativity at this stage is introduced by training the students in solving problems creatively using SCAMPER, which consists of substitute, combine, adapt, modify, put to another use, eliminate, and reverse. Students are asked to ask questions in each of the SCAMPER category and the answers derived from the questions will lead to new ideas and propositions on how the target problem can be solved. The deliverables at this stage consists of a system specification document that consists of project design artefacts, work breakdown structure (WBS), requirements analysis, and system analysis. Embedded into the PBL platform, oneproject is the tool used for WBS input.

In the running example, a back-propagation neural network (BPNN) is designed for the detection of driver fatigue level based on 4 different statistics of HRV. Using SCAMPER, the students try to adapt the conventional BPNN for HRV analysis by modifying the weighted moving average (WMA).

3.4   Implementation

After a solution to the target problem has been designed and analyzed in the design phase, the solution is then implemented and tested on an actual platform. Contradictory elements, if any, are identified during the implementation phase so that creative solutions can be devised. Creativity at this stage is introduced by training the students in TRIZ (Theory of Inventive Problem Solving), where the students are presented with challenging problems that need inventive solutions. Two contradictory elements are presented and the students are asked to resolve the contradiction using a contradiction matrix based on the 40 principles of TRIZ. The deliverables at this stage consists of TRIZ solutions to design contradictions and system design and testing documents.

In the running example, the accuracy of fatigue detection and the real-time processing of ECG signals for HRV and other statistics analysis were contradictory because a higher accuracy required more processing data and time, whereas the requirement for timeliness of data processing resulted in lower degree of accuracy in the final results of detection.

3.5   Operation

The operation stage of iPBL involves an actual online demonstration of the system prototype such that problems in the system that have evaded testing can be identified and resolved before the system is really put online. It is a very important stage for students to understand how their prototype system run in the real world and receive feedback from users as well as failures of the system. However, it received little attention in the past. Thus, in iPBL, students are required to test their system prototype in the real world. The deliverables include reference and user manuals for the project. In the running example, these two manuals are produced for the driver detection system. The reference manual includes details on the implementation of the system. The user manual includes steps by which the system can be deployed for use. Both manuals are improved due to the feedbacks of operating the prototype system. This reflects to the CDIO's final stage, "Operate, uses the implemented product or process to deliver the intended value, including maintaining, evolving and retiring the system."

3.6   Evaluation

In the evaluation stage, the projects designed, implemented, and tested in the previous stages are evaluated by experts. The project teams must submit written reports and an oral presentation. The evaluation experts include computer science domain experts and creative thinking experts. Two kinds of peer assessments are also performed, including intra-group suggestions and consensus forming within a group. Creativity is mainly evaluated at this stage. Deliverables include project demonstration, written reports, oral presentations, peer assessment results.

3.7   Revision

After evaluation, based on the comments from domain and creativity experts, the students are asked to revise their projects such that the comments can all be addressed. The final version of the system and a final project report constitute the deliverables.

4   Evaluation

Contrast to the cPBL, the application of creative thinking instructional strategies, mainly the SCAMPER and six thinking hats methods [2], the proposed iPBL was implemented on an instructional platform for the capstone course of the junior/senior computer science students.

A class of 85 junior students taking the capstone course in our computer science department were the targets for application of iPBL. There were 46 experiment groups and 39 control groups, where each group consisted of 2 or 3 students.

As what were done in 2016 for the cPBL, two checkpoints were also introduced in iPBL in 2017, including before and after the capstone project design. At the first checkpoint, assessments of creativity of students were performed for both the experiment, as well as, the control groups using the Torrance Tests of Creative Thinking (TTCT), with four scales fluency, flexibility, originality, and elaboration. At the second checkpoint, with the same scales, students' capstone projects were evaluated by two external experts and 10 faculty members as internal experts who all were the evaluators of students' projects in cPBL as well. The assessments allowed us to evaluate the effectiveness of iPBL after the application of the pedagogical techniques. The initial assessment was an indication of students' creativity levels before the practical phase of iPBL. The final assessment evaluated the creativity performance revealed from the capstone projects after the application of all pedagogical techniques in iPBL.

In cPBL, creativity scores evaluated from students' capstone projects were significantly higher for the experiment group as compared to the control group [2].

To compare the creativity of iPBL's students with that of cPBL's students, the one-way analysis of covariance method (ANCOVA) was applied using the TTCT scores of both courses' experimental-group students as covariance. The results show that students' creativity scores evaluated from their capstone projects, with the same scales, by the same group of experts, were significantly higher for the iPBL course as compared to the cPBL course (Table 1). In other words, iPBL was even more effective in elevating students' creativity levels than cPBL.

Table 1. ANCOVA of experimental-group students' creativity scores in cPBL and iPBL.

Source	SS	DF	MS	F	P
Covariate	447.012	1	447.012	2.344	.130
Between	1426.643	1	1426.643	7.480**	.008
Within	13542.024	71	190.733		
Total	15415.679	73			

**: $p < .01$

5   Summary and Acknowledgements

In this work, we have proposed an innovative PBL (iPBL) for a capstone course. The application of iPBL to the course demonstrated not only significantly increased creativity, but also a more systematic record and analysis of all creativity tasks.

This work was supported by the Ministry of Science and Technology, Taiwan under project grants MOST-103-2511-S-194-004-MY3 and MOST-103-2511-S-194-003-MY3.

References

1. Shyu, H.: Web-enhanced project-based learning: an implementation for elementary science lessons. In: Proceedings of the International Conference on Problem-Based Learning in Higher Education (2002)
2. Hsiung, P.-A., Hwang, R.-H., Chen, Y.-J.: Introducing creativity into engineering capstone courses. In: Proceedings of the SEFI Annual Conference (2016)
3. Berggren, K.-F., et al.: CDIO: an international initiative for reforming engineering education. World Trans. Eng. Technol. Educ. 2(1), 49–52 (2003)
4. Thomas, J.W.: A Review of Research on Project-based Learning. http://www.bobpearlman. org/BestPractices/PBL_Research.pdf. Accessed 21 July 2017
5. Thomas, J.W., Mergendoller, J.R., Michaelson, A.: Project-based Learning: A Handbook for Middle and High School Teachers. Novato, CA (1999)
6. Intel Teach Program Homepage. http://download.intel.com/education/Common/pk/ Resources/DEP/projectdesign/DEP_pbl_research.pdf. Accessed 21 July 2017
7. Blumenfeld, P., et al.: Motivating project-based learning: sustaining the doing, supporting the learning. Educ. Psychol. 26(3–4), 369–398 (1991)
8. CDIO Homepage. http://www.cdio.org/files/cdio_brief.pdf. Accessed 21 July 2017

Selected Factors Supporting the Learning Organization

Vaclav Zubr[(⊠)] ⓘ and Hana Mohelska ⓘ

Faculty of Informatics and Management, University Hradec Králové,
Hradec Králové, Czech Republic
{vaclav.zubr,hana.mohelska}@uhk.cz

Abstract. Learning organization structure is very important for organizations, it enables to achieve competitive advantages. Some factors with positive effect on learning organization have been found, e.g. organizational culture, teamwork, self-development, learning communities or information sharing. Most of these factors are connected together with learning. With regard to growing use of Internet the e-learning is one of frequently used learning form in learning organization. Therefore the objective of the study was to find out, what type of education the teachers perceive as the most effective and what way of obtaining information is the most effective for them. Based on the characteristics of schools being learning organizations, primary and secondary schools from Hradec Kralove and Pardubice region of the Czech Republic were selected for the study. The questionnaire was sent approximately to 1,000 respondents, less than 10% of e-mails was returned with an error message. After one-month period 272 questionnaires were completed. The most represented were respondents aged 41–50 years old (25.37%) and 51–60 years old (24.63%). Most of respondents (84.19%) work as a teacher at secondary school. The most effective type of learning are individual lessons (47.06%). Only 5.88% of respondents believe to e-learning. The most popular way to get information about education are web pages and e-mail.

This study shows relatively high use of Internet and low confidence of respondents to e-learning. With regard to growing rate of using e-learning is appropriate to repeat this study in future to complete data about the development of e-learning.

Keywords: Learning organization · E-learning · Internet · Knowledge management

1 Introduction

In the management of organizations currently take the central place organizational structure and learning organization. [1] With learning organization are connected the basic principles such as collective thinking, learning and support of employees, continuous improvement of employee skills and dynamic new models of thinking and achievement of wanted results. [2] In a learning organization learning takes place through work, employees make flexible teams, information is captured and shared among all employees, managers facilitate instead of control and typical is formative

© Springer International Publishing AG 2017
T.-C. Huang et al. (Eds.): SETE 2017, LNCS 10676, pp. 195–202, 2017.
https://doi.org/10.1007/978-3-319-71084-6_22

relationship with the external environment. [3–5] Learning organization should continuously change and this organization facilitates the members' learning. [6] The learning organization structure enables organization to achieve competitive advantages against its rivals. [1, 3, 6] Learning of employees can be realized as organizational learning, individual or group learning and the utilization of knowledges in organization can be improved. If the goal is to learn the whole organization, cannot be focus only on individual learning. Is useful to mention that organizational learning is not a simple sum of individual learning. [7] Crossan, Lane and White interconnect the importance of individual, group and organizational learning as the basis for the entire organization. This statement is based on these foundations [8]:

- Organizational learning involves exploration and exploitation.
- Organizational learning takes place at several levels (individual, group and organizational).
- These three levels are connected by intuition, interpretation, integration and institutionalization (4I).
- Cognition influences action and vice versa (Table 1).

Table 1. Levels of organizational learning [8]

Level	Process	Inputs/outcomes
Individual	Intuiting	Experiences
		Images
		Metaphors
	Interpreting	Language
		Cognitive map
		Conversation/dialogue
Group	Integrating	Shared understandings
		Mutual adjustment
		Interactive systems
Organization	Institutionalizing	Routines
		Diagnostic systems
		Rules and procedures

In the business organizations the knowledge management represents the basic knowledge. Knowledge management and learning organization depend on each other on the way to success. Changes in knowledge management are reflected in changes in the organization and vice versa. [9] The introduction of knowledge management has a positive effect on the quality of the speeches and innovation, learning, increase profits and efficiency of the organization and creating new opportunities. [10] From the management point of view the improvement of the organization leads to reduced costs for specific activities, increase sales, increase profitability, ensure uniform draft terms for clients worldwide, more targeted marketing and proactive marketing. Organizational benefits of knowledge management may be primarily intended as financial, marketing and general nature. [11] The benefits for a larger number of organizations with knowledge management monitored K. North, when analysed 48 companies from the Association of German Knowledge Management or Swiss Forum of Knowledge Management. The results show the benefits of implementing organizations observed especially in the area of business processes and employee performance [12].

From different studies targeted to learning organization and organizational learning, the summary of factors with a positive impact on learning organization have been done (Fig. 1).

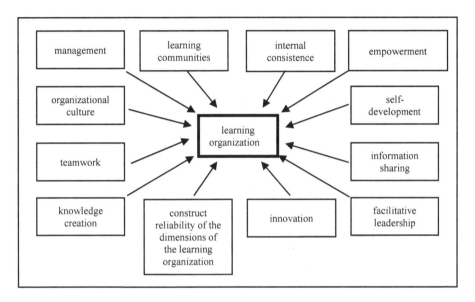

Fig. 1. Factors with positive impact on learning organization

It's necessary to mention that the impact of these factors can be reduced by some barriers. To achieve an effective learning organization should be these barriers avoided. According to some sources, the main barriers in team working is unproductive, poor communication, not clearly defined goals, poor planning and poor leadership [13].

Compared to other factors, the most important role in learning organization plays education and internet as a way to share information and to learn new information. The education in learning organization can be realized as an individual learning or as the learning organization. [14] With regard to some studies [15, 16] is internet an integral part of employees' life. In study from 2010, 69.84% of respondents agree with the statement that using the Internet is an indispensable part of life for them. [15] In another study from 2012 primarily aimed at students and teachers mainly in secondary schools, 53.77% of respondent couldn't imagine learning without Internet. [16] E-learning seems to be very effective way to learn employees because it requires less employee time, increases retention of information, in some companies e-learning led to increase in revenue. [17] However there are exceptions, for example in one large national retailer, 85% of employees wanted traditional instructor (the classes were very interactive and fun). [18] We have to mention, that several modalities as presentations, e-course at www, web-assisted courses or distance education belong to e-learning [19].

In the Czech Republic one of the most common learning organizations are schools. The conditions for use e-learning and internet for searching information have improved in recent years. The growth rate of self-placed e-learning is 27% for the Czech Republic in 2015 [20].

The aim of this study was to find out, what type of education teachers perceive as the most effective and what way of obtaining information on education is the most effective for them. Another aim of this study was to find out what way of obtaining information about education is the most frequently in teachers.

2 Methods

Based on the main characteristics of schools being learning organizations, [21] primary and secondary schools from Hradec Kralove and Pardubice region of the Czech Republic were selected for this study. The selection was based on meet at least five from ten criteria defining school as learning organization [21]:

- Incentive structure that encourages adaptive behaviour.
- Challenging, achievable shared goals.
- Members can accurately identify the organization's stages of development.
- Gathering, processing, and acting upon information in ways best suited to its purposes.
- Institutional knowledge base and processes for creating new ideas.
- Exchange information frequently with relevant external sources.
- Feedback on products and services.
- Continuously refine of basic processes.
- Supportive organizational culture.
- "Open systems" sensitive to the external environment (social, political, economic conditions).

The survey was conducted as a questionnaire research. As the basis of a questionnaire were used the structured interviews with pedagogical workers from February 2013. An electronic questionnaire was compiled using web service of "docs.google.com". The questionnaire was sent approximately to 1,000 respondents whose e-mail addresses were obtained on the websites of selected primary and secondary schools. Less than 10% of all e-mails was returned with an error message regarding to inactive address. After one-month period of collecting data was completed 272 questionnaires.

3 Results

From a total of 272 respondents were the most represented respondents aged 41–50 years old (25.37%), 51–60 years old (24.63%) and 31–40 years old (21.69%). Most of respondents (84.19%) work as a teacher at secondary school (Fig. 2).

Most of respondents consider individual lessons (47.06%) and group lessons (37.13%) as the most effective type of learning. Almost 10% of respondents believe in effectivity of self-study. E-learning is not considered to be an effective type of learning,

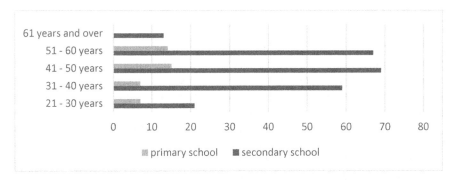

Fig. 2. The number of respondents by age and employment at primary or secondary school.

only 5.88% of respondents believe that is effective. These results can be supported by information from the structured interviews in the beginning of the study. In these interviews some teachers compared their time options at home and priority of e-learning compared to other obligations (Table 2).

Table 2. The most effective type of learning by age.

	E-learning	Individual lessons	Self study	Group lessons
21–30 years	1	14	2	11
31–40 years	8	34	5	19
41–50 years	4	42	8	30
51–60 years	3	34	8	36
61 years and over	0	4	4	5
Total	16	128	27	101

The most popular way to get information about education is by using web pages (185 respondents in total) or via personal or bulk e-mail (134 respondents via personal e-mail and 155 respondents via bulk e-mail in total). Using printed materials for getting information about education is the third most popular way (143 respondents in total). The lowest number of responses were for answers "telephone call" and "intranet". The same result was obtained from structured interviews.

Needed to mention that the question focused to obtaining information about education had multiple choices to answer (Table 3).

Table 3. The way of obtaining information on education

	Personal meeting	Telephone call	E-mail (personal)	E-mail (bulk)	Intranet	Web pages	Printed materials
21–30 years	11	3	10	17	8	20	15
31–40 years	21	8	32	36	16	49	32
41–50 years	33	8	49	51	23	62	51
51–60 years	23	7	37	44	16	45	39
61 y. and over	6	0	6	7	3	9	6
Total	94	26	134	155	66	185	143

4 Discussion

The concept of the learning organization is quite favorable and brings many benefits to learning organizations. However, the number of learning organizations in the Czech Republic is not known. Taking into account certain parameters can be argued that some of Czech schools fulfill the criteria for learning organizations. For the first study focused on learning organizations are schools one of the best samples. We have taken to account relatively high use of information technologies during lessons as well as the fact that e-learning has several modalities as presentations of lectures, placing e-course at WWW, web-assisted courses and distance education. [19] Modalities as presentations of lectures or e-course are quite common in Czech schooling. Theoretically it could be assume that if teachers require these type of learning by pupils, they will use e-learning too. Therefore, it was surprisingly, that only 5.88% of teachers considered that e-learning is an effective type of learning. This may be caused by dominant representation of respondents with higher age. If we compare this result with another similar studies from Czech Republic, they correspond to each other [22, 23].

In our study respondents reported the individual and group lessons as the most effective type of education. This may be explained by age of respondents or by high quality and effectivity of individual and group lessons. If the lessons are interesting, interactive and effective, it is possible that people will not want to change the type of education. [18] The structured interviews show that the effectivity of individual and group lessons may be related to the payment of these lessons and hence greater motivation to attend such courses (and full remittance of the paid money into the acquired education).

Because e-learning and self-study are relatively close to each other it is possible to justify the low outcome of both types of education by their correlation. It is also appropriate to recall that the term "e-learning" can be understood in different ways. Supported with results from structured interviews we can say that in home conditions are usually preferred other obligations than self study in any way. The low value of using e-learning may be due to the fact that the e-learning course does not even start in some cases.

The age distribution of respondents in our study corresponds with general information about teacher's age of the first half of 2016. The data about teacher's age in 2016 were gained from the Ministry of Education in the Czech Republic [24].

From the information gained from the question focused on the way of obtaining information on education we can conclude, that Czech teachers commonly use Internet to get information about new educational events. This fact corresponds with studies from 2010 and 2012 when respondents said that Internet is an indispensable part of life for them and they couldn't imagine learning without Internet. [15, 16] However, teachers do not always search for education on the Internet, more recently are teachers addressed by external companies that offer learning courses via e-mail. Although, the printed material as the way of obtaining information is frequently answer after Internet (web pages and e-mail to be concretely). The explanation may be that printed materials as a source of information about education are periodically delivered to the schools and they are targeted on teachers. The basic structured interviews with pedagogical workers showed low exploitation of intranet and confirmed high use of internet and e-mail. The low use of intranet can be attributed to the small number of teaching staff in many schools, therefore is preferred the personal communication in such schools. Another reason for the low use of the intranet is to replace the intranet by communications over the Internet in bigger schools, as is shown by structured interviews.

Relatively startling is the fact that despite the use of the Internet, some e-mail addresses of respondents were inactive (less than 10%) during the distribution of questionnaires. The cause of outdated e-mail addresses may be outdated school website, which lists former employees and vice versa there may be missing some new employees.

In recent years, the implementation of new e-learning forms such as webinars (online seminars led by a lecturer via videoconference) contributes to improve status of e-learning in the Czech Republic. The increase of e-learning popularity could be supported by providing employees benefits such as more time for self education, financial support of education or a wider range of e-learning courses compared to traditional forms of education.

5 Conclusion

The average age of Czech teachers is relatively higher (41–60 years old). Despite this, Internet is the most favourite way to obtain information about education. Due to relatively high use of the Internet we would expect high use of e-learning. But this study shows the exact opposite. Based on results of this study we can say, that the most effective type of learning are still individual and group lessons with direct contact with the lecturer, e-learning is the least effective according to the answers. Although the popularity of e-learning is very low we can recommend e-learning as a suitable complementary type of learning to individual or group lessons.

With regard to growing rate of using e-learning is appropriate to repeat this study in future to complete data about the development and effect of e-learning.

Acknowledgement. The paper was written with the support of the specific project 2017 granted by the University of Hradec Králové, Czech Republic.

References

1. Kanten, P., Kanten, S., Gurlek, M.: The effects of organizational structures and learning organization on job embeddedness and individual adaptive performance. Procedia Econ. Finan. **23**, 1358–1366 (2015)
2. Senge, P.M.: The Fifth Discipline: The Art and Practice of the Learning Organization, 2nd edn. Random House Business, London (2006)
3. Míka, J.: Co je to "Učící se organizace"? (2016). http://www.personalista.com/pracovni-prostedi/co-je-to-ucici-se-organizace.html. Accessed 10 Apr 2017
4. Smith, K.D., Taylor, W.G.K.: The Learning Organisation Ideal in Civil Service Organisations: Deriving a Measure. MCB University Press, Bradford (2000)

5. Randhir, A.: Benchmarking: a tool for facilitating organizational learning? Public Adm. Dev. **22**(2), 109–122 (2002)
6. Farrukh, M., Waheed, A.: Learning organization and competitive advantage – an integrated approach. J. Asian Bus. Strat. **5**(4), 73–79 (2015)
7. Ropes, D., Thölke, J.: Communities of practice: finally a link between individual and organizational learning in management development programs. In: Proceedings of the European Conference on Intellectual Capital, p. 504 (2010)
8. Crossan, M.M., Lane, H.W., White, R.E.: An organizational learning framework: from intuition to institution. Acad. Manag. Rev. **24**(3), 522–537 (1999)
9. Dust, H.V., Dehaghi, M.K., Demneh, R.S.: Learning organizations and knowledge management: which one enhances another one more? Manag. Sci. Lett. **4**, 325–334 (2014)
10. Bureš, V.: Znalostní management a proces jeho zavádění. Prague (2007)
11. Alavi, M., Leidner, D.E.: Knowledge management systems: issues, challenges, and benefits. Commun. Assoc. Inf. Syst. **1**(7), 1–37 (1999)
12. North, K., Reinhardt, R., Schmidt, A.: The benefits of knowledge management: some empirical evidence. In: The 5th European Conference on Organizational Knowledge, Learning and Capabilities (2004). http://www2.warwick.ac.uk/fac/soc/wbs/conf/olkc/archive/oklc5/papers/a-8_north.pdf. Accessed 13 Apr 2017
13. Incedo, Barriers to Great Teamwork what Makes a Team Ineffective. http://incedogroup.com/barriers-to-great-teamwork-what-makes-a-team-ineffective/. Accessed 01 Apr 2017
14. Šuleř, O.: Manažerské techniky II. Rubico, Olomouc (2003)
15. Šiler, J.: Moderní technologie ve výuce (2010). https://www.vyplnto.cz/realizovane-pruzkumy/moderni-technologie-ve-vyuce/. Accessed 02 Apr 2017
16. Sedláček, D.: Vliv internetu na vzdělávání (2012). https://www.vyplnto.cz/realizovane-pruzkumy/vliv-internetu-na-vzdelavani/. Accessed 01 Apr 2017
17. Gutierez, K.: Facts and Stats that Reveal the Power of eLearning (2016). http://info.shiftelearning.com/blog/bid/301248/15-facts-and-stats-that-reveal-the-power-of-elearning. Accessed 10 Apr 2017
18. Minton, M.C.: Is your organization ready for e-learning? Commun. Project Mag. **3**, 1 (2000)
19. Klímová, B., Poulová, P.: Reflection on the development of eLearning in the Czech Republic. In: Recent Researches in Communications and Computers, pp. 433–437 (2012)
20. Pappas, C.: The Top eLearning Statistics and Facts for 2015 You Need to Know (2015). https://elearningindustry.com/elearning-statistics-and-facts-for-2015. Accessed 10 Apr 2017
21. Brandt, R.: Powerful Learning. Association for Supervision and Curriculum Development, Alexandria (1998)
22. Bartoníková, D.: Paměť a efektivní učení (2013). https://www.vyplnto.cz/realizovane-pruzkumy/pamet-a-efektivni-uceni/. Accessed 03 Apr 2017
23. Tichá, I.: Učící se organizace. Alfa Publishing, Prague (2005)
24. Ministry of education youth and sports: Gender Issues in the Education Staff. http://www.msmt.cz/vzdelavani/skolstvi-v-cr/statistika-skolstvi/genderova-problematika-zamestnancu-ve-skolstvi. Accessed 10 Apr 2017

Factors Influencing Social Media Adoption and Continued Use in Academia: A Case Study at a Traditional University

Liezel Cilliers$^{(\boxtimes)}$ and Obrain Murire

Information Systems Department, University of Fort Hare, Alice, South Africa
lcilliers@ufh.ac.za

Abstract. The popularity of social media amongst university students, has necessitated traditional universities to incorporate these tools in academia. However, few lecturers incorporate these tools in academia for teaching and learning activities. The objective of the study was to identify factors influencing social media integration and continued use in academic setting at a traditional university in the Eastern Cape. The unified theory of acceptance and use of technology was employed as the theoretical foundation in this study. A quantitative survey data collection method making use of a questionnaire was distributed to all the academics at the university, with a response rate of 39%. From these, data was analysed using descriptive statistics and the Pearson Chi-square test was used to establish the relationship between different variables. The results show that the following factors could influence the adoption of social media in teaching and learning amongst lecturers: Performance expectancy is influenced by the age and gender of the lecturer; facilitating condition is influenced by the faculty that the lecturer is employed in, while social influence was significant for age, knowledge of social media, management and the support from the Department of Higher Education. The study therefore recommends that traditional university management should prioritise the use of social media tools as they may be used as a tool to enhance the throughput in order to address critical skills shortage in the economy.

Keywords: Social media · Teaching and learning · Traditional university · Unified theory of acceptance and use of technology

1 Introduction

Traditional universities need to find innovative ways to promote student centered learning. The use of social media in academia can increase student – lecturer interaction and learning. The typical interactions that are improved include engagement, communication, and collaboration as well as learner centered learning environments, hence improving throughput rates of students [1]. Nevertheless, the incorporation of social media such as social networking tools at traditional universities in South Africa is low due to limited knowledge or proficiency required to use social media effectively as a pedagogical tool amongst lecturers [2]. Accordingly, the adoption of social media tools amongst lecturers must be improved in order to realise the benefits that social media tools can bring to teaching and learning.

© Springer International Publishing AG 2017
T.-C. Huang et al. (Eds.): SETE 2017, LNCS 10676, pp. 203–209, 2017.
https://doi.org/10.1007/978-3-319-71084-6_23

The objective of the study was to identify factors that could influence social media integration and continued use in academic setting at a traditional university in the Eastern Cape. The paper is outlined as follows: The first section discusses the literature followed by the methodology used in this study. After which the UTAUT is introduced and a discussion of the results follows. The remaining sections discuss barriers of social media, the contribution of the study and conclusion.

2 Literature

2.1 Social Media Tools in Higher Education

Social media is described as new media applications such as Wikis, Twitter, Facebook and YouTube. These tools provide features that help to manage students and promote student-lecturer interaction [3]. Furthermore, studies have revealed that social media in teaching and learning plays an essential role to increase collaboration and communication in academia [4]. Most of the student population enrolled at higher education institutions are using social media [1]. Therefore, traditional universities should incorporate social media to support student-centred education. Gonzalez [5] asserts that the integration of social media in the traditional university learning environment has increased during the last decade, but despite the popularity of social media, few lecturers use these tools in academia for educational purposes [1, 6]. This is supported by Chen and Bryer [7] who state that not enough lecturers are exploiting social media in teaching and learning in order to create innovative learning environments. The next section will discuss classification of social media in academia.

3 Research Methodology

The paper applied a case study approach which according to Bromley [12] can be defined as a c "systematic inquiry into an event or a set of related events which aims to describe social science and explain phenomenon of interest" (p. 302). In this study the University of Fort Hare, a traditional university in the Eastern Cape Province of South Africa, was used as the test ground with an exploratory case study design. This design allowed the researchers to explore how social media is being used by lecturers for teaching and learning purposes while the results of this study will contribute to the body of knowledge on the subject matter in South Africa.

The university does have a good information and communication infrastructure with WIFI access on campus and 2 computer laboratories that are used for classes. The lecture halls have projectors installed and the lecturers have access to the internet within these halls. The university does have a learner management system (LMS) available for lecturers, but the system is mostly used for administrative purposes to manage big classes, and not for teaching and learning purposes [13].

A quantitative survey tool was used to collect the data at one traditional university. A questionnaire developed by Venkatesh et al. [14] to test technology acceptance was adapted for the study after a thorough literature review. The questions were adapted to reflect the social media context of the study which included using social media in teaching and learning activities by lecturers.

An ethical approval for this paper was acquired from the University Research Ethics Committee (UREC). The study population was limited to full-time lecturers at one traditional university where data was collected, and a convenience sampling method was used as the study made use of the readily available study population. A link to the web-based questionnaire was emailed to the participants with detailed instructions to complete the questions. A total of 116 responses were received. Prior to this, the questionnaire was piloted to 10 lecturers for suitability, user-friendliness and unambiguousness. All responses to the questionnaire were analysed as quantitative variables. Statistical Package for the Social Science (SPSS 22) was used to analyse data. The following section discusses the theoretical foundation of the study.

4 Unified Theory of Acceptance and Use of Technology

The unified theory of acceptance and use of technology (UTAUT) was developed from 8 diverse models with the aim of enhancing the success rate of predicting if technology will be accepted in a specific context [14]. The theory comprises of four key constructs: performance expectancy, effort expectancy, social influence, and facilitating conditions. These constructs are moderated by four facilitating conditions including experience, age, gender and voluntariness of use.

Performance Expectancy refers to "the degree to which an individual believes that using the system will help him or her to attain gains in job performance" [14, p. 447]. Performance expectancy denotes lecturers' belief that integrating social media in academia environment would be an advantage to them as well as to students. Effort expectancy refers to "the degree of ease associated with the use of the system" [14, p. 450]. Effort expectancy refers to the expected amount of ease which lecturers presume while using social media to accomplish their professional goals. Social influence refers to "the degree to which an individual perceives that important others believe he or she should use the new system" [14, p. 451]. Social influence is referred as the impact of colleagues and senior management support or role played by the heads of the institution in inspiring and encouraging lecturers to employ social media in academia to facilitate curriculum delivery. Facilitating conditions describes as "the degree to which an individual believes that an organizational and technical infrastructure exist to support use of the system" [14, p. 453]. Facilitating conditions denotes the extent to which an individual believes that institutional and technical infrastructure exists to support the use of social media [14].

5 Results and Discussion

The paper applied Cronbach's alpha to test reliability. Table 1 shows that several scales of the UTAUT construct attained a good degree of reliability as each was computed above 0.70 [16]. The Cronbach's alpha for facilitating condition construct was the lowest at 0.542, However, Leech, Barrett and Morgan [17] states 0.50 is an acceptable level of reliability. Table 1 below presents reliability analysis of the study.

Table 1. Descriptive statistics for behaviour (n = 83)

	Name of scale	Number of items	Cronbach's alpha
1	Performance expectancy	3	0.833
2	Effort expectancy	3	0.869
3	Social influence	3	0.831
4	Facilitating condition	4	0.542
5	Behavioural intention	3	0.956

5.1 Performance Expectancy

From this study's perspective, performance expectancy denotes lecturers' belief that integrating social media in academia environment would be an advantage to them as well as to students. The findings of this study suggested that performance expectancy is of the factors that affect lecturers' behavioural intention to use social media in academic setting. These findings are consistent with the results from previous study done by Mbodila, et al. [18] at the University of Venda who asserts that performance expectancy is the most influential factor of social media integration in academia. Lecturers indicated that they feel that social networking tools will support learning activities (92.7%), improve collaboration and communication (89.2%) and help them to be more productive (73.5%).

5.2 Effort Expectancy

The results suggested that the majority of lecturers at a traditional university do see the significance of social media in academia activities (59.5%), but some feel that it would be difficult to learn how to incorporate it into their teaching pedagogy 26.5%). However, once the initial learning curve has been overcome, most lecturers agree that social media is easy to use for teaching and learning activities (71.1%). Moreover, results suggest that some lecturers are adopting social media because it is easy to use and are familiar with social networking sites [19].

5.3 Social Influence

Regarding social influence, it was suggested that more than half of the lecturers (54.2%) at the traditional university feel that they are influenced by others (colleagues) to use social media. However, the majority of the lecturers (54.3%) suggested that the senior management does not inspire teachers to employ social media academic setting. Furthermore, 56.6% of the lecturers were positive that the Department of Higher Education supports universities to use of social media in academic environment.

These findings suggest that lecturers at the traditional universities are more prospective to employ social media because they are influenced by colleagues rather than the management of the institution or the Department of Higher Education. Furthermore, these results are consistent with the findings from previous studies done by Oye et al. [20] where social influence was identified as the most prominent predictors of lecturers' adoption of ICT. Therefore, traditional universities ought to develop strategies in order to encourage colleagues to communicate and recommend lecturers to use social media in academic environment.

5.4   Facilitating Condition

The outcomes from the paper suggest that the facilitation condition as a variable influences social media use in academic setting. Lecturers perceive universities has institutional and technical infrastructure to support the use of social media in academia. These results are consistent with the findings from previous studies done by Mbodila et al. [18] who found that facilitating condition was the most influential predictor of lecturers' adoption and use of Facebook in teaching and learning. Additionally, a number of studies has pointed out that there is need for adequate resources to successfully adopt social media in teaching and learning at traditional universities [7]. This entails that lecturers' perception on the resources that support social media use influences their intention to make use of it. Presently, lecturers have access to social media anywhere as they have smart phones. This denotes that social media is suitable for use at traditional universities as a teaching and learning platform that complements mainstream e-Learning. Table 2 provides descriptive statistics for social influence.

Also, ICT access at traditional universities has been prioritised as of late, and connectivity specifically in residences has improved. Thus, a robust network has to be in place all around the university. Additionally, access to the network should not only be on cables as it disturbs the lecturers and students' flexibility in the adoption of social media in teaching and teach [21]. The next section provides descriptive statistics for behaviour.

Table 2. Descriptive statistics for facilitating condition (n = 83)

Facilitating conditions	Strongly agree %	Agree %	Disagree %	Strongly disagree %
I have adequate resources necessary to employ social media tools in academia	15.7	55.4	22.9	6.0
I have adequate knowledge necessary to use social media for teaching and learning	14.5	54.2	26.5	4.8
Using some of the social media in academic setting is not compatible with other lecturing responsibilities that I have	6.0	43.4	39.8	10.8
There is a specific person allocated for assistance if I experience difficulties when using social media in academia	6.0	27.7	44.6	21.7

The majority of lecturers (73.5%) are positive that they will incorporate social media in their teaching and learning activities in the near future. Similarly, 71.1% of the lecturers expect to use social media in teaching and learning in the next 12 months. Furthermore, a majority of the lecturers (75.9%) plan to use social media in academia in the next 12 months. This is because they find social media to be a useful tool, and most of the lecturers are knowledgeable about social media. There is need for management support in order for the lecturers to adopt social media in the near future. The incorporation which is a taking place depends on individual lecturer effort.

6 Conclusion

The results shows that lecturers are familiar with social media and the technology could be incorporated in teaching and learning with an aim to increase communication and interaction amongst lecturers and learners. The analysis found that performance expectancy, social influence, and facilitating condition will have a positive influence on social media adoption and continued use by academics in teaching and learning at traditional universities. Lecturers were positive that they will adopt social media in their teaching and learning activities in the near future.

References

1. Almeshal, T.: Social Media Adoption in Learning and Teaching by Higher Education Faculty, Higher Education Faculty, Madrid, pp. 1–10 (2015)
2. Tarantino, K., McDonough, J., Hua, M.: Effects of student engagement with social media on student learning: a review of literature. eJournal 1, 1–14 (2013)
3. Kaplan, A.M., Haenlein, M.: User's of the world, Unite! The challenges and opportunities of social media. Sci. Direct 53, 59–68 (2010)
4. Kagohara, D.M., et al.: Using iPods® and iPads® in teaching programs for individuals with developmental disabilities: a systematic review. Res. Dev. Disabil. 34(1), 147–156 (2013)
5. Gonzalez, C.: What Do University Teachers Think eLearning is Good for in their Teaching. Routledge, London (2010)
6. Asma, F.: The advantages and disadvantages of technology in the classroom (2012). https://sites.google.com/site/technoeducom/adv-disadv
7. Chen, B., Bryer, T.: Investigating instructional strategies for using social media in formal and informal learning. Int. Rev. Res. Open Distance Learn. 13(1), 87–104 (2012)
8. Cilliers, L.: Wiki acceptance by university students to improve collaboration in Higher Education. Innov. Educ. Teach. Int. 54, 1–9 (2016). https://doi.org/10.1080/14703297.2016.1180255
9. Nakamaru, S.: Making (and not making) connections with web 2.0 technology in the ESL composition classroom, National Council of Teachers of English, London (2011)
10. Heng, L.T., Marimuthu, R.: Let's Wiki in Class. Procedia – Soc. Behav. Sci. 67, 269–274 (2012)
11. Bromley, D.B.: Academic contributions to psychological counselling: a philosophy of science for the study of individual cases. Couns. Psychol. Q. 3(3), 299–307 (1990)
12. Cilliers, L.: Barriers to the implementation of a learner management system in higher education. In: ICERI2014 Conference 2014, Seville, Spain, 18–20 November 2014

13. Venkatesh, V., Morris, M., Davids, G., Davis, F.: User acceptance of information technology: toward a unified view. MIS Q. **27**(3), 425–478 (2003)
14. Khechine, H., Lakhal, S., Pascot, D., Bytha, A.: UTAUT model for blended learning: the role of gender and age in the intention to use webinars. Interdiscip. J. E-Learn. Learn. Objects **10**, 33–52 (2014)
15. Marchewka, J.T., Liu, C., Kostiwa, K.: An application of the UTAUT Model for understanding student perceptions using course management software. Commun. IIMA **7**(2), 93–104 (2007)
16. Leech, N.L., Barrett, K.C., Morgan, G.A.: SPSS for Intermediate Statistics: Use and Interpretation. Lawrence Erlbaum Associates, Mahwah, NJ (2004)
17. Mbodila, M., Ndebele, C., Muhandji, K.: The effect of social media on student's engagement and collaboration in higher education: a case study of the use of Facebook at a South African University. J. Commun. **5**(2), 115–125 (2014)
18. Wiid, J.A., Nell, C.E., Cant, M.C.: Perceptions of lecturing staff on social media networking systems and their use of it. Int. Bus. Econ. Res. J. **14**(3), 395–410 (2015)
19. Oye, N.D., Iahad, N.A., Rahim, N.A.: The history of UTAUT model and its impact on ICT acceptance and usage by academicians. Educ. Inf. Technol. **19**, 251–270 (2014)
20. Munguatosha, G.M., Muyinda, P.B., Lubega, J.T.: A social networked learning adoption model for higher education institutions in developing countries. Horizon **19**(4), 307–320 (2011)
21. Madhav, N., Joseph, M.K., Twala, B.: Creating social learning spaces to enhance the learning experience, pp. 1–15 (2014)

Emerging Technologies Supported Personalized and Adaptive Learning

Generalization of Tooltips: An Assistive Technology Extension

Saira-Banu Adams$^{(\boxtimes)}$, William D. Tucker, and Isabella M. Venter

University of the Western Cape, Cape Town, South Africa
3162887@myuwc.ac.za

Abstract. Software applications use tooltips to assist users to improve their understanding of icons. When hovering over an icon with the cursor, a short text description of the icon appears. Text-based tooltips are helpful for users without any literacy limitations. An extension was created to generalize tooltips for users with low text literacy. In this case study and to explore such generalization, video based tooltips show short South African Sign Language clips to assist those who use South African Sign Language as a first language. When the user hovers over an icon, a video appears with a short description of the icon in South African Sign Language. As a way to abstract tooltips, audio-based tooltips have also been developed, for users with language barriers, reading disabilities and those who are visually impaired. When hovering over an icon, a short audio description of the icon plays. Both audio and South African Sign Language video based tooltips have been pre-recorded. Through a web extension, users are able to select a tooltip preference for their Mozilla Firefox Browser for audio-based or video-based tooltips.

Keywords: Internet services · End-user applications · Software design · Deaf · Tooltip · Mozilla Firefox extension · Sign language

1 Introduction

Most software packages use icons, small visual representations, to represent tools and specific functions located in a toolbar. These icons make the user interface more attractive although the meaning of the icons is not always apparent. Since icons are pictorial rather than text-based, it means that users who understand their meaning can recognize them quickly. The problem arises where multiple icons are needed to represent different functions within a software application, making it challenging for designers to develop easily recognizable icons that represent functionality that may or may not be known to users. To assist users, a user can hover the cursor controlled by the mouse, over an icon, and the meaning of the icon is displayed as a text message. This message disappears immediately once the cursor is moved off the icon [2]. The text message displayed is called a 'tooltip' or 'infotip'. Tooltips provide additional information about an icon or button without crowding the display with too much information, therefore making the interface uncluttered yet helpful to the user [2]. Since tooltips are text-based, they do not benefit all users, especially those who cannot read or understand the tooltip. The size of the tooltip text can also pose a problem for visually

© Springer International Publishing AG 2017
T.-C. Huang et al. (Eds.): SETE 2017, LNCS 10676, pp. 213–222, 2017.
https://doi.org/10.1007/978-3-319-71084-6_24

challenged users. Tooltips can be made more accessible if users have the option to: select the language they prefer; change the size of the tooltip text; receive the text as a video- or audio-message. It was decided to develop video tooltips to assist the Deaf[1] Community of Cape Town (DCCT) and to enhance their ability to access the Internet.

DCCT is a non-governmental welfare organization with the aim to address the needs of Deaf people in the Western Cape. The organization has an active Deaf membership of 1090 members [3]. Projects undertaken by DCCT are mostly intended to develop and empower Deaf people. DCCT has a computer laboratory on their premises which provides the community with access to Information Technology (IT). A certified computer literacy training course called the International Computer Drivers' License (ICDL) is offered to the community in sign language. Besides the IT program, DCCT also offers a variety of other programs with the aim of growing the skills of the Deaf community. South African Sign Language (SASL) is their preferred language [3]. Contrary to popular belief, sign language is not a single language; there exist many variants of sign language and in some cases, such as South Africa, multiple variants can be found in a single region. To assist this community, tooltips needed to be designed in the more widely understood version of SASL.

Internet browsing is a popular activity used daily by many DCCT members. The Mozilla Firefox browser was thus the software package chosen to be extended with assistive, video and audio-based, tooltips. This browser is open source and easy to use; users do not have to be very technically literate to use it.

To ensure that the design of the tooltips met with the needs of the proposed users, participatory design was chosen as the research methodology as it involves the users in the design of an artefact. Data was collected using both qualitative and quantitative methods. The tooltip extensions designed for Mozilla Firefox were tested by a few Deaf participants at DCCT as well as some software experts and was found to be very useful.

2 Literature Review

In a paper by Petrie, Weimann & Weber, visual and video tooltips were created—based on the icons of Microsoft Foundation Classes Toolbar—to assist Deaf people with the understanding of icons [8]. Their solution consists of four tooltips: a sign language video, an enlarged icon with a text description, digital lips and human mouthing clearly speaking the function out for lip reading. These tooltips were tested by a group of deaf users. The sign language video (a) and picture tooltips (d) were rated to be the most beneficial (see Fig. 1)

WordPress developed a plugin called WordPress tooltip. Their tooltip solution is aimed at helping bloggers post tooltips within blog posts and consists of text, images, links, video, radio or mp4 formats. It can also be used as glossary. The WordPress

---

[1] Deaf with a capital 'D' is a cultural designation that denotes people whose first language is sign language.

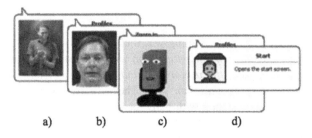

Fig. 1. Augmented Tooltips (a) sign language video, (b) human mouthing, (c) digital lips, (d) enlarged icon with a text description (Petrie, Weimann & Weber). [8]: Page 1132

tooltip provides bloggers with the ability to add related information to their blogs and gives the reader access to this additional information when hovering over text, images or a link [11].

The Mac operating system (macOS) implemented an accessibility feature called VoiceOver for Blind users. Blind students have found VoiceOver to be beneficial as their notes can be read aloud to them [7]. Audio tooltips, using touch sensors, can assist visually impaired users to select the correct controls when using devices. When the user lightly touches a control with a finger, an audio tooltip plays, describing the function of the control [7].

The extensive use of text within most computer software is problematic for Deaf people since most are functionally illiterate. This especially becomes an issue when the Deaf have to access services such as travel information or banking, which now almost always require the ability to use information technology. There is a need for more computer software to be available for Deaf people in their first language, namely, sign language [1]. In a study by Ahmad, he mentions the difficulty of determining user requirements for Deaf people since an interpreter needs to be present. When infor-mation about user requirements, is collected, it is challenging, but necessary, to get this information as accurate and complete as possible since the information is not received from the Deaf person themselves but from an interpreter [1]. This situation may skew the information.

A software solution called the Automatic Translation into sign Languages (ATLAS) project was a project developed with the purpose of enhancing Deaf people's access to the services and content provided by IT [10]. The system developed consists of an automatic sentence translator from Italian text to Italian Sign Language (LIS). The domain of this software is a weather forecast system where LIS translations are signed by a virtual character animation, which uses pre-captured hand animated signs [9].

3   Methods and Materials

To address the question as to whether assistive tooltips would make software more accessible for Deaf users, it was decided to include Deaf participants in the design of the tooltip technology. Participatory design is a methodology that involves stakeholders in the design process in order to ensure that the end product meets the needs of the intended users [6].

Evolutionary cooperative prototyping was thus used to design the prototype since this approach allows *"enhanced communication with end-users, improved incorporation of end-user insights into the prototypes, and stronger collective ownership and collective action-planning by the team"* [6]. The assistive tooltip extension to the browser software was co-designed with participants at DCCT.

The participative design of the tooltip was executed ethically based on Lund's five principles for ethical research [4]: 1. To minimize the risk of harm, the participants were regular users of the equipment in the IT laboratory and thus knew the environment; 2. Informed consent was obtained from each participant; 3. The participants were informed that their responses would be anonymous and the data collected would be confidential; that is, it would only be used by the researcher and would be destroyed once the research had been completed; 4. The researcher took care to avoid deceptive practices; and finally, 5. The participants were given the right to withdraw [4]. Ethical permission for this research was received from the university's ethical committee (number 15/7/232).

Participatory Design is a methodology executed in three phases, (see Fig. 2).

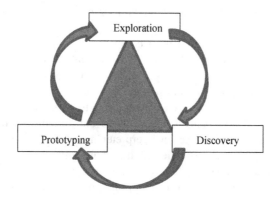

Fig. 2. Participatory design process

3.1   Phase 1: Initial Exploration of Work

During the first stage of this participatory design, the designer met with the users and discussed the users' workflow and their lives in order to grasp an understanding of who the software would be designed for [6]. A SASL interpreter, who is a child of Deaf adults (CODA), was used to assist with this process. Since a CODA's mother tongue is sign language, their interpretation is more useful than the interpretation of a second language sign language interpreter. To refine the prototype, two CODA interpreters and a DCCT member co-designed the tooltip extension in three iterations.

3.2   Phase 2: Discovery Process

This phase normally entails gathering needs from users. The users' needs and goals were analysed and prioritized, and a desired project outcome was agreed upon [6]. The main goal of the tooltips was to ensure that icons and functions would be easily understood by the users. Since the tooltips consist of many technical terms for which no SASL signs have been developed the CODA interpreter, during the first iteration of the design, created her own signed terminology for the icons. In the second iteration, this was reconsidered and it was decided rather to explain the icons in normal SASL terms using analogies. For example: the tooltip "bookmark this page" was signed in SASL as placing a bookmark in a physical book. During the final iteration, through the different phases, all the tooltips were re-recorded. The design team agreed upon how each tooltip would be signed.

3.3   Phase 3: Prototyping

During this stage, a prototype artefact was created to meet the needs of the user and to meet the desired outcome [6]. Using Hypertext Mark-up Language (HTML), Cascading Style Sheets (CSS) and Java Scripting, a prototype for the assistive tooltip extension to the Mozilla Firefox browser was written (see Fig. 3).

Fig. 3. Assistive SASL video tooltip for Mozilla Firefox browser.

This extension allowed either a video clip or an audio clip to be played when the cursor was moved over the icon (mouse-over). Tooltips for eleven standard browser icons were developed for Mozilla Firefox. SASL videos and audio clips were recorded and placed within the extension for each corresponding icon. Interviews were conducted with the participants after this intervention.

To confirm that the prototype was usable and correct, content verification and usability evaluations were done, in the next section the design of the evaluation will be discussed.

3.4   Design of the Evaluation

Deaf and CODA participants (5) checked both content—whether the sign language is signing the correct text translation [5]—and usability. In addition five software experts, randomly chosen, were asked to do a heuristic walkthrough of the software to test the tooltips' usability.

Content
Computer literate SASL signers, who were acquainted with the Firefox browser, were required to do this testing. Eleven video clips were placed in a folder in a random order, and each video was allocated a random number as a file name.

The participants were given a pre-prepared form with the numbers of the video clips and a space next to each number to record the text, as understood by the participant. They were asked to watch each of the eleven video clips and then write down the text translation of the tooltip on the form. The video clip was marked as correct on the form only when the text translation of the video clip reflected the required translation.

Usability
To test the usability, the participants were shown how to use the software and the tooltip extension. The participants were then asked to interact with the software and to fill in a usability testing survey. The survey consisted of questions to provide usability feedback based on the participants experience using the extension. While the participants were testing the software, the researcher observed them.

Heuristic Walkthrough
To further test the usability of the software a heuristic walkthrough by five software experts was done, which according to Preece et al. [9], can identify approximately 75% of usability problems (see Fig. 4). A heuristic walkthrough is an informal testing method using a set of heuristics to evaluate an artefact. The experts were asked to evaluate the tooltip software in terms of the following usability principles:

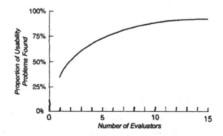

Fig. 4. The curve depicts the ratio of problems within an interface identified by a heuristic evaluation using a range of numbers of evaluators (Preece et al.). [9]. Page 409

- Feedback: feedback about an action.
- Match between the system and the real world: icons resemble the action that they represent.
- Recognition rather than recall: all options and actions are easily visible

- Aesthetic and minimalist design: simple dialogs do not contain any irrelevant information.
- Flexibility and efficiency of use: software caters for experienced and inexperienced users.

4   Results

4.1   Testing by SASL Participants

Content Verification Results

Nine out of the eleven tooltip video clips' were translated correctly by the participants, only video clips 4, 8 and 10 were unclear (see Table 1) since none of the three participants could interpret these tooltips correctly. Although the text translations of Participants 2 and 3 for Videos 1 and 2 are not the exact text translation of the tooltips, the participants' translations were still reasonable descriptions of the functions of the icons. The Deaf participants gave suggestions as to how these unclear videos, could be signed correctly. These videos were then re-interpreted and re-recorded.

Usability Testing

The aim of usability testing was to determine how the users interact with the software; whether the extension developed is user friendly; how easy the software is to use; how easy it is to learn to use the software and how easy it is to navigate the user interface of the software. The testing procedure was explained, the software solution demonstrated to the participants using a tooltip information sheet, and a consent form was signed.

To evaluate the usability of the extension, each participant was handed a pre-designed questionnaire to complete while testing the software. The participants interacted with the software and completed the questionnaire. On analysis of the data the following was found:

User-friendliness. All participants agreed that to make the system more user-friendly, the video tooltip should loop on mouse-over, instead of only playing once. During the concluding interview, a Deaf participant noted that she had always seen the buttons in her browser's toolbar but had never used them because she did not know their functions.

Ease of use. Although participants said that the subtitles on the video clip were clear and easy to read, they felt that subtitles were unnecessary since they only viewed the SASL tooltip. One participant suggested that there should be an option to add subtitles or not. The participants also suggested that the video clips be signed by a native Deaf signer rather than by an interpreter. They felt that then it would be easier for Deaf people to understand.

Learnability. Overall all participants found the software easy to learn. Since many of the tooltip terms are technical, the participants suggested that the tooltip for each button should be described and explained (rather than spelled out) in the video clip.

Table 1. Content verification results

Tip	Tooltip meaning	Participants 1	2	3	4	5
1	Bookmark this page	Bookmark this page	Choose bookmark	Choose book-mark from this page	Choose Bookmark	Select to bookmark the page
2	Show your bookmarks	Show your bookmarks	Bookmarks	This icon shows you the bookmarks	Show your Bookmarks	Show the bookmarks
3	Save to pocket	Save to pocket	Pocket save	This icon is saved pocket save	Save to pocket	Use this icon to save to pocket
4	Display the progress of ongoing downloads	Display the progress of ongoing downloads	Scroll down	Icon is used to download	Use icon to download	Scroll down
5	Mozilla Firefox startpage	Mozilla Firefox startpage	Mozilla homepage	Opens Mozilla homepage	Mozilla homepage	House icon means Mozilla homepage
6	Start a conversation	Start a conversation	Icon to start a chat	Smile is to start a conversation	Smile icon is to start a chat	Smile icon means talk
7	Open menu	Open menu	Press to open menu	This is open your menu	Menu page	Press to open menu
8	Go back one page, pull down to show history	Go back one page, pull down to show history	Open again, show history	You can go back to what you previously opened	Go back to recent	Open to show history
9	Close tab	Close tab	Press button to close	Close this tab	Close tab	Close tab
10	Open new tab	Open new tab	Tabs name is open	This is the open tab button	Open a tab	Open new tab
11	Reload current page	Reload current page	Loading page again	Opens the same page again	Reload page	Loading same page again

Ease of navigation. All participants said that the position of the video tooltip was easy to find and should not be placed anywhere else. All participants felt that navigation between pages was easy.

4.2   Heuristic Walkthrough Results

The software experts were asked to evaluate the tooltip software in terms of specific usability principles:

Feedback. The experts strongly agreed that the user is always aware of what functions they may perform within the extension. Furthermore, they agreed that every video clip appears without any lag on mouse-over.

Match between the system and the real world. The experts strongly agreed that the buttons/icons were easily recognizable and could be related to real world situations. For example, the icon with the house meant "go home" and the cross button meant "close tab".

Recognition rather than recall. Since the icons resembled the functions they were easily recognizable.

Aesthetic and minimalist design. All experts strongly agreed that the layout of the extension was straight forward and the explanations did not contain any unnecessary information. Three experts suggested that the subtitle colour should be changed to yellow rather than white to make it easier for the user to see.

Flexibility and efficiency of use. All experts agreed that they were always aware of where they were, what they could do and where they could go within the extension.

5 Conclusion

The tooltips provided by most software packages are text-based and explain the functionality of buttons or icons with a mouse over. These text explanations are in most cases not useful for Deaf users as many are "textually" illiterate. In order to make assistive tooltips more accessible for Deaf users, it was decided to include Deaf participants from a Deaf community in Cape Town in the design of the tooltip technology and to create SASL video tooltips for the Mozilla Firefox browser. These tooltips were then tested with the Deaf users of DCCT.

It was found that DCCT users preferred the video tooltips. They felt that the text subtitles that were added to videos for further information were superfluous, as they did not read them. In their experiments, Petrie et al. [8] also found that Sign Language tooltips were of more benefit to Deaf computer users than text.

It became evident that there are no SASL signs for technical terms. It was therefore necessary to explain these terms in detail rather than spell them out. It would be useful if SASL translations of technical terms could be developed. These will simplify the video recorded explanations. If assistive tooltips for more applications can be developed, especially for Deaf computer users, these users will learn the meaning of technical terms. Over time this will allow Deaf users to improve their understanding of, and become familiar with, the technical requirements of software. The participants at DCCT positively experienced video tooltips.

There is definitely a need for more assistive technologies for a range of dis abled people. It is clear that without assistive technologies, the Deaf computer users were limited in their use of the features offered on most software applications. Assistive technologies, such as tooltips, will allow them to explore new software applications and it will make the software more user-friendly for Deaf users. Without assistive tooltips these users are unaware of how many features of the software exist and how they function. This became evident from the participants' comments that they were previously ignoring buttons or icons that were present in the Mozilla Firefox browser just because they did not know what the buttons or icons meant or how they functioned.

6 Future Work

Based on our experience with video tooltips for Deaf users, we can safely assume that other types of low literacy end users could benefit from this approach. In order to improve and expand on the assistive tooltips, and to make them more accessible to a range of users, the following can be considered:

- Assistive tooltips can be adapted to be used with different browsers;
- An authoring tool for creating tooltips can be developed with a drag and drop tool where the audios or videos of choice could just be dragged and dropped on the correct icon.
- Where video clips were not correctly understood, the participants suggested how they felt the videos could be signed so that the meaning would be made clearer. These suggestions will be incorporated in the next prototype design and the tooltips will be re-recorded.

References

1. Ahmad, N.: People Centered HMI's for Deaf and Functionally Illiterate Users (2014)
2. Cassezza: Patent No. 9,501,178. Washington, D.C. (2016)
3. DCCT Welcome to Deaf Community of Cape Town—DCCT. http://www.DCCT.org.za. Accessed 08 Mar 2017
4. Lærd Dissertation Principles of research ethics. http://dissertation.laerd.com/principles-of-research-ethics.php Accessed 23 Mar 2017
5. Mothlabi, M.: Usability and content verification of a mobile tool to help the deaf person with pharmaceutical instruction (2014)
6. Muller, M.: Participatory design: the third space in HCI. In: Human Computer Interaction: Development Process, pp. 165–185 (2003)
7. O'Connell, T., Freed, G., Rothberg, M.: Using Apple technology to support learning for students with sensory and learning disabilities, pp. 19–21. WGBH Educational Foundation (2010)
8. Petrie, H., Fischer, W., Weimann, K., Weber, G.: Augmenting icons for deaf computer users. In: Extended abstracts on Human Factors in Computing Systems, pp. 1131–1134 (2004)
9. Preece, J., Rogers, Y., Sharp, H.: Interaction Design: Beyond Human-Computer Interaction. Wiley, Chichester (2015)
10. Vendrame, M., Tiotto, G.: ATLAS project: forecast in Italian sign language and annotation of corpora. In: Proceedings of 4th Workshop on the Representation and Processing of Sign Languages: Corpora and Sign Language Technologies, Valetta, pp. 22–23 (2010)
11. Wordress Tooltips Plugin – Tooltips Pro. http://www.tooltips.org/features-of-wordpress-tooltips-plugin/. Accessed 03 July 2017

An Accurate Brainwave-Based Emotion Clustering for Learning Evaluation

Ting-Mei Li[4], Hsin-Hung Cho[2], Han-Chieh Chao[1,4(✉)],
Timothy K. Shih[2], and Chin-Feng Lai[3]

[1] Department of Computer Science and Information Engineering,
National Ilan University, Yilan, Taiwan
hcchao@gmail.com
[2] Department of Computer Science and Information Engineering,
National Central University, Taoyuan, Taiwan
[3] Department of Engineering Science,
National Cheng Kung University, Tainan, Taiwan
[4] Department of Electrical Engineering,
National Dong Hwa University, Hualien, Taiwan

Abstract. The purpose of this study is to help teachers understand their students' learning situation. Especially in engineering education, Project-based Learning (PBL) is employed to promote self-learning by training thinking. The interaction between students is also an important factor. However, as is well known, traditional examinations and questionnaires only obtain subjective results. In fact, many studies have shown that brain wave data are currently the most reliable and immediate way to analyze human emotions, and are very suitable for use in evaluating things which cannot be quantified, such as the effect of learning, the appeal of music, and so on. Therefore, we boldly assume that the analysis of the brain waves can also help teachers adjust their teaching policy. Currently, most works on the analysis of brain waves, according to the rule of thumb, is to define the policy of using classification algorithms. However, the composition of human emotions is quite complex. Psychologists believe that human emotions are developed on a foundation of several basic emotions. It means that raw data on brain waves must be refined to obtain an accurate understanding of emotions. Therefore, we must focus on the degrees of classification and classification itself to find the trend of each emotion. Since living environments and cultures differ, clustering algorithms should be considered in seeking to improve the accuracy of classification. We have also developed a similarity discovery model, combined with the K-means algorithm, in proposing a more accurate framework for teaching evaluation. Our system can produce each student's KPI. Peer rating can also establish standards. Teachers can learn about the student's learning situations through PBL through our system, including competition among peers, the effectiveness of group discussions, active learning, and so on.

Keywords: Brain wave · Emotion · Learning evaluation · Clustering

© Springer International Publishing AG 2017
T.-C. Huang et al. (Eds.): SETE 2017, LNCS 10676, pp. 223–233, 2017.
https://doi.org/10.1007/978-3-319-71084-6_25

1 Introduction

Life is often influenced by emotions. Paying attention has a great influence on the learning effect of the student learning process, and attention is easily affected by emotions. Students are more likely to improve their attention when enjoying emotional pleasure; conversely, negative emotions easily lead to distraction. In engineering education, students are required to take the initiative to learn and think, so they need to pay greater attention for learning. It is therefore important to provide students with a pleasant situation so that they will learn more. In engineering education, teachers need to improve the quality of their teaching, so we must understand their learning situation. Understand the learning situation of students in order to provide a suitable teaching strategy. The teacher's assessment of the student's learning effect usually includes the use of attention. However, that main goal of PBL is to enhance the willingness of students to take the initiative to learn. It means that keeping a pleasant situation for learning is very important for students. Previously, in order to evaluate students' creativity and effectiveness in PBL, teachers could only use examinations and questionnaires. However, each students' cultures differ, so there are many differences between students. So for students, the use of questionnaires is too subjective and cannot guarantee honest answers. In addition, these examinations and questionnaires do not reveal the emotional state of the students when they are in the course.

In order to solve this problem, some works propose that the use of brain waves can achieve the identification of human emotions [5]. The reason is that the brain waves release currents when the brain's nerve cells are activated. This shows that brain waves are a direct reflection of the psychological state and cannot be tampered with. Based on these ideas, we believe that the emotional characteristics in brainwave data should be extracted through a classification algorithm since the brainwave data, human emotions and physiological conditions are related. However, most recent works on the analysis of the brain waves suggest defining the policy related to the classification algorithm employed. Because the field of brainwave analysis is very novel, no one yet can clearly delineate the actual physical meaning of the brain waves. The current researches can only sort out a few simple emotions, and cannot cope with complex emotional interactions [9] like some different emotions occurring at the same time. In addition, each person's emotional reaction may differ because life experiences and background are not the same. It means that only one classification criterion cannot explain human emotional reactions, so we must admit that only the use of a classification algorithm for emotional classification is inadequate. In order to solve this problem, we designed a clustering algorithm to adaptively find classification criteria, thus improving the accuracy of the classification algorithm. In addition, we propose a similarity model to refine the raw data on brain waves to improve the quality of the found emotional trends. Finally, we used the emotional analysis in the actual course, according to the student's emotional state to derive the most appropriate teaching strategies. The experimental results show that our system can indeed increase the learning efficiency of students.

The rest of the paper is organized as follows. Section 2 introduces background and related works. Section 3 defines the problem, and then we introduce our proposed clustering algorithm and analysis of emotional similarity. The simulation results are presented in Sect. 5. Finally, we summarize the research contributions and discuss future work in last section.

2 Backgrounds and Related Works

2.1 Electroencephalogram

Professor of Physiology Richard Carton detected electric current responses from animal scalps in 1875, and found that this current reaction is produced by the brain [6]. These current response records are called brain waves. Brain neurons produce a current response during their exercise. These reactions are closely related to body movement, emotional response, and physiological status. The body's status every second of the activities will be reflected by the brain waves [3]. Even in the sleep state, brain waves will also be active. So brain waves began to be used in various studies. The International Federation of Societies for Electroencephalography and Clinical Neurophysiology uses the frequency to distinguish between brain waves. The frequency of different brain waves is divided into five different types: alpha wave, beta wave, gamma wave, delta wave and theta wave. Table 1 shows the frequency of each brain wave. The waveforms of different brain waves are shown in Fig. 1. Many scholars believe that the uniqueness of the waves can be used as a basis for digital analysis. Many researches have shown that different emotions will have different permutations and combinations.

Table 1. Brainwave frequency

Band	Frequency (Hz)
Delta	0.1–4
Theta	4–7
Alpha	8–15
Beta	16–31
Gamma	32–100

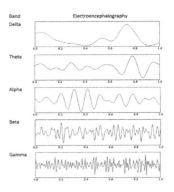

Fig. 1. Types and waveforms of brain waves

2.2 Emotion

Human beings experience many psychological situations. Receiving external stimuli can produce different physical reactions. These reactions may be slight or severe. We call these reactions emotions. Emotions are quite complex. Psychologists believe that human emotions can be divided into two major kinds: several "basic emotions" and "complex emotions" acquired from learning [2]. Basic emotions are generated by physiological factors. Paul Ekman, one of the twentieth century distinguished psychologists believes that there are four basic human emotions [1]: Fear, Anger, Sadness, and Pleasure. Basic sentiment will grow with age. Because of the different degrees of basic emotional experience, new definitions of human emotions began to appear. For example, "pleasure" can also be divided into "happiness", "joy", and so on. "Anger" may be mixed with "sadness" at the same time. These factors make emotional analysis more difficult. Basic sentiment coupled with experience, and the body's reaction to subjective emotions, comprise complex emotions, regarding which people are subject to their own cognitive assessment. Everyone's culture and subjective feelings differ, exacerbating the difficulty of emotional analysis.

2.3   Project-Based Learning (PBL)

Engineering education [7, 8] employs the most popular teaching method, student-centered, to get students to take the initiative to learn in groups in class. Students themselves look for thematic topics, collecting and analyzing information in the process of learning to find and solve problems, through group learning cooperation. PBL and traditional courses are not the same. In the traditional courses, the teaching process is teacher-centered, so that students only need to maintain their concentration to achieve better learning effectiveness. PBL emphasizes that group members interacting with each other, so that students need to accept a variety of different views, and learning directions. This means that only maintaining concentration is not enough; the focus is on whether students are willing to accept new things. This also shows that the relationship between learning and emotions is very close.

3   Problem Definition

Some studies use brain waves to accomplish emotional classification [5, 10]; this shows that brain wave analysis must be a comprehensive procedure because all combinations of brain waves represent cognitive and sensory perceptions. In the other words, a complete analysis of brain waves must include all the waves at the same time slot. In this study, we considered all the eight brain waves: δ wave, θ wave, Low α wave, High α wave, Low β wave, High β wave, Low γ wave and High γ wave, respectively. We believe that all the biological characteristics of the brain waves must be taken into account in order to derive more accurate emotions.

We know that brain waves are characteristics of emotions; all the emotional characteristics are needed in order to use the classification algorithm. There are also many studies [4, 10, 11] that directly use a classification algorithm to classify brain waves, but that's not enough. Brain waves reflect high-dimensional information. In the feature space, they will produce many dense areas, however, the same emotion may not only produce a dense area. We view the feature space from the perspective of two-dimensional space, as shown in Fig. 2. Each of the emotions has multiple dense areas that can influence the judgment underlying the classification; hence, we can see that the line of classification cannot accurately distinguish between the blue points and brown points. Therefore, we need to add the clustering algorithm to help the classification algorithm find the most suitable θ to improve the classification accuracy.

In order to guarantee our proposed cluster algorithm is able to improve the accuracy of classification, a clear problem definition is given by linear programming, as shown in following.

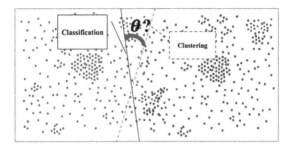

Fig. 2. Feature space

$$arg_C \; Maximum \; \sum_{i=1}^{k} \mu_k$$

s.t.

$$0 < k \le n$$

$$0 < \mu_k \le 100$$

$$|C_{emo_l} - D_{emo_l}| < |C_{emo_l} - C_{emo_{l'}}|$$

First, we set an experimental group $V_D = \{D_1, D_2, D_3, \ldots, D_n\}$ and a control group $V_C = \{C_1, C_2, C_3, \ldots, C_k\}$. Each data point in the data set is a vector of eight dimensions. Each data point in the data set has an emotional label $emo_l = \{fear, angry, sadness, happy\}$. μ_k is the clustering accuracy; finding the maximal μ_k is the main goal of this study. μ_k can be calculated by Eq. 1:

$$\mu_k = \frac{\sum_{i=1}^{n} T_{D_i}}{L_e} * 100\% \qquad (1)$$

where L_e is the number of the brain wave data. T_{D_i} represents whether the data points are grouped correctly, as shown in the following:

$$T_{D_i} \begin{cases} = 0 \; D_i, \textit{The data points are grouped into the wrong cluster} \\ = 1 \; D_i, \textit{The data points are grouped into the correct cluster} \end{cases} \qquad (2)$$

Therefore, we can know that the maximized $\sum_{i=1}^{n} T_{D_i}$ represents that most the data points have the correct emotion label. Some restrictions must be noted. k is the number of clusters; n is the number of data. All the data must be assigned to each cluster. The status of an empty cluster cannot occur. The chances of coverage between clusters are reduced. The distance between the data points of the same emotions and the centroid must be less than the distance between the center of the mass and the centroid. This is mainly used to strengthen its discrimination.

4 Proposed Mechanism

In this study, we chose K-means [13] as our clustering algorithm. In the beginning, we must find the emotion pattern in the raw data on brain waves, to define the position of the centroid. However, raw data on brain waves are very messy so that the found centroid may not ensure the ability to map the defined emotion because we know that each kind of emotion has a degree of difference to the others. With a lower degree, the voltage may be smaller, but they all signify the same emotions. Based on this observation, as long as any two emotional trends are the same, we can regard them as the same emotions. So before the K-means, we designed a similarity discovery model whereby we could find the better centroid position faster.

4.1 Similarity Discovery Model

This study used eight bands of brain waves. We first divided the eight waves into seven groups that is shown in Table 2.

Table 2. Eight waves divided into seven groups

	EEG	Hz
1	Delta–theta	1–7
2	Theta–low alpha	4–9
3	Low alpha–high alpha	8–12
4	High alpha–low beta	10–17
5	Low beta–high beta	13–30
6	High beta–low gamma	18–40
7	Low gamma–high gamma	31–50

We arranged these groups in order, and then drew their curves. Each curve may represent a kind of emotion. The main goal of this part is to identify whether any two curves are similar. We all know that when we are going to judge whether a person's appearance is similar to that of another person, we will compare the local facial features one by one. For example, we sometimes say that your eyes are like one person, and your nose like another person's. The concept of a similarity discovery model is similar to face recognition in that each group means a feature. If most groups are very similar, this means that two curves represent two identical emotions. There are two ways to compare the experimental group and the control group for similarities.

- Judgment by slope
- Judgment by area

Judgment by slope means comparing the line slope between the control group and the experimental group for each group of brain waves to verify if the two lines of the same slope have the same trend. However, sometimes two lines may have the same slope but the distance between them is too large. It may represent that these two lines cannot be regarded as similar. Therefore, we designed another way: determining the size of the rectangular area of the composition of the two lines as shown in the pink part of Fig. 3. If its area is small enough to represent the two lines being very close, even if the two lines of slope differ, we can still regard them as similar. Both of these methods are useful, but only one criterion can be used in each operation. We will hold an optimistic attitude to select the more positive factors. In other words, we define similarity of judgment by slope as J_i and similarity of judgment by area as J_i'; we will then choose $Max(J_i, J_i')$ as the final judgment.

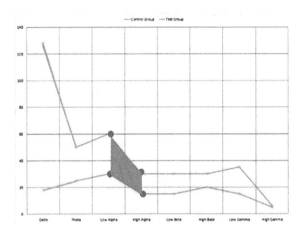

Fig. 3. Drawing

4.2   K-Means Clustering

For clustering algorithm of this study uses the K-means algorithm [12]. At the beginning of the initialization of the cluster center, the original method is to randomly generate the cluster center. But we modify the cluster center by the similarity method. The best point of view is the initial cluster center. Next, we use the Euclidean distance method to calculate the distance D between the material point and the cluster center:

$$D = \sum_{i=1}^{8} C_i - E_i \tag{3}$$

We classify the data points to the cluster of the nearest cluster center., using the data points after the group to calculate the average value of each group of data points as the next cluster center. We repeat the distance and update the cluster center until a stop condition is reached.

5 Experiment

The main goal of the study is to help teachers improve the quality of their teaching. The concept is that the teacher can know whether the student has positive emotions during the process of learning; when they are negative the teacher can provide timely intervention. So, we must first confirm the accuracy of identifying positive and negative emotions. Figure 4 shows that the accuracy of our system judging negative and positive emotions has a correct rate that is more than 90%.

```
The Best old all correctrate : 99.44%
The Best old weight
----------------------------------------
The Best new all correctrate : 99.11%
```

Fig. 4. Emotional judgment accuracy

Figure 5 shows that the cluster algorithm can improve the accuracy of the classification algorithm. The classification algorithm adopted the common k-nearest-neighbor (KNN). The expansion of the experimental data collection represents more and more diversification of each mood. When the emotional diversity increases, the accuracy of the classification will decrease. The rate of error will become high as long as the classification criteria cannot be changed. We can see that since the clustering algorithm can change the classification criteria according to the characteristics of emotions, it is still possible to maintain a high accuracy rate when the amount of data becomes large.

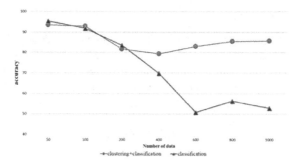

Fig. 5. Comparison classifier and classifier with cluster

Based on the previous two stress tests, we know that our system can accurately inform teachers whether students need help. Before the actual experiment, we will ask the students to wear the brain wave instruments before class; they make a good match with student phones' Bluetooth. During the course, brainwave signals will be sent to our server for analysis. The analysis results will be returned to the student phone and teacher computer that is shown in Fig. 6.

Fig. 6. Experimental flow chart

We set the experimental field as a practical course on metaheuristic algorithms. Each team has to complete a final project to pass this course. We selected two groups of student experiments in the course. Each team is composed of four students. One team used our system during the course, with every student wearing a brainwave instrument. The other group does not. The brainwave instrument transmits the brainwave signal to the computer via Bluetooth. The computer transmits the brainwave information to our system via the Internet. Students' brainwave signals are analyzed by our system; the results are returned to the students' and teachers' computers. Table 3 shows how teachers should help students when students exhibit negative emotions. It means that the teacher will be guided by the students' learning mood, and provide timely intervention via discussion with the students. In other words, if someone in the team encounters difficulties, the teacher will take the initiative to help. The difficulties include disputes, fooling around, and so on. In the other hand, another team did not consider to the emotion of students so that the team cooperation is weaker.

Table 3. How teachers should help students

Positive	Negative
Guide students to embrace more diverse ideas	When students are distracted, ask students to maintain a high degree of concentration
Remind students to reflect on their own methods	When a student is angry or depressed, remind the student to relax and restore their mood

After the experiment, some KPIs are given to help teachers assess students' learning effectiveness. KPIs include: pleasure to learn, learning attention, creation and critical thinking, team communication, self-exploration and responsibility, and project completeness.

In the PBL course the teacher is no longer the leader, but the facilitator. How can teachers help when students learn in their own way? In the experiment, our system will show the emotions of each student. When the team is in turmoil, the delegate needs the help of the teacher. After our experiment, we can find if the use of our system can help teams to discuss activities more often, cooperate more, become keener on learning, and more actively express their own ideas. We can also find if there are fewer exchanges between peers, and if looking for the direction of the problem is relatively simple without our proposed system. The reason is that teachers cannot easily understand the emotions of students during the course so that teachers cannot timely modify the student's thinking direction when students encounter some problems. The details are shown in the following table (Table 4).

Table 4. Comparison with some KPIs

	With proposed system	Without proposed system
Pleasure to learn	75%	50%
Learning attention	100%	75%
Creative and critical thinking	100%	25%
Team communication	100%	50%
Self-exploration and responsibility	75%	50%
Project completeness	100%	50%

6 Conclusion

In engineering education, PBL promotes students' self-learning, by students thinking and peer interactions. Teachers cannot effectively assess the creativity and effectiveness of students under the PBL. Our system helps students via learning emotions, concentration and thinking, improves their exchanges between peers, and aids teachers in guiding students in due course. Our experiments show that the use of our system allows students to learn with a pleasant mood. After the experiment, we found that the use of our system had improved the efficiency of team learning and thinking in more diversified directions.

Acknowledgments. This research was partly funded by the National Science Council of the R. O.C. under grants MOST 106-2511-S-259-001-MY3 and 105-2221-E-197-010-MY2.

References

1. Ekman, P., Friesen, W.V.: The repertoire of nonverbal behavior: categories, origins, usage, and coding. Semiotica 1(1), 49–98 (1969)
2. Lin, Y.P., Wang, C.H., Jung, T.P., Wu, T.L., Jeng, S.K., Duann, J.R., Chen, J.H.: EEG-based emotion recognition in music listening. IEEE Trans. Biomed. Eng. 57(7), 1798–1806 (2010)
3. O'Regan, S., Faul, S., Marnane, W.: Automatic detection of EEG artefacts arising from head movements. In: 32nd Annual International Conference of the IEEE EMBS. Buenos Aires, Argentina, pp. 6353–6356, 31 August–4 September 2010

4. Zheng, W.-L., Santana, R., Lu, B.-L.: Comparison of classification methods for EEG-based emotion recognition. In: Jaffray, D.A. (ed.) World Congress on Medical Physics and Biomedical Engineering. IP, vol. 51, pp. 1184–1187. Springer, Cham (2015). https://doi.org/10.1007/978-3-319-19387-8_287
5. Paul, S., Mazumder, A., Ghosh, P., Tibarewala, D.N., Vimalarani, G.: EEG based emotion recognition system using MFDFA as feature extractor. In: International Conference on Robotics Automation Control and Embedded Systems – RACE 2015, 18–20 February 2015
6. Caton, R.: Electrical currents of the brain. J. Nerv. Ment. Dis. 2(4), 610 (1875)
7. Chua, K.J., Yang, W.M., Leo, H.L.: Enhanced and conventional project-based learning in an engineering design module. Int. J. Technol. Des. Educ. 24(4), 437–458 (2014). https://doi.org/10.1007/s10798-013-9255-7
8. Hung, W., Jonassen, D.H., Liu, R.: Problem-based learning. In: Handbook of Research on Educational Communications and Technology (2008)
9. Arai, K., Mardiyanto, R.: Method for psychological status estimation by gaze location monitoring using eye-based human computer interaction. Int. J. Adv. Comput. Sci. Appl. 4(3), 199–206 (2013)
10. Soleymani, M., Asghari-Esfeden, S., Fu, Y., Pantic, M.: Analysis of EEG signals and facial expressions for continuous emotion detection. IEEE Trans. Affect. Comput. 7(1), 17–28 (2016)
11. Zheng, W.L., Lu, B.L.: Investigating critical frequency bands and channels for EEG-based emotion recognition with deep neural networks. IEEE Trans. Auton. Mental Dev. 7(3), 162–175 (2015)
12. Jain, A.K.: Data clustering: 50 years beyond K-means. In: 19th International Conference in Pattern Recognition (ICPR), vol. 31, no. 8, pp. 654–666, 1 June 2010
13. Hartigan, J.A., Wong, M.A.: Algorithm AS 136: a k-means clustering algorithm. J. Roy. Stat. Soc. Ser. C (Appl. Stat.) 28(1), 100–108 (1979)

System of Evaluation for Reading Based on Eye Tracking

D. Rivas-Lalaleo[1(✉)], V. Luna[1], M. Álvarez[1], V. Andaluz[1],
W. Quevedo[1], A. Santana[1], G. Vayas[2], M. Navas[1], and M. Huerta[3]

[1] Universidad de las Fuerzas Armadas ESPE, Sangolquí 170501, Ecuador
{drrivas,veluna,ralvarez,vhandaluzl,wjquevedo,
amsantana,mlnavas}@espe.edu.ec
[2] Pontificia Universid Catolica del Ecuador, Ambato, Ecuador
gvayas@pucesa.edu.ec
[3] Universidad Politecnica Salesiana, Cuenca, Ecuador
mhuerta@ieee.org

Abstract. The present work aims to develop a non-invasive interactive system by using an eye sensor known as Tobii Eye Tracking to evaluate students in environments such as reading or visual appreciation. Finally, the results obtained are shown graphically showing the trajectories of what the person observes and a statistical weighting close to the normal standard.

Keywords: Learning Assessment · Eye tracking · Visualization

1 Introduction

A key point in the development of the teaching-learning process is evaluation; in recent years, projects have been developed focused on the development of tools for evaluating some type of parameters taking into account that most of them require an interaction with the person; as the electroculogram for the development and analysis of learning problems. [1] Through the evaluation can be determined disorders such as dyslexia, which mainly affects the growth and development of vocabulary in people. This gives rise to 65% of academic failures along with attention deficit disorders [2].

At the moment several visual tests are applied that help to evaluate different types of competences, such as reading, where you can focus on parameters such as memory, attention, perception, coordination and reasoning. In this work an alternative evaluation is given, which consists in using a system that registers the location of the look on a computer screen [3, 4], thus allowing to determine if there is a fluidity in the pattern tracking of reading and areas that register greater attention to the user, obtaining the analysis that determines the correct development of the process teaching-learning [5, 6]. The coordinates provided by the eye tracker and their result are represented in real time [5, 6]. With this system of evaluation the teacher will have the possibility to determine the progress of their students or determine if they may have some disorder.

This article is divided into 5 sections including the Introduction. Section 2 formulates the methodology for development, as well as the architecture of the tool, mainly describing the bilateral communication between MatLab-Unity3D. Then, in

T.-C. Huang et al. (Eds.): SETE 2017, LNCS 10676, pp. 234–241, 2017.
https://doi.org/10.1007/978-3-319-71084-6_26

Sect. 3, the analysis of results is presented. While the conclusions are present in Sect. 4. Finally, the possible future work in Sect. 5 is detailed.

2 Methodology

The present work aims to analyze the visual process that determines values obtained by the ocular sensor to later analyze them and identify the learning problem if it were the case. In addition to establishing guidelines of design regarding the modality of presentation of the information.

2.1 Reading Evaluation or Spatial Positioning

These tests are applied for the analysis that exists between speed and accuracy that the person performs at the time of reading. This test can be monitored if the person has phonological, visual or mixed dyslexia. Taking into account if there are too many errors that may be inversions, substitutions or omissions of words and rotations can be said to be altered phonological route [8].

Since there is difficulty in decoding and uses the visual path to read what it recognizes. And if the reading is too slow but does not have too many errors you can believe that the reader does not use the visual path to read familiar words; one could say that the mechanism is affected. And in turn if you give these two causes it is deduced that both routes are altered and there is mixed dyslexia [9].

2.2 Tobii Eye Tracker 4C

Nowadays, eye tracking technology uses an "Eye - Tracker" device, which is made up of a sensor and infrared cameras. The function of the ocular sensor as shown in Fig. 1 is to illuminate the eyes with infrared light when it comes in contact with the cornea and the pupil generating a reflex, causing an eye frame and delimiting the space to be monitored [10].

For its part, the function of the cameras is to capture the live image of what happens in the delimited space of the gaze. From this a vector is calculated, having the direction

Fig. 1. System implementation

combined with other geometric factors results in being able to control the position of the eyes and to calculate the direction of the gaze on a stimulus [11]. Eye tracking is a technique that provides objective information, not consciously controlled by the user.

2.3 Unity

The acquisition of the signals of the eye sensor were developed in the software Unity, which has an SDK that has the performance of use to obtain the data of Tobii Eye Tracker. And get a fast and robust response to different changes and eye models by adapting the features of precision and accuracy [10].

2.4 Architecture of the Tool

The system is constituted by a data acquisition stage that is performed in Unity, a storage stage and data processing stage that is performed in Matlab. Thus obtaining a statistical analysis of the data.

Figure 2 is described in several blocks: the first block are the inputs corresponding to the eyepiece sensor and input devices (mouse-keyboard) for information input. The

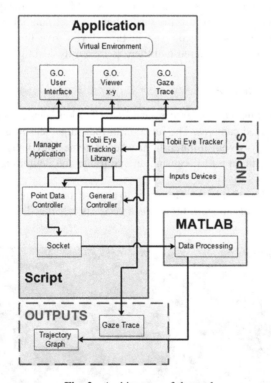

Fig. 2. Architecture of the tool

second block is the application that contains the Game Object that integrate visual objects like User Interface, Gaze Trace and Coordinate Viewer (x-y). The blocks are controlled by script and controllers within the stage script which are separated by functions such as the Tobii. EyeTracking that manages the eye sensor and shows it graphically within the application.

The application manager function controls the user interface and the dot controller shows where the eye's focuses on a place on the screen and in turn uses a socket to send to the Matlab section. In this section we perform the statistical analysis with the x-y coordinates, which yielded two main graphs: Graph of trajectories and Graph in consecutive steps. These graphs and the visual feedback of the Gaze Trace make up the outputs block.

3   Analysis of Results

In order to evaluate the reading the following tool has been developed which was described in the previous sections; the validation of the same was performed with a test group composed of 19 people, 15 men and 4 women in an age range of 24 to 38 years. The experiment consisted in presenting a text on a monitor which each of the people proceeded to read as shown in Fig. 3a; that information is stored in a database and the corresponding processing is performed. Figure 3b shows the pattern obtained by relating the x-y planes, which will be used to determine the correct reading path; Fig. 3c shows the graph that relates the x-y planes in addition to the time that elapses in the development of the test.

Then the standards obtained were contrasted with a second test group which consisted of 5 people, 4 men and 1 woman in the age range of 24 to 26 years; this test is shown in Fig. 4. Tabulating the values yields a result with a correlation factor equal to 0.8 which represents a significant relationship between two quantitative variables, between the test performed and the standard.

This correlation factor does not tend to increase, since the flicker of the eyes that exists at the time of the test makes there is a difference between the trajectories that are generated. Figure 5 shows the correlation between the quantitative variables that resemble each other.

If there are values not similar to the standard as shown in Fig. 6, the correlation factor would have to fall as in this case to 0.23 which represents a weak relation between the test and the standard suggesting as a result a problem in the process of reading.

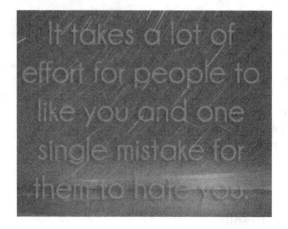

a)

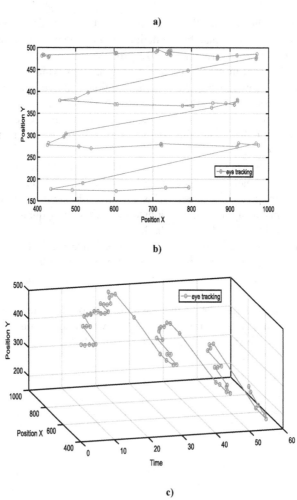

b)

c)

Fig. 3. (a) Image of a particle reading. (b) Graph of the values x-y (Trajectories) (c) Graph of eye tracking in consecutive stages

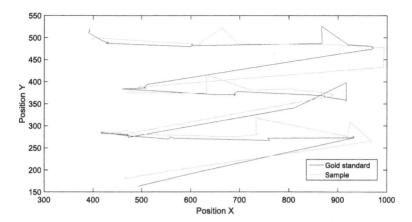

Fig. 4. Graph of a test performed and a standard.

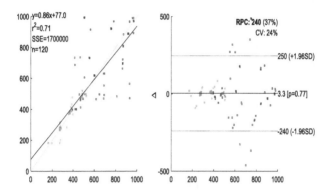

Fig. 5. Graph of the correlation with a factor of 0.8

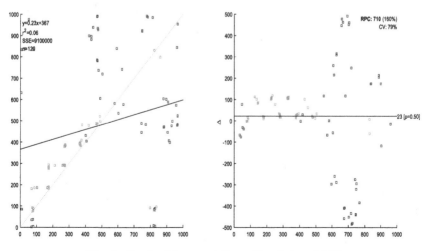

Fig. 6. Graph of the correlation with a factor of 0.23

4   Conclusions

The technique of eye tracking has allowed to develop an alternative evaluation system to the reading process, taking as a metric the special and temporal position where we obtained as results an 80% reliability in the tests performed.

The development of this type of test is considered as non-invasive because it allows the teacher to observe the development of the reading process of the students in a quantitative way.

Obtaining the values generated by this ocular sensor has a greater capacity to evaluate the metric of the vision that is of great importance and at the same time difficult to evaluate.

5   Future Work

The experiments carried out have allowed us to propose new evaluation techniques, which based on machine learning and pattern search, will allow an intelligent evaluation.

In addition, this technology can be used to perform assessments in the field of psychology, marketing and others.

Acknowledgment. The authors thank the Universidad de las Fuerzas Armadas - ESPE for the support to the execution of the project.

References

1. Kaufman, A.E., Bandopadhay, A., Shaviv, B.D.: An eye tracking computer user interface, pp. 120–121 (1993). https://doi.org/10.1109/VRAIS.1993.378254
2. Zapirain, B.G., Zorrilla, A.M., Bartolome, N.A.: Dyslexia diagnosis in reading stage though the use of games at school, pp. 12–17 (2012). https://doi.org/10.1109/CGames.2012
3. Kurzhals, K., Hlawatsch, M., Seeger, C., Weiskopf, D.: Visual analytics for mobile eye tracking. IEEE Trans. Vis. Comput. Graph. **23**, 301–310 (2017). https://doi.org/10.1109/TVCG.2016.2598695
4. Navarro Martínez, Ó., Molina Díaz, A.I., Lacruz Alcocer, M.: Utilización de eye tracking para evaluar el uso de información verbal en materiales multimedia. Pixel-Bit. Revista de Medios y Educación, 51–66 (2016)
5. Peretz, C.A.K.: Basado en un Programa Informático (2011). Obtenido de https://www.cognifit.com/es/evaluacion-cognitiva/test-dislexia
6. Alam, S.S., Jianu, R.: Analyzing eye-tracking information in visualization and data space: from where on the screen to what on the screen. IEEE Trans. Vis. Comput. Graph. **23**, 1492–1505 (2017). https://doi.org/10.1109/TVCG.2016.2535340
7. Mejia, C., Florian, B., Vatrapu, R., Bull, S., Gomez, S., Fabregat, R.: A novel web-based approach for visualization and inspection of reading difficulties on university students. IEEE Trans. Learn. Technol. **10**, 53–67 (2017). https://doi.org/10.1109/TLT.2016.2626292
8. Salamanca, G.H.: Centro de optometría comportamental. San Francisco, 17 de Septiembre de 2015. Obtenido de http://optometriasanfrancisco.es/dislexia-y-vision/

9. Bailet, L.L.: TeensHealth from Nemours, Junio de 2015. Obtenido de https://kidshealth.org/es/teens/dyslexia-esp.html
10. Tobii Eye Tracking, 17 de Mayo de 2017. Obtenido de https://tobii.github.io/UnitySDK/manualgetting-started
11. Brain and Marketing, Febrero de 2016. Recuperado el 28 de Marzo de 2017, de http://brainandmarketing.blogspot.com/2016/02/eye-tracking-neuromarketing.html
12. Shatil, E., Mikulecka, J.: Novel television-based cognitive training improves working memory and executive function. PLOS (2014)
13. Fitzpatrick, V., Reed, T., Gilger, J.: First-year engineering students with dyslexia: comparison of spatial visualization performance and attitudes (2013)
14. Begum, R., Ohene-Djan, J.: Multisensory games for dyslexic children, pp. 1040–1041 (2008). https://doi.org/10.1109/ICALT.2008.98
15. Costa, M., Zavaleta, J., da Cruz, S.M.S.: A computational approach for screening dyslexia (2013)
16. Fujita, A., Todo, N., Sugawara, S., Kageura, K., Arai, N.H.: Development of a reading skill test to measure basic language skills. In: 2016 IEEE Eighth International Conference on Technology for Education, pp. 156–159 (2016). https://doi.org/10.1109/T4E.2016.040

Emerging Technology and Engineering Education

Teaching of IA-32 Assembly Language Programming Using Intel® Galileo

Tan Chee Phang, Shaiful Jahari b. Hashim,
Nurul Adilah bt. Abdul Latiff, and Fakhrul Zaman Rokhani(✉)

University Putra Malaysia, 43400 Serdang, Malaysia
fzr@upm.edu.my

Abstract. Most universities are still using microprocessor training board that equipped with Intel® 8086 to introduce students about assembly language and computer architecture due to its popularity and availability. The Intel® 8086 is the first x86 microprocessor, it is no longer suitable to introduce students to the modern x86 architecture. A new microprocessor that featured modern architecture design is needed to maintain the competency of university students to keep pace with the fast advancing computer technology. Intel® Galileo is a single board computer board that equipped with Intel® Quark™ X1000 SoC. We successfully developed new approach for programming the device using assembly language. Supporting lab materials, example codes, macros, and procedures are developed to incorporate the Intel® Galileo board into the laboratory experiments design for microprocessor course. The proposed laboratory experiments allow undergraduate students to learn IA-32 instruction sets and protected mode programming. The results from pre-post-test and quantitative survey shows that Intel® Galileo board is effective to support the learning of the IA-32 assembly language and computer architecture.

Keywords: Assembly language programming · Intel® Galileo · Intel® Quark™ SoC X1000 · x86 · IA-32 · Computer architecture

1 Introduction

Students major in computer science or engineering are first exposed to high-level language (HLL) such as C++ or Java as an introductory language to computer programming. HLL is important for much faster program development especially in digital era with highly competitive market. However, assembly language is still playing an important role for students to study the underlying computer architecture.

The teaching of assembly language is a challenging task at universities as students might find that the assembly programming is a confusing and difficult process [1]. One of the reasons that demotivate students is they learn the underlying design of the microprocessor architecture based on their imagination in lecture class [2]. Hence, laboratory session plays an important role to help students gaining practical hands-on skill of microprocessor architecture and usage of assembly language.

Complex instruction set computing (CISC) microprocessor is undeniably still dominating the market segments in terms of total computing power, especially x86

© Springer International Publishing AG 2017
T.-C. Huang et al. (Eds.): SETE 2017, LNCS 10676, pp. 245–251, 2017.
https://doi.org/10.1007/978-3-319-71084-6_27

microprocessors from Intel and AMD that can be easily found on desktop, laptop, server center. Hence, in this research we focus on the improvements of hardware-based x86 microprocessor training platform in universities. However, the current x86 microprocessor training kits that adopted by most of the universities still equipped with Intel® 8086, which is a 16-bit architecture and only support real-mode programming [3–5]. Examples of commercial available 16-bit x86 microprocessor training board for educational purpose can be found on [6–8]. This is no longer suitable to introduce students about the modern and newer x86 microprocessor architecture which running in protected mode and have better memory protection mechanism.

In year 2013, Intel® Galileo Gen 1 Board was released targeting maker community, students, and professional developers [9]. The board is based on Intel® Quark™ SoC X1000, a 32-bit Intel® Pentium-class system on a chip for low-power embedded systems integration [10]. The Intel® Galileo board is also Arduino pin-compatible means that plenty of market available Arduino shield board can be used to integrate wide variety of hardware sensors and actuators for project development. In fact, many professors have adopted the Intel® Galileo board into their universities new curricula to allow students engaging in hands-on learning and prototypes building of different subjects ranging from robotics to design, Internet of Things (IoT), art, and computer science [11].

The Intel® Galileo is running on Linux operating systems and can be programmed using Arduino sketch. However, the protective layer of operating system does not allow students to directly program the hardware resources of the Intel® Quark™ SoC X1000 in assembly language. In [12], authors remove protective layer of operating systems and employing only the first-stage bootloader to enable assembly programming on Raspberry Pi, an ARM based SoC single board computer. This project presents the similar approach to modify the firmware that embedded in the on-board flash of the Intel® Galileo to enable assembly language programming. To the best of our knowledge, we are the first in academic to adopt the Intel® Galileo board to teach assembly language programming.

In the next section of this paper, the methodology for the development of both the hardware and software setup included with laboratory materials for microprocessor is described in detail. In Sect. 4, the results from the quantitative survey and pre-post-test are analyzed and discussed to evaluate the effectiveness of the use of Intel® Galileo in teaching assembly language. Finally, the conclusion about this project is presented.

2 Microprocessor Laboratory Setup

The laboratory setup is designed for the microprocessor course (ECC3105) at the University of Putra Malaysia. It is a compulsory course for Computer and Communications Systems Engineering students. In the laboratory session, two students will share one desktop computer running Windows OS and a set of Intel® Galileo Gen 1 board with JTAG debugger as shown in Fig. 1 below.

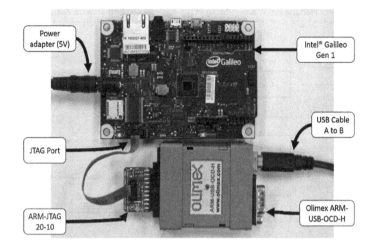

Fig. 1. Intel® Galileo Gen 1 with JTAG debugger

2.1 Hardware Setup

This Intel® Galileo Gen 1 is equipped with Intel® Quark^{TM} SoC X1000 and support JTAG debugging. The firmware embedded in the on-board flash of the Intel® Galileo was modified to remove the built-in small Linux OS. This approach not only allows the board boots to the first-stage bootloader for minimum hardware initialization, but also switch to protected mode. A JTAG debugger that support OpenOCD, Olimex ARM-USB-OCD-H is used to load and debug code and physically access the Intel® Quark^{TM} SoC X1000 internal registers.

2.2 Software Platform

The necessary software for assembly language programming runs on a Windows-based computer. The flow of the assembly language programming is shown in Fig. 2. First, students will create assembly code using text editor, assemble the assembly instruction into object code using NASM assembler. Then, single or multiple object codes will be linked together into an executable code using GNU linker, ld. OpenOCD server runs on the host computer then load the executable code into the random-access memory (RAM) on Intel® Galileo board through JTAG debugger. After that, the EIP register value will be adjusted to set the correct instruction point of the microprocessor where the code located. Finally, GDB command will be sent to resume the Intel® Quark^{TM} SoC X1000 and start executing the assembly code (Fig. 3).

2.3 Lab Manuals

Three lab modules were created for the teaching purpose based on the proposed training board. The first lab module introduces students about the Intel® Galileo based training board, Intel® Quark^{TM} X1000 internal registers and memory addressing and

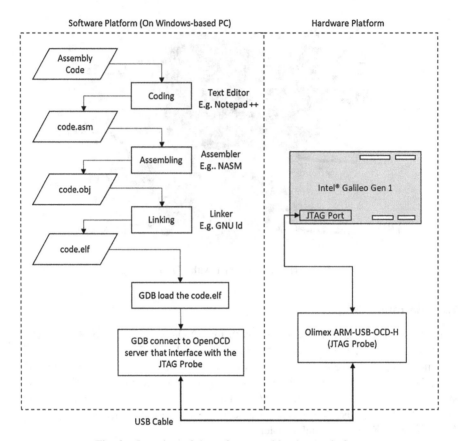

Fig. 2. Overview of the software and hardware platform

procedures for assembly programming. The second lab module help student to learn about the basic execution registers of the IA-32 microprocessor and protected mode programming. In the third module, students were exposed to programming different type of I/O interfaces and peripherals using assembly language to enable hardware sensor and actuator modules integration.

2.4 Example Codes, Macros and Procedures

To guide students to build microprocessor-based project with various sensor and actuator modules, customizable macros and procedures are provided for them to use.

Macros and procedures create an abstraction layer to use the hardware resources of the Intel® Quark^{TM} SoC X1000. This approach helps students to develop assembly program in a much easier way without the hassle process of registers value configuration.

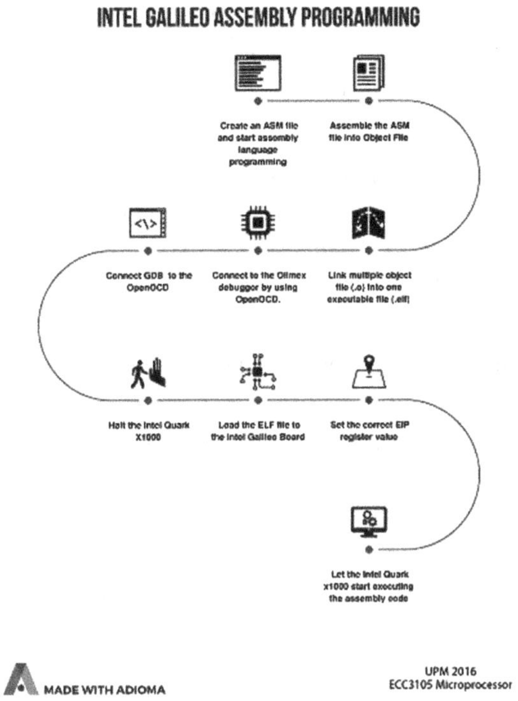

INTEL GALILEO ASSEMBLY PROGRAMMING

Fig. 3. Steps for assembly language programming on the Intel® Galileo board

3 Students Evaluation

In 2016, a total of 44 second year undergraduate students major in Computer and Communication Systems Engineering program were the first batch of students using the Intel® Galileo board to learn assembly language. Students were also arranged into smaller groups, proposed various open-ended projects based on the Intel® Galileo board. Students successfully completed their course project using assembly language programming with integration of different hardware sensors and actuators to the Intel® Galileo board.

To address the question whether the proposed programming approach using Intel® Galileo board help to improve student's knowledge and concept about x86 microprocessor architecture and assembly language, pre- and post-test that each consists of 24 questions were carried out. Paired t-tests was implemented to examine both pre- and post-test score to make sure the two scores are reliably different from each other. From Table 1, the paired t-tests showed significant increase in score, $p < 0.05$. This result suggests that the proposed training board and lab material help students to improve their learning about assembly language and x86 computer architectures.

At the end of the semester, 39 out of 44 students (88.64%) participated the anonymous online survey that based on Likert scale of 1 to 5. Table 1 shows the four of the survey's questions that evaluate the effectiveness of Intel® Galileo board for the

Table 1. Paired t-test for pre- and post-test

Pre-test (mean)	Post-test (mean)	t	p-value
10.907	12.14	−2.688	0.010

teaching of assembly language programming. The overall average rating of the survey's questions is 4.05, with average standard deviation of 0.931. The survey's results showed that the students mostly satisfied with the use of the Intel® Galileo board and able to complete the laboratory exercises and course projects (Table 2).

Table 2. Student evaluation results for the Intel® Galileo board based on Likert scale (1 to 5)

Statement	Average
Intel® Galileo training board stimulated my interest to study assembly language and computer architecture	4.21
Easy to use command prompt (without GUI software) for assembly programming	3.97
Intel® Galileo training board helped to learn assembly language?	4.15
I am satisfied with the use of the Intel® Galileo training board in the laboratories	4.23
I will recommend the use of Intel® Galileo training board to other students	4.18

4 Conclusion

In this paper, we described the innovative approach to enable assembly programming on Intel® Galileo board that equipped Intel® Quark SoC X1000. Compared to the traditional microprocessor training board that equipped with Intel® 8086, the Intel® Galileo board allows undergraduate students to be exposed to modern IA-32 assembly language and protected mode programming. Also, the hardware Arduino-pin compatible design of Intel® Galileo board support plenty of market available Arduino shield board to integrate hardware sensors and actuator modules for project development. The students' evaluation results showed that the Intel® Galileo is suitable to be incorporated into universities laboratory design to support the teaching of IA-32 assembly language and computer architecture.

Acknowledgements. We would like to thank Mr. Ong Wen Jian from Intel Microelectronics Malaysia and Mr. Lim Yang Wei from University Putra Malaysia (UPM), for their participation in this project to enable the assembly programming on the Intel® Galileo board.

References

1. Crookes, D.: Teaching assembly-language programming: a high-level approach. Softw. Microsyst. **2**(2), 40–43 (1983)
2. Hatfield, B., Rieker, M., Jin, L.: Incorporating simulation and implementation into teaching computer organization and architecture. In: Proceedings of Frontiers in Education Conference on FIE, vol. 2005 (2005)

3. Husain, H., Abdul Samad, S., Hussain, A.: Teaching microprocessor course: challenges and initiatives. In: 2010 2nd International Congress on Engineering Education Transformations Engineering Education to Prod. Qual. Eng. ICEED 2010, pp. 215–218 (2010)
4. Gao, F., Wang, J., Zhang, J.: A research on the teaching method of 80X86-based assembly language programming. In: 2009 1st International Workshop on Education Technology and Computer Science, pp. 964–966 (2009)
5. Shan, L.: Exploration of education reform based on 32-bit assembly language programming. In: International Conference on Computer Science & Education, ICCSE, pp. 595–599 (2011)
6. ESA 16 bit Microprocessor Trainers. http://www.esaindia.com/esa-16-bit-microprocessor-trainers.html
7. MTS-86C 8086 Microcomputer Trainer. http://www.kandh.com.tw/products_2.php?prod=205
8. ASICO 8086 Microprocessor Training Kit. http://www.asicoindia.com/8086-microprocessor-training-kit-2651903.html
9. Intel® Galileo Board User Guide. Intel® Corporation, U.S. (2014)
10. Intel® Quark^{TM} SoC X1000 Datasheet. Intel® Corporation, U.S. (2015)
11. Intel® Galileo University Curricula. https://www.intel.com/content/www/us/en/education/university/galileo-university-curricula.html
12. Kawash, J., Kuipers, A., Manzara, L., Collier, R.: Undergraduate assembly language instruction sweetened with the raspberry Pi. In: Proceedings of 47th ACM Technical Symposium on Computing Science Education - SIGCSE 2016, pp. 498–503 (2016)

Identifying Drivers of Remanufacturing in Nigeria

Ifije Ohiomah[(✉)], Clinton Aigbavboa, and Jan-Harm Pretorius

University of Johannesburg, Johannesburg, South Africa
ifije93@gmail.com, {caigbavboa, jhcpretorius}@uj.ac.za

Abstract. Remanufacturing restores end of life products to almost new. It is a form of sustainability. The research set out to identify the drivers of remanufacturing, which could assist with the transition to a green economy. A questionnaire survey was used to establish the drivers of remanufacturing in Nigeria. Data analysis involving the mean item score revealed the creation of job opportunities, achieving low carbon opportunities, the reduction of greenhouse emissions and achieving a landfill reduction as drivers of remanufacturing. Factor analysis reveals six clusters, in the order of importance, as manufacturers' attitude towards achieving green economy, policies to drive remanufacturing, benefits of driving remanufacturing, responses to driving remanufacturing, manufacturers' drive to remanufacturing and economic benefits of remanufacturing as the clusters signifying the classification of remanufacturing drivers in Nigeria. The implication of the findings revealed that the major driver of remanufacturing in Nigeria is the creation of job opportunities, which is vital as Nigeria is presently grappling with a high unemployment rate.

Keywords: Remanufacturing · Sustainability · Nigeria

1 Introduction

Remanufacturing is defined as an industrialized process where parts described as cores, which have reached their end of life, are restored to useful life or almost new [1]. The steps associated with the restoration to useful life are inspection, disassembly, part replacement/refurbishment, cleaning, reassembly and testing to ensure the desired product standard is met [2]. Lund [3] developed seven conditions for remanufacturing. The seven conditions are the following: the product should be durable; the failure of the product should be a functionality failure; the manufactured article is standardised and the components are exchangeable; the remaining value-added is high; the price to acquire the failed manufactured goods is lower as associated to the left-over value added; the expertise for the product is steady; and an awareness of customers that remanufactured goods exist.

In order to develop appropriate strategies and policies for the industry, a good knowledge of the drivers of remanufacturing is necessary [4]. Studies has showed that the common drivers for remanufacturing include EOL regulations, increasing reusability, economic viability, Original Equipment Manufacturers, new markets, product service systems, remanufacturing, new demand, green labelling and certifying

© Springer International Publishing AG 2017
T.-C. Huang et al. (Eds.): SETE 2017, LNCS 10676, pp. 252–259, 2017.
https://doi.org/10.1007/978-3-319-71084-6_28

by associations. There are several examples of research conducted on drivers and barriers of remanufacturing. For example, in Greece Kapetanopoulou and Tagaras [5] concluded that the drivers of remanufacturing are customer service, green image, competition, profitability and legislation.

In Finland Guidat et al. [6] found that the drivers of remanufacturing include profitability, reduction of environmental impact, existing demand for remanufactured products, compliance with legislation and third parties remanufacturing products. In Sweden et al. [7] concluded that the results of the research on drivers of remanufacturing include improving turnover, competition, strategic advantage, green image, asset production, environmental legislation and ecological motivation. The aim of this study is to identify the drivers of remanufacturing in Nigeria.

1.1 Research Methodology

A quantitative methodology was adopted for this study as the aim of this study is to identify and explore the drivers which will motivate the development of remanufacturing in Nigeria. A questionnaire survey method was used to collect the data. The five point Likert scale was used to measure the responses of the respondents. Respondents were requested to indicate the degree of importance of each of the drivers of remanufacturing that play a role in the transition to a green economy based on the five point Likert scale (strongly agree = 5, agree = 4, neutral, = 3, disagree = 2, strongly disagree = 1). Ninety-eight completed questionnaires were received signifying an 81% response rate.

The demographics of the respondents indicated that the majority of the respondents who participated in this survey were within the age range from 26–30 to 31–35 years and had work experience of between 2–5 and 6–10 years in the manufacturing industry.

Data Analysis. Two statistical analysis were carried out using descriptive statistics and factor analysis. The mean item score was used to identify the importance of the variables, whilst factor analysis was used in establishing which of the variables could be measuring the same underlying effect. The procedure, findings and relevant discussion follow.

Mean item score for ranking of drivers for remanufacturing. The mean ranking of each attribute was presented to provide a clearer picture of the measure of agreement reached by the respondents. A summary of the test result is shown in the tables below. The mean for each variable included the standard deviation. The following Table 1 gives a summary of all heading levels.

1.2 Factor Analysis

Factor analysis was employed to establish which of the variables could be measuring aspects of the same underlying dimensions. Factor analysis is useful for identifying clusters of related variables and thus ideal for reducing a large number of variables to a more easily understood framework (Norusis 2006). Tables 2, 3, 4 and 5 present the results. The average communality of the variables after extraction is shown below in Table 2; the Kaizer-Meyer-Olkin (KMO) measure of sampling adequacy achieved a

Table 1.

Drivers of remanufacturing	Mean	Standard deviation	Ranking
Creation of job opportunities	4.76	0.455	1
Achieving low carbon footprints	4.70	0.541	2
Reduction of greenhouse emission	4.64	0.542	3
Improve profitability	4.61	0.671	4
Improve profitability	4.55	0.690	5
Conservation of natural resources	4.55	0.629	5
Implementation of proper waste disposal of all product and services	4.54	0.661	7
Implementation of responsible consumption	4.52	0.597	8
Lower production costs	4.51	0.646	9
Prolonging product lifecycle	4.49	0.647	10
New market development opportunities	4.42	0.911	11
The original state of the product to be remanufactured is retained	4.42	0.930	11
Commitment to maintain environmental balanced	4.40	0.670	13
Pollution control measures	4.39	0.771	14
Remanufactured goods can be sold as new	4.37	0.792	15
Product warranty is assured	4.31	0.901	16
Multiple product is assured	4.28	0.910	17
Implementation of initiatives for conservation of environment	4.22	0.979	18
Creation of a niche market	4.20	0.896	19
Broaden product market reach	4.11	0.940	20
Adequate and timely response to environmental impact	3.98	1.243	21
Portraying green image by organization	3.90	1.089	22
Lower prices	3.89	1.014	23
Targets and reporting for environmental balance	3.76	1.210	24
Training employees for protection of environment	3.51	1.401	25
Safe disposal of harzardous material	3.03	1.395	26

high value of 0.833 as is seen in Table 3, the Bartlett test of sphericity was also significant and suggests that the population matrix was not an identity matrix (Table 3). Thus, the necessary tests in respect to adequacy of the sample size were favorable for the factor analysis to proceed. Cronbach's alpha of 0,867 suggested the reliability of the study instrument used was good.

The data was subjected to principal component analysis (with varimax rotation). The eigenvalue and factor loading were set at conventional high values of 1.0 and 0.5 respectively. As shown in Table 5, six components with eigenvalues greater than 1.00 were extracted using the factor loading of 0.5 as the cut-off point The total variance, as is seen in Table 5 is explained by each component and extracted as follows: factor 1

Table 2. Communalities

	Initial	Extraction
C1.2	0.428	0.674
C2.2	0.315	0.240
C2.3	0.435	0.269
C2.4	0.377	0.434
C2.5	0.417	0.735
C3.1	0.563	0.630
C3.2	0.530	0.503
C3.3	0.454	0.385
C4.2	0.405	0.377
C4.3	0.537	0.517
C4.4	0.366	0.377
C5.1	0.318	0.277
C5.2	0.321	0.269
C5.3	0.439	0.489
C5.4	0.511	0.616
C5.5	0.522	0.573
C5.6	0.410	0.382
C5.7	0.587	0.602
C5.9	0.455	0.430
C5.10	0.557	0.562

Table 3. KMO and Bartlett's test

KMO and Bartlett's test		
Kaiser-Meyer-Olkin measure of sampling adequacy		0.833
Bartlett's test of sphericity	Approx. Chi-square	890.988
	df	253
	Sig.	0.000

(32.925), component 2 (9.041), component 3 (6.970), component 4 (6.191), component 5 (5.040) and component 6 (4.854). The final statistics of the principal component analysis and the components extracted accounted for approximately 65% of the total cumulative variance.

Based on the examination of the inherent relationships among the variables under each component, the following interpretation was made: component 1 was termed *manufacturers' attitude towards achieving green economy*; component 2 was termed *policies to drive remanufacturing*; component 3 was termed *benefits of driving remanufacturing*; component 4 was termed *response to driving remanufacturing*; component 5 was termed *manufacturers' drive to practise remanufacturing* and lastly component 6 was termed *economic benefits of remanufacturing*. These names were

Table 4. Rotated component matrix

	Factor					
	1	2	3	4	5	6
Implementation of responsible consumption	**.677**					
Achieving zero-landfill reduction	**.641**		.420			.280
Implementation of proper waste disposal	**.639**		.262			
Achieving of low carbon footprint	**.566**		.450			
Multiple product lifecycle	**.541**					
Reduction of greenhouse gas emission	**.509**					
Prolong life cycle	**.463**				.447	
Remanufactured goods can be sold as new	**.424**					
Implementation of initiatives for conservation of environment	.298	**.728**				
New market development opportunities		**.713**				
Pollution control measures	.320	**.587**	.399			
Broaden product market reach		**.500**				
Product warranty assured		**.458**				.457
Creation of job opportunities			**.712**			
Conservation of natural resources			**.568**			
Improve profitability	.399		**.517**		.498	
Commitment to maintain environmental balance	.269	.375	**.446**			
Adequate and timely response to environmental impact	.283			**.739**		
Targets and reporting for environmental performance				**.671**		
Creation of a niche market				**.568**		.384
Portraying of green image organization				**.546**	.285	
Lower production costs					**.664**	
Original state of the products to be remanufactured is retained	.292					**.355**

Extraction Method: Principal Axis Factoring 0.
Rotation Method: Varimax with Kaizer Noirmalisation[a].

Table 5. Total variance explained

Factor	Initial eigenvalues			Extraction sums of squared loadings			Rotation sums of squared loadings		
	Total	% of variance	Cumulative %	Total	% of variance	Cumulative %	Total	% of variance	Cumulative %
1	**7.573**	32.95	32.925	7.139	31.039	31.039	3.322	14.443	14.443
2	**2.079**	9.04	41.966	1.620	7.045	38.084	2.500	10.867	25.311
3	**1.603**	6.97	48.936	1.119	4.864	42.948	2.133	9.274	34.585
4	**1.424**	6.19	55.127	.960	4.176	47.124	1.968	8.555	43.140
5	**1.159**	5.040	60.167	.663	2.882	50.006	1.384	6.016	49.156
6	**1.117**	4.854	**65.021**	.646	2.807	52.813	.841	3.657	**52.813**

derived from the components by observation of the components and how closely related the variables are using the highest loading factor.

2 Discussion of Results

Component 1: Manufacturers' attitude towards achieving green economy

The eight extracted barriers of remanufacturing for component 1 were: implementation of responsible consumption with (67.7%), achieving zero-landfill reduction (64.1%), implementation of proper waste disposal of all products and services (63.9%), achieving a low carbon footprint (56.6%), multiple product lifecycle (54.1%), reduction of greenhouse gas emission (50.9%), prolong life cycle (46.3%) and remanufactured goods can be sold as new (42.4%). This cluster accounted for 32% of the variance (see Table 5). These criteria share a common link to *manufacturers' attitude towards achieving green economy*. *Achieving a zero-landfill reduction,* as seen by Fuji Xerox, is an example of a company which achieved zero landfill after Xerox adopted remanufacturing as a principle in the 1980s. Xerox achieved zero landfill in Japan in 2000 by employing a closed loop supply chain where the products are recovered via a customer take-back policy and then sent to the remanufacturing plant (Maslennikova and Foley 2000). *Reduction of carbon footprint* is another driver for remanufacturing. In 2005 Caterpillar Global Remanufacturing Operation collected and reused 43 million tons of core material preventing the emission of 52 million tonnes of CO_2 into the ecosystem (Caterpillar Sustainability Report 2006). In comparison with other forms of product recovery management, the remanufacturing of products will retain all the value (Kim *et al.* 2008), functional characteristics and *multiply the lifecycle of the product.* It therefore potentially has a high level of sustainability and is considered as the best way of recovering products.

Component 2: Polices to drive remanufacturing

The five extracted barriers of remanufacturing for component 2 were: implementation of initiatives for conservation environment (72.8%), new market development opportunities (71.3%), pollution control measures (58.7%), broaden product market research (50.0%) and product warranty is assured (45.8%). This cluster accounted for 9.04% of variance. Subsequently this component was labelled *policies to drive.* Studies have shown that one of the major drivers for remanufacturing is the involvement of government by developing policies to encourage remanufacturing as seen by countries like China and the USA. Remanufacturing can be favourable to manufacturers as they seek to *broaden their market* in search of consumers who cannot pay the high price of new products (Steinhilper 2001). According to Gehin *et al.* (2008), components used for remanufacturing processes are either from the same or from other products. This reduces the use of new components, saves resources, materials, energy and other inputs. Other economic drivers are the *assured warranty*, life expectancy as good as new, high quality products and competitive price which can lead to *new market development opportunities* as remanufacturers target a specific market.

Component 3: Benefits of driving remanufacturing

The four extracted barriers of remanufacturing for component 3 were: creation of job opportunities (71.2%), conservation of natural resources (56.8%), improve prof-itability (51.7%) and commitment to maintain environmental balance (44.6%). This cluster accounted for 6.970% of the variance. Subsequently this component was labelled *benefits of driving remanufacturing*. The sale of remanufactured products can provide profit margins as high as 40% (Lund and Hauser [3]) thus leading to *improve profitability*. Remanufacturing plays a major role in the society as a whole (Lund and Hauser [3]). Products returned are always an economically feasible option (technical and physical upgrade) simultaneously benefiting the society by providing skills in terms of *job creation* (King *et al.* 2006). (King *et al.* 2006) states that remanufacturing products is a means of creating profit for the organization and at the same time bringing about benefits for the environment. This benefit brings about a commitment to maintain an environmental balance.

Component 4: Response to driving remanufacturing

For component four, four drivers were extracted. These were: adequate and timely response to environmental impact (73.9%), targets and reporting for environmental performance (67.1%), creation of a niche market (56.8%) and portraying of green image organization (54.6%). Portraying of green image by an organization is the reason why remanufacturing is adopted by organizations (Sharma *et al.* 2016).

Component 5: Manufacturers' drive to practise remanufacturing

For component five one driver, lower production costs (66.4%), was extracted. Significant lower input cost is an economic driver of remanufacturing since original cores of products are reused in remanufacturing (Bras and McIntosh 1999).

Component 6: Economic benefits of remanufacturing

For component six, one driver namely the original state of the product is retained (35.5%), was extracted.

3 Conclusion

From the primary data, results have shown that the creation of job opportunities is seen as a major driver for the development of remanufacturing in Nigeria to reduce the present high unemployment rate. This is followed by achieving a lower carbon footprint as respondents saw this as a way to transit to a green economy, the reduction of greenhouse emissions and achieving a zero-landfill. Findings from the questionnaire indicated that the creation of job opportunities, achieving a low carbon footprint, the reduction of greenhouse gas emissions and achieving a zero landfill are seen as the most important drivers of remanufacturing. The drivers of remanufacturing can be classified in six clusters namely the manufacturers' attitude towards achieving a green economy, policies to drive remanufacturing, benefits of driving remanufacturing, responses to driving remanufacturing, manufacturers' drive to remanufacturing and economic benefits of remanufacturing. These findings lend support to the possible ways to drive remanufacturing in Nigeria.

References

1. Lund, R.: Remanufacturing: United States experience and implications for development. The World Bank, Washington DC (1983)
2. Sundin, E.: Product and process design for successful remanufacturing. Doctoral dissertation, Linköping University Electronic Press (2004)
3. Lund, R.T. Hauser, W.M.: Remanufacturing - an American perspective responsive manufacturing. In: Green Manufacturing (ICRM 2010), 5th International Conference on IET, pp 1–6 (2010)
4. Ostlin, J., Sundin, E., Bjorkman, M.: Business drivers for remanufacturing. In: LCE 2008: 15th CIRP International Conference on Life Cycle Engineering: Conference Proceedings, CIRP (2008)
5. Kapetanopoulou, P., Tagaras, G.: Drivers and obstacles of product recovery activities in the Greek industry. Int. J. Oper. Prod. Manag. **31**(2), 148–166 (2011)
6. Guidat, T., et al.: A classification of remanufacturing networks in Europe and their influence on new entrants. In: Procedia CIRP, vol. 26, pp. 683–688 (2015)
7. Sundin, E., Bras, B.: Making functional sales environmentally and economically beneficial through product remanufacturing. J. Clean. Prod. **13**(9), 913–925 (2005)
8. Norušis, M.J.: SPSS 14.0 guide to data analysis. Upper Saddle River, Prentice Hall, NJ (2006)
9. Kim, H.J., Severengiz, S., Skerlos, S.J., Seliger, G.: Economic and environmental assessment of remanufacturing in the automotive industry. In: 15th CIRP International Conference on Life Cycle Engineering, Conference Proceedings, LCE 2008, CIRP, p. 195 (2008)
10. Maslennikova, I., Foley, D.: Xerox's approach to sustainability. Interfaces, **30**(3), 226–233 (2000)
11. Steinhilper, R.: Recent trends and benefits of remanufacturing: from closed loop businesses to synergetic networks. In: Proceedings EcoDesign 2001: Second International Symposium on Environmentally Conscious Design and Inverse Manufacturing, pp. 481–488. IEEE (2001)
12. Gehin, A., Zwolinski, P., Brissaud, D.: A tool to implement sustainable end-of-life strategies in the product development phase. J. Cleaner Prod. **16**(5), 566–576 (2008)
13. King, A.M., Burgess, S.C., Ijomah, W., McMahon, C.A.: Reducing waste: repair, recondition, remanufacture or recycle?. Sustainable Dev. **14**(4), 257–267 (2006)
14. Sharma, V., Garg, S.K., Sharma, P.B.: Identification of major drivers and roadblocks for remanufacturing in India. J. Cleaner Prod. **112**, 1882–1892 (2016)
15. Bras, B., McIntosh, M.W.: Product, process, and organizational design for remanufacture–an overview of research. Rob. Comput. Integr. Manuf. **15**(3), 167–178 (1999)

Factors Affecting the Evolution of Welding and Fabrication Education from the Perspective of Engineering Technology Graduates in Nigeria

Eghosa Eguabor[1]([✉]), Clinton Aigbavboa[2], and Jan-Harm Pretorius[1]

[1] Faculty of Engineering and the Built Environment,
Postgraduate School of Engineering Management,
University of Johannesburg, Johannesburg, South Africa
eghosaem@gmail.com, jpretorius@uj.ac.za
[2] Department of Construction Management and Quantity Surveying,
Faculty of Engineering and the Built Environment,
University of Johannesburg, Johannesburg, South Africa
caigbavboa@uj.ac.za

Abstract. The application welding and fabrication principles are at the core of industrial activities. The evolution of welding and fabrication education however is expected to meet the demands of the constantly evolving technology and industrial space. This paper investigates the factors affecting the evolution of welding and fabrication education in Nigeria based on the results of a questionnaire survey from 122 graduates of Welding and Fabrication Engineering Technology of the Petroleum Training Institute Effrun, Nigeria. Data analysis was carried out using the mean item score and factor analysis. Results revealed that the level of awareness of global educational standards and industrialization are the key factors affecting the evolution of welding and fabrication education in Nigeria. The outcome of this investigation is expected to contribute to the continuous development of the welding and fabrication curriculum in learning and also to meet industry requirements.

Keywords: Education · Evolution · Fabrication · Industry · Welding

1 Introduction

Welding (joining) and fabrication serves as a very important process and is involved in about 98% of the manufacturing industry activities [1]. Its application can be found in the construction of nuclear and chemical engineering plants, buildings, bridges, offshore installations, pipelines, shipbuilding, aviation, automobile, military hardware, agriculture and domestic appliances. Today's standard of living and quality of life can largely be credited to the evolution and advancement of welding practices which include the use of laser and plasma arc welding processes [2].

Welding is a process used in joining two or more material parts with the application of heat or pressure or a combination of both heat and pressure to form a permanent homogeneous component [3]. It is generally accepted as the most widely used and

© Springer International Publishing AG 2017
T.-C. Huang et al. (Eds.): SETE 2017, LNCS 10676, pp. 260–268, 2017.
https://doi.org/10.1007/978-3-319-71084-6_29

cost-effective process of joining metallic sections to produce an assembly in the manufacturing industry [2]. Kannatey-Asibu [4] described welding as an ancient science that has been passed down over the centuries. However, very little is known about the origin of welding because different tribes in various continents used the same basic methods of heating metal in fire to attain a plastic state which makes fusion possible.

The evolution of welding can be traced to ancient Egyptian history, through the 1800s and the times of the First and Second World Wars. This evolutionary trend is present in landmark achievements in air, land and sea transportation, space exploration, telecommunications, power generation and distribution, agriculture and mechanization in general. Welding can be comfortably described as the bedrock of engineering and technology [5].

1.1 Welding and Fabrication Education in Nigeria

The nature of technical education is dependent on the educational level and personnel type in demand. It is; however; important to note that vocational and technical education is dynamic in nature and hence its sustainability is dependent on the constant upgrade requisite training skills [6]. Technical and vocational education is meant to equip individuals with the requisite knowledge and skill that can immediately be put to work. The sustainable initiative of vocational education also provides the opportunity for self-employment [7]. Okediran [8] identified the need to improve local research in welding, fabrication and its consumables to enable Nigerian labour force tap into the benefits of the Nigerian Local Content Bill, which empowers Nigerians to be actively involved in the fabrication of steel structures including pipelines, steel facilities, storage tanks, and drilling rigs, a sector predominantly dominated by expatriate work force.

Welding and fabrication education in Nigeria is not isolated from the challenge facing the educational sector in general. The federal government has long identified the need to build the technical and vocational sector of the national education system [18], identifying it as the foundation of the nation's wealth. However, the shortfalls in the technical and vocational education can be traced to poor curricula and implementation of curriculum development and hence a high number of graduates from the Nigerian educational system are unemployable. Osami [9], also highlights the decline in the educational system in Nigeria, especially in the vocational sector.

At the time of this research, welding and fabrication education in Nigeria is at its highest level in polytechnic institutions and mono-technics such as the Petroleum Training Institute in Effurun. These institutions of higher learning are guided by the regulations of the government through the Ministry of Education and the National Board for Technical Education. A review of the National Policy on Education [18] reveals that there is no call for research as part of the deliverables of technology institutions. There is, however, the need to improve the local research in welding in Nigeria to enable Nigerians to benefit from the vast steel fabrication projects in the oil and gas industry [8]. The oil and gas sector, which involves a large number of welded and fabricated facilities, demands a high level of safety, quality and professionalism, a process that can only be achieved by high educational standards in research and specific content of curriculum [10].

2 Research Methodology

Respondents through the survey questionnaire were asked to indicate the degree to which identified factors affected the evolution of welding and fabrication education in Nigeria based on a five point Likert scale (strongly agree = 5, agree = 4, neutral = 3, disagree = 2, strongly disagree = 1). One hundred and twenty- two completed questionnaires were returned completed form the one hundred and fifty distributed, and this signified an 80% response rate. Based on the distribution of the respondents, it was observed that the majority of respondents have between five to fifteen years post graduation work experience and also graduated between the year 2000 and 2009.

2.1 Data Analysis

This paper considered the frequencies and descriptive using the mean item score as well as factor analysis. The mean item score was primarily used to determine the strength of the variables based on the respondents perspective. Factor analysis however, reduces the number of variables to a manageable scale by identifying the relationship between variables with the aim of developing theoretical constructs.

2.1.1 Mean Item Score for Factors Affecting the Evolution of Welding and Fabrication Education in Nigeria

Table 1 revealed the respondents' perspective concerning the factors that affect the evolution of welding and fabrication education in Nigeria. Underdeveloped manufacturing sector in Nigeria with a MIS of 4.23 and SD of 1.225 was ranked first; dependence on foreign expatriates was ranked second with a MIS of 4.11 and SD of .658; rate of Industrialization in Nigeria with a MIS of 4.07 and SD of .729 was ranked

Table 1. Results from mean item score

	Mean	Std. deviation	Ranking
E12.5 Underdeveloped manufacturing sector in Nigeria	4.23	1.225	1
E12.7 Dependence on foreign expatriates	4.11	.658	2
E12.8 Rate of industrialization in Nigeria	4.07	.729	3
E12.13 Global certifications in welding	4.07	.718	4
E12.14 Awareness of welding and fabrication education	4.03	.559	5
E12.6 Underdeveloped re-manufacturing sector in Nigeria	4.03	.574	6
E12.1 Industry demand of welding and fabrication graduates	4.00	.643	7
E12.2 Research	3.98	.616	8
E12.4 Government intervention and funding	3.98	.787	9
E12.10 Cost of welding and fabrication education	3.98	.698	10
E12.3 Location of oil and gas fabrication projects in Nigeria	3.95	.615	11
E12.12 Technology change	3.92	.583	12
E12.9 Social stigmatization of the welding profession	3.91	.668	13
E12.11 Number of welding institutions	3.88	.611	14

third; while global certifications in welding was ranked forth with a MIS of 4.07 and SD of .718; awareness of welding and fabrication education with a MIS of 4.03 and SD of .559 was ranked fifth; underdeveloped re-manufacturing sector in Nigeria was ranked sixth with a MIS of 4.03 and SD .574; industry demand of welding and fabrication graduates with a MIS of 4.00 and SD of .643 was ranked seventh; Research was ranked eighth with a MIS of 3.98 and SD of .616; while government intervention and funding with a MIS of 3.98 and SD of .787 was ranked ninth; cost of welding and fabrication Education was ranked tenth with a MIS of 3.98 and SD of .698; location of oil and gas fabrication projects in Nigeria with a MIS of 3.95 and SD of .615 was ranked eleventh; technology change was ranked twelfth with a MIS of 3.92 and SD of .583, social stigmatization of the welding profession with MIS of 3.91 and SD of .668 was ranked thirteenth and finally number of welding institutions was ranked fourteenth with a MIS of 3.88 and SD of .611.

2.2   Factor Analysis

Factor analysis was carried out to reduce the number of variables to a manageable scale by identifying the relationship between variables with the aim of developing theoretical constructs. The factorability of the correlation matrix is examined. A factorability of 0.3 indicates that approximately 30% of the variables share a lot of variance and the test of correlation becomes impractical. To further verify the strength of inter-correlation among selected variables, the Barlett's test of sphericity and the Kaiser-Meyer-Olkin (KMO) measure of sampling adequacy are used [11]. Factors are then extracted by rotation method. In this study the principal component analysis (PCA) was utilized. Furthermore, the criteria for determining factor extraction were considered and in this study the Kaiser's criteria (eigenvalue > 1 rule) was adopted. Average communality of the variables after extraction is as shown below (Table 2).

Table 3 shows the KMO value of 0.810 which is >0.5; the Bartlett's test of sphericity has an approximate chi-square value of 1692.802 (considering 95% level of significance, $\alpha = 0.05$) and degree of freedom of 66 and a significant value of 0.00 which is <0.05 [11].

Hence, to examine the appropriateness for factor analysis, the Kaiser-Meyer Olkin (KMO) and Bartlett's test measure of sampling adequacy were used. Also, the chi-square approximate was 1692.802 with 78 degrees of freedom, which was significant at 0.05 level of significance. The KMO statistic of 0.810 was also appropriate (>0.50). Therefore, factor analysis is considered as an appropriate technique to further analyze data (Table 4).

Commonalties at extraction range between 0.254 and 0.877 which is >0.3, hence valid, according to Pallant [11]. Using varimax rotation with Kaiser normalisation, two factors were extracted from thirteen variables used in this study. These two extracted factors cumulatively explained 66.522% of the variability on the aspect of the study relating to the factors affecting welding and fabrication education evolution in Nigeria.

Also, the combined percentages show 71% of the total variance before rotation and 66.522%% of total variance after rotation, which was sufficient to explain the composite items of these variables.

Table 2. Communalities

Communalities		
	Initial	Extraction
E12.1	.852	.787
E12.3	.488	.254
E12.4	.801	.573
E12.5	.813	.665
E12.6	.934	.747
E12.7	.742	.453
E12.8	.873	.918
E12.9	.665	.536
E12.10	.736	.574
E12.11	.740	.661
E12.12	.840	.762
E12.13	.931	.877
E12.14	.941	.841

Extraction Method:
Principal Axis Factoring.

Table 3. KMO and Bartlett's test

KMO and Bartlett's test		
Kaiser-Meyer-Olkin measure of sampling adequacy		.810
Bartlett's test of sphericity	Approx. Chi-square	1692.802
	df	78
	Sig.	.000

Table 4. Correlation matrix

Correlation matrix														
		E12.1	E12.3	E12.4	E12.5	E12.6	E12.7	E12.8	E12.9	E12.10	E12.11	E12.12	E12.13	E12.14
Correlation	E12.1	1.000	.456	.681	.657	.730	.481	.619	.558	.710	.631	.801	.840	.842
	E12.3	.456	1.000	.203	.464	.439	.303	.271	.271	.267	.468	.404	.485	.426
	E12.4	.681	.203	1.000	.644	.768	.478	.632	.640	.480	.492	.644	.584	.606
	E12.5	.657	.464	.644	1.000	.664	.757	.682	.644	.528	.488	.606	.731	.668
	E12.6	.730	.439	.768	.664	1.000	.458	.842	.539	.590	.589	.749	.666	.582
	E12.7	.481	.303	.478	.757	.458	1.000	.542	.489	.605	.354	.539	.642	.567
	E12.8	.619	.271	.632	.682	.842	.542	1.000	.376	.647	.322	.725	.570	.536
	E12.9	.558	.271	.640	.644	.539	.489	.376	1.000	.350	.661	.490	.649	.633
	E12.10	.710	.267	.480	.528	.590	.605	.647	.350	1.000	.342	.766	.637	.642
	E12.11	.631	.468	.492	.488	.589	.354	.322	.661	.342	1.000	.574	.689	.695
	E12.12	.801	.404	.644	.606	.749	.539	.725	.490	.766	.574	1.000	.743	.798
	E12.13	.840	.485	.584	.731	.666	.642	.570	.649	.637	.689	.743	1.000	.923
	E12.14	.842	.426	.606	.668	.582	.567	.536	.633	.642	.695	.798	.923	1.000

Table 5. Rotated factor matrix[a]

Rotated factor matrix[a]		
	Factor	
	1	2
E12.13	**.808**	.473
E12.14	**.803**	.443
E12.11	**.790**	
E12.1	**.672**	.579
E12.9	**.666**	.302
E12.3	**.456**	
E12.8		**.946**
E12.6	.437	**.745**
E12.12	.529	**.694**
E12.10	.352	**.671**
E12.5	.546	**.606**
E12.4	.458	**.603**
E12.7	.417	**.528**

Extraction Method: Principal
Axis Factoring.
Rotation Method: Varimax
with Kaiser Normalization.[a]
a. Rotation converged in 3
iterations.

The following variables that were found to be highly correlated with Factor 1, but negligibly correlated with Factors 2 (see Table 5): Global certifications in welding (80.8%), awareness of welding and fabrication education (80.3%), number of welding institutions (79%), industry demand of welding and fabrication graduates (67%), social stigmatization of the welding profession (66%) and location of oil and gas fabrication projects in Nigeria (45%). These variables were thus named: **Awareness of global welding education standards.**

Also, the following variables based on the factor loading scores were considered as Factor 2, but negligibly correlated with Factors 1 (see Table 5):: Rate of industrialization in Nigeria (94.6%), underdeveloped re-manufacturing sector in Nigeria (74.5%), technology change (69.4%), cost of welding and fabrication education (67.1%), underdeveloped manufacturing sector in Nigeria (60.6), government intervention and funding (60.3%) and dependence on foreign expatriates (58.2%). These factors were thus named: **Industrialization and welding technology space in Nigeria** (Table 6).

Table 6. Total variance explained

Total variance explained

Factor	Initial eigenvalues			Extraction sums of squared loadings			Rotation sums of squared loadings		
	Total	% of variance	Cumulative %	Total	% of variance	Cumulative %	Total	% of variance	Cumulative %
1	**8.097**	62.282	62.282	7.802	60.016	60.016	4.325	33.271	33.271
2	**1.139**	8.758	**71.041**	.846	6.506	66.522	4.323	33.251	**66.522**
3	.871	6.702	77.743						
4	.798	6.139	83.881						
5	.729	5.607	89.488						
6	.325	2.502	91.990						
7	.285	2.194	94.185						
8	.236	1.815	96.000						
9	.188	1.447	97.446						
10	.139	1.067	98.513						
11	.094	.724	99.237						
12	.075	.580	99.817						
13	.024	.183	100.000						

Extraction Method: Principal Axis Factoring.

3 Discussion of Results

Component 1: Awareness of global welding education standards.

Based on the responses, global certification requirements related to welding and fabrication education is a key factor for the evolution of welding and fabrication education in Nigeria, stated that the International Institute of welding (IIW) is poised to transfer the world's best practices in welding and fabrication through the implementation of IIW education, training, qualification, and certification through its members to various organizations worldwide. Awareness of welding and fabrication education and social stigmatization of the welding profession in Nigeria is best described by Dehelean [12] in which the perception of the welding profession is considered dirty, dusty and dangerous. Number of welding institutions and the industry demand for welding fabrication graduates as an evolution criteria is best described by Smallbone [13] stating that achieving the required training needed for industry personnel development requires some level of cooperation between the industry and educational institutions offering welding training to properly highlight the necessary modules for training because, the quality of the end products of welding is seriously dependent on the skill and competence of the welding personnel. Also, the local content policy of the Nigerian Government has over the years aimed at improving the local skill content in welding and fabrication to serve the needs of the oil and gas sector [14]

Component 2: Industrialization and welding technology space in Nigeria.

Based on the responses, the rate of industrialization in Nigeria took precedence in this group as a major factor affecting the evolution of welding education in Nigeria. This factor is however closely linked to the lack of manufacturing and re-manufacturing activities in Nigeria and clearly buttressed by Weman and Linnert [1, 2], stressing that welding and fabrication is highly significant to the process of industrialization and also counts as the most important joining process in the manufacturing sector. Also, the cost of welding and fabrication education is an evolutionary factor. Individuals and companies usually bear the cost of welding and fabrication education as leading to employees receiving only required training that will benefit the company [15]. Furthermore the high cost of welding and fabrication education [15, 16] is a call for the Nigerian government intervention to curb the influx of foreign expatriates in the welding and fabrication sector of the economy [8]. Finally, Okediran [17], identified the need to improve local research in welding, fabrication and its consumables to enable Nigerian labour force tap into the benefits of the Nigerian Local Content Bill, which empowers Nigerians to be actively involved in the fabrication of steel structures including pipelines, steel facilities, storage tanks, and drilling rigs, a sector predominantly dominated by expatriate work force.

4 Conclusion

From the primary data, it is evident that underdevelopment of the manufacturing, re-manufacturing and the industrial sector in Nigeria is the major drawback for the evolution of welding and fabrication education in Nigeria. The demand for qualified and certified welders is quite limited to the oil and gas sector and employers tend to provide only the required certification and re-training to suit project requirements. The need to also embrace research and global educational standards in welding and fabrication education is also a contributing factor to the evolution of welding and fabrication education in Nigeria.

References

1. Weman, K..: Metal arc welding with coated electrodes. In: Welding Processes Handbook, pp. 63–67 (2003)
2. Linnert, G.E.: Milestones in welding history. In: Welding Metallurgy - Carbon and Alloy Steels, Fundamentals, 4th edn., vol. I. American Welding Society (AWS) (1994)
3. O'Brien, R.L.: History of welding and cutting. In: Jefferson's Welding Encyclopedia, 18th edn. American Welding Society (AWS Mimi) (1997)
4. Kannatey-Asibu, E.: Milestone developments in welding and joining processes. J. Manuf. Sci. Eng. 119(4), 801 (1997)
5. James, F.: Lincoln Arc Welding Foundation Arc Welding in Manufacturing and Construction: Design, Engineering, Fabrication. James F. Lincoln Arc Welding Foundation, Cleveland (1982)
6. Ukuma, S., Ochedikwu, J.O., Deke, G.N.: Revamping vocational and technical education in Nigeria for sustainable development. Mediterr. J. Soc. Sci. 4(12), 55 (2013)
7. Muchemi, A.K., Muthoni, D.M., Mutahi, I.W., Gunga, S.O., Origa, J.O.: The implications of collaborative industrial attachments for Kenya vision 2030 development programmes. Afr. J. Educ. Technol. 3(1), 57–67 (2013)
8. Okediran, B., Yawas, D.S., Samotu, I.A., Dagwa, I.M., Obada, D.O.: Effects of electrode type on the mechanical properties of weldments of some steel samples produced in Nigeria. World J. Eng. 11(2), 95 (2014)
9. Osami, I.: Implementing vocational and technical education programmes in South-South Nigeria: a case of rivers state. Int. J. Sci. Res. Educ. 6(2), 128–148 (2013)

10. Kah, P., Martikainen, J.: Current trends in welding processes and materials: improve in effectiveness. Rev. Adv. Mater. Sci. **30**, 189–200 (2012)
11. Pallant, J.: SPSS Survival Manual: A Step by Step Guide to Data Analysis using SPSS, 3rd edn. Mc-Graw Hill, New York (2007)
12. Dehelean, D.: Environmental friendly welding - an evolution from 3d (dirty, dusty, dangerous) to 3c (cool, clever and clean). Environ. Eng. Manag. J. (EEMJ) **8**(4), 957–961 (2009)
13. Smallbone, C.: International system for education, training and qualification of welding personnel. Weld. World **46**, 35–37 (2013)
14. Heum, P., Quale, C., Karlsen, J.E., Kragha, M., Osahon, G.: Enhancement of local content in the upstream oil and gas industry in Nigeria: a comprehensive and viable policy approach (2003). <https://brage.bibsys.no/xmlui/handle/11250/164539>. Accessed 22 Apr 2016
15. Tsang, M.C.: The cost of vocational training. Int. J. Manpow. **18**(1/2), 63–89 (1997)
16. Fast, K., Gifford, T., Yancey, R.: Virtual training for welding. In: 3rd IEEE and ACM International Symposium on Mixed and Augmented Reality, ISMAR 2004, pp. 298–299. IEEE (2004)
17. Ovadia, J.S.: Local content and natural resource governance: the cases of Angola and Nigeria. Extract. Ind. Soc. **1**(2), 137–146 (2014)
18. NewsBank: Welding offers great opportunity in oil and gas (2014)

Industry Expectation from Graduates of Welding and Fabrication from the Perspective of Engineering Technology Graduates in Nigeria

Eghosa Eguabor[1(✉)], Clinton Aigbavboa[2], and Jan-Harm Pretorius[1]

[1] Faculty of Engineering and the Built Environment,
Postgraduate School of Engineering Management,
University of Johannesburg, Johannesburg, South Africa
eghosaem@gmail.com, jpretorius@uj.ac.za
[2] Department of Construction Management and Quantity Surveying,
Faculty of Engineering and the Built Environment,
University of Johannesburg, Johannesburg, South Africa
caigbavboa@uj.ac.za

Abstract. The application welding and fabrication principles are at the core of industrial activities. It is however expected that graduates of welding and fabrication are equipped with the right knowledge to meet the demands of the constantly evolving technology and industrial space. This paper investigates industry expectations form graduates of welding and fabrication based on the results of a questionnaire survey from 122 graduates of Welding and Fabrication Engineering Technology of the Petroleum Training Institute Effrun, Nigeria. Data analysis was carried out using the mean item score and factor analysis. Results revealed that graduates are expected to meet the global employability benchmark, competency skills and an appreciable level of safety consciousness. The outcome of this investigation is expected to contribute to the continuous development of the welding and fabrication curriculum in learning and also to meet industry requirements.

Keywords: Education · Employability · Fabrication · Graduates · Industry · Welding

1 Introduction

1.1 Welding and Industry Demands

Welding (joining) and fabrication serves as a very important process and is involved in about 98% of the manufacturing industry activities [18]. Its application can be found in the construction of nuclear and chemical engineering plants, buildings, bridges, offshore installations, pipelines, shipbuilding, aviation, automobile, military hardware, agriculture and domestic appliances. Today's standard of living and quality of life can largely be credited to the evolution and advancement of welding practices which include the use of laser and plasma arc welding processes [7].

© Springer International Publishing AG 2017
T.-C. Huang et al. (Eds.): SETE 2017, LNCS 10676, pp. 269–277, 2017.
https://doi.org/10.1007/978-3-319-71084-6_30

Welding is a process used in joining two or more material parts with the application of heat or pressure or a combination of both heat and pressure to form a permanent homogeneous component [9]. It is generally accepted as the most widely used and cost-effective process of joining metallic sections to produce an assembly in the manufacturing industry [7]. Kannatey-Asibu [3] described welding as an ancient science that has been passed down over the centuries. However, very little is known about the origin of welding because different tribes in various continents used the same basic methods of heating metal in fire to attain a plastic state which makes fusion possible.

Industry in this perspective will be viewed as companies, enterprises and organizations that engage in welding and fabrication practices in one form or the other. The demands includes the personnel, technology and equipment that support welding and its related activities, materials and consumables, labour and skills support services as well as quality control in the form of destructive and non-destructive testing processes. This demand can be found for equipment and personnel in the automobile sector, shipbuilding, power stations and boiler making industries, machinery, metallurgy, construction, chemical, petroleum, transportation and the like.

The success of a company in the new economic era is based on intellectual capital development. Organizations now invest in building competencies, a firm organizational structure and functional customer relationship [13]. However, when businesses have to pay for additional training for their workers, the training cost is reflected in the overall cost of production of goods and services. Secondly, small businesses in need of specialized or skilled workforce cannot afford the cost of retraining which means that employees will only receive the required training that will ultimately benefit the company [4].

A proper control of welding and fabrication operations has positive outcomes in safety, quality and profit and this can best be achieved by an appropriate level of competence in welding technology applications and practices by key personnel involved in operations [14]. On the other hand, mistakes in welding and fabrication can no doubt be catastrophic and cost hundreds of millions of dollars in damage [20]. Additional survey reports shows that it costs 500–600% of the initial cost of welding and fabrication to repair an unacceptable weld during production [14]. It is therefore pertinent for organizations involved in welding and fabrication activities to only engage the services of qualified and competent personnel.

An individual needs to attain a certain level of knowledge for employability. This knowledge should be verifiable, and backed by an official and respected certificate as a proof of capability in the labour market [2]. This knowledge possessed by the individual should also be assessable to the employing company, backed by the company's policy to develop this knowledge to meet evolving trends and achieve future success in the business [2].

Achieving the required training needed for industry personnel development requires some level of cooperation between the industry and educational institutions offering welding training to properly highlight the necessary modules for training because the quality of the end products of welding is seriously dependent on the skill and competence of the welding personnel [17]. Bhaduri et al. [1, p. 396] describes welded joints as the weakest links in structural failures in the industry. To achieve the required quality of weld demands a clear understanding of service requirements and this must be considered during design and fabrication of components [1].

To ensure that welding and fabrication activities in industry are under proper control, it is recommend the strict adherence to competence requirements of ISO 3834 and ISO 14731. The issue of competence in welding and fabrication personnel is, however, the responsibility of welding education providers, manufacturers and the commitment of individuals being trained.

Zuga [19] stresses the need for researchers to focus on the effectiveness of technology education through a dynamic and integrated curriculum research to meet the professional needs of industry. These needs can best be achieved by a systematic approach to collecting and sharing data concerning welding key players and could help towards optimizing the quality of welds, improving design, reducing cost and ultimately creating the required platform for improved research [15].

2 Research Methodology

Respondents through the survey questionnaire were asked to indicate the degree to which they agree on the expectations of industry form welding and fabrication graduates based on a five point Likert scale (strongly agree = 5, agree = 4, neutral = 3, disagree = 2, strongly disagree = 1). One hundred and twenty-two completed questionnaires were returned completed form the one hundred and fifty distributed, and this signified an 80% response rate. Based on the distribution of the respondents, it was observed that the majority of respondents have between five to fifteen years post graduation work experience and also graduated between the year 2000 and 2009.

2.1 Data Analysis

This paper considered the frequencies and descriptive using the mean item score as well as factor analysis. The mean item score was primarily used to determine the strength of the variables based on the respondents perspective. Factor analysis however, reduces the number of variables to a manageable scale by identifying the relationship between variables with the aim of developing theoretical constructs.

2.1.1 Mean Item Score for Industry Expects the Following from Welding and Fabrication Graduates

Table 1 revealed the respondents' perspective concerning industry's expectation from graduates of welding and fabrication in Nigeria. Health and safety consciousness was ranked first with a MIS of 4.36 and SD of .705 while interpret project drawings was ranked second with a MIS of 4.25 and SD of .687; experience in industry welding and fabrication activities with a MIS of 4.21 and SD of .658 was ranked third; technical knowledge related to welding and fabrication was ranked forth with a MIS of 4.20 and SD of .655; ability to do project costing with a MIS of 4.12 and SD of .722 was ranked fifth; ability to identify and operate equipment was ranked sixth with a MIS of 4.11 and SD of .614; evaluate technical bids and tenders with a MIs of 4.09 and SD of .750 was ranked seventh; professional certifications from the American Welding Society

(AWS) was ranked eight with a MIS of 4.08 and SD of .638; ability to assess damages and cost repairs with a MIS of 4.07 and SD of .652 was ranked ninth; prepare technical bids and tenders was ranked tenth with a MIS of 4.02 and SD of .710; professional certifications from The Welding Institute (TWI) UK with a MIS of 4.02 and SD of .596 was ranked eleventh; professional certifications from the International Institute of Welding (IIW) was ranked twelfth with a MIS of 4.02 and SD of .649 and finally automation in welding and fabrication with a MIS of 4.01 and SD of .698 was ranked thirteenth.

Table 1. Results from mean item score

	Mean	Std deviation	Ranking
F13.3 Health and safety consciousness	4.36	.705	1
F13.8 Interpret project drawings	4.25	.687	2
F13.4 Experience in industry welding and fabrication activities	4.21	.658	3
F13.1 Technical knowledge related to welding and fabrication	4.20	.655	4
F13.6 Ability to do project costing	4.12	.722	5
F13.5 Ability to identify and operate equipment	4.11	.614	6
F13.10 Evaluate technical bids and tenders	4.09	.750	7
F13.12 Professional certifications from the American Welding Society (AWS)	4.08	.638	8
F13.7 Ability to assess damages and cost repairs	4.07	.652	9
F13.9 Prepare technical bids and tenders	4.02	.710	10
F13.11 Professional certifications from The Welding Institute (TWI) UK	4.02	.596	11
F13.13 Professional certifications from the International Institute of Welding (IIW)	4.02	.649	12
F13.2 Automation in welding and fabrication	4.01	.698	13

2.2   Factor Analysis

Factor analysis was carried out to reduce the number of variables to a manageable scale by identifying the relationship between variables with the aim of developing theoretical constructs. The factorability of the correlation matrix is examined. A factorability of 0.3 indicates that approximately 30% of the variables share a lot of variance and the test of correlation becomes impractical. To further verify the strength of inter-correlation among selected variables, the Barlett's test of sphericity and the Kaiser-Meyer-Olkin (KMO) measure of sampling adequacy are used [10]. Factors are then extracted by rotation method. In this study the principal component analysis (PCA) was utilized. Furthermore, the criteria for determining factor extraction were considered and in this study the Kaiser's criteria (eigenvalue > 1 rule) was adopted. Average communality of the variables after extraction is as shown below (Table 2).

Table 2. Communalities

Communalities		
	Initial	Extraction
F13.1	.937	.890
F13.2	.861	.718
F13.3	.841	.766
F13.4	.944	.859
F13.5	.960	.824
F13.6	.978	.942
F13.7	.979	.888
F13.8	.929	.874
F13.9	.980	.877
F13.10	.980	.934
F13.11	.963	.754
F13.12	.973	.815
F13.13	.942	.790

Extraction Method: Principal Axis Factoring.

Table 3 shows the KMO value of 0.797 which is >0.5; the Bartlett's test of sphericity has an approximate chi-square value of 2946.294 (considering 95% level of significance, $\alpha = 0.05$) and degree of freedom of 78 and a significant value of 0.00 which is <0.05 [10].

Table 3. KMO and Bartlett's test

KMO and Bartlett's test		
Kaiser-Meyer-Olkin measure of sampling adequacy		.797
Bartlett's test of sphericity	Approx. chi-square	2946.294
	df	78
	Sig.	0.000

Hence, to examine the appropriateness for factor analysis, the Kaiser-Meyer Olkin (KMO) and Bartlett's test measure of sampling adequacy were used. Also the chi-square approximate was 2946.294 with 78 degrees of freedom, which is significant at 0.05 level of significance. The KMO statistic of 0.797 was also appropriate (>0.50). Therefore, factor analysis is considered as an appropriate technique to further analyze data (Table 4).

Commonalties at extraction range between 0.718 and 0.942 which is >0.3, hence valid, according to [10]. Using varimax rotation with Kaiser normalisation, two factors were extracted from thirteen variables used in this study. These two extracted factors

Table 4. Correlation Matrix

Correlation matrix

		F13.1	F13.2	F13.3	F13.4	F13.5	F13.6	F13.7	F13.8	F13.9	F13.10	F13.11	F13.12	F13.13
Correlation	F13.1	1.000	.466	.859	.818	.747	.663	.762	.894	.665	.585	.792	.831	.708
	F13.2	.466	1.000	.548	.643	.788	.801	.707	.599	.750	.835	.476	.463	.766
	F13.3	.859	.548	1.000	.830	.770	.659	.667	.867	.560	.595	.707	.724	.631
	F13.4	.818	.643	.830	1.000	.863	.831	.814	.902	.714	.764	.745	.805	.703
	F13.5	.747	.788	.770	.863	1.000	.865	.808	.817	.734	.787	.739	.695	.803
	F13.6	.663	.801	.659	.831	.865	1.000	.912	.786	.897	.956	.608	.678	.822
	F13.7	.762	.707	.667	.814	.808	.912	1.000	.755	.943	.867	.655	.722	.895
	F13.8	.894	.599	.867	.902	.817	.786	.755	1.000	.682	.725	.752	.801	.672
	F13.9	.665	.750	.560	.714	.734	.897	.943	.682	1.000	.928	.624	.690	.860
	F13.10	.585	.835	.595	.764	.787	.956	.867	.725	.928	1.000	.569	.641	.794
	F13.11	.792	.476	.707	.745	.739	.608	.655	.752	.624	.569	1.000	.931	.619
	F13.12	.831	.463	.724	.805	.695	.678	.722	.801	.690	.641	.931	1.000	.694
	F13.13	.708	.766	.631	.703	.803	.822	.895	.672	.860	.794	.619	.694	1.000

cumulatively explained 84.1% of the variability on the aspect of the study relating to the industry expectations from the graduates of welding and fabrication.

Also, the combined percentages show 86.5% of the total variance before rotation and 84.1% of total variance after rotation, which was sufficient to explain the composite items of these variables.

The following variables that were found to be highly correlated with Factor 1, but negligibly correlated with Factors 2 (see Table 5): Evaluate technical bids and tenders (90.2%), ability to do project costing (86.4%), prepare technical bids and tenders (85.0%), automation in welding and fabrication (80.4%), ability to assess damages and cost repairs (79.0%), professional certifications from the International Institute of

Table 5. Rotated factor matrix[a]

Rotated factor matrix[a]

	Factor	
	1	2
F13.10	**.902**	.347
F13.6	**.864**	.441
F13.9	**.850**	.393
F13.2	**.804**	.266
F13.7	**.790**	.514
F13.13	**.759**	.463
F13.5	**.664**	.619
F13.1	.338	**.881**
F13.12	.369	**.824**
F13.8	.459	**.815**
F13.11	.322	**.806**
F13.3	.356	**.799**
F13.4	.541	**.752**

Extraction Method: Principal Axis Factoring.
Rotation Method: Varimax with Kaiser Normalization.[a]

Table 6. Total variance explained

Factor	Initial eigenvalues			Extraction sums of squared loadings			Rotation sums of squared loadings		
	Total	% of variance	Cumulative %	Total	% of variance	Cumulative %	Total	% of variance	Cumulative %
1	**9.956**	76.581	76.581	9.802	75.400	75.400	5.554	42.725	42.725
2	**1.294**	9.951	**86.533**	1.127	8.668	84.068	5.375	41.343	**84.068**
3	.533	4.097	90.629						
4	.358	2.751	93.380						
5	.303	2.327	95.707						
6	.174	1.339	97.047						
7	.113	.871	97.917						
8	.106	.817	98.734						
9	.082	.633	99.367						
10	.035	.267	99.634						
11	.031	.238	99.872						
12	.010	.079	99.951						
13	.006	.049	100.000						

Extraction Method: Principal Axis Factoring.

Welding (IIW) (75.9%) and ability to identify and operate equipment (66.4%). These variables were thus named: **Global employability and competent ready graduates.**

Also, the following variables based on the factor loading scores were considered as Factor 2, but negligibly correlated with Factors 1 (see Table 5): Technical knowledge related to welding and fabrication (88.1%), professional certifications from the American Welding Society (AWS) (82.4%), interpret project drawings (81.5%), professional certifications from the Welding Institute (TWI) UK (80.6%), health and safety consciousness (79.9%) and experience in industry welding and fabrication activities (75.2%). These variables were thus named: **Standardized certifications and "additional skills"** (Table 6).

3   Discussion of Results

Component 1: Global employability and competent ready graduates.

Based on the responses, industry expects graduates of welding and fabrication to have the ability to evaluate technical bids and tenders and this is closely related to the ability to do project costing as well as ability to assess damages and cost repairs. This can however be described as graduates having the employability skills. Knight and Yorke [6, p. 4] defined employability as "…a set of achievements, skills, understandings and personal attributes that make graduates more likely to gain employment and be successful in their chosen occupations which benefits themselves, the workforce, the community and the economy". The dynamic trends in technology demand the need for students to be readily equipped with the necessary knowledge to fit into employment positions after academic work [5]. According to research findings, internships, part-time employment and related professional association membership are strategies that can be employed by institutions to help improve graduate employability

[5]. This further buttress the advantage of membership and certification with global professional bodies related to welding and fabrication.

Component 2: Standardized certifications and "additional skills".

Based on the responses, technical knowledge related to welding and fabrication as a prerequisite for welding and fabrication graduates cannot be overemphasized. Also the need for global certification has been highlighted in component one above. However, the need for graduates to have the required knowledge of safety consciousness has been describe as the most important aspect of welding and fabrication education [12]. This need is also backed by policies concerning welding and fabrication relate to the health and safety of welding personnel [11], as well as equipment emissions and environmental impacts [16].

4 Conclusion

From the primary data, it is evident that the industry expectations from graduates of welding and fabrication engineering technology are centered on competence and employability skills. The need for safety consciousness can be attributed to the high level of risk and precision associated with welding and fabrication activities. Technical knowledge is also an expectation and the need for global certification body serves as a benchmark to measure competency.

References

1. Bhaduri, A., Albert, S., Ray, S., Rodriguez, P.: Recent trends in repair and refurbishing of steam turbine components. Sadhana **28**(3–4), 395–408 (2003)
2. Hirvonen, L., Veijalainen, E., Orpana, V.: The role of a university in the continuous competence development of Master's level engineers. In: Proceedings of International Conference on Production Research, vol. 19, no. 4, pp. 1–4 (2000)
3. Kannatey-Asibu, E.: Milestone developments in welding and joining processes. J. Manuf. Sci. Eng. **119**(4), 801 (1997)
4. Kerr, A., McDougall, M.: The small business of developing people. Int. Small Bus. J. **17**(2), 10–11 (1999)
5. Kinash, S., Crane, L., Judd, M., Knight, C.: Discrepant stakeholder perspectives on graduate employability strategies. High. Educ. Res. Dev. **35**, 1–17 (2016)
6. Knight, P.T., Yorke, M.: Employability and good learning in higher education. Teach. High. Educ. **8**(1), 3–16 (2003)
7. Linnert, G.E.: Milestones in welding history. In: Welding Metallurgy - Carbon and Alloy Steels, Fundamentals, 4th edn., vol. I. American Welding Society (AWS) (1994)
8. O'Brien, R.L.: Appendix 1: history of welding and cutting. In: Jefferson's Welding Encyclopedia, 18th edn. American Welding Society (AWS Mimi) (1997)
9. O'Brien, R.L.: Welded sculpture. In: Jefferson's Welding Encyclopedia, 18th edn. American Welding Society (AWS Miami) (1997)
10. Pallant, J.: SPSS Survival Manual: A Step by Step Guide to Data Analysis Using SPSS, 3rd edn. Mc-Graw Hill, New York (2007)

11. Pellerin, C., Booker, S.M.: Reflections on hexavalent chromium: health hazards of an industrial heavyweight. Environ. Health Perspect. **108**(9), A402 (2000)
12. Popescu, M., Mocuta, E., Vartolomei, M.: Welding: integrated quality, environment and safely management system. In: Annals of DAAAM & Proceedings, pp. 977–979 (2009)
13. Prahalad, C.K., Hamel, G.: The core competence of the corporation. In: Hahn, D., Taylor, B. (eds.) Strategische Unternehmungsplanung—Strategische Unternehmungsführung. Springer, Heidelberg (2006). https://doi.org/10.1007/3-540-30763-X_14
14. Quintino, L., Ferraz, R., Fernandes, I., Jessop, T.: European welding federation: recent achievements and future challenges In: IIW International Congress in Central and East European Region, 14–16 October 2009, Slovakia, High Tatras, Stará Lesná (2008)
15. Rippey, W.: We need better information connections for welding manufacturing. NIST White paper (2004)
16. Schischke, K., Nissen, N.F., Lang, K.: Welding equipment under the energy-related products directive. J. Ind. Ecol. **18**(4), 517–528 (2014)
17. Smallbone, C.: International system for education, training and qualification of welding personnel. Weld. World **46**, 35–37 (2013)
18. Weman, K.: Metal arc welding with coated electrodes. In: Welding Processes Handbook, pp. 63–67 (2003)
19. Zuga, K.F.: An analysis of technology education in the United States based upon an historical overview and review of contemporary curriculum research. Int. J. Technol. Des. Educ. **7**(3), 203–217 (1997)
20. Mendez, P.F., Eagar, T.W.: Penetration and defect formation in high-current arc welding. Weld. J. **82**(10), 296 (2003)

Benefits of Minimised Wastage in Construction Sites: A Gauteng Province Case Study

Godfey Shai Thaphelo[⊠], Clinton Aigbavboa, and Ohiomah Ifije

University of Johannesburg, Johannesburg, South Africa
godfrey.thaphelo@gmail.com, caigabvaboa@uj.ac.za,
ifije93@gmail.com

Abstract. The construction industry is notorious for its large production of waste and large consumption of energy and natural resources. This has led to tight regulations and a conscious effort by government to make the environment better has led to the construction industry to battle with the scourge of wastage. The causes of this waste stems from design, procurement and amongst other processes involved with the construction project. This study aim to seek the benefits of minimised wastage in construction sites using South Africa as a case study. The data used for this research was from both primary and secondary sources. The secondary sources was from detailed review of related literature. The primary data was gathered through a questionnaire, which was distributed to both registered and non-registered professionals. The statistical approach used for this study was the mean item score, which ranks the questions according to the level of agreement of the respondents. This study revealed that clean and safe environment, avoiding cost over-runs are one of the many benefits of minimising wastage in construction sites. Further discussed was the implications of findings that revealed that the South African construction industry is environmentally driven to better their environment and constant argument on who to bore the cost will be reduced as one of the benefits of minimised wastage in construction sites.

Keywords: Wastage · Construction · Construction sites

1 Introduction

The construction industry is an essential player in the economy of South Africa [1]. The seasonally adjusted real gross domestic product at market prices for the fourth quarter of 2011 increased by an annualized rate of 3.2% during the third quarter of 2011. The formation of projects is thus the principal force in the dynamics of change in the built environment. The construction industry, however, faces some serious challenges in its struggle to deliver infrastructure projects successfully. Construction companies face many problems when delivering construction projects. One of the dominant problems faced by many construction companies is that of material wastage on construction sites and this leads to a loss of profit.

Construction waste has a negative effect on the environs, the increasing generation of construction waste has a major impact on the environment and has stimulated

T.-C. Huang et al. (Eds.): SETE 2017, LNCS 10676, pp. 278–283, 2017.
https://doi.org/10.1007/978-3-319-71084-6_31

increasing public worry in the community at large [2]. With the demands in executing projects, alongside many commercial building and housing projects program, a huge amount of waste is being generated by the construction sector.

Waste minimization, prevention and management are sometimes used interchangeably. Jacobsen and Kristofferson [3] in their report on waste minimization practices in Europe gave a clear distinction between the three concepts and defined waste minimization as a set of three options prioritized according to the waste hierarchy. The first priority is waste prevention, the second is waste reuse and the third priority is waste recycle.

Reducing the waste generated at source is considered as the first option to be implemented for better protection of the environment, and for better economic savings. A review of the literature suggests the following measures as the main solutions for efficient prevention of material waste on construction sites:

Logistics management
It has been the subject of many reports published by the Waste and Resources Action Program in the UK where they emphasize the importance of implementation of a sophisticated Material Logistics Plan on-site for better waste reduction. In fact, logistics management is proven to prevent double handling and ensure the adequate handling of equipment to minimize damage to materials on-site [4].

Supply chain management
It is based on long-term commitment with suppliers and subcontractors and on the win2win arrangements [5]. A good supply chain management can help to achieve just-in-time delivery in order to avoid waste due to long storage or to ordering unneeded materials [5–7].

Modern construction methods
A study published by WRAP (Waste & Resources Action Programme) in January 2007 shows that 'the substitution of some modern methods of construction for traditional building methods resulted in a net reduction in waste levels' [7]. Dainty and Brooke [9] have reported the same finding in their survey of waste minimization measures implemented in the UK; they stated that there is an increased use of off-site prefabrication to control waste and damage on-site.

Training and incentivizing
A number of studies and government guides insist on staff training as one of the first steps in dealing with construction waste. Increasing the awareness could be through using toolbox talks or waste posters about the benefits and rules of waste on-site [10]. In addition, incentives for good performers can contribute to meet the waste targets [11]. Reuse and recycling are usually treated together in the literature. Both these practices require a separation of waste streams in order to be accomplished [12]. In fact, the good practice of waste minimization involves segregation of key waste streams namely: timber, plasterboard, packaging, general waste, inert waste, metal and hazardous by using clearly labelled skips or bins [10]. Once the waste material is segregated, the possibilities of reuse or recycling on-site must be investigated before considering any off-site recovery or disposal [12].

The Aim of this is to determine the benefits of minimised wastage in construction sites in the Gauteng region, South Africa.

1.1 Methodology

The research methodology used for this study is the quantitative methodology; the instrument used to gather the data was the questionnaire survey. A total of one hundred and fifty three was returned out of two hundred representing a 77% return. The statistical approach used to analyse the data gathered was the mean item score.

A five-point Likert scale was used to determine the benefits of minimised wastage in construction; a case of Gauteng South Africa with regards to the identified factors from the reviewed literature. The adopted scales were as follows: 1 = strongly disagree; 2 = Disagree; 3 = Neutral; 4 = Agree and 5 = strongly agreed.

The five-point scale was transformed to mean item score for each variable as assessed by the respondents. The indices were then used to determine the rank of each item. The ranking made it possible to cross compare the relative importance of the items as perceived by the respondents. This method was used to analyse the data collected from the questionnaires survey. The mean item score was calculated for each item as follows;

$$MIS = 1n1 + 2n2 + 3n3 + 4n4 + 5n5 \qquad (1.0)$$

$\sum N$ Where;

N1   = Number of respondents for factor number 1
N2   = Number of respondents for factor number 2
N3   = Number of respondents for factor number 3
N4   = Number of respondents for factor number 4
N   = Total number of respondents.

After the mathematical computations, the factors were then ranked in descending order of their mean item score (from the highest to the lowest).

2 Results

Table 1 reveals the responses from the respondent, on the benefits of minimising wastage in construction waste with having a clean and safe site condition ranked first with a mean of 4.03 and a SD of 0.910; avoid cost overruns was ranked second with a mean of 3.97 and a SD of 0.983; ranked third was avoiding schedule overruns with a mean of 3.96 and a SD of 1.006; protection of the environment was ranked third with a mean of 3.96 and a SD of 0.999; enhancing the image of the company as a green contractor was ranked fifth with a mean of 3.90 and a SD of 0.951; increased profit was ranked sixth with a mean of 3.88 and a SD of 1.028; Furthermore saving cost of disposal and transport was ranked seventh with a mean of 3.88 and a SD of 0.993;

Table 1. Benefits of minimized wastage in construction sites

Heading level	Mean	Standard deviation	Ranking
Clean and safe site condition	4.03	0.910	1
Avoid cost overruns	3.97	0.983	2
Avoid schedule overruns	3.96	1.006	3
Protection of the environment	3.96	0.999	4
Enhancing the image of the company as a green contractor	3.90	0.951	5
Increased profit	3.88	1.028	6
Saving cost of disposal and transport	3.88	0.993	7
Shortened construction time	3.80	1.047	8
Avoid dispute	3.50	1.052	9
Avoid budget over run	3.33	1.141	10

Shortened construction time was ranked eighth with a mean of 3.80 and a SD of 1.047; Avoiding dispute was ranked ninth with a mean of 3.50 and a SD of 1.052; lastly avoiding budget overrun was ranked tenth with a mean of 3.33 and a SD of 1.141.

Also analysed was the reliability of the scale, the cut-off-alpha adopted for this study was 0.70 (Table 2).

Table 2. Theoretical reliabilities

Objectives	No of questions	Cronbach alpha
What are the benefits of minimized wastage in construction sites	10	0.890

3 Findings

In answering the research question on data related to the benefits of minimised wastage in construction sites revealed that clean and safe environment is one of the benefits of minimised waste in construction sites with a MIS of 4.03 and a SD of 0.910; avoidance of cost overrun is one of the benefits of minimised waste in construction sites which was ranked second with a MIS of 3.97 and a SD of 0.983; ranked third is the avoidance of schedule overruns with a MIS of 3.96 and a SD of 1.006 which was ranked third; ranked joint third is the protection of the environment with a MIS of 3.96 and 0.999; enhancing the image of the company as a green contractor was ranked fifth with a MIS of 3.90 and a SD of 0.951.

3.1   Discussion of Findings

Empirical findings from this research question revealed that cleaner and safer condition was ranked as first. This indicates that the health and safety issues in South Africa are more than moderately important for the industry. This is line with findings from [13] who went about observing project sites and found out that there is an increasing interest and awareness in health and safety issues in UAE. The next benefit is the saving cost of disposal and transport, this finding is line with findings from Assem Al-Hajj and Karima Hamani [13] that the cost of disposal of landfill are not very high in the UAE and represent a minimal incentive for material minimisation. Protection of the environment is one of findings from the survey which is not in line with one of the findings of Assem Al-Hajj and Karima Hamani (2011) as in South Africa it is fairly ranked high while which means the environment is cared for as compare to the contractors in the UAE who care less about the environment. Also the image of the company as a green contractor is very important to the South African professionals as they care about the state of their environment as compared to the finding of [13].

3.2   Implications of Findings

From the findings it was revealed that the benefits of minimised wastage in construction sites revealed that the respondents put clean and safe site condition as the topmost of their response as they worry about their environment therefore putting the drive for profit low as seen in the result ad it was ranked sixth. Avoidance of cost over runs and schedule over runs are also seen as benefit of minimising waste in the construction sites. Protection of the environment is also seen as very important for the respondents.

4   Conclusion of Findings

Findings from literature revealed that the many benefits of minimised wastage in construction sites include the following; clean and safe condition, avoiding cost overruns, avoid schedule overruns, protection of the environment, enhancing the image of the company as a green contractor and saving cost of disposal and transport.

Findings from the questionnaire survey results obtained from the respondents revealed clean and safe condition, avoiding cost overruns, avoid schedule overruns, protection of the environment, enhancing the image of the company as a green contractor and saving cost of disposal and transport. Therefore the research objective was met.

For citations of references, we prefer the use of square brackets and consecutive numbers. Citations using labels or the author/year convention are also acceptable. The following bibliography provides a sample reference list with entries for journal articles [1], an LNCS chapter [2], a book [3], proceedings without editors [4], as well as a URL [5].

References

1. Thwala, W.D., Monese, L.N.: Motivation as a tool to improve productivity on the construction site. In: 5th Post Graduate Conference on Construction Industry Development (2006)
2. Shen, L.Y., Tam, V.W.Y.: Implementation of environmental management in the Hong Kong construction industry. Int. J. Project Manag. **20**(7), 535–543 (2002)
3. Jacobsen, H., Kristoffersen, M., Tsotsos, D.: Case Studies on Waste Minimisation Practices in Europe. European Environment Agency, Copenhagen (2002)
4. WRAP: Reducing Material Wastage in Construction, Waste Resources Action Programme, Brandbury (2017)
5. Ofori, G.: Greening the construction supply chain in Singapore. Eur. J. Purch. Supply Manag. **6**(3), 195–206 (2000)
6. Mcdonald, B., Smithers, M.: Implementing a waste management plan during the construction phase of a project: a case study. Constr. Manag. Econ. **16**(1), 71–78 (1998)
7. Chartered Industry of Building: Sustainability and the Construction Industry (2004)
8. Department for the Environment, Food and Rural Affairs: Non-statutory Guidance for Site Waste Management Plans, London (2008)
9. Dainty, A.R.J., Brooke, R.J.: Towards improved construction waste minimisation: a need for improved supply chain integration? Struct. Surv. **22**(1), 20–29 (2004)
10. Waste and Resources Action Program: Reducing Material Wastage in Construction (2007b)
11. Lingard, H., Gilbert, G., Graham, P.: Improving solid waste reduction and recycling performance using goal setting and feedback. Constr. Manag. Econ. **19**(8), 809–817 (2001)
12. CIRIA: Waste Minimisation and Recycling in Construction - A Review, Construction Industry Research and Information Association (CIRIA) Special Publication, London (1995)
13. Al-Kaabi, N., Hadipriono, F.: Construction safety performance in the United Arab Emirates. Civil Eng. Environ. Syst. **20**(3), 197–212 (2003)

Introduction of Construction Experience to the Classroom: What Approaches Should Be Adopted

Aliu John[✉] and Aigbavboa Clinton[✉]

Department of Construction Management and Quantity Surveying,
University of Johannesburg, Johannesburg, South Africa
Ajseries77@gmail.com, caigbavboa@uj.ac.za

Abstract. The present day construction industry is characterized by a wide range of factors influencing it. Factors such as globalization, technological innovations, client base and expectations, increased project based work, amongst others have led to the increased need for higher education to improve their curriculum to adequately prepare graduates to meet the needs of the 21st century construction industry. Construction experiences are known to expose students to various convolutions of construction regarding its challenges, dynamics and limitations. This paper identifies the various approaches of introducing construction experiences into the lecture room in a bid to improve the level of construction pedagogy delivered to future construction professionals. An extant review of literatures was conducted from databases such as Taylor and Francis online, Springer, Emerald, Scopus, ASC conference proceedings amongst others. One of the primary finding stemming from the study revealed that construction site visits/field trips, hosting of guest speakers from the construction industry to deliver lectures and role-playing teaching are some of the key approaches by which HEI's curricula could be improved with construction experiences. Hence, the findings of this paper provides a basis for integrating more construction experiences into HEI curricula to better equip the future employees of the construction industry.

Keywords: Construction education · Construction industry · Higher education institutions · Employability skills · Construction experience

1 Introduction

Transitioning from academia to industry life is never an easy ride; it is like moving from a zone of comfort to a zone of work. Graduates of today step in to their professional stride with high hopes of getting huge motivational rewards based on their academic qualifications and knowledge. It is a well-known fact that construction professionals of today are saddled with the responsibility of developing the built environment which improves the quality of life for any society. Their responsibilities which involves the creation and sustainability of infrastructures through industrial activities has seen their functions in economic development become a vital one. Factors such as the environmental problems, climate changes, technological innovations and

© Springer International Publishing AG 2017
T.-C. Huang et al. (Eds.): SETE 2017, LNCS 10676, pp. 284–294, 2017.
https://doi.org/10.1007/978-3-319-71084-6_32

depletion of natural resources have seen the present day society plagued with various forms of challenges. In solving these problems, there is a growing demand for skilled graduates to provide solutions which intensifies the need for Higher Education Institutions (HEIs) to make conscious efforts in their approach to fortify construction education.

Generally, it is the aim of HEIs through its curricula to improve students understanding of the fundamentals of construction and professional practice through innovative ways of construction pedagogy (Wiezel 2006). Several educators and researchers argue that an early step to prepare the future construction professionals for the industry is to ensure a flexible education that improves the overall quality of the undergraduate programs (Christodoulou 2004; Arcila 2006). Arcila (2006) opines that HEIs are also tasked with ensuring that education delivered to students at the early stage equips them for challenges not just in construction but in other fields. This can be achieved through defining and re-shaping the curriculum of construction education, reviewing the course work and introducing activities that can develop students holistically (Carrato and Haryott 2003). Overtime, the HEIs have been crucial in developing the next generation of construction professionals for societal and economic growth. It has witnessed a paradigm shift which has seen its function as an education provider transcend into a human capital provider as its activities are key in providing competent workforce for the construction industry. This role in enhancing future construction professionals makes it a 'development hub' (Hansen and Lehmann 2006), which further increases the need to examine vital approaches in achieving its functions. Sewell and Dacre Pool (2010) suggested that a major aim of HEIs is to ensure that construction pedagogy is delivered in a way that the gap between industry expectations and the actual abilities of students should be minimal. The introduction of construction activities which heightens classroom experience through student-oriented and project-based learning are key in improving the creativity, innovativeness and curiosity of the students (Lucko 2006).

According to Toor and Ofori (2008), one of the ways in enhancing learning experiences in the classroom is through the effective use of information and communication technology (ICT). An example of this is CIVCAL, a multimedia pedagogical package which is used in Hong Kong to support undergraduate learning in construction education. This online portal enables students to embark on a virtual construction site visit through videographic and photographic application to learn more about ongoing and completed projects. Apart from these innovative functions of ICT, classroom teaching could be complemented by construction site visits, group projects, involvement in research activities and programs, participation in academic symposiums and conferences, introduction of construction courses and international exchanges among HEIs. These pedagogical approaches in improving the learning outcomes of students develops their problem solving skills, communication skills, creativity, decision making skills, leadership and team building skills (Biggs and Tang 2011). Bhattacharjee and Ghosh (2013) further highlights some strategic pedagogical approaches HEIs can employ in facilitating the desired learning outcomes among construction students. They include collaborative teaching, problem-based teaching, peer-tutoring, case study-based teaching, simulation based teaching and involving students in project presentations (Bhattacharjee and Ghosh 2013). Most of these learning approaches improves the students holistically as they actively participate in these activities unlike when compared to conventional teaching approaches (Mayer and Chandler 2001).

From the various aims of the HEIs above in preparing students for the world of work, the need to complement classroom lectures with construction experiences plays a crucial role in upscaling construction education. Kuennen and Pocock (2003) states that construction practices equips the students with a broader understanding of theoretical lectures delivered by construction educators. The benefits of skilled construction graduates cannot be quantified as these key approaches by HEIs provides students with an up-to-date information of the construction industry (Batra 2010). According to Kuennen and Pocock (2003), some of these practical activities includes construction site/field visits, the use of footages and photographs for illustration, practical experiences in lecture rooms, inviting guest speakers from the construction industry amongst others. Other practical activities are team-based projects and class room presentations (Gunhan 2014). These practical activities improves the employability of students for the industry by developing skills such as communication, team work, problem solving, analytical, organizational, leadership, self-confidence amongst others.

In reference to the various approaches in introducing construction experiences to the classroom, this paper argues the importance of revisiting the curricula of HEIs to further improve the holistic education of students. Considering the fact that the future construction graduates are to be engaged in various capacities in design and supervisory roles, this study is germane in helping them succeed in the future of the construction industry. This paper reviews literature from various sources including conference papers, journals and government reports to highlight the importance of such practical activities. With the aid of search engines such as Googlescholar, as well as databases including Taylor and Francis online, Springer, Emerald, Scopus and ASCE, related literatures were key in this review. Therefore, the aim of this paper is to examine the benefits of practical activities that improves the classroom experience for construction students ahead of fitting into the construction industry. This study will lay emphasis on the benefits of construction-site visits, inviting guest speakers from the construction industry into class rooms and role-playing teaching as successful approaches in introducing construction experiences into the classroom.

2 Literature Review

2.1 Construction Site Visits

In enhancing the development of the future construction industry professionals, the inclusion of construction site visits in HEI curricula is key in improving learning experience and developing various skills in students which the industry require (Gunhan 2014). These visits encourages individuals to work in teams which creates a perfect environment to collaborate and learn from each other thereby improving interpersonal and leadership skills. This type of learning acquired through site visits is called 'collaborative learning'. According to Koehn (2001), 'collaborative learning' occurs when individuals act cooperatively with others to become knowledgeable in some specific subject matter. The skills developed during construction site visits are necessary because the present day construction industry thrives on professionals with team building and leadership skills. The importance of these skills were amplified in a study by Ahn et al. (2012) which found out that 'affective competency skills' which comprises collaborative, leadership and interpersonal skills are the most desired by construction industry employers. In today's construction industry, there is an increased importance attached to collaborative skills because projects are becoming highly demanding from a professional point of view. This requires various professionals to work in a team to meet up high expectations of clients or employers. For example, the concept of 'sustainability' which is a major concept requires the collaboration of various experts throughout the life cycle of construction projects. This further requires the close collaboration of key industry players such as the contractors, clients, designers amongst others (Korkmaz 2012).

In broadening the overall pedagogical experience of students, the infusion of construction site visits must be encouraged. Stepping out of the classrooms to construction sites increase students observation, memorizing abilities and real-life experiences as they are exposed to the tangible aspects of construction education. Robertson (2003) pointed out that in achieving the utmost benefits of construction site visits, it is necessary to integrate it into the HEIs curricula and not be an isolated activity. This infers that construction site visits improves construction education as it is vital in providing a real preview into what the industry entails and helps to ease transition from classroom to industry after graduation. These benefits therefore helps students to be proactive as they know what to expect right after graduation. This attribute is critical in construction education, because one of the characteristics of possessing leadership skills is possessing a proactive personality. Findings from various studies including Mason (1980); Gunhan (2014) shows that these visits increases the learning scope of students and are more effective than conventional lectures. The studies also indicates that field visits are good supplementary pedagogical methods which can be used in tandem with other methods to improve learning experiences among students. By providing an opportunity for social interaction, construction site visits facilitates 'learner-centered pedagogy' as highlighted by (Rebar 2009). This aligns with the observation of Martin (2004) that learning during construction site visits develops the student's identity and improves social skills.

From the above benefits of construction site visits, it can be deduced that it is an approach which is instrumental in engaging students with practical issues pertaining to construction. This means that it is crucial for HEIs to introduce it into their curricula to complement course content. According to Arain (2010), a construction program curricula should be designed in such a way to promote activities that could provide project-based learning, active learning and student interaction which points to the need for construction site visits to be instilled. This approach further provides a fascinating, unforgettable and stimulating experience not obtainable during conventional lectures. In improving construction education, Tatum (2010) outlined three different approaches to bolster HEI curricula. They include: traditional/conventional, cooperative/active and integrated learning approaches. Construction site visits are part of the cooperative/ active methods which amplifies the need for its inclusion into the curricula of HEIs (Tatum 2010). By providing students the opportunities to observe various construction processes, construction site visits provide an insight into their professions (Sanromán et al. 2010). This implies that students are further provided with a deeper understanding of the theoretical aspects of construction education when they are exposed to real life industry situation. It is also reinforces concepts learnt during lectures and further stimulates students interest (Forest and Rayne 2009).

2.2   Guest Speakers From Construction Industry in Class Rooms

In further enhancing the lessons taught in classrooms, hosting guest speakers with an ample wealth of experience from the construction industry to share ideas with students plays a key role in improving construction education. They can form a valuable real-world adjunct to lecture room pedagogy in construction which can enhance the overall learning curve of students. Various researchers have stated the benefits of this medium as they can help induce construction interest in students. Miller et al. (2009) states that it provides the students with an up-to-date information of the industry which stimulates them rather than scare them. Payne et al. (2003) also states that guest speakers have the tendency to open the minds of students to various viewpoints around a specific matter which affects the student's perceptions and attitudes in positive ways. During these lectures, talks and occasional visits, guest speakers convey their experiences in a way that would inspire students in readiness for the industry challenges (Schmidt et al. 2008). Through this inspiring talks, guest speakers can act as mentors and provide industry knowledge which generally improves the mind-set and employability of students (Phillips 2002; Hogan 2009).

Apart from making construction related topics come alive, guest speakers from the construction industry are a potential source for enlightening students and helping them realize the essence of their field of study. This was asserted by Robinson and Kaleka (2006) who states that the use of guest speakers from the construction industry is key in fostering an active learning scenario. This approach is seen by various researchers as an 'active learning' alternative using interactive methods of explaining to students the intricacies of their academic disciplines. It is further seen as an instrument in 'spicing' up the lecture room, supplementing other teaching tools such as lectures by educators and providing 'creativity in education' (Robinson and Kaleka 2006; Zdravkovic 2010). Furthermore, the use of guest speakers from the construction industry can lead to networking opportunities for students, as well as provide industry with an avenue to scout for employable students who might meet their expectations.

2.3   The Concept of Role-Playing Teaching

This approach provides students the opportunity to take up different roles of construction project stakeholders in solving real life problems that have been replicated in the classrooms. Bhattacharjee and Ghosh (2013) describes the concept of role-playing teaching as a holistic pedagogical approach that instills the process of critical thinking, prompts emotions and moral values, and informs the students about the world of work. Driscoll (2005) opines that this teaching approach is derived from the idea that knowledge is constructed in individuals by attempting to understand their experiences. This shows that the efficacy of learning experience is ensured through this teaching approach. Learning has been described as a process by which knowledge is obtained through acquired information that can be processed and utilized when necessary. Effective learning transcends conventional read and memorizing activities as it requires a deeper insight of situations and occurrences (Bhattacharjee and Ghosh 2013). In achieving this, the use of drama is vital as the educators not only conveys the subject idea but can also portray a more vivid image of reality to buttress classroom lectures. Cherif et al. (1998) divided role-playing teaching into four stages: preparation and clarification of the activity by the educator; preparation of the activity by the students; role-playing actions to further understand the situation and discussing the entire process. Poorman (2002) posited that these experiential learning activities improves students' understanding of the course contents as their interests are stimulated in the subject matter. This reiterates the assertion made by Fogg (2001) who stresses that students' involvement in role-playing increases their enthusiasm for learning. This can be attributed to the fact that role-playing ensures that students are actively involved in the process of information exchange.

Furthermore, as multiple stakeholders are actively involved in a typical construction project, it is the responsibility of the construction manager to solve arising critical problems that is encountered during supervision. This highlights the importance of role-playing teaching in class rooms as it replicates the real life industry setting as students assume various roles which offers a valuable realistic experience. Therefore, role-playing teaching stimulates an exciting learning experience for students and develop key skills like communication and problem solving. Bhattacharjee and Ghosh (2013) adds that it also trains students to understand real life industry professionals and their roles by placing them in similar roles.

3 Research Methodology

This research study was conducted with reference to extant literatures published in government reports, conference papers and journals articles in order to review the various approaches in introducing construction experiences to classrooms to enhance the quality of future construction professionals. It is noteworthy that various graduate and undergraduate programs instill different knowledge, expertise and skills through the introduction of several activities. Students are trained and engaged with various tasks which are based on their specific career fields. In order to understand the vital approaches, extensive literature searches were carried out over several weeks in June and July 2016, covering the major academic databases including Emerald, Science Direct, ISI Web of Knowledge, ASC, EBSCO, and GoogleScholar. A number of construction education databases distilled includes the Association of Researchers in Construction Management, Associated Schools of Construction conference proceedings (ASC), the European Conference on Education Conference Proceedings, the American Society for Engineering Education (ASEE), Springer, Taylor and Francis Online, Emerald and ICE Virtual Library. In order to develop an initial shortlist of key pedagogical approaches, a preliminary survey of five sources was done- ASC, ASEE, Taylor and Francis Online, ScienceDirect and Emerald which identified a number of key pedagogy approaches from 63 articles/book sections which was relevant to this study. An inclusion/exclusion criteria was then adopted in the preliminary survey which targeted specific approaches that benefits construction students the most. In the second stage of the study, based on a robust literature review and preliminary survey results, a comprehensive skill table was developed to determine which approaches directly stimulates the following skills/attributes construction industry require from graduates. These key areas included: (1) technical skills; (2) communication skills; (3) interpersonal skills; (4) managerial and leadership skills; (5) teamwork skills; (6) critical thinking skills; and (7) problem solving skills. At this stage, it was also decided that only those approaches which stimulates at least 90 percent of the listed skills directly will be included in the review. From the 63 shortlisted articles, the works of Cherif et al. (1998); Poorman (2002); Payne et al. (2003); Robertson (2003); Martin (2004); Miller et al. (2009); Hogan, (2009); Bhattacharjee and Ghosh (2013) and Gunhan (2014) were drawn upon in the study of identifying key approaches in introducing construction experiences into the classroom. From the review of the literatures in this study, HEIs are required to be proactive in their pedagogy approach to improve the quality of the future construction professionals.

4 Benefits of Introducing Construction Experience to Classroom

From the various literatures reviewed, the following benefits can be deduced:

- The activities encourages students to utilize higher order thinking skills.
- They help students to apply what they have learned in other subject areas.
- The activities encourages brain-storming, creativity, problem solving and innovation among students.
- They help to facilitate cooperative learning and teamwork among students.
- The activities are engaging, stimulating and motivating.
- Helps students to understand better what is difficult in textbooks.

5 Lessons Learnt

From the reviewed literature, the scope of the construction industry have increased and have become multi-disciplinary in nature with the effect of inventions and innovations making it dynamic. This implies that construction professionals have to be more aware of the environmental and social impacts of technology, and be prepared to work in complex teams to solve arising industry challenges. One of the pedagogical approaches identified was the introduction of site visits into the HEI curricula. From a broad viewpoint, it has been identified as a major collaborative learning experience for students. The experience garnered from this visits exposes the students to the requirements and rigors of the construction industry. For example, by embarking on a to a visit to mechanical factory, construction students are provided with a hands-on-equipment experience which reinforces the theoretical aspect of the lectures acquired in the classroom which improves their learning process. Similarly, by visiting an on-going construction site, students are provided the opportunity to interact with various construction professionals and seek clarifications where necessary. Students can also be furnished with a proper understanding of site drawings, project documents, schedules, bills amongst others which can broaden their holistic understanding of the construction industry and its activities. In summary, construction site visit is an integral part of construction education as it helps bridge the gap between the lecture room and the construction industry. Several literatures Robertson (2003); Kuennen and Pocock (2003); Rebar (2009) and Gunhan (2014) all gave various benefits of construction site/field visits and they are summarized below:

- Helps students to learn new concepts in thinking
- Improves articulation and communication skills among students
- Improves cooperation and interaction among students thereby boosting teaming skills
- Broadens the mindset of students
- Improves their problem solving skill as they are faced with real-life situations and tasks
- Encourages creativity and inventiveness among students
- Helps to discover students personality as they are exposed
- Helps students to easily focus and memorize factual information
- Provides a break from the usual lecture room setting
- Exposure to a variety of other related construction professions
- Helps students to appreciate the importance and relevance of the lecture room
- Helps improve critical thinking skills and tolerance among students

Literature also examined the benefits of HEIs inviting guest speakers to lecture room as another key approach in introducing construction experience into their curricula. The benefits of guest speakers from industry also enhances student learning as well as improved collaborations between the HEIs/industry and industry/community. Various literatures highlights that the invitation of guest speakers to classrooms provides the opportunity for students to ask real-time industry questions. Guest speakers from industry also give a different perspective of issues which provides students with a variety of possible ideas. Finally, through discussions, guest speakers can inspire students which is key in building their self-confidence ahead of working in the construction industry.

Finally, due to the construction industry complexities and involvement of multiple stakeholders in the successful completion of construction projects, role-playing can be an effective pedagogical approach. By playing the roles of different industry stakeholders, students are actively engaged which improves their skills and creates a wonderful pedagogical experience.

6 Conclusions

The construction industry is continually evolving as a result of new trends, technologies and improved delivery methods which increases the need for adequately prepared construction graduates. Despite the importance of technical skills and acumen, industry employers today are seeking graduates with good communication, leadership, interpersonal and collaborative skills. These skills cannot be fully acquired from conventional lectures but from key teaching approaches which necessitates the reason for this study. This paper contributed to the body of knowledge by examining various pedagogical approaches in introducing construction experience into the classroom in a quest to develop better graduates for the construction industry. A review of extant literature was undertaken to explore these approaches. The studies revealed that an integral part of construction pedagogy is the introduction of construction site visits in HEI curricula. These visits helps to improve their communicative, technical, leadership, team building and critical thinking skills. In developing a clear link between classroom and the industry, the students are enhanced as they value the thrill of reality. The study also revealed that hosting of guest speakers from the industry plays a key role in construction pedagogy. This approach has the tendency to broaden the industry horizon of students, enhance their learning curve and provide a source of inspiration and mentorship for them. Students are also provided with the latest industry information through this teaching approach. Further findings revealed that role-playing teaching provides a great opportunity for students to be actively involved as they assume roles of various industry project stakeholders in a replicated classroom setting. This approach improves their creativity, problem solving, communication, decision making skills and critical thinking skills. It is therefore recommended that HEIs ensure that the future construction professionals are engaged in the role-playing teaching approach since the theoretical knowledge taught will be transferred to the practical field someday. These approaches discussed in this study are extremely beneficial to construction students, but their implementation is completely dependent on the HEIs and its educators.

References

Ahn, Y.H., Annie, R.P., Kwon, H.: Key competencies for US construction graduates: industry perspective. J. Prof. Issues Eng. Educ. Pract. **138**(2), 123–130 (2012)

Arain, F.M.: Construction Research Congress. Conference Proceedings of the Xth Conference Held in Y (2010)

Arcila, J.L.: Proceedings: CIB W107 International Symposium on Construction in Developing Economies: New Issues and Challenges. Conference Proceedings of the Xth Conference Held in Y (2006)

Batra, J.: Knowledge management: emerging practices in IT industry in NCR. IUP J. Knowl. Manag. **8**(1/2), 57 (2010)

Bhattacharjee, S., Ghosh, S.: ASC Annual International Conference Proceedings, Associated Schools of Construction. Conference Proceedings of the Xth Conference Held in Y (2013)

Biggs, J.B., Tang, C.: Teaching for Quality Learning at University: What the Student Does. McGraw-Hill Education, New York City (2011)

Carrato, P., Haryott, R.: Building leaders of a global society. J. Prof. Issues Eng. Educ. Pract. **129**(3), 125–128 (2003)

Cherif, A.H., Verma, S., Somervill, C.: From the Los Angeles zoo to the classroom: transforming real cases via role-play into productive learning activities. Am. Biol. Teach. 613–617 (1998)

Christodoulou, S.: Educating civil engineering professionals of tomorrow. J. Prof. Issues Eng. Educ. Pract. **130**(2), 90–94 (2004)

Driscoll, M.P.: Psychology of Learning for Instruction (2005)

Fogg, P.: A history professor engages students by giving them a role in the action. Chron. High. Educ. **48**(12) (2001)

Forest, K., Rayne, S.: Thinking outside the classroom: integrating field trips into a first-year undergraduate chemistry curriculum. J. Chem. Educ. **86**(11), 1290 (2009)

Gunhan, S.: Collaborative learning experience in a construction project site trip. J. Prof. Issues Eng. Educ. Pract. **141**(1), 04014006 (2014)

Hansen, J.A., Lehmann, M.: Agents of change: universities as development hubs. J. Clean. Prod. **14**(9), 820–829 (2006)

Hogan, C.: Making the most of visiting speakers (for everyone involved). Train. Manag. Dev. Methods **23**(4), 371 (2009)

Koehn, E.: Assessment of communications and collaborative learning in civil engineering education. J. Prof. Issues Eng. Educ. Pract. **127**(4), 160–165 (2001)

Korkmaz, S.: Case-based and collaborative-learning techniques to teach delivery of sustainable buildings. J. Prof. Issues Eng. Educ. Pract. **138**(2), 139–144 (2012)

Kuennen, S.T., Pocock, J.B.: Construction Research 2003, ASCE Conference Proceedings. Conference Proceedings of the Xth Conference Held in Y (2003)

Lucko, G.: 2nd Specialty Conference on Leadership and Management in Construction. Conference Proceedings of the Xth Conference Held in Y (2006)

Martin, L.M.: An emerging research framework for studying informal learning and schools. Sci. Educ. **88**(S1), S71–S82 (2004)

Mason, J.L.: Annotated bibliography of field trip research. Sch. Sci. Math. **80**(2), 155–166 (1980)

Mayer, R.E., Chandler, P.: When learning is just a click away: does simple user interaction foster deeper understanding of multimedia messages? J. Educ. Psychol. **93**(2), 390 (2001)

Miller, B.K., Bell, J.D., Palmer, M., Gonzalez, A.: Predictors of entrepreneurial intentions: a quasi-experiment comparing students enrolled in introductory management and entrepreneurship classes. J. Bus. Entrepr. **21**(2), 39 (2009)

Payne, B.K., Sumter, M., Sun, I.: Bringing the field into the criminal justice classroom: field trips, ride-along, and guest speakers. J. Crim. Justice Educ. **14**(2), 327–344 (2003)

Phillips, C.R.: Allied Academies International Conference. Academy of Educational Leadership Proceedings. Conference Proceedings of the Xth Conference Held in Y. Jordan Whitney Enterprises, Inc. (2002)

Poorman, P.B.: Biography and role playing: fostering empathy in abnormal psychology. Teach. Psychol. **29**(1), 32–36 (2002)

Rebar, B.M.: Evidence, explanations, and recommendations for teachers' field trip strategies (2009)

Robertson, A.M.: A case study in collaboration in science education [electronic resource]: integrating informal learning experiences into the school curriculum (2003)

Robinson, C.F., Kakela, P.J.: Creating a space to learn: a classroom of fun, interaction, and trust. Coll. Teach. **54**(1), 202–207 (2006)

Sanromán, M., Pazos, M., Longo, M.: Efficient planning and assessment of field site visits in science and engineering undergraduate studies. In: EDULEARN 2010 Proceedings, pp. 1839–1843 (2010)

Schmidt, S., Ralph, D., Buskirk, B.: The effective marketing class: enhancing student learning. J. Am. Acad. Bus. **13**(2), 52–57 (2008)

Sewell, P., Dacre Pool, L.: Moving from conceptual ambiguity to operational clarity: employability, enterprise and entrepreneurship in higher education. Educ. Train. **52**(1), 89–94 (2010)

Toor, S.R., Ofori, G.: In quest of leadership in the construction industry: new arenas, new challenges (2008)

Tatum, C.B.: Proceedings of the Construction Research Congress (CRC), Banff, Canada. Conference Proceedings of the Xth Conference Held in Y (2010)

Wiezel, A.: Proceedings of the 2nd Specialty Conference on Leadership and Management in Construction. Conference Proceedings of the Xth Conference Held in Y. PM Publishing Louisville, CO. (2006)

Zdravkovic, N.: Spicing up information literacy tutorials: interactive class activities that worked. Public Serv. Q. 6(1), 48–64 (2010)

SpeL (International Workshop on Social and Personal Computing for Web-Supported Learning Communities)

A Platform for Developing and Maintaining Competences in PBL Supervision

Dorina Gnaur[1] and Hans Hüttel[2(✉)]

[1] Department of Learning and Philosophy, Aalborg University,
Aalborg, Denmark
dg@learning.aau.dk
[2] Department of Computer Science, Aalborg University, Aalborg, Denmark
hans@cs.aau.dk

Abstract. One of the emerging challenges in academia is that of developing and maintaining teaching qualifications in a setting where teaching staff is often temporary and with diverse backgrounds. At Aalborg University, project-organized problem-based learning is at the heart of all degree programmes and supervision within this format has particular challenges. We propose a crowd-sourcing approach to developing teaching competence within this format. PBL Exchange is a question/answer-based platform that is currently being rolled out to help teaching staff share and discuss their experiences as project supervisors.

1 Introduction

A major challenge in providing high-quality learning at universities is that of developing professional competence for the teaching staff, and here it is essential to be able to capture and maintain the experience and expertise that are the results of teaching practice. At Aalborg University problem-based learning (PBL) is at the heart of all degree programmes in the form of problem-based projects carried out by groups of students, and it has often turned out to be a challenge to ensure that the competencies related to this particular approach to university pedagogy do not wither away.

Maintaining good teaching practice at a PBL university. An illustrative example of this is that of the changes that occurred to the examination of projects at Aalborg University. From the inception of the university in 1974 to 2007, projects were assessed via group-based oral exams. However, this form of oral exam was explicitly banned by the Danish government in 2007. When the ban was lifted in 2011 and group-based project exams re-introduced, a generation of students and teaching staff had emerged with no knowledge of and a large amount of scepticism towards an examination practice that had been at the core of PBL practice for a long time [3]. It became a major task to re-create good project exam practice and to ensure that it would be maintained.

In a previous paper we have argued [4] that one of the dangers of a lack of reflection and explicit maintenance of good teaching practice is that ritualization may set in: supervision practice and student projects can become rituals that live up to the official requirements but lose touch with the actual problem-based approaches to learning.

© Springer International Publishing AG 2017
T.-C. Huang et al. (Eds.): SETE 2017, LNCS 10676, pp. 297–303, 2017.
https://doi.org/10.1007/978-3-319-71084-6_33

A further challenge is that there is now a large throughput of temporary teaching staff with short academic careers and little teaching experience. Many of these members of staff come to see the role as project supervisor as an isolated one and end up thinking that the problems that they face are theirs alone. Moreover, an increasing percentage of temporary teaching staff (as well as a sizeable fraction of the permanent staff) have no previous exposure to PBL as practiced at Aalborg University, while it is often tacitly taken for granted that anyone can supervise student projects.

Aalborg University offers courses on PBL supervision for teaching staff, and there is a large body of literature on PBL practice available from the local PBL Academy [12] that is being used for competence development in these courses and can be consulted. However, the sources are often not based in current experience but are either normative descriptions of how PBL should be carried out or retrospective studies.

Developing teaching practice via crowdsourcing. Crowdsourcing is now advocated as a powerful strategy for mobilizing creative knowledge development and problem-solving [5] and as an approach to peer learning [14, 15]. So far there has been little research on how to apply this approach in the area of competence development. The focus appears to be on competence development in non-academic organizations (see e.g. [6]). Our hypothesis is that crowdsourcing can make it easy to bring to light the challenges that arise for teaching staff as they happen, can be used to develop professional competencies for teaching in higher education and can supplement the existing body of knowledge on PBL.

In this paper we describe our development of and ongoing experiences with PBL Exchange, a web site whose goal is to facilitate the transfer and development of competences with the field of PBL project supervision by means of a web-based crowdsourcing approach that makes it easy to exchange one's experiences with project supervision. PBL Exchange should be thought of as a *closed expert crowdsourcing* forum in the sense that experts are guiding other experts towards solving the problems that they have: The users of the system will all be project supervisors at Aalborg University.

2   Crowdsourcing as Knowledge Generation

Crowdsourcing is a form of collaborative user-generated creation of knowledge made possible by the World Wide Web. The term itself was initially used in the context of product development by companies [1, 5]. but it now also describes a strategy for general knowledge development and exchange. A particularly well-known example is that of Wikipedia [19].

Following Stonebraker and Zhang [16], we distinguish between two dimensions in crowdsourcing: Strategies can be *open* and *closed* – i.e. they can apply to an open community or to a limited, well-defined one. Moreover, one can speak of *course* and *expert-based* crowdsourcing; the former appeals to a wide community, whereas the latter limits itself to experts within the problem domain.

From a learning and (professional) development perspective, crowdsourcing expertbased exchanges, including wikis, are used to facilitate virtual collaborative learning. This strategy of Computer-Supported Collaborative Learning evolved in the 1990s as a means to help educators seize the possibilities offered by the new technologies in facilitating online learning by using a collaborative approach. Central notions here are those of peer interaction and the sharing and building of knowledge and expertise among virtual groups or communities of learners [10]. In this setting, learning is learner-centered, investing participants with equal rights and responsibility for the mutually shared learning objectives [9].

There are now several examples of uses of crowdsourcing in educational settings. Crowdsourcing approaches are often problem-based and demand-driven and take the form of question/answer-based fora. In a formal Danish educational context, VIA University College runs VIA Connect [18] which is a customized crowdsourced platform featuring challenge scenarios produced in collaboration with external stakeholders that invite students to present their solutions.

StackExchange [7] has over the past few years become recognized as an important means of establishing crowd-sourced knowledge in a question/answer-based format and with a large user community. StackExchange fora cover a wide variety of subject areas; they are open and expert-based and are becoming increasingly popular with students in higher education as well as with professionals [17]. At their heart is a *gamification* principle: Any user can pose a question and other users can now answer the question. The community can upvote or downvote questions as well as answers or comment on questions and answers. Answers of particular importance can be added to a special community wiki.

At present, fairly little is known about how crowdsourcing can be used in the context of competence development. An example of related work is that of King [8] who studied how social media such as Facebook and virtual communities that arise in these settings can shape the professional development of a mental health therapist. In the setting of higher education, Coto Chotto and Dirckinck-Holmfeld [2] describe how teachers across geographically dispersed local campuses at the National University of Costa Rica can form communities to help them develop their teaching competences with the aid of the virtual community UNA-Virtual.

3   The PBL Exchange Platform

Since the PBL Exchange platform is aimed at a well-defined target group, namely the teaching staff at Aalborg University, we are dealing with a closed and expert-based approach. Moreover, in a PBL setting we find it natural to focus on problems and the search for solutions to them; our approach is therefore inspired by StackExchange [7].

For the PBL Exchange platform we have decided to use Question2Answer [13] as our outset; this is an open-source piece of software written in PHP and using a mySQL database. Question2Answer already supports quite a few of the features that we consider important. In particular, it is easy to support a categorization of questions, and here we have decided to shape the pre-defined categories based on the understanding of PBL common to Aalborg University [12] with categories such as *Problem analysis*, *Group formation*, *Cooperation within the project group* and *Assessment*. Users can tag their questions to provide a classification is orthogonal to that of the pre-defined categories.

Question2Answer also already supports a kind of gamification in the form of a reputation-based voting system similar to that used by StackExchange. Questions and answers can be upvoted and downvoted, and users are then ranked wrt. their privileges according to how many points they receive.

While several aspects of Question2Answer can therefore be reused, other aspects have had to be adopted and added to the software. Most importantly, the PBL Exchange system must be able to interface with other systems related to teaching activities at Aalborg University. Here, the main platform is that of Moodle [11], and the common gateway to Moodle and to other web-based services is that of a single sign-on feature that enables a user to log on to several services through a common entry point.

Our initial version of PBL Exchange became operational in the autumn of 2016. A screenshot can be seen in Fig. 1.

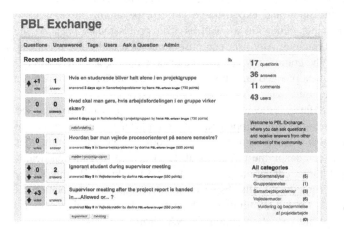

Fig. 1. Screenshot of the PBL Exchange platform

A feature currently being developed is that of multilingual support. This is a natural requirement in a university setting with staff members of many nationalities and one, in which both Danish and English are widely used. This is already handled at the level of reserved keywords (such as menu headings) but must also be dealt with at the level of content and in tagging. We have chosen to use the machine translation service offered by Google Translate to auto-translate questions and answers.

We will also extend the gamification aspect further by a notion of challenges within PBL Exchange, inspired by StackExchange. The challenges represent particularly "wicked" problems within project-organized PBL, that is, problems with no definite solution. Examples are group formation and handling different roles in supervision.

4   Experiences

The present version of PBL Exchange is a prototype version that has been rolled out to a small community that we deemed to be receptive, and the next version, to be introduced to a much larger community of teaching staff in the autumn of 2017, will take the initial user experience into account.

A survey of the first version. During the initial phase we involved a total of 40 test users and have asked them to evaluate their experience with PBL Exchange in the form a mixed quantitative/qualitative survey. We have sought to involve a diverse set of users from several faculties with both experienced and less experienced supervisors. In particular we have targetted the participants of the pedagogical course that is mandatory for junior lecturers at Aalborg University.

To start with, we wanted to know whether the users found PBL-Exchange useful, so far. The responses reveal that this is indeed the case. See Fig. 2.

How useful do you find the present version of PBL Exchange?

14 responses

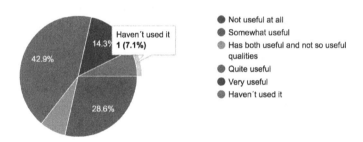

Fig. 2. Responses to: *How useful do you find the present version of PBL Exchange?*

One user writes

Of cause [sic] the answers are nice and I have tried to implement several answers into my supervision. Besides, it's nice to know that other people are having the same questions, challenges etc.

We asked the question *How could we get more people to contribute to PBL Exchange?* and the following reply in the survey is typical.

Maybe through integration in existing systems, e.g. notifications when logging onto Moodle. [...] When a new system is introduced, it must fit in as seamless as possible (i.e. limited disturbance of existing work processes and habits), it must also be stated from up the hiearachy that this system is to be used.

It turns out that a particular concern, that we did not foresee, is one of anonymity both for questions and for answers. This may be related to the fact that there seems be a particular interest in problems related to collaboration, as these will often involve person-sensitive issues.

Taking PBL Exchange to the wider community. Based on our initial, small-scale survey involving the first, prototype version PBL Exchange is currently being revised and as users in the initial survey point out, a particular challenge is that there are several other systems relating to teaching activities at Aalborg University. Another is to ensure that PBL Exchange will become widely used and accepted.

Every semester the boards of studies at Aalborg University appoint a semester coordinator for each semester class within every degree programme. A coordinator should be a project supervisor at the semester and must discuss issues related to project supervision with their supervisor colleagues. Our next step is therefore to integrate PBL Exchange into the practice of semester coordinators.

This integration will involve Moodle, since this system as used at Aalborg University organizes its content following the way degree programmes are organized, that is, according to schools, study boards and semesters. For instance, the 4th semester of the undergraduate programme in computer science is found under the Study board of Computer Science within the School of Information and Communication Technology.

In order to use help users of our crowdsourcing platform, PBL Exchange will therefore be re-organized using the same structure, such that users can visit PBL Exchange directly from Moodle and such that PBL Exchange offers a collection of sub-fora with the same classification as that used by Moodle. Moreover, which subfora will be accessible to a user will be determined by which of the corresponding semesters and schools are available to the user on Moodle. At the implementation level this requires a fairly low-level interaction using the Moodle API; the use of school- and semester-specific sub-fora can be achieved by using specific tags.

A longer-term effort will be to integrate PBL Exchange into the current competence development activities, including the pedagogical course for assistant professors at Aalborg University, such that teaching staff can use it for continuing their competence development.

5 Conclusions and Further Work

In this paper we have presented the PBL Exchange platform and our work in the first phase of introducing the platform. PBL Exchange is a step towards the development of professional competences in the area of PBL project supervision by means of crowdsourcing. To the best of our knowledge, this is a new application of the principle.

The work on developing PBL Exchange is continuing. Many of the software development issues point toward this leading to a new, restructured version of the Question2Answer codebase. At the level of applications to competence development, an important task is that of ensuring that PBL Exchange will be taken up by the teaching staff at Aalborg University and continue to be used.

A further development will be one of using PBL Exchange as a basis for similar fora at other higher education institutions that use forms of problem-based learning. In particular, there are now universities in several countries that take up forms of PBL similar to that used at Aalborg University; we belive that the PBL Exchange platform can be of particular value in settings where a new teaching practice is to be built from the ground up.

Acknowledgements. The work on PBL Exchange described here is funded by an Aalborg University grant for developing PBL practice.

References

1. Brabham, D.C.: Crowdsourcing as a model for problem solving: an introduction and cases. Converg.: Int. J. Res. New Media Technol. **14**(1), 75–90 (2008)
2. Coto Chotto, M., Dirckinck-Holmfeld, L.: Facilitating communities of practice in teacher professional development, vol. 1, pp. 54–60. Lancaster University (2008)
3. Dahl, B., Kolmos, A.: Students' attitudes towards group based project exams in two engineering programmes. J. Probl. Based Learn. High. Educ. **3**(2), 62–79 (2016)
4. Gnaur, D., Huttel, H.: If PBL is the answer, then what is the problem? J. Probl. Based Learn. High. Educ. (2017, to appear)
5. Howe, J.: The rise of crowdsourcing. Wired **14**(6) (2006). http://www.wired.com/wired/archive/14.06/crowds.html
6. Jayanti, E.: Open sourced organizational learning: implications and challenges of crowdsourcing for human resource development (HRD) practitioners. Hum. Resour. Dev. Int. **15**(3), 375–384 (2012)
7. Keller, J.: Stack overflow's crowdsourcing model guarantees success. The Atlantic, 18 November 2010
8. King, K.: Professional learning in unlikely spaces: social media and virtual communities as professional development. Int. J. Emerg. Technol. Learn. (iJET) **6**(4), 40–46 (2011)
9. Lehtinen, E.: Computer supported collaborative learning: an approach to powerful learning environments. In: De Corte, E., Verschaffel, L., Entwistle, N., Van Merriboer, J. (eds.) Unraveling Basic Components and Dimensions of Powerful Learning Environments, pp. 35–53. Elsevier, Amsterdam (2003)
10. Lipponen, L.: Exploring foundations for computer-supported collaborative learning. In: Proceedings of the Conference on Computer Support for Collaborative Learning: Foundations for a CSCL Community, CSCL 2002, pp. 72–81. International Society of the Learning Sciences (2002)
11. Moodle. https://moodle.org
12. The Problem-Based Learning Academy at Aalborg University. http://www.pbl.aau.dk
13. Question2Answer - Free Open Source Q&A Software for PHP. http://www.question2answer.org/
14. Rice, S., Gregor, M.N.: E-Learning and the Academic Library: Essays on Innovative Initiatives. McFarland, Incorporated Publishers, Jefferson (2016)
15. Stonebraker, I., Zhang, T.: Crowdsourcing reference help: using technology to help users help each other. Libraries Faculty and Staff Scholarship and Research (2015)
16. Stonebraker, I., Zhang, T.: Participatory culture and e-learning. In: Rice, S., Gregor, M.N. (eds.) E-Learning and the Academic Library: Essays on Innovative Initiatives, pp. 201–213. McFarland, Jefferson (2016)
17. Vasilescu, B., Capiluppi, A., Serebrenik, A.: Gender, representation and online participation: a quantitative study of stackoverflow. In: 2012 International Conference on Social Informatics, pp. 332–338, December 2012
18. VIA University College: VIA Connect (2017). http://www.viaconnect.dk
19. Wikipedia. https://www.wikipedia.org/

Website Analysis in the Context of Practicing Geography: From First Impression to Recommendation – Case Study

Miloslava Cerna(✉)

University of Hradec Králové,
Rokitanského 62, 500 03 Hradec Králové, Czech Republic
Miloslava.cerna@uhk.cz

Abstract. The paper deals with the interdisciplinary field of developing geography knowledge and digital competences in university students via usability testing of geography websites by students themselves. The paper brings description of the process of website analysis from first impression, through specially tailored tasks, evaluation based on the level of satisfaction to the final recommendations. Suitability and potential pitfalls of incorporation of such an innovative didactic method into the educational process of Cultural Studies subject of Tourism management is discussed.

Keywords: Geography · Games · Website analysis · Satisfaction · Motivation · Case study

1 Introduction

The 'endless' Internet provides space for unlimited amount of both professional and unprofessional websites from various areas. Usability testing of websites serves predominantly for commercial purposes. User's satisfaction with the web design together with their ability to smoothly and quickly grasp offered functions of the site has crucial influence on user's behaviour [1].

In this paper the issue of usability testing is presented from different perspective, as a beneficial educational tool. This study discusses an innovative didactic approach where university students of Tourism Management Bachelor study programme explore recommended websites via running usability tests within the subject Africa and India Cultural studies and its e-learning supportive course. Individual chapters of the e-course are accompanied with a set of sources. The approach which is here presented as a potential way of websites exploration is shown on two educational websites comprising geography games. Links to these websites are placed in the first chapter of the e-course on geography of Africa; see Fig. 1 which brings the authentic print-screen from the e-course. The website analysis was run through individual stages of the completion of the assessment form on usability testing from the first impression to user satisfaction. The website analysis was enriched with a follow-up discussion dealing with findings and further implications.

© Springer International Publishing AG 2017
T.-C. Huang et al. (Eds.): SETE 2017, LNCS 10676, pp. 304–313, 2017.
https://doi.org/10.1007/978-3-319-71084-6_34

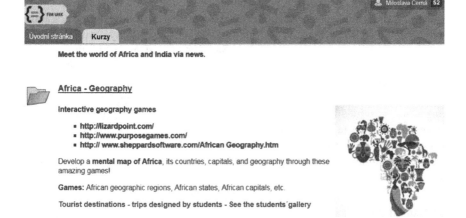

Fig. 1. E-course - entry to geography

The paper is divided into following chapters: Methodological background encompassing entry into usability testing, history on usability testing within English language classes in brief at the Faculty Informatics and Management, University of Hradec Kralove, literature review with definitions of key usability phenomena, objectives and research questions, description of the applied method and accessible research sample, the core chapters are Findings and Conclusion with practical implications.

2 Methodological Frame

Usability evaluation issue plays its distinctive role in various corners of our everyday lives. Web usability has been developed since the Internet beginnings in the 1990s; the time of recognized fame is connected with the renowned web design and usability engineering authority Nielsen [2]. Out of a long queue of Nielsen's followers Hodgson [3] might be mentioned, his approach is simplified and more explanatory. Completely different approach to usability testing was worked out by Gerardo Martinez in his blog. Usability testing is perceived as a medical examination, the author works with hyperbole. Martinez uses formal 'written usability reports' and 'audio think aloud recordings' as tools of usability testing. He found out that written reports which were in structured manner didn't correspond to the rather chaotic think aloud recordings. He diagnosed the problem in testers' focus on particulars [4]. A deep insight into the last decade contributions on Web site usability is brought by a review of 199 studies aiming to identify the trends in this field. User-based usability Evaluation Methods were applied in most studies, a questionnaire and usability testing domineered [5]. An inspirational study fitting our purposes was the mixed-method approach to elaboration of analysis procedure by Raban et al. [6]. The stages of their study were: identification of needs, identification of websites, assessment of website content and user testing of websites including qualitative interviews. The other influential paper corresponding to our research was the paper dealing with usability assessment of the library website [7]. This study approaches website usability assessment strictly following the traditional principles stated by Nielsen [2, 8] not omitting any of the usability attributes Usefulness, Efficiency, Effectiveness, Learnability, Satisfaction and Accessibility.

As for our research, *usability*, *utility* and *usefulness* are 3 key terms that represent the quality attributes. Usability assesses how easy user interfaces are to use. Utility refers to the design's functionality. Usability and utility are sides of one coin determining whether something is useful [9]. Out of five quality components three were incorporated into the research: *Learnability*: How easy is it for users to accomplish basic tasks the first time they encounter the design?, *Efficiency*: Once users have learned the design, how quickly can they perform tasks?, *Satisfaction*: How pleasant is it to use the design?

2.1   State of Art

Usability testing in this study is another try of scholars to get students involved into the study process, to provide them with a new technique which combines development of a subject knowledge and mastering computer competence. The implementation of usability testing method at the Department of Applied Languages has ten years old history, originally it started by testing of English websites by secondary and tertiary English language teachers and English foreign language (EFL) students within a wide project on analysis of web language educational sites and their services with focus on navigation and ease of use [10]. Two years ago this method of exploration of selected websites based on students' need analysis was conducted with all students of Professional English language subject at the Faculty of Informatics and Management, University Hradec Králové. Practicing of website exploration via usability testing proved to be beneficial with students of computer studies [11].

A follow up stage of the research is presented in this paper. The specific user testing method has been implemented into the subject that ranks into the Tourism Management field of study which isn't purely information one so that different perceptions and different approach from students might have been expected. The paper aims to evaluate the usability of two educational websites. The websites were selected to fit the needs of the geography chapter in the Cultural studies subject. Usability testing of geography websites is a multimethod approach. It comprises development of geography knowledge, language competences and computer literacy.

2.2   The Goal and Sub-goal

The objective of the study is to describe individual phases of the whole assessment process of one of two selected geography educational websites called Lizard Point and Purpose Games in detail according to time-proven Usability Testing with Five Users method [8, 12]. This testing is supposed to reveal potential pitfalls which could be detected so that user testing of websites by students of Tourism management could be adapted accordingly to reflect needs and abilities of students with different computer competences, with different experience and behaviour.

The sub-goal is to compare the outcomes and determine suitability of incorporation of websites into the process of education and define possible modifications in the content and structure of usability forms.

The discussion raises questions relating to adaptation of user-testing forms, selection and a number of analyzed websites.

2.3   Research Sample, Research Area, Research Questions, Stages of the Research

Research sample consisted of full-time students of the Tourism management Bachelor study programme attending Cultural studies of Africa and India subject in summer semester 2017. The age span was 20 to 22 years. Five usability forms assessing Lizard Point website and five forms testing Lizard Point website are analyzed in this study.

Usability testing with Five users' is based on Five users who are able to detect more than 78% of information about usability of the design, more users generate small amount of new data [12].

Several research questions from four thematically connected areas were stated. The paper deals with studying via playing on-line games so it is important to know students' experience with playing educational computer games as a starting point before approaching usability testing itself.

Students' actual experience with computer games from previous studies represents the first questioned area. Students were asked two relevant questions:

1. Do you have any experience from earlier studies with playing educational computer games?
2. Would you recommend any other geographical computer games?

The second area refers to the willingness to work in an unknown environment area. The crucial fact is that students are not computer experts and have no experience with usability testing.

3. Will this way of website analysis be difficult to manage or even bothering?

The third area relates to educational targets comprising computer competence and mastering geography games.

4. Will students be able to describe functionalities of web-sites?
5. Will students be able to find and play the selected geography games according to the tasks in the user testing form?

The last explored area focuses on the level of satisfaction with the websites and students' opinion whether to incorporate this way of 'studying/playing' into university studies.

6. What is your level of satisfaction with the assessed websites? Could you justify your opinion?
7. Would you incorporate game websites into the university education or not?

The multimethod approach on usability testing of web sites consisted of two parts. The first core part was run in the way of applying usability testing form with elaborated set of general and expert tasks followed by a semi-structured discussion with the students who participated in the testing and their classmates. The procedure of the completion of the assessment form on testing of websites consisted of four stages: The first impression from websites, General and Expert tasks, Acquainted user stage, User's satisfaction with websites.

During the follow-up discussion the research questions were raised, selected games were played and gained findings with diagnosed troubles with the design of websites were discussed. The aim was to discuss pros and contras of implementation of this way of website exploration into the subject Cultural studies.

3 Procedure and Findings

Forms on usability testing of Lizard Point and Purpose Games geography websites were analyzed. The procedure and gained findings are described in this chapter.

The first two questions related to students experience with studying via playing on-line games and whether they would recommend any geographical games. Five students out of ten whose usability tests were analyzed had experience with computer educational games from both primary and secondary school. As for geography games, blind maps had domineered, followed by games on states and capital cities. Only one student could remember and recommend one website with geography games. http://online.seterra.net/cs?img=1. During the discussion it was found out that the ratio of students who had had experience with geography games was even lower, all of them had had experience with English on-line tests so none of them was novice in on-line testing.

Following section brings findings from individual stages of usability testing from the first impression via general and expert tasks, to the acquainted expert and finally to the level of satisfaction stage in detail. Testers were asked in the first part of the usability testing form to determine the main mission of the websites from their first one-minute stay in the new environment. The Table 1 shows their statements from their impression in both analyzed websites. (Note: the statements are students' ones).

During the first and second phase of the exploration of websites *two significant problems were diagnosed in the web-design*. As for Lizard Point, web two testers out of five expressed dissatisfaction with *lack of information on the homepage*. The other website also faces quite important trouble in the design. Purpose Games website offers sharing via Facebook, Twitter or Google+ but surprisingly only one tester out of five found the *links to social nets* in Purpose Games website. During the follow up discussion in the classes accompanied with the demonstration of tasks on the websites students themselves couldn't understand that they hadn't found the links.

From the second stage of work on the usability testing of websites one game as an expert task from the set of tasks in the usability form was selected and analyzed in this paper. In the Purpose Games website testers were asked to find and play the game 'The countries of Africa' and to describe the way to the game. All respondents managed the task within 3–10 min, all respondents copied the web address of the required game into the usability form, all of them noted down that they found the game within 1 min and

Table 1. What is the main mission of the website?

Purpose Games	Lizard Point
1. The server focuses mainly on quizzes. The topics are both school and everyday life. On the home page, you can see the latest games added	1. The server focuses on quizzes and activities for both entertainment and education. Nothing more from the homepage can be read. The homepage seems empty, more information is needed
2. Playing games and ranking according to popularity. Creation of games	2. In my opinion, the main mission of the server is to learn or improve in the knowledge of geography in a fun way, especially through various forms of quizzes
3. I think the main mission are quizzes. Quizzes are of all kinds, there are common themes, as well as topics that are taught in schools	
4. Practice knowledge by playing the games and competitions	3. I think the main missions are quizzes. There is no more information on the homepage
5. The game-oriented server contains lots of games in different areas, probably targeted at children and youth	4. To refresh knowledge of geography
	5. To remember where states of Africa are situated ☺

four of them used a search field to find the game. In the Lizard Point website testers were asked to find and play the game Africa: countries quiz in a 'Quiz mode' and describe how they proceeded. Three testers completed the game within 6–10 min, one tester tried three times and finally lost the game and one student selected an easier mode to succeed.

Troubles which the testers faced in accomplishing the tasks in the 'Lizard Point' website got reflected in their answers on the question from the last web testing stage 'Did you have troubles with accomplishing the tasks?' The brief students' comments follow: *(1) Some quizzes are harder. For example, to guess some states of West Africa at first try is nearly impossible, (2) Yes, (3) I used a lot of tries to find solution, (4) Big problems, (5) Yes, because I am not good at finding states.*

Troubles with accomplishing tasks in the 'Lizard Point' website didn't get reflected in the level of Satisfaction section. Respondents realized that it was their lack of knowledge and not the problem of the website itself. This issue was discussed with other students during face to face classes and the games were done together.

After the phase of meeting with the website and doing the tasks in a new environment the testers might be called 'acquainted users' as they enter the Acquainted user stage. At this stage the testers were asked to give their updated view of the websites: What is the mission of the portal? For whom the websites are designed? Are the games categorized, If so, how? What are positives and negatives of the websites? What functionalities does the website have? All users stated that games and quizzes represent the main mission and described their categorization in detail. Out of functionalities all mentioned: search field, registration/sign in-sign up, tournaments with charts and scores and possibility to create own game.

In spite of the fact that the testers' major is Tourism management and not Informatics, they were able and eager to enumerate various beneficial functionalities of websites. Two following Tables 2 and 3 bring findings on perceived positives and negatives of evaluated websites.

Table 2. Positives and negatives of Purpose Games website stated by web-usability testers

Positives	Negatives
6. There is a great variety and a big number of games 7. I like the games on the main page which are sorted according to the ones that are most often played, and they are ranked according to users/members rating. On the right side there is also the Top Ten feature section, which is very original. You do not have to click through each game 8. Variety and number of quizzes 9. No note 10. The pages are graphically nicely processed, simple, easy to orientate. There are a lot of options: register and manage own stuff, evaluate individual games. The biggest plus is a responsive design (displayed differently depending on the size of the display)	1. I miss classification according to categories. It is not possible to play the games on older, slow computes 2. No note 3. Quizzes aren't sorted out according to categories 4. Deeper categorization is needed 5. The site is likely to be funded by advertising. I use the AdBlock Plugin for Google Chrome, and what happened? The webpage was redirected to the site: http://www.purposegames.com/adblock which prevents the use of the site until you turn the plugin off. In all other cases, I would leave the site immediately, but I wanted to do the tasks, so I stayed, anyway I was discouraged and disgusted by this redirection. I understand that for some servers the ads are vital but I would rather choose a recommending announcement in the header or in the place of the ads. The ads are unpleasant and ruin the impression of a fairly elaborate site

Testers positively assessed variety and a number of games. They missed the standard division of games according to categories but on the other hand the specific approach to the layout of games which is ranked according to users rating on the main page was highly appreciated. Proper display of websites on various devices was highlighted. Very important issue is a disturbing ad element.

Table 3 brings perceived positives and negatives of the Lizard Point website.

There is also a consensus in the evaluation. Each tester expressed briefly positive characteristics of the web. Dissatisfaction with the home page dominates in the negative assessment. Diagnosed dissatisfaction with the Lizard Point home page was so significant that the first user gave the lowest evaluation (+2 points) in the level of Satisfaction rating which anyway was high on the scale −5 to +5.

Final stage of the usability testing represents user's satisfaction with websites. User's satisfaction with the websites consisted of quantitative and qualitative parts. Testers defined their level of satisfaction on the scale from minus 5 points to plus 5 points, see Fig. 2. Both websites reached very good results.

Then students were asked to justify their assessment; actual contribution to education or fun. The educational benefit is mentioned as of main importance in both websites. Only one tester noted down that the web is mainly for fun, 'its role in the education is just for refreshing knowledge'. Three more illustrative extracts from written comments follow and show how the testers perceive the websites: 'The benefit to education is in learning and expanding information; The page is really for education

Table 3. Positives and negatives of Lizard Point website stated by web-usability testers

Perceived positives	Perceived negatives
1. Good division of tests into individual categories 2. There are a lot of quizzes and information about certain areas of a given country or continents 3. Good division games according to topics 4. It is a clear website 5. It is good for better knowledge	1. Negative is the home page of the server with only a few links, otherwise the page is empty 2. I would make the pages clear from the first page 3. The home page is 'negative' because there is no information 4. No note 5. But it is not well arranged

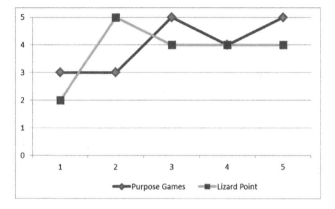

Fig. 2. Level of Satisfaction in Purpose games and Lizard Point websites

so it is very good to spend our time there; A lot of games are fun to use for education, others are not so great, but because there are plenty of them so surely everyone will find something interesting ☺'.

The last but one of the key issues deals with the students' view of incorporation of similar game websites into the university education. This question concluded the section on tester's level of satisfaction with the website. The answers varied from unambiguous acceptance to indifference. The answers from both websites are given in the Table 4.

During the follow up discussion not only those students who completed the usability testing forms but all the class got involved. Individual tasks both general and specific were tailored to fit the needs of the Geography chapter in the Cultural studies subject. When the pages were explored together students were even more open to incorporating gaming into university studies but all of them voted for the voluntary activity in an e-course.

Table 4. Incorporate game websites into the university education or not?

Purpose Games	Lizard Point
1. If there is time in the classes why not to include it in? 2. Since the games have different categories (listed in the previous question), for those subjects with certain themes, these games can be useful, for example, at the end of the lesson so that the student recalls what he actually learned and what he had taken from the lesson 3. I don't know, maybe not 4. Yes 5. Yes, to variegate the classes	1. Definitely – Yes 2. I think so. Students will not be bored only with lectures☺, but they can practice their knowledge and compare (compete) with their classmates in this way 3. Yes 4. If time allows 5. I don't think so

4 Conclusion

Based on the literature review and the author's experience, a usability assessment tool for geography websites was developed. Usability testing form which was completed by five representative users comprised 4 stages: First impression, General and Expert tasks, Acquainted user stage and User's satisfaction. All raised questions supporting the accomplishment of the goal and sub-goals were answered and step by step presented in the chapter Procedure and findings.

The educational benefit was noted down as of main importance in both analyzed websites. No connection was found between students' experience with playing educational computer games and willingness to participate in the voluntary activity on usability testing of selected educational websites. Even if the students got into troubles with accomplishing the task 'play the game' which was tailored to fit the content of the subject chapter on Geography, they didn't blame the websites and did the task during the discussion phase in classes. All testers described their troubles but no-one mentioned that in their final assessment on the level of satisfaction.

Key finding influencing the further stage of the research is that website analysis was an interesting and enriching experience for the participants, no-one was discouraged by tasks on navigation or web-functionalities. The opposite is true; usability testers were able to aptly describe functionalities and even highlight their beneficial features for studying, like proper display of website content on various devices or suggestion on website design improvement relating to disturbing amount of advertisements.

Several limitations of the study were identified. The crucial obstacle is time. Usability testing is a time-consuming activity. The following issues have to be considered in the future phase of the project like shortening the usability testing form and removing selected tasks on general view of websites. Another area of researchers' tasks relates to the selection of at least one appropriate coherent website out of the set of regularly updated websites accompanying each chapter of the subject and its e-course. Consequently researchers will design usability testing forms with thoughtfully tailored tasks. The activity of running usability tests is designed as optional activity enabling students master desired subject knowledge in an enjoyable and exploratory way.

Measuring the efficiency of actual subject knowledge gaining will be in focus of the next phase of the research on utilization of user testing method in non-informative subjects.

Acknowledgment. The paper is supported by the SPEV Project.

References

1. Nielsen, J., Norman, D.: Usability Is Not a Luxury, Jnd.org Don Norman: Designing For People. http://www.jnd.org/dn.mss/usability_is_not_a_l.html. Accessed 10 May 2017
2. Nielsen, J.: Usability Engineering. Morgan Kaufmann, Burlington (1993)
3. Hodgson, P.: Is Usability a Science? Eserfocus. http://www.userfocus.co.uk/articles/is-usability-a-science.html. Accessed 10 May 2017
4. Martinez, G.: Website Analysis: a look behind the screen, Gerardomatinezjr. https://gerardomartinezjr.wordpress.com/2014/02/28/website-analysis-a-look-behind-the-screen/. Accessed 10 May 2017
5. Ugras, T., Gülseçen, S., Çubukçu, C., İli Erdoğmuş, İ., Gashi, V., Bedir, M.: Research trends in web site usability: a systematic review. In: Marcus, A. (ed.) DUXU 2016. LNCS, vol. 9746, pp. 517–528. Springer, Cham (2016). https://doi.org/10.1007/978-3-319-40409-7_49
6. Raban, M., et al.: Evaluation of web-based consumer medication information: content and usability of 4 Australian websites. Interact. J. Med. Res. **5**(3), 2–14 (2016)
7. Pant, A.: Usability evaluation of an academic library website: experience with the Central Science Library, University of Delhi. Electron. Libr. **33**(5), 896–915 (2015)
8. Nielsen, J.: Usability 101: Introduction to Usability. Nielsen Norman Group. http://www.nngroup.com/articles/usability-101-introduction-to-usability/. Accessed 10 Aug 2016
9. User experience basics, Usability.gov. https://www.usability.gov/what-and-why/user-experience.html. Accessed 10 May 2017
10. Cerna, M., Poulova, P.: User testing of language educational portals. E+M Ekonomie Manag. **12**(3), 104–117 (2009)
11. Cerna, M., Svobodova, L.: Development of financial and language competences via on-line games and tests. In: European Conference on E-Learning, ECEL 2015. Academic Publishing, Reading (2015)
12. Nielsen, J.: Why You Only Need to Test with 5 Users. http://www.nngroup.com/articles/why-you-only-need-to-test-with-5-users/. Accessed 10 May 2017

Adaptive Practising Using Mobile Touch Devices

Libor Klubal[✉], Katerina Kostolanyova, and Vojtech Gybas

Pedagogical Faculty, University of Ostrava, Ostrava, Czech Republic
libor.klubal@osu.cz

Abstract. Mobile touch devices are a separate set of devices that can be used in education. Especially from the point of view of their personal nature, they can be used advantageously in the field of adaptive elearning. The work deals with the analysis of the use of mobile devices in fixation of the subject with adaptive elements. It turns out that there is acquiring skills of pupils who are not sufficiently trained in the subject. There is also an effect of easier control of such a device.

Keywords: Adaptive e-learning · Practising · Mobile device

1 Introduction

Modern technologies must become an integral part of education process. As ICT tools become common same as fundamental part of all activities of the human world, it is not possible to insist on models which ignore such ICT benefit. Intentional use of specific ICT tools demonstrably brings increase of effectiveness of teaching-learning process (Major et al. 2017). However, it is necessary to follow the validated methodologies and use ICT tools where it really makes sense.

The goal of the work is to evaluate possibilities of the mobile touch screen devices in the course of the subject matter and to compare benefits of the mobile devices, mainly in comparison with other ICT tools, like computers and notebooks. Methods of adaptive e-learning along with methods of adaptive practising with regard to specifics of the mobile devices shall be taken into account.

2 Fixation of a Knowledge

The teaching-learning process itself can be divided into several stages. The first stage is a motivation when the teacher struggles to capture pupil's attention in relation to the content. The second stage - an exposition when new findings are passed and bases as for skills and habits are created. The last stage is a consolidation (also labeled fixation) - revision and consolidation of knowledge and skills. Fixation methods are divided upon the fact we fix the knowledge or the skills (Hennessy et al. 2006).

One type of fixation form used is practising. Our research in schools shows, that this form is used mainly in the teaching-learning of the foreign languages and

T.-C. Huang et al. (Eds.): SETE 2017, LNCS 10676, pp. 314–319, 2017.
https://doi.org/10.1007/978-3-319-71084-6_35

mathematics. Partial skills get consolidated and fixed by such repeated practising. As for the mathematics, there is a multiplication of single digits when once the multiplication via addition found out, step-by-step transfer from a skill to knowledge is being carried out. Knowledge is then built up by practising which is sometimes called a drill. Thanks to this fact, the brain capacity of the pupil is released so that he could solve more demanding tasks and gain more complicated skills (Gathercole et al. 2004; Hejny and Kurina 2015). As for the foreign languages, we can mention building vocabulary. Method of drill is often used here as one of the basic tools of the curriculum fixation.

An essential part of the practising is to gain feedback, both for the teacher and for the pupil. Especially for the pupil the immediate reaction is very important. If we consider use of tools without ICT components as typical form of practising, then the feedback comes late, usually when corrected by another person or via searching of the correct response in different part of the working material (usually on the end of material). Use of ICT brings advantage, i.e. immediate correction of the result and gaining of the feedback at the time when the pupil's attention is fully focused on specific knowledge. Existing researches show that in case of electronic practising the efficiency increases significantly, mainly with the pupils who have not reached needed knowledge yet.

3 Adaptive E-learning

Main principle of adaptive teaching-learning systems is respecting and reacting on needs of each specific user (a pupil). Theory of adaptive teaching-learning process comes mainly from the theory of programme learning (Kostolányová 2012). As for the purposes of adaptive teaching-learning process, a basic idea of division of the learnt material into smaller parts is introduced. Verification of partial knowledge along with reaction on result of such verification becomes a part of each whole.

Contrary to the programme learning as described by Tollingerova et al. (1968), the adaptive teaching-learning process contains further features. In the framework of the programme learning the system reacts just on the pupil's response and upon the correct and incorrect replies the teacher sets further course of the teaching-learning process via branching. Furthermore, amendment of educational materials occur in the adaptive teaching-learning process. Individual wholes of the curriculum are processed in more variants and they reflect different styles of the teaching-learning process. So called virtual teacher plays his role in the adaptive e-learning. He suggests optimized teaching-learning materials upon the study results of an individual pupil.

3.1 ICT Tools and Adaptive E-learning

From the common e-learning point of view, it is not important which ICT tools are used in the teaching-learning process. This can be a very broad scope as ICT are defined, for example, by Zounek (2002). He defines ICT as technological means intended for data and information processing. In general terms, ICT tools belong to the group of learning aids which Průcha et al. (2013) describes as traditional marking for the objects, subjects imitating reality, helping wider illustrative purposes same as facilitating the teaching-learning process. It further specifies that, for didactic technique, we consider a set of labels of technical devices used for educational purposes and are understood either by devices or their programs, which are usually distinguished from traditional and modern.

From today's perspective, ICT tools can be divided into the following groups:

- all types of classical desktop or portable computers equipped with operating system;
- mobile touch screen devices with operating system;
- projection technlogy and visualization technology;
- experimental sets for science teaching with possibility of data processing;
- production technology;
- network infrastructure.

It is clear that from the adaptive e-learning perspective we are interested mainly in tools which are focused on work of an individual person. If we should change the teaching-learning environment upon individual needs, the technology must be able to monitor behaviour of a person directly the teaching-learning process or, eventually, it must be able to set conditions of the teaching-learning process upon the test carried out in advance.

Adaptation of teaching-learning process is based on processing of the learning content by small parts and it incorporates several variants of the adjusted learning content. That is why we must focus on ICT applications equipment more than on the ICT tool itself.

3.2   Adaptive Practising

As for the adaptive e-learning we hit further sphere - an adaptive practising. It is a way of practising of certain knowledge via adequately selected questions. This sphere is being usually divided into intelligent and adaptive systems (Brusilovsky and Peylo 2003) with possible overlap of both spheres. Adaptive practising term comes from English "Computer Adaptive Practice" and it is a technique where the system learns the difficulty of the content directly during practice while adapting the questions asked to the needs and abilities of the student (Klinkenberg 2011). Adaptive practising fits mainly where the pupil has to gain memorable knowledge (facts, factographic data, foreign languages). The advantage is time saving as no learning material which the pupil already knows gets practised. Another advantage is maximization of pupil's interest and higher probability of increase of his motivation same as increase of the time spent on the task fulfillment (Eggen and Verschoor 2006).

One of the adaptive practising methods is so called distributed revision using the effect of distribution of the repeated learning material into longer time period. This term is described in English as "spacing effect" and the study was published by Vlach and Sandhofer in the year 2012. They describe planning algorithm which upon the correct answers determines further time plan of asking the same questions. This method, however, does not solve difficulty of questions and that is why it meets elements of adaptability within one part only.

Theory of modelling of the student's knowledge focuses on the possibilities of adaptive practising much more. We try to answer the question of what the likelihood is that the student knows the certain fact. Basic modelling is carried out via the Rasch model (Klinkenberg 2011) being clarified via PFA method (performance factor analysis). Furthermore, Pelánek et al. (2016) describe advantages of ELO method which leads us to similar results as when compute-intensive methods used. ELO method was used by authors in the system of web applications intended for practising of factographic knowledge. The Elo rating system was originally developed for rating chess players, nowadays it is widely used for ranking players of many other games (Pelánek 2016).

3.3 Adaptive Teaching-Learning Process and Mobile Devices

A tablet and mobile phone equipped with operating system are usually considered mobile touch screen devices (Kostolányová and Klubal 2014). Simply said - a desktop computer integrated into one device without need of further peripheries to be linked (a keyboard, PC mouse, monitor). Mobility, integration of mode devices and possibility of individual adjustment are the elements considered to be significant advantage of using mobile devices. From the adaptive e-learning perspective, we mainly focus on character of such a device. Tablet same as a mobile phone are devices which are intended for use of one user only. He adjusts his device upon his needs and it is supposed that the device is used more often in shorter time intervals contrary to a desktop computer where longer time period of work is expected. Such way of using can be used to advantage during practising with "Spacing effect" being mentioned above. We can find this access for example in Duolingo application which asks its user to practice very short parts of to-be-learned material in regular intervals.

Use of mobile touch screen device can be found useful for adjustment of learning materials upon individual learning style of a student. Viewing/displaying of textual materials and playing of multimedia files is a sure thing. But we actually may use further tools as for example reading of any texts. At present, this function is fully integrated in iOS system and, with certain limitations, in Android and Windows systems.

Most publications dedicated to adaptability in education deal with the use of a classical desktop or laptop computer. There are fewer articles about mobile devices published, nevertheless, there is one significant study from 2003 which was carried out in Finland. Ketamo (2003) describes influence of use of mobile devices and of adaptive geometrical game during teaching-learning process of mathematics (6-year-old pupils). Comparison was carried out in three situations. There was combined use of a tablet, PDA device and interactive geometrical game. This game was adjusted in the last phase of the experiment for analysis of the pupil's result in the course of the process. Obtained results clearly show that the use of touch screen device and use of adaptation significantly increases effectiveness of results, mainly with the pupils which belong to the group with low level acquisition of tested skills. It is interesting that already in the year 2003 the authors used a combination of a mobile touch screen device along with a web application with which individual devices were combined. Similar access is visible even within mobile applications, thus 14 years later.

Regardless of adaptation, the similar conclusion was confirmed even while using of mobile device during fixation of mathematics curriculum. There was confirmed as well that use of practice application significantly increases effectiveness mainly with pupils who have not reached needed abilities and knowledge so far (Kostolányová and Klubal 2015). We may suppose that the synthesis of input and output device surface is a reason of such results and orientation in practice application gets much easier for a pupil. This influence has already been proved with pupils with lower intellect (Klubal and Gybas 2015) when need for necessary hand-eye coordination for use of classical keyboard-mouse-monitor system was eliminated.

In relation to the mobile device we may even mention BYOD concept as well. It is a model when the pupils bring to the school their own portable devices (Neumajer 2016). Pupils may find such planned and well prepared BYOD concept highly useful. It presents them another dimension of how to use their own devices. And that way closer interconnection of school and home environment is ensured. Even though the BYOD concept was originally described for all mobile devices, even the laptops, it is clear that mobile devices predominate. Researches show that the laptops are not owned by the second level primary school pupils as much as the mobile devices. (Klubal and Kostolányová 2016).

4   Conclusion

Adaptive e-learning represents one of the time-tested trends of ICT use in education. Thanks to wide accessibility of ICT tools the use of adaptation has become much more accessible than ever before. Adaptation can be ensured by adaptation to specific learning style of a pupil, specifically by offering of such teaching-learning materials which are much more suitable for his personal profile. Concerning the teachers, this kind of adaptation calls for higher requirements of the whole educational programme to be prepared. In some cases, we can use functions of mobile devices even here and, for example, we can read classic textual materials automatically. Another way where adaptive e-learning findings can be applied is curriculum fixation via practising. It is suitable mainly when the pupil must fix the given schemes or when he has to acquire factographic data. In such cases, the choice of a mobile device is suitable from the perspective of its personal nature.

References

Brusilovsky, P., Peylo, Ch.: Adaptive and intelligent web-based educational systems. Int. J. Artif. Intell. Educ. (IJAIED) **13**, 159–172 (2003). <hal-00197315>

Eggen, T., Verschoor, A.: Optimal testing with easy or difficult items in computerized adaptive testing. Appl. Psychol. Meas. **30**(5), 379–393 (2006)

Gathercole, S., Pickering, S., Knight, C., Stegmann, Z.: Working memory skills and educational attainment: evidence from national curriculum assessments at 7 and 14 years of age. Appl. Cogn. Psychol. **18**(1), 1–16 (2004)

Hejny, M., Kurina, F.: Dítě, škola a matematika: konstruktivistické přístupy k vyučování. Portal, Praha. Pedagogická praxe (Portál) (2015). ISBN 978-80-262-0901-0

Hennessy, S., Wishart, J.M., Whitelock, D., et al.: Pedagogical approaches for technology-integrated science teaching. Comput. Educ. **48**, 137–152 (2006)

Ketamo, H.: An adaptive geometry game for handheld devices. Educ. Technol. Soc. **6**(1), 83–95 (2003)

Klinkenberg, S.: Computer adaptive practice of maths ability using a new item response model for on the fly ability and difficulty estimation. Computers **57**(2), 1813–1824 (2011). [acc. 30. prosince 2015]. https://doi.org/10.1016/j.compedu.2011.02.003. ISSN 0360-1315

Klubal, L., Gybas, V.: Organizační formy výuky z pohledu integrace mobilních dotykových technologií v základní škole speciální. In: MMK 2015, pp. 1345–1350. Magnanimitas, Hradec Králové (2015). ISBN 978-80-87952-12-2

Klubal, L., Kostolányová, K.: Forms of the materials shared between a teacher and a pupil. In: Sánchez, I.A., Isaías, P. (eds.) Proceedings of the 12th International Conference on Mobile Learning 2016, Vilamoura, Algerve, Portugal, p. 4. IADIS (2016). ISBN 978-989-8533-49-4

Kostolányová, K.: Teorie adaptivního e-learningu, 1. vyd, 118 p. Ostravská univerzita, Ostrava (2012). ISBN 978-80-7464-014-8

Kostolányová, K., Klubal, L.: iPad integration in to the current professional practice of teachers in primary and secondary schools. Scientia iuvenis. Constantine the Philosopher University in Nitra, Nitra, pp. 450–455 (2014). ISBN 978-80-558-0650-1

Kostolányová, K., Klubal, L.: Practicing in mathematics using a tablet. In: European Conference on e-Learning Conference Proceedings, ACPI 2015, pp. 714–719 (2015). ISBN 978-1-910810-70-5

Major, L., Haßler, B., Hennessy, S.: Tablet use in schools: impact, affordances and considerations. In: Marcus-Quinn, A., Hourigan, T. (eds.) Handbook on Digital Learning for K-12 Schools, pp. 115–128. Springer, Cham (2017). https://doi.org/10.1007/978-3-319-33808-8_8

Neumajer, O.: BYOD – bring your own device to school. Wolters Kluwer ČR a. s., Prague, roč. 13, č. 12, pp. 20–22 (2016). ISSN 1214-8679

Pelánek, R.: Applications of the Elo rating system in adaptive educational systems. Comput. Educ. (2016). https://doi.org/10.1016/j.compedu.2016.03.017

Průcha, J., Walterova, E., Mares, J.: Pedagogický slovník. 7., Portál, Prague (2013). ISBN 9788026204039

Tollingerova, D., Knezu, V., Kulic, V.: Programované učení. SPN, Prague (1968)

Vlach, H.A., Sandhofer, C.: Distributing learning over time: the spacing effect in children's acquisition and generalization of science concepts. In: Child Development, vol. 83, no. 4, pp. 1137–1144 (2012). http://doi.org/10.1111/j.1467-8624.2012.01781.x. ISSN 1467–8624

Zounek, J.: Počítac, Internet a multimédia v práci ucitele. In: Novotný, P., Pol, M. (eds.) Vybrané kapitoly ze školní pedagogiky. Brno, pp. 61–73 (2002)

Using Social Media to Enhance Student Engagement

Audrey J.W. Mbogho[(✉)]

Pwani University, P.O. Box 195-80108, Kilifi, Kenya
a.mbogho@pu.ac.ke

Abstract. Lack of enthusiasm for learning is a major problem in higher education. We have found in our experience that often students are more interested in passing the course than in engaging deeply with the content. Low student engagement has occupied educators for some time, and a large body of research exists into the possible causes of this problem and how it may be tackled. Here, we report on our own experience with this problem at Pwani University in Kenya. Further, we propose the use of social networking as a means of addressing the problem of student apathy. We postulate that young people's propensity for social networking can be a distraction on the one hand, but, on the other hand, it can be harnessed to provide strong support for active learning, boost learner participation and improve academic performance. This is a preliminary report, and its intent is to explore possibilities and lay the foundation for future work in enhancing active learning among our students.

1 Introduction

Student engagement [1] refers to the extent to which students are invested in their own learning. There are three types of student engagement defined in the literature, namely behavioral engagement, affective engagement and cognitive engagement [2]. Behavioral engagement has to do with a student's actions and habits, for instance one student might obey university rules while another might flout them. The former is an example of a behaviorally engaged student while the latter is non-engaged. Affective engagement has to do with the emotions: how the student feels about various aspects of university life. A student who is unhappy about the courses he or she is studying or one who feels that the university is hostile towards students is showing affective disengagement. On the other hand, a student who has strong affective engagement may enjoy favourable interactions with fellow students, lecturers and administrative staff and find university life enriching. Cognitive engagement refers to how involved a student is in the learning process. If he or she is interested in the material, is keen to do assignments, then he or she has strong cognitive engagement.

Evidence of student engagement includes paying attention in class, asking for clarification during the lecture, answering questions posed by the lecturer, doing assignments well and submitting them on time, consulting with the teacher outside of the lecture period and discussing course topics with peers. The opposite of these activities is indicative of student disengagement.

T.-C. Huang et al. (Eds.): SETE 2017, LNCS 10676, pp. 320–325, 2017.
https://doi.org/10.1007/978-3-319-71084-6_36

At Pwani University, lecturers report frustration with widespread student non-engagement. Mbogho and Hassanali [3] have noted a mismatch between what is said and what is heard, what is shown and what is seen, what is taught and what is learnt. A lecturer asks a recall question about something she has just explained and is met with blank stares. The author recalls asking students in an E-Learning Technologies class to go and look up the acronym MOOC and report back on what it means the next week. No student bothered. These were third year students, which, alarmingly, suggests the problem of apathy can persist throughout the years a student spends at university.

There are many approaches to address this problem, but in this paper we focus only on those which are amenable to integration with social media. Other scholars have also considered this use of social media given its prevalence in society, and especially among young people (see, for example, Junco [4] and Purvis et al. [5]). Tess [6] reviewed the literature on leveraging social media for educational good. He found the evidence to be mostly anecdotal and the empirical backing weak.

In this paper, we look at some factors that we have observed in our environment that may contribute to the problem of student apathy, and then suggest some solutions based on social media. Our aim is to add to the anecdotal evidence, and to lay the groundwork for a proper scientific investigation to be carried out in future.

2 Factors Contributing to Student Disengagement at PU

In first year, students are still in high school mode and are unprepared for university level studies. The work is more challenging both intellectually and physically. There is a need to manage time, to multi-task and to be self-motivated. These qualities are critical, but even when they are present, the workload in some courses is excessive, leaving students overworked and unable to cope or to concentrate in class. Such students then lack confidence and are timid in class and will not even attempt to answer simple questions. They are overwhelmed by the risk of getting it wrong and embarassing themselves. It is important, therefore, that teachers create a safe environment in the classroom in which students know it's okay to get the answer wrong as part of the learning process. Classroom response systems, discussed below, may provide this sense of safety.

The teaching styles of some lecturers contribute to the problem. There are lecturers who dictate notes and do not interact with the students in any way at all. It is an easy way of teaching, involving little preparation and requiring no teaching tools such as a laptop and projector or whiteboard markers and erasers. Some universities in Kenya which face perennial financial struggles and are unable to provide teaching tools force lecturers to resort to such modes of delivery.

Plagiarism is prevalent, especially for take-home assignments, where we have witnessed rampant and blatant copying from peers or from the online sources. Universities lack the resources to crack down on this practice, leading to its normalisation. Students who copy and those from whom they copy do not see this as morally wrong, but explain that a degree is "harambee", a Swahili word meaning "communal work". In other words, they feel that it is not possible to fulfill all the academic requirements alone; students must assist each other. A student who makes a habit of copying is a disengaged student since he or she makes only superficial contact with the subject matter. They do not have to work hard on an assignment or even pay too much attention in class because they see themselves as having an alternative way out.

Large classes having 300 students or more are particularly vulnerable to the problem of student disengagement. For example, it is not possible for the lecturer to go at a pace that is suitable for everyone. Students at the back of the lecture hall may struggle to hear what the lecturer is saying or see what he or she is writing on the board. One on one interaction with the lecturer is not possible. These conditions leave a large proportion of the class feeling left out, and the inevitable outcome is massive failures for the challenging courses and too many failures or low grades in easy courses which should have none.

3 Student Engagement and Academic Achievement

There is strong evidenced that increased student engagement leads to higher academic achievement. Reyes et al. [7] found that an emotionally supportive classroom environment enhanced learner engagement, which in turn boosted academic performance among fifth and sixth graders in the United States. Similarly, in a study performed at a university in Turkey [8], Gunuc found a positive correlation between student engagement and academic achievement. The study found that all three forms of student engagement (behavioral, emotional and cognitive) together explained academic achievement with a rate of 10%. When it came to emotional engagement, it was positive, affirming relationships with faculty rather than with peers that were found to contribute significantly to better academic performance. Lee [9] conducted a large study involving 121 US schools and more than 3,000 students. She found a strong link between behavioural engagement and reading performance.

Given these findings, it is clear that educators should make it a priority to find ways to foster student engagement. One class of promising approaches is active learning [10]. Active learning is a set of pedagogical methods which seek to make students active participants in their own learning rather than passive recipients of knowledge imparted to them by the lecturer. The educator then becomes a "guide on the side" rather than a "sage on the stage". Furthermore, collaboration is an important component of active learning. In this paper, we look at some active learning approaches which are amenable to implementation using social media, taking advantage of the inherently collaborative nature of social networking platforms.

4 Addressing Disengagement with Active Learning

Active learning [11] has been shown to be very effective in combating low student engagement. We propose that digital technologies, specifically social media, can provide effective means of implementing a number of active learning methods. Taking cognisance of the digital generation from which today's university students are drawn, we believe leveraging social media can increase the effectiveness of active learning among digital natives. Such intervention must be kept as natural as possible, as excessive control has been found to be counterproductive [12]. Therefore, students should be allowed to use social media the way they normally use them, not in some modified way for data collection or some other purpose that does not directly benefit them.

We will now describe some active learning techniques that are amenable to digital implementation. We discuss in tandem those digital technologies that can be used and how they can be used as part of active learning to combat disengagement.

Good [13] found that in using Facebook for teaching and learning, students were more engaged when they were allowed to be content creators rather than just content consumers. This finding underscores the value of social media for student engagement. By their very nature, social media are participatory–it is not likely that any student would just read posts and not share thoughts of their own from time to time. For those who are too shy to post any thoughts, social media provide a number of low-risk options for participation:

Like (or show several other emotions) by just clicking on an icon
Follow another member
Share another's post
Share links from elsewhere on the Web.

All of these actions are forms of participation and engagement that are not possible in the traditional non-digital classroom.

4.1 Simple Active Learning Techniques

There are simple techniques for active learning which can be easily implemented using social media. These techniques foster collaboration, which is known to boost active learning and engagement. We provide modifications to the way the techniques are described in the literature in order to incorporate the use of social media.

Pause Procedure. It has been shown that on average students maintain focus for brief periods, after which they become distracted and are no longer listening to the lecture [10]. A pause procedure [10] involves pausing for a minute or two after every fifteen minutes or so during the course of a lecture. During the pause, students may be directed to write down what they remember from what has been presented so far. Alternatively, in a form of the technique known as a clarification pause, students think about what has been presented and discuss key points with three or four other classmates. This discussion may bring out an issue that needs to be clarified. One person in the group can share this issue on a WhatsApp forum set up for the course. On resuming the lecture, the lecturer addresses the issues raised and clarifies points of confusion before proceeding.

Think-Pair-Share. In this technique introduced by Lyman [14], the lecturer poses a question which the students spend a few moments thinking about individually. They then discuss their ideas with someone sitting next to them and come up with a joint solution, which they share with the class. Similar to the pause procedure, the sharing can be easily achieved with social media such as WhatsApp.

Classroom Response Systems (CRS). In the developed world, classroom response systems (or clickers) have been found to be very effective in fostering active learning and student engagement [15]. However, our university may not be inclined to acquire such a system due to the costs involved. We propose that a mobile app such as Doodle can be used to the same effect. Doodle is a polling app normally used to schedule meetings, but is flexible enough for any use requiring participants to vote. The lecturer prepares a multiple choice question in advance on Doodle. During a pause such as the one described above, the lecture shares the link on WhatsApp and asks the students to follow the Doodle link and select an answer. Doodle automatically tallies the number of people who have selected each choice, providing a quick way to see which way the class is leaning. As with a normal CRS, the lecturer now has the opportunity to revisit the relevant material if the results show widespread misconceptions. The poll can also arouse interest ("Why was my answer wrong?") and prompt discussion.

Posing a Question. When a student raises his or her hand, they can post their question or comment on the forum. This way, everyone can see it, thus eliminating the problem common in large classes where much of the class gets left out when a conversation is taking place between the teacher and a particular student.

An additional benefit of using social media in the various ways described above is that the content created is preserved. In a normal lecture, the questions asked or comments made are lost when the lecture ends. Assessment of class participation can be greatly aided as there is now a record of it.

5   Conclusion and Future Work

We have discussed the extent of student disengagement at Pwani University in Kenya and looked at some published solutions. We have discussed ways these solutions can be modified to incorporate digital technologies which many of our students have access to. In particular, we believe that social media can play an important role in implementing collaborative active learning, fostering student engagement and improving academic achievement. In future we plan to test these ideas out and subject them to proper scientific study.

References

1. Kuh, G.D.: Assessing what really matters to student learning: inside the national survey of student engagement. Change **33**(3), 10–17 (2001)
2. Fredricks, J.A., Blumenfeld, P.C., Paris, A.H.: School engagement: potential of the concept, state of the evidence. Rev. Educ. Res. **74**(1), 59–109 (1982)
3. Mbogho, A., Hassanali, J.: Tackling classroom apathy among undergraduate students in a developing world context at Pwani University. In: INTED 2017 Proceedings, pp. 2337–2340 (2017)
4. Junco, R.: The relationship between frequency of Facebook use, participation in Facebook activities, and student engagement. Comput. Educ. **58**(1), 162–171 (2012)

5. Purvis, A., Rodger, H., Beckingham, S.: Engagement or distraction: the use of social media for learning in higher education. Stud. Engagem. Exp. J. **5**(1) (2016)
6. Tess, A.T.: The role of social media in higher education classes (real and virtual)–a literature review. Comput. Hum. Behav. **29**(5), A60–A68 (2013)
7. Reyes, M.R., Brackett, M.A., Rivers, S.E., White, M., Salovey, P.: Classroom emotional climate, student engagement, and academic achievement. J. Educ. Psychol. **104**(3), 700 (2012)
8. Gunuc, S.: The relationship between student engagement and their academic achievement. Int. J. New Trends Educ. Implic. **5**(4), 216–231 (2014)
9. Lee, J.S.: The relationship between student engagement and academic performance: is it a myth or reality? J. Educ. Res. **107**(3), 177–185 (2014)
10. Prince, M.: Does active learning work? A review of the research. J. Eng. Educ. **93**(3), 223–231 (2004)
11. Bonwell, C.C., Eison, J.A.: Active learning: creating excitement in the classroom. ASHE-ERIC Higher Education Report, No. 1 (1991)
12. Phillips, T.M.: Learning with mobile technologies: considering the challenges, commitments and quandries. Commun. ACM **60**(3), 34–36 (2017)
13. Good, D.J.: A course Facebook page increases student engagement with course content. In: Conference on Higher Education Pedagogy (CHEP 2015) Proceedings, pp. 83–84 (2015)
14. Lyman, F.T.: Think-pair-share, thinktrix, thinklinks, and weird facts: an interactive system for cooperative learning. In: Enhancing Thinking Through Cooperative Learning, pp. 169–181. Teachers College Press, New York (1992)
15. Fies, C., Marshall, J.: Classroom response systems: a review of the literature. J. Sci. Educ. Technol. **15**(1), 101–109 (2006)

Evaluation of the Blended Learning Approach in the Course of Business English – A Case Study

Blanka Klimova[✉]

University of Hradec Kralove,
Rokitanskeho 62, Hradec Kralove, Czech Republic
blanka.klimova@uhk.cz

Abstract. At present, blended learning seems to be a commonly used methodology in all educational settings. The purpose of this study is to analyze and evaluate the blended learning approach and its learning materials in the Course of Business English taught at the Faculty of Informatics and Management in Hradec Kralove, Czech Republic, and discuss its efficacy as far as the learning outcomes are concerned within a wider international setting. The methods include a method of literature search of available sources describing this issue in the world's acknowledged databases Web of Science, Scopus, and ScienceDirect, and a method of comparison and evaluation of the findings from the selected studies on the research topic. In order to analyze and evaluate the blended learning methodology used in the Course of Business English, a case study approach, as well as a questionnaire survey and online course reports were used. Although the findings of this study and other research studies confirm the prevalence of the use of blended learning, its effectiveness is still rather inconclusive. Therefore more experimental studies on the effectiveness of the blended learning approach are needed.

Keywords: Blended learning · Business English · Survey · Learning materials · Effectiveness

1 Introduction

Currently, the blended learning approach is a well-established methodology, used at all types of educational institutions, but especially at the institutions of higher learning [1]. Although there are many definitions of blended learning, the most common perceives blended learning as a combination of traditional, face-to-face teaching and online learning [2, 3]. The main characteristics of the blended learning approach is as follows:

- it enhances personalized learning, which means that it tries to meet students' learning needs [4, 5];
- it promotes students' intrinsic motivation [1];
- it gives flexibility both for students and teachers in terms of lesson planning, preparation, modification of materials, pace, place of learning, and timing [6, 7];
- it provides targeted and continuous feedback [8];

© Springer International Publishing AG 2017
T.-C. Huang et al. (Eds.): SETE 2017, LNCS 10676, pp. 326–335, 2017.
https://doi.org/10.1007/978-3-319-71084-6_37

- it contributes to the broadening, practicing and revision of students' knowledge and skills by offering them additional examples and exercises [9];
- it enhances students' autonomous learning if students are well motivated in their studies [10];
- it can also promote creative problem solving [11];
- it is especially suitable for foreign language teaching since no online course can substitute the role of face-to-face conversation [12];
- it can suit those who are not able to participate in class due to different reasons such as illness or workload in the case of distant students [13, 14];
- it is a cost-effective approach; [15] but
- it may be also time-demanding on its preparation and management [3];
- it may demotivate students who are not motivated enough and self-disciplined in making e-learning a powerful option which allows them to work independently on their own pace [16].

The wide dissemination of the use of the blended learning approach can be illustrated by a number of research articles on this topic found in ScienceDirect between 2000 and 2016. Figure 1 below provides an overview of an increase in the number of the articles on this topic [17].

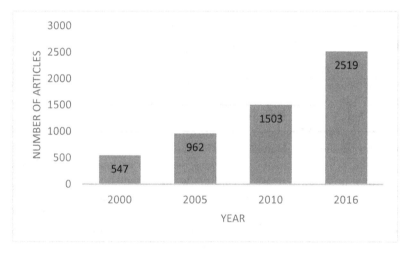

Fig. 1. A number of articles on the blended learning approach in ScienceDirect from 2000 to 2016 (author's own processing, based on the data from [17])

2   Methods

The theoretical background to this article is based on the method of a literature search of available sources on the research topic in the world's acknowledged databases Web of Science, Scopus, Springer and ScienceDirect, especially in the period of 2010 till the end of the year of 2016 in order to provide the latest information on the use of the blended learning approach. However, older studies are also discussed in order to compare the findings.

In order to analyze and evaluate the blended learning (BL) methodology used in the Course of Business English, a case study approach was implemented [18]. Moreover, the results of the questionnaire survey from the BL course distributed among the participants of the course were analyzed and evaluated. The author also took advantage of the course evaluation reports from the corresponding Blackboard online course.

The author of this study set the following research questions:

1. *Do distant students really welcome the blended learning approach?*
2. *Are the learning materials in the online course relevant for the blended learning approach?*
3. *How much effective is the blended learning approach with respect to the learning outcomes?*

Thus, the purpose of this study is to analyze and evaluate the blended learning approach and its learning materials in the Course of Business English taught at the Faculty of Informatics and Management in Hradec Kralove, Czech Republic, and discuss its effectiveness as far as the learning outcomes are concerned.

3 Survey

3.1 Description of the Sample and the Course

At the end of the winter semester of 2016/2017, 35 distant students participated in the survey in the Course of Business English (KOBA 1). Their age ranged from 20 to over 50 years. Majority of students were females (80%), while only 20% were males.

The Business English course is an obligatory one-semester course taught for the distant students of the Management of Tourism in the third year of their study at the Faculty of Informatics and Management (FIM) of the University of Hradec Kralove, Czech Republic. The course is run in the winter semester each year. The entry level of these students is usually at B2 according to the Common European Reference Framework for languages. After passing this course, students obtain two credits. This course is aimed at the distant students who come to study to the faculty on Fridays and Saturdays during the semester. The teacher meets the students just twice during the semester for a six-hour block. However, s/he must manage to convey the same amount of learning material as in the traditional classes. In this respect, s/he tries to motivate them to use the on-line course which contains the material discussed during the face-to-face blocks, but also additional materials and exercises for further practicing. Since the course tries to meet the students' needs which the real business situations require, no particular textbook is used and all the materials in the on-line course are constantly modified [19].

The main topics and skills which are trained in KOBA 1 are described in the course syllabus and listed on the screen from the online blackboard course (Fig. 2).

The learning outcomes are then measured by the written test which consists of several tasks such as reactions to the questions dealing with the main topics described

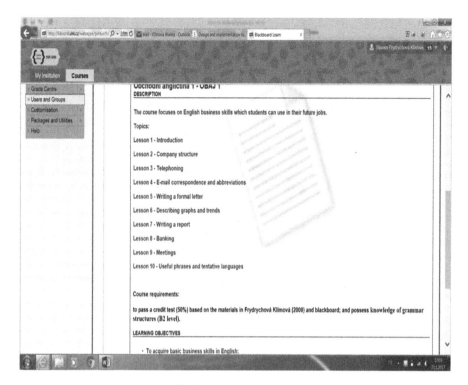

Fig. 2. Course topics [20]

above, finding synonyms, finding verb collocations to the topic nouns, translating several phrases into target language, i.e., English, and writing a formal letter of complaint. The pass mark set by the management of the faculty is 50%. Students have two attempts for passing this credit test.

3.2   Findings

In the survey students were asked if they preferred blended classes (i.e. a combination of traditional/face-to-face classes and online classes) or only traditional classes or online classes only in order to answer research question 1. Figure 3 below shows that majority of them (66%) prefers the blended learning approach, 29% would rather have the traditional, face-to-face classes and only 5% would study online.

Furthermore, the learning materials play an important and irreplaceable role in students' learning and they also reflect students' motivation to study. In fact, they are usually the most exploited content tools in the online courses [8–10]. In the Course of Business English they created 96% of all hits into the online course [21]. Therefore the second research questions focused on the usefulness of these materials for the distant students. The survey revealed that 97% of the course respondents found the learning materials placed in the online course useful and only 3% of them considered them not particularly useful. Figure 4 then illustrates the key features students appreciated in these learning materials.

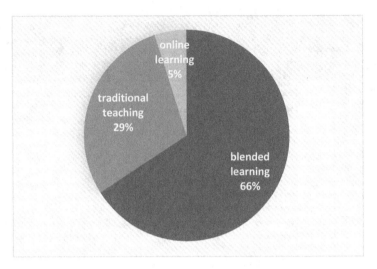

Fig. 3. Students' preferences about classes (author's own processing)

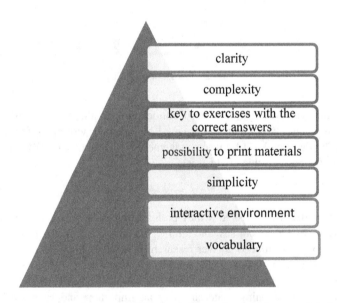

Fig. 4. Students' opinions on the positive features of the online learning materials (author's own processing)

On the contrary, students would welcome more exercises for practicing and audio recordings. Interestingly, overall, majority of the respondents (57%) prefer the printed materials.

Figure 5 below then shows students' activities in the online course materials. It is obvious that the distant students do not study on a regular daily basis, but they do access the materials when they have their lectures or before the credit test as it is demonstrated in Fig. 5. The first contact class was run on 25 November 2016 and the following contact class when students did the written test was held on 18 January 2017. As one can observe, students mostly accessed the materials during the six days before the test and during the first face-to-face class.

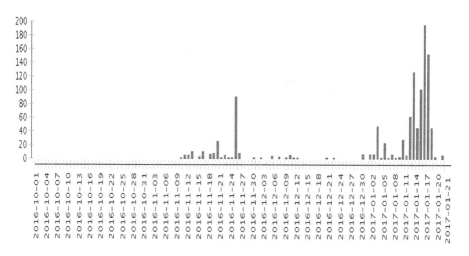

Fig. 5. Students' activity in the online course materials [21]

With respect to the learning outcomes, it was also discovered that 43% of the respondents had had some kind of business input before attending this Course of Business English, while 57% had not had any. In addition, distant students are working people and that is why some of them also use English at work, especially if they are employed in multinational companies. As they stated in the questionnaires, they mostly exploit business English in writing e-mails and reports, communicating or negotiating with clients, telephoning, or making presentations. This was the case of 51% of the respondents. During the credit test 57% of the students passed the test on the first attempt, while 43% failed and had to retake the test for the second time.

4 Discussion

The findings of this study reveal that the blended learning approach is welcomed by the distant students. This also confirms the results of the previous studies published by other teachers of FIM on this topic [6–10, 22–24]. The reason is that the distant students are working people and sometimes they are unable to come even to those two-block face-to-face sessions. Therefore they appreciate having access to all the course materials online although as this and the previous research on the learning materials indicate [22], students mostly prefer the printed materials. And this is not the problem either since they can print out a user-friendly version of the online materials from the online course from anywhere and at any time.

This leads to the second research question on the relevancy of the online course materials. The findings indicate that the learning materials are very positively evaluated by the distant students for their clarity, complexity and the answer key to all exercises. However, students would still welcome more exercises for practicing the newly acquired words and phrases or skills. They would also include more audio recordings.

The most problematic, however, seems research question number 3, which deals with the effectiveness of the whole course. So far there have not been many studies on the effectiveness of the blended learning approach. And if there were, they did not bring conclusive results. For example, Dziuban et al. [25] compared all three modalities, i.e., face-to-face teaching, blended learning and online learning and concluded that the blended learning approach contributed to better learning outcomes than the fully online approach. In addition, in some subjects the blended learning approach was better than the traditional one. The positive results as far as the learning outcomes are concerned, were also confirmed by Bakor Nordin and Alias [26] in their study on the use of blended learning in history classes. Some modest improvement in students' learning performance was revealed in the study by Garrison and Kanuka [27]. On the contrary, the study by Reasons et al. [28] indicates that the best modality is the fully online learning.

Furthermore, the results of this study are in compliance with the study by Tosun [16], which also revealed that the blended learning strategy did not improve the students' vocabulary achievement although students were satisfied with the proposed blended learning strategy in teaching vocabulary and prefer it to the traditional classroom based learning. As, for example, Siew-Eng and Muuk [29] state, the BL approach in English classes is especially used to improve students' writing, reading and speaking skills.

Thus, the findings of this study, according to the students' activity in the online course and the results of the outcome measures in the form of the end semester test do not show much effectiveness. Nevertheless, the author of this study taught the same course face-to-face to present, full-time students who did not have any experience in business English. They also used the materials from the online course but only as the support to their every week's 90-min classes. Their learning outcomes of the same test showed that the traditional, face-to-face classes during which they could practice the new business English words and phrases and skills, had been effective. In this traditionally taught course only one student failed the first attempt and the reason was that he did not attend the course on a regular weekly basis.

Overall, both present and distant students enjoyed the Course of Business English enormously, which they stated in their questionnaires. However, the problem is that the distant students are both working and in some cases they have to take care of their own families. That is why they study towards the set deadlines such as the terms of the tests. And it is not simply enough because the process of retention of new words and phrases lasts longer than just a few days before the test. The new words and phrases need revision several times and to maximize the students' potential, all senses should be employed because because one remembers:

- 10% of what one has read,
- 20% of what one has heard,
- 30% of what one has seen,
- 50% of what one has heard and seen,
- 70% of what one has said,
- 90% of what one has done [30].

Therefore to make blended learning more powerful, other media delivery types may be implemented, for example, YouTube, video, animation, or social media books [31].

One of the possibilities to enhance students' learning performance might be also the inclusion of additional face-to-face tutorials, which might be substituted by a more flexible mode of participation, the so-called blended synchronous learning environments - contexts where distant students can participate in face-to-face classes through the use of rich-media synchronous technologies such as video conferencing, web conferencing, or virtual worlds [14]. However, this approach requires to select adequate technologies according to representational and communication requests, as well as to prepare the environment and people for blended synchronous learning activity such as pedagogical assistants as it is the case in all other educational settings [32].

5   Conclusion

Although the findings of this study and other research studies confirm the prevalence of the use of blended learning, its effectiveness is still rather inconclusive. Therefore more experimental studies on the effectiveness of the blended learning approach are needed in order to elaborate successful strategies which would enhance learning outcomes in blended learning such as the one described above.

Acknowledgments. This review study is supported by SPEV project 2017/18 run at the Faculty of Informatics and Management, University of Hradec Kralove, Czech Republic. The author especially thanks Josef Toman for his help with data processing.

References

1. Klimova, B., Poulova, P.: Learning technologies and their impact on an educational process in the Czech Republic. In: Proceedings of the International Conference on Computer Science and Information Engineering (CSIE 2015), pp. 429–434. Destech Publications, Lancaster (2015)
2. Buran, A., Evseeva, A.: Prospects of blended learning implementation at technical university. Procedia Soc. Behav. Sci. **206**, 177–182 (2015)
3. Frydrychova Klimova, B.: Blended learning. In: Mendez Vilas, A., et al. (eds.) Research, Reflections and Innovations in Integrating ICT in Education, vol. 2, pp. 705–708. FORMATEX, Spain (2009)
4. Poulova, P., Simonova, I.: Flexible e-learning: online courses tailored to student's needs. In: Proceedings of the 9th International Scientific Conference on Distance Learning in Applied Informatics (DIVAI 2012), pp. 251–260. UKF, Nitra (2012)

5. Herlo, D.: Improving efficiency of learning in education master programs. Procedia Soc. Behav. Sci. **191**, 1304–1309 (2015)

6. Hubackova, S., Semradova, I.: Comparison of on-line teaching and face-to-face teaching. Procedia Soc. Behav. Sci. **89**, 445–449 (2013)

7. Frydrychova Klimova, B., Hubackova, S., Semradova, I.: Blended learning in a foreign language learning. Procedia Soc. Behav. Sci. **28**, 281–285 (2011)

8. Frydrychova Klimova, B., Poulova, P.: ICT in the teaching of academic writing. Lectures Notes in Management Science, vol. 11, pp. 33–38 (2013)

9. Klimova, B.: Assessment in smart learning environment – a case study approach. In: Uskov, V., Howlett, R.J., Jai, L.C. (eds.) Smart Innovation, Systems and Technologies, vol. 41, pp. 15–24 (2015)

10. Frydrychová Klímová, B., Poulova, P.: Pedagogical issues of online teaching: students' satisfaction with on-line study materials and their preferences for a certain type. In: Cao, Y., Väljataga, T., Tang, J.K.T., Leung, H., Laanpere, M. (eds.) ICWL 2014. LNCS, vol. 8699, pp. 187–194. Springer, Cham (2014). https://doi.org/10.1007/978-3-319-13296-9_21

11. Sophonhiranraka, S., Suwannatthachoteb, P., Ngudgratokec, S.: Factors affecting creative problem solving in the blended learning environment: a review of the literature. Procedia Soc. Behav. Sci. **174**, 2130–2136 (2015)

12. Hubackova, S.: Blended learning – new stage in the foreign language teaching. Procedia Soc. Behav. Sci. **197**, 1957–1961 (2015)

13. Mustapa, M.A.S., Ibrahim, M., Yusoff, A.: Engaging vocational college students through blended learning: improving class attendance and participation. Procedia Soc. Behav. Sci. **204**, 127–135 (2015)

14. Bower, M., Dalgarno, B., Kennedy, G.E., Lee, M.J.W., Kenney, J.: Design and implementation factors in blended synchronous learning environments: outcomes from a cross-case analysis. Comput. Educ. **86**, 1–17 (2015)

15. Porter, W.W., Graham, C.R., Spring, K.A., Welch, K.R.: Blended learning in higher education: institutional adoption and implementation. Comput. Educ. **75**(6), 185–193 (2013)

16. Tosun, S.: The effects of blended learning on EFL students' vocabulary enhancement. Procedia Soc. Behav. Sci. **199**, 641–647 (2015)

17. ScienceDirect: Blended learning approach (2016). http://www.sciencedirect.com/science?_ob=ArticleListURL&_method=list&_ArticleListID=-1122069391&_sort=r&_st=13&view=c&md5=2f2a4b412ff7d4c33545e2c92303bdb1&searchtype=a

18. Yin, R.K.: Case Study Research: Design and Methods. Sage, Newbury Park (1984)

19. Klimova, B.: University Business English learners and their needs. In: Proceedings of INTED 2015 Conference, pp. 560–564. IATED, Spain (2015)

20. Course Topics (2016). http://bboard.uhk.cz/webapps/portal/frameset.jsp?tab_tab_group_id=_2_1&url=%2Fwebapps%2Fblackboard%2Fexecute%2Flauncher%3Ftype%3DCourse%26id%3D_3426_1%26url%3D

21. Overall Summary of User Activity (2016). http://bboard.uhk.cz/webapps/portal/frameset.jsp?tab_tab_group_id=_2_1&url=%2Fwebapps%2Fblackboard%2Fexecute%2Flauncher%3Ftype%3DCourse%26id%3D_3426_1%26url%3D

22. Frydrychova Klimova, B., Poulova, P.: Forms of instruction and students' preferences - a comparative study. In: Cheung, S.K.S., Fong, J., Zhang, J., Kwan, R., Kwok, L.F. (eds.) ICHL 2014. LNCS, vol. 8595, pp. 220–231. Springer, Cham (2014). https://doi.org/10.1007/978-3-319-08961-4_21

23. Simonova, I., Kostolanyova, K.: The blended learning concept: comparative study of two universities. In: Cheung, S.K.S., Kwok, L.-f., Shang, J., Wang, A., Kwan, R. (eds.) ICBL 2016. LNCS, vol. 9757, pp. 302–311. Springer, Cham (2016). https://doi.org/10.1007/978-3-319-41165-1_27

24. Černá, M.: User evaluation of language websites as a way of students' engagement into blended learning process case study. In: Cheung, S.K.S., Kwok, L.-f., Shang, J., Wang, A., Kwan, R. (eds.) ICBL 2016. LNCS, vol. 9757, pp. 269–280. Springer, Cham (2016). https://doi.org/10.1007/978-3-319-41165-1_24

25. Dziuban, C., Hartman, J., Moskal, P., Sorg, S., Truman, B.: Three ALN modalities: an institutional perspective. In: Bourne, J., Moore, J.C. (eds.) Elements of Quality Online Education: Into the Mainstream, pp. 127–148 (2004)

26. Bakor Nordin, A., Alias, N.: Learning outcomes and student perceptions in using of blended learning in history. Procedia Soc. Behav. Sci. **103**, 577–585 (2013)

27. Garrison, D., Kanuka, H.: Blended learning: uncovering its transformative potential in higher education. Internet High. Educ. **7**(2), 95–105 (2004)

28. Reasons, S., Valadares, K., Slavkin, M.: Questioning the hybrid model: student outcomes in different course formats. J. Asynchronous Learn. **9**(1), 83–94 (2005)

29. Siew-Eng, L., Muuk, M.A.: Blended learning in teaching secondary schools' English: a preparation for tertiary science education in Malaysia. Procedia Soc. Behav. Sci. **167**, 293–300 (2015)

30. Klimova, B.: Developing ESP study materials for engineering students. In: Proceedings of 2015 IEEE Global Engineering Education Conference (EDUCON 2015), pp. 52–57. Tallinn University of Technology, Estonia (2015)

31. Joshi, A.: Multimedia: a technique in teaching process in the classroom. Curr. World Environ. **7**, 33–36 (2012)

32. Reid, E., Horvathova, B.: Teacher training programs for gifted education with focus on sustainability. J. Teach. Educ. Sustain. **18**(2), 66–74 (2016)

Modeling a Peer Assessment Framework by Means of a Lazy Learning Approach

Maria De Marsico[1], Andrea Sterbini[1], Filippo Sciarrone[2], and Marco Temperini[2(✉)]

[1] Department of Computer Science, Sapienza University,
Via Salaria, 113, 00189 Rome, Italy
{demarsico,sterbini}@di.uniroma1.it
[2] Department of Computer, Control and Management Engineering,
Sapienza University, Via Ariosto, 25, 00184 Rome, Italy
sciarro@dia.uniroma3.it, marte@dis.uniroma1.it

Abstract. Peer-assessment entails, for students, a very beneficial learning activity, from a pedagogical point of view. The peer-evaluation can be performed over a variety of peer-produced resources, the principle being that the more articulated such resource is, the better. Here we focus, in particular, on the automated support to grading open answers, via a peer-evaluation-based approach, which is mediated by the (partial) grading work of the teacher, and produces a (partial, as well) automated grading. We propose to support such automated grading by means of a method based on the K-NN technique. This method is an alternative to a previously studied and implemented one, based on Bayesian Networks. Here we describe the new approach and provide the reader with a preliminary evaluation.

Keywords: Peer assessment · Open-ended answers · Machine Learning

1 Introduction, and Related Work

Peer-assessment is generally deemed to be a very beneficial activity for students, from a pedagogical point of view. It is the task, given to students, to assess the products of other students (the peers), and entails a learning activity placed at the highest cognitive level [1]. It allows for both testing and challenging the learner's knowledge and level of understanding about a subject. Moreover, as an happy addition, it helps achieving high metacognitive capabilities [10, 13] As a matter of fact, the use of peer-assessment may even become just necessary, when the number of students to manage is too big, such as when a teacher is given a large class, or when *Massive Open Online Courses* (MOOCs) are the learning playground [8, 9]. The peer-evaluation can be performed over a variety of peer-produced resources, such as project report documents, essays, open answers in a questionnaire; the principle is that the more articulated the answer is, the better [12].

In this paper we focus, in particular, on the automated support to grading open answers, via a peer-evaluation-based approach, which is mediated by the (partial) grading work of the teacher. *OpenAnswer* is a didactic system where a classic n-tier web application allows students for peer assessment and teachers to monitor the overall

T.-C. Huang et al. (Eds.): SETE 2017, LNCS 10676, pp. 336–345, 2017.
https://doi.org/10.1007/978-3-319-71084-6_38

learning process through some didactic actions [4]. In it a *Bayesian Network* (BN) [11], implemented as an external module, acts as the inference engine: students are modeled by means of their Knowledge level K on the question topic and by the effectiveness of their evaluations, denoted as Judgment level J (a variable depending on K). In the BN, the answers of a single student have an estimated Correctness C (a variable depending on K as well). The values of K, J and C are represented by probability distributions and can be updated by evidence propagation through a learning algorithm. Here we present the design of a new inference engine for the OpenAnswer system, obtained as a KNN-based module. *K-NN* is an Instance-Based Learning technique, belonging to *lazy learning* methods, where instances can be represented as points in an Euclidean space. Learning consists of simply storing the presented training data [11], while inference is represented by the association of an instance (a point) to the nearest point(s), in such a way to classify the instance basing on the classification of the nearest point(s). In this module we basically maintain the structure of the student model as it is in *OpenAnswer*: $SM = \{K, J\}$, being K the student's knowledge level and J the student's judgment capability to assess and grade tasks (answers) performed by peers. The K-NN module has to fulfill the usual OpenAnswer's goal: inferring the grade that a student should receive, basing on the data coming from the peer-evaluation, the learning algorithm, and the grades added by the teacher over a subset of the students' answers.

The process starts with the peer-evaluation of the answers given by the class. Then the system assigns initial values for each student's K and J, basing on the peer-evaluation data. At this stage, the data related to each student are (1) her K and J values, computed basing on the marks received by the peers, and (2) the marks given by the student to the answers she peer-evaluated. So K is determined basing on the marks received by the student's answer; and J is determined basing on the agreement of her evaluations with the marks given to the answers she evaluated. Then the teacher gets involved in the process. A choice algorithm determines the most convenient answer to grade (i.e. whose grading would release as much information as possible in the system), and that answer is graded by the teacher. The teacher's grading is iterated on as many answers as it is needed (according to a termination condition). Each new grading contributes to progressively build a *core* group of graded answers, in which the precision of the grading is maximal (as the grading was given by the teacher). Basing on the model of a student, she can be represented as a point in the (K, J) space. Some of these points will be in the *core* group. Once the *core* group is not empty anymore, for each non-core point (i.e. student not included in the *core* set) the system can find the points in the *core* set that are nearest to it, and then it can use such proximity to infer over the student's model. After each additional graded answer, the whole system evolves, and new values for the student models are computed, as well as new distances between the points are determined, and new core-nearest-neighbors for the non-core students can be defined. Eventually, when a new grading is not going to change significantly the distances among the points in the system, the grade of each non-core student's answer can be computed, basing on the state of her model.

Our main research question in this paper, is to see whether the approach sketched above is viable and feasible. From a computational point of view we already know that the new approach has advantages over the BN-based one. We think that this new approach could be able to present the teacher with a relevant additional advantage: it can give significant help while facing big peer-communities, where it would be impossible to grade all the assignments. In Sect. 2 we describe the K-NN based module mentioned above. Then, in Sect. 3 an evaluation and discussion of the approach is given. Finally, in Sect. 4 conclusions are drawn.

1.1 Related Area

Open answers are answers to open-ended questions; they are given usually under the form of an essay, or, anyway, not in the closed form of the more widely adopted multiple choice questionnaires. The automated grading of open answers, is in fact important in various research fields. For instance in [14] an application to marketing analysis and support is discussed: customers' opinions are extracted, in order to get a fix over product reputation, by means of data mining techniques and natural language processing. However the topic is of particular relevance in the educational field, where a variety of techniques have been applied. In [2] the evaluation of answers is done basing on ontology models of the knowledge domain of interest, and semantic web technology is used to support the annotation of the questions (and, consequently, of the answers). An important contribution, related to the study of mathematics, is in [5], where the text/graphic documents produced by the students through a web editor are analyzed to uncover learner's misconceptions, and devise a treatment.

[3] use Bayesian Network techniques to maintain and manage the student model, in the framework of an Intelligent Tutoring System (ITS). In [7] the K-NN algorithm is applied with educational aims, in order to perform text-based categorization over the essays submitted by students in an English language course. In [6], Naive-Bayes and K-NN are used to generate dynamically questions about English language, out of the content of resources taken from Internet (BBC.com web pages).

2 The Learning Process

The inference module is based on a *learning* algorithm: K-NN. This is a *Lazy Learning* approach [11], also referred to as *Instance Based* learning: basically, in order to *learn* better classifying elements, the algorithm adapts the classification to each further instance of the elements, that becomes part of the training set. Each training instance is represented as a point in the n-dimensional space of the instance attributes.

The above mentioned elements are of course students, which we represent by a two-variables Student Model (SM): $K \equiv [1, 10]$ and $J \equiv [0, 1]$. K represents her competence (*Knowledge level*) about the question domain; J is a measure of her assessing capability (*Judgement*). By such attributes, each student is in turn represented as a point in the (K, J) space. Furthermore, the community of students is, at any given moment, dynamically parted into two groups: the *Core Group* (CG), and its complement. CG is composed by the students whose answers have been graded directly by the teacher; for them K is given (fixed); in the following we also call this set as S^+, and call its elements the s^+ students. On the contrary, S^- is the set of students whose grade is to be inferred (so, they have been graded only by peers).

Once the whole peer-evaluation has been completed, and no teacher's grading has yet been performed, our module's overall learning process starts with an initialization step: the students' SMs are initialized basing solely on the peer-evaluation data. Then, the learning process continues: at each following step, some answers from the S^- students are graded by the teacher, and consequently some students are extracted from S^- and added to S^+, and the *SMs* are recomputed: in particular, at each step the positions of the points representing S^- students, in the (K, J) space, do change, implying a new classification for them, which depends on their distance from points in S^+, according to the K-NN protocol.

At each step the module *learns* to (hopefully) better classifying the students in S^-, until a termination condition suggests to stop cycling, and the S^- students *SMs* become the grades finally inferred by the module.

2.1 Student's Model Initialization

The SM of each student is first initialized in the (K, J) space. This process goes by the following steps:

- The teacher assigns an open-ended question to all the students;
- Each student provides an answer;
- Each student grades the answers of n different peers, and her answer receives m peer grades;
- each s_l^- student model, $SM_l = \{K_l, J_l\}$, is initialized as follows:

$$K_l^- = \frac{\sum_{i=1}^m K_i^-}{m} \tag{1}$$

where K_i^- is the grade received by the $i - th$ of the n peers who graded the $s_l^- -$ student. In this way, the K_l value is initialized with the mean of all received grades. The rationale is that in this step we do not know the differences among students' true assessment capabilities, and so we give to each of them the same weight. For each s_l^- student, J_l^- is initialized as follows:

$$J_l^- = \frac{1}{1 + \sum_{i=1}^n \Delta_i^2} \tag{2}$$

$\Delta_i^2 = (\overline{K_{lj}} - \overline{K_j})^2$, being K_{lj} the grade assigned by the student s_l to the student s_j and K_j the arithmetic mean, i.e., the initial K^- of the student s_j, computed by Eq. 1. So, if a student grades her n peers with values always equal to their K^- values, her J^- value gets maximal: 1 (here we haven't teacher's grades available, so we have to do with the peer evaluations only).

2.2   The Learning Engine

After the initialization process, the students are represented in the (K, J) space. Our module's learning process, then, goes by the following steps, and it is now that teacher's grading takes place (grading one, or more, answers from s^- students):

- The teacher is suggested a ranked list of students/answers to grade, done basing on the variance in the peers evaluations;
- The teacher selects a group of students/answers in the ranked list, and grades them. Such grades are the new, final, K^+ values for such students;
- The graded students become s^+ students, and their position in the (K, J) space changes, as well as the positions of those students that peer-evaluated them.

In the following we will use K_{min} and K_{max} to denote the minimum and maximum values for K (i.e. here resp. 1 and 10). I_{max} will denote the maximum difference between two values of K, i.e. here 9. Moreover J_{min} and J_{max} will denote the minimum and maximum values for J (i.e. here resp. 0 and 1).

The new position (K^+, J_{new}^+) is computed by the following equations:

$$K^+ = K_{teacher} \tag{3}$$

being $K_{teacher}$ the grade assigned by the teacher,

$$
\begin{aligned}
J_{new}^+ &= J_{old} + \alpha(J_{max} - J_{old}) \ (0 \leq \alpha \leq 1) \\
J_{new}^+ &= J_{old} + \alpha J_{old} \ (\alpha < 0) \\
\alpha &= \frac{K_{teacher} - K_{old}^-}{I_{max}}
\end{aligned} \tag{4}
$$

Notice, in Eq. 4:

1. A convex function has been adopted for J update, providing the two cases according to the possible value of α. In particular J_{old} could stand for J_{old}^+ or J_{old}^-, depending on the student being already in S^+ (case J_{old}^+), or being just entering in S^+ (case J_{old}^-) or remaining in S^- (case J_{old}^- again).
2. In general we assume that the assessment skill of a student depends on her K, so the J value is a function of K. In the case $K_{teacher} = K_{old}^-$, no change is implied for J. Also notice that the difference $K_{teacher} - K_{old}^-$ is normalized with respect to I_{max}.

Once such a position has been computed for a student, all the students, s^+ or s^-, who graded this student, have their J value changed, according to Eq. 4 (for s^+) and to Eq. 6 (for s^-).

- Finally, each SM is updated, i.e. the (K_{new}^-, J_{new}^-) values are computed as in the following two equations (if and only if at least one of its k nearest students has changed with respect to the previous k-NN learning step):

$$K_{new}^- = K_{old}^- + \alpha(K_{max} - K_{old}^-)(0 \le \alpha \le 1)$$
$$K_{new}^- = K_{old}^- + \alpha K_{old}^-(\alpha < 0)$$
$$\alpha = \frac{1}{I_{max}} \frac{\sum_{i=1}^{k} \frac{1}{d_i}(K_i^+ - K_{old}^-)}{\sum_{i=1}^{k} \frac{1}{d_i}} \tag{5}$$

where:

1. d_i is the Euclidean distance between the s_{old}^- student under update, and the $i - th$ student in the Core Group (s_i^+);
2. The K_{new}^- value is given as a convex function, to keep K in [1, 10];
3. The acronym K-NN features a K, possibly misleading here, so we are using k for the number of nearest neighbors to be used in the learning algorithm.

$$J_{new}^- = J_{old}^- + \frac{(K_{new}^- - K_{old}^-)}{I_{max}} J_{old}^- (\beta = 0 \wedge J_i^+ = J_{old}^-, i = 1...k)$$
$$J_{new}^- = J_{old}^- + \beta(J_{max} - J_{old}^-)(0 \le \beta \le 1)$$
$$J_{new}^- = J_{old}^- + \beta J_{old}^-(\beta < 0) \tag{6}$$
$$\text{with } \beta = \frac{(K_{new}^- - K_{old})}{I_{max}} \frac{\sum_{i=1}^{k} \frac{1}{d_i}|J_i^+ - J_{old}^-|}{\sum_{i=1}^{k} \frac{1}{d_i}}$$

Where:

1. As mentioned earlier, we assume J depending on K: this is expressed through the difference between the K_{new}^- value, obtained by Eq. 5, and the K_{old}^- value.
2. d_i is the Euclidean distance between the s_{old}^- student under update, and the $i - th$ student in the Core Group (s_i^+);
3. The J_{new} value is given as a convex function, to keep J in its normal range [0,1];
4. k is as explained in the previous equation.
5. About the coefficient β, some notices are due, for the cases when $\beta = 0$. On the one hand, when the J^+ of the k nearest neighbors is equal to the J_{old}^- value of the s_i^- student under update, J_{new}^- is computed by the difference between K_{new}^- and K_{old}^- only. The rationale is that when the s^- student changes her K^- value, her assessment skill should change as well (by the assumption of dependence of J on K). On the other hand, when the K^- value for the student under update is not changed, the assessment skill stays unchanged as well.

In Fig. 1 an example of the application of the Eqs. 5 and 6 is shown.

So, every time the teacher grades a student, the network configuration changes in the (K, J) space according to Eq. 4 through 6. The teacher can execute these steps until the stop condition is met.

Two last details have to be dealt with: First, which students, not yet in the CG, could be profitably graded by the teacher? We have two alternatives: either the s^- student is directly chosen by the teacher, or it is suggested by the system. The module allows for the second strategy: a ranked list of s^- students is computed, basing on the

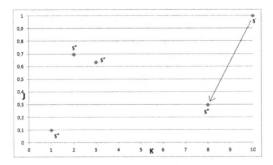

Fig. 1. Sample application of Eqs. 5 and 6. Here we have a 3-NN case. The s^- student changes her position, (K, J), according to the 3 associated s^+ neighbors. She becomes in turn a s^+ student. In particular, the teacher graded the s^- student with $K = 3$, while she had $K = 10$ from peers and $J = 1$. As a consequence, the SM changed from $(10, 1)$ to $(3, 0.63)$

variance among the grades given them by peers. In fact, if a student s^- shows a high variance in the received grades, the teacher's grade could be useful to get rid of a high error rate in the peer evaluation. Second, which termination condition could be applied, to stop the process? We propose a geometric rule, as a stop condition: the process stops when, after a teacher's grading step, the distances among the points in the network do not change significantly.

3   Evaluation

In this section we show the network dynamics, as it evolves according to the definitions given in Sect. 2. The learning process is managed directly by the teacher: every time she grades an answer, the SMs of all students change, resulting in a new configuration of the (K, J) space. This process ends when no significant change happens in the configuration. In the following we use a dataset composed by 26 students answering a question about Physics, at high School level. We run only one step of k-NN, with the aim to see the framework at work, and still appreciate its effects. Figure 2 shows the initial (K, J) distribution, according to peer data only.

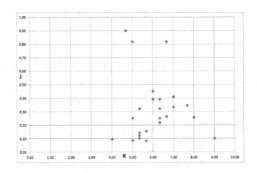

Fig. 2. The sample representation of the students (*SMs*)in the (K, J) space.

The peer assessment consisted of 3 evaluations for each student. Table 1 shows a subset of the ranked list of answers/students to be graded by the teacher. Each s^- student's rank follows the variance of the received marks. The teacher could select any student(s) in the list, however, the rank is devised in order to suggest the *best* answer(s) to grade, to get the greatest amount of information.

Table 1. The ranked list of the first six s^- students together with their received grades.

Student	$1 + \sum_{i=1}^{n} \Delta_i^2$	Peer Assessment	Teacher Assessment	J_{old}	J_{new}
26	4.67	8	8	0.26	0.26
27	3.56	6.33	7	0.22	0.28
30	3.56	7.67	6.5	0.35	0.30
34	3.56	5.67	6	0.16	0.19
21	2.67	5		0.08	0.09
3	2.00	6.5		0.41	0.41

In this experiment, the teacher decides to grade the first 4 s^- students: 26, 27, 30, 34: they become s^+ students; their final grades (the teacher's ones) are shown in table. Their positions in the plane change, as well as the positions of those s^- and s^+ students who graded them. Figure 3 shows the new configuration of the community in the space. In bold the new s^+ students.

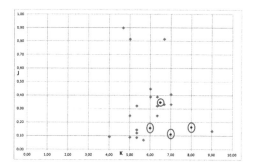

Fig. 3. The (K, J) space after the first teacher assessment.

The following part of the process goes now through the K-NN algorithm. Notice that we used $k = 1$ here, due to the limited extent of the experimentation, and of the available paper space. Figure 4 shows the new students distribution in the (K, J) space. Some points changed their position according to Eqs. 5 and 6.

In order to verify the termination condition, at each step the difference between the two spatial distributions has to be computed. Provisionally, here we computed this difference by the ratio of the sums of the distances of all the points from the origin of the K, J axes, before and after the update. As a threshold value for such difference we used 5%. In our case we had a difference of 3%, as shown in Table 2, which allowed us to stop after the single iteration described above.

Table 2. Distances between the two steps.

$Step_0$	$Step_1$	%
130	134	3.5%

For a final consideration, we show in Table 3 data related to the distribution of the assessments, given by the teacher, the peers, and by the framework's inference (initial step and k-NN step). The teacher gave a 5.85 mean grade, and the peers a more generous 6.05. Then the bare initialization of the system produced a 5.89 mean, then developed to 6.09 after the k-NN step. One key point, in our opinion, is in the standard deviation of the assessments, which is dramatically diminishing with the k-NN step. This seems encouraging, as it suggests that the framework can improve on the pure peer-evaluation, and also produce more stable assessment distributions.

Table 3. Arithmetic means of the assessments distributions.

$\mu_{teacher} - \sigma$	$\mu_{students} - \sigma$	$\mu step1 - \sigma$	$\mu step2 - \sigma$
5.85 − 0.7	6.05 − 1.17	5.89 − 1.10	6.09 − 0.39

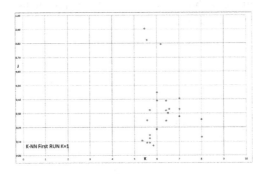

Fig. 4. The (K, J) space after the first K-NN step.

4   Conclusions and Future Work

We have presented a logical framework, based on a K-NN technique, devised to support semi-automated grading of peer-evaluated answers to open ended questions. The basic idea consists in modeling the individual student (by competence and assessing capability) and enhancing the peer-evaluation results by teacher's grading (of part of the answers). This proposal stems from a previous approach, based on Bayesian Networks, aiming to improving with respect to feasibility and computational costs. This is a first formalization of the new framework, and we have presented a preliminary evaluation of its effectiveness, on a dataset used to analyze the previous approach. Results appear to be promising, and a further, deeper experimentation seems in order. In terms of future work, we see that a main research problem is in how to build the Core

Group of students (on which the teacher's grading happened). The definition of an initial state of the CG, different than empty, and the ways of its growing, by further teacher's grading, is a relevant aspect. Possible solutions would entail to choose this set according to the results of preceding sessions (so passing the student modeling from a question to the next, contrary to starting over at each new question). An interesting investigation will also be on using the model without the teacher, to see if and how the pure peer-evaluation is positively affected by the sole use of the framework.

References

1. Bloom, B.S., Engelhart, M.D., Furst, E.J., Hill, W.H., Krathwohl, D.R.: Taxonomy of educational objectives: the classification of educational goals. In: Handbook I: Cognitive Domain. McGraw-Hill Inc., New York (1956)
2. Castellanos-Nieves, D., Fernandez-Breis, J., Valencia-Garcia, R., Martinez-Bejar, R., Iniesta-Moreno, M.: Semantic web technologies for supporting learning assessment. Inf. Sci. **181**(9), 1517–1537 (2011)
3. Conati, C., Gartner, A., Vanlehn, K.: Using Bayesian networks to manage uncertainty in student modeling. User Model. User-Adap. Inter. **12**, 371–417 (2002)
4. De Marsico, M., Sciarrone, F., Sterbini, A., Temperini, M.: The impact of self- and peer grading on student learning. EURASIA J. Math. Sci. Technol. Educ. **13**(4), 1085–1106 (2017)
5. El-Kechaï, N., Delozanne, É., Prévit, D., Grugeon, B., Chenevotot, F.: Evaluating the performance of a diagnosis system in school algebra. In: Leung, H., Popescu, E., Cao, Y., Lau, Rynson W.H., Nejdl, W. (eds.) ICWL 2011. LNCS, vol. 7048, pp. 263–272. Springer, Heidelberg (2011). https://doi.org/10.1007/978-3-642-25813-8_28
6. Hoshino, A., Nakagawa, H.: A real-time multiple-choice question generation for language testing - a preliminary study. In: Proceedings of 2nd Workshop on Building Educational Applications Using NLP, pp. 17–20 (2005)
7. Li, B., Lu, J., Yao, J.-M., Zhu, Q.-M.: Automated essay scoring using the KNN algorithm. In: Proceedings of International Conference on Computer Science and Software Engineering (2008)
8. Limongelli, C., Lombardi, M., Marani, A., Sciarrone, F.: A teacher model to speed up the process of building courses. In: Kurosu, M. (ed.) HCI 2013. LNCS, vol. 8005, pp. 434–443. Springer, Heidelberg (2013). https://doi.org/10.1007/978-3-642-39262-7_50
9. Limongelli, C., Lombardi, M., Marani, A., Sciarrone, F., Temperini, M.: A recommendation module to help teachers build courses through the moodle learning management system. New Rev. Hypermed. Multimed. **2**(1–2), 58–82 (2015)
10. Metcalfe, J., Shimamura, A.P.: Metacognition: Knowing About Knowing. MIT Press, Cambridge (1994)
11. Mitchell, T.M.: Machine Learning, 1st edn. David McKay, New York (1997)
12. Palmer, K., Richardson, P.: On-line assessment and free-response input-a pedagogic and technical model for squaring the circle. In: Proceedings of 7th CAA Conference, pp. 289–300 (2003)
13. Sadler, P.M., Good, E.: The impact of self- and peer-grading on student learning. Educ. Assess. **11**(1), 1–31 (2006)
14. Yamanishi, K., Li, H.: Mining open answers in questionnaire data. IEEE Intell. Syst. **17**, 58–63 (2002)

ADOILS (Application and Design of Innovative Learning Software)

A Framework Design for On-line Human Library

Tien-Wen Sung[1], Ting-Ting Wu[2(✉)], and Yi-Chen Lu[2]

[1] Fujian Provincial Key Laboratory of Big Data Mining and Applications,
Fujian University of Technology, Fuzhou, China
tienwen.sung@gmail.com
[2] Graduate School of Technological and Vocational Education,
National Yunlin University of Science and Technology, Douliou, Taiwan
ttwu@yuntech.edu.tw, luange10520@gmail.com

Abstract. A human library is an activity or event held to improve understanding between different individuals and reduce intergroup prejudice by a face-to-face conversation. For the purpose of promoting the advantages and improving the convenience and availability of the human library, this paper proposes an on-line human library system framework that can be applied to the implementation of moving human libraries from the real world to the digital world.

Keywords: Human library · Human book · On-line library · Framework

1 Introduction

A library usually plays an important role in providing people a rich knowledge or information source. It collects books, periodicals, multimedia, etc. and makes them accessible to people for reference or borrowing. Nowadays, on-line libraries make services convenient to readers via the Internet. On the other hand, there has been a kind of library activity, namely, human library. A human library activity usually takes place in a given venue. Readers read books at the place. However, the books are human beings, namely, living books. The reading behavior is a conversation with a living book. Thus, a human library is just like a conventional library, but readers borrow a living book (a person) to read (get into conversation). A human library is only active in a limited period of time because living books are not always on a bookshelf for borrowing. Since a human library is usually limited to the location and duration, it is not convenient for people to access and be benefited. Accordingly, this paper proposes a system framework for designing an on-line human library. The framework can be used to assist developers in designing an Internet-based human library.

2 Literatures

The original name of Human Library is Living Library, however it was changed in 2010 from Living Library to Human Library by the organizers in Denmark due to an international copyright contravening [1]. The first human library was founded in

T.-C. Huang et al. (Eds.): SETE 2017, LNCS 10676, pp. 349–354, 2017.
https://doi.org/10.1007/978-3-319-71084-6_39

Denmark by the *Stop The Violence* organization in 2000 [2]. The purpose of the activity is to reduce prejudices and stereotypes among different kinds of people by face-to-face conversations, and thus promote understanding and prevent conflicts between groups. The concept of a human library activity have globally spread to more than 70 countries [3], such as Australia [4] and Thailand [5]. There has been a literature indicating that a human library can be utilized to transfer and share tacit knowledge [6]. Although tacit knowledge is difficult to be expressed and presented in a formal real book, it can be easy to transfer by face-to-face conversations in a human library activity. In addition to promoting understanding and preventing conflicts between background-different groups, the literature [7] indicated that human libraries can also benefit human books and readers with seven altruistic and self-focused dimensions. The dimensions are helping others, teaching, making connections, learning, self-expression, reflection, therapeutic, and personal enjoyment.

3   System Architecture

Nowadays the human libraries are organized in the form of an activity event. Thus an event period and an activity location will be designated and announced prior to the event. These conditions cause people who would like to participate in the activity a great inconvenience. In addition to the inconvenience to the possible participants, the arrangement and management for human libraries are also heavy works. There is still a lack of on-line system to support the management and human book reading func-tionalities for human libraries. To make a progress towards a more convenient human library and facilitate the interaction between human books and readers, a system framework for an on-line human library is proposed in this work.

Figure 1 shows the system architecture for the on-line library. The system service must be based on Internet connections. The worldwide network environment makes communications easy for participants who come from different countries or regions. This is the aim to set up an on-line human library. A three-tier architecture can be a good model of the platform. The front-end tier is user clients, and the users can be categorized into three types: human books, readers, and librarians. There should be a functionality of on-line face-to-face chat between a human book client and a reader client. The clients can be either a web browser for a web-based system or a software for a client-server system. This paper merely describes a framework, thus both a web-based and a client-server system are applicable in a realized implementation. Moreover, not only a desktop computer but also a mobile device can be a user client platform since book reading could not be limited to a fixed location. The middle tier is an application server of the human library. It provides all the service functionalities required for the users of the three types. In addition, the application server has an ability to access the database server. The database server belongs to the back-end tier in the architecture and it is located behind the application server. All the database accesses should be done via the application server. This can avoid directly exposing the database to users for security concerns. There are three major databases included in the back-end database server for storing the data about users, lending records, and comments respectively.

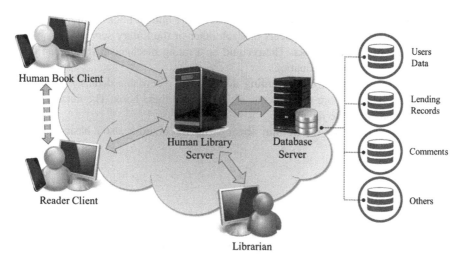

Fig. 1. The system architecture for the on-line human library.

4 Functionality Requirements

Although conducting information and network technologies into an on-line human library implementation is partially similar to an Internet-based website system for a general public library, there are still quite different between these two types of library systems. For example, the presentation and classification of the books. In this section, it is attempted to give the functionality requirements for the on-line human library. The fundamental requirements for the system are listed and briefly described as follows:

(1) **Electronic shelves for human books.** Human books are unlike printed books because they are human beings and not put on real shelves. The human book shelves should be presented virtually on the user interface of the system.

(2) **Classification for human books.** Human books should be categorized by a scheme which is different from the conventional classification schemes such as Dewey Decimal Classification (DDC) and Chinese Library Classification (CLC).

(3) **Introduction to human books.** An introduction to a printed book could be a concise summary with a table of contents while the introduction to a human book could be the living experiences or the profession owned by the person, or even a short biography.

(4) **Human books searching.** Some searching conditions are not appropriate for human book, for example, book name, publisher, ISBN number, etc.

(5) **Human book reservation or borrowing.** The reservation and borrowing should be fitted to the pre-defined and time-limited availability of the person. It is unlike a printed book that always on the book shelves.

(6) **On-line interaction between human books and readers.** Reading a human book is actually a behavior of conversation. The functionality of instant messaging or on-line chatting is essential.

(7) **Commentary functionality.** After finishing the human book reading, the book and reader can give comments on each other or the library service.

(8) **Rating of human books.** There could be a rating mechanism for human book encouragement or evaluations.

(9) **Records of human book lending details.** The recordable details of lending a human book is more than the one of lending a printed book. The details should be recorded in the database.

(10) **Bulletin board for the human library.** Bulletin board is also a basic service in a human library.

5   Framework Design

In this section, it is attempted to give a design of system framework for an on-line human library. The following Fig. 2 shows the block diagram of the framework. It can be utilized for the implementation of an on-line human library system. There are eight major modules in the diagram that described as follows.

(1) **Human Book.** This module presents the function components for the human book client. Both of the components of *Register* and *Login/Logout* are basic and necessary. A user should provide personal information to the system for a human

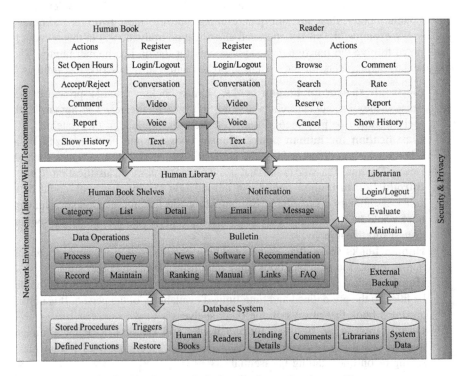

Fig. 2. The framework design for the on-line human library.

book evaluation. Once the registration is approval, the user can login the system with his/her ID and password as a human book. A human book uses *Set Open Hours* function to arrange available times for readers to borrow or reserve. *Accept/Reject* function can help a human book to respond to the actions of borrowing or reservation from readers. The book can use the *Comment* function to make a feedback on a reading event. The *Report* function is used to accuse the reader of violating regulations. *Show History* allows human books to list the past book lending details. *Conversation* is an important component to enable the human book and user to communicate, that is, reading the book. The conversation can be achieved with a medium of video, audio, or text.

(2) **Reader.** Several components in the module of reader client are similar to the human book module, but the other components are not. Readers can use *Browse* or *Search* function to find a human book of interest and can *Reserve* the book according to the human book open hours. Also, a *Cancel* of the reservation is allowed. The *Rate* function provides readers to give a rating for the human book after the conversation with the book.

(3) **Librarian.** The *Evaluate* component in this module is used to support librarians to accept or reject the registration of a new human book. It is also possible to remove an existing book with negative ratings. The *Maintain* component supports fundamental operations for human library data processing and management.

(4) **Human Library.** This module provides interactions and services for the three clients above. The component of *Human Book Shelves* deals with the category, list, and detail information of the human books evaluated and available in the library. *Data Operations* provide the functionalities of data processing, recording, query, and maintenance for the user clients or database system. The *Notification* component can support the function of notifying users a reminder, new information, a warning, etc. by an email or message. *Bulletin* component is used to make some information public. The information includes news, human book recommendations, human book ranking, downloadable software, manuals, and others such as related links and FAQs.

(5) **Database System.** This module serves as a back-end server to support data storage, in-system data processing, and the responses to the requests from the human library module given above. *Stored Procedures, Defined Functions,* and *Triggers* are previously built to achieve the processing. *Restore* function is required once a database damage happens. Moreover, the data can be categorized into human books, readers, librarians, lending details, comments, and system data.

(6) **External Backup.** This module performs a necessary and useful backup plan to avoid the loss of data caused by damage. An external storage device is required to automatically store a duplicate data for the system.

(7) **Network Environment.** This module includes hardware, software, communication systems, mechanisms, and protocols to support reliable inter-module and intra-module data transfers for the system. The technology and infrastructure of Internet, WiFi, and telecommunication systems such as 3G and 4G can be utilized.

(8) **Security and Privacy.** The content of a printed book is public, but some detail information about a human book could be secret or not public. Data stored in an

on-line human library should be protected. A user admission control to the system, firewall deployment for inter- and intra-networks, and encryption scheme for data should be involved in security concerns. Data also should be accessed, maintained, and managed under a privacy strategy.

6 Conclusion

To facilitate the utilization of a human library, it is essential to migrate a real world human library to a digitalized human library system. This paper proposes a system framework of an on-line human library with a three-tier system architecture. The system is composed of the modules of human book, reader, librarian, human library, database system, external backup, network environment, security and privacy. The framework can be utilized to implement an Internet-based human library system for eliminating the limitations of event location and duration in the real world human library activities. It can improve the availability and benefit the promotion of a human library.

Acknowledgments. This work is partially supported by the Fujian Province Education Science Thirteen-Five Plan 2016 Cross-strait Vocational Education Special Research Project, China (FJJKHX16-031) and partially supported by Ministry of Science and Technology, Taiwan under grant MOST 104-2511-S-224-003-MY3 and MOST 105-2628-S-224-001-MY3.

References

1. Dreher, T., Mowbray, J.: The Power of One on One: Human Libraries and the Challenges of Antiracism Work. UTSePress, Sydney (2012)
2. Garbutt, R.: The living library: some theoretical approaches to a strategy for activating human rights and peace. In: Proceedings of Activating Human Rights and Peace Conference 2008, pp. 270–278, Southern Cross University, Byron Bay, Australia (2008)
3. The Origin of the Human Library. http://humanlibrary.org/about-the-human-library/. Accessed 17 Apr 2017
4. Kinsley, L.: Lismore's living library: connecting communities through conversation. Australas. Public Libr. Inf. Serv. **22**(1), 20–25 (2009)
5. Charoensak, R., Vongprasert, C.: Public libraries in Thailand in the context of living library model for lifelong learning in the community. Asia Pacific J. Libr. Inf. Sci. **3**(2), 1–10 (2013)
6. Zhai, Y., Zhao, Y., Wang, R.: Human library a new way of tacit knowledge sharing. In: Zhu, M. (ed.) Business, Economics, Financial Sciences, and Management, vol. 143, pp. 335–338. Springer, Heidelberg (2012). https://doi.org/10.1007/978-3-642-27966-9_46
7. Dobreski, B., Huang, Y.: The joy of being a book: benefits of participation in the human library. In: Proceedings of the 79th ASIS&T Annual Meeting: Creating Knowledge, Enhancing Lives through Information & Technology, American Society for Information Science Silver Springs, Copenhagen, Denmark (2016)

Design and Evaluation of Mobile Cuisine Guiding System for English Learning Applications

C.-H. Hunag, J.-F. Fang, H.-R. Chen(✉), P.-H. Tseng, and J.-J. Chang

Department of Digital Content and Technology,
National Taichung University of Education, Taichung 403, Taiwan
hrchen@mail.ntcu.edu.tw

Abstract. English has become the international dominant language, but English learning in Taiwan still focuses on traditional oral teaching and digital leaning method. Without the guidance of actual life situation, such English learning method has the difficulty in arousing English learning motivation. Gradually, scholars have put forward the idea that situational experience in mobile learning is used to improve English learning motivation. In order to achieve mobile learning, it is necessary to rely on location-aware technology and the development of GPS is the most popular among the numerous location-aware technologies. Therefore, this research implemented a set of system combining food guide and English mobile learning and applied Technology Acceptance Model (TAM) to discuss the usage acceptance of this system. Research results show that in regard to the usage of learners' mobile device, the factor of "anxiety" is the most important to system acceptance and the factor of "perceived usefulness" has the highest correlation with the factor of "system usage acceptance".

Keywords: Context-aware · Mobile Technology · English learning

1 Introduction

With the development of economy and evolution of transportation tool, communication between countries is extremely easier. In this case, English has become the main language for communication between each other. Although English learning has become the topic valued by all the people, English teaching still adopts traditional teaching model in most cases. The so-called traditional English teaching model means that a general teacher teaches students to learn English. In this teaching mode, teachers need to spend lots of time in preparing teaching materials or making teaching tools and students have difficulty in arousing learning interest for lack of actual feeling to cause lower learning effectiveness [1]. With the development of science and technology, rapid prevalence of the Internet, advancement of multimedia technology and improvement of broadband, the learning model gradually evolves into new digital learning and many researchers have also been engaged in this field. For instance, establish online dynamic English reading and learning platform and use acceptance evaluation [2]; online English teaching system provides a tool for oral practice and

© Springer International Publishing AG 2017
T.-C. Huang et al. (Eds.): SETE 2017, LNCS 10676, pp. 355–362, 2017.
https://doi.org/10.1007/978-3-319-71084-6_40

online English teaching system considering both listening and pronunciation [3]. The above-mentioned research has gotten rid of traditional English teaching model to digitize English teaching materials and establish English learning website in combination with multimedia assisted teaching. After the establishment, the learning effectiveness is evaluated in these researches. Compared with learning effectiveness in traditional teaching, the digitization of teaching materials can achieve higher learning effectiveness and improve students' learning interest [4, 5]. Moreover, thanks to the rapid development of current mobile device and higher wireless network technology, scholars further propose mobile learning, emphasizing learn whenever and wherever possible. Therefore, mobile learning has been developed into major appeal in many researches; for instance, design the learning system to assist in English oral reflection ability and mobile English situation assisted learning system. In conclusion, the research results show that as for English learning, mobile learning can achieve higher learning effectiveness than general digital learning and better arouse students' learning motivation.

Although mobile learning has solved the problem of usage position limitation, the learning motivation cannot be improved effectively if English teaching website is only transferred into the model used by mobile device without changing the teaching materials according to the different learning environments. If English teaching and learning materials related to situation can be provided on the basis of specific location, the learning motivation can certainly be improved effectively. At present, priority is given to navigation model centering on specific location in most researches integrating GPS mobile navigation system: for instance, the research into applying the combination of RFID and GPS to electronic inspection system and the research into mobile navigation situation and interface in campus on the basis of proactive service; in these researches, GPS is mainly applied to campus [6]. People feel it enjoyable and happy to taste the snacks and most students often spend great mental efforts and much money enjoying local snacks, but the exact position for this snack cannot be expressed accurately. Therefore, every time students go there, they must ask the local residents for the position or rely on the classmates who are more familiar with the local path to lead the way; sometimes they may fail to find that store and return in low spirits due to the road maintenance or the changes of surroundings. In that situation, if a set of food navigation system is developed out with the center of local famous snacks, the unpleasant emergency events will be avoided to truly enjoy the local snacks.

This study aims to design mobile English learning and food navigation system to improve English learning motivation through students' favor for local snacks. Meanwhile, GPS positioning technology is combined to plan the path and guide students to the location of the snacks, so as to avoid the event that they cannot find the store and return in low spirits. Therefore, the purposes of this research are shown as below: (1) To develop out a set of mobile English learning & food navigation system with the mobile device as the platform by combining the digitalized English teaching materials and local snacks and integrating GPS positioning technology to plan the path. (2) To conduct situational English learning for students in life food. (3) To evaluate Technology Acceptance Model of mobile English learning & food navigation system.

2   Literature Review

The [7] considered that mobile learning can occur whenever and wherever possible and the mobile device used can present the learning contents required by user and provide the communication channel between teacher and student. However, the [8] thought that mobile learning refers to the learning whenever and wherever possible through mobile device in combination with location-aware technology and digital learning. The [9] held that as long as the learning occurs through any mobile device without the limitation of time and place, it can be called mobile learning. There are 3 necessary elements for mobile learning: 1. The communication infrastructure: user can use such communication infrastructure to access digitalized learning materials and communicate or discuss with other users. 2. The learning activity model: indoor or outdoor individual or team learning activity. 3. The mobile learning device: mobile learning device is the most important for mobile learning to realize learning whenever and wherever possible. In addition to all the features owned by digital learning, mobile learning also has its own unique features, such as urgency for learning demand, initiative for knowledge acquisition, maneuverability for learning site, interaction during learning process, contextualization of teaching activity and integrality of teaching contents [10].

Technology Acceptance Model (TAM) is developed by [11] on the basis of Theory of Reasoned Action (TRA) of social psychology. Proposed by [12], TRA's main purpose is to predict and understand human's behavior. Basically assume that human's behaviors are produced under the control of reason and their own will, i.e. individual behavior is the activity adopted after the systematic and rational thinking based on the acquired information. In order to effectively explain and predict user's behavior of using information technology, Davis modifies TRA to make it conform to the application situation of information technology, i.e. TAM. Davis considered that perceived usefulness and perceived ease of use are the two important factors in TAM because the extrinsic variable affecting user's information technology acceptance behavior produces the actual system usage behavior through perceived usefulness and perceived ease of use as well as the effect on using attitude and using behavior intention.

3   Methodology

3.1   Design of Mobile English Learning and Food Navigation System

In this study, GPS positioning tool is matched with mobile device to establish a set of mobile English learning & food navigation system, so as to improve English learning motivation through food navigation and evaluate this system by TAM. The system structure can be divided into 2 parts: GPS positioning program for assistant position system as well as administration page side and user side of main system. Besides, in terms of data communication, this system must rely on wireless network and database to transfer data under the environment of wireless network and the acquired information is transmitted to user's mobile device by means of wireless network. The function option and navigation in the system are all presented in English to achieve the research purpose of situational English learning. The main function planning is divided into 2 parts: user side and administrator page. In user side, there are 5 functions, including food information navigation, food path planning, food recommendation, error reporting, and real-time message exchange; while in administrator page, there are 3 functions, including updating food information, new addition of food resorts and deletion of food resorts, as shown in Figs. 1 and 2.

Fig. 1. The framework of mobile English learning and food navigation system

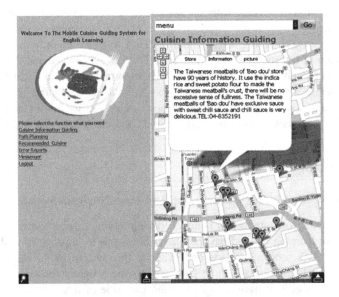

Fig. 2. The screenshot of cuisine information guiding for English learning

3.2 Evaluation and Process

In this study, the questionnaire design is divided into 6 dimensions, respectively including information literacy, familiarity with the usage of mobile device, anxiety for the usage of mobile device, perceived usefulness, perceived ease of use and system usage acceptance. The questionnaire content is divided into 2 parts: Part 1 is the basic information, including gender, length of schooling and experience of using mobile device. Part 2 respectively includes information literacy, familiarity with the usage of mobile device, anxiety for the usage of mobile device, perceived usefulness, perceived ease of use and system usage acceptance. Likert 7-point scale was adopted as the measurement method. The questionnaire contents were prepared mainly through collection of relevant data and summary of relevant literature. This study used convenience sampling to select participates. In total, 131 valid surveys remained for analysis. Hypotheses tested by this study are presented as follows.

H1a: user's information literacy has the significantly positive effect on the system of perceived usefulness

H1b: user's information literacy has the significantly positive effect on the system of perceived ease of use

H2a: user's familiarity with the usage of mobile device has the significantly positive effect on the system of perceived usefulness

H2b: user's familiarity with the usage of mobile device has the significantly positive effect on the system of perceived ease of use

H3a: anxiety for the usage of mobile device has the significantly positive effect on the system of perceived usefulness

H3b: anxiety for the usage of mobile device has the significantly positive effect on the system of perceived ease of use

H4: the system perceived ease of use has the significantly positive effect on system perceived usefulness

H5a: system perceived usefulness has the significantly positive effect on system usage acceptance

H5b: system perceived ease of use has the significantly positive effect on system usage acceptance.

The study used Pearson Correlation Coefficient to analyze whether the correlation among the 6 factors, including information literacy (IL), familiarity with the usage of mobile device (FD), anxiety for the usage of mobile device (AD), perceived usefulness (PU), perceived ease of use (PE) and system usage acceptance (SA) in this questionnaire is significant as shown in Table 1. The correlation coefficient for the 6 dimensions in this questionnaire lies between 0.365 and 0.654, achieving the significant level. This research adopted Kaiser-Meyer-Olkin (KMO) and Bartlett sphericity test to verify the correlation between the dimensions. According to the verification results, KMO is 0.888, signifying the correlation between dimensions in this questionnaire is good; besides, the Approx. Chi-Square of Bartlett sphericity test is 1851.862 and its result achieves the significant level, signifying that this questionnaire is suitable for factor analysis.

Table 1. Pearson correlation

Factor	IL	FD	AD	PU	PE	SA
IL	1					
FD	.452**	1				
AD	.365**	.542**	1			
PU	.495**	.502**	.395***	1		
PE	.528**	.654**	.394**	.438**	1	
SA	.492**	.653**	.417**	.443**	.597**	1

*<.05, **<.01, ***<.001

4 Results

After factor analysis as shown in Table 1, the first factor is the "anxiety for the usage of mobile device", and its eigenvalue is 3.067; the second factor is the "perceived ease of use" and its eigenvalue is 3.007; the third factor is the "information literacy" and its eigenvalue is 2.515; the fourth factor is the "system usage acceptance" and its eigenvalue is 2.268; the fifth factor is the "perceived usefulness" and its eigenvalue is 2.242; the sixth factor is the "familiarity with the usage of mobile device" and its eigenvalue is 2.146. In terms of explained variance, the factor of "anxiety for the usage of mobile device" is 10.954%, the factor of "perceived ease of use" is 10.741%, the factor of "information literacy" is 8.984%, the factor of "system usage acceptance" is 8.099%, the factor of "perceived usefulness" is 8.006%, and the factor of "familiarity with the usage of mobile device" is 7.664%, i.e. the explained variance totals 54.448%.

The path analysis results are shown in Fig. 3. The β coefficient between factor of "information literacy" and "perceived usefulness" is 0.675, the β coefficient between factor of "information literacy" and "perceived ease of use" is 0.689, the β coefficient between factor of "familiarity with the usage of mobile device" and "perceived usefulness" is 0.682, the β coefficient between factor of "familiarity with the usage of mobile device" and "perceived ease of use" is 0.720, the β coefficient between factor of "perceived ease of use" and "perceived usefulness" is 0.721, the β coefficient between factor of "perceived usefulness" and "system usage acceptance" is 0.735 and the β coefficient between factor of "perceived ease of use" and "system usage acceptance" is

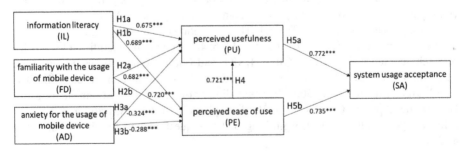

Fig. 3. Path analysis

0.772, all having the significantly positive relationship. But the β coefficient between factor of "anxiety for the usage of mobile device" and "perceived usefulness" is -0.324 and the β coefficient between factor "anxiety for the usage of mobile device" and "perceived ease of use" is -0.288, having the significantly negative relationship. Therefore, when user's anxiety for the usage of mobile device is lower, the user's system perceived usefulness and perceived ease of use will be higher. It can be seen that user's information literacy will have a direct effect on user's system perceived usefulness and perceived ease of use, user's familiarity with the usage of mobile device will positively affect user's system perceived usefulness and perceived ease of use, and user's perceived ease of use towards system will also directly affect user's system perceived usefulness. Moreover, user's system perceived usefulness and perceived ease of use will have significantly positive effect on user's system usage acceptance.

5   Conclusion

In terms of factor "information literacy, research H1a and H1b are true. The research result conducted by [13] that information literacy has the significantly positive effect on perceived usefulness and perceived ease of use, is consistent with the result of this study. In terms of factor "familiarity with the usage of mobile device", research H2a and H2b are true. The research result conducted by [2] that familiarity with the usage of mobile device has the significantly positive effect on perceived usefulness and perceived ease of use, is consistent with the result of this study. In terms of factor "anxiety for the usage of mobile device", research H3a and H3b are true. The anxiety for the usage of mobile device shown in the research results of [14] has no significant effect on perceived usefulness and perceived ease of use, which is different from the results in this study. In terms of factor "perceived ease of use", research H4 and H5b are true. In the end, in terms of factor "perceived usefulness", research H5a (system perceived usefulness has the significantly positive effect on system usage acceptance) is true.

References

1. Shiuan, T.-s., Liu, W.-y.: Investigating the influence of teaching methods on students' english learning from the perspective of multiple intelligences. J. Natl. Taipei Teach. Coll. **18**(1), 151–182 (2005)
2. Shi, B.-Y.: The research of the development of an on-line english reading environment and acceptance evaluation. J. Natl. Pingtung Univ. Educ. **24**, 521–554 (2006)
3. Hung, Y.-C., Lai, Y.-L., Chen, J.-H.: Online English classroom-with speaking practicing. J. Natl. Chiayi Univ. **76**, 157–165 (2005)
4. Wang, C.-C.: Mobile English situated assistant learning system about campus living environment. Master dissertation, National Pingtung University, Taiwan (2007)
5. Huang, C.-H.: A system for assisting english oral proficiency - a case study of the elementary level of general English proficiency test in Taiwan. Master dissertation, Chinese Culture University, Taiwan (2008)

6. Hung, I.-C., Yang, X.-J., Fang, W.-C., Hwang, G.-J., Chen, N.-S.: A context-aware video prompt approach to improving students' in-field reflection levels. Comput. Educ. **70**, 80–91 (2014)

7. Bekkestua: Mobile Education - A Glance at the Future (2003). http://www.dye.no/articles/a_glance-at_the_future/introduction.html. Accessed 12 Mar 2013

8. Harris, P.: Goin' Mobile (2001). http://www.astd.org/LC/2001/0701harris.htm

9. Chabra, T., Figueiredo, J.: How to Design and Deploy and held Learning (2002). Http://www.empoweringtechnologies.net/eLearning/eLearning_expov5_files/frame.htm. Accessed 9 Nov 2009

10. Hwang, G.-J., Chen, T.-W.: Future classroom, mobile and ubiquitous technologies-enhanced learning. High Education Publisher (2014)

11. Davis, F.D., Bagozzi, R.P., Warsaw, P.R.: User acceptance of computer technology: a comparison of two theoretical models. Manag. Sci. **35**(8), 983–1003 (1989)

12. Fishbein, M., Ajzen, I.: Belief, Attitude, Intention, and Behavior: An Introduction to Theory and Research. Addison-Wesley, Reading (1975)

13. Zou, H.-y.: Personal factors' influences on behaviors of using instructional resources websites-taking Miaoli County elementary school teachers as examples. Master dissertation, Chung Hua University, Taiwan (2008)

14. Lo, J.-L.: Study on mobile learning device - technology acceptance model. Master dissertation, National Central University, Taiwan (2004)

The Development of an Affective Tutoring System for Japanese Language Learners

Yu Chun Ma$^{(\boxtimes)}$ ⓘ and Hao-Chiang-Koong Lin ⓘ

National University of Tainan, Tainan, Taiwan
coldlavender@gmail.com

Abstract. In this time of internationalization, learning a second language is now a mainstream trend, but, learning a new language can be something frustrating and annoying for most people. This research applied Affective Computing into Intelligent Tutoring System in order to make learning fun and interesting. The system will be set up in cloud drives (cloud storage sites), so the learner can avoid the time and space limitation, providing them an adaptive learning environment. Additionally, we will also be discovering the difference between the learners with different learning style, and we will also be using Emotional Recognition Method to understand the learner's emotion while learning in order to promote learner's learning efficiency.

Keywords: Affective Computing · Affective Tutoring Systems · Chinese language semantic recognition · Second language learning · VAK learning style

1 Introduction

1.1 Research Background and Motivation

As technology progress rapidly day by day, technology tends to develop in order to fulfill the needs of mankind. It does not only change the human lifestyle, but also provided more ways to learn. It is an important aid for teachers to use technology as a teaching method to increase learning efficiency. In the other hand, knowing a second language is almost a "must" in today's society, but learning second language is not an easy task for everyone, Krashen (1981) pointed out the "affective filter hypothesis" on second language learning, that a negative attitude and lack of enthusiasm for learning will decrease the learner's ability to receive and process the message, and then affect the learning efficiency of learning the second language. We all hope to understand the learner's emotion and help them to stay positive while learning, since affective computing can use any sensor to capture human's facial expression, body movement, semantics...etc. to identify emotional state and give it the best response. This research combines affective computing with tutoring system, and second language as the learning content, and apply the cloud drives to increase its accessibility, hoping the learner can effectively improve learning efficiency with this system.

© Springer International Publishing AG 2017
T.-C. Huang et al. (Eds.): SETE 2017, LNCS 10676, pp. 363–371, 2017.
https://doi.org/10.1007/978-3-319-71084-6_41

1.2 Research Purpose

This research adds intelligent tutoring systems (ITS) into affective computing, creating affective tutoring system (ATS), and uses this system on learning Japanese language. In addition, an interactive agent is set up to aid learners with difficulties, it also uses Chinese language semantic recognition to detect learner's emotion while using the system and provide feedback, and analyze it through message encoding in order to study the emotion changes with different learning style.

2 Literature Review

2.1 Affective Computing

Natural Language Processing. Natural Language Processing (NPL) is a language similar to what human kind uses, it involves the cross-domain technology in computer science and linguistics, NPL mainly studies the problems of words and phrases, can effectively help in analyzing word and sentence structure. Zhang (2003) uses Hidden Markov Model (HMM) to get five different marks from five different layers of participles, and converge it into a complete word segmentation system. Asahara et al. (2005) increases the system's ability by combining two learning algorithm, SVM and CRF. In addition, Goh (2005) uses SVM to practice combining information with maximum matching algorithm, increasing SVM's segmentation ability and other features.

Emotion Classification System. Russell (1980) constructed a planar emotion model, diving emotion into four quadrant, with the total of eight emotions: joy, surprise, calmness, bored, fear, anger, sadness, and disgust as shown on Fig. 1.

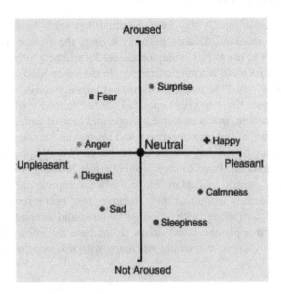

Fig. 1. James Russell's circumplex model (Russell1980)

Shaver et al. (1987) used user report and listed out 135 emotion adjective, dividing it into six emotions: love, happiness, surprise, anger, sadness and fear. In Plutchik's (1991) published works stated that emotion is caused by the surrounding environment and physiological or psychological reactions, so by creating emotion classification module can present the relationship of each emotion, as shown below (Fig. 2).

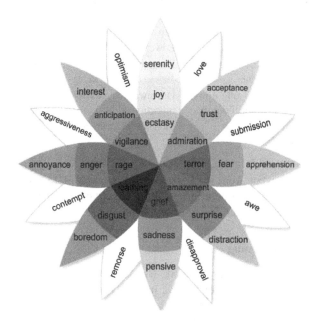

Fig. 2. Robert Plutchik's wheel of emotions (Plutchik 1991)

Emotional Recognition System. Emotional Recognition System uses a variety of detecting method to correctly determine learner's emotion while participating in activities, so voice recognition is also part of research, Murray and Arnott (1993) made a research on the relation between emotion and voice, and the result is shown in the Table 1 below.

Also, Ren (2009) uses words, voices, facial movement as signal of recognition, letting the system know it's emotion and give feedback; secondly, word is a part worth discussing, because word itself contains emotion, combining words with different emotions can create other emotions, plus, the sentence combined by words can also bring out another emotion.

Semantic Recognition System. Emotional Recognition through word is a system often used in detecting emotion, in identification rate analysis, Yang, Chao, Lin and Chang (2013) analyzed the negative and positive emotion, by accuracy of Bayesian is 78.30%, SVM 78.67%, Conditional Random Field (CRF) 82.27%. Lin et al. (2012) used SVM and SeCeVa to enhance the analysis on emotion adjectives and semantic structure, by using these semantic clues: privative, conjunction, and transitional word,

Table 1. Emotions and speech relations (Murray and Arnott 1993)

	Anger	Happiness	Sadness	Fear	Disgust
Speech rate	Slightly faster	Faster or slower	Slightly slower	Much faster	Very much faster
Pitch Average	Very much higher	Much higher	Slightly lower	Very much higher	Very much lower
Pitch Range	Much wider	Much wider	Slightly narrower	Much wider	Slightly wider
Intensity	Higher	Higher	Lower	Normal	Lower
Voice Quality	Breathy, chest	Breathy, blaring tone	Resonant	Irregular voicing	Grumble chest tone
Pitch changes	Abrupt on stressed	Smooth, upward inflections	Downward inflections	Normal	Wide, downward terminal inflects
Articulation	Tense	Normal	Slurring	Precise	Normal

the recognition rate went from 40.3 to 65.15%. According to ontology's analysis methods, it uses the distance between emotion adjectives to calculate the emotion's strength, furthermore, calculate the emotion of the phrase.

2.2   Emotion and Learning

Emotion and learning is closely related, Barker (1992) mentioned that cognitive emotion state and learning environment is interactive; from the research of Graesser et al. (2004), they discovered that the student's emotion in a learning environment s relative to it's action and learning. Through ontology, Eyharabide and Amandi (2012) predicted the student's emotion while learning, and pointed out that positive emotions can help increase the ability of problem solving. All these related research proves the relation between emotion and learning.

2.3   Teaching System

Intelligent Tutoring System (ITS) consist of four basic components: domain model, student model, tutoring model and user interface model (Nwana 1990; Freedman 2000; Nkambou and Bourdeau 2010), this system gives feedback and proper study content according to the learner's level, the affective tutoring system (ATS) can determine the learner's learning state and identify it's emotion state, give it an emotion feedback to guide the learner's emotion (Mao and Li 2010). With ITS combined with emotion recognition system, hoping to help the learner by giving him emotion feedback like a real person would, hence increase the learning efficiency. (Sarrafzadeh et al. 2004)

2.4   Learning Style

How a learner process the information learned is called learning style, it can define an individual's learning style by how the learner process information and how he solves problems. This research's participants learns with the system, mainly with Japanese video and Japanese textbooks as teaching materials, and this research uses VAK learning style test as learning style classification.

3   Research Methods

3.1   Research Subject

The purpose of this research is to investigate the satisfaction rating of the learners with different learning style while using ITS, and if these learners' emotion throughout the learning process will affect the learning efficiency. 73 people with education level above college volunteered to use this system, with 41 people being male and 32 female.

3.2   Design of Experiment

Learner uses this system to do the learning style classification test, then began to operate the system after the test. The system's learning materials includes graphic textbook reading and video learning, the learner are free to choose its learning materials. While operating, the system will collect the data between the interaction of the learner and system and the learner's emotion, the learner will also complete the system's system usability scale (SUS) and questionnaire for user interaction satisfaction (QUIS).

3.3   Learning Style Scale

This research uses VAK learning style scale, this scale divides learning style into three types: visual, auditory and kinesthetic. Visually-dominant learner absorbs and retains information best when it is presented in pictures, texts or charts. An auditory-dominant learner responds best to voices, prefers to listen to what is being presented. A kinesthetic-dominant learner prefers to learn through physical experience, a "hands-on" activity will be the most efficient way for them to learn.

3.4   System Usability Scale (SUS)

In 1986, John Brooke published system usability scale (SUS), which is used to evaluate the user's satisfaction after using the product. In this research, the scale is used to measure the user's emotion, then fractionalize the results in order to use it in statistical analysis.

3.5   Questionnaire for User Interaction Satisfaction (QUIS)

The QUIS is mainly used for user to give feedback for the overall system satisfaction, measuring the multimedia, learning factor, terminology and system feedback, system performance and many other factors. Likert Scale is used as rating scale, the user will fill out the QUIS from a scale from 1–7, with 1 being very unsatisfactory and 7 being very satisfactory.

3.6   Information Encoding

In this research, while the user is learning through the system, the semantic recognition system will collect the emotion data, then after every user is finished, it will start information encoding analysis, the data collected will be divided into Ekman's six emotion: contentment, sadness, fear, anger, surprise and grossness. After that, an encoding analysis will be done in order to determine if the changes in emotion and the learner's learning style classification is related.

4   Research Result and Analysis

4.1   System Usability Scale (SUS) Analysis

This research uses reliability analysis to process SUS and the result value of Cronbach's Alpha is 0.830, so this research's SUS is credible. The SUS was used to analyze by category, and it was found that the both the high score group and low score group's SUS were significant. Also, by using ANOVA for one-way analysis of variance, the average score of the three different learning style: visual, auditory and kinesthetic was 70.18, 74.40, 77.5. Kinesthetic-dominant's usage was higher than visually-dominant's, its significance was $P = .136 > .05$, the three types of learning style has no significance difference, so the system is acceptable for all the users.

4.2   Questionnaire for User Interaction Satisfaction (QUIS) Analysis

This research uses reliability analysis to process QUIS and the result value of Cronbach's Alpha is 0.924, so this research's QUIS is credible. After calculating the result of QUIS, we can get the assessment of user's point of view and interaction with the system, data shows that user' system usability of this system's average is 5.14, with the median 5.14, mode being 4, standard deviation of .609. With the median of 5.14 means that all user was satisfied interacting with the system. Also, by using ANOVA for one-way analysis of variance to analyze if different learning style shows differences while interacting with the system, the average score of the three different learning style: visual, auditory and kinesthetic was 4.92, 5.21, 5.34. In the interaction between the system and the three different learning style user, its significance was $P = .035 < .05$, which means that the interaction between the system and different learning style user were significant.

4.3   Information Encoding Analysis

While using the Japanese Affective Tutoring System to learn, the users' emotion changed frequently, for example: before entering the system they would feel happy due to excitement, nervous to fear while learning, helpless, sadness and anger also shows while having trouble learning. All the emotions mentioned above can be determined by the semantic recognition to let the system know the user's current emotion. After processing the data of different learning style user through information encoding analysis, for auditory-domain user, the learning efficiency is lower than other style learners, it can be explained as auditory-domain user's emotion is harder to turn back to positive emotion; besides, while the kinesthetic-domain user uses the system, emotion changing into happiness (A) was significant, so it achieved in guiding the emotion into positive emotion, that is why kinesthetic-domain user and the system's interaction is better than other learning style users.

5 Conclusion

As the technology improves every day, internet is now easy access, this system is set up on cloud drive and adds emotional recognition system into tutoring system, eliminates the time and space limitation of learning. At the same time, this research emphasizes on the satisfaction and feelings of the users of different learning styles after the usage of the system. The system is acceptable for all of the different learning style users, and different learning style's interaction satisfaction with the Japanese affective tutoring results in kinesthetic-domain user being better than visual-domain user.

References

Anderson, J.R., Corbett, A.T., Koedinger, K.R., Pelletier, R.: Cognitive tutors: lessons learned. J. Learn. Sci. **4**(2), 167–207 (1995)

Arnold, M.B.: Emotion and Personality. Columbia University Press, New York (1960)

Asahara, M., Fukuoka, K., Azuma, A., Goh, C.L., Watanabe, Y., Matsumoto, Y., Tsuzuki, T.: Combination of machine learning methods for optimum Chinese word segmentation. In: Proceedings of 4th SIGHAN Workshop on Chinese Language Processing (2005)

Bakeman, R.: Observing Interaction: An Introduction to Sequential Analysis. Cambridge University Press, Cambridge (1986)

Barker, P.: Electronic books and libraries of the future. Electron. Libr. **10**, 139–141 (1992)

Ben Ammar, M., Neji, M., Alimi, A.M., Gouardères, G.: The affective tutoring system. Expert Syst. Appl. **37**(4), 3013–3023 (2010)

Ekman, P.: Facial expression and emotion. Am. Psychol. **48**(4), 384 (1993)

Ekman, P., Friesen, W.: Facial action coding system: a technique for the measurement of facial movement. Consulting Psychologists, San Francisco (1978)

Ekman, P., Friesen, W.V.: Constants across cultures in the face and emotion. J. Pers. Soc. Psychol. **17**(2), 124 (1971)

Eyharabide, V., Amandi, A.: Ontology-based user profile learning. Appl. Intell. **36**(4), 857–869 (2012)

Felder, R.M., Silverman, L.K.: Learning and teaching styles in engineering education. Eng. Educ. **78**(7), 674–681 (1988)

Franklin, S., Graesser, A.: Is it an agent, or just a program?: a taxonomy for autonomous agents. In: Müller, J.P., Wooldridge, M.J., Jennings, N.R. (eds.) ATAL 1996. LNCS, vol. 1193, pp. 21–35. Springer, Heidelberg (1997). https://doi.org/10.1007/BFb0013570

Freedman, R., Ali, S.S., McRoy, S.: Links: what is an intelligent tutoring system? Intelligence **11**(3), 15–16 (2000)

Frijda, N.H.: The Emotions. Cambridge University Press, Cambridge (1986)

Goh, C.L., Asahara, M., Matsumoto, Y.: Chinese word segmentation by classification of characters. Comput. Linguist. Chin. Lang. Process. **10**(3), 381–396 (2005)

Graesser, A.C., Lu, S., Jackson, G.T., Mitchell, H.H., Ventura, M., Olney, A., Louwerse, M.M.: AutoTutor: a tutor with dialogue in natural language. Behav. Res. Methods Instrum. Comput. **36**(2), 180–192 (2004)

Horwitz, E.K., Horwitz, M.B., Cope, J.: Foreign language classroom anxiety. Mod. Lang. J. **70** (2), 125–132 (1986)

Hsu, S.C., Wong, W.K., Wu, S.H., Lin, M.D., Hsu, W.L.: A web-based diagnosis system with cognitive knowledge for problem posing. In: Proceeding of 10th Conference on Artificial Intelligence and Applications, Kaoshiung, Taiwan (2005)

Kim, K.H., Bang, S.W., Kim, S.R.: Emotion recognition system using short-term monitoring of physiological signals. Med. Biol. Eng. Comput. **42**(3), 419–427 (2004)

Kolb, D.A.: Learning Style Inventory Technical Manual. Mcber and Company, Boston (1976)

Koo, D.M., Ju, S.H.: The interactional effects of atmospherics and perceptual curiosity on emotions and online shopping intention. Comput. Hum. Behav. **26**(3), 377–388 (2010)

Krashen, S.D.: Second Language Acquisition and Second Language Learning. Oxford University Press, Oxford (1981)

Lin, H.C.K., Hsieh, M.C., Loh, L.C., Wang, C.H.: An emotion recognition mechanism based on the combination of mutual information and semantic clues. J. Ambient Intell. Humaniz. Comput. **3**(1), 19–29 (2012). https://doi.org/10.1007/s12652-011-0086-7

Mao, X., Li, Z.: Implementing emotion-based user-aware e-learning. In: CHI 2009 Extended Abstracts on Human Factors in Computing Systems, pp. 3787–3792. ACM (2009)

Mao, X., Li, Z.: Agent based affective tutoring systems: a pilot study. Comput. Educ. **55**(1), 202–208 (2010)

Metri, P., Ghorpade, J., Butalia, A.: Facial emotion recognition using context based multimodal approach. Int. J. Emerg. Sci. **2**(1), 171 (2012)

Mitsuyoshi, S., Ren, F., Tanaka, Y., Kuroiwa, S.: Non-verbal voice emotion analysis system. Int. J. Innov. Comput. Inf. Control **2**(4), 819–830 (2006)

Murray, I.R., Arnott, J.L.: Toward the simulation of emotion in synthetic speech: a review of the literature on human vocal emotion. J. Acoust. Soc. Am. **93**(2), 1097–1108 (1993)

Murray, I.R., Arnott, J.L.: Applying an analysis of acted vocal emotions to improve the simulation of synthetic speech. Comput. Speech Lang. **22**(2), 107–129 (2008)

Nkambou, R., Bourdeau, J.: Advances in Intelligent Tutoring Systems. Springer, Heidelberg (2010)

Norman, D.A.: The Design of Future Things. Basic Books, New York (2007). https://doi.org/10. 1007/978-3-642-14363-2

Nwana, H.S.: Intelligent tutoring systems: an overview. Artif. Intell. Rev. **4**(4), 251–277 (1990)

Ortony, A., Turner, T.J.: What's basic about basic emotions? Psychol. Rev. **97**(3), 315 (1990)

Picard, R.: Affective Computing. MIT Press, Cambridge (1997)

Plutchik, R.: The Emotions. University Press of America, Washington, DC (1991)

Reid, J.M.: Perceptual learning style preference questionnaire. In: Learning Styles in the ESL/EFL Classroom, pp. 202–204 (1984)

Ren, F.: Affective information processing and recognizing human emotion. Electron. Notes Theoret. Comput. Sci. **225**, 39–50 (2009)

Russell, J.A.: A circumplex model of affect. J. Pers. Soc. Psychol. **39**(6), 1161 (1980)

Sarrafzadeh, A., Chao, F., Dadgostar, F., Alexander, S., Messom, C.: Frown gives game away: affect sensitive tutoring systems for elementary mathematics. In: International Conference on Systems, Man and Cybernetics (2004)

Seki, Y., Evans, D.K., Ku, L.W., Chen, H.H., Kando, N., Lin, C.Y.: Overview of opinion analysis pilot task at NTCIR-6. In: Proceedings of 6th NTCIR Workshop Meeting on Evaluation of Information Access Technologies, pp. 265–278 (2007)

Shaver, P., Schwartz, J., Kirson, D., O'Connor, C.: Emotion knowledge: further exploration of a prototype approach. J. Pers. Soc. Psychol. **52**(6), 1061–1086 (1987)

Goh, T.-T., Huang, Y.-P.: Monitoring youth depression risk in Web 2.0. J. Inf. Knowl. Manag. Syst. **39**(3), 192–202 (2009)

Wong, W.K., Hsu, S.C., Wu, S.H., Lee, C.W., Hsu, W.L.: LIM-G: learner-initiating instruction model based on cognitive knowledge for geometry word problem comprehension. Comput. Educ. **48**(4), 582–601 (2007)

Xue, N.: Chinese word segmentation as character tagging. Comput. Linguist. Chin. Lang. Process. **8**(1), 29–48 (2003)

Yan, J., Bracewell, D.B., Ren, F., Kuroiwa, S.: The creation of a chinese emotion ontology based on HowNet. Eng. Lett. **16**(1), 166–171 (2008)

Yang, Y.F., Chao, C.J., Lin, Y.L., Chang, C.K.: Usability testing of Japanese captions segmentation system to scaffold beginners to comprehend Japanese videos. Int. J. Cyber Soc. Educ. **6**(1), 1–14 (2013)

Zhang, H.P., Yu, H.K., Xiong, D.Y., Liu, Q.: HHMM-based Chinese lexical analyzer ICTCLAS. In: Proceedings of 2nd SIGHAN Workshop on Chinese Language Processing. vol. 17, pp. 184–187. Association for Computational Linguistics (2003)

A Study on the Behavioral Patterns Formed by Subjects with Different Cognitive Styles in Playing Augmented Reality Interaction Games

Meng-Chun Tsai[✉] [iD] and Hao-Chiang-Koong Lin[iD]

Department of Information and Learning Technology,
National University of Tainan, Tainan, Taiwan
cherrybearpipi@gmail.com

Abstract. The study aims at designing an augmented reality interaction game to realize its usability, user interaction satisfaction, and the behavioral differences among users with different cognitive styles. The research tools used here are Study Preference Questionnaire (SPQ), Questionnaire for User Interaction Satisfaction (QUIS), System Usability Scale (SUS), and Sequence Analysis. The research subjects are 52 seventh graders of some junior high. Research has found that, both the 17 students categorized as with Holist Cognitive Style, and the 35 with Serialist Cognitive Style have high, positive usability and interaction satisfaction with our system. In terms of behavior, the serialist testees operate and familiarize themselves with the system first before another problem comes. In the state where written words are used as a means of communication, many learners answer correspondingly as they observe the way this system has given them feedback. The holist cognitive testees ask and operate simultaneously. Most testees, however, deliberately give wrong answers to observe how the system gives feedback.

Keywords: Augmented Reality · Cognitive Style · Interactive Technology · System Usability Scale (SUS) · Questionnaire for User Interaction Satisfaction (QUIS)

1 Introduction

These years, as mobile devices become popular, education has never been traditional as it embraces scientific technology. Education Ministry started its "Promotion Project of Junior-and-Senior-High-School Mobile Learning" in 2013, which, up to 2016, over 200 schools have been involved in. The application of mobile devices to teaching in class has been more and more highly regarded. It has been more frequently seen that mobile devices are used to compensate for the deficiencies of traditional education. There were researchers who put digital games into the course design, combining learning with play [8]. A study showed that a game which interests students can positively influence their learning [13, 14, 20] because digital games can help stimulate the curiosity in students [7, 17]. Digital games, therefore, have contributed much in

© Springer International Publishing AG 2017
T.-C. Huang et al. (Eds.): SETE 2017, LNCS 10676, pp. 372–381, 2017.
https://doi.org/10.1007/978-3-319-71084-6_42

students' learning [3]; even abstract ideas can be concretized. Mobile devices help explain more easily and make the class more interactive; this boost learning and team spirit. The easy access to information can help data collection, from whose analysis a timely feedback can be given immediately and data integrated accordingly. A more suitable and individualized teaching method can therefore be developed.

Augmented reality is here combined with human feelings to develop a game that can interact with the user. Through the using process, both the usability, interaction satisfaction of the system, and the behavioral patterns of holist and serialist cognitive students can be detected. The questions list as follows:

1. What is the respective usability of augmented reality interaction games for holist and serialist cognitive learners?
2. What is the respective interaction satisfaction of augmented reality games for holist and serialist cognitive learners?
3. Is there any behavioral difference for the holist and serialist cognitive learners when playing an augmented reality game?

2   Literature Review

2.1   Augmented Reality

Augmented reality is more popular and widely used today. It is a technique combining the real with the imaginary, and creates a surprisingly fantasy world by adding pictures and other materials to a device. The user can interact with the virtual interface. Augmented reality has been applied in education, research, entertainment, and other aspects of life. With its unique visual effect, intuitive interaction, and flexibility it can give to a user, it is easy to become addicted. Applied in education, it can often achieve great learning results [1].

2.2   Interaction

In devising an interactive system, the user should always be kept in mind. The two goals of interaction design as defined by Jennifer Preece, Yvonne Rogers, and Helen Sharp in their book Interaction Design are 1. Usability: this has to contain effectiveness, efficiency, safety, utility, learnability, and memorability, and 2. Experience: it has to be satisfying, enjoyable, fun, entertaining, helpful, motivating, aesthetically pleasing, supportive of creativity, rewarding, and emotionally fulfilling. This study aims at the latter in the development of the system, and the whole interaction design is based on the four interactive elements: 1. Make sure and create a need, 2. Develop optional plans and choose the ideal one, 3. Make the interaction pattern, and 4. Design and evaluate.

2.3   Cognitive Style

The study categorizes holist and serialist cognitive styles through the operation interaction of the augmented reality game and the learner. Cognitive style means the habit formed when one gets a message and responds; it is also the top priority one may have in expressing personal feelings, thinking, memorizing, and problem shooting [16]. It is a standard by which one evaluates the difference of each learner, know their basic psychological difference, and offers another teaching method based up the difference. The application of cognitive style in education helps researchers understand that different cognitive styles lead to variant performances [19].

Holistic-serialist cognitive style as developed by Pask [18] and his group has been regarded as one of the most influential methods. Holist cognitive thinkers, in learning, tend to adopt an overall strategy and "make assumptions," while serialist cognitive ones tend to focus and go "step by step". Holist-serialist cognitive style shows an individual's perceptual difference, which is related to one's personality. In a freer learning environment, the serialist cognitive style likes to pay attention to the detail and is prone to subdivide a major problem into minor ones before trying to solve them. On the contrary, a holist cognitive one likes to see a problem in its entirety and solve it accordingly. Holist cognitive learners are passive but panoramic in learning. Whereas, the serialist cognitive ones are active, narrow but in-depth [19]. Though these two types have different patterns in learning, they understand things in their own separate ways [18].

3 Methodology

3.1 Augmented Reality Interaction Game System

Vuforia for Unity SDK package is used in the research to design an augmented-reality-based interaction game. Figure 1 shows the menu of this game. The buttons can switch one screen setting to another different one and let the agent and learner interact. Chatting through texting familiarizes both the agent and the learner while data are collected (see Figs. 2 and 3).

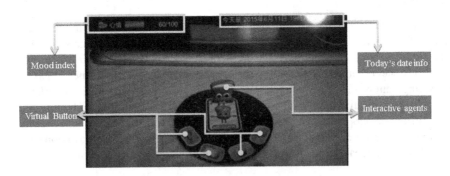

Fig. 1. Interaction game menu.

Fig. 2. Chatting through texting and interaction game.

holist		serialist	
characteristic	behavior	characteristic	behavior
passive	strengthening the mental structure using a conceptual map in mind	active	being fond of using index pointers
whole-oriented	panoramic	analysis-oriented	in-depth
inwardly	non-linear; flexible reading strategy	outwardly	linear; scheduled reading strategy

Fig. 3. Holist-serialist cognitive styles [15].

3.2   Research Tools

Study Preference Questionnaire (SPQ). SPQ is adopted to differentiate between holist and serialist cognitive styles [6]. Designed by Ford [9], it uses 18 pairs of descriptive statements to tell the holistic from the serialistic. Ford and Chen [10, 11] hold the view that holist cognitive learners try to grasp the whole framework before going in-depth, while serialist cognitive ones focus on the detail and parts before understanding things as a whole, as shown in Fig. 3. In SPQ, the testee intuitively chooses one from the two statements that better describes him or her. The testee can be of the holistic when the number of statements demonstrating the holist cognitive characteristics are chosen; otherwise, the testee can be of the serialist cognitive one.

System Usability Scale (SUS). Designed by Digital Equipment Co Ltd. in 1986, SUS uses ten questions to check the usability of a system. It adopts Likert Scale in asking testees from reverse aspects to measure the objected evaluations. It turns, through a formula, into data the different scale testees choose for each question. The higher the score, the higher the system usability. This is reliable, efficient, and low cost [4]. The higher score one gets, the more user friendly the system is.

Questionnaire for User Interaction Satisfaction (QUIS). QUIS was designed by Human-Computer Interaction Lab (HCIL) at Maryland University. It is a reliable, valid measurement in evaluating the subjective satisfaction when one interacts with a system [5]. Based on the seven-scale evaluation of Likert scale, QUIS gives points from the user perspective, and the range goes from 1 to 7. This study revises the questionnaire and integrates the seven aspects into 25 questions: overall impression about the interface, outlook of the interface, system jargons and data, system learning, system function, interface usability, and user experience.

Behavior Coding-Sequence Analysis. The behavior oriented sequence analysis is performed through a series of events. After an experiment, it observes the interaction behavior of the learner and starts its coding process [2]. It checks the sequence conversion of every act, and collects from it a large sum of statistic data, and finally comes up with a chart of sequence relationship to help explain the behavior of the learner. Every sequence is not raw, unhandled simple ratios or numbers, but a well calculated analysis. What turns out is, therefore, descriptive data worthy to be discussed and offered as suggestions [12]. This study records the whole using process of the learner. When one finishes, the researcher starts to analyze the difference in terms of behavior between each learner and categorize between holist and serialist, as seen in Table 1.

Table 1. Operation behavior coding.

Coding	Behavior	Example
Q	Raise questions	Ask the teacher
B	Touch the cellphone buttons on the screen	Back to the main menu, continue, leave
V	Push the virtual button on target	Selection of game settings
E	Unintentionally push the virtual button on target	Tough the wrong button, two buttons were detected touched simultaneously
M	Move the agent	
T	Words entry	
N	Nonsensical answers	The blank is empty still, or key in unidentifiable answers
O	Operate at the wrong moment	Push target at the wrong time
S	Interested in the system environment	Would want to touch the virtual character in real life

4 Results

4.1 Cognitive Styles

This study has categorized the learners into holist and serialist cognitive styles according to learning preferences. Among the 52 valid samples, 17 of them are of the holist, while the other 35 are serialist cognitive learners.

4.2   System Usability Scale (SUS)

In the 52 valid samples, Cronbach's Alpha value is 0.802, which means the system usability scale is reliable. In Table 2, the usability mean of holist cognitive style is 75.88, the median is 87.50, the standard deviation is 22.89, and the maximum and minimum is 100 and 32.5. respectively. The usability mean of serialist cognitive style is 76.43, the median is 82.50, the standard deviation is 17.34, and the maximum and minimum is 100 and 37.5. The usability mean for this system is 75.88 and 76.43, indicating the usability for both holist and serialist is satisfying.

Table 2. Statistic result of the usability scale of holist and serialist cognitive styles displayed as figures.

Type	Sample number	Median	Minimum	Maximum	Mean	Standard deviation
Holist	17	87.50	32.50	100.00	75.88	22.89
Serialist	35	82.50	37.50	100.00	76.43	17.34

4.3   Questionnaire for User Interaction Satisfaction (QUIS)

The Cronbach's Alpha value got through QUIS is 0.954. Seven levels of the statistical analysis are shown in Table 3. Holist cognitive style gets 4.94 in system efficiency, and is more than 5 on every other level. The mean is 5.66, the standard deviation is 1.23. For serialist cognitive style, satisfaction is over 5 on every level. The mean is 5.65, and the standard deviation is 1.11, which means the interaction satisfaction is high.

Table 3. Statistic result of the usability scale of holist and serialist cognitive styles displayed as figures.

Level	Type	Sample number	Mean	Standard deviation
Overall interface use	Holist	17	5.43	1.02
	Serialist	35	5.68	1.05
Interface presentation	Holist	17	5.69	1.15
	Serialist	35	5.69	1.09
System jargons	Holist	17	5.97	1.24
	Serialist	35	5.37	1.23
Operation learning	Holist	17	5.74	1.61
	Serialist	35	5.83	1.27
System efficiency	Holist	17	4.94	1.76
	Serialist	35	5.47	1.19
Interface usability	Holist	17	6.08	0.87
	Serialist	35	5.81	1.01
User experience	Holist	17	5.76	0.97
	Serialist	35	5.70	0.94
Mean	Holist	17	5.66	1.23
	Serialist	35	5.65	1.11

4.4   Sequence Analysis Based on Behavior Coding

Sequence analysis of holist cognitive style. Analyzed from the frequency of behavior conversion, as seen in Fig. 4, holist cognitive testees operate the system in two ways: the first one goes as follows: V (correctly push the virtual button) to S (show interest in the system) to B (push the screen button) to T (text messages) to N (nonsensical answers) to B (push the screen button). The other is: E (push the wrong button) to Q (raise questions) to B (push the screen button) to T (text messages) to N (nonsensical answers) to B (push the screen button). The researcher finds the learners become interested after they correctly press the button and enter into the system, and they would like to touch in real life the virtual agent the system has created. When they push the wrong one, they ask the teacher for help. In the state where the learners text to interact with the agent, they give nonsensical answers as a response. It takes a longer process because holist cognitive learners tend to have an overall strategy to grasp first the whole idea. They passively learn but ask for help while encountering problems. The reason they reply nonsensically is that the way a holist cognitive learner responds is non-lineal and hypothesis-oriented.

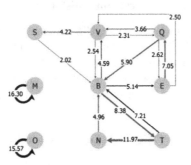

Fig. 4. Behavior conversion—holist style holds the highest frequency.

Sequential analysis of serialist cognitive style. Analyzed from the frequency of behavior conversion, as seen in Fig. 5, when serialist testees operate the system, two ways have been found to convert to high frequency: the first one is: E (push the wrong button) to Q (raise questions) to B (push the screen button) to T (text messages) to B (push the onscreen button). The other is: V (press the correct virtual button) to B (press the screen button) to T (text messages) to B (push the button). According to what the researcher has observed, when the learners press the wrong button, they go to the teacher for help. When they interact with the agent through texting, they reply according to what they are asked. The process is comparatively much shorter because serialist cognitive learners are in focus and tend to pay attention to the detail, and they will divide a major problem into small ones before solving them. They actively learn and even fumble their way when they don't know how to use it. They also responds to the question and answer accordingly; serialist cognitive learners tend to go step by step and have a lineal response pattern.

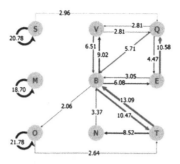

Fig. 5. Behavior conversion-serialist style holds the highest frequency.

Analysis of behavior conversion illustrations. The red lines in Fig. 6 show the behavior the serialist cognitive learners lack. Some learners push the correct button after they have tried the wrong one. After pressing the correct button, they start to show interest. Figure 7 shows in red lines the behavior the holist cognitive learners never have. Some learners show interest in the environment of the system and raise further questions, while others don't even bother to ask when they push the wrong button; they quietly operate the system and touch repeatedly the screen, wanting to shorten the time and switch quickly to another environmental setting.

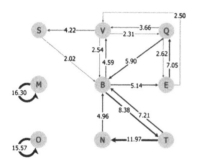

Fig. 6. Difference of behavior conversion— holist (Color figure online)

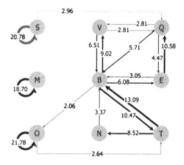

Fig. 7. Difference of behavior conversion— serialist (Color figure online)

5 Conclusion

Based upon the research, the conclusion has been reached and listed as follows:

1. What is the respective usability of augmented reality interaction game system for holist and serialist cognitive learners?
   The usability for the holist cognitive learners is 75.88, and 76.43 for the serialist. Both are within the range of "GOOD".
2. What is the satisfaction and interaction of the augmented reality interaction game system for both cognitive learners?

The mean interaction satisfaction is 5.66 for the holist cognitive style, and 5.65 for the serialist cognitive one. Both are over 4, which indicates both have high satisfaction and interaction.

3. What is the behavioral difference between the holist and the serialist when they operate the augmented reality interaction game system?

Through observation, behavior coding and high behavior conversion, the researcher has found that the holist cognitive learners are interested in the system when pushing the right button and entering into the system, and they would want to touch with their hands the virtual agent. The learners ask the teacher for help when they push the wrong button, and answer nonsensically to try to understand how the system responds. The process is longer because the holist cognitive learners adopt an overall strategy in learning and tackle the problem as a whole. They are passive learners but ask questions when they have one. The holist cognitive learners reply nonsensically because their cognitive style are nonlinear and hypothetic. On the other, the serialist cognitive learners, when pushing the wrong button, enter into the state of raising questions, and respond accordingly. The process is obviously shorter, which is because serialist cognitive learners are in focus and like to pay attention to the detail. They try actively to find a solution when encountering problems, and answer accordingly, which is the characteristic of the lineal, step-by-step serialist cognitive learners.

References

1. Asai, K., Kobayashi, H., Kondo, T.: Augmented instructions-a fusion of augmented reality and printed learning materials. In: 5th IEEE International Conference on Advanced Learning Technologies, ICALT 2005, pp. 213–215. IEEE, July 2005
2. Bakeman, R., Gottman, J.M.: Observing Interaction: An Introduction to Sequential Analysis. Cambridge University Press, Cambridge (1997)
3. Braghirolli, L.F., Ribeiro, J.L.D., Weise, A.D., Pizzolato, M.: Benefits of educational games as an introductory activity in industrial engineering education. Comput. Hum. Behav. **58**, 315–324 (2016)
4. Brooke, J.: SUS-A quick and dirty usability scale. Usabil. Eval. Ind. **189**(194), 4–7 (1996)
5. Chin, J.P., Diehl, V.A., Norman, K.L.: Development of an instrument measuring user satisfaction of the human-computer interface. In: Proceedings of SIGCHI Conference on Human Factors in Computing Systems, pp. 213–218. ACM (1988)
6. Clarke, J.: Cognitive style and computer-assisted learning: problems and a possible solution1. Assoc. Learn. Technol. J. **1**(1), 47–59 (1993)
7. Dickey, M.D.: Game design and learning: a conjectural analysis of how massively multiple online role-playing games (MMORPGs) foster intrinsic motivation. Educ. Tech. Res. Dev. **55**(3), 253–273 (2007)
8. Dorji, U., Panjaburee, P., Srisawasdi, N.: A learning cycle approach to developing educational computer game for improving students' learning and awareness in electric energy consumption and conservation. Educ. Technol. Soc. **18**(1), 91–105 (2015)
9. Ford, N.: Learning styles and strategies of postgraduate students. Br. J. Educ. Technol. **16**(1), 65–77 (1985)
10. Ford, N., Chen, S.Y.: Individual differences, hypermedia navigation and learning: an empirical study. J. Educ. Multimedia Hypermedia **9**(4), 281–312 (2000)

11. Ford, N., Chen, S.Y.: Matching/mismatching revisited: an empirical study of learning and teaching styles. Br. J. Educ. Technol. **32**(1), 5–22 (2001)
12. Hou, H.T., Chang, K.E., Sung, Y.T.: Analysis of problem-solving based online asynchronous discussion pattern. Educ. Technol. Soc. **11**(1), 17–28 (2008)
13. Ke, F.: A qualitative meta-analysis of computer games as learning tools. In: Handbook of Research on Effective Electronic Gaming in Education, vol. 1, pp. 1–32 (2009)
14. Kebritchi, M., Hirumi, A., Bai, H.: The effects of modern math computer games on learners' math achievement and math course motivation in a public high school setting. Br. J. Educ. Technol. **38**(2), 49–259 (2008)
15. Mampadi, F., Chen, S.Y., Ghinea, G., Chen, M.-P.: Design of adaptive hypermedia learning systems: a cognitive style approach. Comput. Educ. **56**(4), 1003–1011 (2011)
16. Messick, S.: Individuality in Learning, pp. 4–23. Jossey-Bass, San Francisco (1976)
17. Papastergiou, M.: Digital GBL in high school computer science education: impact on educational effectiveness and student motivation. Comput. Educ. **52**(1), 1–12 (2009)
18. Pask, G.: Styles and strategies of learning. Br. J. Educ. Psychol. **46**(2), 128–148 (1976)
19. Saracho, O.N.: Research directions for cognitive style and education. Int. J. Educ. Res. **29**, 287–290 (1998)
20. Wu, W.H., Chiou, W.B., Kao, H.Y., Hu, C.H.A., Huang, S.H.: Re-exploring game-assisted learning research: the perspective of learning theoretical bases. Comput. Educ. **59**(4), 1153–1161 (2012)

Exploration of Learning Effectiveness, Cognitive Load and Attitude on Mobile E-book Introduced in Nursing Education

Lei Chang[1], Ting-Ting Wu[1(✉)], Chih Wei Chao[1], and Jim-Min Lin[2]

[1] Graduate School of Technological and Vocational Education, National Yunlin University of Science and Technology, Douliu, Taiwan
zegxiazhang@gmail.com, ttwu@yuntech.edu.tw,
bluejit23@gmail.com
[2] Department of Information Engineering and Computer Science, Feng Chia University, Taichung, Taiwan
jimmy@fcu.edu.tw

Abstract. Nursing education is a professional subject field, which is also an important part for cultivation the national nursing talent. Currently, most of nursing education used traditional lecture teaching, but it is important to use information technology as a tool in the convenient technology era. Therefore, this research adopted the e-learning method which introduced mobile devices and e-books into the nursing education course. The main purpose of this research is to explore the learning effectiveness, learning attitude, and the degree of cognitive load after using e-books system.

Keywords: Nursing education · E-book · Cognitive load · Mobile learning

1 Introduction

With the progress of information technology and vigorous development of internet and wireless sensor technology, learning style changes and becomes more diverse, Learning content is also more varied. E-learning has been the global trend of education and learning and applied in elementary schools, secondary schools and universities. In recent years, E-learning model changes from web-based learning to mobile learning and even ubiquitous learning. In such environment, learners should learn to adopt different techniques and devices in different types of learning. Although educational method makes progress and changes constantly, at present, nursing education is still mostly based on traditional lecture instruction. Knowledge construction relies on interaction between environment and learners [1]; thus, when learning in one situation, students' knowledge constructed might be restricted. Nursing education is the professional education which cultivates medical and caring talents. The education concept, model and practice pattern are continuously updated and changed. In order to adapt to progress of nursing model, students must possess broad knowledge and offer proper care to every patient in order to become professional nursing personnel in terms of both theory and practice. Current nursing education is based on traditional lecture instruction

T.-C. Huang et al. (Eds.): SETE 2017, LNCS 10676, pp. 382–390, 2017.
https://doi.org/10.1007/978-3-319-71084-6_43

and several students are taught by one teacher. Besides the limitation of learning environment, clinical courses cannot meet all students' questions and demands. Hence, the researcher intends to introduce nursing education by mobile learning and include different elements in nursing education through e-book to activate the courses and cultivate students with the proper information literacy beyond textbooks in the era of E-learning. The main purpose of this study is to probe into correlation between e-book introduced in nursing education and learning effectiveness, learning attitude and teaching material cognitive load of students in Department of Nursing of university.

2 Literatures

2.1 Nursing Education

The mother of modern nursing is Ms. Nightingale who promoted professional image and spirit of nursing to the world and reinforced students' nursing education by establishing nursing school. The purpose of nursing education is to instruct students with more professional competence and literacy in order to offer better care and concern for patients. In recent years, the countries around the world actively promote educational nursing associations and provide more nursing knowledge and evaluation to enhance quality of nursing education. Development of nursing education is associated with human beings and environment. In the past years, nursing personnel's severe training system and nursing examination system lead to professional performance of nursing. Nursing personnel cope with the job associated with humans' lives and errors are not tolerated; besides, nursing personnel must play the role as the carers of patients, fight for the rights of patients and protect them. Therefore, in order to cultivate excellent nursing personnel, school education becomes extremely important. In modern nursing environment, in order to become registered nurses, they must first participate in clinical oral test. The test is the clinical situation of live person stimulation and it evaluates nursing students' assessment on patients, inquiry of case history, clinical inference and decision-making and communication competence. Nursing education not only pays attention to knowledge and skill practice, but also cultivates students' human literacy and affective knowledge, reinforces students' professional attitude and social justice and responsibility in order to allow students to possess the competence to acquire and organize knowledge. Research in recent years gradually includes technology in medical system of nursing. As to students' learning, regarding distant teaching, in Taiwan, some scholars apply Mind Map to encourage students to develop creative questions and problem-solving competence. By radioactive thinking, students present the concepts acquired by images to result in more clear thoughts and enhanced memory. There are scholars allowed students to have simulated learning in the situation by high-fidelity patient [2].

2.2 Cognitive Load Theory

Cognitive load was derived from the field of ergonomics and subsequently extended to education for the research. Cognitive load is defined as individuals' load of cognitive system in specific activities and tasks. [3] The scholars stated that main factors of cognitive load include learners' characteristics, learning procedure, time limit, etc. [4] According to theory of cognitive load, there are 3 types of cognitive load in learning, as shown in Table 1:

Table 1. Three types of cognitive load in learning.

Type of cognitive load	Source	Effect on learning
Intrinsic cognitive load	Field complexity prior knowledge	Overly high intrinsic cognitive load might result in overload of cognitive resources and it is harmful for learning
Extraneous cognitive load	Inappropriate instructional design	Harmful or ineffective
Germane cognitive load	Supportive instructional design	Helpful or effective

2.2.1   Intrinsic Cognitive Load

Intrinsic cognitive load mainly depends on difficulty of instructional materials and learners' degree, including personal competence and prior knowledge. When teaching materials are too difficult or learners' degree or prior knowledge is insufficient, learners should place great amount of knowledge in working memory zone of the brain and result in higher intrinsic cognitive load.

2.2.2   Extraneous Cognitive Load

Extraneous cognitive load is mainly influenced by presentation and design of teaching material content or teaching activities. Thus, inappropriate instructional design influences learners' extraneous cognitive load. Since extraneous cognitive load is additional, it can be improved by revising instructional content. Therefore, many researchers are devoted to the study on instructional content and materials which lower extraneous cognitive load.

2.2.3   Germane Cognitive Load

It is also called effective cognitive load and it means learners' efforts in learning process. It thus constructs learning schema and enhances automation of schema. Although it is cognitive load, in fact, it can strengthen learners' concentration and it reinforces learners' learning ability. However, there is limitation of germane cognitive load. It is positively effective when intrinsic and extraneous cognitive load are not beyond learners' cognitive scope. Sweller reorganized research findings of cognitive load in different fields in recent years and proposed the principles of instructional design as follows: Goal-free effect, Worked example effect, Completion problem effect, Split-attention effect, Modality effect, Redundancy effect, Variability effect [5].

2.3   Multimedia Learning Theory

Multi- denotes "many, varied and diverse", media means "media and medium". The combination of two words represent multimedia.

Multimedia instruction includes words, pictures, sound, animation, images, etc. It is based on themes and is learner-centered design. It allows learners to select appropriate learning method or environment and choose the course schedule according to personal situations. It offers repetitive use and review [6]. Mayer proposed multimedia learning cognition theory and emphasized that relationship between designs of instructional media and learning problem solving would directly influence learners' learning effectiveness [7]. In meaningful learning, there are 3 basic cognitive processes, including selection, organization and integration. In learning process, through selection of sensory organs, learners organize and systematize the messages received to integrate them in memory. According to several scholars' concepts, Mayer proposed 3 hypotheses of multimedia cognition [8]:

1. Dual Channels: when receiving messages by "hearing" and "vision", learners cope with messages by different channels.
2. Limited Capacity: when learners cope with messages received, the message volume processed at the same time and in the same channel is limited.
3. Active Processing: learners are actively aware of the messages in the channel; they select and organize them and integrate them with individuals' prior related knowledge.

3   Research Methodology

This study treated the juniors of Department of Nursing in one university of Taiwan as experimental subjects and introduced e-book teaching material in "Community Health Nursing", the obligatory course of the juniors in the said department. The subject was obligatory in national examination of registered nurse and it was expected that students' learning attitude should be positive and active.

The teacher was an experienced Department of Nursing Associate Professor, who has had nursing education experience for years and published nursing related work. The specialty was Community Health Nursing, nursing research, elderly nursing, community development, health promotion, chronic disease nursing, etc.

Instructional unit of this study included 7 chapters. There were 3 sections every week for the 9-week experiment. It included 32 subjects. As to learning effectiveness, in the first class, learners received "Learning effectiveness test" designed by the teacher as pretest and midterm exam as posttest. In order to complete functions of e-book, this study adopted Google questionnaire, including two parts: "e-book cognitive load scale" after the course of each chapter and "e-book instructional attitude scale" after posttest. The experiment procedure is shown in Fig. 1.

In the first week of experiment, the researcher conducted pretest with experimental subjects in the university. 32 subjects were individually distributed with one tablet computer, installed with e-book reading APP and e-book of course in this experiment.

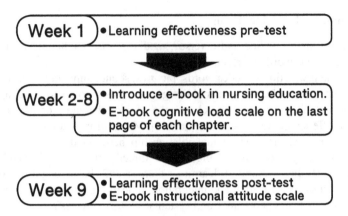

Fig. 1. Experiment procedure

From Week 2 to Week 8, this study conducted experiment to introduce e-book in nursing education. The teacher projected the content on tablet computer to the screen by wireless projector and proposed key point marks and reminders through e-book noting system. In Week 9, it practiced midterm exam as posttest and invited students to fill in e-book attitude instruction scale to respond to the attitude and view toward the learning.

4   Research Tools

4.1   E-book System

E-book software employed by this study is the product of HAMASTAR Technology Company: SimMagic eBook interactive e-book editing program. By simple steps, it inputs primitive materials such as PDF and PPT in editing program and integrates several multimedia components, including images, pictures and words. E-book of the course in the study includes 7 chapters. It was made by briefing of new content and course of Community Health Nursing of Yeong Dah Book. The units include health policy, health care system, epidemiology, life statistics, health education, health promotion, community health evaluation and community health development. At the end of each chapter, the related practices are attached for students. System interface is shown in Fig. 2.

4.2   Learning Effectiveness Test

The researcher invited the nursing teacher to design questions of learning effectiveness test. The scope is chapter 1 to 7 of this study. Since participants had received related programs before this experiment, they had certain degree of prior knowledge. The questions are multiple choices which include 40 questions showing on Google sheets, and students filled in the answers and showed the scores automatically. Post-test used the same questions, but order of the questions are changed in the midterm exam after the course.

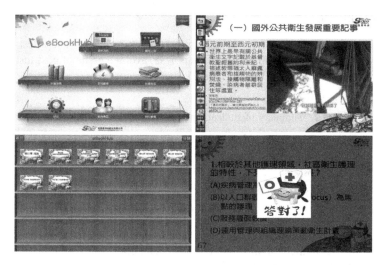

Fig. 2. System interface

4.3   E-book Cognitive Load Scale

E-book cognitive load scale employed by this study is based on Huang's cognitive load scale. The purpose is to measure students' perceived difficulty, confidence and engagement in e-book teaching materials. Among others, Item 2 is the reverse question which can be applied to screen valid questionnaires. The scale is scored by Likert 5-point scale (from 1 to 5). Strongly agree is 5 and strongly disagree is 1. The feedback is based on Google sheets. On the last page of each chapter in e-book, connection and QR codes are attached. Thus, students can immediately respond to the questions after learning.

4.4   E-book Instructional Attitude Scale

Attitude scale employed by this study is based on Huang's multimedia learning attitude scale. By three dimensions, this study probes into learning attitude toward e-book introduced nursing education: "attitude toward e-book instructional activity", "attitude toward e-book teaching materials" and "learners' views toward e-book". There are 17 Question. Among others, Item 2, 4 and 6 of "attitude toward e-book instructional activity", Item 6 of "attitude toward e-book teaching materials" and Item 2 and 3 of "learners' views toward e-book" are reverse questions. They serve as criteria to select valid questionnaires. The scale is scored by Likert 5-point scale (from 1 to 5). Strongly agree is 5 and strongly disagree is 1. Feedback is based on Google sheets. Students filled in the questions after midterm exam (posttest).

5   Results and Findings

After e-book introduced nursing education experiment, this study conducted posttest test and learning attitude scale on learners and collected the data for analysis and statistics.

5.1   Learning Effectiveness Test

According to descriptive statistics effectiveness of learning effectiveness test, average grade of pre-test is 59.61, standard deviation is 7.35, average grade of post-test is 85.31 and standard deviation is 8.63 (see Table 2).

Table 2. Summary of students' perceptions of the learning game.

	N	M	SD	df	t	p
Pre-test	32	59.609	7.3537	31	−13.534	.000***
Post-test	32	85.313	8.6311			

*p < .05 ***p < .001

After dependent sample t-test, in Table 2, this study demonstrates that $p < .001$. It reveals that it is extremely significant. That is to say, after receiving e-book and PBL introduction instruction, students' learning effectiveness is relatively significant.

5.2   Scale of Cognitive Load

As to scale of cognitive load, after the course of each chapter, this study invited learners to fill in the questions. Since Google sheet is the same, in terms of samples, there are repetitive responses and the number lower than learners. In the analysis of cognitive load scales, it shows that the grades mainly fall in "neutral" and "satisfied" (3–4). Hence, the e-book instructional tool reveals certain degree of cognitive load for students. However, in the statistics of the highest and lowest values, it reveals that with the progress of course, number of 1 point becomes less. However, in the design of reverse questions, it shows that few students did not pay attention to change of questions. According to Table 3, standard deviations of the chapters decrease progressively. It means that learners' difference on cognitive load is reduced. That is to say, after being familiar with the instructional model, the students' difference of acceptance becomes less significant. Even learners who had difficulty at the beginning are gradually familiar with the system and instructional model.

Table 3. The descriptive statistics of cognitive loads in each chapter

Items	N	Min.	Max.	M	SD
CH1	144	1	5	3.57	.994
CH2	160	1	5	3.78	.977
CH3.1	128	1	5	3.67	.843
CH3.2	176	1	5	3.67	.858
CH4	104	2	5	3.80	.659
CH5	136	1	5	3.73	.725
CH6	128	1	5	3.66	.726
CH7	132	1	5	3.83	.796

5.3 Scale of Learning Attitude

In the analysis of learning attitude scales, the question with the lowest mean is Question 2-1 "words of e-book teaching materials draw my attention and are helpful for the learning". The score is 3.89. The questions with the highest mean are Question 2.3 "interactive function of e-book teaching materials draws my attention and is helpful for learning", Question 2.5 "design of units in e-book teaching materials matches instructional goals and content and is helpful for learning", Question 2.6 "I do not prefer learning community health nursing by e-book and even dislike the words, pictures or interactive function in teaching materials". The score is 4.14. Among others, Question 2.6 is a reverse question. In terms of total scores, learners' learning attitude toward e-book instruction is generally satisfied. The most attractive content refers to interactive function. Attraction of words is lower. According to Question with secondary scores, Question 1.1 "in comparison to traditional teaching, e-book instruction is more interesting" and Question 1.3 "e-book instruction in the classroom enhances the fun of the topics", in comparison to traditional instruction, e-book teaching is relatively attractive. In addition, as to the lowest score, except for reverse questions, the lowest value is 3. The question with the lowest value as 1 are reverse questions. Thus, when filling in the questions, learners might not pay attention to the content of questions.

6   Conclusion

This study introduces e-book in nursing education and probes into effect of e-book on learning effectiveness, cognitive load and learning attitude. Throughout the whole experiment, it reveals that after e-book instruction, students' overall learning effectiveness is significantly enhanced. However, teaching materials still lead to learners' cognitive load. Besides, according to analytical result of learning attitude, it should enhance interaction of teaching materials and properly reduce the number of words in order to result in learners' more significant learning effectiveness. E-learning continuously makes progress with time. In the coming future, we expect that E-learning can be more applied in nursing education and there will be more original research findings.

Acknowledgments. This work was supported in part by the Ministry of Science and Technology (MOST), Taiwan, ROC, under Grant MOST 104-2511-S-224-003-MY3, and MOST 105-2628-S-224-001-MY3.

References

1. Brown, J.S., Collins, A., Duguid, P.: Situated cognition and the cultural of learning. Educ. Res. **18**(1), 32–42 (1989)
2. Parker, B.C., Myrick, F.: A critical examination of high-fidelity human patient simulation within the context of nursing pedagogy. Nurse Educ. Today **29**(3), 322–329 (2009)
3. Sweller, J., van Merriënboer, J.J.G., Paas, F.G.W.C.: Cognitive architecture and instructional design. Educ. Psychol. Rev. **10**(3), 251–297 (1998)

4. Gerjets, P., Seheciter, K., Cierniak, G.: The scientific value of cognitive load theory: a research agenda based on the structural view of theories. Educ. Psychol. Rev. **21**(1), 43–54 (2009)
5. Sweller, J.: Cognitive load during problem solving: effect on learning. Cogn. Sci. **12**, 257–285 (1988)
6. John, M.: Multimedia-why and why not. Comput. Teach. **22**, 16–18 (1995)
7. Mayer, R.E., Moreno, R.: Aids to computer-based multimedia learning. Learn. Instr. **12**, 107–119 (2002)
8. Mayer, R.E., Moreno, R.: A split attention effect in multimedia learning: evidence for dual processing system in working memory. J. Educ. Psychol. **90**(2), 312–320 (1998)

The Ideal and Reality of Implementing Technology into English Language Teaching: A Case Study of Using a Peer Review System

Wei-Wei Shen[1(✉)], Ming-Hsiu Michelle Tsai[1],
and Jim-Min Lin[2]

[1] Department of Foreign Languages and Literature,
Feng Chia University, Taichung, Taiwan
{wwshen,mhtsai}@fcu.edu.tw
[2] Department of Information Engineering and Computer Science,
Feng Chia University, Taichung, Taiwan
jimmy@fcu.edu.tw

Abstract. Although research into peer review claimed some convenience and benefits of executing online or computer-mediated-communication peer revisions in writing courses, few of them mentioned the control of the peer reviewing process via the help of technology. This paper depicts a possibility of creating a controlling online system on the one hand, and the process of executing it on the other. Using the subjects who were studying English as a foreign language, the preliminary study has shown some merits but raised some precautions of conducting this system for future studies.

Keywords: Computer assisted language learning · English language teaching · Writing · Peer review

1 Introduction

There is an increasing yearning of using technology in the teaching of English as a second/foreign language (L2) due to the proof of learning effectiveness based on the fast growing research. To name but a few, technology can not only increase learners' motivation but reduce teachers' burden [7, 10].

In particular, using technology to assist how to write in English should be favored because writing is considered difficult and complicated. Students have lots of demands but teachers may find it hard to fulfill whatever students want [22]. So it is a good idea that technology can be employed to teach writing. However, it is worthwhile pondering how to make this happen and what technology can do to help the teaching job appropriately.

This paper intends to present a case study on the teaching of writing at a university in Taiwan and show some benefits and problems regarding how an online system may or may not assist the peer-review processes. Examining the advantages and disadvantages together may be beneficial for future research design and the teaching of English writing in similar L2 learning settings.

© Springer International Publishing AG 2017
T.-C. Huang et al. (Eds.): SETE 2017, LNCS 10676, pp. 391–399, 2017.
https://doi.org/10.1007/978-3-319-71084-6_44

2 Related Work

It is very normal to hear from instructors who are teaching English as an L2 language that correcting students' writings is very time-consuming and there are plenty of mistakes [23]. Although in the context of teaching writing at the university level in Taiwan, students are getting familiar with the concept of peer correction, they may not execute this function themselves before they submit their writings to teachers if this is not a compulsory task.

On the other hand, more often than not, quite a few teachers still choose to conduct peer review on the printouts in class to ensure that no single one student can escape away from completing this activity. In a way, this type of teacher-centered management of the class is still very common in this L2 context. Therefore, using peer review via the help of technology may be appreciated by teachers to reduce students' errors in the drafting process. This section highlights the major development in these two research fields.

2.1 The Advantages and Disadvantages of Peer Review

Among all the teaching techniques that can help students improve their writings, peer review has been frequently researched and theoretically grounded [11, 12].

Executing peer review process in a writing class may fulfill Vygotsky's theory of zone of proximal development because learning can be developed by interaction. There are four beneficial aspects of peer review listed as follows [20]:

- For the cognitive development, this activity can give students helpful suggestions including content, rhetoric and writing skills.
- Linguistically, peer review helps with the training of vocabulary and grammar.
- Regarding the meta-cognitive development, it enhances learners' independent and critical thinking skills.
- By interacting and sharing thoughts with other peers, social relationships and supports can be easily developed and maintained.

However, despite the obvious advantages of using peer review, some scholars concerned that learners' insufficient knowledge may provide incorrect comments, surface or rough corrections. Besides, peers may feel hesitated to point out their classmates' mistakes [18], so there is a need to consider the skills of applying this activity to different cultures. For example, many Chinese learners from the settings of teacher-centered learning styles may not be used to this strategy because they depend more on teachers to do corrections than peers. Moreover, they do not normally find peer review useful or enjoyable. This is perhaps an obviously cultural form of learning in Chinese contexts [14].

2.2 Computer Technology Assisted Peer Review

There is a rapid growing research interest investigating the effectiveness of using peer review via the computer-mediated-communication (CMC) method because this mode is beneficial to do peer revision outside of the classroom, or it can avoid some awkwardness when peers have to pick up each other's writing faults face to face [3, 5, 8].

Although scholars have been attempting to identify the best mode of online peer revision, such as using Word document, Blackboard platform [5] or Blogs [21], not much has mentioned about creating a tool of computer technology to govern the flow of the peer review process. Meanwhile, although there are some published websites, such as *Pigaiwang* or *Grammarly* to pick up grammatical and vocabulary mistakes, not many can be used to guide a systematic peer review [24]. One recent online writing system designed by Kuo [15] for university students aimed at helping learners' composing and reviewing practices, but it is still different from the only and focused control of the reviewing steps as claimed in our system in this study. In addition, although another similar title of the online peer review system was found in 2011 [16], not much has shown regarding its implementation and evaluation in their study.

Since there are benefits of peer review as long as the shortcomings may be eliminated, the main objective of this paper is to show, first, there is an approach to creating a computer-assisted blind review system to deal with the shortcomings of peer review mentioned above. Then, the paper is to further evaluate the implementation of this system.

2.3 Approach to Creating the System

As mentioned, partly because computer-assisted learning is a trend and partly because buying a commercial software program may be a financial burden, this paper will show writing teachers, especially for those who are working at a university, that it is possible to make an online system based on personal teaching needs to control students' peer-review processes as long as language teachers can collaboratively work with technology programmers. First, the writing teacher can inform the programmer the major required functions based on the current principles of teaching writing because the programmer may not necessarily know them. Then the programmer can use the system with operating software MS-Windows 7/8 32x/64x, the software tools including IIS 7, MySQL Server 5.5, MySQL ODBC 5.3 and the programming tools including Dreamweaver CS6, PHP, HTML, JAVASCRIP, AJAX. Finally, about six man-months, the peer review system can be set up as a Web-based application [13, 17].

This system supports several learner functions: (1) a login page; (2) writers' and reviewers' records; (3) a writing page for writers to draft and calculate written words; (4) a grading rubric page showing the IELTS band descriptors. The writer's page and the reviewer's page are shown in Figs. 1 and 2 respectively. There are also teacher functions to group students, find their writings and comments and grade their writings.

The system is strict to put four students together because each writer can read three different writings to increase enough but not exhaustive reading. Moreover, three peer reviewers may increase the objectivity of the comments in the 2-stage review process. The first stage is for peer reviewers to give feedback on the first received draft based on the two general criteria: local (i.e. grammatical mistakes) and global (i.e. content or meaning errors), and return the first feedback to the writer for further modification. Next, after the writer sends back a new revised draft, the reviewer reads again to check

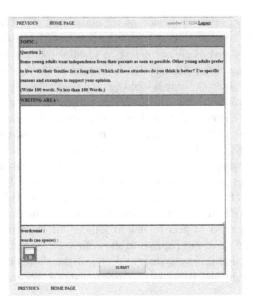

Fig. 1. Writing page-drafting, calculating written words, saving the writing

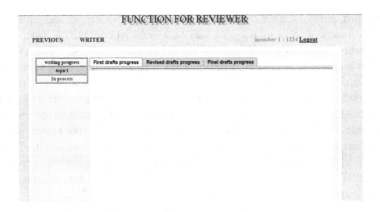

Fig. 2. Reviewer's page

if the corrections are appropriately done. If the reviewer is not satisfied with the new revision, the writing can be returned to the writer again. Then the teacher can intervene at this stage to find out the problems to help the writers. Finally, when every writing in a group successfully passes the peer examination, teachers can give a score to the writing.

The system also has different storage functions that can keep the records of learners' practices and teachers' feedback. The learners' background information, account numbers and reviewing processes can be classified into different categories, sheets or tables in the system. Every category records learners' original writing, revisions after two peer-reviews and their final edition of writings. Peer suggestions are also saved in one file. The system can also show the grouping data and writing topics assigned by the instructor. All of these data can be kept for teaching and researching purposes.

3   The Implementation of the System

At first, the system programmers designed the system in Chinese version, but the writing teachers as researchers considered it important to use English as an international language, so the system was modified further. It is worthwhile mentioning that the change of the language caused some bugs and designers had to solve the problems. After the system was ready, the teachers and students were required to test it to see if there were any technical faults.

We then formally tested the system in public originally in March 2015 on 36 voluntary participants who were first-year English majors and they got involved in the first round test. In the trial phase, according to our observations, when students wrote, they really engaged in composing attentively. However, during the reviewing process, based on the oral feedback of users, due to the constraint of team-work and students' time management problems, in the second, third and fourth rounds of peer reviewing meetings by the end of December 2015, only about 12 students, i.e. 3 groups, could still show their enthusiasm for helping with the following research tests. Therefore, finally these 12 well motivated students were chosen to be observed and reported the ways they used the peer review system.

3.1   Research Design

Twelve university students mentioned above studying English language as their majoring subject in the central area of Taiwan had agreed to be involved in this peer review process. They were required to write at least 100 words for two writing topics chosen from the TOEFL test bank [9], and each of which took them 20 minutes to write at the same time, and then they played as a reviewer following the processes in the system. It took longer time to finish the review process of the first topic because the subjects were required to finish the process on their own. As a result, when conducting the second topic, the researchers could only require students to complete the review process in 50 minutes followed by composing the content.

Two writing topics were done in this research as follows.

- Some young adults want independence from their parents as soon as possible. Other young adults prefer to live with their families for a long time. Which of these situations do you think is better?
- Do you agree or disagree with the following statement? Always telling the truth is the most important consideration in any relationship.

The study intended to explain the following three questions by analyzing the quantitative and qualitative data stored in the peer review system.

1. How much can students' writing quality change based on the record of the system?
2. In what ways the users' reviewing styles may show?
3. What may be the disadvantages of using the online reviewing system?

3.2   Results and Discussions

Based on the profiles of students' writings, the data regarding the writing length in Table 1 show that, first, there is an obvious growth across the first and second drafts and across two different topics. For example, there were only 53 words in the initial writing of the first topic, and then its second draft could increase almost a double size. Moreover, regarding the writings of the second topic, students could write at least 300 words for both versions. More importantly, the increase of the writing length for the two different topics has reached the statistical significance (p = .005) calculated by SPSS.

Table 1. The word counts of the two topics

	First topic	Second topic	Mean	Standard deviation
The first draft	53	310	179.54	92.474
The second draft	95	321	212.43	72.577

Therefore, the answer to the first question is that the system can easily store students' written works in different timings and show the significant change of students' writing length. It is possible that the more students can write, the more details of the ideas can be written. In addition to the change of the writing length that can be easily detected via the system, students modified frequently on the grammar and vocabulary which result in less obvious written mistakes and more complex sentence structure so the readability was increased in the second draft. Such findings are consistent with the ones of the past research [6, 15]. Thus, if this big change of their writing quality can be shown in class, students may be even more motivated to write and cooperate with other students via the help of the peer review system.

When examining other qualitative data that the reviewers wrote in the system to find out their reviewing patterns, apart from frequent indications of the grammatical, vocabulary or punctuation mistakes, we noticed that quite a few positive comments were given to the content *per se*. For example, peers normally gave kind comments such as "I agree with you", "good idea", and "your writing has no big problems", etc. Therefore, the answer to the second research question is that peers' feedback can be very encouraging and helpful for creating a harmonious learning atmosphere. Nevertheless, reviewers did not always keep agreeing with writers' ideas. Occasionally, the reviewers would also respond to the authors when they had different viewpoints. For instance, one writer expressed her main reason to live with her familiy because they were her closest relationship in the world. This writer then assumed that if one cannot develop in harmony with the families who care and understand him/her the most, then he/she cannot get along with other people outside of the families. Interestingly, one student reviewer expressed a different viewpoint by mentioning that "I think this is not about how good you get along with your family because sometimes getting along with friends and families can be two different things!" Such feedback shows students' different ideas which can be valuable starting points to do follow-up discussions in class.

However, despite the merits of improving students' writing qualities mentioned above, the past research had warned that using technology or an online writing system is not a panacea, but good classroom management and understanding of individual learning differences can be crucial [1–4]. Thus it is necessary to ask students' concerns after the use of the peer review system. Based on the interview data and written reflections, students mentioned quite a lot about the flexibility and feasibility of the peer corrections by the support of the system. First, the system had to put the same four students together without a chance to change, so as long as one of the four students did not constantly or persistently continue the composing, reviewing and revising process, the completion of the whole group work became impossible. Similarly, some students said that their motivation of completing the teamwork process required by the system may be easily demotivated because of some long waiting for others in the same group. Second, few students commented on the system design and showed their preferences to mark, highlight or correct directly on the content area instead of using a separate electronic feedback sheet. This kind of correcting habits matched with these subjects' real learning experiences because they told the researchers that conventionally and frequently teachers gave them writers' printouts and they did corrections directly on the paper in class.

4   Conclusion

The paper has shown that, on the one hand, a peer review system could be created to follow up the ideal of peer review training process proclaimed by former studies so that it was expected to reduce teachers' burden when guiding the peer review process in class. Our system has the benefits of keeping students' writings and reviewing records all together in a paperless manner. It can also provide an anonymous and blind reviewing process to solve the problem that peers, especially living in the broader concept of Chinese culture, normally hesitate to indicate their classmates' mistakes in class.

On the other hand, although this research on the system implementation has only collected a small size of the data, it has identified its limitations in reality for further improvement and has been in line with quite a few studies done in the past. First, using computer or technology to assist peer review does not mean that teachers can just sit back and relax behind the system without structuring the reviewing schedule carefully because not all students can be eager to do the writing and reviewing tasks. In the original pilot test of the system, our study had 36 voluntary students at first but many of them found this peer reviewing process time-consuming, and then only 12 students were left to show their willingness of collaborating with blind reviewers continually. Hence, what researchers can do is to prove that there are benefits of conducting peer review, but course teachers still play a key role to make it work [4–6, 15]. Second, some students who tended to work faster and more eagerly may lose patience waiting for other slower writers and reviewers to submit their work, so teachers can set up the submission deadline strictly and clearly. Third, more writing topics to be conducted in a formal class will be needed to see obvious progress in giving feedback on the meaning and content comparing to the one without using the peer review technique. Meanwhile, for learners such as the ones from more teacher-centered learning styles, it is better to inform them first about the advantages of having peer review activities, and then make this writing exercise be part of the course requirement because abilities of peer review need training to be more effective [19].

Because this preliminary research presented in this paper did not intend to show the causative relationship between the effectiveness with or without the use the system, future study may be still needed to make a firmer proclaim for this aspect. Nevertheless, comparing to the current reality of teaching writing in university courses with a very high frequency of using traditional pen and paper format to give teacher or peer feedback, there is no doubt that it is not easy to quickly display and integrate peers' comments further as class activities shown earlier. Overall, in view of this, our peer review system must be helpful for teachers to save their time, energy and paper.

Acknowledgments. We are grateful for the funds of the Ministry of Science and Technology of the Republic of China under the contract numbers MOST 102-2221-E035-068, MOST 103-2221-E035-051, MOST 103-2511-S-468-002 and MOST 105-2511-S-035-002-MY2.

References

1. Breuch, L.A.K., Racine, S.J.: Developing sound tutor training for online writing centers: creating productive peer reviewers. Comput. Compos. **17**(3), 245–263 (2000). https://doi.org/10.1016/S8755-4615(00)00034-7

2. Breuch, L.A.K.: Thinking critically about technological literacy: developing a framework to guide computer pedagogy in technical communication. Tech. Commun. Q. **11**(3), 267–288 (2002). https://doi.org/10.1207/s15427625tcq1103_3

3. Breuch, L.A.K.: Virtual Peer Review: Teaching and Learning About Writing in Online Environments. State University of New York Press, Albany (2004)

4. Breuch, L.A.K., Rendahl, M.: Toward a complexity of online learning: learners in online first-year writing. Comput. Compos. **30**(4), 297–314 (2013). https://doi.org/10.1016/j.compcom.2013.10.002

5. Chang, C.F.: Peer review via three modes in an EFL writing course. Comput. Compos. **29**(1), 63–78 (2012). https://doi.org/10.1016/j.compcom.2012.01.001

6. Chang, C.F.: Fostering EFL college students' register awareness: writing online forum posts and traditional essays. Int. J. Comput. Assist. Lang. Learn. **2**(3), 17–34 (2012)

7. Chin, K.Y., Hong, Z.W., Huang, Y.M., Shen, W.W., Lin, J.M.: Courseware development with animated pedagogical agents in learning system to improve learning motivation. Interact. Learn. Environ. **24**(3), 360–381 (2016). http://www.tandfonline.com/doi/full/10.1080/10494820.2013.851089

8. Ertmer, P.A., Richardson, J.C., Belland, B., Camin, D., Connolly, P., Coulthard, G., Lei, K., Mong, C.: Using peer feedback to enhance the quality of student online postings: an exploratory study. J. Comput. Mediated Commun. **12**, 412–433 (2007). https://doi.org/10.1111/j.1083-6101.2007.00331.x

9. ETS.: The Official Guide to the TOEFL Test, 4th edn. McGraw Hill Education, Singapore (2012)

10. Hong, Z.W., Huang, Y.M., Hsu, M., Shen, W.W.: Authoring robot-assisted instructional materials for improving learning performance and motivation in EFL classrooms. Educ. Technol. Soc. **19**(1), 337–349 (2016)
11. Hyland, K.: Second Language Writing. Cambridge University Press, Cambridge (2003)
12. Hyland, K., Hyland, F.: Feedback in Second Language Writing: Contexts and Issues. Cambridge University Press, Cambridge (2006)
13. Jhong, Y.F., Lin, J.M., Shen, W.W., Hong, Z.W.: An online peer review learning system for English writing class. In: Taiwan Conference on Software Engineering (2014)
14. Jin, L., Cortazzi, M. (eds.): Researching Inter-Cultural Learning: Investigations in Language and Education. Palgrave, Macmillan, Houndmills (2013)
15. Kuo, C.H.: Designing an online writing system: learning with support, 285–299 (2008). http://journals.sagepub.com/doi/abs/10.1177/0033688208096842
16. Lan, Y.-T., Wang, J.-H., Hsu, S.-H., Chan, T.-W.: Peer feedback in online writing system. In: Chang, M., Hwang, W.-Y., Chen, M.-P., Müller, W. (eds.) Edutainment 2011. LNCS, vol. 6872, pp. 126–129. Springer, Heidelberg (2011). https://doi.org/10.1007/978-3-642-23456-9_23
17. Lin, J.M.: Demonstration of an online English writing peer review system. In: 51st Annual International IATEFL Conference and Exhibition, Glasgow (2017)
18. Min, H.T.: Why peer comments fail? Engl. Teach. Learn. **27**(3), 85–103 (2003)
19. Min, H.T.: Training students to become successful peer reviewers. System **33**, 293–308 (2005). https://doi.org/10.1016/j.system.2004.11.003
20. Min, H.T.: The effects of trained peer review on EFL students' revision types and writing quality. J. Second Lang. Writ. **15**, 118–141 (2006). https://doi.org/10.1016/j.jslw.2006.01.003
21. Pham, V.P.H., Usaha, S.: Blog-based peer response for L2 writing revision. Comput. Assist. Lang. Learn. **29**(4), 724–748 (2016). http://www.tandfonline.com/doi/full/10.1080/09588221.2015.1026355
22. Shen, W.W.: Your wish is my command. Engl. Teach. Prof. **79**, 26–28 (2012)
23. Shen, W.W., Chou, M.L.: Empower EFL students to reduce their L2 lexical errors caused by L1 semantic interference. Humanising Lang. Teach. **13**(5) (2011). http://www.hltmag.co.uk/oct11/mart02.htm
24. Shen, W.W., Lin, J.M.: Training L2 writer autonomy via an electronic peer review system. In: 50th Annual International IATEFL Conference and Exhibition, Birmingham, UK (2016)

Digital Storytelling and Mobile Learning: Potentials for Internationalization of Higher Education Curriculum

Andreja Istenic Starcic[1,2,3(✉)], Po-Sen Huang[4],
Roza Alexeyevna Valeeva[3], Liliia Agzamovna Latypova[5],
and Yueh-Min Huang[4]

[1] Faculty of Civil and Geodetic Engineering,
University of Ljubljana, Ljubljana, Slovenia
andreja.starcic@gmail.com
[2] Faculty of Education, University of Primorska, Koper, Slovenia
[3] Institute of Psychology and Education, Kazan Federal University,
Kazan, Russia
valeykin@yandex.ru
[4] Department of Engineering Science, National Cheng Kung University,
Tainan, Taiwan
phuang@tajen.edu.tw, huang@mail.ncku.edu.tw
[5] Institute of Management, Economics and Finance, Kazan Federal University,
Kazan, Russia
melilek@yandex.ru

Abstract. The professions are becoming global and required are intended students' learning outcomes to ensure intercultural communication; therefore, the prospective students' learning outcomes include those for working in international and multicultural environments. Higher education needs to be responsive to students' cultural background and to engage them in intercultural exchange by creating authentic cultural contexts guaranteeing authentic learning, which requires integration of students' authentic social practices. Mobile technology providing instant information access and connectivity supports new types of learning relationships, connecting students outside the immediate classroom context. Mobile technology is transforming social practices and facilitates learning embedded in social practices. Students are engaged in cross-cultural learning and thus develop knowledge, skills and attitudes from within the context meeting other cultures. Social networking sites for collaborative learning are recognized as useful and allow students to experience authentic cultural and authentic social practices that they use in non-academic activities and as such merging formal and informal learning. Digital storytelling was applied in computer supported collaborative international learning. The collaborative learning took place in academic year 2016/17 involving two Slovenian, two Taiwanese and one Russian class.

Keywords: Digital storytelling · Mobile learning · Computer supported collaborative learning · Internationalization of curriculum · Higher education

T.-C. Huang et al. (Eds.): SETE 2017, LNCS 10676, pp. 400–406, 2017.
https://doi.org/10.1007/978-3-319-71084-6_45

1 Introduction

With Bologna reform, the internationalization of curriculum was conducted on the levels of transparent and comparable curriculum structures internationally with students and teachers mobility aiming at European common labor market and global competitiveness. Knight defines two pillars of internationalization, abroad and at home, which are interdependent [2]. Intended students' learning outcomes include those for working in international and multicultural environments. The professions are becoming global and intercultural competences are required for communication to work abroad or at home. Erasmus mobility programme offers mobility on average to app. 4.5% of all students in Europe [21], therefore, internationalization at home is required to provide to all students possibility to develop competences for work in international contexts.

Digitalization carries a potential for internationalization at home [3] and emergent is collaborative online international learning (COIL) facilitating students' global awareness with engagement in cross-cultural learning activities online under supervision of teachers within their home university courses [4]. The design and implementation of internationalized curriculum includes consideration of four dimensions: learning outcomes, learning resources, learning and teaching methods and learning environments. The model of the internationalized curriculum design and implementation is designed by Istenic Starcic and includes four elements (Fig. 1). The key components of four elements are listed in order to support teachers to provide diverse international learning experience for students at home. Different kinds of international experiences at home could be supported by digital technology and resources. Increasing potential is identified in digital storytelling and in social networking which both facilitate students' agency. Digital storytelling facilitates students' acting as producers of digital contents and is proven to be effective in multimodal design and

Fig. 1. Internationalization of curriculum: design and implementation

delivery integrating technical, pedagogical and content knowledge [11]. Computer supported collaborative learning (CSCL) enables international collaboration. Applied were mobile learning and social networking. The research findings suggest that social networking practices are more student-driven and have as such potential for engaged and autonomous learning [5] and also professional development [7]. Required competences include intercultural interaction and collaboration which is dependent of digital environments. The two competences in focus are intercultural competency and digital competency. Students are involved in intercultural learning developing knowledge, skills and attitudes [7] from within the context meeting other cultures.

To meet the requirements, teaching and learning methods apply CSCL in international environments. Two dimensions should be met: being responsive towards students' cultural background [17] and engaging them in cross-cultural exchange, which guarantees authentic cultural contexts and authentic learning activities that require integration of students' authentic social practices. The inclusion of students' social practices has been found beneficial for students' engagement [2]. Social practices predominantly involve web activities, however, research findings indicate that students are still more consumers than producers of contents. Digital competency has transformed from being oriented towards assimilative to productive activities [12]. In this study involved are student-teachers who require competences to work with ICT in teaching and learning.

The article describes the project initiated by the universities of Slovenia, Taiwan and Russia: University of Primorska, National Cheng Kung University, Taien University and Kazan Federal University. Under the project digital storytelling was conducted to develop student-teachers' competences within the course of educational technology in two study programs for primary and pre-primary school teachers. By means of Facebook digital stories made by student-teachers in Slovenia were shared with and evaluated by students from Taiwan and Russia.

In the article we discuss digital storytelling and social networking in learning addressing the following research question:

RQ: How do student-teachers develop technical, pedagogical and content knowledge utilizing multimodal digital storytelling and create narratives according to the rubric sharing story in a community of students from Taiwan and Russia?

Slovenian students were designing stories applying technological, pedagogical and content knowledge and sharing digital stories on Facebook in an international community with students from Taiwan and Russia. The rubric was applied to conduct a content analysis and assessment [10].

2 Student-Teacher from Consumer to Producer of Digital Contents

Digital storytelling support creative expression, reflection, individual perspective and insight and self-presentation utilizing multimodal narrative. Students' personal experiences are shaped with digital practices and within the framework of the project student-teachers examined the opportunities offered for teaching. Experiences on digital storytelling show that students *"perceived digital storytelling as a strategy and means for empowering the "student voice" and the active construction of knowledge"* [10].

Examining teachers' and student-teachers' competences for technology supported learning the Technological, Pedagogical Content Knowledge model (TPACK) introduced by Mishra and Koehler [8]. Within the internationalization of curriculum, CSCL offers students and teachers international and intercultural experiences. Mobile technology providing instant information access, hyper connectivity and new sense of space [18] supports new types of learning relationships, connecting students outside the immediate classroom context [14]. Mobile technology transforms social practices and facilitates learning embedded in social practices.

An "app" or "application" is "a software program, often designed to run on a mobile device that allows the user to carry out one or more operations" [8]. Apps are applied in learning to facilitate students' engagement [20]. Research findings indicate that emotional engagement with technology facilitates motivation, satisfaction and achievement [9]. Mobile technology facilitates short time sequences for learning [19] with mobile apps as significant genre. Mobile apps are pervasive within mobile technology. They integrate a number of technologies and tools and are among fastest growing features of IT affecting education and informal life [13]. The availability of commercial apps expands the affordability of mobile devices and also affordance of mobile learning in education [16].

Application of social networking sites for collaborative learning proved to be useful providing students with authentic cultural and authentic social practices, which they use in non-academic activities and as such merging formal and informal learning. Research findings of [1, 6] suggest that social network sites (SNSs) practices are more student-driven: students can share their experience, thoughts, perspective, information and knowledge and therefore have potential for engaged and autonomous learning. In teaching and learning SNSs foster effectiveness of students' learning process in terms of knowledge sharing, on-line interaction and discussion in comparison with traditional learning management tools and conventional face-to-face learning environment [1]. Students' engagement in SNSs is done in the way of developing narratives and publishing them, which makes it more learner-centered compared to learning management or traditional face-to-face classroom learning that are more under control of the institution and more institution-centered. SNSs have potential for transforming students' academic experiences integrating informal and formal academic experiences and facilitating self-regulated learning [6] when engaging in SNSs as a source of learning and experiences. It is crucial to know how students are aware of SNSs in support of their interaction and agency internationally or globally and if they utilize the potential for global networking. Introducing social networking sites in formal learning of student-teachers is preparing them for bridging to professional context. With the international dimension in the classroom and the professional context becoming globalized, student-teachers are facing contemporary challenges of diverse cultural settings.

3 Methods

3.1 The Context of the Study: Internationalization of the Curriculum

The study was conducted within the course of Educational technology in programs for pre-primary and primary school teachers. The course of educational technology curriculum reflects international dimensions at the four levels: learning content/resources, teaching methods, learning environment and intended learning outcomes.

The rapid development and application in the area of educational technology is distributed and proliferated globally. Learning contents, learning, and teaching methods are international and common across study programs globally. The international dimension presented within study was addressed at the level of learning outcomes and learning environment. To prepare students for work in international and diverse cultural settings requires learning in authentic contexts of learning environments where diverse cultures meet and interact. The authenticity is provided by social practice in SNSs and cultural settings of the classes from three national contexts involved. Within the bilateral project between Slovenia and Russia (BI-RU/16-18-020) and agreement of collaboration between Slovenia and Taiwan, the computer supported collaborative learning took place in academic year 2016/17 involving two Slovenian, two Taiwanese and one Russian class. The objective of the study is to pilot setting of international learning environments consisting of teaching and learning tasks conducted in team teaching of teachers from Slovenia, Taiwan and Russia. Students applied mobile apps for digital storytelling. Intended learning outcomes are: multimodal design of digital learning contents for international community, sharing and communicating the digital learning contents in social networking with peer professionals from diverse cultural settings (Slovene, Taiwanese, and Russian).

3.2 Research Design, Data Collection and Analysis

The case study was conducted in academic year 2016/17. Within this research paper, presented is the content analysis of digital stories produced by 120 students from Slovenia. Pre-service teachers aged 19–21 participated in the project. To answer the research question, the rubric applied in content analysis and assessment of digital stories were conducted by means of the following rubrics (verbal, visual, spatial, auditory, dynamics) [10].

4 Results and Discussion

4.1 Content Analysis of Digital Stories

Students are engaged in cross-cultural learning developing knowledge, skill s and attitudes from within the context meeting other cultures. Through the design of multimodal digital stories, students developed pedagogical, technical and content knowledge. Intercultural communication by multiple modes in digital storytelling was utilised through the following modes: verbal, visual, auditory and dynamics presented in Table 1.

Table 1. Modalities in digital storytelling based on adapted rubrics

	Modality	Assessment criteria	M	SD
1	Verbal	Cohesion of narration type	2.24	0.44
2		Cohesion of theme and the cohesion of elements following the learning objectives	2.78	0.69
3		Formulation of text and the vocabulary in relation to students' developmental level of children	3.86	0.77
4	Visual	Digital elements	2.74	0.43
5		Non-digital elements	3.54	0.71
6	Spatial	Screen presentation and organisation	3.97	0.73
7	Auditory	Sound, music	3.42	0.55
8		Voice over	3.73	0.69
9	Dynamics	Dynamic images	3.56	0.86
10		Transmodal elements	3.86	0.87
11		Transitions between sequences	4.44	0.71
12		Interactive tasks	4.34	0.75

5   Conclusions

The paper presents the development of pre-service teachers' digital and inter-cultural competence by means of digital storytelling sharing on Facebook. Sharing digital stories on Facebook in an international community with students from Taiwan and Russia demonstrated that students were designing their stories applying technological, pedagogical and content knowledge. The rubric was applied to conduct a content analysis and assessment [10]. The content analysis of digital stories according to the rubrics identified the sufficient alignment with all dimensions (verbal, visual, spatial, auditory, dynamics). Relationship between students' social practices with SNSs and TPACK factors involved in the digital content design had effects on narrative and digital content design.

Acknowledgments. The authors acknowledge the financial support from the Slovenian Research Agency within a bilateral project BI-RU/16-18-020 and research program ARRS P2-0210.

References

1. Eid, M.I.M., Al-Jabri, I.M.: Social networking, knowledge sharing, and student learning: the case of university students. Comput. Educ. **99**, 14–27 (2016)
2. Cakir, H.: Use of blogs in pre-service teacher education to improve student engagement. Comput. Educ. **68**, 244–252 (2013)
3. Knight, J.: Higher Education in Turmoil: The Changing World of Internationalization. Sense, Rotterdam (2008)
4. Higher Education in the World (2013). http://eur-lex.europa.eu/legal-content/EN/TXT/?uri=CELEX:52013DC0499

5. Rubin, J., Guth, S.: Collaborative online international learning: an emerging format for internationalizing curricula. In: Moore, A.S., Simon, S. (eds.) Globally Networked Teaching in the Humanities: Theories and Practices, pp. 15–27. Routledge, New York (2015)

6. Dabbagh, N., Kitsantas, A.: Personal learning environments, social media, and self-regulated learning: a natural formula for connecting formal and informal learning. Internet Higher Educ. 12(1), 3–8 (2015)

7. Deradorff, D.: The identification and assessment of intercultural competence as a student outcome of internationalisation of institutions of higher education in the United States. J. Stud. Int. Educ. 10(3), 241–266 (2006)

8. Gardner, H., Davis, K.: The App Generation. Yale University Press (2013). [Kindle version]. http://www.amazon.com

9. Hatzigianni, M., Gregoriadis, A., Fleer, M.: Computer use at schools and associations with social-emotional outcomes – a holistic approach. Findings from the longitudinal study of Australian children. Comput. Educ. 95, 134–150 (2016)

10. Istenic Starcic, A., Cotic, M., Solomonides, I., Volk, M.: Engaging preservice primary and preprimary school teachers in digital storytelling for the teaching and learning of mathematics. Br. J. Educ. Technol. 47(1), 29–50 (2016)

11. Istenic Starcic, A., Barrow, M., Zajc, M., Lebenicnik, M.: Students' attitudes on social network sites and their actual use for career management competences and professional identity development. Int. J.: Emerg. Technol. Learn. 12(5), 65–81 (2017)

12. Istenic Starcic, A., Turk, Z.: Ubiquitous learning and digital literacy practices connecting teacher and learner. In: WWW 2016 Companion, International World Wide Web Conference, 11 to 15 April 2016, Montreal, Canada, cop. 2016, pp. 823–827. ACM Digital Libray: Association for Computing Machinery, New York (2015)

13. Johnson, L., Adams, S., Cummins, M.: The NMC Horizon Report: 2012 Higher Education Edition. The New Media Consortium, Austin, Texas (2012)

14. Merchant, G.: Mobile practices in everyday life: popular digital technologies and schooling revisited. Br. J. Educ. Technol. 43(5), 770–782 (2012)

15. Mishra, P., Koehler, M.J.: Technological pedagogical content knowledge: a framework for teacher knowledge. Teach. Coll. Rec. 108(6), 1017–1054 (2006)

16. Mouza, C., Barrett-Greenly, T.: Bridging the app gap: an examination of a professional development initiative on mobile learning in urban schools. Comput. Educ. 88, 1–14 (2015)

17. Olneck, M.R.: Immigrants and education. In: Banks, J.A., Banks, C.A.M. (eds.) Handbook of Research on Multicultural Education. Macmillan, New York (1995)

18. Parry, D.: Mobile perspectives: on teaching mobile literacy. Educause Rev. (2011). http://net.educause.edu/ir/library/pdf/ERM1120.pdf

19. Peng, H., Su, Y.-J., Chou, C., Tsai, C.-C.: Ubiquitous knowledge construction: mobile learning re-defined and a conceptual framework. Innov. Educ. Teach. Int. 46(2), 171–183 (2009)

20. Zhang, M., Trussel, R.P., Gallegos, B., Asam, R.R.: Using math apps for improving student learning: an exploratory study in an inclusive fourth grade classroom. TechTrends 59(2), 32–39 (2015)

21. Klemenčič, M., Flander, A.: Evaluation of the Impact of Erasmus Programme on Higher Education in Slovenia. CMEPIUS, Ljubljana (2014)

SLEEP (International Workshop on Smart Learning by Emerging Educational Paradigm)

Using Educational Robotics to Support Elementary School Students' Electrical Engineering Knowledge: A Preliminary Analysis

Pan-Nan Chou[1]([⊠]) and Yen-Ning Su[2]

[1] National University of Tainan, Tainan, Taiwan
pnchou@gm2.nutn.edu.tw
[2] Shengli Elementary School, Tainan, Taiwan

Abstract. This study aimed to investigate how elementary school students used Arduino-based educational robotics to support their electrical engineering learning. A maker education program (Robot MakerSpace) as one of afterschool clubs was created in a public elementary school. 15 students voluntarily participated in the program. A qualitative case study approach was used to collect required data. A preliminary analytical results indicated that the educational robotics were effective instructional tools to teach varied types of engineering concepts. In addition, Students might increase their systematic thinking, problem solving, and logical thinking skills during robotics programming.

Keywords: K-6 engineering education · Maker education · Educational robotics

1 Introduction

Since 2014, the Engineering Education Lab (EEL) at the National University of Tainan in Taiwan has created a long-term learning partnership with local elementary schools to introduce emerging technologies into classrooms. Under this cooperative scheme, technological resources in the college can be employed to promote teacher professional development in engineering instruction, as well as to increase student interest in studying engineering in K–6 educational environments [1]. In 2016, EEL received a three-year research grant entitled "A Case Study of Little Engineers" from Ministry of Science and Technology in Taiwan. In the first year of the project, we collaborated with one public elementary school and created an after-school maker program in which students (being a little electrical engineer) operated a low-cost Arduino-based educational robotics to learn fundamental engineering concepts.

Makerspaces are defined as "informal workshop environments located in community facilities or education institutions where people immerse themselves in creative making and tinkering activities" [2]. In this study, the maker program is an after-school informal club located in one public elementary school where students engaged in different engineering learning activities by manipulating educational robotics. Through children's hand-on making experiences, we reported preliminary findings regarding

T.-C. Huang et al. (Eds.): SETE 2017, LNCS 10676, pp. 409–412, 2017.
https://doi.org/10.1007/978-3-319-71084-6_46

how educational robotics might be used to support students in learning engineering knowledge.

2 Research Method

We adopted Yin (2003)'s qualitative case study methodology to collect required data since case study allowed the researcher to observe how students used emerging technologies (i.e. educational robotics) to participated in engineering design learning. The data collection sources contained field observation report, teaching notes, course learning material, and informal interviews with children and the schoolteacher.

Overall, 15 elementary school students were recruited to participate in the study. Student participants completed weekly 3-h engineering design lessons in the after-school maker program. Basically, in each learning unit during one semester, students should use Scratch coding language to import required actions into electrical board embedded in the educational robotics (MBot). Figure 1 shows a learning activity in the maker program.

Fig. 1. Students using the programming tool to control robotics

3 Preliminary Findings

A summary of preliminary research results was listed as follows:

1. Students were extremely attracted by educational robotics, which in turn directly motivated students to learn varied levels of engineering concepts.

2. Programming language (Scratch) supported students to develop logical thinking skills. In particularly, engaging de-bug learning activities enabled students to increase their problem solving skills.
3. During assembling and manipulating educational robotics, students clearly understood the importance of systematic structure (thinking), which is a critical element in engineering design process.
4. Being a little electrical engineer, students not only understood fundamental engineering concepts, but also attempted to capture electrical engineering related knowledge.
5. Students might apply their math and science knowledge that already learned in class into robotics programming. Such learning activities provided students a learning opportunity to link their prior knowledge in STEM.

4 Concluding Remark

Our preliminary research results indicated that the educational robotics were effective instructional tools to teach varied types of engineering concepts. In addition, Students might increase their systematic thinking, problem solving, and logical thinking skills during robotics programming.

Appendix (Teaching Schedule in Robot MakerSpace)

Week	Learning unit (3 h)
1	Orientation and programming practice (mBlock)
2	Programming practice (mBlock)
3	Platform assembling and motor
4	Switch and resistor control
5	Buzzer
6	LED light
7	Light sensor
8	Ultrasound sensor
9	Sound sensor
10	Gas sensor
11	LED matrix
12	Temperature sensor
13	Remote control (Infrared)
14	Remote control (Bluetooth)
15	Competition practice
16	Robot competition (Maze Pass)

References

1. Katehi, L., Pearson, G., Feder, M.: Engineering in K–12 Education. The National Academies Press, Washington, D.C
2. The Horizon Report. http://cdn.nmc.org/media/2016-nmc-cosn-horizon-report-k12-EN.pdf. Accessed 11 Nov 2016

Understanding Students' Continuance Intention to Use Virtual Desktop Service

Yong-Ming Huang[1(✉)] and Chien-Hung Liu[2]

[1] Department of Multimedia and Entertainment Science,
Southern Taiwan University of Science and Technology, Tainan, Taiwan, R.O.C.
ym.huang.tw@gmail.com
[2] Shanghai Lida Polytechnic Institute, Shanghai, China
lchienhung@qq.com

Abstract. As a cloud computing application, virtual desktop service has attracted increasing attention from educational institutes because it allows students to learn outside the confines of specific time and place by granting them access to authorized software which was previously inaccessible off campus. In other words, students can continue their learning by using the authorized software after leaving the campus. Hence, understanding students' continuance intention to use such kind of service will enhance its prospects in educational institutes. The information systems continuance model was employed in this study to achieve this goal. The research findings of this study revealed that students' continuance intention is primarily influenced by perceived usefulness; while perceived usefulness is mainly affected by confirmation. It implies that students' expectation confirmation is the key factor to the success of this service.

1 Introduction

In recent years, virtual desktop service has garnered increasing attention from educational institutes [1, 2]. As a kind of cloud computing applications, virtual desktop service gives users, mainly by using computers, mobile devices or browsers, a direct access to remote computers. Different from traditional remote desktop applications (e.g. the built-in functions of Windows), virtual desktop service consists of many high-end servers and storage systems in which the virtualization technology is applied to provide several virtual host computers that allow users to access virtual desktops [3]. The users are thus able to use these virtual desktops directly on the Internet without having to take additional steps like software installation and interface setting. As far as educational institutes are concerned, virtual desktop service allows teachers or students to use given software outside the confines of time and space. On a more specific basis, educational institutes may usually purchase some pieces of authorized software such as Photoshop (a commercial image-editing software) for the need of teaching and install them in the computers which can be used on campus. However, students cannot install the authorized software in their PCs and use them after leaving the campus because the software allows limited installation attempts. This is an unfavorable situation for students because they can only take practice on campus. Their learning processes are forced to be disrupted after they go home. Helping students transcend the confines of

© Springer International Publishing AG 2017
T.-C. Huang et al. (Eds.): SETE 2017, LNCS 10676, pp. 413–419, 2017.
https://doi.org/10.1007/978-3-319-71084-6_47

time and space, virtual desktop service has been thrust into the educational spotlight and applied to teaching activities. Students are ergo able to use the authorized software at home through this service.

Nevertheless, the effectiveness of virtual desktop service in facilitating students' learning rests on students' continuance intention to use it; otherwise it would become useless no matter how powerful its function is. Specifically speaking, examining users' continuance intention to use educational technology has been gradually construed as a crucial issue. Since students may accept a certain technology at the beginning but fail to use it continuously [4], this kind of examination is therefore regarded as a critical indicator for assessing the success of an educational technology [4, 5]. Virtual desktop service requires a fortiori systematic examination on students' continuance intention to use it because this sort of emerging technologies demands greater scholarly efforts to measure their value in education. For example, Tan and Kim identified perceived usefulness and satisfaction as the crucial factors behind students' continuance intention to use Google Docs [6], a cloud service used for word processing that supports students in collaborative writing. Different from previous studies, Huang developed a more comprehensive research model that incorporates technological and social factors to pinpoint the reasons for students' continuance intention to use Google Docs [7]. He found that attitude toward using is the most influential factor behind students' continuance intention, and social presence directly and significantly influences their attitude toward using. Despite the massive accumulation of related studies, the issue of students' continuance intention to use virtual desktop service has received surprisingly little scholarly attention. As a result, educational institutes are in urgent need for investigation into this issue in order to promote this service.

This study developed an information systems (IS) continuance model [8] as the tool for the investigation. We firstly applied Horizon, a famous virtual desktop service developed by the VMware Inc., to a course offered by a university in Taiwan. Based on the IS continuance model, we then designed a questionnaire concerning students' opinions about the service. The data collected from the questionnaire were used for testing the model as well as the hypotheses, thereby we can identify the influential factors behind students' continuance intention to use the service. From the research findings we finally made several concrete and important suggestions for experts and scholars in this field, with the aim of promoting the development and application of virtual desktop service in education.

2   Research Design

2.1   Research Model and Hypotheses

Figure 1 shows the research model adapted from the IS continuance model [8]. Five hypotheses are formulated accordingly and explicated below.

Developed by Bhattacherjee [8], the four-construct IS continuance model has been widely used in examining users' continuance intention to use a given technology. The four constructs of this model include confirmation, perceived usefulness, satisfaction, and continuance intention. Derived from expectation confirmation theory [9], confirmation

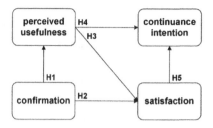

Fig. 1. Research model

means that users firstly hold some expectations about a given product when they start to use it, and then assess the degree to which these expectations are confirmed by the performance of this product [8]. Perceived usefulness refers to "the degree to which a person believes that using a particular system would enhance his or her job performance" [10]. Satisfaction refers to "a psychological or affective state related to and resulting from a cognitive appraisal of the expectation-performance discrepancy (i.e. confirmation)" [8]. Continuance intention refers to "the degree to which a person is willing to continue using an information system" [7]. Based on these definitions, Bhattacherjee further formulated the following hypotheses to explore the relationships among these constructs, so as to identify the determinants of users' continuance intention to use the technology. First, confirmation has a positive influence on perceived usefulness and satisfaction. Second, perceived usefulness has a positive influence on satisfaction and continuance intention. Third, satisfaction has a positive influence on continuance intention [8]. This means that the IS continuance model is an effective tool for understanding the subjects' continuance intention to use virtual desktop service, through which we can measure the value of this technology. Accordingly, this study formulated the following five hypotheses:

H1. Confirmation has a positive effect on perceived usefulness.
H2. Confirmation has a positive effect on satisfaction.
H3. Perceived usefulness has a positive effect on satisfaction.
H4. Perceived usefulness has a positive effect on continuance intention.
H5. Satisfaction has a positive effect on continuance intention.

2.2 Virtual Desktop Service

Figure 2 illustrates Horizon, a virtual desktop service developed by the VMware, Inc. [11]. VMware provides users with the service by dividing a powerful computing and storage center into several virtual machines with virtualization technology. To put it more specifically, Horizon allows users to use virtual desktops through mobile devices or the applications or browsers on their PCs. Figure 2(a) shows the scene when users log in Horizon through their browsers. Users can access the authorized software installed in the virtual machines outside the confines of time and place. Figure 2(b) is the scene in which users use Adobe Photoshop on a virtual desktop. The service allows students to use the software either on campus or at home, ensuring them an uninterrupted learning process.

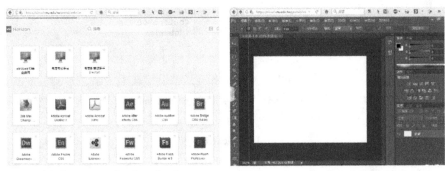

(a) the scene after logging in   (b) the scene of using Adobe Photoshop
                                            on a virtual desktop

Fig. 2. Virtual desktop service

2.3   Measurement and Data Collection

To collect the data on the subjects' opinions about the virtual desktop service, a structured questionnaire was developed on the basis of an extensive review of previous studies [7, 8, 10, 12, 13]. The questionnaire includes four constructs; to wit, confirmation, perceived usefulness, satisfaction, and continuance intention. The final questionnaire was distributed to the subjects who were asked to indicate their level of agreement with the statements using a five-point Likert scale.

The subjects who volunteered to participate in this study were 167 students enrolled in a university in Tainan, Taiwan. The subjects took a course in 3D model design in which the teacher instructed them to construct 3D models with the software such as 3ds Max. The subjects could practice through Horizon at home. In the final week of the two-month course, the subjects were required to fill in the questionnaire about their experiences of using the virtual desktop service.

3   Results

This study employed the partial least squares approach to analyze the data collected from the questionnaire, and applied the SmartPLS 3.0 software to perform the approach, which includes the measurement model and the structural one.

3.1   Measurement Model

This study assessed the measurement model in terms of item loadings, reliability of measures, convergent validity, and discriminant validity. An item would be viewed as reliable if its loading is greater than 0.70 [14]. The reliability of measures was evaluated by composite reliability with its minimum value of 0.7 and Cronbach's alpha with its minimum value of 0.6 [15]. We employed the average variance extracted (AVE) to assess the convergent validity, and the value has to exceed the standard minimal level of 0.5 to make the assessment significant and acceptable [15]. The

Table 1. The item loadings of the measurement model

Construct	Items	Loading	Standard error	P-value
Confirmation	CO1	0.87	0.05	0.00
	CO2	0.92	0.02	0.00
	CO3	0.91	0.02	0.00
Perceived usefulness	PU1	0.95	0.01	0.00
	PU2	0.94	0.01	0.00
	PU3	0.93	0.02	0.00
Satisfaction	SA1	0.93	0.03	0.00
	SA2	0.96	0.01	0.00
	SA3	0.93	0.02	0.00
Continuance intention	CI1	0.96	0.01	0.00
	CI2	0.95	0.01	0.00

Table 2. The reliability and convergent validity of the measurement model

Construct	Reliability of measure		Convergent validity
	Composite reliability	Cronbach's alpha	AVE
Confirmation	0.93	0.88	0.81
Perceived usefulness	0.96	0.93	0.88
Satisfaction	0.96	0.93	0.88
Continuance intention	0.96	0.91	0.91

Table 3. The discriminant validity of the measurement model

Construct		1	2	3	4
Confirmation	1	0.90			
Perceived usefulness	2	0.74	0.94		
Satisfaction	3	0.82	0.79	0.94	
Continuance intention	4	0.69	0.73	0.77	0.96

discriminant validity was assessed by the square root of AVE and latent variable correlations. To make the assessment significant and acceptable, each construct's square root of AVE must exceed its correlation coefficient with the other constructs in the model [16]. Tables 1, 2 and 3 indicate that the results delivered by the measurement model are significant and acceptable, since all the values meet the required standards.

3.2   Structural Model

The structural model was employed to test the hypotheses developed in the research model. The test was based on the path coefficients and the R^2 values, in which the former served as the indicator for the statistical significance of the hypotheses, and the latter revealed the model's ability to explain the variation in the dependent variables [14]. Figure 3 shows the results of the structural model that highlighted the acceptance

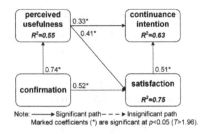

Note: ———▶ Significant path– – – ▶ Insignificant path
Marked coefficients (*) are significant at $p<0.05$ ($T>1.96$).

Fig. 3. The results of the structural model

of all the five hypotheses. It also illustrates that this model explained 55% of the variation in perceived usefulness, 75% in satisfaction, and 63% in continuance intention.

4 Conclusion

This study applied the IS continuance model to analyze students' continuance intention of using virtual desktop service. Our research findings demonstrated that (1) perceived usefulness is mainly influenced by confirmation; (2) confirmation and perceived usefulness simultaneously affect satisfaction; and (3) perceived usefulness has a greater influence than confirmation and satisfaction on continuance intention. To sum up, confirmation significantly influences perceived usefulness, the decisive factor behind continuance intention. Based on these research findings, we suggest educational institutes to reconcile the expectation-performance discrepancy regarding virtual desktop service. For example, teachers should not so much exaggerate its functions as introduce it appropriately. In this way, students tend to perceive the service as useful insofar as to confirm their expectations when they actually use it, and are therefore willing to continue using it.

Acknowledgements. We would like to express sincere gratitude to the lecturer Mr. Cheng-Xuan Lan who agreed to apply the virtual desktop service to the course he teaches and assisted us in collecting the subjects' opinions about the service. Besides, the authors would also like to thank the Ministry of Science and Technology of the Republic of China, Taiwan for financially supporting this research under Contract No. MOST 103-2511-S-041-002-MY3.

References

1. González-Martínez, J.A., Bote-Lorenzo, M.L., Gómez-Sánchez, E., Cano-Parra, R.: Cloud computing and education: a state-of-the-art survey. Comput. Educ. **80**, 132–151 (2015)
2. Sultan, N.: Cloud computing for education: a new dawn? Int. J. Inf. Manag. **30**(2), 109–116 (2010)
3. Deboosere, L., Vankeirsbilck, B., Simoens, P., Turck, F.D., Dhoedt, B., Demeester, P.: Efficient resource management for virtual desktop cloud computing. J. Supercomput. **62**(2), 741–767 (2012)

4. Lee, M.C.: Explaining and predicting users' continuance intention toward e-learning: an extension of the expectation–confirmation model. Comput. Educ. **54**(2), 506–516 (2010)
5. Lin, K.M.: e-Learning continuance intention: moderating effects of user e-learning experience. Comput. Educ. **56**(2), 515–526 (2011)
6. Tan, X., Kim, Y.: Cloud computing for education: a case of using Google Docs in MBA group projects. In: Proceedings of the 2011 International Conference on Business Computing and Global Informatization, pp. 641–644 (2011)
7. Huang, Y.M.: The factors that predispose students to continuously use cloud services: social and technological perspectives. Comput. Educ. **97**, 86–96 (2016)
8. Bhattacherjee, A.: Understanding information systems continuance: an expectation-confirmation model. MIS Q. **25**(3), 351–370 (2001)
9. Oliver, R.L.: A cognitive model of antecedents and consequences of satisfaction decisions. J. Market. Res. **17**(4), 460–469 (1980)
10. Davis, F.D.: Perceived usefulness, perceived ease of use and user acceptance of information technology. MIS Q. **13**(3), 319–340 (1989)
11. VMware: VMware Horizon (2017). Accessed 22 Mar 2017. http://www.vmware.com/products/horizon.html
12. Huang, Y.M.: Exploring the factors that affect the intention to use collaborative technologies: the differing perspectives of sequential/global learners. Aust. J. Educ. Technol. **31**(3), 278–292 (2015)
13. Huang, Y.M.: Exploring students' acceptance of team messaging services: the roles of social presence and motivation. Br. J. Educ. Technol. (in press). https://doi.org/10.1111/bjet.12468
14. Chin, W.W., Newsted, P.R.: Structural equation modeling analysis with small samples using partial least squares. In: Hoyle, R. (ed.) Statistical Strategies for Small Sample Research, pp. 307–341. Sage Publications, California (1999)
15. Hair, J.F., Black, W.C., Babin, B.J., Anderson, R.E., Tatham, R.L.: Multivariate Data Analysis, 6th edn. Prentice-Hall, New Jersey (2006)
16. Fornell, C., Larcker, D.F.: Evaluating structural equation models with unobservable variables and measurement error. J. Market. Res. **18**(1), 39–50 (1981)

Exploring the Development and Evaluation of Integrating Emerging Technology into a STEAM Project

Yu-Kai Chen[(⊠)] and Chi-Cheng Chang

Department of Technology Application and Human Resource Development,
National Taiwan Normal University, Taipei, Taiwan
frank.kai6812@gmail.com, samchang@ntnu.edu.tw

Abstract. Recently, an important trend of engineering education is involving the design process into students' learning cycle. The design process is more aesthetically and artistically motivated. The purpose of this study is to develop and evaluate a truss tower STEAM project that integrates emerging technology of 3D printing and cloud technology. The design research method was adapted and a three-phase framework guided the process of this study. We proposed some critical tasks for each phase and thus to manage the STEAM project. Suggestions on revising the project are proposed in this study.

Keywords: 3D printing · Cloud technology · Design research method · STEAM

1 Introduction

Recently, an important trend of engineering education is involving the design process into students' learning cycle. In addition, the design process is more aesthetically and artistically motivated (Bequette and Bequette 2012; Hall 2013; Metz 2016; Rolling 2016). The arts have been proposed as a means to engage individuals in STEM education, resulting in the concepts of STEAM. Evidences suggest that art may improve STEM learning (Crayton and Svihla 2015; Ghanbari 2015). Thus, from STEM to STEAM is reframing the meaning of making education (Bazler and Van Sickle 2017; Crayton and Svihla 2015; Ghanbari 2014; Glass and Wilson 2016; Gross and Gross 2016). Less is known about the enactments of STEAM education, and there have been calls for understanding on how specific models of STEAM education that support learning. In addition, as the scholar claimed that STEM education should teach the students using current tools and techniques (Sahlin and Lobera 2016), the stakeholders of STEAM education should consider it. Thus, the purpose of this study is to develop and evaluate a STEAM project that integrates emerging technology on 3D printing and cloud technology.

T.-C. Huang et al. (Eds.): SETE 2017, LNCS 10676, pp. 420–424, 2017.
https://doi.org/10.1007/978-3-319-71084-6_48

2 Integrating Emerging Technology into the STEAM Project

2.1 3D Printing

Today, 3D printing in education seems to be mainstream. By doing so, a computer-based three-dimensional object is printed by a sequential, layered deposition of material to construct a physical model (Lipson and Kurman 2013; Martin et al. 2014). A critical mode through which a 3D printer could be used in a classroom setting is to allow an educator to produce physical models that students can touch, feel, and test under different physical conditions (Martin et al. 2014). In addition, a 3D printer could produce particular parts that students may physically inspect and further have immediate effects on the overall design process. In this study, a 3D printer plays such a role on producing the trusses that constitute a tower.

2.2 Cloud Technology

Cloud computing is a model for enabling ubiquitous, convenient, on-demand network access to a shared pool of configurable computing resources that can be rapidly provisioned and released with minimal management effort or service provider interaction (Mell and Grance 2011). One of the critical service model is the platform that provides to the consumer to deploy onto the cloud infrastructure consumer-created or to acquire applications created using programming language, services, and tools supported by the provider (Mell and Grance 2011; Weber 2016). For STEM education, the use of cloud computing as a platform for bridging and supporting the distance learning and for providing tools to enhance the STEM experience in multiple areas (Sahlin and Lobera 2016). In this study, a cloud platform is provided for students to have the platform sharing their knowledge learning, and to have the mechanism reflecting their learning (designing) processes.

3 Integrating Emerging Technology into the STEAM Project

A design research method that blends design, research, and practice concurrently was adopted in this study (Anderson and Shattuck 2012; Kelly et al. 2008; Luckin et al. 2013; McKenney and Reeves 2014; Plomp and Nieveen 2010; Sandoval 2014). According to McKenney and Reeves (2012), a three-phase framework of conducting the design research method was adapted to guide the process of this study (as shown in Fig. 1). Phase 1 emphasizes on investigating of context and analyzing of literature and learning theory that informs draft design principles. Phase 2 emphasizes on development and construction of the resource for the specific context. Phase 3 emphasizes on evaluation and reflection. The phase 3 results are leading to modification of the designed solution and refinement of design principles.

A class that consists of 40 students is involved in this research and the context is a senior high school in Taipei, Taiwan. The research team consists of the researchers and practitioners, and the close collaboration is the key to the continuous refinement of the project in this study. The data collection includes (1) the open-ended questionnaire that

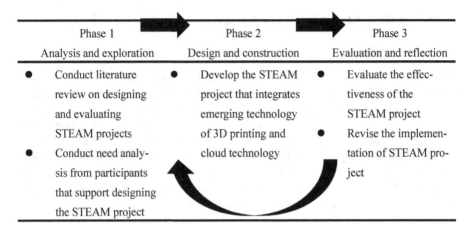

Fig. 1. The three-phase research framework

asks students to describe the gains, difficult from the project, and suggestions for future implement; (2) semi-structured interviews from the teacher and five volunteer students after the end of the project.

4   Results

4.1   What Did We Do in the Analysis and Exploration Phase?

In this phase, we carried out an examination on students to realize what they need in such a STEAM project. In light of the need analysis results, three critical issues may be proposed while considering the project design. Firstly, most of the students are provided sufficient subject knowledge, however, insufficient on providing the opportunities to train the engineering practices. Secondly, most of the students lack for practice experiences on 3D printing. Thirdly, what the students want to learn should be closely related with their daily life. By considering the needs, several decisions were made in this phase that includes (1) engineering design should be trained within this project; (2) Constructing the prior knowledge and its applications of the emerging technology adopted in this research; (3) due to the natural location of Taiwan, truss tower may be a suitable project context.

4.2   What Did We Do in the Design and Construction Phase?

Three mainly types of activities were planned in the truss tower project (as shown in Fig. 2). The introduction activity aims to introduce the rules, equipment, and the project goal and limitations for students. The four fundamental activities aim to supply the students' prior knowledge and skills for finishing the project. Due to the results of phase 1, introducing 3D printing and cloud technology thus become parts of the fundamental activities. In addition to this, each basic activity consists of a hands-on unit which provides the opportunities for students to train related engineering practices and apply what they learned. The three advanced activities aim to support the students plan, design, fabricate, and modify their truss tower.

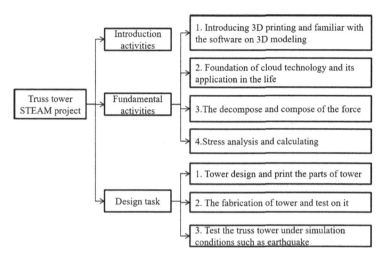

Fig. 2. The framework of a truss tower STEAM project

4.3   What Did We Do in the Evaluation and Reflection Phase?

According to the data analysis, we found more than 90% of students (N = 37) gained from the truss tower STEAM project, including the basic knowledge of truss, the principles of the building structure, and the skills of adapting engineering design. In addition, 80% of students (N = 32) mentioned the positive 'hands-on' experiences during the implementation of the project. 75% of students (N = 30) have positive experience on 3D printing. However, 60% of students (N = 24) felt difficult to learn in this project. We found that the 15 of the 24 students felt difficult due to the frequent hands-on activities. According to the teacher's interview, this result revealed that some Taiwan students used to receive traditional lecturing from teacher.

5   Conclusion and Recommendation

The aim of this study is to develop and evaluate a STEAM project that integrates emerging. In light of the results, the design research method is appropriate to manage the STEAM project. Further studies may be suggested to compare the effects on some specific skills (abilities) between the STEAM project and normal classroom setting.

Acknowledgement. The authors greatly appreciate the financial support provided by Ministry of Science and Technology, R. O. C. and also appreciate for the efforts of the reviewers.

References

Anderson, T., Shattuck, J.: Design-based research: a decade of progress in education research. Educ. Res. **41**(1), 16–25 (2012)

Bazler, J., Van Sickle, M.: Cases on STEAM Education in Practice. IGI Global, Hershey (2017)

Bequette, J.W., Bequette, M.B.: A place for art and design education in the STEM conversation. Art Educ. **65**(2), 40–47 (2012)

Crayton, J., Svihla, V.: designing for immersive technology: integrating art and STEM learning. STEAM J. **2**(1) (2015)

Ghanbari, S.: STEAM: the wave of the future embedded in ideals of the past. STEAM J. **1**(2), 27 (2014)

Ghanbari, S.: Learning across disciplines: a collective case study of two university programs that integrate the arts with STEM. Int. J. Educ. Arts **16**(7), 1–21 (2015)

Glass, D., Wilson, C.: The art and science of looking: collaboratively learning our way to improved STEAM integration. Art Educ. **69**(6), 8–14 (2016)

Gross, K., Gross, S.: Transformation: constructivism, design thinking, and elementary STEAM. Art Educ. **69**(6), 36–43 (2016)

Hall, N.: Merging science and art: the bigger picture. STEAM J. **1**(1), 9 (2013)

Kelly, A., Lesh, R., Baek, J.: Handbook of Design Research Methods in Education: Innovations in Science, Technology, Engineering, and Mathematics Learning and Teaching. Routledge, New York (2008)

Lipson, H., Kurman, M.: Fabricated: The New World of 3D Printing. Wiley, New York (2013)

Luckin, R., Puntambekar, S., Goodyear, P., Grabowski, B.L., Underwood, J., Winters, N.: Handbook of Design in Educational Technology. Routledge, New York (2013)

Martin, R.L., Bowden, N.S., Merrill, C.: 3D printing. Technol. Eng. Teach. **73**(8), 30–35 (2014)

McKenney, S., Reeves, T.C.: Conducting Educational Design Research. Routledge, Oxon (2012)

McKenney, S., Reeves, T.C.: Educational design research. In: Spector, J., Merrill, M., Elen, J., Bishop, M. (eds.) Handbook of Research on Educational Communications and Technology, pp. 131–140. Springer, New York (2014). https://doi.org/10.1007/978-1-4614-3185-5_11

Mell, P., Grance, T.: The NIST definition of cloud computing: special publication 800-145 (2011). http://nvlpubs.nist.gov/nistpubs/Legacy/SP/nistspecialpublication800-145.pdf

Metz, S.: Science and the arts. Sci. Teach. **83**(7), 6 (2016)

Plomp, T., Nieveen, N.M.: An introduction to educational design research. In: Proceedings of the Seminar Conducted at the East China Normal University, Shanghai (PR China), 23–26 November 2007, SLO (2010)

Rolling, J.H.: Reinventing the STEAM engine for Art + design education. Art Educ. **69**(4), 4–7 (2016)

Sahlin, J.P., Lobera, K.: Cloud computing as a catalyst for change in STEM education. In: Chao, L. (ed.) Handbook of Research on Cloud-based STEM Education for Improved Learning Outcomes, pp. 12–30. IGI Global, Hershey (2016)

Sandoval, W.: Conjecture mapping: an approach to systematic educational design research. J. Learn. Sci. **23**(1), 18–36 (2014)

Weber, A.S.: Strategic planning for cloud computing adoption in STEM education: finding best practice solutions. In: Chao, L. (ed.) Handbook of Research on Cloud-based STEM Education for Improved Learning Outcomes, pp. 1–11. IGI Global, Hershey (2016)

Inference of Learning Creative Characteristics by Analysis of EEG Signal

Shih-Yeh Chen[1], Chin-Feng Lai[2(✉)], Ren-Hung Hwang[3],
Chu-Sing Yang[4], and Ming-Shi Wang[2]

[1] Department of Computer Science and Information Engineering,
National Taitung University, Taitung, Taiwan
[2] Department of Engineering Science, National Cheng Kung University,
Tainan, Taiwan
cinfon@ieee.org
[3] Department of Computer Science and Information Engineering,
National Chung Cheng University, Chaiyi, Taiwan
[4] Department of Electrical Engineering, National Cheng Kung University,
Tainan, Taiwan

Abstract. In recent years, more and more researches on evaluating student's creativity has been discussed in the field of science and technology education. According to the past research results, we can find more alpha wave among electroencephalogram signals from the high creative students. In other words, the process of generating creative ideas is accompanied by increasing the alpha wave. The main goal of this study is to observe the relationship between the four characteristics of creativity (fluency, originality, refinement and flexibility) and the alpha wave variation, and we also observe the creative thinking method is able to improve the creation of students at the same time. The experimental results show the original play the most important role in the four characteristics of creativity. It means the students with relatively high originality will be measured more alpha wave in the creative thinking activity. On the contrary, if the students' creative character lacks originality, then the alpha wave may not increase as expected. By the way, we also get the result a relatively high alpha wave is measured when the students try to use the creative thinking method for solving problems.

Keywords: Creative characteristics · Learning inference · EEG signal

1 Introduction

In general, the creativity may be innate or developed through training. It always is difficult to be evaluated although we can feel it exists. With the beginning of the 1950, human beings slowly opened the mystery of creativity by studying the creativity. More and more scholars were getting started to join the creative researches and let the creativity shine in various fields. Until today, although creativity has been spread all over our daily life, it has always been very abstract. What is called creativity? How is it called creativity? How to evaluate creativity? These questions so far lack one recognized answer because scholars in the various fields have their unique perspectives to

© Springer International Publishing AG 2017
T.-C. Huang et al. (Eds.): SETE 2017, LNCS 10676, pp. 425–432, 2017.
https://doi.org/10.1007/978-3-319-71084-6_49

creativity. The early researches on creativity primarily evaluated the degree of individual creativity through the scales or tests. For example, as Torrance's creativity test, the creative process checklist proposed by Ghiselin et al. (1964), the creative five-item test proposed by Wallach and Kogan (1965) and so on.

With the maturity of the scales and tests of evaluating creative, the recent researches of creativity gradually are tried to combine other technologies or theories, one of which is the combination of creativity and physiological signals to observe the relevance between each other. The main research objectives include:

(A) Is the method of guiding creative thinking effective?
Because this study imports creative thinking in the course, we would compare and analysis the degree variety of creative thinking of students in each stage. We will measure the electroencephalogram signal of students before and after the stage of importing creative thinking, then analysis the signal for the research objective.

(B) The students' creative thinking degree variety in each stage.
At the beginning of the semester, Torrance Tests of Creative Thinking (TTCT), the traditional creativity test method, was used to initially evaluate the creativity degree of all students. After a semester of importing creative thinking, we try to evaluate the students' creativity degree again at the end of the semester to observe the variety of their creativity degree.

(C) Are there any differences in electroencephalogram signal among students with different creative characteristics during creative thinking?
We try to evaluate the degrees of four creative characteristics according to the students' final project demo and report, while observing their original electroencephalogram signal variety in the creative thinking stage.

2   Related Works

As the researches of probing the relation between creativity and brain waves are mostly in the discussion of Alpha wave, the brief summary about the Alpha wave and creativity will be introduced. In this study, the experiments of this study are mainly carried out experiments and data analysis with the Alpha wave.

Martindale 1975 divided 22 subjects into four groups for brainwave test according to the scores of remote associates test and alternate uses test that are the imagination measurement methods. The results of the experiment showed that the group with the high scores almost presented high alpha wave during the experiment course. The group with high scores in the remote associates test presented diverse degrees of alpha wave variations in the whole experiment. The imagination test showed high alpha wave values, but the intelligence test showed a high and low amplitude of the alpha wave. The alternate uses test and Scamper are the same as divergent creative thinking tests, so we assume that alpha waves are positively correlated with creativity in this experimental. In addition, Martindale carried out two experiments in 1978 to observe the relationship between creativity and alpha waves. The first experimental results showed that creative people got higher alpha wave values in the inspiration phase (as thinking about an innovative story) than in the stage of elaboration (as writing down this story).

But there are not the same results to the subjects with the relatively low creativity. In the second experiment, the subjects were divided into the experimental and control groups. The experimental group was asked to try their best to present the imagination as much as possible during the experiment course, while the control group was not required. And the results showed that the experimental group had higher Alpha wave values. Therefore, we assume that alpha waves are positively correlated with creativity in this study.

Fink (2007) tried to carry out brainwave experimental analysis for the Insight task (assuming some special and unusual situation, then ask the subjects to answer the relevant questions), Utopian Situation task (for example, if all the doors are not locked, what will happen or what things will be changed?), Alternative Uses task and Word Ends task (provide suffix, then ask the subjects write the complete word). The experimental results show that subjects with three tasks of IS, US, and AU arouse more alpha wave amplitude. In other words, the alpha wave has a positive synchronization relationship with these three tasks, and the results found that the WE task that always needs more intelligence gets the least alpha wave increase. To sum up, the tasks that need more creative always make the subjects to produce more alpha waves, on the contrary, the tasks that need more intelligence suppress the increase of alpha waves.

The relevance of the following two theories made Fink and Neubauer to present the relationship between inward and outward personality traits and creativity in 2008. The first theory is Martindale's low arousal theory of creativity, which means that the level of creativity of a person can be determined by observing the awakening of the brain prefrontal lobe. It means the persons with higher the creativity arouse the lower degree of awakening of brain prefrontal lobe. The second is Eysenck's arousal theory, referring to the more outgoing people will arouse the lower level of the awakening of the brain frontal lobe. So the two scholars decided to combine these two theories and assumed that there is a correlation between outgoing personality traits and creativity. In the experimental results, the persons with the outgoing personality traits and highly creative arouse high alpha waves, and vice versa. Razumnikova (2009) analyzed high alpha waves (10–13 Hz) and low alpha waves (8–10 Hz) for creative thinking in college students. There are 30 students classified in the highly creative group, 16 students of which were given the topics of three words in one group and were asked to come up with a topic-related creative words. The other 14 students were given the topics of three words in one group and were asked to use the three words come up with a creative sentence. On the other hand, low-creativity group include 35 students divided into 22 and 13 students to do the same experiments with high creativity group. The experimental results show that (1) the high-creativity group arouse more low alpha waves (2) the high-creativity group show more high alpha waves than the low-creativity group in the anterior, parietal and cortical regions of the brain.

Regarding of the relationship of creativity and alpha waves, the following four phenomena were found based on the above research results.

(1) The individuals with more creativity arouses more alpha waves.
(2) The process of producing creative thinking will be accompanied by the increase in alpha waves, especially the right hemisphere is more obvious.

(3) The task of different levels of creativity will have different alpha wave presentation, in other words, when the creative thinking task requires more creativity, the alpha wave will be increased more obviously.

(4) Most of the researches focus on analyzing the entire frequency of alpha waves, but it is still controversy that creativity is associated with high alpha or low alpha waves. Some scholars believe that creativity is correlated with the high alpha wave, but others think low alpha wave is highly correlated.

3 Methodology

This section will introduce the design of the entire research and experiment, including research hypothesizes, subjects, tools and experimental processes.

3.1 Hypothesizes

Hypothesis 1: Creativity has a positive correlation with alpha waves
There are many factors that affect the change in the alpha wave. In this experiment, we try to exclude other possible factors and ask the subjects to focus on the thinking of creativity. Therefore, this experiment assumes that the biggest factor of affecting the variety of the alpha wave is the creative thinking of the subjects. In addition, according to the previous researches of discussing creativity and brain wave, this experiment also assumes that creativity and alpha wave has a positive correlation. When the measured alpha wave increases, it means that the subjects use more creativity in the creative thinking or the subjects themselves have high creativity.

Hypothesis 2: Two subjects within one group have the same contribution to the final project
The workload of developing the final project is relatively large, thus the final project always is done by a group of two people and the score of the final project is evaluated by a group. In this experiment, we assume that the group of two subjects have the same contribution to the final project.

Hypothesis 3: The non-creativity external factors that affect alpha waves have been minimized as much as possible
Although the previous researches point out that creativity has a high association with alpha waves, there are many factors that can affect alpha waves, and it is very difficult to completely rule out. We try to reduce the non-creativity factors to interference the experiment results and ask the subjects to focus on creative thinking.

3.2 Participants

The participants are the 22 to 25-year-old students in the course of developing creative internet of things application, including 19 boys and 3 girls who have never been trained by relevant creative thinking before. Every student must participate the pre-test and post-test of measuring brain wave, but the final project is developed by a group of two people. There are totally 11 groups in this experiment. In contrast to the general experimental approach, the study did not divide the 22 students into experimental and control groups to carry out the experiment. We take the pre-test of all students as a control group and post-test as the experimental group. The reason is that this experiment is based on a semester course, students cannot be split into two classes, which also means that it is impossible for half of the students to be taught by the traditional teaching method (control group), the other half of students to be taught by the creative teaching method (experimental group).

3.3 Procedure of Experiment

This section describes the process of the experiment. The whole experiment is carried out from the beginning of the semester of the creative internet of things application course to the end of the semester. Through the introduction of the internet of things technology and creative thinking, the students are asked to make the presentation about the generation processes of finding final project topics and developing problems solutions by creative thinking methods, and demo the final project. The following items are described as follows:

(1) TTCT creativity pre-test:
    At the beginning of semester, the TTCT creativity test (about 20 to 30 min) was conducted by the TA of education college, which was used to determine the original creativity degree of the students. More creative individuals have higher test scores.
(2) Teaching for internet of things technologies:
    In addition to creativity pre-test, brain wave pre-test, brain wave post-test and the final project demo & creative thinking presentation, the remaining number of courses are used for teaching internet of things technologies, including basic concept of internet of things and practice labs, that make students are able to develop the final project by themselves.
(3) Introduction to the experimental process and electroencephalography device:
    One week before the midterm, we will introduce the experimental process to the students, as well as the use of EEG devices and measurement system teaching, mainly to let the students understand how to do the experiment and how to use the EEG device.
(4) Brain wave pre-test:
    After confirming that the students are aware of how the experiment is going and how to operate the EEG device, we will carry out the brainwave pre-test without any teaching of creative thinking methods. The students are asked to wear a EEG device then write down the concept idea of final project. The pre-test time is 10 min and gets the students' brain wave values.
(5) Brain waves post-test:
    Before the brain wave post-test, the teacher will teach the students what is the creative thinking. The teacher aslo introduces the concept of SCAMPER and provides the relevant SCAMPER examples to enable the students to understand the meaning of the creative thinking methods and how to use SCAMPER to help

Fig. 1. Scenario of measuring brain waves

themselves think creatively. The brain waves post-test is roughly the same as the pre-test, but the difference is the brainwave post-test will provide the SCAMPER creative thinking document for assisting the students doing the creative thinking. The brain waves were measured as shown in Fig. 1.

(6) Final project demo and Creative Thinking Presentation:
At the end of the semester, students will be asked to make the pretention for their project. The focus of this final project is to understand students hot to present their creativity by developing the project. In order to avoid creativity is limited since the development is too difficult to be implemented, we will ask the students to prepare a creative thinking presentation that is mainly to put forward the unrealized creative ideas. Finally, the teachers will evaluate the students' comprehensive creativity by the final project demo and creative thinking presentation.

(7) Satisfaction Questionnaire:
In addition to the final project and creative thinking presentation, the students are asked to fill in a questionnaire with five items, using the Likert five-point scale as a scoring method to understand the students' feelings to this experiment. After collecting the questionnaire results, the teachers will have a simple interview with the students for detail answers.

(8) Creativity post-test scores:
Since the TTCT creativity test has only one question bank, the same TTCT creativity test will not be taken again as creativity post-test. Therefore, we replace creativity post-test score by the comprehensive score of final project demo and creative thinking presentation.

4 Results and Discussion

The first step in the data analysis is to calculate the average number of alpha wave values measured from each student during the course of the experiment, and then we use the SPSS software to compare the difference of the average focus index between the pre-test and post-test by the paired sample t test analysis. The measured alpha wave values can be split into two parts: Low Alpha wave and High Alpha wave. The analysis result contains (1) Table 1: Average Low Alpha Sample Statistic (2) Table 2: Average Low Alpha Pairwise Sample Verification (3) Table 3: Average High Alpha Samples Statistic (4) Table 4: Average High Alpha Pair Samples. Tables 1 and 3 show that the resulting values of post-test are higher than the values of the pre-test, either the average low alpha or the average high alpha.

Table 1. Average low alpha pair sample statistics.

Paired samples statistics		Mean	N	Std. deviation	Std. error mean
Pair 1	(Pre-test) AverageLowAlpha	2.020441E6	22	6.3271697E5	1.3489571E5
	(Post-test) AverageLowAlpha	2.586724E6	22	7.9094640E5	1.6863034E5

Table 2. Average low alpha pair samples.

Paired samples test		Paired differences					t	f	Sig. (2-tailed)
		Mean	Std. deviation	Std. error mean	95% Confidence interval of the difference				
					Lower	Upper			
Pair 1	(Pre-test) AverageLowAlpha – (Post-test) AverageLowAlpha	−5.6628217E5	8.9604324E5	1.9103706E5	−9.6356549E5	−1.6899885E5	−2.964	1	.007

Table 3. Average high alpha pair sample statistics.

Paired samples statistics		Mean	N	Std. deviation	Std. error mean
Pair 1	(Pre-test) AverageHighAlpha	1.807913E6	22	7.2362365E5	1.5427708E5
	(Post-test) AverageHighAlpha	2.512937E6	22	9.3414509E5	1.9916040E5

Under the assumption that alpha waves are positively related to creativity, the above results show that the students' creativity can be improved when using SCAMPER to guide the students to do creative thinking. However, there are a small number of students in the case of alpha wave decline, we speculate that SCAMPER may not be suitable for them, which can not lead to creative thinking and cause alpha wave decline.

Table 4. Average high alpha pair samples.

Paired samples test

		Paired differences					t	df	Sig. (2-tailed)
		Mean	Std. deviation	Std. error mean	95% Confidence interval of the difference				
					Lower	Upper			
Pair 1	(Pre-test) AverageHighAlpha – (Post-test) AverageHighAlpha	−7.0502357E5	9.8493633E5	2.0998913E5	−1.1417199E6	−2.6832727E5	−3.357	1	.003

5 Conclusion

The main finding of this study is that when using creative thinking method to help the participants to think, we can find the increase of alpha wave and focus from the subjects, and inference creative thinking guide method can help enhance their creativity indirectly. Through this creative thinking guide, we also find that the creative score of end of semester almost is higher than the creative score of beginning.

References

Kohn, S., Hüsig, S.: Computer aided innovation – state of the art from a new product development perspective. J. Comput. Ind. **60**, 551–562 (2009)

Petrova, I., Zaripova, V.: Systems of teaching engineering work on base of internet technologies. Int. J. Inf. Technol. Know. **1**, 89–95 (2007)

Thagard, P., Steward, T.C.: The AHA! experience: creativity through emergent bonding in neural networks. Cogn. Sci. **35**, 1–33 (2011)

Mesquita, D., Alves, A., Fernandes, S., Moreira, F., Lima, R.M.: A first year and first semester project-led engineering education approach. In: Anais: Ibero–American Symposium on Project Approaches in Engineering Education 2009, Guimarães, Portugal, pp. 181-189 (2009)

Lima, R.M., Silva, J.M., Janssen, N., Monteiro, S.B.S., Souza, J.C.F.: Project-based learning course design: a service design approach. Int. J. Serv. Oper. Manag. **11**(3), 293–313 (2012)

Graff, E., Kolmos, A.: Characteristics of problem–based learning. Int. J. Eng. Educ. **17**(5), 652–657 (2003)

Developing a Curriculum of Maker Education in Taiwan Higher Education

Tien-Chi Huang[1], Shu-Hsuan Chang[2], Vera Yu Shu[2(✉)],
Preben·Hansen[3], and Sung-Lin Lee[1]

[1] National Taichung University of Science and Technology, Taichung, Taiwan
[2] National Changhua University of Education, Changhua, Taiwan
shc@cc.ncue.edu.tw, vera.yushu@gmail.com
[3] Stockholm University, 106 91 Stockholm, Sweden
preben@dsv.su.se

Abstract. Maker Education is a practice-oriented movement that has risen in the last decade, and emphasizes more on innovation, creativity and problem solving. Maker Education is based on knowledge, directed by creation, and is aimed at solving problems. This study, aimed at the curriculum of the Department of Information Management, expects to develop a systematic information Maker curriculum. This curriculum, combined with the 3D printing machine and Arduino open hardware configured with the STEM education framework, is designed to explore the impact of the introduction of Maker education to information curriculum of technical or vocational colleges on attitude differences and learning of STEM. Two courses, 3D model design and Arduino programming, are implemented, after the end of which, students' achievements are evaluated. The result is that male still have higher interests in science, engineering and technology than women, but Maker curriculum is multifaceted and foundational so that many people can spend a little time in learning and use various skills to produce their own works. Therefore, there is little difference between women and men in scores of achievement test.

Keywords: Arduino · Maker education · STEM education · 3D printing

1 Introduction

Maker Education is a practice-oriented Movement that has risen in the last decade, and emphasizes more on innovation, creativity and problem solving. The acronym STEAM (Park and Kim 2012), referring to science, technology, engineering, art and mathematics, is a framework to which Engineering Education has attached importance in recent years. STEAM emphasizes the integration of interdisciplinary knowledge to solve practical problems and is suitable for higher education to achieve Maker spirit; Maker Education is based on knowledge, directed by creation, and is aimed at solving problems (Martinez and Stager 2014).

This study, aimed at the curriculum of the IT domain, expects to develop a systematic information Maker course. Accordingly, this study integrates courses already in place to develop unique information Maker curriculum, such as 3D model design, C

© Springer International Publishing AG 2017
T.-C. Huang et al. (Eds.): SETE 2017, LNCS 10676, pp. 433–437, 2017.
https://doi.org/10.1007/978-3-319-71084-6_50

language programming, Android programming, human-machine interface design and so on.

Among the many technologies used in Maker education, 3D printing is particularly attractive. In the early days, the 3D printing technology was not popular because of its high cost and patent, but in recent years, because of its patent expiration and low pricing, 3D printing technology has begun to be popularized. 3D printing is not only used for customized production (Rayna and Striukova 2015). 3D printing machines allow designers to print their own designs, reduce the differences and costs caused by virtual models and entities, and even can protect intellectual property rights by enabling them to implement their own ideas. Since 3D printing depends on 3D modeling as the foundation, it is a prerequisite for colleges to consider how to improve the ability of modeling. Some scholars propose assisting students with their study of 3D modeling in a way of 3D printing (Huang and Lin 2017). Therefore, 3D printing not only changes customized products, but also indirectly assists students' ability of learning 3D modeling.

Secondly, open-source hardware was one of the courses that undergraduate students took. Arduino open hardware has the advantage of being understood quickly by people with non-electrical backgrounds. Programming is the core competency of the Department of Information Management. The simple use of Arduino enables students to create entity tools in a short time by integrating hardware and software (Mesas-Carrascosa et al. 2015). This course, combined with the 3D printing machine and Arduino open hardware configured with the STEM education framework, is designed to explore the impact of the introduction of Maker education to information curriculum of technical or vocational colleges on attitude differences and learning of STEM.

2 Literature Review

STEM is the acronym of the four subjects: science, technology, engineering and math. Instead of simply putting the four disciplines together, the educational framework of STEM stresses the cross-integration of multi disciplines—the disciplines originally scattered are integrated to form a new one. Students apply what they learn to life, develop their ability to innovate and practice, and think from different perspectives, and have multiple cross-field communication skills (Land 2013).

The features of STEM education includes interdisciplinary, situational, collaborative, designed, experienced, empirical and technology-enhanced activity. For example, science and mathematical logic at elementary-school level are combined into a new system, enabling students to get in touch with space and pixel art, and stimulating interest in engineering, mathematics and science (Roberts 2014). Practicing theory in books is more likely to arouse students' learning willingness than only reading books.

This study aims to cultivate students' ability of solving problems by the assembly of 3D printing machines and teaches them the ability to use and manufacture 3D model, and design concept, to cultivate students into talents with self-creativity (Ko et al. 2012). The study allows students to learn science, mathematical logic and teamwork, expression and acceptance in the team, and think and solve problems together.

3 Methodology

The participants and setting: In this study, a single group design was adopted; the curriculum lasted for 18 weeks; a total of 46 subjects were college students from the Department of Information Management. The process of the curriculum to be implemented was as follows: before class, students were required to complete a form of STEM attitude scale and a test of preliminary knowledge to understand the willingness, attitude to STEM and the past related learning experience or cognition of the students before class.

The task: Then the modeling courses for four weeks were taken; the students were led to design the body shells of self-propelled vehicles for future courses, and understand its structure; during that time interviews were made to understand the students' learning situations. But after the modeling courses, students had to use their spare time to print the finished self-propelled vehicle model in two weeks, and started the Arduino curriculum which introduces the basic concepts of Arduino and App Inventor, and their combination with self-propelled vehicles. In the eighteenth week, the students' class knowledge of the semester was tested.

4 Results and Conclusions

The results of the study are as follows: in respect of gender differences in achievement test, Table 1 shows that there is little difference in preliminary Arduino knowledge of different gender subjects. And it may only slightly different in each subject test for different genders after they learn Maker curriculum.

Table 1. t test for all kinds of test scores grouped by gender

	性別 gender	N	Mean	SD	df	t值 t-value	p值 p-value
Arduino test of preliminary Arduino knowledge	Male	30	65.57	15.624	44	−0.280	0.781
	Female	16	67.06	19.988			
Subject test-3D model design	Male	30	47.36	13.715	44	0.536	0.594
	Female	16	44.95	16.059			
Arduino subject test-Arduino	Male	30	61.50	24.458	44	0.124	0.902
	Female	16	60.75	16.267			

*$p < .05$

According to the form of STEM attitude scale completed by students, different attitudes of different genders towards STEM are analyzed, and data on math, science, engineering and technology are specially discussed. Students of different genders have significantly different attitudes towards science as well as engineering and technology, but no significantly different attitude towards math (Table 2). This result suggests that the female students do not have great interests in science, engineering and technology

Table 2. Kruskal-Wallis test of STEM attitude scale grouped by gender

	Gender	N	Average	Chi-square	p-value
Math	Male	30	25.80	2.572	0.109
	Female	16	19.19		
Science	Male	30	28.40	11.571	0.001**
	Female	16	14.31		
Engineering and technology	Male	30	28.73	13.201	0.000**
	Female	16	13.69		

$*p < .05$, $**p < .01$

before they take these courses. The possible reasons are that the female students of Department of Information Management have no ambition and strong employment intention for science, engineering and technology or there were no good learning experiences in these courses before. Therefore, all that influenced the present choice. But after the curriculum, female students are still willing to strive to learn and complete it. According to this interview, the reason is that Maker curriculum is different from the previous courses in physics and chemistry and emphasizes the practice of the curriculum, allowing students to have actual output and learn the results of practicing formula code after studying the courses, which improve the students' interests and willingness.

In this study, we found that women, after learning the curriculum, gradually accept engineering subjects, partly because Maker curriculum is somewhat different from ordinary industry courses. In Maker curriculum, students' understanding of the basic principle and the operation of the machine is based on the goals of application and practice, and personal works can come out. On the contrary, industry courses focus on theoretical knowledge and general machine operation. In contrast, Maker curriculum is multifaceted and foundational so that many people can spend a little time in learning, and use various skills to produce their own works. Therefore, the acceptance of Maker curriculum by female is higher than expected.

References

Huang, T.C., Lin, C.Y.: From 3D modeling to 3D printing: development of a differentiated spatial ability teaching model. Telemat. Inform. **34**(2), 604–613 (2017)

Ko, Y., An, J., Park, N.: Development of computer, math, art convergence education lesson plans based on smart grid technology. In: Kim, T., Stoica, A., Fang, W., Vasilakos, T., Villalba, J. G., Arnett, K.P., Khan, M.K., Kang, B.-H. (eds.) SecTech 2012. CCIS, vol. 339, pp. 109–114. Springer, Heidelberg (2012). https://doi.org/10.1007/978-3-642-35264-5_15

Land, M.H.: Full STEAM ahead: the benefits of integrating the arts into STEM. Procedia Comput. Sci. **20**, 547–552 (2013)

Martinez, S., Stager, G.: The maker movement: a learning revolution. ISTE (2014). https://www.iste.org/explore/articledetail?articleid=106

Mesas-Carrascosa, F.J., Santano, D.V., Merono, J.E., de la Orden, M.S., García-Ferrer, A.: Open source hardware to monitor environmental parameters in precision agriculture. Biosyst. Eng. **137**, 73–83 (2015)

Park, N., Kim, Y.: Development and application of STEAM teaching model based on the Rube Goldberg's invention. In: Yeo, S.S., Pan, Y., Lee, Y., Chang, H. (eds.) Computer Science and its Applications, vol. 203, pp. 693–698. Springer, Dordrecht (2012). https://doi.org/10.1007/978-94-007-5699-1_70

Rayna, T., Striukova, L.: From rapid prototyping to home fabrication: how 3D printing is changing business model innovation. Technol. Forecast. Soc. Change **102**, 214–224 (2015)

Roberts, S.J.: ENGage: the use of space and pixel art for increasing primary school children's interest in science, technology, engineering and mathematics. Acta Astronaut. **93**, 34–44 (2014)

A Real-Time Assessment of Programming Through Debugging Log Analytic

Yu-Lin Jeng[1]($\boxtimes$), Qing Tan[2], Yu Shu[3], and Sheng-Bo Huang[1]

[1] Department of Information Management,
Southern Taiwan University of Science and Technology, Tainan, Taiwan
jackjeng@mail.stust.edu.tw, ma490106@stust.edu.tw
[2] School of Computing and Information Systems, Athabasca University,
Athabasca, Canada
qingt@athabascau.ca
[3] Department of Industrial Education and Technology,
National Changhua University of Education, Changhua, Taiwan
vera.yushu@gmail.com

Abstract. Computer programming learning is an important course for students to foster critical thinking and logical thinking ability. However, most students don't have enough debugging skill when encountering programming error. With the development of information technology, researches apply the technology and pedagogy to achieve the diversity of programming learning research topics. In order to provide a real-time assessment from students, this research proposes an integrated learning environment of mobile APP programming learning to generate learning analytic results for teachers. In the proposed system, it can provide programming error type of students in real-time manner and help teacher to tune the teaching strategy dynamically. The analytic results give helpful information for teachers to implement right teaching strategy on specific learning concept.

Keywords: Programming learning · Learning concept · Teaching strategy

1 Introduction

With the rapid advancement of mobile technology, intelligent mobile devices have become increasingly prevalent, such as smartphone, tablet PC, etc. In this trend, the development and application of mobile APP program has gradually become a hot topic in the fields of software development and mobile learning. Particularly, some schools also take advantage of intelligent mobile devices to develop E-book system for the enhancement of teaching efficiency [1]. The great importance of mobile APP programming has been gradually recognized and the talent cultivation in mobile programming has been valued by many countries. Under such circumstance, it has become a very important issue in Taiwan how to cultivate our software talents having the ability in designing and programming mobile APP correctly and efficiently to further strengthen the competitiveness of Taiwan's science and technology industry.

© Springer International Publishing AG 2017
T.-C. Huang et al. (Eds.): SETE 2017, LNCS 10676, pp. 438–445, 2017.
https://doi.org/10.1007/978-3-319-71084-6_51

Nevertheless, for most students in vocational college or university, it is not that easy to learn programming. In addition to the necessary training for the logic thinking skill, students also need to learn various syntax and commands of program languages. To the beginners, the syntaxes and commands could be too abstract and fuzzy, which the students might have the difficulty to connect them with real objects. Therefore, the students could suffer a setbacks during the process then eventually give up their learning. To some extent, these program syntax and commands tend to become one of the obstacles for students to learn program design [2]. Additionally, the traditional lecture style is still used for programming courses, in which a teacher deliver the lecture in class then students practice what they have learned after class. However, students may understand the lecture in class but they still cannot design and code properly and independently after class. Thus, it is not an effective teaching mode for programming courses. To solve this problem, there is a better approach that students are allowed to go on hands-on practice immediately after teachers' explanation. However, being limited in lecture time, not all students can complete the hands-on practice in class. Moreover, there are too many students in one class and one teacher has the difficulty to answer all the students' questions. On the other hand, students' problems cannot be solved in real time in after class practice, which makes students be stuck in one problem then give up the practice. Also, in such practice, students are easily led to only focus on learning specific syntax then ignore the development of logical ability and problem-solving skills, which results students put program codes together wrongly to just complete the homework [3]. When it happens, students do not learn concepts related to the programming, later they will run into more obstacles and their learning willingness will also get lower gradually. Consequently, students will escape learning from suffering the setbacks in programming courses that are essential for the program design in the curriculum. Thus, reducing the difficulties of learning program language in the curriculum through effective methods is the way to enhance, students' learning motivation and learning willingness as well as to improve learning effectiveness [4].

In this paper, we propose a real-time assessment programming environment for students to learn programming. The proposed environment aims to collect students' developing log and to provide real-time analysis results to teachers. Teachers can implement a dynamic teaching strategy in classroom according to the results.

The rest of the paper is organized as follows: the related works are reviewed in the following section, then the proposed real-time assessment programming environment is introduced in the Sect. 3. Next the debugging log analytic results and the discussion are presented in Sect. 4. Finally, the conclusions of this study are given in Sect. 5.

2   Related Works

In order to make students learn program design smoothly, many researchers have studied how to help students apply problem-solving skills to program design. [5] indicated that program design process is to firstly know about the problem, then analyze, design and plan the program and at last actually write down the program code and debug it. Therefore, at the time of program design, students must firstly know about the problem, then analyze the problem, and lastly find out the solution. In other words, problem-solving ability is indispensable to the learning of program development. Among the discussions on problem-solving ability, [3] pointed out that students have basically learned the methods or tools of problem solving in program development, but they have no idea how to apply the skills in practices. The main problem existing in the teaching of program development lies in that teachers merely focus on program syntax and fail to teach students how to apply problem solving skills to program development. In order to address this problem, Linn & Clancy adopted case study as teaching method to divide the sample applications compiled by experts into several blocks and give relevant concept instructions, so that students can observe experts' problem solving skills and learn the analysis and planning skills to complete design and coding of program smoothly. Similarly, [6] also indicated that program development experts can make good use of program planning skills, including using their own knowledge and strategies to fulfill their program development and implementation. Therefore, [6] advises students to adopt top-down method for problem solving. They should firstly set a goal and then analyze the strategies to be used prior to concepts and knowledge to be mastered in order to smoothly complete program development. In addition to helping students apply problem solving skills to program development, some researchers also discussed that different learning theories are applied to the program development curriculum. In terms of the application in collaborative learning, [7] found that two students learning in one group can gain better achievements than student alone in program development. Two students in one group are able to describe their design contents more confidently. Such concept is characterized by collaboration: one student plays the role of a programmer, in charge of program writing; the other one plays the role of observer, in charge of reviewing and thinking about program codes written by the programmer [8]. [9] further stated that the application of paired program development mode in teaching is helpful to students' learning of program development, including (1) students can write higher-quality program, (2) students can write the program with less time, (3) students can have a better understanding of program running process, (4) students can increase the fun of learning program, (5) students' learning effectiveness can be improved. In terms of the application in cognitive development theory, [10] emphasized the importance of actual practice in program development curriculum and proposed a web program learning system to help students' cognitive development in program learning. In conclusion, the applications of different learning theories and problem-solving ability can improve learning effectiveness in program development and enable students to become more confident in program development courses.

In learning program development courses, students need to write, compile and execute program codes on their own. Without an integrated coding development environment, these steps would have become extremely troublesome and complicated, which may discourage students to learn programming. Therefore, most teachers adopt Integrated Development Environment (IDE) as the environment of learning program development curriculum. IDE is a kind of application software used to assist programmers to develop software and it usually includes program language editor, compiling program/language interpreter, self-built tools and log debugger. There are many kinds of IDEs supported different program languages. This research mainly focuses on courses of mobile APP program development based on Android platform. Eclipse is used as program development environment, which is an open source IDE designed for Java and its function can be extended by installing plug-in. A plug-in application embedded in IDE can provide function to trace the implementation log in real-time manner. Figure 1 is the interface of Eclipse and the outer frame area with red line refers to LogCat, one of Eclipse's plug-in modules. This research uses not only Eclipse as program design and development environment but also develops a plug-in as the main approach for real-time assessment application.

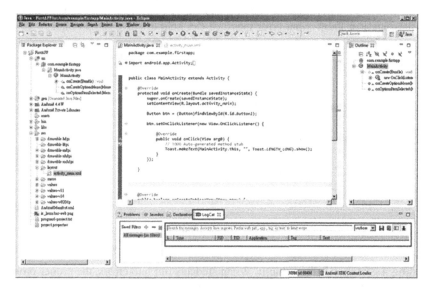

Fig. 1. Eclipse IDE and its plug-in.

3 The Real-Time Assessment Programing Environment

3.1 System Design

The main purpose of this research is to embed a self-built plug-in module with real-time feedback function into the Android APP's integrated development environment - Eclipse. This self-developed plug-in module will provide relevant coding assistance for students in case of any errors. The information of plug-in module includes the error types, important error prompts, and learning assistance information. The detailed contents are described respectively as below:

Error Type: This module provides the compile error and run-time error for each student. Thus, students can be aware of their current error types and make the connection between program error and its error type. Besides, the error information will also be sent to server side application for teachers to be aware of the learning status of students.

Important Error Prompt: When the IDE detects run-time error, the Stack Trace will be printed out for students to debug their code. Stack Trace means that a series of methods called during the process when APP program goes wrong are printed out, and its example is shown in Fig. 2 錯誤! 找不到參照來源。. However, for students or beginners in programming, such message is still too complicated. Therefore, the proposed plug-in will help students mark the important error prompt so that students will not give up understanding error contents upon seeing much complicated error information. The plug-in error prompt effects are shown in Fig. 2. By means of highlight effect in different colors, students can know the more important ones among numerous error messages, or know what error message can help to solve the problem.

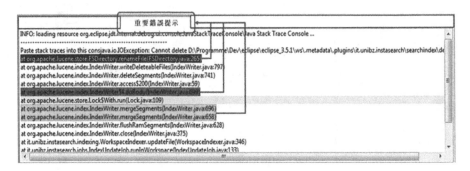

Fig. 2. Interface of important error prompt.

Learning Assistance Information: When students run into errors, the proper prompt, guidance or demonstration can help them construct knowledge and make reflection. Consequently, after the proposed plug-in detects error types and important errors mentioned above, it will automatically help students search the relevant solutions on the network and put several important links together in one function module, making students understand search direction and solution when errors occur. In this way, students can establish knowledge links according to errors and solutions. The purpose of this module is to verify whether the proposed learning environment can help students learn mobile APP development or not.

According to the function modules mentioned above, this research will provide the mobile APP programming learning environment shown in Fig. 3. The users are divided into students, teachers and the Expert Group. With the proposed plug-in module, client side used by students and server side used by teachers are keeping connected to collect students' development log in real time manner. Server side can also push learning assistance resources to client side in real time. The teachers can browse students' learning status in the courses of their teaching or after class, including program error occurring during the process of students' coding, learning process, etc., which will be further used as the basis for improving the teaching strategy.

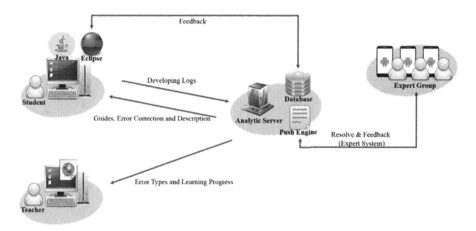

Fig. 3. The proposed real-time assessment programming environment

4   Experimental Results and Discussions

We collected the developing log from students in an Android Development course using the proposed IDE plug-in. Students don't need to learn extra learning tool to attend this experiment. The proposed plug-in doesn't affect the coding steps or operational behavior to students. There are total 60 students in the classroom and each experiment lasts for 150 min to collect developing log for a learning concept. In the end of the experiment, we collected 8 learning concepts in mobile APP development course to understand the coding issues of the students. For each learning concept, we collected three types of developing log, they are Compile Error, Run-time Error, and Logic Error. Each type of error collection is an independent event which means there could be up to 60 students have Compile error and 60 students have Logic error in a learning concept. Therefore, the total collection counts of each learning concept which contains three error types are 180 students. Table 1 shows the analysis results of this experiment.

In Table 1, it reveals that students get compile error when doing the IDE interface operation. Taking basic component as an example, students learn how to drag the user interface component into main activity layout file. Then they need to register those component in Java file. In these steps, compile error includes Java syntax typo, assigning incomplete component ID, and finding the wrong component in layout file. According to Table 1, there are four types of learning concepts belonging to this kind of compile error, including basic component, messaging component, selection and dropdown spanner, and Imageview. Besides, run-time error is mostly happened in learning concepts of Listview, Intent, File Management, and Database. Run-time error usually happens when the student is not familiar with the Java language. Therefore, teachers should put extra effort on Java language when teaching those learning concepts.

Table 1. The analysis results in the experiment.

Learning concepts	Error types			
	Compile error	Run-time error	Logic error	Collected counts
Basic component	70%	50%	20%	84
Messaging component	67%	47%	14%	76
Selection and dropdown spanner	59%	42%	17%	70
Imageview	64%	35%	14%	67
Listview	50%	75%	34%	95
Intent	45%	70%	30%	87
File management	52%	64%	17%	79
Database	55%	75%	20%	90

5 Conclusions

This research proposed and implemented a real-time assessment programming environment through debugging log. We developed a plug-in, embedded and implemented it into the Android IDE, Eclipse to collect students' developing log. According to the analysis results, there are two learning types of students. The first is operational learning type that focuses on the IDE interface operation and its manipulating steps. The second is programming logical learning type that focuses on the programming ability and logical coding style. Teachers can use different teaching strategy to help students for programming learning and meet students' different needs according to the analysis results from the proposed system. In future work, we will collect the learning performance of students to verify whether the proposed system provide sufficient learning assistance information for them.

Acknowledgement. The authors would like to thank the Ministry of Science and Technology of the Republic of China, Taiwan, for financially supporting this research under Contract No. MOST 105-2511-S-218-003-MY2.

References

1. Huang, Y.M., Liang, T.H., Su, Y.N., Chen, N.S.: Empowering personalized learning with an interactive E-book learning system for elementary school students. ETR&D-Educ. Technol. Res. Dev. **60**(4), 703–722 (2012)
2. Kelleher, C., Pausch, R.: Lowering the barriers to programming. ACM Comput. Surv. **37**(2), 83–137 (2005)
3. Linn, M.C., Clancy, M.J.: The case for case studies of programming problems. Commun. ACM **35**(3), 121–132 (1992)
4. Huang, W.H., Huang, W.Y., Tschopp, J.: Sustaining iterative game playing processes in DGBL: the relationship between motivational processing and outcome processing. Comput. Educ. **55**(2), 789–797 (2010)

5. Pea, R.D., Kurland, D.M.: On the cognitive effects of learning computer programming. New Ideas Psychol. **2**, 137–168 (1984)
6. Soloway, E.: Learning to program = learning to construct mechanisms and explanations. Commun. ACM **29**(9), 850–858 (1986)
7. Bagley, C., Chou, C.C.: Collaboration and the importance for novices in learning Java computer programming. ACM SIGCSE Bull. **39**(3), 211–215 (2007)
8. Williams, L., Upchurch, R.: In support of student pair programming. ACM SIGCSE Bull. **33** (1), 327–331 (2001)
9. Preston, D.: Pair programming as a model of collaborative learning: a review of the research. J. Comput. Sci. Coll. **20**(4), 39–45 (2005)
10. Hwang, W.Y., Wang, C.Y., Hwang, G.J., Huang, Y.M., Huang, S.: A web-based programming learning environment to support cognitive development. Interact. Comput. **20**, 524–534 (2008)

Using Facial Expression to Detect Emotion in E-learning System: A Deep Learning Method

Ai Sun[1], Ying-Jian Li[2(✉)], Yueh-Min Huang[1], and Qiong Li[2]

[1] Department of Engineering Science,
National Cheng Kung University, Tainan, Taiwan
sun_ai@hotmail.com, huang@mail.ncku.edu.tw
[2] School of Computer Science and Technology,
Harbin Institute of Technology, Harbin, China
hitlyj@stu.hit.edu.cn, qiongli@hit.edu.cn

Abstract. E-learning system is becoming more and more popular among students nowadays. However, the emotion of students is usually neglected in e-learning system. This study is mainly concerned about using facial expression to detect emotion in e-learning system. A deep learning method called convolutional neural network (CNN) is used in our research. Firstly, CNN is introduced to detect emotion in e-learning system based on using facial expression in this paper. Secondly, the training process and testing process of CNN are described. To learn about the accuracy of CNN in emotion detection, three databases (CK+, JAFFE and NVIE) are chosen to train and test the model. 10-fold cross validation method is used to calculate the accuracy. Thirdly, we introduce how to apply the trained CNN to e-learning system, and the design of e-learning system with emotion detection module is given. At last, we propose the design of an experiment to evaluate the performance of this method in real e-learning system.

Keywords: E-learning · Emotion detection · Facial expression · Deep learning

1 Introduction

In recent years, with the development of e-learning technology, more and more students choose to learn knowledge using the e-learning system. With e-learning system, people can learn what they need at any time and at anywhere, as long as there is network around them. As a result, learning through the e-learning system is becoming more and more popular.

One of the differences between e-learning and face-to-face education (traditional education) is the lack of affective factors. It is well known that emotion plays an important role in learning process [1, 2]. For example, the learning efficiency could be higher if the learner is in happy state and be lower if the learner is sad. In face-to-face education, instructors can observe the motion of students and adjust the teaching strategies in time. However, in e-learning system, teachers are usually separated from

© Springer International Publishing AG 2017
T.-C. Huang et al. (Eds.): SETE 2017, LNCS 10676, pp. 446–455, 2017.
https://doi.org/10.1007/978-3-319-71084-6_52

students. In this case, it is difficult for the teachers to feel the emotion of students and detect the problems especially incurred by the confusion or sadness.

Due to the important influence of emotions on different areas, lots of approaches are proposed to detect emotions. All these approaches can be divided into two kinds: (1) using off-the-shelf software (FaceReader [3, 4], Xpress Engine or other alternative products) [5]; (2) using other technologies instead of software [6–9].

Moridis and Economides [5] used FaceReader to observe the emotions of students. The best advantage of using these off-the-shelf products is that the researchers don't need to learn about how to implement a classifier because the software does that automatically. However, the shortage is the recognition rate is not high enough. Brodny et al. [10] tested the performance of different softwares, the recognition rates of FaceReader on CK+ database [11] and MMI database [12] were 77.59% and 56.10%, while Xpress Engine achieved 87.60% and 45.12%, respectively.

Some researchers were not satisfied with the result of off-the-shelf software and proposed various kinds of approaches to classify emotions. Some common approaches are speech-based method [6], text-based method [7], facial-expression-based method [8, 9] and multi-modal-based method [13]. Chi-Chun et al. [6] applied decision tree, a kind of machine learning model, to detect emotions in speech, it was found the testing performance was improved by 3.37%. The emotions in text were evaluated by Chan and Chong [7] with a sentiment analysis engine. Decision tree approach was applied to classify emotions on CK+ database using facial expression by Salmam et al. [8] and the accuracy rate was 90%. Lee et al. [9] used SVM, another machine learning model, to evaluate the emotions on CK+ database and JAFFE database [14].The recognized rates were 94.39% and 92.22%, respectively. Han and Wang [13] used multi-modal signals to detect emotions. As we can see, different approaches may result in various performances. The performance can be different when using different machine leaning models. This suggests that the recognition rate can be improved if we use reasonable machine leaning models. Motivated by this finding, we want to try more effective approaches to detect emotions.

In the past few years, deep learning has become a popular research area. For classification tasks, the basic of using general machine learning methods is feature extraction. Different features would result in different accuracy rates. However, feature extraction is complicated work. How many features should be extracted? What kinds of features are the most effective for classification? These are important questions that should be noticed. Fortunately, deep learning technology can learn the features automatically instead of extracting features manually. Lots of work using deep learning has been done till now and excellent result has been achieved in various areas [15–17]. In speech recognition domain, Dahl et al. [15] applied deep learning technology in large vocabulary speech recognition and the accuracy rate was improved by 9.2%. In machine translation area, Devlin et al. [16] proposed a deep learning method to improve the recognition rate of sentences and was regarded as the best paper in ACL in 2014. In digital image processing area, Convolutional Neural Networks (CNN), a kind of deep learning model, is widely accepted due to its wonderful performance. Sun et al. [17], applied CNN to implement face recognition and the accuracy was 99.53% (even better than that of human beings). So what if we apply deep learning technology (CNN) to detect emotion in e-learning system is the research purpose for this paper.

According to the analysis above, the main ideas of this research are as follows:

(1) Introduce CNN to detect emotions based on using facial expression in e-learning system.
(2) Design the framework to detect emotions using facial expression in e-learning system.
(3) Design the experiment to test the performance of CNN in real e-learning system.

2 Related Works

In this section, some works that has been done by pioneers in facial expression recognition are going to be introduced.

2.1 Common Approaches in Facial Expression Recognition

Ekman et al. [18] proposed that facial expressions could be divided into six basic emotions: happiness, surprise, sadness, fear, anger, and disgust. Together with natural, these seven emotions are usually used in facial expression recognition. Three key crucial parts were included in facial expression recognition: (1) face detection; (2) feature extraction; (3) facial expression (emotion) classification. The frame work of emotion detection using facial expression is showed in Fig. 1.

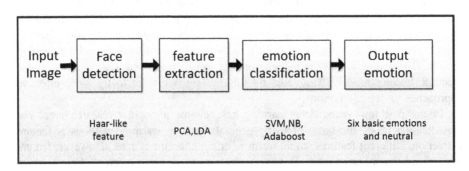

Fig. 1. The frame work of emotion detection using facial expression

Even in nowadays, lots of work has been done in facial expression recognition followed these three crucial parts. Face detection is a preprocess step of facial expression recognition. To describe the variance of facial expression, the FACS system was proposed by Friesen and Ekman [20]. They defined 44 Action Units (AU) and group of AU were used to describe a certain facial expression. Principal Component Analysis (PCA) and Linear Discriminant Analysis (LDA) are two usually used methods to extract features. PCA prefers the best features that can maintain the information of data while LDA chooses the features that can benefit classification well. There are various kinds of classifiers that can be used to complete facial expression classification task. SVM was applied on CK+ database by Lee et al. [9]. Eskil and Benli

[19] used SVM, Naive Bayesian (NB) and Adaboost methods to classify emotions using facial expression.

2.2 Deep Learning in Emotion Facial Expression Recognition

Because of the excellent performance in different areas, deep learning technology was employed to detect facial expressions by some researchers [21–24]. Soleymani et al. [21] applied Long-short-term-memory recurrent neural networks (LSTM-RNN) and conditional random fields (CCRF) to classify emotions using facial expression, as well as electroencephalogram (EEG) signals. The best result was 0.043 ± 0.025 measured by RMSE using facial features. Lv et al. [22] proposed to classify emotions using only facial components. In their work, deep belief network (DBN) was trained to learn important components first. After that, tanh function was applied to divide emotions into seven classes. In order to achieve the same purpose, two kinds of deep learning structures, deep neural network (DNN) and CNN, were implemented by Jung et al. [23]. There are two main differences between DNN and CNN: (1) CNN has Convolution kernel; (2) There are less parameters in CNN. As a result, CNN is easier to train compared with DNN. Liu et al. [24] proposed Deep Networks (AUDN) to achieve facial expression recognition.

2.3 Emotion Detection in E-learning System

In this subsection, some methods to classify emotions of students in e-learning system are introduced.

In order to detect the emotions of students in e-learning system, different kinds of signal were used, such as text [25, 26], facial [27, 28] and so on. Ortigosa et al. [25] presented Sentbuk, a Facebook application, to achieve emotion analysis with a accuracy of 83.27%. With Sentbuk, emotional change can also be detected. They described the usefulness of their work in e-learning system at the end of the paper. Qin et al. [26] paid special attention to negative emotion. Interactive text was used to detect negative emotion, after which music was selected to regulate the emotion of student. Sun et al. [27] trained a SVM classifier using images from CK database. 265 facial images of 42 people were used as testing sets and the accuracy was 84.55%. Most e-learning systems are mainly focus on single user detection. However, Ashwin et al. [28] proposed multi-user face detection based on e-learning system using SVM. It was the first work on multi-user face detection for e-learning Systems. The proposed method was tested on three databases: LFW, FDDB and YFD, and the accuracy were between 89% and 100%. To speed up the processing, Central Processing Unit (CPU) and Graphics Processing Unit (GPU) were used.

3 Method Description

In this section, the design of CNN is introduced first. Then, the way how to train and test the CNN is described. The framework of emotion detection in e-learning system is also given in this part. Finally, a rough design of testing the performance of CNN in e-learning is proposed.

3.1 Design of CNN

CNN has been used in many tasks by researchers. The different CNNs are with different parameters, such as the depth, the size of convolution kernel, the choice of activation function and so on. The structure of our CNN is shown in Fig. 2. There are three convolution layers with RELU (a kind of activation function), three pooling layers and two fully connected layers in our CNN. The convolution kernels are set at size of 5 * 5. In each pooling layer, we choose max pooling as pooling method. The size of pooling window and pooling stride are set at 3 * 3 and 2, respectively. The number of units in the first fully connected layer is set as 1024. In the last layer, there are 7 units with softmax function and each one is stand for a certain kind of emotion. The output is the probability of the input image's emotion.

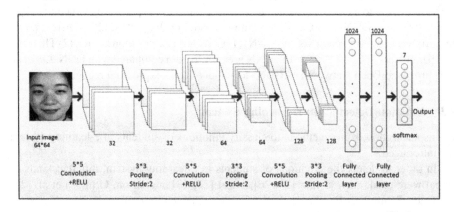

Fig. 2. Structure of our CNN

3.2 Training and Testing Framework Design

The same as other machine learning method, the use of CNN is divided into two steps: training step and testing step. The two steps are described in this subsection.

Training Step

In the training step of CNN, we decide to use stochastic gradient descent (SGD) algorithm. The advantage of SGD is SGD can reduce the over fitting phenomenon. To speed up the training process, the following methods can be used:

(1) Use a batch of images to regulate the weight in CNN every time instead of a single one.

(2) Use GPU. GPU is faster than CPU in image processing. There are many deep learning frameworks supporting GPU, such as Tensorflow, Caffe and Theano.

(3) Detect the location of face and cut it out of the image before training. Using OpenCV library can implement this idea. The faces for training are put into training data set and others are put in testing data set.

The training process is shown in Fig. 3. CNN training needs lots of images with emotion labels. We aim at training a CNN that can be generally used to all kinds of faces. As a result, the training images should include both eastern faces and western faces. In our research, CK+ database, JAFFE database and NVIE database are chosen.

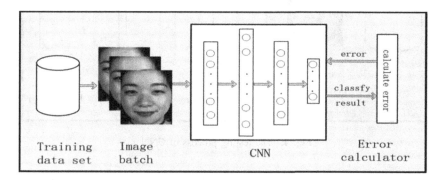

Fig. 3. The training process of CNN using SGD

CK+ database consist of 593 sequences from 123 subjects. There are eight kinds of emotions in this database: neutral, happy, surprise, angry, disgust, fear, sadness and contempt. In our research, however, we are going to use all the images but those with contempt emotion.

JAFFE database contains 213 facial expression images from 10 Japanese women. The extension of each image is "tiff" and the resolution ratio is 256 * 256. There are seven emotion labels in this database: happy, surprise, angry, disgust, fear, sadness and neutral.

NVIE database [29] consists of natural visible and infrared facial expressions. In this database, there are lots of images from about 100 subjects under front, left and right illumination. The emotion is activated by eliciting videos. The number of emotion labels is 6. They are happy, surprise, angry, disgust, fear and sadness.

Testing Step

In order to learn about the performance of CNN on the data set, 10-fold cross validation is designed. The testing process of each image is shown in Fig. 4.

The classification result is compared with the label of the image and is recorded if the result is correct. The accuracy if the ratio of correct-classified number and testing set size. In 10-fold cross validation, the average of ten accuracy rates is set as the final accuracy rate.

3.3   Application in E-learning Systems

In this subsection, we introduce how to apply the trained CNN to detect emotion in e-learning system.

The e-learning system with emotion detector can be divided into two modules, emotion detection module and teaching strategy regulation module. At the beginning, the teacher teaches the students with a certain strategy. The emotion state of students

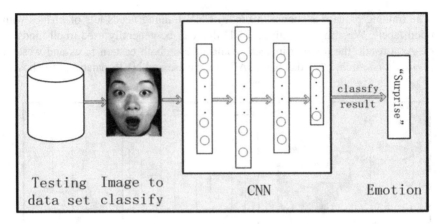

Fig. 4. The testing process of CNN

will be detected by emotion detection module. The detected emotion returns to teacher as feedback. The teacher regulates his teaching strategy and content according to the emotion of most students. The whole system is shown in Fig. 5.

In emotion detection module, the learners' facial expressions are shot by a camera first and we can get the image sequence. Second, we use OpenCV library to detect and cut the face area out of each image. All of the face areas form the face sequence. After that, the faces in face sequence are fed to CNN one by one. The emotion of each student was obtained.

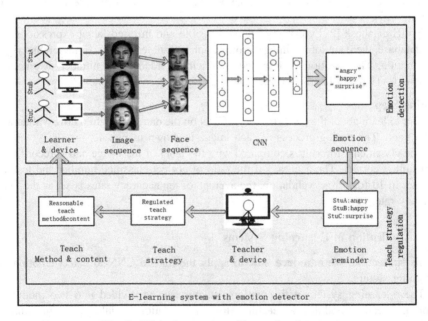

Fig. 5. E-learning system with emotion detector

In teaching strategy regulation module, the emotion sequence obtained from emotion detection module is input into the emotion reminder. The emotion reminder is a device that can remind the teacher of the students' emotion state. The teaching strategy is regulated by the teacher according to the emotion of students. After teaching strategy regulation, new emotion may arise among students. The new emotion can be detected and sent to teacher and the teaching strategy may be changed further. As a result, this is a dynamic process. The advantage of this kind of e-learning system is that it can improve the efficiency of learning.

In our research, we are concerned the accuracy rate of the CNN in emotion classification in e-learning system. In last subsection, we designed 10-fold cross validation to test the performance of CNN on the testing dataset. However, how the CNN will perform in real e-learning system is not tested. The rough design of this idea is given as follows:

(1) Choose 50 college students to learning a course via e-learning system.
(2) For each student (for example, StuA), the testing process can be described by Fig. 6. StuA learn the course via computer or other electrical device. In the process of learning, his facial expression is recorded by a camera every 20 s. On one hand, the face area is cut out of each photo and is fed to CNN. We can get the classification result by CNN. On the other hand, the recorded photos are classified by SutA manually. We can get the classification result by human. The two results are compared and the number of correctly-classified photos is recorded.

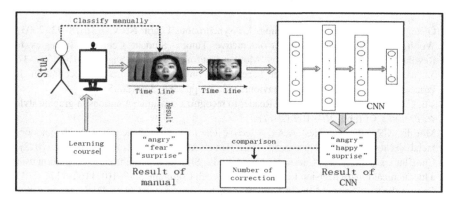

Fig. 6. Testing in real e-learning system

(3) Calculate the accuracy using the following formula.

$$accuracy = \frac{N_{correct}}{N_{all}},$$

where $N_{correct}$ is the sum of correctly- classified photos for all students and N_{all} is the number of all recorded photos.

4 Conclusion and Future Work

E-learning systems are becoming more and more popular nowadays. However, emotion, an important factor in learning process, is often ignored in e-learning system. In this paper, we are mainly concerned about the emotion detection in e-learning system using facial

Due to the excellent performance of CNN, we introduced this model to detect emotion in e-learning system. First, we characterize the structure of our CNN. After that, the training and testing process of CNN was described. To train the CNN, three facial expression databases (CK+, JAFFE and NVIE) were selected. The working process of CNN in e-learning system was showed. At last, the rough design to test the accuracy in e-learning system is offered.

There are some questions left in this paper: (1) How does the proposed CNN perform on the testing data set and in e-learning system? (2) How long does it take to train this CNN? In near future, we are going to focus on these questions. For the first one, we are going to implement the CNN. The accuracy of CNN should be tested on testing data set given in this paper. Also, we will carry out the experiment in e-learning system according to the design from Subsect. 3.3. For the second question, CNN training may take a long time if we use CPU only. As a result, we are going to use GPU to speed up the training process and record the training time.

References

1. O'Regan, K.: Emotion and e-learning. J. Asynchronous Learn. Netw. **7**(3), 78–92 (2003)
2. Woolf, B.P.: Building Intelligent Interactive Tutors: Student Centered Strategies for Revolutionizing E-Learning, vol. 59. Morgan Kaufmann Inc., Burlington (2010). 337–379
3. Yi, M.J.D., Kuilenburg, H.V.: The FaceReader: online facial expression recognition. In: Proceedings of the Measuring Behaviour, vol. 30, pp. 589–590 (2005)
4. Yu, C.Y., Ko, C.H.: Applying FaceReader to recognize consumer emotions in graphic styles ⋆. Procedia Cirp **60**, 104–109 (2017)
5. Moridis, C.N., Economides, A.A.: Affective learning: empathetic agents with emotional facial and tone of voice expressions. IEEE Trans. Affect. Comput. **3**(3), 260–272 (2012)
6. Chi-Chun, L., Emily, M., Carlos, B., Sungbok, L., Shrikanth, N.: Emotion recognition using a hierarchical binary decision tree approach. Speech Commun. **53**(9–10), 1162–1171 (2011)
7. Chan, S.W.K., Chong, M.W.C.: Sentiment analysis in financial texts. Decis. Support Syst. **94**, 53–64 (2017)
8. Salmam, F.Z., Madani, A., Kissi, M.: Facial expression recognition using decision trees. In: IEEE International Conference on Computer Graphics, Imaging and Visualization, pp. 125–130 (2016)
9. Lee, S.H., Kostas, P.K.N., Yong, M.R.: Intra-class variation reduction using training expression images for sparse representation based facial expression recognition. IEEE Trans. Affect. Comput. **5**(3), 340–351 (2014)
10. Brodny, G., Kołakowska, A., Landowska, A., Szwoch, M., Szwoch, W., Wróbel, M.R.: Comparison of selected off-the-shelf solutions for emotion recognition based on facial expressions. In: IEEE International Conference on Human System Interactions, pp. 397–404 (2016)

11. Lucey, P., Cohn, J.F., Kanade, T., Saragih, J., Ambadar, Z., Matthews, I.: The extended Cohn-Kanade dataset (CK+): a complete dataset for action unit and emotion-specified expression. In: IEEE Computer Vision and Pattern Recognition Workshops, vol. 36, pp. 94–101 (2010)

12. Valstar, M.F., Pantic, M.: Induced disgust happiness and surprise: an addition to the MMI facial expression database. In: Proceedings of the International Workshop on Emotion Corpora for Research on Emotion & Affect, pp. 65–70 (2010)

13. Han, Z.Y., Wang, J., Bohai University: Emotion visualization method for speech and facial expression signals. Electron. Des. Eng. **24**, 146–149 (2016)

14. Lyons, M., Akamatsu, S., Kamachi, M., Gyoba, J.: Coding facial expressions with Gabor wavelets. In: 1998 IEEE International Conference on Automatic Face and Gesture Recognition Proceedings, pp. 200–205 (1998)

15. Dahl, G.E., Yu, D., Deng, L., Acero, A.: Context-dependent pre-trained deep neural networks for large-vocabulary speech recognition. IEEE Trans. Audio Speech Lang. Process. **20**(1), 30–42 (2012)

16. Devlin, J., Zbib, R., Huang, Z., Lamar, T., Schwartz, R.M., Makhoul, J.: Fast and robust neural network joint models for statistical machine translation. In ACL (1), pp. 1370–1380 (2014)

17. Sun, Y., Liang, D., Wang, X., Tang, X.: Deepid3: face recognition with very deep neural networks. arXiv preprint arXiv:1502.00873 (2015)

18. Ekman, P., Rolls, E.T., Perrett, D.I., Ellis, H.D.: Facial expressions of emotion: an old controversy and new findings. Philos. Trans. R. Soc. B: Biolog. Sci. **335**(1273), 63–69 (1992)

19. Eskil, M.T., Benli, K.S.: Facial expression recognition based on anatomy. Comput. Vis. Image Underst. **119**, 1–14 (2014)

20. Friesen, E., Ekman, P.: Facial action coding system: a technique for the measurement of facial movement, Palo Alto (1978)

21. Soleymani, M., Asghari-Esfeden, S., Fu, Y., Pantic, M.: Analysis of EEG signals and facial expressions for continuous emotion detection. IEEE Trans. Affect. Comput. **7**(1), 17–28 (2016)

22. Lv, Y., Feng, Z., Xu, C.: Facial expression recognition via deep learning. In: IEEE International Conference on Smart Computing (SMARTCOMP), pp. 303–308 (2014)

23. Jung, H., Lee, S., Park, S., Kim, B., Kim, J., Lee, I., Ahn, C.: Development of deep learning-based facial expression recognition system. In: IEEE Korea-Japan Joint Workshop on Frontiers of Computer Vision, pp. 1–4 (2015)

24. Liu, M., Li, S., Shan, S., Chen, X.: Au-inspired deep networks for facial expression feature learning. Neurocomputing **159**, 126–136 (2015)

25. Ortigosa, A., Martín, J.M., Carro, R.M.: Sentiment analysis in Facebook and its application to e-learning. Comput. Hum. Behav. **31**, 527–541 (2014)

26. Qin, J., Zheng, Q., Li, H.: A study of learner-oriented negative emotion compensation in e-learning. Educ. Technol. Soc. **17**(4), 420–431 (2014)

27. Sun, J.M., Pei, X.S., Zhou, S.S.: Facial emotion recognition in modern distant education system using SVM. In: IEEE International Conference on Machine Learning and Cybernetics, vol. 6, pp. 3545–3548 (2008)

28. Ashwin, T.S., Jose, J., Raghu, G., Reddy, G.R.M.: An e-learning system with multifacial emotion recognition using supervised machine learning. In: IEEE International Conference on Technology for Education, pp. 23–26 (2015)

29. Wang, S., Liu, Z., Lv, S., Lv, Y., Wu, G., Peng, P., et al.: A natural visible and infrared facial expression database for expression recognition and emotion inference. IEEE Trans. Multimedia **12**(7), 682–691 (2010)

Maker Movement Influence on Students' Learning Motivation and Learning Achievement – A Learning Style Perspective

Jan-Pan Hwang[(✉)] [ID]

Fortune Institute of Technology, Kaohsiung, Taiwan (R.O.C.)
jphwang.academic@gmail.com

Abstract. In recent years, the development of maker movement is very prosperous with the emergence and wide application of digital fabrication equipment and open source hardware, the maker movement, featuring cooperative innovation and user self-production, is a new trend around the global. It close development with STEAM education is also very exciting. This article focus on maker movement to understand what differences between students with different learning achievement and motivation from the perspective of learning style. The research question is what influence of maker movement on the motivation and achievement of primary students' learning. The participants are sixth grade primary school students from southern of Taiwan, a total of 95 people, and teaching activities for a period of eight weeks and a total of 16 h. The results show that students of different learning styles, gender have significant differences in the dimension of motivation. The result is discussed in the article, and implications for maker movement has also put forward our views.

Keywords: Maker movement · STEAM · Learning achievement · Learning motivation

1 Introduction

With the emergence and wide application of digital fabrication equipment and open source hardware, the maker movement, featuring cooperative innovation and user self-production, is a new trend around the global [1]. The main core spirit "Learning by doing" originated from Dewey [2], it focuses on personal use of IT products (or technology) to play creative, integrate existing resources, collaborative, and then solve the problems.

The US president Barack Obama proposed a competitive upgrade program and advocate STEM for engineering education. The educator are sparing to promote integration with science and technology education, in order to show the importance of STEM concept [3]. Recently, the promotion of humanistic qualities are also combined with STEM, widely known as STEAM (Science, Technology, Engineering, Art, and Math). With this trend of STEAM, not only driven by the ability such as computing thinking, interdisciplinary integration, teamwork…and so on, but also by the public attention and scholars into the research [4].

© Springer International Publishing AG 2017
T.-C. Huang et al. (Eds.): SETE 2017, LNCS 10676, pp. 456–462, 2017.
https://doi.org/10.1007/978-3-319-71084-6_53

In Taiwan, Microsoft collaborated with the Dept. of Electrical Engineering of National Taiwan University to launch the "Coding Summer Camp" in 2015 [5], which has been followed by many colleges and universities until now. And the relevant departments of government has also promoted the "vMaker" action plan, and dispatched a "Fab Truck" tour full of 189 senior high school, that expect to take root from the campus, nurturing the maker talent of next generation. Those plan let students will be able to start training and contact with creative thinking and hands-on spirit of practice in school. In the implementation process, they might give the product a higher value, also to create more added value, and extensive application [5], and establish learning confidence and enhance their motivation.

The most commonly used theoretical framework for improving learning motivation was the ARCS Model [6, 7]. There are four steps for promoting and sustaining motivation in the learning process: *Attention, Relevance, Confidence, Satisfaction* [8, 9].

In view of foregoing, it can be understood that the cultivation of talent with creative thinking and the overall national competitiveness is closely related. Therefore, the domestic education system not only need to cultivate professional and technical functions of the staff, but also improve the development of related industries. How to make the Internet of Things and Maker Movement to improve for related industries, how to nurture creative thinking of talent for the service value, should be more widely concerned by the community. This study focus on the STEAM topic, to primary school children as the object, supplemented by ARCS model for the teaching of the spindle, in order to enhance learning motivation and achievement.

2 Methodology

2.1 Participants

There are 105 students participated in this research. They filled out the ILS (Index of Learning Style) questionnaire [10] under the guidance of the teacher for identified their learning style. Based on research considerations and requirements, students who are not full participation in the competition will be excluded. Accordingly, 10 students were excluded. The following Table 1 gives a summary of all students' learning style.

Table 1. Summary of learning styles. (n = 95)

Learning style	Active	Reflective	Sensing	Intuitive	Visual	Verbal	Sequential	Global
Numbers	49	46	55	40	79	16	44	51

2.2 Research Tools

There are two kinds of tools used in this experiment, ARCS learning motivation scale and learning achievement test, as described below.

ARCS Learning Motivation Scales. This is a Likert's five-point scale design, 5point for "very agree", sequentially to 1 point for "very disagree". The ARCS questionnaire is divided into four factors, which 6 questions (items) for each factors, a total of 24 questions. The score of the four factors as their learning motivation indicators. The higher score means stronger the motivation for learning. In contrast lower score means negative for learning motivation. Separated by six weeks for pretest and posttest.

Learning Achievement Test. The test was compiled by three senior teachers. The contents of the test is the basics of learning topics, background knowledge. A total of 20 multiple choice questions in questionnaire, and higher score represents the higher achievement.

In addition, there are two consents document signed by the guardian for participated experiment and collected personal data.

2.3   Experimental Process

The 8 weeks teaching experimental activities are arranged in the survey class. The implementation period of this activities may refer to Fig. 1.

In week 1, before the experimental activities, the students implemented the pre-test. The contents of the test is the basic knowledge of the course. The main purpose of the pre-test is to determine that all students have the same basic knowledge before participating in the activity. Week 2, for later solving learning task, students must understand how devices used and operated. From week 3 to 7, students challenge different level of learning task, from elementary to advance. Last, student filled out the post-test for better understanding the change of learning motivation and achievement.

3   Data Analysis

In order to understand the changes in the learning motivation and achievement of all the students after 8 weeks of experimental activity, they were tested by pre-test and post-test for learning motivation and achievement, and the score were measured by dependent sample t-test. Then we find the relationship between motivation and achievement from a learning style perspective. The following will be divided into three parts for the results analysis.

3.1   ARCS

For better understanding the differences between pre-test and post-test, we use dependent sample t-test for examine.

Overall Motivation. The result was shown in Table 2, the pre-test *Mean* of overall motivation is 88.16(SD = 13.59), and post-test is 94.79(SD = 12.99). The post-test *Mean* is higher than the pre-test *Mean*. At the same time with the significant differences $(t = -2.94, p < .05)$. Next, to analyze ARCS each factors in the same way.

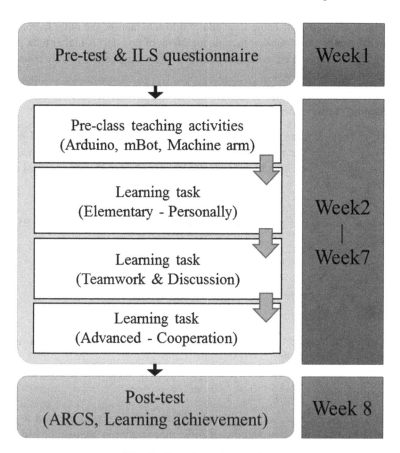

Fig. 1. Experimental procedure

Table 2. Summary of ARCS in dependent sample *t*-test. (n = 95)

Factors	Test	*Mean*	S.D.	*t*-value
Overall	Pre-test	88.16	13.59	−2.94*
	Post-test	94.79	12.99	
Attention	Pre-test	22.18	3.95	−2.69*
	Post-test	25.19	3.84	
Relevance	Pre-test	20.29	4.01	−2.23*
	Post-test	21.99	3.93	
Confidence	Pre-test	22.58	3.94	−2.13*
	Post-test	23.95	4.11	
Satisfaction	Pre-test	23.11	4.26	−0.85
	Post-test	23.67	3.97	

*$p < .05$, S.D. = Standard deviation.

Each Factors. As shown in Table 2, in addition to satisfaction, the other factors else is significant differences. In *Attention* factors, the *Mean* of post-test is higher than pre-test, and the same result also appears in other factors. Only satisfaction is only a small gap between post-test and pre-test.

3.2   Learning Achievement

As shown in Table 3, there is a significant differences between pre-test and post-test ($t = -9.31$, $p < .001$). The results indicate that there is a significant difference in the overall learning achievement, which post-test (45.58) is higher than the pre-test (54.95) by the *Mean*.

Table 3. Summary of learning achievement in dependent sample *t*-test. (n = 95)

	Test	Mean	S.D.	t-value
Overall	Pre-test	45.58	6.76	−9.31***
	Post-test	54.95	7.24	

***$p < .001$, S.D. = Standard deviation.

Then we try to analyze the learning motivation and learning achievement from the perspective of learning style.

3.3   Learning Style

As shown in Table 4, there is a significant differences between *Active* and *Reflective* ($t = -2.36$, $p < .05$), and other significant differences between *Sequential* and *Global* ($t = -2.16$, $p < .05$). The results indicate that there is a significant difference in the gain score of learning motivation, which post-test is higher than the pre-test by the *Mean of gain score*.

Table 4. Summary of learning style with gain score of learning motivation. (n = 95)

Learning style	Mean	S.D.	t-value
Active	13.25	2.13	−2.36*
Reflective	16.35	1.95	
Sensing	14.55	2.26	0.68
Intuitive	13.20	2.15	
Visual	15.85	2.17	0.96
Verbal	14.75	2.39	
Sequential	16.04	2.93	−2.16*
Global	18.84	3.07	

*$p < .05$, S.D. = Standard deviation.

As shown in Table 5, there is a significant differences between *Active* and *Reflective* ($t = 2.44$, $p < .001$), and other significant differences between *Sensing* and *Intuitive* ($t = 2.62$, $p < .001$). The results indicate that there is a significant difference in the gain score of learning achievement, which post-test (9.98; 9.99) is higher than the pre-test (5.97; 5.38) by the *Mean of* gain score.

Table 5. Summary of learning style with gain score of learning achievement. (n = 95)

Learning style	Gain score *Mean*	S.D.	*t*-value
Active	9.98	4.12	2.44***
Reflective	5.97	3.23	
Sensing	9.99	4.21	2.62***
Intuitive	5.38	2.94	
Visual	8.10	4.15	0.11
Verbal	7.81	4.74	
Sequential	8.41	3.64	0.39
Global	7.74	4.48	

***$p < .001$, S.D. = Standard deviation.

4   Conclusions

In the study, the students after teaching activities can increase the learning motivation, and also significantly improve learning achievement. In ARCS model, *Attention, Relevance, Confidence, Satisfaction* all have significant differences between pre-test and post-test of motivation.

In perspective of learning style, learning attitude (*Active/Reflective*) have significant differences in learning motivation and achievement. The students of *Reflective* have higher motivation then *Active*. In learning achievement, the students of *Active* have higher score then *Reflective*. And thinking way (*Sequential/Global*) have significant differences in learning motivation. The students with *Global* have higher motivation then *Sequential*. Last, learning manner (*Sensing/Intuitive*) also have significant differences in learning achievement. The students with *Sensing* have higher motivation then *Intuitive*.

Overall, the maker movement can enhance the learning motivation and achievement. And, the students with difference learning style, there will be significant differences in motivation and achievement, except for sensory type (*Visual/Verbal*).

5   Future Work

For future researchers, it is recommended that the experimental sample can be more diversified, not limited to primary school students.

Second, we can consider quasi-experimental design to carry out research, try to compare the differences between motivation and achievement in detail.

Finally, the curriculum design reintegrates into more theories and techniques, such as cognitive load, AI, etc.

Acknowledgement. This research is partially supported by the Ministry of Science and Technology (MOST), Taiwan (R.O.C.) under grant no MOST-106-2511-S-268-001. In addition, I want to give a special thanks to Dr. Yen-Ning Su who is an information team leader in Sheng-Li primary school for help the experimental activities carried out smoothly.

References

1. Tan, M., Yang, Y., Yu, P.: The influence of the maker movement on engineering and technology education. World Trans. Eng. Technol. Educ. **14**(1), 89–94 (2016)
2. Dewey, J.: The Educational Situation, p. 104. University of Chicago Press, Chicago (1904)
3. Kalil, T., Miller, J.: Announcing the first white house maker faire. The White House Blog (2014)
4. Hatch, M.: The Maker Movement Manifesto. McGraw-Hill Education, New York City (2014)
5. NTUEE (2016). https://www.ee.ntu.edu.tw/hischool/exercise.html
6. Chang, N.-C., Chen, H.-H.: A motivational analysis of the ARCS model for information literacy courses in a blended learning environment. Libri **65**(2), 129–142 (2015)
7. Aşıksoy, G., Özdamlı, F.: Flipped classroom adapted to the ARCS model of motivation and applied to a physics course. Eurasia J. Math. Sci. Technol. Educ. **12**(6) (2016)
8. Keller, J.M.: Motivational Design for Learning and Performance: The ARCS Model Approach. Springer Science & Business Media, Berlin (2009). https://doi.org/10.1007/978-1-4419-1250-3
9. Keller, J.M.: Development and use of the ARCS model of instructional design. J. Instr. Dev. **10**(3), 2–10 (1987)
10. Felder, R.M., Soloman, B.A.: Index of learning styles (1991)

Synchronous Collaboration in English for Tourism Classes

YiChun Liu[(⊠)]

Chia Nan University of Pharmacy and Science, Tainan 717, Taiwan
ycliu715@gmail.com

Abstract. Cloud-based projects have drawn the attention of many researchers in recent years. This current project is designed to assist students to acquire specific knowledge and expressions in English for Tourism through cloud-based collaborative courses. The study explores synchronous collaboration, using free software *Google Documents* to support project-based learning (PBL). Students participate in group discussions as they prepare to use English to introduce their hometown's tourist attractions. Approximately 60 sophomores from 2 classes participated in this project at a technological university. The experimental group applies *Google Documents* as the learning platform, while the control group uses the e-learning platform offered by the university. The different characteristics of the two collaboration formats are examined, and the challenges of carrying out such activities through the two formats are discussed in terms of how a synchronous collaborative group project has the potential to enhance the effectiveness of learning in English for Tourism classes. Data is analyzed from pre- and post-tests, students' editing of group projects, brochures, and questionnaires. In summary, it is hoped this project will be helpful for English teachers interested in computer-assisted language learning who would like to take advantage of free online resources *Google Documents* to foster student collaboration and VoiceTube for English learning.

Keywords: Synchronous · Asynchronous · Collaborative learning · Cloud-based technology

1 Introduction

CALL is a field that is characterized by a learner-centered approach, providing vivid and real-life materials on the screen and interactive activities [2]. There are generic technologies that have been applied in language teaching, such as email and mobile phones [4]. Furthermore, CALL practitioners and researchers have developed online reciprocal peer review systems for college students' writing [6, 7]. Due to the increasing range of technologies available and the rise of information communication technologies (ICTs), CALL offers effective ways for learning.

Since the mid-1980s, the research direction in this field has been shifting from a product-oriented to a more process-oriented approach. There has been a number of studies that have investigated how technology supports language learning. Reference [8] assessed and investigated the effectiveness of technology in improving language

© Springer International Publishing AG 2017
T.-C. Huang et al. (Eds.): SETE 2017, LNCS 10676, pp. 463–468, 2017.
https://doi.org/10.1007/978-3-319-71084-6_54

education in his review of recent developments in technology and language learning research. He found that CALL was as or more effective than human teachers when applying technology-supported language learning. Chang and Lin [1] focused on the effect of web-based strategy instruction in Taiwan on English achievement. Based on their findings, they recommended strategies for web-based English instruction including (a) predicting, summarizing, self-questioning and clarifying; (b) text annotation with pictures and (c) glossing. Peer interaction has a larger effect than teacher interaction in computer-mediated communication (CMC) settings and the opinion exchange facilitated by CMC tasks contributes to a larger effect [3].

2 Related Work

In addition, for low English level college students, introducing Taiwan's tourist attractions and accommodation in a region as a tour guide and comparing these with those in a foreign place regarding local and ethnic culture is a challenging task. In order to assist students individually in undertaking this task, it is proposed in the current study that learners work collaboratively in order to build confidence and basic communicative skills before attempting to undertake tasks individually. Online tools such as *Google Documents* make it possible for learners to work collaboratively, and through this type of collaborative activity, it is proposed that learners will be able to develop their skills to make them more efficient in the brainstorming process.

However, little attention has been paid to teach Taiwanese students how to introduce Taiwan's features to foreigners in English. Without training, technological university students will encounter difficulties while communicating with foreigners, especially in the workplace. Moreover, this is one of the most required "soft" skills, since Taiwan keeps expanding its tourism and hospitality industry. We usually ignore teaching the basic information regarding our own country. In this way, specifically, students are offered opportunities to discover and engage in learning adventures developed from their own hometown related to local tourism and hospitality, which in turn expands Taiwan's tourism industry. Students are able to communicate interculturally with foreigners and introduce Taiwan to foreigners. It is believed that this will provide substantial motivation for students to learn English. English can be interesting, especially when it connects to students' daily lives. Thus, the study focuses on Taiwanese culture embedded in the English for Tourism class to help students to be more familiar with our homeland in order to promote Taiwan to foreigners. At the same time, students are able to use practical English in their daily lives. It is also an attempt to supplement the findings of earlier studies.

The purpose of this project is twofold: (1) to examine how a teacher in the role of facilitator can help peer interaction work, using synchronous and asynchronous collaboration in English for Tourism classes; (2) to investigate what challenges students encounter in the process of a project-based learning activity. This study is guided by the following research question:

3   Methodology

3.1   Research Question

(1) Is an asynchronous approach to collaboration in students' project-based learning as effective as a synchronous approach?

3.2   Participants

Two individual classes of English for Tourism were conducted at a technological university in Southern Taiwan. Sixty students took part in the experiment and were investigated in this study. These two classes were made up of sophomores from the Department of Applied Foreign Languages. The aim of the class is to assist students to acquire domain knowledge through oral training and the reading of English texts related to tourism and hospitality.

3.3   Collaborative Learning Tool

Google Docs is being used as a collaborative learning tool to support students in group projects. It is a well-known cloud service on which users are able to use a word processing service. *Google Docs* also enables users to collaboratively edit their documents in the cloud. During the working process, they can utilize a "Track Changes" function to record changes and compare the differences between different versions. Therefore, *Google Docs* can be applied to assist students to work collaboratively in the same group project in the English Tourism class, as shown in Fig. 1.

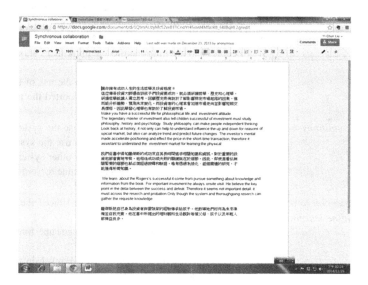

Fig. 1. Google documents

3.4   Measurement Tool

The measurement tool is a questionnaire used to measure users' perceptions of utilizing technology systems and their usage behaviors. The questionnaire is modified from the Unified Theory of Acceptance and Use of Technology (UTAUT) proposed by [5]. The UTAUT consists of four subscales: performance expectancy, effort expectancy, social influence, and the facilitation of conditions. Users' perceptions of using technology systems and their usage behaviors are affected by these four main variables. For this study, the researcher has modified and deleted some items; the modified UTAUT has 25 items as shown in Table 1 [5]. These four variables are intended to understand learners' perceptions of intentions to use the VoiceTube online learning community.

Table 1. Questionnaire items used in this study [5]

Constructs	Questionnaire items
Performance expectancy	PE 1. I would find the system useful in my English learning PE 2. Using the system enables me to accomplish tasks more quickly PE 3. Using the system increases my productivity PE 4. If I use the system, I will increase my learning chances
Effort expectancy	EE 1. My interaction with the system would be clear and understandable EE 2. It would be easy for me to become skillful at using the system EE 3. I would find the system easy to use EE 4. Learning to operate the system is easy for me
Social influence	SI 1. People who influence my behavior think that I should use the system SI 2. People who are important to me think that I should use the system SI 3. The VoiceTube has been helpful in the use of the system SI 4. In general, the organization has supported the use of the system
Facilitating conditions	FC 1. I have the resources necessary to use the system FC 2. I have the knowledge necessary to use the system FC 3. The system is not compatible with other systems I use FC 4. A specific person (or group) is available for assistance with system difficulties
Behavioral intention to use VoiceTube online learning community	BI 1. Given the opportunity, I would use VoiceTube for learning English BI 2: I will recommend others to use VoiceTube for learning English BI 3: I intend to use VoiceTube to learn English in the future BI 4. I will reuse this system for relevant English learning activities BI 5. I will use the e-learning system on a regular basis in the future

3.5   Procedures

The collected data in the project includes the pre- and post-tests, the students' three-round group project editing via Microsoft Office Word document and *Google Docs* to track their learning progress, and the questionnaires. At the beginning of the learning activity, the students took the pre-test. The purpose of the pre-test is to evaluate students' English language proficiency and to examine whether the two classes have similar English proficiency level. After the pre-test, the two classes of students went through learning activities approximately a total of 60 min each time, where they conducted project-based learning activity in English for Tourism class. Each week, students were also asked to do the assigned homework before coming to class, that is, to watch video clips from VoiceTube website with English subtitles and then click one of the channels to answer questions.

During the learning activity, the students of two classes were grouped randomly consisting of 3–4 people in a group. In the control group, each group member used the desktop computer to work on the group project via Microsoft Office Word, in other words, they were not able to edit the project synchronously. However, at least e-learning platform has the function of discussion forum that they can chat online. After they have worked for 1 h, they have to submit the file via e-learning, in which the online system is offered by university for all classes on campus. On the other hand, in the experimental group, every student of each group has a desktop computer to use *Google Docs* so that they can synchronously revise the group project. Both groups have at least three rounds of editing. At the end of the semester, students were expected to present their product-brochure by using Microsoft Publisher. They could share the works via Facebook so that they could receive feedbacks from more audiences. Once the whole presentation is completed, the students took the post-test to track their learning outcomes and fill out the UTAUT questionnaire to find out their intentions.

4   Difficulties

The difficulties are the instructor may not be unfamiliar with *Google Documents* and VoiceTube, let alone the participants. Thus, instructors are trained before the experiment takes place. Also, students whose English proficiency level is low may not be willing to work together and affect other peers' working process and progress since the project-based learning activity may be time-consuming for them to complete the group project. The solution will be the promotion from the instructor and the department. The instructor will encourage and explain to those students that it is a meaningful project. If they perform well, they will receive extra credits.

5   Conclusion

The study contributes to students who acquire specific knowledge and expressions in the related fields of tourism and hospitality. Students learn how to use English to introduce Taiwan and talk about the local culture, festivals, and food in simple English as a travel guide or a local host. Oversea traveling related practices facilitate real communication opportunities abroad. Through the project-based learning and conversation practicing, this project enhances students' abilities in oral English to introduce Taiwan to foreigners or for individual's traveling to a foreign country. (1) The results could contribute to the teaching of English literature studies. (2) The research outcome could be applied to ESP (English for Specific Purposes) courses. (3) New teaching approaches could be derived from the data analysis.

References

1. Chang, M.-M., Lin, M.-C.: Strategy-oriented web-based English instruction-a meta-analysis. Australas. J. Educ. Technol. **29**(2), 203–216 (2013)
2. Chapelle, C.A.: Multimedia CALL: lessons to be learned from research on instructed SLA. Lang. Learn. Technol. **2**(1), 22–34 (1998)
3. Lin, H.: Establishing an empirical link between computer-mediated communication and SLA: a meta-analysis. Lang. Learn. Technol. **18**(3), 120–147 (2014)
4. Stockwell, G.: A review of technology choice for teaching language skills in the CALL literature. ReCALL **18**(2), 105–120 (2007)
5. Venkatesh, V., Morris, M.G., Davis, B., Davis, F.D.: User acceptance of information technology: toward a unified view. MIS Q. **27**(3), 425–478 (2003)
6. Yang, Y.-F.: Developing a reciprocal teaching/learning system for college remedial reading instruction. Comput. Educ. **55**, 1193–1201 (2010)
7. Yang, Y.-F.: A reciprocal peer review system to support college students' writing. Br. J. Educ. Technol. **42**(4), 687–700 (2011)
8. Zhao, Y.: Recent developments in technology and language learning: a literature review and meta analysis. CALICO J. **21**(1), 7–27 (2003)

The Jacobian Matrix-Based Learning Machine in Student

Yi-Zeng Hsieh[1(✉)], Mu-Chun Su[2], and Yu-Lin Jeng[3]

[1] Department of Electrical Engineering, National Taiwan Ocean University,
Keelung, Taiwan
yzhsieh@mail.ntou.edu.tw
[2] Department of Computer Science and Information Engineering,
National Central University, Taoyuan, Taiwan
[3] Department of Information Management,
Southern Taiwan University of Science and Technology, Tainan, Taiwan

Abstract. The student learning performance is analyzed that we adopted the proposed Jacobian Matrix-based Learning Machine (JMLM). It is significant for establishing prediction machine learning model for student learning performance and these tool can help teacher to analyze the student data not difficult to analyze. Correct rate of our model is 87% and 86% better than traditional machine learning models.

Keywords: Machine learning · Student performance · Parameter based methods · Structure based methods

1 Introduction

In adaptation stage is education and learning is more and more growing into opening approachable to one and all (by on-line courses, google, etc.) and learning is improved by many givers instead of only one editor [1, 2]. Then, fresh technology permitted of individual learning qualifying pupils to study more effectively and letting advisors to help each student personally if wanted, although the group is extensive [3].

There are many machine learning methods for predication such as multi-layer perceptron, radial basis function, support vector machine etc., To depend on association with these prediction methods, we can analyze the major reward from the raw data. Now, the fitness of students can be predicted in many campus and machine learning is more significant for supporting teachers on class. Through the machine learning tools many students will help for learning course before entering the campus, and it is also helpful of predicting their career in the future. Today, advisors can support the students in many ways and advance student's ability. It is significant for establishing prediction machine learning model for student learning performance and these tool can help teacher to analyze the student data not difficult to analyze. For example, the professional special education teacher can execute more remedial grades for powerless students.

In many computer-based systems, prediction methods such as function approximation or pattern recognition issues generally put on an important stage. One of the

© Springer International Publishing AG 2017
T.-C. Huang et al. (Eds.): SETE 2017, LNCS 10676, pp. 469–474, 2017.
https://doi.org/10.1007/978-3-319-71084-6_55

promising approaches to solving these kinds of problems is the use of neural networks or learning machines. The major objective of machine learning methods is to build an input-output transforming from a set of knowledge data. The accomplishment of a machine learning methods very trusts to if transforming from a set of knowledge data is success or not. There are two functions of learning problem included of using machine learning methods to figure out a different of problems: (1) the parameter based methods and (2) the structure based methods [4]. While the parameter based methods include the renewing neural network of the connecting weights, the structure learning focuses on the decision of the network structure like layers' numbers and the neural nodes of each layer. These two types of learning issues can be either explained together or respectively. Each type of methods has its own engaging characteristic and constraints. In this paper is organized that the Sect. 2 is related work, and Sect. 3 introduces our proposed Jacobian Matrix-based Learning Machine (JMLM). Section 4 is experiments result, and finally the conclusion is described.

2 Related Work

Many researches have explored the worth of normal experiments [5–7] professional tests [8] and GPA in many schedules [6] in presaging the scientific attainment of students in campus. They accept a definite reference among these accomplishment grades like GPA. In addition, normal experiments, the connection of other parameters for predicting learners' GPA have been explored, usually bringing on the completion that GPA from previous instruction and measures in some topics. [9] have a powerful definite reference machine learning methods has its spacious studies in the range of many domains. In field of education it has great quantity of studies been surveyed. This great expansion is from the magnificent accession to profession of students and better their results as the symbol of many researchers perform in this domain to search living platform and better result. Not many connected performance are scheduling to be improved reason of occurring in the further expansion. Stamos and Andreas [10] offer their platform that it is more confronting and more correct prediction than other platforms. The analysis for the result that a few data was measured for each learner, and then that was the first time trying to put on the new ideas such as meaningful discussion of the machine learning methods for recognizing the parameters that effect learning results. The student learning performance is analyzed that we adopted the proposed Jacobian Matrix-based Learning Machine (JMLM) [11] is to incrementally search for a set of appropriate sampling points in such a way that their function values are known and corresponding first-order derivatives are computed. The student data is as points, and we find the corresponding first-order derivatives. Then the input-output transforming function value at any position can be approached by the first-order Taylor series expansion at the sampling point and it is the nearest sampling point to that specific position. The execution of the proposed JMLM fully relies on the choosing of the sampling points and the effective measurements of the Jacobian matrices at the choosing sampling points.

3   A Jacobian Matrix-Based Learning Machine

The linear Taylor system can be functioned to vector-valued function cases such as:

$$F(x) \cong F(p) + J(p)(x - p) \tag{1}$$

The function value of a data point **x** is found **such as** (1) can be approached by the linear Taylor expansion at one data position **p** which is very near the data position **x**.

Hence, if we can store up some sampling data in a kind of way. That their correlating function values and Jacobian matrices are known then the input-output mapping function weight at any position in the data domain can be approached by the linear Taylor system at the specific sampling data which is the closet sampling data to that testing data position.

On the basis of the steepest decent algorithm, we have the following updating function for **J**:

$$J(\text{new}) = J(\text{old}) - \eta \frac{\partial E}{\partial J} = J(\text{old}) - \eta(\Delta F - J(\text{old})\Delta p)(\Delta p)^{T} \tag{2}$$

$$\Delta F = J(p)\Delta p = \begin{bmatrix} J_{11} & \cdots & J_{1n} \\ \vdots & \ddots & \vdots \\ J_{m1} & \cdots & J_{mn} \end{bmatrix} \Delta p \tag{3}$$

where

$$\Delta p = \begin{bmatrix} x_1 - p_1 \\ \vdots \\ x_n - p_n \end{bmatrix}$$

The measurement of the approaching via the linear Taylor system relies on the values of the Jacobian matrices and the choosing of the sampling data. We also adopt the LMS methods like Eq. (8) to calculate the homologous Jacobian system.

4   Experiments

Our student data, there are the secondary education containing for 3 years, and also preliminary basic education for 9 years after following higher education in Portugal. There are many learners connecting the public and free learning organization. Several courses such as Sciences and Technologies, Visual Arts distribute major topics like the Language and Mathematics. It is similar with other countries such as France or Venezuela, defining a 20-point grading scale, and 0 is the minimum grade and 20 is the better score. Hence, among the school year, students are estimated among three parts like G3 of Table 1.

Table 1. The parameter of student data set

1	School	Student's school	16	Schools up	Extra educational support
2	Sex	Student's sex	17	Famsup	Family educational support
3	Age	Student's age	18	Paid	Extra paid classes within the course subject (Math or Portuguese)
4	Address	Student's home address type	19	Activities	Extra curricular activities
5	Famsize	Family size	20	Nursery	Attended nursery school
6	Pstatus	Parent's cohabitation status	21	Higher	Wants to take higher education
7	Medu	Mother's education	22	Internet	Internet access at home
8	Fedu	Father's education	23	Romantic	With a romantic relationship
9	Mjob	Mother's job	24	Famrel	Quality of family relationships
10	Fjob	Father's job	25	Free time	Free time after school
11	Reason	Reason to choose this school	26	Go out	Going out with friends
12	Guardian	Student's guardian	27	Dalc	Workday alcohol consumption
13	Travel time	Home to school travel time	28	Walc	Weekend alcohol consumption
14	Study time	Weekly study time	29	Health	Current health status
15	Failures	Number of past class failures	30	Absences	Number of school absences
31	G3	Final grade (pass if G3 > 5, else fail;)			

We also test our performance with the multi-layer perceptron, radial basis function. The MLP is with one hidden layer and hidden neurons number is 10 and the RBF is with 10 hidden neurons. Our method has 2 neurons. The iteration are all 100, and learning rate is all 0.1. Then, all models use 10 folders and 50% data number is for training and 50% is for testing. The performance result show as Table 2.

The information (e.g., the Jacobian matrix and the coordinates of the sampling data) about the two generated sampling scores is as follows:

$$\text{If } \mathbf{x} \text{ is close to} \begin{pmatrix} 1.00, 0.48, 15.69, 0.85, \\ 0.74, 0.90, 2.89, 2.68, \\ 2.47, 2.80, 1.27, 0.32, \\ 1.44, 2.00, 0.38, 0.22, \\ 0.68, 0.40, 0.55, 0.83, \\ 0.94, 0.83, 0.27, 4.01, \\ 3.27, 3.09, 1.36, 2.04, \\ 3.73, 2.10 \end{pmatrix}^T$$

Table 2. Performance result

Machine learning model	Our model	MLP	RBF
Training correct rate	$87.85 \pm 1.25\%$	$75.81 \pm 3.5\%$	$74.47 \pm 2.73\%$
Testing correct rate	$86.38 \pm 0.79\%$	$73.97 \pm 2.6\%$	$74.67 \pm 1.58\%$

$$\begin{aligned}
\textbf{\textit{Then }} F_1(x) = & \ 0.00000000 * (X_1 - 1.00) + 0.01892120 \\
& * (X_2 - 0.48) + 0.00632927 * (X_3 - 15.69) \\
& + 0.02320544 * (X_4 - 0.85) - 0.03920942 \\
& * (X_5 - 0.74) - 0.04515686 * (X_6 - 0.90) \\
& + 0.04619556 * (X_7 - 2.89) - 0.06162033 \\
& * (X_8 - 2.68) + 0.01559720 * (X_9 - 2.47) \\
& - 0.02117583 * (X_{10} - 2.80) + 0.00284465 \\
& * (X_{11} - 1.27) + 0.04505280 * (X_{12} - 0.32) \\
& - 0.03234805 * (X_{13} - 1.44) + 0.02749322 \\
& * (X_{14} - 2.00) - 0.12927421 * (X_{15} - 0.38) \\
& + 0.08564614 * (X_{16} - 0.22) - 0.05544262 \\
& * (X_{17} - 0.68) + 0.16518648 * (X_{18} - 0.40) \\
& + 0.03887072 * (X_{19} - 0.55) + 0.00266129 \\
& * (X_{20} - 0.83) - 0.01833940 * (X_{21} - 0.94) \\
& - 0.06005664 * (X_{22} - 0.83) - 0.09066509 \\
& * (X_{23} - 0.27) + 0.04829510 * (X_{24} - 4.01) \\
& + 0.07166188 * (X_{25} - 3.27) - 0.07362436 \\
& * (X_{26} - 3.09) - 0.06631100 * (X_{27} - 1.36) \\
& + 0.05741631 * (X_{28} - 2.04) - 0.02045861 \\
& * (X_{29} - 3.73) + 0.05012248 * (X_{30} - 2.10)
\end{aligned} \tag{4}$$

5   Conclusion

This paper introduces our proposed JMLM machine learning method to predict elementary student grades with two major courses (Mathematics and Portuguese) and use the following parameters like past school grades (first and second grades), demographic, social and other school related data. The, a well-training JMLM play a role as a real number transformed in the interpreting way.

Acknowledgement. This paper was partly supported by the Ministry of Science and Technology, Taiwan, R.O.C, under 106-2511-S-019-003-, and 105-2218-E-008-014-.

References

1. Baraniuk, R.: Open education: new opportunities for signal processing. In: Plenary Speech, 2015 IEEE International Conference on Acoustics, Speech and Signal Processing (ICASSP) (2015)
2. Meier, Y., Xu, J., Atan, O., Der Schaar, M.V.: Predicting Grades. IEEE Trans. Sig. Process. **64**(14), 959–972 (2016)
3. Openstax college. http://openstaxcollege.org/. Accessed 7 May 2015
4. Lin, C.-T., Lee, C.S.G.: Neural Fuzzy Systems: A Neuro-fuzzy Synergism to Intelligent Systems. Prentice-Hall International Inc., Upper Saddle River (1996)
5. Kuncel, N.R., Hezlett, S.A.: Standardized tests predict graduate students success. Science **315**, 1080–1081 (2007)
6. Cohn, E., Cohn, S., Balch, D.C., Bradley, J.: Determinants of undergraduate GPAs: Sat scores, high-school GPA and high-school rank. Econ. Educ. Rev. **23**(6), 577–586 (2004)
7. Julian, E.R.: Validity of the medical college admission test for predicting medical school performance. Acad. Med. **80**(10), 910–917 (2005)
8. Gallagher, P.A., Bomba, C., Crane, L.R.: Using an admissions exam to predict student success in an ADN program. Nurse Educ. **26**(3), 132–135 (2001)
9. Gorr, W.L., Nagin, D., Szczypula, J.: Comparative study of artificial neural network and statistical models for predicting student grade point averages. Int. J. Forecast. **10**(1), 17–34 (1994)
10. Karamouzis, S.T., Vrettos, A.: Sensitivity analysis of neural network parameters for identifying the factors for college student success. In: World Congress on Computer Science and Information Engineering, pp. 671–675 (2009)
11. Su, M.C., Hsieh, Y.Z., Wang, C.H., Wang, P.C.: A jacobian matrix-based learning machine and its applications in medical diagnosis. IEEE Access **5**, 1 (2017)

UMLL (International Symposium on User Modeling and Language Learning)

Lexical Bundle Investigation for Automated Scoring of Business English Writing

Shili Ge[1,2], Xue Yu[1], and Xiaoxiao Chen[1(✉)]

[1] School of English for International Business,
Guangdong University of Foreign Studies, Guangzhou 510420, China
geshili@gdufs.edu.cn, {yuxue020,gracekot}@qq.com
[2] Guangdong Collaborative Innovation Center for Language Research
and Service, Guangdong University of Foreign Studies,
Guangzhou 510420, China

Abstract. Business English (BE) writing teaching and assessment are important in college level English teaching. Automated essay scoring (AES) is already widely accepted in English writing evaluation and should be applied in business English teaching. One of the key steps of AES is the selection of scoring features. In order to explore the effect of lexical bundles applied in AES research, the relationship between lexical bundle amount and business English writing quality is investigated. Two business English corpora were constructed: BE writing textbook corpus and college students' composition corpus. Target lexical bundles were extracted from the textbook corpus. The correlation coefficients between writing scores and target lexical bundles from students' writing were calculated. The results show that the amount of three-word bundles and the number of total bundles have a moderate correlation with writing scores, which means these two features should be covered in AES study of BE writing.

Keywords: Business English writing · Lexical bundles · Automated essay scoring · Feature selection

1 Introduction

Business English (BE) education aims at meeting the requirements of occupational life which includes various aspects of business activities. BE is the application of English language in business world. It is a combination of business knowledge and English language. It is also an important subfield of English education in China with the large-scale development of higher education. By the end of 2016, there are already 323 colleges or universities recruiting students of BE major. A vast amount of BE professionals are trained every year. However, similar to English major education, writing, or more specifically, BE writing teaching is a hard nut to crack. Along with the fast development of AI research, the study of automated essay scoring (AES) has made significant progress and many systems have been adopted in practical applications including some large-scale language tests such as GMAT and TOEFL [1].

The teaching of BE writing should take advantage of the technology, too. One of the important steps in AES study is scoring feature selection [2]. This research explores the

© Springer International Publishing AG 2017
T.-C. Huang et al. (Eds.): SETE 2017, LNCS 10676, pp. 477–484, 2017.
https://doi.org/10.1007/978-3-319-71084-6_56

possibility of involving lexical bundles as one feature in scoring, by investigating the correlational relationship between the usage of lexical bundles and BE writing quality.

2 Related Works

2.1 Business English Writing and Assessment

Business English writing, an important course for Business English majors in colleges and universities, has drawn much attention from teachers and researchers. It is already listed as one of the top 10 hot topics in Business English studies in China as indicated by Wang and Li [3]. These studies mainly lie in three fields. The first is the pedagogical practice of writing teaching; the second is the study of status quo and development of textbooks and teaching materials; and the last field is discussion on the education and advancement of Business writing ability [4].

Though business English writing is considered important, there is almost no specific study on its assessment. Yan defines the three writing skills required in Test for Business English Majors (Band 8) and describes the detailed scoring procedures [5]. Ge et al. study the relationship between business terms in writing and the writing quality [2]. They find that the numbers of certain types of terms used in business writing are significantly correlated with writing scores, which means that term using, at least some types of terms, can be an effective feature in determining writing quality, especially in the automated scoring of business writing.

2.2 Automated Essay Scoring and Feature Selection

Automated essay scoring (AES) has been a promising area of study for more than half a century since the development of PEG [6, 7, 8]. And since then, many AES systems have been studied or developed, such as IEA, E-Rater and BETSY [9]. The common procedures are summarized by Ge et al. [2] as following:

(1) Collect a set of essays and obtain their scores by human raters.
(2) Divide the scored essay set into a training set and a testing set, and construct a scoring model by fitting the values of textual features from the training set with the scores of essays.
(3) Test the scoring model on the testing set essays and apply it when it meets the requirement of scoring.

In the model construction process, textual feature selection is a fundamental stage as many researchers indicated [1, 10], especially for providing feedback of writing.

Most AES systems or studies adopt lexical features according to Valenti et al. [9]. The earliest system, PEG, takes essay length, i.e., total word number of an essay, number of different types of words, such as prepositions, relative pronouns and other parts of speech, as the main features [6]. The IEA system adopts knowledge content, instead. That means all the words in an essay are considered as its feature set [11]. E-rater V.2 adopts two key lexical features: lexical complexity and prompt-specific vocabulary usage [1].

Ge combines lexical and phrasal features in AES of college students' writing and achieves a higher total scoring accuracy [12]. In fact, phrase is one type of lexical feature, too. Another lexical feature studied in business English AES is terminological feature by Ge et al. [2]. The result shows that certain types of terms have a moderate correlation with writing scores. Terminological features, covered in business AES feature set, can improve the performance of AES systems and facilitate BE learners' writing proficiency. Terms may contain one or more words, and phrasal terms may have at least two words. Another similar lexical feature is lexical bundle, which is well studied in corpus linguistics but not noticed by AES researchers, yet.

2.3   Lexical Bundles

More and more corpus-based studies show that "much of our everyday language use is composed of prefabricated expressions" [13]. The so called "every language use" exists not only in spoken language, but also academic writing, such as writing by university students as studied in [13–16] etc. "Multi-word sequences have been studied under many rubrics, including 'lexical phrases', 'formulas', 'routines', 'fixed expressions', prefabricated patterns' (or 'prefabs'), and 'lexical bundles'" [13].

Sinclair points out that words do not occur at random in a text, "The choice of one word affects the choice of others in its vicinity" [17]. In other words, "the language user has available to him a large number of preconstructed or semi-preconstructed phrases that constitute single choices, even though they appear to be analyzable into segments" [18]. Though there are still disagreements in theoretical definition, identification and classification of this linguistic unit, researchers believe that "flexible use of typical conventionalized lexical sequences to achieve communicative purpose is an important component of native speakers' language ability" [19]. An investigation of lexical bundles in Chinese English learners also indicates that learner's writing of different proficiency shows different features in term of lexical bundle usage [20]. Therefore, it is worthwhile to investigate lexical bundle usage in relation to business English writing quality in AES.

3   Data and Methodology

3.1   Corpus Data

Data for the study consist of two corpora of written texts. One comprises written samples from three business English writing textbooks (Table 1) and the other comprises university students' business English writing compositions.

The construction of the composition corpus was based on a writing task from the second part of writing module in authentic Business English Certificate (BEC) Higher examination. Business English majors were invited to join the writing practice. 80 compositions were collected and scored according to the scheme of BEC higher writing test, assessed within the range of 0 to 10. The detail of the corpus can be seen in Table 2.

Table 1. Information of the textbook corpus.

Title	Number of samples	Tokens
Business English writing	59	12157
Practical business English writing	52	11320
Up-to-date business correspondence for import & export	92	15010
Total	203	38420

Table 2. Information of the composition corpus.

Score	No. of comp.	No. of tokens	Ave. comp. len.
3	2	429	214.5
4	2	494	247
5	7	1647	235.29
6	31	7765	250.48
7	27	6888	255.11
8	11	3038	276.18
Total	80	20261	253.26

3.2   Identification and Extraction of Target Bundles

As teaching outcomes, lexical bundles contained in writing samples of textbooks should be acquired and used in students' writing. Therefore, they are defined as the target bundles investigated in this study. A computer program was coded with Python 3.6 in the identification and extraction of lexical bundles in the textbook corpus. The target bundles, including three- and four-word combinations, investigated in the research are defined as those which occur four times or more in at least three writing samples in the textbook corpus. The criteria are quite conservative just like [20] due to the exploratory effort and small corpus sizes.

The bundle extraction algorithm is as following:

```
Read in all writing samples from textbook corpus
for each sample in the corpus:
   for each sentence in a sample:
      for each punctuation separated clause:
         Count all three- and four-word lexical bundles
      Add 1 to the sample amount of the bundles
Output the results of bundles and sample amounts of the
bundles
```

There are 212 types of 4-word bundles and 650 types of 3-word bundles in the output. The top 10 recurrent strings are presented in Table 3.

It is obvious that some three-word bundles are part of four-word ones, such as many examples of "thank you for" are from "thank you for your" and all "you for your" are the latter part of "thank you for your". Yet, three-word strings still need to be extracted

Table 3. Top 10 bundles in textbook corpus.

4-word bundles	Freq.	3-word bundles	Freq.
Thank you for your	37	Thank you for	47
We look forward to	21	Travel and entertainment	44
We thank you for	18	Look forward to	41
Shall be borne by	14	You for your	37
The total contract price	14	Terms and conditions	26
As soon as possible	12	Letter of credit	25
Look forward to hearing	12	Of the goods	24
To hearing from you	12	We look forward	22
The terms and conditions	12	We thank you	21
Arrival of the goods	12	The other party	20

because many of them are independent from longer structures and have their own functions, such as "letter of credit" and "the other party".

4 Analysis of Bundles in Students' Writing

Another Python 3.6 program was coded to identify and extract all three- and four-word target bundles from 80 students' business English writing compositions. There are 284 three-word bundles and 34 four-word ones, with the total number of 318 bundles. Top 10 target bundles in students' writing are presented in Table 4.

Table 4. Top 10 target bundles in composition corpus.

4-word bundles	Freq.	3-word bundles	Freq.
As soon as possible	4	Would like to	23
Forward to hearing from	4	To apply for	18
To hearing from you	4	One of the	15
We would like to	3	To be a	11
To inform you that	3	As well as	10
Hearing from you soon	3	To deal with	8
Look forward to your	2	Am writing to	8
Look forward to hearing	2	Forward to your	8
Hope that you will	1	In the future	8
With a view to	1	In the world	7

Comparing target bundles from textbook corpus and composition corpus, it is clear that among top 10 four-word bundles from students' writing, three appear in the top 10 bundles from textbook corpus and four in top 20. This indicates that students are adept at using high-frequency four-word bundles. Yet, the small total number of four-word bundles in composition corpus indicates that only a few students, maybe a few high proficient ones, can take advantage of the long lexical device in writing. However, among top 10 three-word target bundles, only two appear in the top 20 from textbook corpus and others are all low-frequency ones. The large amount of three-word target bundles in students' writing means that most English learners, though relatively high proficient in English, cannot master the most frequent used three-word strings.

In order to verify the effect of these features applied in AES of business writing, the correlation coefficients are calculated between composition scores and amounts of target bundles in students' writing as listed in Table 5.

Table 5. Correlations between bundle numbers and BE writing scores (n = 80).

	3-word bundles	4-word bundles	Total bundles
Pearson correlations	0.48	0.41	0.52
P	0.00	0.00	0.00

Table 5 shows that the numbers of three-word, four-word and total bundles have a moderate correlation with scores while the total amount of bundles has a higher correlation coefficient. The number of four-word bundles has a relatively lower correlation coefficient with writing scores, which is not expected because the high-frequency four-word target bundles are used in students' writing as mentioned above. These bundles should be the indication of high proficiency of writing. Yet, further analysis shows that only a small portion of compositions adopt this type of lexical device, which leads to a low calculated correlational value. To make the best of this device, we may need larger textbook and composition corpora.

The number of three-word bundles and especially the number of total bundles have relatively high coefficients with writing scores, which are even higher than the relationship between total term amount and writing score of 0.42 [2].

This result shows that there is a possibility that the numbers of three-word target bundles and total bundles can have a relatively high correlational relationship with writing scores or quality, which means they can be tested or even applied in AES process.

5 Conclusion and Limitation

This research shows only a moderate correlation between composition scores and the number of bundles. However, lexical bundles, especially three-word bundles and the total number of three- and four-word bundles, should be covered in the AES feature set for automatic evaluation of BE writing. From the correlational study, it is obvious that some types of lexical bundle using, as an automated scoring feature, can definitely reflect BE writers' confidence and proficiency. At the same time, the involvement of bundle features will provide specific feedback so as to improve Chinese college EFL learners' writing accuracy, and finally improve their writing skills and communicative ability in business context.

The tentative exploration of lexical bundles in BE writing and its relationship with writing quality arrives at a positive conclusion, but there is still more work to do. First, the result needs to be tested on larger BE textbook and composition corpora with more business writings in different genres, which may lead to insight into the effect of four-word bundles in research. Moreover, lexical bundles should be further analyzed and divided into different functional groups as studied in [21, 22] and structural groups as in [14]. The relationship between lexical bundles of different groups and writing quality is worth further probing, for instance, terminological study of different categories in the AES study of business writing [2].

Acknowledgements. This work is financially supported by the National Social Science Fund (No. 13BYY097).

References

1. Attali, Y., Burstein, J.: Automated essay scoring with e-rater® V.2. J. Technol. Learn. Assess. **4**(3), 1–30 (2006)
2. Ge, S., Zhang, J., Chen, X.: Corpus-based correlational study of terms and quality in business english writing. In: Wu, T.-T., Gennari, R., Huang, Y.-M., Xie, H., Cao, Y. (eds.) SETE 2016. LNCS, vol. 10108, pp. 349–358. Springer, Cham (2017). http://doi.org/10.1007/978-3-319-52836-6_37
3. Wang, L., Li, L.: The developments of business english research in China from 2002 to 2011. Foreign Lang. World **4**, 2–10 (2013)
4. Chen, X., Ge, S.: An exploration of procedural business english writing ability from the perspective of business communication. Foreign Lang. Res. **2**, 58–62 (2016)
5. Yan, M.: Business english competence: construct definition and test development. Contemp. Foreign Lang. Stud. **2**, 23–28 (2012)
6. Page, E.B.: Project essay grade: PEG. In: Shermis, M.D., Burstein, J. (eds.) Automated Essay Scoring: A Cross-Disciplinary Perspective, pp. 43–54. Lawrence Erlbaum Associates, Mahwah (2003)
7. Shermis, M.D., Burstein, J., Leacock, C.: Applications of computers in assessment and analysis of writing. In: MacArthur, C.A., Graham, S., Fitzgerald, J. (eds.) Handbook of Writing Research, p. 403. Guilford Press, New York (2005)
8. Dikli, S.: Automated essay scoring. Turk. Online J. Distance Educ. **7**(1), 49–62 (2006)
9. Valenti, S., Neri, F., Cucchiarelli, A.: An overview of current research on automated essay grading. J. Inf. Technol. Educ. **2**, 319–330 (2003)
10. Huang, Z., Xie, J., Xun, E.: Study of feature selection in HSK automated essay scoring. Comput. Eng. Appl. **50**, 118–122 (2014)
11. Landauer, T.K., Laham, D., Foltz, P.W.: Automated scoring and annotation of essays with the intelligent essay assessor. In: Shermis, M.D., Burstein, J.C. (eds.) Automated Essay Scoring: A Cross-Disciplinary Perspective, pp. 87–112. Lawrence Erlbaum Associates, Inc., Publishers, New Jersey (2003)
12. Ge, S.: Automatic scoring of english writing based on joint of lexical and phrasal features. In: Yang, Y., Ma, M., Liu, B. (eds.) ICICA 2013. CCIS, vol. 391, pp. 182–192. Springer, Heidelberg (2013). http://doi.org/10.1007/978-3-642-53932-9_18
13. Biber, D., Conrad, S., Cortes, V.: If you look at…: lexical bundles in university teaching and textbooks. Appl. Linguist. **25**(3), 371–405 (2004)

14. Cortes, V.: Lexical bundles in published and student disciplinary writing: examples from history and biology. Engl. Specif. Purp. **23**, 397–423 (2004)
15. Salazar, D.: Lexical Bundles in Native and Non-native Scientific Writing. John Benjamins Publishing Company, Amsterdam/Philadelphia (2014)
16. Durrant, P.: Lexical bundles and disciplinary variation in university students' writing: mapping the territories. Appl. Linguist. **38**(2), 165–193 (2017)
17. Sinclair, J.: Corpus, Concordance, Collocation. Oxford University Press, Oxford (1991)
18. Partington, A.: Patterns and Meanings: Using Corpora for English Language Research and Teaching. John Benjamins, Amsterdam (1998)
19. Sun, F.: The usage pattern of english lexical bundles in research articles by Chinese scholars. Foreign Lang. Educ. **36**(1), 69–74 (2015)
20. Chen, Y.H., Paul, B.: Investigating criterial discourse features across second language development: lexical bundles in rated learner essays, CEFR B1, B2 and C1. Appl. Linguist. **37**(6), 849–880 (2016)
21. Hyland, K.: As can be seen: lexical bundles and disciplinary variation. Engl. Specif. Purp. **27**, 4–21 (2008)
22. Csomay, E.: Lexical bundles in discourse structure: a corpus-based study of classroom discourse. Appl. Linguist. **34**(3), 369–388 (2013)

Designing Interactive Exercises
for Corpus-Based English Learning
with Hot Potatoes Software

Xiaowen Wang[1] and Tianyong Hao[2(✉)]

[1] School of English and Education, Guangdong University of Foreign Studies,
Guangzhou, China
annie_mogi@qq.com
[2] School of Information Science and Technology,
Guangdong University of Foreign Studies, Guangzhou, China
haoty@126.com

Abstract. Hot Potatoes is a popular software which can be conveniently used to create interactive Web-based educational exercises. Though there have been a number of studies on the use of this software in designing English learning exercises, no one has reported its application in designing corpus-based learning exercises to our knowledge. In the corpus-based English learning project carried out in a university in mainland China, English teachers with limited computer knowledge feel hard to design autonomous learning exercises to encourage students' data-driven learning, so we find it necessary to resort to self-authoring softwares such as the Hot Potatoes. Therefore, in this paper we explore how to design interactive exercises for corpus-based English learning with embedded programmes in Hot Potatoes, namely, JQuiz, JCloze, JMix, JMatch, and the Masher. It is found that this software is very helpful in designing online exercises for students to carry out autonomous English learning based on corpora, but it would be more useful for data-driven learning if it could allow the direct loading of self-built corpora.

Keywords: Hot Potatoes · Corpora · Data-driven learning · English learning

1 Introduction

With the development of computer technology and the internet, foreign language teaching is undergoing a transform from traditional teaching-centred classroom teaching to computer-assisted language teaching (CALT) (Wang and Wu 2010). In the computer-assisted language pedagogy revolution, the use of corpora - large databases of texts collected through random sampling of naturally occurring texts built under certain linguistic principles (Yang 2002:33), has become one of the most significant areas (Wang, Ge and Wang 2013, Wang and Hao 2017). Therefore, the Data-driven learning (DDL) approach put forward by Johns (1988, 1991) - an advanced learning model based on direct application of corpus, has become more and more popular in language teaching, especially English teaching at the university level. The corpus approach to language e-learning is based on the assumption that "the use of authentic

© Springer International Publishing AG 2017
T.-C. Huang et al. (Eds.): SETE 2017, LNCS 10676, pp. 485–494, 2017.
https://doi.org/10.1007/978-3-319-71084-6_57

language together with a concordancer will enable learners to gain insights into the language used in real-life situations" (Li 2015), and it emphasizes on the student-centred inductive learning based on corpus concordancing. In view of this, a project is currently carried out in a university in Mainland China for data-driven English learning in English teaching classrooms and ESP (English for Specific Purposes) practices. As part of its teaching experiments in a course named "Learning English through Movies" (hereinafter named "Movie English" for short) offered to non-English major freshmen and sophomores, teachers want to guide students to do online autonomous data-driven learning. However, due to lack of training on computer programming, English teachers are not familiar with the design of Web-based exercises for such kind of data-driven learning. Under such a condition, we find it necessary to resort to self-authoring softwares such as the Hot Potatoes.

Developed by the research and development team at the Humanities Computing and Media Centre in University of Victoria, Hot Potatoes is a popular software which can be conveniently used by teachers to create interactive Web-based educational exercises that "can be easily accessed by learners at any place through connection with internet with any standard Web browsers" (Sadeghi and Soleimani 2015). Although all of the exercises adopt JavaScript and HTML for their functionality, Hot Potatoes is highly user-friendly in that Web pages can be created automatically based on the input data from teachers so that the teachers do not have to understand JavaScript or HTML. There have been a number of studies on the use of this software in designing English learning exercises; however, no one has reported its application in designing corpus-based learning exercises to our knowledge. Then, could Hot Potatoes be effectively used to design data-driven learning exercises? In this paper we take the initiative to explore this question. We will discuss how to design interactive exercises for corpus-based English learning with the programmes included in this software, namely, JQuiz, JCloze, JMix, JMatch, and the Masher, and we adopt the exercises for the Movie English class for example.

2 Background

Hot Potatoes is a suite of programmes created by Stewart Arneil, Martin Holmes, and Hilary Street, and the commercial aspects are handled by Half-Baked Software Inc. Initially creating for their own need to support language programmes in 1997, the creators' main objective was to "provide interactive self-access materials in support of language courses" (Arneil and Holmes 1999). They released the first version as integrated suite of programmes (version 2.0) in 1998 (Soleimani and Raeesi 2015). It soon became popular and by March 1999, over 3600 people and institutions in 76 countries had registered as its users (Arneil and Holmes 1999). Currently, the Hot Potatoes suite includes six programmes, enabling users to create interactive multiple-choice, short-answer, jumbled-sentence, crossword, matching/ordering and gap-fill exercises for the World Wide Web. They are: JQuiz, JCloze, JCross, JMix, JMatch, and the Masher (Half-Baked Software 2017, Hot Patatoes 2017).

Considering that it is "generally used by ordinary instructors who would not otherwise be able to build interactivity into their sites" (Arneil and Holmes 1999), we especially choose Hot Potatoes among other self-authoring softwares with similar functions as our tool. Of course, other softwares with similar templates may also suit our needs, but comparison of such softwares is not essential in this paper.

Although there have been great number of publications about the use of Hot Potatoes, no one has focused on how it can be used to support corpus-based language teaching to our knowledge. Some scholars review this software (Sadeghi and Soleimani 2015; Solermani and Raeesi 2015; Winke and MacGregor 2001), and comment on its advantages and disadvantages. They all agree that this is an excellent resource for creating on-line, interactive language learning exercises that can be used in or out of the classroom and could be beneficial to language instructors to facilitate online assessment and teaching practices. For one thing, it is easy to use and does not need much technical knowledge on the part of the users. For another, it can create exercises which may be used by students as supplementary classroom work so that students can work on their own pace without much press any time during the day, and students can get quick feedback to every single question. However, scholars also find some limitations. It is limited to only options and applications to produce tests and exercises, and is not meant to teach language directly and interactively (Solermani and Raeesi 2015).

Researchers have applied the software to design various exercises for language classes, including English teaching classes in China. Ward (2004) discusses additional uses of CALL in the endangered language context with modified Hot Potatoes templates. Shawback (2002) outlines a course using films to study language and culture with the help of online interactive exercises designed by Hot Potatoes. In China, Liu (2004); Wang and Wu (2010) introduce how to use this software to create interactive English learning exercises. Zhang, Gao and Song (2010) describe how to use it for listening comprehension, compound dictation and reading comprehension so as to help students adapt to the new 4/6 CET assessment model. However, they focus more on the form-focused tasks, and no one has ever reported application of Hot Potatoes in support of the advanced teaching model of data-driven learning. As Solermani and Raeesi (2015) state, the efficiency and usefulness of it to a great extent depends on the creativity and skills of the teachers who use it to create exercises, so it can only reach all its potential once it is being used innovatively by creative teachers. Therefore, this paper tries to explore the potential of Hot Potatoes by creatively designing interactive exercises for data-driven learning tasks.

3   The Design of Interactive Exercises with Hot Potatoes

As mentioned above, there are 6 programmes in Hot Potatoes: JCross, JQuiz, JCloze, JMix, JMatch, and the Masher. However, as JCross is more suitable for word spelling training, so in the following we focus on the other five programmes which we think are most practical for creating data-driven learning exercises. Below we describe how to use them to design interactive DDL exercises one by one. In Movie English class, the corpora that teachers recommend to students are the online corpus resources by Mark Davies (http://corpus.byu.edu/, 2017) and a self-built corpus of English movie scripts, so we mainly design exercises making use of those corpora.

On the whole, JQuiz, JCloze, JMix, and JMatch all provide teachers with basic templates to work out certain types of exercises by simply typing in the content text, setting the answers and feedbacks, saving them and then exporting to create a Web page. Teachers can also add a separate reading text by typing manually or importing from a HTML file. Moreover, graphics, sounds, videos can all be loaded into the exercises. Once a student finishes a question, he can check the answer, and the feedback set by the teacher for that answer turns out automatically. The system gives the student a hint if he clicks the "hint" button, for example, for the next correct letter in a quiz, gap-fill, or jumbled-sentence exercise. The programmes also allow teachers to set time limits for the exercises, so these texts can be set to disappear after a pre-specified amount of time (Winke and MacGregor 2001). All the programmes allow teachers to customize the appearance of output Web pages, such as colour and font of texts, by setting the "configuration output" in the option menu.

Finally, the Masher gathers a number of Hot Potatoes exercises into units. It enables teachers to launch the Hot Potato programmes they need, load the file into it, set the same colours and appearance settings, and compile the Web page. An index page is created for the unit as a whole so that students can get access to the exercises.

3.1   Designing Multiple-choice, True-False, Short-Answer Quizzes with JQuiz

JQuiz is used for creating question-based quizzes of unlimited numbers of questions. After entering the questions and answers, the teacher can choose to make one type of quiz from the four types of options given by the programme: "multiple-choice", "short-answer", "multi-select", and "hybrid". While the multiple-choice question asks students to click the button to choose only one answer, the multi-select question allows the student to select several of a specific set of options. The short-answer question asks students to answer a question by typing text into the answer box. Interestingly, the hybrid question integrates a short-answer question and a multiple-choice question together in one exercise. The exercise is a short-answer question in the beginning, but it turns to be a multiple-choice question if the student cannot correctly answer it after a pre-specified number of tries. Of course, a true or false question can also be made through the template of multiple-choice question if the answers to be chosen are set as T and F.

For example, Fig. 1 shows a hybrid exercise and Fig. 2 is its design interface. At first (on the left in Fig. 1), the students are asked about the country in which the phrase "no offense" is most often used. A link to the website of the corpus of Global Web-based English (GloWbE) (Davies 2017) is given. To answer the question, students need to search for "no offense" and "no offence" in GloWbE (Davies 2017) - a unique online corpus that supports comparisons between different varieties of English. If they carry out corpus-based comparative investigation successfully, they will find that the Americans often use "no offense", but the British people often use "no offence" instead. However, if the student fails to type in the right answer ("America") after three tries, he will find that five options appear (on the right in Fig. 1). In this way, he only needs to choose one among the five options, which lowers the difficulty of the exercise for him. This exercise is designed to guide students to independently use an online

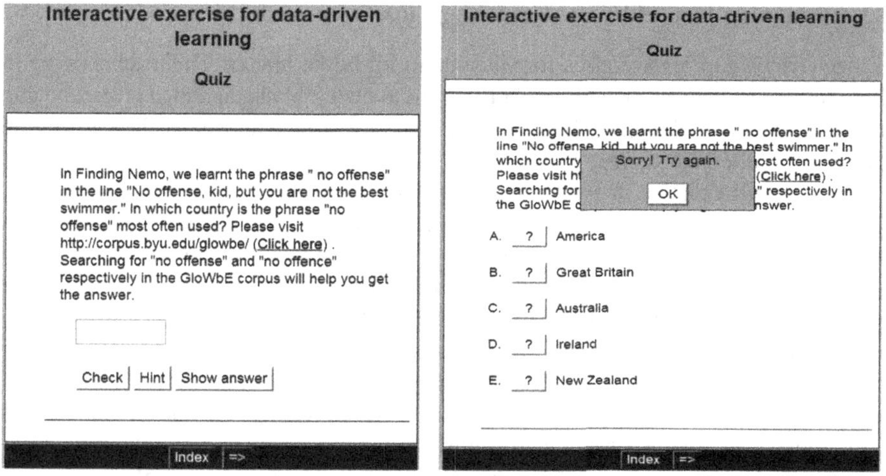

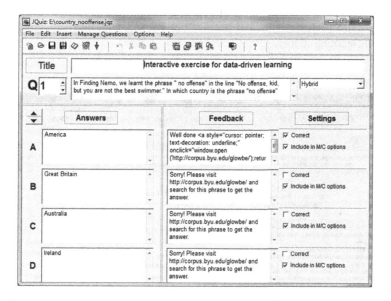

Fig. 1. An example of the short-answer question (left) and multiple-choice question (right) in a hybrid exercise designed with JQuiz

Fig. 2. A screenshot of the user interface of JQuiz in the design of the hybrid exercise

corpus to distinguish the different usages of idiomatic expressions between American and British English. With JQuiz, similar quizzes such as multiple-choice, true-false, short-answer and hybrid quizzes can be made to practise data-driven learning for an idiomatic expression, like the countries or time periods it is often used in, the context it is used in, and the meaning it conveyed.

3.2 Designing Gap-Fill Exercises with JCloze

JCloze creates gap-fill exercises for students to fill in the blanks. The teachers type in passage(s) or ordered sentences, select the word to be left blank, and then create the gap by pressing the "gap" button. For each gap, the programme allows teachers to set the clue and the alternate correct answers.

The gap-fill exercise in Fig. 3 is designed for DDL learning on the sentence patterns concerning "different" or "difference". Normally, when asked how to make a sentence with "different" or "difference" in class, our students could only think of the patterns of "be different from", and "the difference between ..and ...is..", which are commonly adopted in English teaching textbooks. However, they do not know how to make a sentence with "different" or "difference" flexibly with various adverbial or adjective modifiers. Therefore, when designing the exercise (Fig. 4), the teacher presents a text showing the key word in context (KWIC) results of a concordance in the Corpus of Contemporary American English (COCA) (Davies 2017) - the only large and balanced online corpus of American English so far. Then, five English sentences involving "different" or "difference" and the translation of them in Chinese are given, but the modifiers of "different" or "difference" are kept blank. After observing sentences in the text that the teacher made, the students enter answers into the gaps, and then they can check the answers by pressing the "check" button so that the incorrect answers are left in place for them to change. Such kind of exercises enable students to learn from concordance results and practice out immediately, thus strengthening students' DDL learning ability.

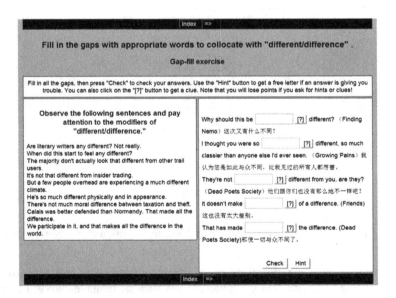

Fig. 3. An example of the gap-fill exercise designed with JCloze

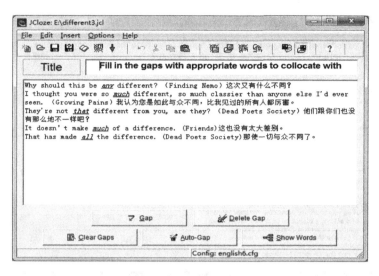

Fig. 4. A screenshot of the user interface of JCloze in the design of the gap-fill exercise

3.3   Designing Jumbled-Sentence Exercises with JMix

JMix, the programme to create jumbled sentence exercises can also be used for DDL practice. The teacher breaks up the sentence by putting each segment on a separate line. There are two output formats: standard, and drag-drop. For the former, students click on the segments (words or letters) sequentially to put the text together; for the latter, they drag and drop the sentence segments to put them in order.

For example, Fig. 5 shows an exercise designed for DDL study on the usages of "chance" in standard format. On the left, the concordance lines for the node word "chance" from a corpus of English movie scripts built by the first author is demonstrated for reference. On the right, the Chinese equivalence to the English sentence "The chances of us getting out of here are a million to one, but there is still a chance" is given, and the students are asked to put the scrambled English words in this sentence into right order. After learning the usages of "chance" from the concordance lines on the left, they may understand that the word "chance" can be followed by "to + verb" or "of + verb + ing" to express the meaning of opportunity or possibility. Based on such understanding, they can try out forming the sentence by clicking the words on the right column one by one in order, and then the words appear in the answer box.

3.4   Designing Matching Exercises with JMatch

JMatch is another useful programme for creating interactive exercises to support DDL learning. It creates matching exercises which allow users to match up items on one side with those on the other side. Figure 6 shows such an exercise designed to learn the collocation of the word "pull". The teacher input the items and insert the pictures, keeping each pair of items on the same line, but the programme shuffles the items on the right when the output Web page is generated. To work out the answer, i.e., "to pull up stakes", "to pull off a major victory", and "to pull down an old house", the students are

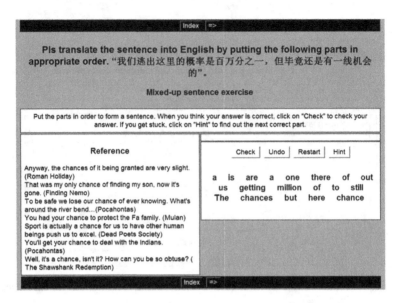

Fig. 5. An example of the jumbled-sentence exercise designed with JMix

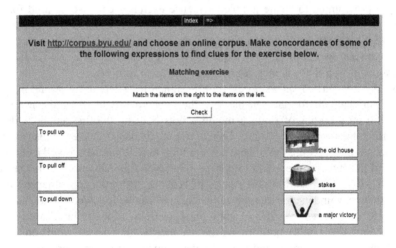

Fig. 6. An example of the matching exercise designed with JMatch

asked to visit an online corpus, input key words, and independently make concordances to test their intuition about the collocation. After getting clues out of DDL learning, they drag the items on the right to match the corresponding items on the left one by one. If they fail to make it correct, a window pops up showing the score as well as the feedback that the teacher has input beforehand - "Sorry! Look up the words in the corpus and try again. Incorrect matches have been removed." And when they successfully complete the exercise, they get the encouraging feedback - "Correct! Well done." In such kind of interactive Web-based DDL practice, students discover patterns of English language through independent inductive learning under the guidance of teachers' instructions, which helps to increase their interest and confidence in English study.

4 Discussion

As shown above, Hot Potatoes can be used to support DDL learning and teaching by creating Web pages for various interactive exercises, and we find students quite interested in doing such exercises in initial teaching experiments. Solermani and Raeesi (2015) comment that this software still has limitations in its degree of interaction, and suggests that it is better to "provide exercises in the form of tasks, in which the negotiation of meaning get the primary focus, then the teachers can provide more pedagogical tasks". In our design, we apply Hot Potatoes in corpus-based learning while relating the exercises with various DDL tasks. Students not only learn the meaning and usages of idiomatic expressions through the exercises, but also improve their ability of independent DDL learning in which they explore patterns of language by themselves with corpora. In this way, we extend the potential of this software in terms of its application field and degree of interaction.

However, in the process of designing exercises, we find it inconvenient in the following aspects:

(1) In most of the templates, the concordance results cannot be listed in the way we like in the Web pages, like allocating sentences centred on node words.
(2) It is hard to mark key words in the concordance lines, which is important for observing the KWIC (key word in context) results in corpus-based learning. The appearance for the text we input are set as a whole, so we cannot set the font of certain words as bold or underlined, nor can we set the colour of picked words.
(3) Most importantly, although links to online corpora can be inserted into the exercises which allows students to open a new window to work on the online corpus, self-built corpora cannot be directly uploaded to the exercise.

Hot Potatoes files that teachers have created can be automatically uploaded to the www.hotpotatoes.net hosting service, be posted to an online teaching module such as a class weblog or course website, or simply be sent to the students. The Web-based exercises can be used as complimentary assignments for students to access outside of the classroom either before or after a lesson, helping students make better preparation for the lesson or reinforce the knowledge they have learnt in class.

5 Summary

Hot Potatoes is a user-friendly software and the templates in most of its programmes are suitable for DDL language training. As no study on the application of this software in data-driven learning has been found in literature, this paper takes the initiative to present how to design corpus-based interactive exercises with five programmes included in Hot Potatoes - JQuiz, JCloze, JMix, JMatch and the Masher. The software indeed helps the teachers in designing Web pages for autonomous DDL learning of

English language. However, there is still space for improvement, and it would be more useful for data-driven learning if it could allow the direct loading of self-built corpora.

Acknowledgements. This paper is supported by the Science and Technology Planning Project of Guangdong Province, China (2016A040403113).

References

Arneil, S., Holmes, M.: Juggling Hot Potatoes: decisions and compromises in creating authoring tools for the Web. ReCALL **11**(2), 12–19 (1999)

Johns, T.: Whence and whither classroom concordancing? In: Bongarerts, T., de Haan, P., Lobbe, S., Wekker, H. (eds.) Computer Applications in Language Learning, pp. 9–35. Foris, Dordrecht (1988)

Johns, T.: Should you be persuaded: two samples of data-driven learning materials. Engl. Lang. Res. J. **4**, 1–16 (1991)

Li, L.: An empirical study of English corpus as a reference tool for PhD students. In: Li, L., Mckeown, J., Liu, L. (eds.) Proceedings of the 9th International Conference of Asian Association of Lexicography, pp. 331–343. Hong Kong (2015)

Liu, M.: Using Hot Potatoes to create interactive English exercises. Comput. Assist. Foreign Lang. Educ. **2**, 73–76 (2004)

Sadeghi, A., Soleimani, H.: A description and evaluation of Hot Potatoes web-authoring software in educational settings. Theory Pract. Lang. Stud. **5**(11), 2407–2415 (2015)

Shawback, M.: Online interactive courseware: using movies to promote cultural understanding in a CALL environment. ReCALL **14**(1), 85–95 (2002)

Soleimani, H., Raeesi, A.: Hot potatoes: the merits and demerits. Theory Pract. Lang. Stud. **5**(6), 1291–1295 (2015)

Ward, M.: The additional uses of CALL in the endangered language context. ReCALL **16**(2), 345–359 (2004)

Wang, X., Ge, S., Wang, Q.: Corpus-based teaching in college "movie English" class in China. In: Lecture Notes in Management Science, vol. 18, pp. 120–125 (2013)

Wang, X., Hao, T.: An empirical study of corpora application in data-driven english lexical learning. In: Wu, T.-T., Gennari, R., Huang, Y.-M., Xie, H., Cao, Y. (eds.) SETE 2016. LNCS, vol. 10108, pp. 370–381. Springer, Cham (2017). https://doi.org/10.1007/978-3-319-52836-6_39

Wang, Q., Wu, Z.: An application of Hot Potatoes in foreign language teaching. Mod. Educ. Technol. **20**(2), 62–64 (2010)

Winke, P., MacGregor, D.: Hot Potatoes, version 5. Lang. Learn. Technol. **5**(2), 28–33 (2001)

Yang, H.: An Introduction to Corpus Linguistics. Shanghai Foreign Language Education Press, Shanghai (2002)

Zhang, K., Gao, Z., Song, H.: Using Hot Potatoes to create questions in English IBT simulation. Softw. Guide (Educ. Technol.) **4**, 94–95 (2010)

Half-Baked Software. http://www.halfbakedsoftware.com/. Accessed 2017

Hot Patatoes. http://hotpot.uvic.ca/. Accessed 2017

Davies, M.: http://corpus.byu.edu/. Accessed 2017

The corpus of Global Web-based English (GloWbE) created by Davies, M.: http://corpus.byu.edu/glowbe/. Accessed 2017

The Corpus of Contemporary American English (COCA) created by Davies, M.: http://corpus.byu.edu/coca/. Accessed 2017

An Explicit Learner Profiling Model for Personalized Word Learning Recommendation

Di Zou[1], Haoran Xie[2(✉)], Tak-Lam Wong[2], Fu Lee Wang[3],
Reggie Kwan[4], and Wai Hong Chan[2]

[1] Department of English Language Education, The Education University of
Hong Kong, Hong Kong, China
[2] Department of Mathematics and Information Technology, The Education
University of Hong Kong, Hong Kong, China
hrxie2@gmail.com
[3] Caritas Institute of Higher Education, Hong Kong, China
[4] Open University of Hong Kong, Hong Kong, China

Abstract. Word knowledge is the foundation of language acquisition for second language learners. Due to the diversity of background knowledge and language proficiency levels of different learners, it is essential to understand and cater for various needs of users in an e-learning system. A personalized learning system which meets this requirement is therefore necessary. Users may also be concerned about the possible risk of revealing their private information and prefer controls on the personalization of a system. To leverage these two factors: personalization and control, we propose an explicit learner profiling model for word learning task recommendation in this paper. This proposed profiling model can be fully accessed and controlled by users. Moreover, the proposed system can recommend learning tasks based on explicit user profiles. The experimental results of a preliminary study further verify the effectiveness of the proposed model.

Keywords: Language acquisition · Word learning · User modeling · Task recommendation

1 Introduction

As widely acknowledged among linguists, word knowledge is the foundation of language acquisition for second language learners [2]. The development of digital devices and information technologies provides language learners with various convenient ways to learn vocabulary, one of which is word learning systems. Due to the diversity of background knowledge and language proficiency levels of different learners, it is essential to understand and cater for various needs of users in an e-learning system. A personalized learning system which meets this requirement is therefore necessary. Many computer-assisted word learning systems [1, 3, 5, 9, 10] have been developed for personalized learning.

T.-C. Huang et al. (Eds.): SETE 2017, LNCS 10676, pp. 495–499, 2017.
https://doi.org/10.1007/978-3-319-71084-6_58

However, an important factor, whether users have control over the personalization [4], is neglected in these personalized learning systems. Users may also be concerned about the possible risk of revealing their private information and prefer controls (e.g., modification or deletion of personal profiles) on the personalization of a system. Therefore, in this article, we suggest that the design of personalized systems should enable users to have controls of the personalization. The contributions of this paper are listed as follows.

- To leverage personalization and control, we propose an explicit learner profiling model, which can be fully accessed and controlled by the users, for word learning task recommendation.
- To recommend learning tasks, a method for task recommendation is developed based on the explicit learner profiling model.
- To verify the effectiveness of the proposed model, a preliminary study on a small scale is conducted.

The remaining sections of this article are structured as follows. In Sect. 2, we introduce both the explicit learner model for the word learning system and the adapted method for word learning task recommendation. The experimental results are reported in Sect. 3. In Sect. 4, we summarize this study and suggest some future research directions.

2 Methodology

One of the important factors which need to be considered while designing word learning systems is the pre-knowledge of a user, as it influences his or her learning effectiveness [6]. The pre-knowledge of a user involves both depth and breadth of his or her vocabulary knowledge. In this paper, we use the number of words a learner knows and the levels of mastery of each word to represent a learner's profile, as follows.

Definition 1. *A **learner profile**, denoted by L_i, is a vector of the value pairs:*

$$L_i = (w_1 : \varepsilon_1^i; w_2 : \varepsilon_2^i; \ldots; w_n : \varepsilon_n^i), \tag{1}$$

where w_a is a target word in the collection of vocabulary a learner knows, n denotes the total number of the vocabulary, ε_a^i represents the degree of mastery level of word w_a by user i, which is in the interval of $[0,1]$, that is, $\forall i, a, \varepsilon_a^i \in [0,1]$. A larger value of ε indicates a higher mastery level of a target word.

To measure the pre-knowledge of a user about the target vocabulary, the explicit method is adopted. To simplify the process, the target words are divided into word sets based on their levels of difficulty, e.g. the frequency of use. As illustrated in Fig. 1, the vocabulary is represented by a nested model. Formally, we define the vocabulary nest as follows.

Definition 2. *Let V be the vocabulary, and a **vocabulary nest** for V, denoted by P, is defined as:*

$$P = \{A_1, A_2, \ldots, A_k, (A_1 \subset A_2 \ldots \subset A_k = V)\}, \tag{2}$$

where k represents the total number of sets in a vocabulary nest; that is, k can be regarded as the number of levels in this vocabulary V semantically.

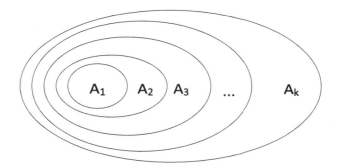

Fig. 1. The nested model for the vocabulary

According to the definition of the **vocabulary nest**, we further define the **word rank** of each word as follows.

Definition 3. *Given a word w_a, the word rank for w_a, denoted by $r(w_a)$, is defined as:*

$$r(w_a) = \begin{cases} n, & w_a \in A_n, w_a \notin A_{n+1} - A_n \\ k, & w_a \notin A_{k-1}, w_a \in A_k \end{cases} \quad (3)$$

where A_n ($1 \leq n \leq k$) is a vocabulary set and indicates a specific level of difficulty.

Through the definition of the **vocabulary nest**, users can specify their mastery level m generally, rather than have to input the mastery level for each word in V. Moreover, m meets the conditions of $1 \leq m \leq k$, and $A_m \in A_n$, so what a learner states explicitly constitutes a set of word Am in the vocabulary. To initialize the learner profile by the given parameter m, we use the **explicit acquisition** method as follows.

Definition 4. *Given learner i and word w_a, and user-specified mastery level m, the mastery level of ε_a^i is obtained by the **explicit acquisition function** below:*

$$\varepsilon_a^i = \begin{cases} 1 - \alpha^{m - r(w_a) + 1}, & r(w_a) \leq m \\ 0, & r(w_a) > m \end{cases} \quad (4)$$

where $r(w_a)$ denotes the rank of w_a, α is the damping factor to give different degrees of mastery according to the difficulty levels. For example, suppose a learner specifies that his/her mastery level is 3, and the degrees of mastery levels are $1 - \alpha^3$, $1 - \alpha^2$ and $1 - \alpha$ for A_1, A_2 and A_3 respectively. These values are in decreasing order given that the parameter is in the interval of $[0,1]$.

Based on the above explicit user model, we adapt the recommendation method of our previous research studies from [5]. A major concern of this method is **word coverage**, and it tends to recommend word learning tasks that include unknown target words to the learners. This process of task recommendation involves selecting learning tasks with the maximal word coverage.

Definition 5. *Given learning task t and learner i,* **word coverage** *is a function θ to measure the degree of unfamiliarity of all target words in t of learner i.*

$$\theta(t, i) = \sum_{\forall w_a \in t} \varepsilon_a^i \tag{5}$$

where w_a is a target word in the task t, and ε_a^i is the mastery level of the learner. A greater value of θ(t, i) indicates greater unfamiliarity of the learner about the target word.

3   Experimental Results

29 intermediate language learners (with IELTS scores of around 5.5) were invited to participate in the study. They were randomly divided into two groups, with 15 and 14 learners in Group A and B respectively. To examine the effectiveness of the word learning system, tasks were randomly assigned to learners in Group A, while tasks were recommended to learners in Group B by employing the explicit learner model. The design of learning tasks and the marking criteria follow the ones used in [7, 8].

The overall experimental processes include three steps. The first step involves conducting a pre-test among the participants of the two groups. The pre-test includes 20 target words at the rank m in the corpus where m is the word rank with which all participants had least prior knowledge. The second step is the learning stage, after inputting their explicit profiles, members in group B were given three recommended tasks based on their profiles. Meanwhile, members in group A were randomly given three learning tasks from the system. Each learning task was set to be completed within 10 min. The last step focuses mainly on the post-test, which examined the participants' learning of the 20 target words. As demonstrated in Fig. 2, the average score of Group B

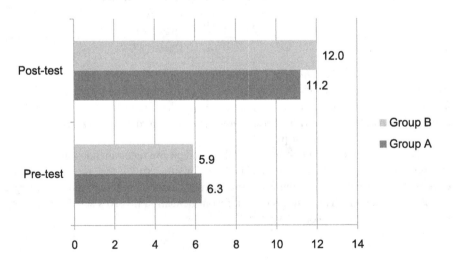

Fig. 2. The pre-test and post-test results in group A and B

(5.9) was a bit lower than Group A in the pre-test, but was higher in the post-test (12.0). Such preliminary results showed that the explicit learner model is effective and useful.

4 Conclusion and Future Work

In this article, we proposed an explicit learner profiling model for word learning systems and adapted the recommendation method by using the metric of word coverage from our previous study. A preliminary experiment was conducted among two groups of learners, the results of which verified the effectiveness of the proposed learner model. For future research, we plan to continue the study in two directions: (i) to compare the explicit model with implicit models, and (ii) to conduct experiments on a larger scale.

Acknowledgement. The work described in this paper was fully supported by a grant from Research Grants Council of Hong Kong Special Administrative Region, China (UGC/FDS11/ E06/14), the Internal Research Grant (RG 66/2016-2017) and the Start-Up Research Grant (RG 37/2016-2017R) of The Education University of Hong Kong.

References

1. Chen, C.-M., Chung, C.-J.: Personalized mobile english vocabulary learning system based on item response theory and learning memory cycle. Comput. Educ. **51**(2), 624–645 (2008)
2. Landau, B., Smith, L.B., Jones, S.S.: The importance of shape in early lexical learning. Cogn. Dev. **3**(3), 299–321 (1988)
3. Lu, M.: Effectiveness of vocabulary learning via mobile phone. J. Comput. Assist. Learn. **24** (6), 515–525 (2008)
4. Wu, D., Im, I., Tremaine, M., Instone, K., Turoff, M.: A framework for classifying personalization scheme used on e-commerce websites. In: Proceedings of the 36th Annual Hawaii International Conference on System Sciences, 2003, p. 12-pp. IEEE (2003)
5. Xie, H., Zou, D., Lau, R.Y.K., Wang, F.L., Wong, T.-L.: Generating incidental word-learning tasks via topic-based and load-based profiles. IEEE Multimed. **23**(1), 60–70 (2016)
6. Yeung, A.S.: Cognitive load and learner expertise: split-attention and redundancy effects in reading comprehension tasks with vocabulary definitions. J. Exp. Educ. **67**(3), 197–217 (1999)
7. Zou, D.: Comparing dictionary-induced vocabulary learning and inferencing in the context of reading. Lexikos **26**(1), 372–390 (2016)
8. Zou, D.: Vocabulary acquisition through cloze exercises, sentence-writing and composition-writing: extending the evaluation component of the involvement load hypothesis. Lang. Teach. Res. **21**(1), 54–75 (2017)
9. Zou, D., Xie, H., Li, Q., Wang, F.L., Chen, W.: The load-based learner profile for incidental word learning task generation. In: Popescu, E., Lau, R.W.H., Pata, K., Leung, H., Laanpere, M. (eds.) ICWL 2014. LNCS, vol. 8613, pp. 190–200. Springer, Cham (2014). https://doi. org/10.1007/978-3-319-09635-3_21
10. Zou, D., Xie, H., Rao, Y., Wong, T.-L., Wang, F.L., Wu, Q.: A comparative study on various vocabulary knowledge scales for predicting vocabulary pre-knowledge. Int. J. Distance Educ. Technol. (IJDET) **15**(1), 69–81 (2017)

Mobile-Assisted Language Learning: Using WeChat in an English Reading Class

Nana Jin[✉]

School of Foreign Languages, Shenzhen University, Shenzhen, China
nanajin7@163.com

Abstract. This study is based on mobile-assisted language learning and specifically focuses on the interaction diversity between English teachers and TESOL students. A smartphone app WeChat is applied in three English Reading classes for undergraduate English major students at Shenzhen University, China. The results indicate that all participants stay on line with WeChat all day long and are interested in using it in English learning. Especially in class, students enjoy taking multi-step directions with WeChat, asking for help in time, and, the most importantly, sharing their opinions or reports more willingly than in traditional class. Besides, the application of WeChat extends the interaction between students and teachers from classroom to wherever they go, from class time to anytime convenient for them, which builds a strong connection and narrows the mental distance between students and teachers. The study offers a successful teaching case: a mobile-assisted English Reading class in China.

Keywords: Mobile-assisted language learning · WeChat · English Reading class

1 Introduction

In-class learning is a tradition to all courses. However, traditional classroom teaching methods have been being challenged and reformed with various modern technologies. It has been changed from the teacher-oriented way to students-oriented way, from a single direction instruction to active interaction between teachers and students. With the development of modern technology, many TESOL teachers are pursuing the most efficient ones in language teaching. However, a successful language learning involves not only modern technology but also feedbacks from students. A successful class reaching pays a lot attention to students' learning motivations, their desires to study anywhere and anytime, their favorite ways of communication, etc. and the influence they will bring to the result of language learning. Therefore, it is necessary for teachers to consider how to give instructions with modern technology, how to activate students' performance in class with modern technology, and how to extend and monitor students' learning after class.

College students in China now are very open minded, and they are confident of choosing diversified and suitable learning methods for themselves, course credits they need and/or they can easily get high scores. All in all, they have a lot of freedom in study. They may even choose not to attend classroom learning, but taking MOOC

© Springer International Publishing AG 2017
T.-C. Huang et al. (Eds.): SETE 2017, LNCS 10676, pp. 500–506, 2017.
https://doi.org/10.1007/978-3-319-71084-6_59

courses instead. All the tempts and technology convenience induce more and more college students to leave classroom, which at the same time challenges teachers to create a more attractive and efficient classroom teaching. The aims of the classroom teaching reform are not only to win students back to class, but also to combine the benefits of traditional classroom teaching and modern technology to bring out better learning results than before. After all, MOOC course learning itself has a lot of shortcomings, such as high percentage of course dropout.

TESOL teaching is basically a language skill-based course, involving four major skills: listening, speaking, reading and writing, which demands a lot of practice, in-time correction and role-play team exercise on spot. Thus, classroom teaching for TESOL students is indispensable and important. However, a content-based course, i.e. infinitesimal calculus, quantum physics, microeconomics, focuses on knowledge cognition and application, which demands less oral practice, role-play exercise than language course, and it may be taken place by on-line courses. Therefore, modern technology and its application in TESOL classroom teaching has a long-term prospect.

MALL could be applied widely on campus due to the popularity of advanced mobile devices and convenience of accessible Wi-Fi. Both teachers and students find it more usable and attractive [1–3]. Researchers have found that mobile technologies have the potential to provide new learning experiences for students in teacher education [4, 5]. Previously Mobile phones were simply used as an electronical dictionary in language learning. However, smartphone devices are now found attractive learning tools for language learners [6–8], and therefore may result in positive language learning experiences [9].

This study is to investigate the benefits of teaching with mobile technology for English Reading class and to explore students' participation and perceptions of MALL.

2 Instructions and Feedbacks in English Reading Class

English Reading class is not only to let students read articles by themselves, but also to improve their reading ability with appropriate instructions before reading, conscious reading strategies while reading, and in-time feedbacks after reading.

How do teachers give appropriate instructions before reading? Teachers may choose to write it on whiteboard, project it on screen, give handouts, or simply speak it out. All the methods are teacher initiated and students obedient.

How do students give feedbacks in class? College students are far less active than primary students, and it's hard to get their feedbacks in time, let alone collecting all students' feedbacks.

How do teachers and students interact in class? In most cases, teachers are initiators, and students are led by a bunch of questions thrown by teachers. On the one hand, some students are very good at sharing their answers and opinions in class, but not all students have the ability and courage, especially for TESOL students. On the other hand, it's impossible to let every student share answers in class, for it is time consuming.

How do teachers know students' learning after class? In most cases, there is almost no contact between teachers and students after class. When students have questions after class, most of them would wait to ask in the next class. Some students lose the curiosity of answering the questions while waiting for the next class.

To solve most of the problems listed above and to achieve a better learning outcome, MALL strategies are introduced into classroom teaching. However, MALL is at the early stage of application. Researchers are still in process of looking for appropriate directions and teachers' training. Some researchers [5] did a pilot study on MALL experiences, and found three critical and practical recommendations for effective mobile learning experiences: effective instructional strategies, training or professional workshop development, and ongoing technical support and assistance.

An active participation in class is what a successful class teaching is pursuing. Pure language leaning easily makes students feel far from social activities, feel bored, and passive in class. Effective language learning is characterized by active and constructive production of thoughtful linguistic artifacts in authentic social settings [10]. This supports the strategy: connect social activities with language learning in class.

The most popular social media nowadays in China is the application WeChat developed by Tencent. Unlike other popular social media, i.e. Facebook Messenger, WhatsApp, WeChat is multifunctional, including instant messaging, commerce and payment services etc. It was first released in 2011. WeChat had over 889 million Monthly Active Users in 2016 90% of whom were Chinese [11]. For comparison, Facebook Messenger and WhatsApp (two other competitive international messaging services better-known in the West) had about 1,000 million Monthly Active Users in 2016 but did not offer most of the other services available on WeChat [12]. In 2017 it was reported that more than half of WeChat's users spend over 90 min a day on the app [13].

WeChat's popularity is everywhere in China, from countryside to metropolis, from kids to the elderly, from street venders to officials, from private sharing to company meetings, from entertaining to learning, etc. It is considered as an indispensable part of daily life. How to use WeChat effectively in language learning is worth of investigating and trying.

3   Methodology

A case study design was used to describe and interpret TESOL students' mobile learning experiences, specifically WeChat learning experiences in college English Reading class.

In the class, the teacher built a WeChat course group and students who attending the class were required to join the group for course data handouts, assignments announcement, submitting homework, conducting discussion, etc. All participants were required to complete a pre-study test, which was taken at the first class, i.e. a week before the WeChat course group building. At the end of the semester, all students were asked to take a post-study test. The two tests were analyzed to evaluate the differences in students' reading comprehension at the beginning and the end of the semester.

After one semester (16 weeks) teaching with WeChat course group, student reflections were collected. The qualitative data from students' reflection on WeChat course group were used to supplement the quantitative findings and to show students' learning experiences with the mobile application WeChat.

In September 2016, we invited Chinese college students who are learning English as a second language to participate in the study. A total of 79 students from three different classes in an urban public university in China participated in the study during the Autumn semester. All the participants use WeChat every day, i.e. they are WeChat active users, and their smartphones (e.g., Android phones, iPhones) have access to campus free Wi-Fi. The focus is on how to take good advantage of the technology that is frequently used by students for the purpose of facilitating their language learning.

The pre-study test was comprised of 35 listening questions (35 credits), 20 reading comprehension questions (40 credits), 20 cloze questions (15 credits) and 15 vocabulary questions (10 credits). It is a campus wide set test used to evaluate freshmen's overall English proficiency. The post-study test shared the same format with the pre-study test, and it was not more difficult or easier than the pre-study test. The post-study test was used to assess, in comparison with the pre-study one, how much progress students would have achieved after a semester's study.

Students' reflection on WeChat assisted learning was collected from a questionnaire of 6 choice questions and an open-ended question. The questions are ranked on a scale of "yes", "not sure", and "no". The rank "yes" is represented by number "1", "not sure" by "0", and "no" by "−1". The brief scale of answers is to look for students' major inclinations of using WeChat in language learning, instead of a detailed classification of it.

4   Results

The study involved both collecting and analyzing quantitative and qualitative data in the pre-study test, the post-study test and the questionnaire. The qualitative data consisted of a 3 scale of answers, short sentences and phrases, which provide a holistic picture of WeChat course group in language learning.

Table 1 is one of the three classes' tests report. Both the pre-study test and the post-study test contain 20 reading comprehension questions (40 credits). As shown in Table 1, most students (20 out of 25 students) make a great progress in the reading part of post-study test. There are more than half of students (13 out of 25 students) whose progress percentages in reading overpass 20%; and 6 students whose progress percentages in reading overpass 30%. The table clearly shows the progress that the participants have made in reading and it also testifies that the WeChat assisted learning in class does no harm to reading class. To know specifically how WeChat functions in class, we need to check the questionnaire.

Table 2 shows 46 students' reflections on WeChat course group in English Reading class.

As shown in Table 2, it is obvious that most students hold a positive view toward using WeChat in English Reading class and in other courses as well. A few students are not sure about it. Only two students hold a negative view toward it. All these answers clearly indicate that students like WeChat course group in language learning and think it helpful. Besides the 6 choice questions, there is an open-ended question for students:

Table 1. A comparison of the pre-study test and the post-study test

Student no.	Pre-test scores in reading part	Post-test scores in reading part	Reading score difference in the tests	Progress percentage in reading part	Progress percentage in the whole test
2016###001	16	30	14	35%	25%
2016###002	20	28	8	20%	19%
2016###003	30	34	4	10%	6%
2016###004	20	32	12	30%	16%
2016###006	14	22	8	20%	22%
2016###007	16	30	14	35%	48%
2016###008	24	32	8	20%	15%
2016###009	14	26	12	30%	32%
2016###011	18	24	6	15%	18%
2016###012	24	22	−2*	−5%*	4%
2016###017	26	34	8	20%	23%
2016###018	26	22	−4*	−10%*	−4%*
2016###020	22	22	0	0%	−22%*
2016###021	20	26	6	15%	16%
2016###022	20	32	12	30%	28%
2016###025	24	28	4	10%	6%
2016###027	24	22	−2*	−5%*	5%
2016###029	20	28	8	20%	20%
2016###030	30	32	2	5%	4%
2016###031	34	32	−2*	−5%*	2%
2016###032	10	28	18	45%	21%
2016###034	28	26	−2*	−5%*	2%
2016###035	24	32	8	20%	13%
2016###036	26	32	6	15%	29%
2016###039	26	36	10	25%	22%

Note: "" means "no progress, but recession"*

what else does WeChat influence your language learning? 33 out of 46 students said that WeChat is very convenient for teachers to notify students of messages, and send course materials, etc. There are some disadvantages shown from students' questionnaires:

  i. Simply ignore some important information or directions in WeChat;

  ii. Too much irrelative information to individuals in the WeChat course group;

  iii. Once check on WeChat, it is easy to be distracted by mobile games.

Table 2. Students' reflection on WeChat course group in English Reading class

Questions	Yes	Not sure	No
1. Is it good to introduce WeChat course group in English Reading Class?	34 (74%)	11 (24%)	1 (2%)
2. Does WeChat help strengthen the relation between teacher and students, and build a sense of belonging?	30 (64%)	16 (35%)	0
3. When you have a question after class, will you use WeChat to ask for help?	21 (46%)	24 (52%)	1 (2%)
4. Does it make you feel less stressed when you use WeChat to display your work in class	29 (63%)	17 (37%)	0
5. Do you prefer your teacher send course data to the WeChat course group than to your personal mailbox or class mailbox?	40 (87%)	6 (13%)	0
6. Do you think the WeChat assisted learning model should be promoted to other courses?	40 (87%)	6 (13%)	0

5 Conclusion

Students participating in this study benefit from the use of mobile application WeChat. Their positive learning experiences offer a pilot study of WeChat assisted language learning in and outside of the classroom. While in most cases, the participants expressed their positive perception about using WeChat in class, there are mobile game temptation existing when participants watch their smartphones.

For language learning, this research provides a mobile assisted method, specifically with the most popular social media WeChat in China. Language learners may use the software to ask for help whenever they come across a question, check course data in time, share comments and feelings, etc. The best practice is to use WeChat to make students feel less stressed and more willing to share their work in class with their favorite expressing style.

WeChat penetrates every corner of our life in China, communicating with friends, even visually, buying food, clothes, books, etc., paying bills, even applying for visa. People in China stay with WeChat 90 min a day on average. If WeChat is effectively embedded with language learning, an active WeChat user could also be an active language learner.

Acknowledgments. The author acknowledges the financial support by Guangdong Academy of Education Project, 000008; Shenzhen University Project, 0000240912; the Ministry of Education, Humanities and Social Science Planning Project, 14YJA740036; Shenzhen Science and Technology Innovation Community Basic Project, NCYJ2014041809143526.

References

1. Cochrane, T.: Exploring mobile learning success factors. Res. Learn. Technol. **18**(2), 133–148 (2010)

2. Martin, F., Ertzberger, J.: Here and now mobile learning: an experimental study on the use of mobile technology. Comput. Educ. **68**, 76–85 (2013)
3. Wu, W., et al.: Review of trends from mobile learning studies: a meta-analysis. Comput. Educ. **59**(2), 817–827 (2012)
4. Baran, E.: A review research on mobile learning in teacher education. J. Educ. Technol. Soc. **17**(4), 17–32 (2014)
5. Kim, D., et al.: Mobile assisted language learning experiences. Int. J. Mob. Blended Learn. **9** (1), 49–60 (2017)
6. De Jong, T., Specht, M., Koper, R.: A study of contextualized mobile information delivery for language learning. J. Educ. Technol. Soc. **13**(3), 110–125 (2010)
7. Ducate, L., Lomicka, L.: Going mobile: language learning with an iPod Touch in intermediate French and German classes. Foreign Lang. Ann. **46**(3), 445–468 (2013)
8. Hsu, C.K., Hwang, G.J., Chang, C.K.: A personalized recommendation-based mobile learning approach to improving the reading performance of EFL students. Comput. Educ. **63** (1), 327–336 (2013)
9. Kukulska-Hulme, A.: Will mobile learning change language learning? Eur. Assoc. Comput. Assist. Lang. Learn. **21**(2), 157–165 (2009)
10. Ellis, R.: Task-based research and language pedagogy. Lang. Teach. Res. **4**(3), 193–220 (2000)
11. http://www.techinasia.com/wechat-blasts-700-million-monthly-active-users-tops-chinas-popular-apps. Accessed 22 Mar 2017
12. http://www.economist.com/news/business/21703428-chinas-wechat-shows-way-social-medias-future-wechats-world. Accessed 8 Aug 2016
13. http://m.ftchinese.com/a/story/001072637/en. Accessed 18 May 2017

Discovering the Recent Research in Natural Language Processing Field Based on a Statistical Approach

Xieling Chen[1], Boyu Chen[2], Chunxia Zhang[4],
and Tianyong Hao[2,3(✉)]

[1] School of Economics, Jinan University, Guangzhou, China
shaylyn_chen@163.com
[2] School of Information Science and Technology,
Guangdong University of Foreign Studies, Guangzhou, China
joeyChenby@163.com, haoty@126.com
[3] Collaborative Innovation Center for 21st-Century Maritime Silk Road Studies,
Guangdong University of Foreign Studies, Guangzhou, China
[4] School of Software, Beijing Institute of Technology, Beijing, China
cxzhang@bit.edu.cn

Abstract. With the purpose of discovering the recent status of natural language processing research field, this paper presents a data-driven statistical method by utilizing bibliometrics and social network analysis on related publications. On 3,222 academic publications retrieved from *Web of Science core collection* during year 2007-2016, this paper explores literature distribution characteristics using descriptive statistical method, research hotspots using *k*-means clustering method, and cooperation relationships among authors and affiliations using network analysis method. The findings provide relevant learners and researchers with information to keep abreast of the research status of NLP field.

Keywords: Natural Language Processing · Distribution characteristics · Research hotspots · Cooperation relationships

1 Introduction

Natural Language Processing (NLP), also known as computational linguistics, emerged in the 1950s with an initial attempt at automatic Russian-to-English translation [1]. As an interdisciplinary research of linguistics and artificial intelligence, NLP concerns with the interactions between computers and natural language, i.e., applying computational techniques to learn, understand, and produce natural language content [2]. Early computational methods for language research centered on the automatic analysis of linguistic structure and the development of fundamental technologies, e.g., machine translation, speech recognition and synthesis. Gradually, researchers also focus on the applications of relevant tools in solving real-world problems, e.g., spoken dialogue systems, speech-to-speech translation engines, as well as sentiment analysis. NLP technologies with application potentials are becoming increasingly widespread [3].

© Springer International Publishing AG 2017
T.-C. Huang et al. (Eds.): SETE 2017, LNCS 10676, pp. 507–517, 2017.
https://doi.org/10.1007/978-3-319-71084-6_60

In academia, the research of NLP has been always of an extensive concern. Researchers have published a great amount of NLP publications for reporting their research findings. These research publications can to a certain extent reflect the development of NLP frontier, which benefits NLP researchers and new learners in understanding the latest research and directions. However, it is far from expectation through traditional manual retrieval when facing with such a big number of NLP publications. For example, there were more than 500 publications in 2016 with the exact NLP as keyword in Web of Science, not mention the much big number of conference publications. Therefore, it is necessary to explore an automated, accurate, scientific, and visualized approach to continuously analyzing the research status of NLP field.

Bibliometrics analysis is capable of assessing and evaluating research output quantitatively using mathematics and statistical techniques [4]. Knowledge mapping analysis is a method of mining and analyzing knowledge with visualization technology displaying the development progress and the structure relationship [5]. As a specific application of graph theory, social network analysis can be regarded as a scientific community where individuals and other social actors are represented by points and their social relations are represented by lines [6, 7]. To a certain degree, bibliometrics, knowledge mapping analysis and social network analysis can be regarded as complements for one another, and the combination of them can bring about more sound and comprehensive understanding of research publications.

To that end, this paper proposes a data-driven statistical approach combined with bibliometrics, knowledge mapping, and social network analysis to analyze the NLP-related publications for discovering the recent research status in NLP field. We conduct literature distribution characteristics analysis, research hotspots analysis, and cooperation relationship analysis among authors and affiliations using the techniques of descriptive statistics, k-means clustering, and network analysis, respectively. The findings may benefit NLP researchers and learners in keeping abreast of the research status of NLP, determining hot research topics, and monitoring new scientific or technological activities.

2   Related Work

Bibliometrics, knowledge mapping, and social network analysis have been applied widely in research output evaluation. Cobo et al. [8] presented a thorough bibliometric analysis of the research using the publications on Journal Knowledge-Based Systems during 1991–2014. Newman [9] discussed and compared the scientific co-authorships patterns through network analysis on researches covering biomedical, physics, and mathematics. Through citation and collaboration network analysis using various statistical measures, Radev et al. [10] investigated the publications published by the Association for Computational Linguistics (ACL) with a purpose of identifying the most central papers and authors. Cobo et al. [11] applied performance analysis and science mapping in analyzing and visualizing conceptual subdomains to quantify and visualize the thematic evolution for a given research field. Merigó et al. [12] provided a general overview of fuzzy sciences research with the application of bibliometric indicators for identifying the most influential and fundamental research in the field. Muñoz-Leiva et al. [13] presented a bibliometric and visual study of consumer behavior research during 1966–2008. Co-word analysis has also been used for detecting and visualizing the conceptual structure of a given research field [14, 15].

There is a limited number of studies concerning with NLP-related research output evaluation using bibliometrics, knowledge mapping, and social network analysis. Zhu [16] analyzed the frequency distributions of authors, journals, affiliations and keywords of NLP publications in China with traditional bibliometrics method. Similar work has also been done by Li and Xu [17]. However, the existing relative studies seldom apply the combined methods of bibliometrics, knowledge mapping, and social network analysis to provide more comprehensive analysis.

Therefore, this study aims at presenting a detailed evaluation of the NLP-related research literature from the *Web of Science* during 2007–2016 by a data-driven statistical method. With the combination of bibliometrics, knowledge mapping, and social network analysis methods, we quantitatively study the publications in the following aspects: (1) descriptive statistics for acquiring literature distribution characteristics, (2) *k*-means clustering for acquiring research hotspots, and (3) network analysis for acquiring cooperation relationships among authors and affiliations.

3 The Statistical Approach

We propose a statistical approach with the combination of bibliometrics, knowledge mapping, and social network analysis on NLP-related literature to provide a detailed evaluation of the recent research status of NLP. Figure 1 shows the whole analyzing procedure. The relevant publications were retrieved from *Web of Science*. We analyzed the literature distribution characteristics with descriptive statistical methods. After that, research hotspots were analyzed with a *k*-means clustering analysis, while cooperation

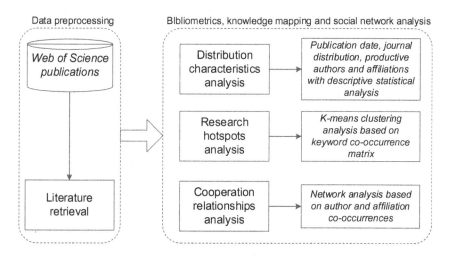

Fig. 1. The procedure of the statistical apporach for analyzing the research status of NLP

relationships among authors and affiliations were discovered with a network analysis method. Software R was used as analyzing tool. Specifically, the procedure contains the following stages:

Literature retrieval: The relevant publications were directly retrieved from *Web of Science Core Collection* in May, 2017 with the searching criteria: (1) "Science citation index expanded (SCI-EXPANDED)" as citation index to keep high literature quality; (2) "Natural Language Processing" and its extended words, e.g., "NLP", "Computational Linguistics", as retrieval topics; (3) "2007" to "2016" as publication year; and (4) "Article" as document type. 3,222 documents were finally obtained for further analysis.

Distribution characteristics analysis: Based on the documents, we used descriptive statistical methods to acquire the literature distribution characteristics with publication date, journal distribution, and productive authors and affiliations included. Take publication journal distribution as an example, the journals were ranked according to their decreasing order of productivity in number of publications.

Research hotspots analysis: The recent research hotspots of NLP was acquired based upon keywords co-occurrence matrix, the specific steps of which are as follows: (1) String case conversion: all the string cases of keywords were converted into uppercase letters for unified representation at the very beginning; (2) Keywords standardization: standardizations of keywords was necessary resulted from some non-standard and inconsistent writings of keywords, e.g., unifying "Natural language processing", "NLP", "Natural language processing (NLP)", "Natural language process", "Natural language process analysis" as "NLP"; (3) The standardized keywords were then ranked and sorted according to their frequency; (4) A co-occurrence matrix of keywords with most frequency was acquired; (5) A keywords correlation matrix was calculated using *Ochiai* correlation coefficient with the basis of the co-occurrence matrix; (6) With the keywords correlation matrix, k-means clustering analysis was realized.

Cooperation network analysis: With the consideration of all the authors and affiliations participating in one publication, we firstly converted the data of authors and affiliations of high prolificacy generated with descriptive statistical method into the form of one-to-one cooperation, and then the cooperation networks of authors and affiliations were acquired respectively using network analysis.

4   Results and Discussions

During the distribution characteristics analysis stage, we took into account of the publication date and journal distribution as well as the productive authors and affiliations. The statistical number of NLP publications by year and its annual growth rate during 2007–2016 is shown as Table 1. The result presents that there were 3,222 NLP publications on *Web of Science core collection* in the last ten years and the annual growth rate reached 13.61% on average. Based on the statistical distributions, we built a log-linear model of the number of publications as $E(y) = \exp(c + \sum \beta_i x_i)$ with time as an independent variable. We obtained the two parameters and set the regression formula as $y = \exp(-252.7 + 0.12847x)$ with AIC equaling to 93.876. The fitted

Table 1. The number and growth rate of publications by year during 2007–2016

Year	# publications	# cumulative publications	Growth rate (%)
2007	181	181	N/A
2008	203	384	12.16
2009	237	621	16.75
2010	222	843	−6.33
2011	245	1,088	10.36
2012	313	1,401	27.76
2013	392	1,793	25.24
2014	398	2,191	1.53
2015	482	2,673	21.11
2016	549	3,222	13.90
Average	322.2	N/A	13.61

parameter of the variable time is 0.12847 with significance test value $P < 2e-16$, indicating the significant influence of variable time on the number of publications. With the log-linear model, we can infer the future research output, e.g., the predicted number of publications in 2017 is as exp(−252.7 + 0.12847*2017) = 616.46.

Table 2 is the top 10 most productive journals accounting together for 21.57% of the total publications, and the top 3 in order were: *Journal of the American Medical Informatics Association*, *Journal of Biomedical Informatics*, and *BMC Bioinformatics*. All of the three belong to medical informatics field. Table 2 indicates the inter-research of NLP with other fields, especially, the needs and applications of NLP in medical is increasing prominent. Table 3 shows the top 10 most productive authors, 5 among which came from *Vanderbilt University*. The top 3 in order were: Denny, Joshua C. from *Vanderbilt University* with 56 publications, *Biegler, Lorenz T.* from *Carnegie Mellon University* with 24 publications, and *Khorasani, Ramin* from *Harvard*

Table 2. Top 10 most productive journals

Journals	# publications	Proportion %	Cumulative proportion %
Journal of the American Medical Informatics Association	130	4.035	4.035
Journal of Biomedical Informatics	121	3.755	7.790
BMC Bioinformatics	66	2.048	9.839
Expert Systems with Applications	66	2.048	11.887
Computers & Chemical Engineering	56	1.738	13.625
Language Resources and Evaluation	56	1.738	15.363
Industrial & Engineering Chemistry Research	54	1.676	17.039
PLOS One	54	1.676	18.715
Computational Linguistics	47	1.459	20.174
Natural Language Engineering	45	1.397	21.570

Table 3. Top 10 most productive authors

Rank	Authors	Affiliations	# publications
1	*Denny, Joshua C.*	*Vanderbilt University*	56
2	*Biegler, Lorenz T.*	*Carnegie Mellon University*	24
3	*Khorasani, Ramin*	*Harvard University*	18
4	*Liu, Hongfang*	*Mayo Clinic*	16
5	*Matheny, Michael E.*	*Vanderbilt University*	16
6	*Solti, Imre*	*Cincinnati Children's Hospital Medical Center*	15
7	*Speroff, Theodore*	*Vanderbilt University*	15
8	*Pouratian, Nader*	*University of California*	14
9	*Roden, Dan M.*	*Vanderbilt University*	14
10	*Xu, Hua*	*Vanderbilt University*	14

University with 18 publications. Top 8 most productive first author affiliations and total author affiliations are shown in Table 4, indicating that *Carnegie Mellon University* ranked both the top 3. Generally, the most productive authors and affiliations contributed the most in NLP research field. Therefore, by following up their research directions, NLP researchers and learners could quickly master the research priority and development trend.

Table 4. Top 8 most productive first author affiliations and total author affiliations

Rank	First author affiliations	# pub.	Rank	Total author affiliations	# pub.
1	**Carnegie Mellon University**	38	1	*Harvard University*	86
2	*Vanderbilt University*	33	2	**Carnegie Mellon University**	67
3	*Columbia University*	28	3	*University Utah*	57
4	*Zhejiang University*	27	4	*Vanderbilt University*	54
5	*University Utah*	26	5	*Columbia University*	49
6	*Mayo Clinic*	25	6	*Mayo Clinic*	45
7	*University Pittsburgh*	21	7	*Brigham & Women's Hospital*	40
8	*University Tokyo*	20	8	*Zhejiang University*	36

For analyzing the research hotspots of the current NLP research, we used publication keywords since they generally represented main points of publications. Due to the limited space, 22 keywords with frequency greater than or equaling to 76 are shown in Table 5. The top 3 were in turn: "NLP" with frequency of 985, "System" with frequency of 369, and "Optimization" with frequency of 246. In order to meet the requirements of k-means clustering analysis, a co-occurrence matrix was created to generate keywords correlation matrix. The co-occurrence matrix was a symmetric matrix. The values on the non-main diagonal indicated the co-occurrence frequency between two different

Table 5. Keywords with frequency greater than or equaling to 76

Rank	Keyword	Freq.	Freq.% / pub.	Rank	Keyword	Freq.	Freq.%/ pub.
1	NLP	985	30.571	12	Text mining	130	4.035
2	System	369	11.453	13	Information	129	4.004
3	Optimization	246	7.635	14	Nonlinear programming	113	3.507
4	Algorithm	245	7.604	15	Electronic health record	107	3.321
5	Model	228	7.076	16	Knowledge	107	3.321
6	Text	187	5.804	17	Information retrieval	103	3.197
7	Information extraction	177	5.493	18	Network	90	2.793
8	Classification	173	5.369	19	Identification	86	2.669
9	Machine learning	142	4.407	20	Language	79	2.452
10	Ontology	142	4.407	21	Management	78	2.421
11	Design	132	4.097	22	Sentiment analysis	76	2.359

keywords, and the values on the main diagonal represented the frequency of the keywords. On the basis of the top 22 keywords, a co-occurrence matrix with 22 rows and 22 columns was created, partial of which can be seen in Table 6.

Table 6. Co-occurrence matrix of top 10 keywords

Keyword	Algorithm	Classification	Information extraction	Machine learning	Model	NLP	Ontology	Optimization	System	Text
Algorithm	245	13	8	9	41	56	3	45	35	9
Classification	13	173	13	17	18	64	3	2	16	20
Information extraction	8	13	177	17	8	103	12	0	37	28
Machine learning	9	17	17	142	11	89	7	0	20	17
Model	41	18	8	11	228	58	8	29	40	16
NLP	56	64	103	89	58	985	53	20	122	90
Ontology	3	3	12	7	8	53	142	0	23	15
Optimization	45	2	0	0	29	20	0	246	30	0
System	35	16	37	20	40	122	23	30	369	48
Text	9	20	28	17	16	90	15	0	48	187

Based on the co-occurrence matrix, we generated a keyword correlation matrix using *Ochiai* correlation coefficient as a measurement of the distance between two keywords. The calculation formula is expressed as: $O_{ij} = A_{ij}/\sqrt{A_iA_j}$. O_{ij} ranging from 0 to 1 indicated the co-occurrence probability of keyword W_i and W_j. A_{ij} indicated the co-occurrence frequency of keyword W_i and W_j. A_i and A_j indicated the frequency of the keyword W_i and W_j, respectively. The larger the value of the correlation matrix was between two keywords, the smaller the distance was between them. With the correlation matrix, *k*-means clustering analysis was done, the results of which can be seen in Fig. 2.

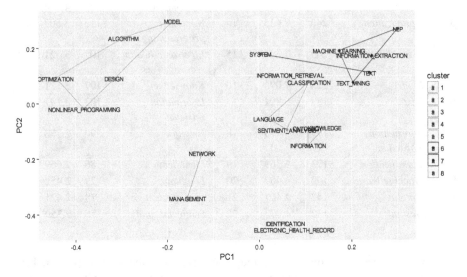

Fig. 2. Clustering results of *k*-means clustering (*k* = 8)

22 keywords were finally subdivided into 8 categories, i.e., (1) *NLP, Machine Learning, Information Extraction, Text Mining*; (2) *Ontology, Knowledge, Information*; (3) *Network, Management*; (4) *Electronic Health Record, Identification*; (5) *Language, Classification, Sentiment Analysis*; (6) *Design, Model, Algorithm, Optimization, Nonlinear Programming*; (7) *Text, System*; and (8) *Information Retrieval*.

Furthermore, in order to measure the closeness the cooperation among authors or affiliations on NLP research, we conducted cooperation network analysis. By including all authors or affiliations in the same publications, we considered the cooperation among authors and affiliations. Figure 3 shows the cooperation network of authors with publications larger than or equaling to 5 (access via the link[1]). Figure 4 shows the cooperation network of affiliations with publications larger than or equaling to 10 (access via the link[2]). In the network, authors or affiliations were represented by the black nodes, and the cooperation relationships were represented by the lines. The cooperation relationship with other authors or affiliations is closer for a specific author or affiliation with more connected lines surrounded. Moreover, one can explore the cooperation relationship for a specific author or affiliation through dynamically dragging and dropping.

---

[1] http://www.zhukun.org/haoty/resources.asp?id=UMLL2017_author_5.

[2] http://www.zhukun.org/haoty/resources.asp?id=UMLL2017_affiliation_10.

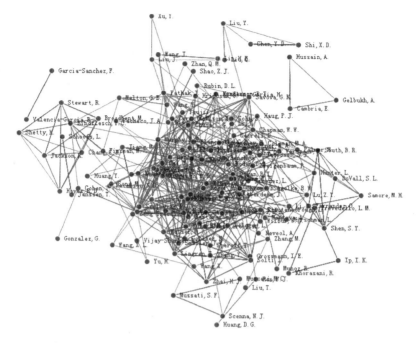

Fig. 3. The cooperation network of authors with publications > = 5

Fig. 4. The cooperation network of affiliations with publications > = 10

5 Summary

This paper proposes a data-driven statistical method based on bibliometrics, knowledge mapping, and social network analysis with an aim of acquiring the recent research status of NLP from 2007 to 2016. Literature distribution characteristics, research hotspots, and cooperation relationships among authors and affiliations were acquired with the analysis methods of descriptive statistics, k-means clustering, and network analysis, respectively. Our work is potential for assisting NLP researchers and learners in keeping abreast of the research status of NLP, delimiting research areas, determining scientific research topics, as well as monitoring new scientific or technological activities.

Acknowledgements. This work was supported by National Natural Science Foundation of China (Nos. 61403088 and 61672098) and Innovative School Project in Higher Education of Guangdong (No. YQ2015062).

References

1. Chaudhari, P.R., Gangurde, P.C., Kulkarni, N.L.: Study of methodologies for utilizing Sanskrit in computational linguistics. Int. J. Electron., Commun. Soft Comput. Sci. Eng., 1–4 (2015)
2. Hirschberg, J., Manning, C.D.: Advances in natural language processing. Science **349** (6245), 261–266 (2015)
3. Bird, S., Klein, E., Loper, E.: Natural Language Processing with Python: Analyzing Text with the Natural Language Toolkit. O'Reilly Media Inc, Sebastopol (2009)
4. Harande, Y.I., Alhaji, I.U.: Basic literature of diabetes: a bibliometrics analysis of three countries in different world regions. J. Libr. Inf. Sci. **2**(1), 49–56 (2014)
5. Zhu, Z., Li, Y., Zhang, Y., Wu, Z.: A method of constructing the mapping knowledge domains in Chinese based on the MOOCs. In: Bao, Z., Trajcevski, G., Chang, L., Hua, W. (eds.) DASFAA 2017. LNCS, vol. 10179, pp. 411–416. Springer, Cham (2017). https://doi.org/10.1007/978-3-319-55705-2_33
6. Freeman, L.: The Development of Social Network Analysis. A Study in the Sociology of Science. Empirical Press, Vancouver (2004)
7. Hanneman, R.A., Riddle, M.: Introduction to Social Network Methods. University of California, Riverside (2005)
8. Cobo, M.J., Martínez, M.A., Gutiérrez-Salcedo, M., et al.: 25 years at knowledge-based systems: a bibliometric analysis. Knowl.-Based Syst. **80**, 3–13 (2015)
9. Newman, M.E.J.: Coauthorship networks and patterns of scientific collaboration. Proc. Natl. Acad. Sci. **101**(suppl 1), 5200–5205 (2004)
10. Radev, D.R., Joseph, M.T., Gibson, B., Muthukrishnan, P.: A bibliometric and network analysis of the field of computational linguistics. J. Am. Soc. Inf. Sci. Technol. **1001**, 48109–1092 (2009)
11. Cobo, M.J., López-Herrera, A.G., Herrera-Viedma, E., Herrera, F.: An approach for detecting, quantifying, and visualizing the evolution of a research field: a practical application to the fuzzy sets theory field. J. Inf. **5**(1), 146–166 (2011)
12. Merigó, J.M., Gil-Lafuente, A.M., Yager, R.R.: An overview of fuzzy research with bibliometric indicators. Appl. Soft Comput. **27**, 420–433 (2015)

13. Muñoz-Leiva, F., Viedma-del-Jesús, M.I., Sánchez-Fernández, J., López-Herrera, A.G.: An application of co-word analysis and bibliometric maps for detecting the most highlighting themes in the consumer behaviour research from a longitudinal perspective. Qual. Quant. **46**(4), 1077–1095 (2012)
14. Cobo, M.J., Chiclana, F., Collop, A., de Ona, J., Herrera-Viedma, E.: A bibliometric analysis of the intelligent transportation systems research based on science mapping. IEEE Trans. Intell. Transp. Syst. **15**(2), 901–908 (2014)
15. Dehdarirad, T., Villarroya, A., Barrios, M.: Research trends in gender differences in higher education and science: a co-word analysis. Scientometrics **101**(1), 273–290 (2014)
16. Zhu, Q.S.: Bibliometric Analysis of Natural Language Processing in China. J. Inf. **28**(2), 32–34 (2009)
17. Li, Y., Xu, P.Y.: Research on natural language processing in China: a bibliometric analysis. Chin. J. Med. Libr. Inf. Sci. **21**(2), 65–70 (2012)

A CRFs-Based Approach Empowered with Word Representation Features to Learning Biomedical Named Entities from Medical Text

Wenxiu Xie[1], Sihui Fu[1], Shengyi Jiang[1(✉)], and Tianyong Hao[1,2(✉)]

[1] School of Information Science and Technology,
Guangdong University of Foreign Studies, Guangzhou, China
vasiliky@outlook.com, sihuifu93@gmail.com,
jiangshengyi@163.com, haoty@gdufs.edu.cn
[2] Collaborative Innovation Center for 21st-Century Maritime Silk Road Studies,
Guangdong University of Foreign Studies, Guangzhou, China

Abstract. Targeting at identifying specific types of entities, biomedical named entity recognition is a fundamental task of biomedical text processing. This paper presents a CRFs-based approach to learning disease entities by identifying their boundaries in texts. Two types of word representation features are proposed and used including word embedding features and cluster-based features. In addition, an external disease dictionary feature is also explored in the learning process. Based on a publically available NCBI disease corpus, we evaluate the performance of the CRFs-based model with the combination of these word representation features. The results show that using these features can significantly improve BNER performance with an increase of 24.7% on F1 measure, demonstrating the effectiveness of the proposed features and the feature-empowered approach.

Keywords: Biomedical Named Entity Recognition · CRFs · Word representation features

1 Introduction

Biomedical nmed entity recognition (BNER) is an essential task in biomedical natural language processing (NLP). BNER aims to find out those biomedical concepts, such as diseases, proteins, drugs, treatments, etc. from biomedical texts. Generally, it mainly contains two stages including the identification of entity mention boundaries and the classification of these mentions into their corresponding semantic classes [1].

Due to the complexity of biomedical texts, BNER has more difficulties than other general domains for several reasons [2]. A biomedical named entity may have many various forms (e.g., "Miscarriage" versus "Spontaneous abortion"). A large number of abbreviations (e.g., "AP" for "Abdominal pain") are frequently used. In addition, the same word or phrase may denote different types of entities, i.e., the ambiguity problem. Athenikos and Han [2] have summarized the difficulties in the biomedical domain as

© Springer International Publishing AG 2017
T.-C. Huang et al. (Eds.): SETE 2017, LNCS 10676, pp. 518–527, 2017.
https://doi.org/10.1007/978-3-319-71084-6_61

more than three points including: (1) there exists highly complex domain-specific terminology; (2) domain-specific concepts and ontology need to be dealt with by means of corresponding resources; (3) tools and approaches specifically for exploiting the underlying semantic information are needed. Though there are plenty of existing researches on BNER [1, 3, 4], the performance of NER on unstructured text is still unsatisfactory, particularly in the biomedical domain.

Conditional Random Fields (CRFs) model is frequently used in NER tasks. There are also existing works by applying CRFs to BNER, e.g., [2]. However, these works seldom make full use of abundant unlabeled biomedical texts. The unlabeled biomedical texts are easy to obtain and can potentially provide useful features in the identification of named entity boundaries. Consequently, in this paper, we explore two types of word representation features from the unlabeled online publication dataset by National Institutes of Health (NIH) and integrate the features into our CRFs-based model. These two different types of word representation features are complementary to each other, as revealed by [5]. In addition, we try to add domain dictionaries as an external resource to optimize the performance of the model. Based on the publically available NCBI (National Center for Biotechnology Information) disease corpus with human annotations, we compare the performance of the CRFs-based model combined with different types of word representation features. The results show that the proposed word representation features are able to help improve the BNER performance with an increase of 24.7% on F1 measure. Besides, the external dictionary as features can also enhance the model with an increase of 1.5% on F1 measure.

In the following section, the related work of BNER is presented in Sect. 2. Section 3 describes the formulation of BNER as a sequence labeling problem, the CRFs model, and the used features. Section 4 demonstrates the experiment, including the dataset, the evaluation metrics and the results, while Sect. 5 concludes the work.

2 Related Work

The commonly used methods for BNER can be divided into three types: dictionary-based methods, rule-based methods and machine learning based methods [6]. With a continual appearance of new biomedical entities which do not follow any nomenclature, dictionary-based methods encounter low recall challenge [7]. Moreover, for the dictionary-based and rule-based methods, they usually need large human labor and are faced with the low-coverage limitation, while machine learning based methods in turn integrate the former two methods and compensate for the weakness. For the rapid development of biomedical literature, which are expanding at an exponential rate, a large scale of redundant and unlabeled data has been a challenge. To tackle this problem, Fries et al. [8] proposed a framework for building biomedical named entity recognition systems without manually annotated data. Viewing biomedical resources as function primitives, they used a generative model to unify supervision which showed competitive performance with state-of-the-art benchmarks.

Zhang and Elhadad [9] proposed an unsupervised approach to extracting named entities and a stepwise solution to the entity boundary detection and entity type classification challenges without any hand-crafted rules, heuristics, or annotated data. The experiment result showed that the proposed method yielded competitive results on two popular biomedical datasets and outperformed a dictionary matching approach.

Kazama et al. [1] proposed a Support Vector Machines based method for BNER and explored word cache as new features. Their experiments showed that the proposed method and features were useful for improving accuracy. Later in Kuksa and Qi [10], they proposed a novel semi-supervised method, namely Word-Codebook Learning, for bio-named entity recognition which learned the class of word-level feature embeddings or word label patterns from a large unlabeled corpus. The proposed method was proved to be yielding state-of-the-art performance and great improvements over supervised baselines.

More recently, Semi-supervised learning (SSL) techniques and deep neural network approaches are investigated to perform BNER learning task. Munkhdalai et al. [11] proposed an SSL method, named Active Co-training (ACT), for BNER based on two different feature sets iteratively learning from informative examples that have been queried from the unlabeled data. Their experiment results verified that the ACT method outperformed the traditional co-training approaches. Later in their 2015 work [12], they extended BANNER with the proposed SSL method which efficiently exploited unlabeled data and did not rely on any lexicon nor any dictionary. The extended system BANNER-CHEMDNER could be applied to chemical and drug NER or biomedical NER learning and showed a remarkable performance in both chemical and biomedical NER tasks. As for Gridach [13], they claimed that they were the first to utilize deep neural networks for BNER tasks. With the combination of CRFs, word embeddings and character-level representation, their approach obtained state-of-the-art performance.

In this paper, we propose a CRF-based machine learning method for biomedical named entity learning and introduce two types of word representation features and an external dictionary feature for expansion.

3   The Method and Features

3.1   The Research Problem

Generally, NER can be regarded as a sequence labeling problem, which is as follows: given a sequence of input tokens $x = \{x_1 \dots x_n\}$ and a set of labels L, determine a sequence of labels $y = \{y_1 \dots y_n\}$ such that each x_i can map to $y_i \epsilon L$, for $1 \leq i \leq n$. In the case of NER, labels mainly fall into two parts: the type of entities and the position of a token (i.e. whether the token is inside or outside the entity). In this paper, we intend to learn the position of a token of the entities and treat it as a classification task. For a better understanding of the position of a token, widely used model *IOBEW* is introduced as the label set. Defined by the model, *I* denotes that the token is inside the entity; *O* denotes that the token is outside the entity; *B* stands for the beginning of the entity; *E* represents the end of the entity, and *W* is the one-word entity. Figure 1 shows a sentence example annotated by the *IOBEW* notation. According to Vlachos [14], the *IOBEW* model can provide better discriminative capability than other models.

> **Sentence:**
> *A 9-year-old woman with paroxysmal nocturnal haemoglobinuria (PNH) was found to have an inherited deficiency in the ninth complement component (C9).*
> **Entities:**
> *paroxysmal nocturnal haemoglobinuria*
> *PNH*
> *inherited deficiency in the ninth complement component*
> **Tags:**
> A/O 9-year-old/O woman/O with/O paroxysmal/B nocturnal/I haemoglobinuria/E (/O PNH/W)/O was /O found/O to/O have/O an/O inherited/B deficiency/I in/I the/I ninth/I complement/I component/E (/O C9/O)/O ./O

Fig. 1. An example sentence annotated using *IOBEW* notation

3.2 Features

To perform classification, CRFs takes features as input which are the numerical representations of the words to be classified and their context. In general, suppose that H is a set of hypothesis (i.e. any predefined conditions) and T is a set of possible labels, the feature function is thus defined in Eq. (1), where $h_i \in H$ and $t_j \in T$.

$$f(h, t) = \begin{cases} 1, & \text{if } h = h_i \text{ is satisfied and } t = t_j \\ 0, & \text{otherwise} \end{cases} \tag{1}$$

Features generated from similar hypothesis can be grouped together. We usually refer such groups as feature templates. For instance, a Part-of-Speech (POS) feature template denotes the characteristics of the features which are the POS tags for specific words. Table 1 presents the feature templates used in our model.

Table 1. The defined feature templates in our model

Type	Feature	Function
Unigram	$w_n(n = -1, 0, 1)$	The previous n, current, and next n words
Prefix	$p_n(w_0), n = 1, 2, 3, 4$	The first n letters in the current word
Suffix	$s_n(w_0), n = 1, 2, 3, 4$	The last n letters in the current word
POS	$POS(w_0)$	The POS tag of the current word
Bigram	$t(w_{-1})$	The predicted tag of the previous word

Since data annotation is labor-intensive while a large amount of unlabeled text is easy to obtain, researchers paid more and more attention to extracting features from unlabeled corpora. Word representation (WR) takes advantage of large-scale unlabeled data to transform a word into a certain kind of representation implying underlying syntactic/semantic information of that word by means of an unsupervised learning algorithm. As evidenced by Tang et al. [5], three different types of word representation features for BNER were investigated and all the features were able to improve the performance of machine learning-based BNER systems.

In this paper, we explore two types of word representation features. The first is word embedding features. Word embedding, also called distributed word representation, aims to convert words into high dimensional real-valued vectors by neural network language model. While each element in a vector denotes a syntactic/semantic component, words that are syntactically/semantically similar usually share similar vectors. The distances among words can be estimated using similarity measures, e.g., cosine. Here, we adopt GloVe [15] to generate vector representations for words, since it is regarded as state-of-the-art [16]. After words are represented as vectors, we then use k-means clustering algorithm to cluster them into k clusters, and add the feature template GC_i, where $GC_i(w_0)$ is the i th cluster that the current word w_o belongs to.

Another is the cluster-based feature. The basic idea of cluster-based representation is that words sharing similar surroundings can be grouped into the same or close clusters and therefore a word can be represented by the cluster it belongs to. Brown clustering, a bottom-up hierarchical clustering algorithm, is utilized. The new feature template BC_i is defined, where $BC_i(w_0)$ is the i th cluster that the current word w_o belongs to.

Apart from word representation features, external dictionary information is also considered, as used in Chinese word segmentation by Zhao et al. [23]. Assume that W stands for the longest entity in which the current word w_0 occurs, the feature template Lt_0 is added, where L is the number of words and t_0 is the boundary tag of w_0 in W.

3.3   The CRFs Model

The toolkit we used is CRF++[1], which is a simple, customizable, and open source implementation of Conditional Random Fields (CRFs) [17]. CRFs-based methods have been applied to various domains and have achieved comparable results to previous rule-based methods [17–19]. CRFs is a probabilistic framework for labeling and segmenting structured data, such as sequences, trees and lattices. The underlying idea is to define a conditional probability distribution over label sequences given a particular observation sequence, rather than a joint distribution over both label and observation sequences. The primary advantage of CRFs against Hidden Markov Models (HMMs) is its conditional nature, resulting in the relaxation of the independence assumption required by HMMs in order to ensure tractable inference. Additionally, due to CRFs' linear-chain structure, it effectively overcomes the problem of the implicit condition of the HMM and avoids the label bias problem which is a weakness exhibited by maximum entropy Markov models (MEMMs) and other conditional Markov models based on directed graphical models [20]. CRFs outperforms both MEMMs and HMMs on a number of real-world tasks in many fields, including bioinformatics, computational linguistics and speech recognition.

For a chain-structured CRF in which each label sequence is augmented by start and end states, y_0 and y_{n+1}, the probability $p(y|x, \lambda)$ of label sequence y given an observation sequence x may be efficiently computed using matrices [21]. Letting Y be the alphabet from which labels are drawn and y and y' be labels drawn from this alphabet, a

---

[1] http://taku910.github.io/crfpp/.

set of $n + 1$ matrices $\{M_i(x)|i = 1,. ..., n + 1\}$ is defined, where each $M_i(x)$ is a $|Y \times Y|$ matrix with elements of the form

$$M_i(y', y \mid x) = exp \sum_j \lambda_j f_j(y', y, x, i) \tag{2}$$

Given observation sequence x, the unnormalized probability of label sequence y may be written as the product of the appropriate elements of the $n + 1$ matrices for that pair of the sequence. For observation sequence x, the normalization factor $Z(x)$ may be computed from the set of $M_i(x)$ matrices using closed semirings, an algebraic structure that provides a general framework for solving path problems in graphs.

$$p(y \mid x, \lambda) = \frac{1}{Z(x)} \prod_{i=1}^{n+1} M_i(y_{i-1}, y_i \mid x) \tag{3}$$

4   Experiment and Evaluation

4.1   Datasets

In order to evaluate the effectiveness of our method, a publically available standard dataset - NCBI disease corpus [22] is used in the experiment. The corpus contains 793 abstracts from PubMed, a free source developed and maintained by NCBI, at the U.S. National Library of Medicine (NLM), located at NIH.[2] In this corpus, all disease names and their corresponding concepts have been manually annotated. The released corpus is divided into training, development and testing data sets. The distribution of the datasets is shown in Table 2.

Table 2. The distribution of the NCBI disease corpus

Dataset	# of abstract texts	# of disease mentions
Training	592	5145
Development	100	787
Testing	100	960

4.2   Evaluation Metrics

The evaluation measures to assess the method performance are three widely used statistical classification measures: precision, recall and F1-measure. The corresponding equations are shown in Eqs. (4), (5) and (6).

---

[2] https://www.ncbi.nlm.nih.gov/pubmed/.

$$\text{Precision} = \frac{TP}{TP + FP} \qquad (4)$$

$$\text{Recall} = \frac{TP}{TP + FN} \qquad (5)$$

$$F1 = \frac{2 * \text{Precision} * \text{Recall}}{\text{Precision} + \text{Recall}} \qquad (6)$$

TP (True Positives) denotes the number of named entities that the system correctly recognized, *FP* (False Positives) the number of named entities that the system incorrectly recognized, and *FN* the number of non-named entities the system incorrectly recognized as named entities.

4.3   Results

While using CRF++ to train our model, we retain the default settings of the parameters since there is no apparent optimization of performance when tuning the regularization term and cut-off threshold for features on our development set. GENIA tagger[3] is used to obtain POS features. To generate word representation features, 927,238 abstracts in year 2013 and 484,205 abstracts in year 2016 are extracted respectively from the NIH publication dataset as the unlabeled biomedical text. For word embedding, GloVe from the official website[4] is applied. Each word is represented by a 200-dimension vector and the number of iteration is set to be 30. To cluster these word vectors, we use *k*-means clustering algorithm and Brown clustering (use the implementation provided by Liang[5]). In terms of external dictionary features, we build a disease dictionary comprised of 17,865 disease entities, by means of an online disease list provided by PharmGKB[6].

At the beginning, we set unigram and bigram features as mentioned in Sect. 3.2 as our baseline. After that, we conduct three experiments to evaluate the effectiveness of the proposed feature sets. The first experiment is to evaluate how WR features contribute to classification performance. For word embedding features, we test two different sizes of the training corpus as well as two different numbers of word clusters. The experiment results are shown in Table 3. As the results illustrate, compared with the baseline, for word embedding plus *k*-means clustering (KC) features, more data leads to significantly higher precision, recall and F1. However, according to our inspection on the development set, it seems there is no relationship between word cluster numbers and performance, since more clusters lead to performance decrease on the 2013 NIH corpus but increase on the 2016 NIH corpus using all the three measures. With regard to Brown clustering (BC) features, we set the number of clusters to be 500

---

[3] http://www.nactem.ac.uk/GENIA/tagger/.

[4] https://nlp.stanford.edu/projects/glove/.

[5] https://github.com/percyliang/brown-cluster/.

[6] https://www.pharmgkb.org/downloads/.

Table 3. The performance of CRFs-based model using k-means clustering and Brown clustering features on the development set

Features	Datasets for feature generation	Precision	Recall	F1
Baseline	N/A	0.7301	0.6048	0.6616
Baseline + k-means clustering	2013 NIH corpus (500 clusters)	0.7698	0.7052	0.7361
	2013 NIH corpus (1000 clusters)	0.7587	0.6950	0.7255
	2016 NIH corpus (500 clusters)	0.7446	0.6595	0.6995
	2016 NIH corpus (1000 clusters)	0.7581	0.6811	0.7175
Baseline + Brown clustering	2013 NIH corpus (500 clusters)	0.7546	0.6760	0.7131
	2016 NIH corpus (500 clusters)	0.7681	0.6862	0.7248
Baseline + KC + BC	2013 NIH corpus (500 clusters) + 2016 NIH corpus (500 clusters)	0.7871	0.7471	0.7666

since larger cluster number usually requires more training time[7]. The result shows that BC features are beneficial to the model, while more data does not suggest better performance. Hence, we combine the two word representation features for the better utilization, where KC features (500 clusters) are generated from 2013 NIH corpus and BC features (500 clusters) are from 2016 NIH corpus. The results indicate that these two types of features are complementary to each other.

The second experiment is to test the effectiveness of the described features and to find out the optimal combination of features for the named entity learning. Taking unigram and bigram as baseline features, the results on the development set are presented in Table 4. Compared with the other features, POS tags seem to be less effective. The affix features have significantly improved the performance with an increase of F1 from 0.6616 to 0.7629. It shows that the combination of POS and other features does not produce better performance than affix alone. When affix, BC, KC and dictionary features (Dict) are used, the learning achieves the best precision of 0.8026. However, the performance in terms of recall and F1 turns to be slightly lower when Dict features are included.

Table 4. The performance of CRFs-based model with different features on the development set

Features	Precision	Recall	F1
Baseline + affix	0.7849	0.7420	0.7629
Baseline + POS	0.7462	0.6239	0.6796
Baseline + dictionary	0.7375	0.6353	0.6826
Baseline + affix + POS	0.7844	0.7395	0.7613
Baseline + affix + BC +KC	0.8010	0.7827	0.7918
Baseline + POS + BC + KC + Dict	0.7788	0.7382	0.7580
Baseline + affix + BC +KC + Dict	0.8026	0.7751	0.7886

---

[7] For 2013 NIH corpus, it takes about 19 h to cluster words into 500 clusters, but 89 h into 1000 clusters on a machine with i5 CPU and 8 GB memory.

The last experiment compares the performance of our CRFs-based method on the testing dataset with the above two feature combinations. The results, as shown in Table 5, present that Dict features slightly improves the entity learning performance with an increase around 1.5% on all evaluation metrics. Moreover, with the help of the feature combinations, the performance has a significant improvement with 24.7% increase on F1 measure, demonstrating the effectiveness of the proposed feature sets.

Table 5. The performance of CRFs-based model with feature combinations on the testing set

Features	Precision	Recall	F1
Baseline	0.7131	0.5333	0.6103
Baseline + affix + BC + KC	0.7634	0.7292	0.7459
Baseline + affix + BC +KC + Dict	0.7801	0.7427	0.7609

5 Conclusion

This paper introduces our work on learning biomedical named entities from the NCBI disease corpus, through a CRFs-based method. In addition to standard features, we propose to integrate word representation features considering that there exists a large scale unlabeled biomedical corpora. Moreover, we also exploit extra information from existing domain dictionaries. Based on a standard NCBI corpus, results of our experiments suggest the effectiveness of the features for improving the performance of the CRFs-based BNER method.

Acknowledgements. The work was substantially supported by the National Natural Science Foundation of China (Nos. 61572145 and 61403088), the Frontier and Key Technology Innovation Special Grant of Guangdong Province (No. 2014B010118005), the Public Interest Research and Capability Building Grant of Guangdong Province (No. 2014A020221039), and the Innovative School Project in Higher Education of Guangdong Province (No.YQ2015062).

References

1. Kazama, J., Makino, T., Ohta, Y., Tsujii, J.: Tuning support vector machines for biomedical named entity recognition. In: Proceedings of the ACL Workshop on Natural Language Processing in the Biomedical Domain, vol. 3, pp. 1–8 (2002)
2. Athenikos, S.J., Han, H.: Biomedical question answering: A survey. Comput. Methods Prog. Biomed. **99**, 1–24 (2010)
3. Leaman, R., Gonzalez, G.: BANNER: an executable survey of advances in biomedical named entity recognition. In: Pacific Symposium on Biocomputing, vol. 13, pp. 652–663 (2008)
4. Yao, L., Liu, H., Liu, Y., Li, X., Anwar, M.W.: Biomedical named entity recognition based on deep neural network. Int. J. Hybrid Inf. Technol. **8**(8), 279–288 (2015)
5. Tang, B., Cao, H., Wang, X., Chen, Q., Xu, H.: Evaluating word representation features in biomedical named entity recognition tasks. Biomed. Res. Int. 1–6 (2014)

6. Wang, X., Yang, C., Guan, R.: A comparative study for biomedical named entity recognition. Int. J. Mach. Learn.Cybern., 1–10 (2015)
7. Li, K., Ai, W., Tang, Z., Zhang, F., Jiang, L., Li, K., Hwang, K.: Hadoop recognition of biomedical named entity using conditional random fields. IEEE Trans. Parallel Distrib. Syst. **26**(11), 3040–3051 (2015)
8. Fries, J., Wu, S., Ratner, A., Ré, C.: SwellShark: a generative model for biomedical named entity recognition without labeled data (2017). arXiv preprint arXiv:1704.06360
9. Zhang, S., Elhadad, N.: Unsupervised biomedical named entity recognition: experiments with clinical and biological texts. J. Biomed. Inf. **46**(6), 1088–1098 (2013)
10. Kuksa, P.P., Qi, Y.: Semi-supervised bio-named entity recognition with word-codebook learning. In: Proceedings of the 2010 SIAM International Conference on Data Mining, pp. 25–36. Society for Industrial and Applied Mathematics (2010)
11. Munkhdalai, T., Li, M., Yun, U., Namsrai, O.E., Ryu, K.H.: An active co-training algorithm for biomedical named-entity recognition. JIPS **8**(4), 575–588 (2012)
12. Munkhdalai, T., Li, M., Batsuren, K., Park, H.A., Choi, N.H., Ryu, K.H.: Incorporating domain knowledge in chemical and biomedical named entity recognition with word representations. J. Cheminf. **7**(1), 1–8 (2015)
13. Gridach, M.: Character-level neural network for biomedical named entity recognition. J. Biomed. Inf. **70**, 85–91 (2017)
14. Vlachos, A.: Tackling the BioCreative2 gene mention task with conditional random fields and syntactic parsing. In: Proceedings of the Second BioCreative Challenge Workshop, pp. 85–87 (2007)
15. Pennington, J., Socher, R., Manning, C.D.: GloVe: global vectors for word representation. In: Proceedings of the 2014 Conference on EMNLP, pp. 1532–1543 (2014)
16. John, V.: A survey of neural network techniques for feature extraction from text (2017). http://arxiv.org/abs/1704.08531
17. Lafferty, J., McCallum, A., Pereira, F.C.N.: Conditional random fields: Probabilistic models for segmenting and labeling sequence data. In: Proceedings of the Eighteenth International Conference on Machine Learning, vol. 8, pp. 282–289 (2001)
18. Jain, D.: Supervised named entity recognition for clinical data. CLEF 2015 Online Working Notes (2015)
19. Wang, S.K., Li, S., Chen, T.: Recognition of Chinese medicine named entity based on condition random field. J. Xiamen Univ. **48**(3), 359–364 (2009)
20. Zweig, G., Nguyen, P., Van Compernolle, D., et al.: Speech recognition with segmental conditional random fields: a summary of the JHU CLSP 2010 summer workshop. In: IEEE International Conference on Acoustics, Speech and Signal Processing, pp. 5044–5047 (2011)
21. Wallach, H.M.: Conditional random fields: an introduction. University of Pennsylvania (2004)
22. Doğan, R.I., Leaman, R., Lu, Z.: NCBI disease corpus: a resource for disease name recognition and concept normalization. J. Biomed. Inf. **47**, 1–10 (2014)
23. Zhao, H., Huang, C.-N., Li, M.: An improved chinese word segmentation system with conditional random field. In: Proceedings of the Fifth SIGHAN Workshop on Chinese Language Processing, pp. 162–165 (2006)

Computer-Assisted Content Analysis in Risk Identification of Public-Private Partnership Projects

Yingying Qu[✉]

School of Business, Guangdong University of Foreign Studies,
Guangzhou, China
yingyinqu2@126.com

Abstract. Public-private partnership (PPP) is increasingly popular around the world. The success in implementation of PPP is affected by the identification of the wide range of risks which exist in the different stages of PPP life cycle. Content analysis is a qualitative data analysis method, which is adopted in this study, since it can assist in understanding of the meaning of the texts, classifying the texts, and reducing to more relevant and manageable bits of data. In this study, a computer-assisted content analysis system is developed based on the part-of-speech and syntax-tree algorithm to exact and annotate keywords/ phrases, and build up coding framework to help users to identify PPP risks more efficiently and conveniently. The computer-assisted content analysis system is simulated by 20 secondary PPP cases. Finally, the results indicated that the computer-assisted content analysis system is having good potential in assisting users to identify PPP risks with great efficiency and convenience.

Keywords: Computer-assisted · Content analysis · PPP · Risk identification

1 Introduction

Public-Private Partnerships (PPPs) are growing in popularity throughout the world. This is a response to the need to invest in infrastructure as well as the constraints on public budgets. In this way, PPP is deployed to reduce public expenditure and increase cost-efficiency in infrastructure provision [1]. Many studies have shown that over the past 40 years, PPP projects are more efficient in service delivery. For example, the privately funded M4 freeway in Sydney which was completed 6 months ahead of schedule, the third runway at Sydney Airport which was completed 15 weeks ahead of schedule and $30 million under budget, offering a total saving of $200 million and, Junee Prison in Australia which was completed 3 months ahead of schedule and under budget saving an estimated $3 million in procurement costs. Private enterprises may also have more professional know-how in management, operating procedures, and use of appropriate technology [2, 3].

However, the process of delivering PPP involves distribution of responsibility and authority across a broad range of participants. This process has been generally characterized by the review of multiple objectives including quality performance, public

© Springer International Publishing AG 2017
T.-C. Huang et al. (Eds.): SETE 2017, LNCS 10676, pp. 528–538, 2017.
https://doi.org/10.1007/978-3-319-71084-6_62

satisfaction, financial return, environmental performance and safety performance [4]. These objectives indicate that the implementations of PPPs are affected by a wide range of risks that exist in different dimensions and at different stages in PPP project life cycle. The failure to identify these risks may lead to serious consequences including poor quality, programming delays, budget over-runs, environmental pollution and prolonged contractual disputes. Therefore, a number of studies have been undertaken to identify the risks that affect the performance of PPP projects [5–8].

Content analysis is a summarizing, qualitative analysis of messages that relies on the scientific method, including an observance of the standards of objectivity, a priori design, reliability, validity, generalizability, reliability, and hypothesis testing [9]. The content analysis is adopted in this study to identify risks in PPP projects, since it can assist in understanding of the meaning of the texts, classifying the texts, and reducing to more relevant and manageable bits of data. However, the content analysis is usually done by manual work, which is redundant, tedium and inefficient. There is little literature on the exploration of computer-assisted content analysis in PPP risk identification. Based on the part-of-speech and syntax-tree algorithm, in this study, a computer-assisted content analysis system is developed to exact and annotate keywords/phrases, and build up coding framework to help people identify PPP risks more efficiently and conveniently.

The remainder of the paper is organized as follows. In Sect. 2 literature on the PPP risk framework is reviewed. Section 3 presents the model of computer-assisted content analysis. The application of computer-assisted content analysis in PPP risk identification is reported in Sect. 4, by use of 20 secondary PPP cases. Finally concluding remarks are presented in Sect. 5.

2 PPP Risk Framework

Given the complexity, size and time frame of concession contracts, there are an enormous range of potential risks which can affect the expected PPP outcomes. The simple and valid method of risk identification is the development of a risk checklist [10].

Tiong (1990) classified risks according to the phases of PPP project, which include pre-investment, implementation, construction, operation, and transfer [11]. Combined with the nature of risk and phrase of project, UNIDO (1996) developed a checklist classifying risks in two major categories: general/country risks and specific project risks [12]. Political risks, commercial risks and legal risks are classified in the first category, whereas developmental risks, construction/completion risks and operating risks fall into the second category. Akintoye et al. (1998) have done risk assessment in private finance initiative (PFI) projects in UK [13]. The 10 most important risk factors identified are design risk, construction cost risk, performance risk, risk of delay, cost overrun, commissioning risk, volume risk, operating/maintenance risk, payment risks and tendering cost risks. Kumaraswamy and Zhang (2001) identified several risks in PPP, such as social and political risks, economic risks, legal and regulatory framework, political environment, state credibility, domestic capital market, competitive bidding, land acquisition, options of government guarantees [9]. Grimsey and Lewis (2002) identified nine risks in PPP: technical risks, construction risk, operating risk, revenue risk, financial risks, force majeure risk, regulatory/political risks, environmental risks and project default [14]. While, two years later, they reduced to six categories: public risk; asset risk, operating risk, sponsor risk, financial risk and default risk [6]. Li et al. (2005) proposed a 3-level risk classification, by which risks are grouped into three categories: macro-, meso-, and micro-level risks [15]. The macro-level risks are exogenous, i.e., external to the project itself. The risks at this level are often associated with political and legal conditions, economic conditions, social conditions and weather. The meso-level risks are endogenous to the project, which represent the PPP implementation problem, such as project demand/usage, location, design and construction and technology. The micro-level risks comprise the risks in the stakeholder relationships during the procurement process, due to the inherent differences between the public and private sectors in contract management. This classification was adopted by Shen et al. (2006) [4], Ke et al. (2010) [8], since it provided a comprehensive overview of risk factors in PPP projects.

We identify the PPP risk framework by mapping the three previous work: (1) Kumaraswamy and Zhang [5], (2) Grimsey and Lewis [6], and (3) Li et al. [15], since these three framework are considered as relatively mature, and are adopted by other researches for exploring PPP risks. The identified framework is shown in Table 1.

Table 1. The proposed PPP risk framework

No.	Type of risk	1	2	3
	Financial risk			
1	Interest rate (i.e. financial cost)	√	√	√
2	Inflation rate volatility	√	√	√
	Economic risk			
3	Market demand forecast	√	√	√
4	Rate of investment return	√	√	√
5	Change in taxes, tariffs		√	
6	Residual asset risk		√	√
	Design risk			
7	Design deficiency (from fault intender specification, contractor design fault, etc.)		√	√
	Site risk			
8	Site preparation (i.e. land acquisition, material/labour availability, site redemption, tenure, pollution/discharge, community liaison, pre-existing liability, etc.)	√	√	√
9	Site condition (i.e. ground conditions, supporting structures, etc.)		√	
10	Land use		√	
	Construction risk			
11	Construction cost overrun (i.e. contract variation, change in scope of work)		√	√
12	Construction time overrun (i.e. late design change, default of sub-contractors/suppliers etc.)		√	√

(continued)

Table 1. (*continued*)

No.	Type of risk	1	2	3
13	Construction quality (i.e. technical risk)		√	√
	Operation risk			
14	Operation cost overrun (i.e. project company request for change in practice; industrial relations, repairs, occupational health and safety, maintenance, other costs, government change to output specifications, etc.)		√	√
15	Operation time overrun (i.e. operator default in low operation productivity, government delays in granting or renewing approvals, providing contracted inputs, etc.)		√	√
16	Quality of operation service		√	
	Political risk			
17	Unstable government and government policy	√	√	√
18	Political intervention (i.e. breach/cancellation of licence; expropriation; failure to renew approvals, discriminatory taxes, import restrictions, political opposition, etc.)	√	√	√
	Legal risk			
19	Change in law	√	√	√
20	Change in legal and regulatory framework			√
21	Legal support	√		
22	**Force majeure** (i.e. floods, earthquake, riots, strikes)		√	√

3   Model of Computer-Assisted Content Analysis

Content analysis is a summarizing, qualitative analysis of messages that relies on the scientific method, including an observance of the standards of objectivity, a priori design, reliability, validity, generalizability, reliability, and hypothesis testing [9]. The content analysis is adopted in this study to identify risks in PPP projects, since it can assist in understanding of the meaning of the texts, classifying the texts, and reducing to more relevant and manageable bits of data. Content analysis measures variables as they "naturally" occur, as it focuses on the words, the message component as the unit of data collection or analysis, by simply counting how many times the variables occur. However, the content analysis in PPP risk identification is usually done by manual work, which is redundant, tedium and inefficient. There is little literature on the exploration of computer-assisted content analysis in PPP risk identification.

Table 2. The types of computer-assisted qualitative analysis systems

Text retrievers – search for words or phrases
Text base managers – sort and organize data
Code and retrieve – support coding and reporting by codes

There are several types of computer-assisted qualitative analysis systems (in Table 2). The first type tended to focus on data management. It was the common experience of researchers carrying out qualitative analysis in the days before computers that such work required careful and complex management of large amounts of texts, codes or notes [16]. The second type could manage the large amounts of data they created, maintain links between the chunks of data and ensure that important ideas could always be tracked back [17]. The third type combines the word processor and simple database, which enabled researchers to search texts and store the results of any extracted chunks in a way that could be easily manipulated. The attaching of labels to chunks of text, called coding, is a central activity in much qualitative analysis. Such code-and-retrieve function make it was not only to select chunks of text and apply codes to them, but also to retrieve all similarly coded text without losing any information about where it came from and to work with it in further analyses. In this sense, the computer-assisted content analysis is to build up the coding framework to search texts and store the results of the extracted chunks, and usually it is achieved by annotation.

Based on the part-of-speech and syntax-tree algorithm, a computer-assisted content analysis system is developed to exact and annotate keywords/phrases, and build up coding framework to help people to identify PPP risks more efficiently and conveniently.

Table 3. The algorithm for syntax-tree-based phrase extraction

```
#------------------POS tagging
tokens = nltk.word_tokenize(sentence)
tagged = nltk.pos_tag(tokens)
#------------------ tree parsing
grammar = r"""
   NBAR:
       # Nouns and Adjectives, terminated with Nouns
       {<JJ><NN.*>*<NN.*>}
       {<NN.*>*}
   NP:
       {<NBAR>}
       # Above, connected with in/of/etc...
       {<NBAR><IN><NBAR>}
   VB:
       {<V|VB|VP>}
   """

#------------------ tree matching
cp = nltk.RegexpParser(grammar, loop=2)
cp_tree = cp.parse(tagged)
#------------------ phrase generation
phrases = get_terms(cp_tree)
```

(1) Part-Of-Speech-based keywords extraction. This algorithm has the following main steps: (1) pre-processing, clearing, and splitting; (2) sentence splitting; (3) Part-Of-Speech tagging based on the word tokenization using NLTK; (4) stop words filtering; (5) word matching with predefined tag list (e.g., NN, NNS, NNP, VB, and VBP).
(2) Syntax-tree-based phrase extraction. This algorithm has the following main steps: (1) pre-processing, clearing, splitting; (2) sentence splitting; (3) Part-Of-Speech tagging based on the word tokenization using NLTK; (4) syntax tree generation; (5) tree matching with rules using a Regexp Parser; (6) phrase generation according to matched trees. The core steps of the algorithm are represented as Table 3. In the algorithm, for example, "{<JJ> <NN.*> *<NN.*>}" is a typical rule to extract noun phrases including "adjective noun", "adjective noun noun", etc.

4 Application of Computer-Assistant Content Analysis in PPP Risk Identification

The existing publications relevant to PPP projects on the following leading construction management journals were used: *International Journal of Project Management*, *Journal of Construction Engineering and Management*, *Construction Management and*

Table 4. The list of 20 secondary PPP cases

No.	PPP case	Country	Year of PPP
1	Dulles Greenway	US	1995
2	Tampa Bay Seawater Desalination Project	US	2003
3	The Alberta Special Water Management System	Canada	1987
4	The Highway 407 Express Toll Route	Canada	1993
5	Chile Highway Projects	Chile	1998
6	Venezuelan Oil Project	Venezuela	2007
7	The Ngone Bridge Project, LAO PDR	LAO PDR	1994
8	Channel Tunnel Rail Link Project	UK	1994
9	Taiwan Electronic Toll Collection (ETC) Program	Tai Wan	2003
10	Water and Sanitation Project in Tucuman	Argentina	1995
11	Malaysia's Sewerage System	Malaysia	1993
12	Highway infrastructure in Central America and Mexico	Mexico	1995
13	Mexican Highway	Mexico	1990
14	Mexican National Railways	Mexico	1996
15	Airport Project in Lima	Lima	2001
16	Buenos Aires Water and Sanitation Project	Argentina	1993
17	Colombia Airport Concession	Columbia	1995
18	Samana Highway Project in the Dominican Republic	Dominican Republic	2002
19	Port Concession in Peru	Peru	1999
20	Water and Sanitation Concession in Bolivia	Bolivia	1999

Economics. The selection of these journals was based on the highest scores in quality rating. The researcher followed the method of Tang et al. [18] to employ a systematic search to identify papers with the following phrases in titles, keywords, or abstracts: ["Public Private Partnership" AND ["Risk"]. The search focuses on the case studies, with the papers published from 2000 to 2014. Finally 20 PPP cases were selected randomly and listed in Table 4.

Based on part-of-speech and syntax-tree algorithm, the keywords and phrases of the Case 1 are extracted in, as well as how many times these keywords and phrases occurred. Based on the risk framework summarized in Table 1, the annotations of these keywords and phrases in Case 2 for content analysis are shown in Fig. 1. The coding framework for content analysis in risk identification of these 20 PPP cases is shown in Fig. 2.

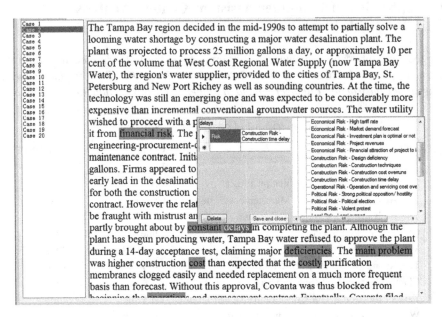

Fig. 1. Annotation for computer-assisted content analysis in PPP risk identification

Figure 3 shows the results of computer-assisted content analysis in risk identification of these 20 secondary PPP cases. The number in Fig. 3 represents the PPP Case Number. The results generated by the system are the same as the manual work in Table 5, which indicated that the computer-assisted content analysis system is having good potential in assisting parties to identify PPP risks with great efficiency and convenience.

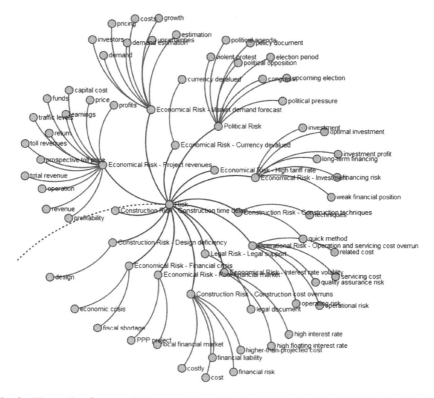

Fig. 2. The coding framework for computer-assisted content analysis in PPP risk identification

Financial Risk - Interest rate	14,15,12		14,15			
Financial Risk - Inflation rate volatility						
Economic Risk - Market demand forecast	3,8,12,13,14,15	3,17,18	8,14,15	13	6,19	1,7
Economic Risk - Rate of investment return	3,12,13	3,18,4	4	13	19	1,7,20,11
Economic Risk - Change in taxes, tariffs				10		
Economic Risk - Residual asset risk						
Design Risk - Design deficiency	12,13	4	4	13		
Site Risk - Site preparation						
Site Risk - Site condition						
Site Risk - Land use						
Construction Risk - Construction cost overrun	12,13	4	4	13	5	
Construction Risk - Construction time overrun						
Construction Risk - Construction quality	12	9,16		16		
Operation Risk - Operation cost overrun		4,9,17	4	11		
Operation Risk - Operation time overrun						
Operation Risk - Quality of operation service		16		11,16	10	20
Political Risk - Unstable government and government policy						
Political Risk - Political intervention	8	4,17,18	8,4	11	6,10,19,2	5,7,20
Legal Risk - Change in law						
Legal Risk - Change in legal and regulatory framework						
Legal Risk - Legal support		9		11		
Force Majeure						

Fig. 3. Results of computer-assisted content analysis in risk identification of 20 secondary PPP cases

Table 5. Results of manual work of risk identification of 20 secondary PPP cases

No.	Risk	1	2	3	4	5	6	7	8	9	10	11	12	13	14	15	16	17	18	19	20
	Financial risk																				
1	Interest rate												√		√	√		√	√		
2	Inflation rate volatility												√					√	√		
	Economic risk																				
3	Market demand forecast	√		√			√	√	√				√	√	√	√		√	√	√	
4	Rate of investment return	√		√	√			√			√	√	√					√	√	√	√
5	Change in taxes, tariffs	√						√			√		√			√					√
6	Residual asset risk																				
	Design risk																				
7	Design deficiency				√								√	√							√
	Site risk																				
8	Site preparation land acquisition				√																
9	Site condition																				
10	Land use																				
	Construction risk																				
11	Construction cost overrun		√		√	√							√	√							
12	Construction time overrun		√																		
13	Construction quality		√						√				√				√				
	Operation risk																				
14	Operation cost overrun	√			√				√		√				√		√				
15	Operation time overrun														√						
16	Quality of operation service								√	√							√				√
	Political risk																				
17	Unstable government and government policy								√												

(*continued*)

Table 5. (*continued*)

No.	Risk	1	2	3	4	5	6	7	8	9	10	11	12	13	14	15	16	17	18	19	20
18	Political intervention		√		√	√	√	√	√		√	√						√	√	√	√
	Legal risk																				
19	Change in law																				
20	Change in legal and regulatory framework																				
21	Legal support								√		√										
22	**Force majeure**																				

5   Conclusions

This paper discusses the computer-assisted content analysis in PPP risk identification.

Based on the part-of-speech and syntax-tree algorithm, the computer-assisted content analysis system is developed to exact and annotate keywords/phrases, and build up coding framework to help people to identify PPP risks more efficiently and conveniently. The system is simulated by 20 secondary PPP cases. The results generated by the system are the same with the manual work. Therefore, it is indicated that the computer-assisted content analysis system is having good potential in assisting parties to identify PPP risks with great efficiency and convenience.

References

1. Albalate, D., Bel, G., Paula, B., Geddes, R.R.: Risk mitigation and sharing in motorway PPPs: a comparative policy analysis of alternative approaches. J. Comparat. Policy Anal.: Res. Pract. **17**(5), 481–501 (2015)
2. Akintoye, A., Beck, M., Hardcastle, C.: Public-Private Partnerships—Management Risks and Opportunities. Blackwell Science, Oxford (2003)
3. Ryan, M., Menezes, F.: Public-private partnerships for transport infrastructure: some efficiency risks. New Zealand Econ. Pap. **49**(3), 276–295 (2015)
4. Shen, L., Platten, A., Deng, X.P.: Role of public private partnerships to manage risks in public sector projects in Hong Kong. Int. J. Project Manag. **24**, 587–594 (2006)
5. Kumaraswamy, M.M., Zhang, X.Q.: Governmental role in BOT-led infrastructure development. Int. J. Project Manag. **19**, 195–205 (2001)
6. Grimsey, D., Lewis, M.K.: Public Private Partnership: The Worldwide Revolution in Infrastructure Provision and Project Finance. Edward Elgar, Cheltman (2004)
7. Ng, A., Loosemore, M.: Risk allocation in the private provision of public infrastructure. Int. J. Project Manag. **25**, 66–76 (2007)
8. Ke, Y.J., Wang, S.Q., Chan, A.P.C.: Risk allocation in public-private partnership infrastructure projects: comparative study. J. Infrastruct. Syst. **16**(4), 343–351 (2010)
9. Hwang, B., Zhao, X., Gay, M.J.S.: Public private partnership projects in Singapore: factors, critical risks and preferred risk allocation from the perspective of contractors. Int. J. Project Manag. **31**, 424–433 (2012)

10. Broadbent, J., Gill, J., Laughlin, R.: Identifying and controlling risk: the problem of uncertainty in the private finance initiative in the UK's National Health Service. Crit. Perspect. Account. **19**(1), 40–78 (2008)
11. Tiong, R.L.K.: BOT projects: risk and securities. Constr. Manag. Econ. **8**(3), 315–328 (1990)
12. UNIDO: Guidelines for Infrastructure Development Through BOT Projects. United Nations Development Organization, Vienna (1996)
13. Akintoye, A., Taylor, C., Fitzgerald, E.: Risk analysis and management of private finance initiative projects. Eng. Constr. Archit. Manag. **5**(1), 9–21 (1998)
14. Grimsey, D., Lewis, M.K.: Evaluating the risks of public private partnerships for infrastructure projects. Int. J. Project Manag. **20**, 107–118 (2002)
15. Li, B., Akintoye, A., Edwards, P.J., Hardcastle, C.: The allocation of risk in PPP/PFI construction projects in the UK. Int. J. Project Manag. **23**, 25–35 (2005)
16. Marshall, H.: Horses for courses: facilitating postgraduate research students' choice of Computer Assisted Qualitative Data Analysis System (CAQDAS). Contemp. Nurse **13**(1), 29–37 (2002)
17. Noble, H., Smith, J.: Qualitative data analysis: a practical example. Evid. Based Nurs. **17**(1), 2 (2014)
18. Tang, L.Y., Shen, Q., Cheng, E.W.L.: A review of studies on public-private partnership projects in the construction industry. Int. J. Project Manag. **28**, 683–694 (2010)

Pedagogical Principle Based E-learning Exploration: A Case of Construction Mediation Training

Yingying Qu[1], Zhiwen Yu[2], Hao Cong[2], and Tianyong Hao[3(✉)]

[1] School of Business,
Guangdong University of Foreign Studies, Guangzhou, China
yingyinqu2@126.com
[2] School of Computer Science and Engineering,
South China University of Technology, Guangzhou, China
zhwyu@scut.edu.cn, 1015558062@qq.com
[3] School of Information Science and Technology,
Guangdong University of Foreign Studies, Guangzhou, China
haoty@126.com

Abstract. E-learning increasingly serves institutes as a fundamental infrastructure that enables teachers to provide students with diverse knowledge and to strengthen interactions between teachers and students. In the implementation of e-Learning, one of the most essential prerequisites is the understanding of underlying pedagogy. Most e-learning providers perceive themselves as mere providers of technology. They seldom inform learners how to select learning materials to teach and learn. The learning path, as a routine to guide learner to select the appropriate learning material, is therefore a significant issue for considering any single learning path cannot adapt to all learners. Therefore, this paper proposes a new pedagogical principle-based e-learning framework for identifying customised learning paths. Based on the framework, a construction mediation training system is introduced. The system has pioneered such a learning path to guide learners to start at preferred position and make efficient bargaining exchange to achieve "win-win" settlement. The experimental results demonstrate the effectiveness of the e-learning system.

Keywords: Pedagogical principle · E-learning · Mediation training · Framework

1 Introduction

All recent advancements in Information and Communication Technology (ICT) have produced a great impact on many aspects of daily life, especially on education and training [1]. It is now applicable to different modes of education, for example, distance education and web-based education. Over the past decades, e-learning has been developed at such a rapid rate that they are commonly accepted as an increasingly popular alternative to traditional face-to-face education [2]. One of the most crucial prerequisites for successful implementation of e-Learning is the need for careful

© Springer International Publishing AG 2017
T.-C. Huang et al. (Eds.): SETE 2017, LNCS 10676, pp. 539–547, 2017.
https://doi.org/10.1007/978-3-319-71084-6_63

consideration of the underlying pedagogy, or how learning takes place [3]. In practice, however, this is often the most neglected aspect in effort to implement e-Learning [4]. For example, Hirumi [5] summarized several guidelines for development of quality e-learning programs, which include (1) Statement of the regional accrediting commissions on the evaluation of electronically offered degree and certificate program [6], (2) Quality on the line: Benchmarks for success in Internet-based distance education [7], (3) Guiding Principles for Distance Learning in Learning Society [8], (4) Distance Education: Guidelines for Good Practice [9], (5) Standards in open and distance education [10].

Although, these guidelines addressed some important instructional variables, such as objectives, events, assessment, feedback, but the e-learning pedagogical principles are seldom deliberated. As a result, most e-learning providers perceive themselves as mere providers of technology. For example, they provide learning materials only without telling educators the way to select learning materials. Generally, inappropriate learning materials may lead a learner to cognitive overload or disorientation during the learning processes, thus it results in reducing learning performance. The learning path is defined as a routine to guide learner to select the appropriate learning material and achieve the best learning performance. The learning path is an important issue for e-learning system, because no fixed learning path is appropriate for all learners. In this regard, the customized learning path will be developed and applied in this paper.

In the next section, the problems in current e-learning practice are identified and the pedagogical principle-based e-learning framework is built up to identify the customised learning paths. The framework is then applied and illustrated by an e-learning construction mediation training system in Sect. 3. Section 4 comes with a summary.

2 The Pedagogical Principle-Based E-learning Framework

Pedagogical principles are theories that govern and deliver quality education practice. "Seven Principles of Good Practice" [11], which was first published by the American Association for Higher Education, developed a great model for both quality collegiate education and technology-based distance education [12, 13]. It described some essential components that were important in constituting effective learning environments including student-faculty contact, cooperation among students, students' active learning, etc. Based on Jonassen [14], Ruokamo and Pohjolainen [15] summarised seven qualities of learning containing active in learning process, collaborative with each other in learning, willing to achieve the intended learning objectives, able to apply the knowledge they learnt into practice, etc. All these qualities are interactive, interrelated, and interdependent with each other. Govindasamy [3] proposed another five pedagogical attributes for successful e-learning: developing content, storing and managing content, packaging content, student support, and assessment. Based on the previous studies, the problems in current e-learning practice are summarized in Table 1, including achievable intended learning outcomes, constructive learning material, involvement and interaction in learning, learning progress tracking and measurable evaluation for learning outcome.

Table 1. The summary of E-learning instruments, problems, and E-learning attributes

E-learning Instruments based on the pedagogical principles	Problems in current E-learning practice	Pedagogical principle-based E-learning attributes
(1) Determine learning objectives that students are active and willing to achieve [16]	Achievable intended learning outcomes	Intended learning outcomes
(2) Instructional events, design and delivery, instructional methods and e-learning system [14]; (3) Learning material is easy to download and easy to read [3, 15]; (4) Construct new knowledge on the basis of their previous knowledge; instructional design and delivery [17]; (5) Instructional sequencing of learning interaction [5]; (6) Innovative teaching with technology enhanced study [18]	Constructive learning material	Learning material
(7) Engage students in active learning process; students have great involvement in the learning process [14]; their involvement can be increased with the teaching and learning modules [15]; Encourage collaboration among students [19]; (8) Learning tasks are situated in a meaningful real world tasks or introduced through case-based or problem-based real life examples [20]; (9) Students are able to use the knowledge they learnt [3]; (10) Learners articulate what they have learned and reflect on the processes and decisions entailed by the process [11, 17]	Involvement and interaction in learning	Learning interaction
(11) Students feedback and response [12]; (12) Easy for students to track learning progress [21, 22]; (13) Students can feel in control of their study [17]; (14) Encourage student-faculty contact [11]	Learning progress tracking	Learning performance
(15) Assessment is to test whether the learning performance achieve the learning objectives [23]; (16) Assessment and evaluation of student learning and performance outcomes [17, 18]	Measurable evaluation for learning outcome	

The corresponding pedagogical principle-based e-learning attributes summarized in Table 1 are intended learning outcomes, learning material, learning interaction, and learning performance. The inappropriate learning materials may lead a learner to cognitive overload or disorientation during the learning processes, thus reducing learning performance. The learning path is defined as a routine to guide learner to select the appropriate learning material and achieve the best learning performance. The learning path is considered as an important issue for e-learning system, since any single learning path cannot be appropriate for all learners. In this paper, the customized learning path will be proposed, based on the learners' intended learning outcomes and their personal preferences indicated in learning interactions. The pedagogical principle-based E-learning framework is shown in Fig. 1.

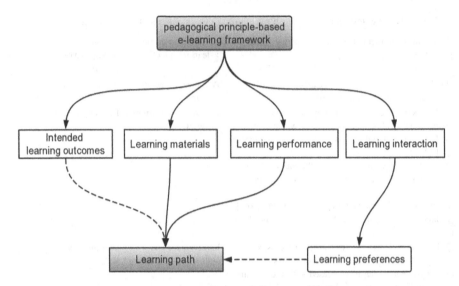

Fig. 1. The pedagogical principle-based E-learning framework

3   Case Study: Construction Mediation Training

In the recent twenty years, conflicts and disputes have been increasing common in construction projects. Mediation has been regarded as an effective informal means for resolving disputes, and it even has become an integral part of dispute settlement provisions in most standard forms of construction contract [24]. Therefore, there is a cogent need to provide mediation training to support its wider use. With the advance in information technology in the last few decades, the use of network technology to deliver training is the latest trend, and has been remarked as the 'e-learning revolution'. In this regard, a E-learning construction mediation training is designed to assist negotiators and mediators to achieve "win-win" settlement. The following attributes will be discussed: Intended Learning Outcomes, Learning Interaction and Learning Path.

(1) Intended Learning Outcomes
The E-learning construction mediation training provides customized learning paths for students to assist them to achieve "win-win" settlement in mediation. On completion of this training course, the students shall be able to reach a "win-win" agreement by themselves (Fig. 2).

(2) Learning Interaction
Learning interaction is one area where the e-learning course is remarkably different from the traditional classroom instruction. In traditional classroom instruction, student learning can be addressed on a supply-and-demand basis. In e-learning training, student learning is interactive with the visual instructional systems. From Laurillard's Conversational theory, it is indicated that a teaching strategy based on the interactions between

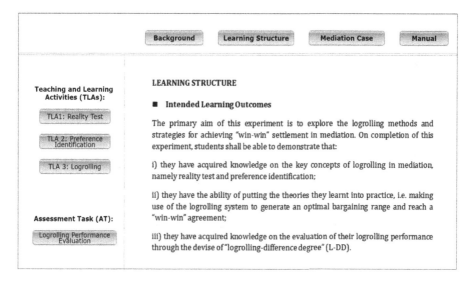

Fig. 2. E-learning construction mediation training – intended learning outcomes

instructor and learners are much more effective than the unilateral actions by the teachers [3]. Thus in this e-learning mediation training, role play is used to enhance the students' involvement and interactions in teaching and learning process. As shown in Fig. 3, the students were randomly assigned to the roles of Mediator, Contractor and Client.

In this E-learning construction mediation training system, it allows learners to choose subjects and to provide their affordable concession rate in mediation. For example, in Fig. 3, the Contractor is inputting the concession rate first. Mediator and Client will receive the Contractor's information, followed which Client responses a corresponding concession rate. Mediator will make a judgment whether the concession rate is within the potential win-win agreement zone or not, based on both Contractor and Client' affordable concession rate. The judgment will be delivered to Contractor and Client separately. Moreover learners also provide their personal preferences of the subjects to the system. The whole information will be submitted to the server, and the training system will compute and display the learning path, depending on those parameters.

(3) Learning Path

Generating learning path is widely studied by many researchers, such as, concept map [25], ontology [26], and learning path graph [27]. In this E-learning construction mediation training system, the learning path is developed to provide effective routes to guide students to achieve "win-win" settlement. The path is proposed through which students, who represent different parties in mediation, could improve joint value by bargaining exchange and get convergence along the efficient frontier. On the efficient frontier, parties could uphold their contracts when one party achieve its profits and the other party would still be better off. In other words, both parties move along the efficient frontier towards Pareto-optimal solution.

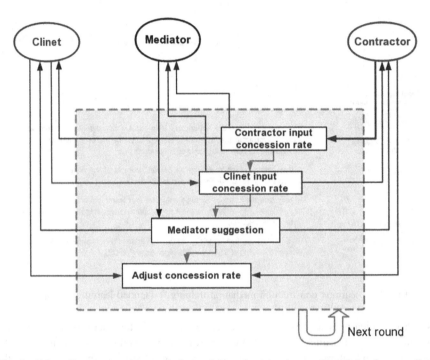

Fig. 3. E-learning construction mediation training - learning interaction (Color figure online)

In this mediation training, the students are recommended to begin at their most preferred position. The system will compute key points and display the learning path. In other words, the system will provide suggestions for students to make efficient bargaining exchange, through which each party concedes at minimum loss while maximum benefit to the other party. For example, as shown in Table 2, the student was recommended to begin at his most preferred position on issue 1 [523673k] and issue 2 [343725k], respectively. In each round, the system will provide a suggestion on the bargaining exchange on each issue. In the first round, the student was recommended to keep no change on issue 1, but increase to the bargaining alternative [351326k] on issue 2. In the second round, the student was recommended to increase to the bargaining alternative [534673k] on issue 1 and increase to the bargaining alternative [356123k] on issue 2. In the third round, the student was recommended to keep no change on issue 1 again, and increase to the bargaining alternative [3600417k] on issue 2. In the fourth round, the student was recommended to increase to the bargaining alternative [538721k] on issue 1 and keep no change on Issue 2. These suggestions involve (1) when (in which round) to concede, (2) on which issue, and (3) how much should be conceded. The student needs to decide whether he accept the suggestion or not. If the student rejects the suggestion, he needs to decide how to make efficient bargaining exchange and on which issue by himself.

In this mediation training course, the system displays the learning path for students. One student played the role of Client, and one student played the role of Contractor. The system's suggestions are marked in red and the students learning path is marked in

Table 2. E-learning construction mediation training – system suggestions

Round	Issue 1	Issue 2
0	[523673k]	[343725k]
1	No change	Increase to the bargaining alternative [351326k]
2	Increase to the bargaining alternative [534673k]	Increase to the bargaining alternative [356123k]
3	No change	Increase to the bargaining alternative [3600417k]
4	Increase to the bargaining alternative [538721k]	No change
	[538721k]	[3600417k]

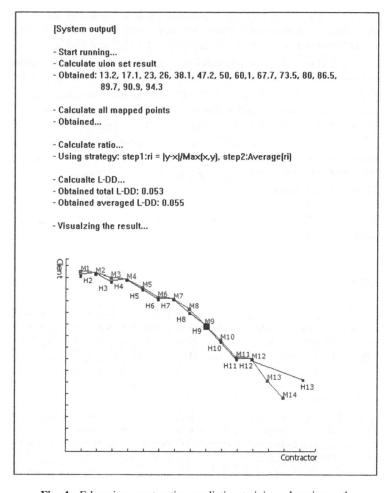

Fig. 4. E-learning construction mediation training - learning path

blue. M represents the system's suggestions and H represents students' actual movements. Client began at point H2, and Contractor began at point H13. It is found that although the students did not always follow the system's suggestions, they were still guided to achieve a win-win solution at H9 finally, which was also the efficient point calculated by the system as M9. The students' learning path was displayed in Fig. 4.

In addition, the system also calculates the difference degree between students' actual learning path and the system's suggested learning path. In Fig. 4, the difference degree between the students' actual learning path and the system's suggested learning path was 5%. The average difference degree of all the students participated in this e-learning training course was 5.5%. Thus this pair of students' learning performance was better than the average level.

4   Summary

The urgency of e-learning education is coming up in a rapid rate as it shows the advantages of removing the limitation of learning time, and space. Considering the importance of learning path in guiding learners to select appropriate learning material and achieve expected learning performance, this paper proposes an e-learning framework based on the summarized pedagogical Principle-based e-learning attributes. The framework is applied and illustrated by a construction mediation training system to develop the customized learning path. The learning path takes in account a number of parameters like the learners affordable concession rate in mediation, their preferences on issues. The system has been proved to be able to generate a learning path to guide learners to achieve "win-win" settlement during the mediation training. The case study presents the whole process of training and learning and it demonstrates the effectiveness of the proposed framework.

Acknowledgements. This work was supported by Innovative School Project in Higher Education of Guangdong (No. YQ2015062).

References

1. Basu, P., Bhattacharya, S., Roy, S.: Online recommendation of learning path for an E-learner under virtual university. In: Hota, C., Srimani, P.K. (eds.) ICDCIT 2013. LNCS, vol. 7753, pp. 126–136. Springer, Heidelberg (2013). https://doi.org/10.1007/978-3-642-36071-8_9
2. Connolly, T.M., MacArthur, E., Stansfield, M.H., McLellan, E.: A quasi-experimental study of three online learning courses in computing. Comput. Educ. **49**, 345–359 (2014)
3. Govindasamy, T.: Successful implementation of e-learning pedagogical considerations. Internet High. Educ. **4**, 287–299 (2002)
4. Bixler, B., Spotts, J.: Screen design and levels of interactivity in web-based training (2000). http://www.clat.psu.edu/homes/jds/john/research/ivla1998/ivla98.htm
5. Hirumi, A.: In search of quality: an analysis of e-learning guidelines and specifications. In: Orellana, A., Hudgins, T.L., Simonson, M. (eds.) The perfect online course: best practices for designing and teaching, pp. 39–67. IAP, Information Age Publishing, Charlotte (2009)

6. Council of Regional Accrediting Commissions: Statement of the regional accrediting commissions on the evaluation of electronically offered degree and certificate programs (2000). http://www.wiche.edu/telecom/guidelines.htm

7. Institute for Higher Education Policy: Quality on the line: benchmarks for success in Internet-based distance education, Twigg (2000). http://www.ihep.com/quality.pdf

8. American Council on Education: Guiding principles for distance learning in the learning society (1997). http://www.acenet.edu. Accessed 3 Oct 2002

9. American Federation of Teachers: Distance education: guidelines for good practice (2000). http://www.aft.org/pubs-reports/higher_ed/distance.pdf

10. Open and Distance Learning Quality Council: Standards in open and distance education (2001). http://www.odlqc.org.uk/stint.htm. Accessed 3 Oct 2002

11. Winona State University: The seven principles for good practice (2003). http://www.winona.msus.edu/president/seven.htm. Accessed 1 Nov 2003

12. Chickering, A.W., Gamson, Z.F.: Seven principles for good practice in undergraduate education. Am. Assoc. High. Educ. Bull. (1987, reprinted with permission). http://learningcommons.evergreen.edu/pdf/Fall1987.pdf

13. Sorensen, C.K., Baylen, D.M.: Learning online: adapting the seven principles of good practice to a web-based instructional environment. In: Orellana, A., Hudgins, T.L., Simonson, M. (eds.) The Perfect Online Course: Best Practices for Designing and Teaching, pp. 69–86. IAP, Information Age Publishing, Charlotte (2009)

14. Jonassen, D.H.: Supporting communities of learners with technology: a vision for integrating technology with learning in schools. Educ. Technol. **35**(4), 60–63 (1995)

15. Ruokamo, H., Pohjolainen, S.: Pedagogical principles for evaluation of hypermedia-based learning environments in mathematics. J. Univers. Comput. Sci. **4**(3), 292–307 (1998)

16. Berge, Z.: Active, interactive, and reflective elearning. Q. Rev. Distance Educ. **3**(2), 181–190 (2002)

17. Rubic for Online Instruction (2004). http://www.csuchico.edu/celt/roi/index.shtml

18. McLaren, A.C.: Designing effective e-learning: guidelines for practitioners. In: Orellana, A., Hudgins, T.L., Simonson, M. (eds.) The Perfect Online Course: Best Practices for Designing and Teaching, pp. 229–245. Information Age Publishing, Charlotte, IAP (2009)

19. Alexander, S.: E-learning developments and experiences. Education+Training **43**(4/5), 240–248 (2001)

20. Mason, R.: Time is the New Distance? An Inaugural Lecture. The Open University (2001). http://kmi.open.ac.uk/projects/stadium/live/berrill/robin_mason.html

21. Yacci, M.: Interactivity demystified: a structural definition for distance Education and intelligent computer-based instruction. Educ. Technol. **40**(4), 5–16 (2000)

22. Rosenberg, M.J.: E-Learning: Strategies for Delivering Knowledge in the Digital Age. McGraw-Hill, New York (2001)

23. Welsh, E.T., Wanberg, C.R., Brown, K.G., Simmering, M.J.: E-learning: emerging uses, empirical results and future directions. Int. J. Train. Dev. **7**(4), 1360–3736 (2003)

24. Cheung, S.O.: Construction mediation landscape in the civil justice system in Hong Kong. J. Legal Aff. Disput. Resolut. Eng. Constr. **2**(3), 169–174 (2010)

25. Chen, C., Peng, C.: Personalized E-learning system based on ontology-based concept map generation scheme. In: 7th IEEE International Conference on Advanced Learning Technologies (ICALT 2007) (2012)

26. Chang, M., Chang, A., Heh, J.S., Liu, T.: Contextaware learning path planner. WSEAS Trans. Comput. **7**(4), 49–70 (2013)

27. Karampiperis, P., Sampson, D.: Adaptive learning resources sequencing in educational hypermedia systems. Educ. Technol. Soc. **8**(40), 128–147 (2015)

An Approach to Constructing Sentiment Collocation Dictionary for Chinese Short Text Based on Word2Vec

Jianfeng Zhou, Boyu Chen, and Yangqing Lin[⊠]

Guangdong University of Foreign Sudies, Guangzhou, China
{Zhoujf1986,linyangqing0324}@foxmail.com,
joey94666@163.com

Abstract. The sentiment analysis of short texts is an important research hotspot in natural language processing. Based on the word features, this paper constructs a binary sentiment dictionary for a Chinese short text corpus using statistical methods. Then we calculate the sentiment value of the dictionary by Word2Vec algorithm and seed words. To evaluate the effectiveness of the dictionary, we manually annotated sentiment of the dictionary and compared with the calculation result. We also compared the performance effects of using different emotional dictionaries for the sentiment classification. The results show that the sentiment collocation dictionary is performed well in the emotional classification of Chinese short texts.

Keywords: Sentiment collocation dictionary · Chinese short text · POS features · Word2Vec

1 Introduction

Short texts are one of the main expressions of the Internet today and the mining of users' emotional tendencies from short texts plays an important role in the discovery of public opinion event and an important reference in the management of social networking platform. A short text is a refined cohesive text which has a shorter length, usually no more than 140 characters, such as micro-blog, news comments and forum comments. Emotional classification of short texts refers to "the classification of short texts contained in the subjective emotional positive and negative tendencies, so as to achieve understanding of the user psychology, supervision and guidance of public opinion and other purposes" [1].

The analysis of short texts emotional tendencies relies on high-quality short texts sentiment dictionaries. Therefore, the construction of sentiment dictionaries is a fundamental and essential research work. At present, the representative results include the Italian English sentiment dictionary SentiwordNet [2, 3], Chinese sentiment dictionary NTUSD by Taiwan University [4], emotional ontology by Dalian University of Technology [5], etc. Using numerical labels to quantify the emotional intensity of the words, these dictionaries divide the emotions from words into positive, neutral, and negative classes. However, the traditional sentiment dictionaries are just for the

T.-C. Huang et al. (Eds.): SETE 2017, LNCS 10676, pp. 548–556, 2017.
https://doi.org/10.1007/978-3-319-71084-6_64

emotional bias division of individual words, ignoring the grammar and contextual relationships. Besides, a short text, which is an unknown type or contains new words, is difficult to be analyzed by the dictionaries without flexibility. Consequently, how to construct an emotion dictionary for Chinese short texts has become an important research problem in the current NLP field.

In order to solve this problem, we proposed a method which is based on Chinese short text corpus to extract collocations according to the characteristics of part-of-speech tags (POS), word order, word frequency statistics, etc. [1]. This method uses Word2Vec algorithm to obtain word vector of each word in the binary collocation. By calculating the distance between each word and the seed emotion word, the emotion vector of the binary collocation phrase is acquired and the sentiment collocation dictionary can be constructed. Experiments show that our method has better accuracy of emotion classification results than the baseline methods.

The paper is organized as follows: Sect. 2 introduces the relevant work in the field of emotional classification of Chinese short texts. In Sect. 3, the construction of Chinese sentiment collocation dictionary is presented. The validity of the method is verified by experimental verification in Sect. 4, while Sect. 5 concludes the paper.

2   Related Work

There are some existing researches on text emotional classification. Yang et al. [6] used the PMI (pointwise mutual information) algorithm with the co-occurrence of the search engine to calculate the emotional weight of the emotional word, and carried on this weight in the Chinese emotional classification. Zhou et al. [7] used the context entropy of the cyber language discovery strategy, through the TF-IDF (term frequency inverse document frequency) for secondary filtering to get the set of candidates, and applied SO-PMI algorithm to the label word's emotions. Zhou et al. [8] got emotional comment words and seed words based on news commentary corpus and basic sentiment dictionary. Then, judging the polarity of the emotional lexicon and calculating its intensity according to the proposed method based on the PageRank algorithm, they constructed the news commentary sentiment dictionary and verified the accuracy and classification performance of the emotional word. Utilizing PMI-IR algorithm, Zhou [9] calculated the emotional tendencies of collocated words and determined the validity of collocation by using the C4.5 algorithm.

Hamdan et al. [10] built a state-of-the-art system for sentiment analysis in short texts, using a supervised classifier trained on several groups of features including n-gram, sentiment lexicons, negation, Z-score and semantic features. They compared the differences between the features and proved the validity of the sentiment lexicons. Zhang et al. [11] determined sentence's sentiment based on word dependency, and aggregated sentences to predict the document sentiment.

Google released the Word2Vec tool [12] in 2013 for training word vector [13], which can re-express words into vector forms according to a given corpus through a training model. The emergence of Word2Vec not only solves the problem of vector space model in traditional text vectorization, but also introduces semantic features, which contribute to short texts classification. Zhang et al. [14] used Word2Vec to capture the semantic features in selected domain and Chinese language, and used Word2Vec again and SVM to classify the comment texts.

Most researches regard words as features, but ignore the semantics and grammatical features. How to express grammar and semantic information of words has become a hot topic in the text classify field. Therefore, this paper presents a method based on Word2Vec algorithm for emotion calculation of collocation, and the construction of the emotion collocation dictionary.

3 The Construction of Binary Sentiment Collocation Dictionary

We proposed an automatic extraction model of binary collocation which combined linguistic knowledge with statistical information based on grammatical POS tagging, co-occurrence frequency statistics and word order, and then calculated the emotional weights of binary collocation by Word2Vec algorithm and seed emotion word set. We used the dictionary with high accuracy in our previous studies as the Chinese seed emotion word set.

3.1 The Construction of Binary Collocation Dictionary

Collocation is a combination of arbitrary and repeated words with a certain grammatical relationship, including fixed collocations and free collocations [15]. The fixed collocations are less, generally included in the various dictionaries. By contrast, the free collocations, which belong to the small particle size of the language knowledge, have a large number, and therefore need to be acquired and analyzed. Because of the unstructured characteristics of the internet text and in order to make the collocation dictionary with self-expansion, the collocations in this paper are mainly free-form models.

We established an effective binary collocations dictionary with the following clauses:

1. Grammatical structure information, the POS tagging features. According to the statistical analysis of the corpus data, on the basis of several kinds of words collocation patterns proposed in literature [16], we put forward to the pattern of nine models: $a + n$ (adjective + noun), $a + v$ (adjective + verb), $a + a$ (adjective + adjective), $v + n$ (verb + noun), $v + v$ (verb + verb), $v + a$ (verb + adjective), $n + a$ (noun + adjective), $n + n$ (noun + noun) and $n + v$ (noun + adjective).
2. Word order, with a structural, is relatively fixed expressed in the relationship between a pair of words. Suppose that the collocation $C_1 = \{W_1, W_2\}$, $C_2 = \{W_2, W_1\}$, then C_1 is called as left collocation and C_2 is called as right collocation. C_1 and C_2 join the word set as a separate combination phrase.
3. The relevance of words is also known as the coexistence of words. The two words have a high correlation when they appear many times at the same time. We defined the correlation and stability of the collocated words by the statistics of the coexistence of words.

Based on the three clauses proposed above, according to the study of linguistic research, this paper build the filtering model based on the combination of statistical model and linguistic knowledge, using the basic collocation word set extracted by POS tagging and word order, and constructed a binary collocation dictionary.

Extraction method of collocations:

1. We used the "JIEBA" segmentation tool to segment the corpus. Then we deleted those words that the POS tags are string(x), punctuation (w), auxiliaries (u), numerals (m) since they have the reverse effect to the correct rate of collocation of words.

   For example, the word segmentation result is: 都/d 是/vshi wifi/x 惹/v 的/ude1 祸/n !/wt. The filtered sentence is expressed as: 都/d 是/vshi 惹/v 祸/n.

   Set the extraction window to 5, 5 words as a binary collocation phrase according to the POS tagging are extracted each time. Suppose the sentence is $S = \{w_1, w_2, ..., w_n, ..., w_m\}$, where w_1 is the first word of the sentence, w_m is the mth word of the sentence, then the generated collocations include $S` = [w_1, w_2], [w_1, w_3], [w_1, w_4], [w_1, w_5], [w_1, w_6], ..., [w_n, w_{n+1}], [w_n, w_{n+2}], [w_n, w_{n+3}], [w_n, w_{n+4}], [w_n, w_{n+5}], ..., [w_{m-1}, w_m]\}$.

   The phrase being extracted in the above example is {[是/vshi 祸/n],[惹/v 祸/n]}.

2. Calculate the co-occurrence frequency of each collocation in the corpus, filter high frequency words and construct the candidate collocation set.

3.2   The Calculation of Sentiment Weight of Binary Collocation

Word2Vec [9] adopts continuous bag-of-words (CBOW) model and continuous skip-gram model to learn the vector representations of words. The CBOW architecture predicts the current word based on the context, and the skip-gram predicts surrounding words given the current word [17].

In the Word2Vec algorithm, the size of the cosine distance between the word vectors represents the relevance between the words. When the word is closer to the positive emotional word, it expresses the positive emotion at a higher probability in the text; when the word is closer to the negative emotional word, it expresses negative emotions at a higher probability in the text. Therefore, based on the Word2Vec algorithm, this paper proposed a EVC (Emotional Value of Collocation) method to calculate the average cosine distance of words of collocation and seed emotional word set to obtain its emotional weight value. The calculation steps are as follows:

1. Calculate the distance between the words in the collocation and the emotional word set of the positive and negative seeds.

$$f_p(Em_p, word) = \frac{\sum_{i=1}^{y} Cos(W_{pi}, word)}{y} \qquad (1)$$

$$f_n(Em_n, word) = \frac{\sum_{i=1}^{y} Cos(W_{ni}, word)}{y} \qquad (2)$$

$$f(Em, word) = f_p(Em_p, word) - |f_n(Em_n, word)| \tag{3}$$

In formula (1), E_{mp} is the average cosine distance of word between positive seed emotional word set $W_p = \{W_{p1}, W_{p2}, ..., W_{py}\}$, where W_{pi} is the i th word in the positive seed emotional word set. In formula (2), E_{mn} is the average cosine distance of word between negative seed emotion word set $W_n = \{W_{n1}, W_{n2}, ..., W_{ny}\}$, where W_{ni} is the i th word in the negative seed emotional word set. When $E_m > 0$, the emotional tendencies of words are positive, and the weight value represent their emotional tendencies; When $E_m = 0$, the emotional tendencies of the words are neutral; when $E_m < 0$, the emotional tendencies of the words are negative, and the weights represent their emotional tendencies.

2. Calculate the emotional weight value of collocation phrases by linear weighting metho

$$EVC(Em_c, Collocation) = a \times f(Em_{word_1}, word_1) + b \times f(Em_{word_2}, word_2) \tag{4}$$

In formula (4), Em_c is the emotional weight of collocation, where a is the emotional weight of $word_1$, b is the emotional weight of $word_2$, $f(Em_{word_1}, word_1)$ is the emotional weight value of $word_1$, $f(Em_{word_2}, word_2)$ is the emotional weight value of $word_2$.

When $Em_c > 0$, the emotional tendencies of collocations are positive, and weights represent their emotional intensity. When $Em_c = 0$, the emotional tendencies of collocation phrases are neutral. When $Em_c < 0$, the emotional tendencies of collating phrases are negative, and weights represent their emotional intensity. Filter the collocations by Em_c, and then remove the collocations that the emotional tendency is not clear (Em_c close to 0) to reduce the dictionary dimension.

4   Experiments and Results

In the experiments, the emotional classification results from the collocations are manually labeled, while the emotional tendency of Chinese short texts is calculated by the linear weighting method which is designated as our benchmark algorithm.

4.1   Experimental Tools and Data

The Word2Vec model used in the experiment was trained using the Gensim [4] tool in conjunction with the micro-blogging public articles [18]. Gensim is a professional theme model Python toolkit which has plays an important role in Word2Vec implementation [19]. The Word2Vec Model used 8 million articles as training data and extracted 352196 words.

After the analysis and filtration of the Taiwan University sentiment dictionary, Xsimilarity sentiment dictionary and Dalian University of Technology emotional vocabulary ontology dictionary, the lexical vocabulary dictionary from Dalian University of Technology [4] was used as the source of the seed emotion words. The words with the highest polarity were selected as the seed emotion words and then we obtained 1139 seed positive emotion words and 975 negative seed emotion words.

The related comments from the Sina micro-blogging and the Tencent microblogging are the main components of experimental corpus which had annotated by three researchers. Besides, 4000 train data from NLPCC 2013 were added into this corpus. Finally, with 7339 data we obtained a total of 96339 collocation(C_1) after calculation, including 16764 positive collocations and 79614 negative collocations. In C_1, the lowest collocations frequency was 1 and the highest was 262. Figure 1 shows the proportions. We used word frequency as a filter with a threshold of 1. Then we obtained 10176 collocations (C_2) include 1105 positive collocations,9037 negative collocations and 34 neutral collocations. In the experiment, we compared the effects of C1 and C2. Figure 1 also shows us that the emotional distribution negative collocations occupy a higher proportion. The experiment would reflect its influence. In Fig. 1, cf means collocations frequency.

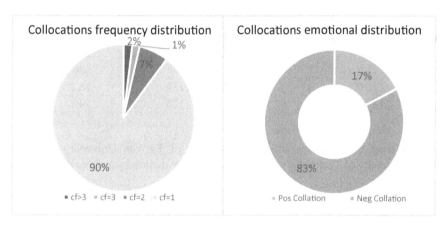

Fig. 1. Collocations distribution

4.2 The Results and Analysis

The highest emotional weight value was 0.062 (positive) and the lowest value was 0.127 (negative) in the collocations. We manually annotated the emotional tendency of our dictionary. The first team marked the dictionary without reading corpus. The result showed that manual tagging and auto computing matching rate was about 60%. After analyzing the multiple mismatched collocations, it is found that when the collocation does not have an emotional word, and both words are neutral words, they are prone to ambiguity, such as [事情/n 发生/v], [湖南省/ns 永州市/ns], [大巴/n 司机/n] and so on. The second artificial annotation was carried out, the researchers read the corpus in first and then labeled the collocations, the matching rate was up to 81%. Mismatched collocation mainly came from neutral corpus.

As this article only focused on the dictionary, so we used the linear weighting method to calculate sentiment weight of the texts. That is, the emotional weight of the text added by the sentiment weight of word or the emotional weight of the collocations together.

$$EM_{Text} = \{EM_{word1} + EM_{word2} + \ldots + EM_{wordn}\} \tag{5}$$

We used another dataset from Chinese micro-blog in the same subject with training dataset as the test dataset. It included 1417 positive texts and 5992 negative texts. We illustrated the performance and efficiency comparisons between the C_1 and C_2 in text sentiment classification. As shown in Table 1, we found that C_1 did better than C_2 in unidentified corpus because C_1 can found more collocations. But C_2 performed better in text sentiment classification with identified corpus because C_2 removed the collocations noise and enhanced the dictionary quality. Also C_1 took about 4 h for text classification that it's about ten times as much as C2. In order to identify corpus as much as possible that we used C_1 as our dictionary in the next experiment.

Table 1. Compare of collocations dictionaries

Dictionary	Unidentified corpus rate	Identified corpus		
		Accuracy rate	Positive recall rate	Negative recall rate
C_1	2.3%	76%	15%	88.2%
C_2	47%	82%	12%	94%

Paper used the Chinese sentiment dictionary of TaiWan University (NTUSD), Dalian University of Technology vocabulary ontology dictionary and our dictionary for comparison.

As shown in Table 2, the experimental results demonstrated that the sentiment collocation dictionary had a better effect in three kinds of dictionaries. The accuracy rate was 71.05%, which the positive recall rate was just 13.43%. The negative recall rate was 84.17%. First of all, imbalances training led to unbalanced collocation dictionary. In the dictionary, negative collocations were 13 times more than positive collocations in the acquired collocations, resulting in the fitting of the dictionary and the negative corpus.

Table 2. Comparison of dictionaries

Dictionary	Accuracy rate	Positive recall rate	Negative recall rate
CollocationDict	**71.05%**	13.43%	**84.17%**
NTUSD	46.25%	**44.10%**	46.50%
DUTIR	53.27%	43.65%	55.90%

In addition, we analyzed an error example by our method:

The original sentence: "开车一定要小心啊!祝福受伤的人早日康复!". (positive).

Included collocations: "开车/v 要/v,开车/v 小心/n,要/v 小心/n,要/v 祝福/nr,小心/n 祝福/nr,小心/n 受伤/v,祝福/nr 受伤/v,祝福/nr 人/n,受伤/v 人/n".

Collocations value: "−0.04157, −0.06263, −0.06334, −0.00279, −0.02385, −0.0776, −0.01705, −0.00533, −0.05908".

The example was one of the comments on the topic of the accident. After added by the emotional weight of the collocations that the emotional value of the text was −0.16754. It meant the emotional tendency of text was negative but our researchers labeled it as positive. After analysis and discussion, we found there was no positive collocation in the text but there were many positive words. According to average size of the cosine distance between word and the seed emotion word set, Word2Vec algorithm gained the emotion value of word. Even the word's emotion value was positive but it didn't mean the collocation consisting of these words would positive too. For example, the emotion value of "祝福" was 0.018351, emotion value of "小心" was −0.0422 and emotion value of "开车" was −0.02043 so that the emotional values of combination collocations were all below 0. So it caused a calculation error. In our next study, we would focus on the issue of how to combine words into collocation and gain the emotional value of it.

Even we used a very simple method to calculate the sentence polarity, our dictionary has a high performance, especially in the negative corpus. That's because a lower percentage of positive collocations. According to the collocation sentiment dictionary, the sentence polarity is dependent on the emotion score add by emotion value of collocations. Emotion value of collocations is affected by Word2Vec model, MVC algorithm and training data. Also negative corpus all account for a rather high percentage in the data set so that it may lead to generate a negative over-fitting phenomenon. In the experiments, our dictionary and method played well in the negative corpus so that we would raise the positive recall rate by increase percentage of positive corpus in the computational procedure that to improve the classification accuracy.

5   Conclusion

This paper established the collocations automatic extraction model combined with statistical information and language knowledge, based on grammatical POS tagging, word frequency statistics and word order. The method calculated the emotional weight value of binary collocation by Word2Vec algorithm and seed emotion word set to constructed the binary sentiment collocation dictionary. Experiments showed that the binary sentiment collocation dictionary can effectively improve the effect of Chinese short texts emotional classification.

Acknowledgments. The work was supported by the University Innovative Talent Project of Guangdong Province (2013).

References

1. Redman, S., Ellis, R.: A way with words. Book 1. Cambridge University Press, Cambridge (1989)
2. Esuli, A., Sebastoamo, F.: Sentiwordnet: a publicly available lexical resource for opinion mining. In: Proceedings of LREC Genoa-Italy: LREC, pp. 417–422 (2006)
3. Baccianella, S., Esuli, A., Sebastiani, F.: SentiWordNet3.0: an enhanced lexical resource for sentiment analysis and opinion mining. In: International Conference on Language Resources and Evaluation, pp. 83–90 (2010)
4. Tang, D.: Nation Taiwan University: simplified Chinese emotional dictionary (2013). http://www.datatang.com/data/11837
5. Xu, L., Lin, H.F., Pan, Y., et al.: Constructing the affective lexicon ontology. J. China Soc. Sci. Tech. Inf. **27**(2), 180–185 (2008)
6. Yang, A.M., Lin, J.H., Zhou, Y.M.: Method on building Chinese text sentiment lexicon. J. Front. Comput. Sci. Technol. **7**(11), 1033–1039 (2013)
7. Zhou, Y.M., Yang, A.M., Lin, J.H.: Construction method of sentiment lexicon for news reviews. J. Shandong Univ. (Eng. Sci.) **44**(3), 36–40 (2014)
8. Zhou, Y.M., Yang, A.M., Yang, J.N.: A method of building Chinese microblog sentiment lexicon. Comput. Sci. **41**(8), 67–70 (2014)
9. Zhou, J.F., Yang, A.M., et al.: Micro-bolg sentimental feature selection based on bigram collocation. Comput. Eng. **40**(6), 162–165 (2014)
10. Hamdan, H., Bellot, P., Bechet, F.: Sentiment lexicon-based features for sentiment analysis in short text. In: International Conference on Intelligent Text Processing and Computational Linguistics (2015)
11. Zhang, C., Zeng, D., Li, J., Wang, F.Y., Zuo, W.: Sentiment analysis of Chinese documents. J. Assoc. Inf. Sci. Technol. **60**(12), 2474–2487 (2009)
12. Tomas, M.: Word2Vec project (2014). https://code.google.com/p/Word2Vec/
13. Zhang, D., Xu, H., Su, Z., Xu, Y.: Chinese comments sentiment classification based on Word2Vec and SVM perf. Expert Syst. Appl. **42**(4), 1857–1863 (2015)
14. Joseph, T., Lev, R., Yoshua, B.: Word representations: a simple and general method for semi-supervised learning. In: Proceedings of the 48th Annual Meeting of the Association for Computational Linguistics, pp. 384–394 (2010)
15. Chen, Y.J.: The Automatic Extraction Method of Collocation of Words in Modern Chinese. East China Normal University (2005)
16. Wang, S., Yang, A.: A method of collocation orientation identification based on hybrid language information. J. Chin. Motion Process. **24**(3), 69–74 (2012)
17. Mikolov, T., Chen, K., Corrado, G., Dean, J.: Efficient estimation of word representations in vector space. In: Proceedings of Workshop at ICLR (2013)
18. Su, J.: Incredible Word2Vec.trained models (2017). http://spaces.ac.cn/archives/4304/comment-page-1
19. Řehůřek, R.: Gensim: Topic modelling for humans (2017). http://radimrehurek.com/genism

A Construction Method for the Semantic Relation Corpus of Traditional Chinese Medicine

Jing Chen[1], Haitao Wang[2], Liangliang Liu[2], Xiaoru Zhang[1], Jing Zhao[2], Fan Zhang[2], and Xinyu Cao[3(✉)]

[1] School of Computer Science and Engineering,
Jiangsu University of Science and Technology, Zhenjiang, China
[2] China National Institute of Standardization, Beijing, China
[3] Institute of Basic Research in Clinical Medicine,
Chinese Academy of Chinese Medical Sciences, Beijing, China
cxy8202@163.com

Abstract. It is difficult to use a search engine to acquire knowledge directly due to the complexity of Web resources. In this paper we proposed a method for semantic relation corpus construction of traditional Chinese medicine based on combination of multiple encyclopedias. For a known conceptual pair, we got some search results by automatically constructing search requests based on URLs' characteristics of the encyclopedia search engine, and used regular expressions to extract meaningful texts from the search results to form semantic relation corpus. The experiment result shows that the precision and recall are 92.1% and 65.3%, respectively.

Keywords: Corpus construction · Knowledge acquisition · Traditional Chinese medicine

1 Introduction

How to effectively combine traditional Chinese medicine with modern discipline and promote development is a research that has attracted much attention in recent years. The identification of the entity and the extraction of the relationship have always been an important work in the informationization of Chinese medicine, while the construction of the corpus is the prerequisite for these studies. Web resources contain a lot of domain knowledge, but only through the analysis and processing of resources to be useful, can constitute a professional domain of corpus. Professional high quality Chinese medicine corpus is the basis of high quality research of Chinese medicine information.

Semantic relations extraction is as important as the entity of identification work. How to obtain the semantic relation efficiently depends on the semantic relation extraction method, and also depends on the quality of the corpus. The corpus used in relations extraction, mostly structured statement, semantic expression of clear text, the quality and scale of corpus to a large extent determine the success or failure of natural

© Springer International Publishing AG 2017
T.-C. Huang et al. (Eds.): SETE 2017, LNCS 10676, pp. 557–564, 2017.
https://doi.org/10.1007/978-3-319-71084-6_65

language processing [1]. At present in the field of foreign medical information research, the English language as the carrier of biomedical literature research, has been more mature [2, 3]. In the domestic, Chinese medicine has a unique medical system. In the process of information technology, the use of the corpus is divided into clinical record and Chinese classical medical books, but the field of traditional Chinese medicine still doesn't have open large-scale corpus [4, 5]. The reason is that high-quality corpus needs to be manually marked, time-consuming, low efficiency, and batch labeling algorithm is still semi-supervision, in a state of continuous improvement [6]. To extract the domain concept in the medical record depending on the format in medical records that structured data corresponds to free text to find the location of the domain concept [6]. However, the structured data format in electronic medical records limits the extraction of semantic relationships. There is a concept pair with some semantic relationship, it's difficult to analyze and classify this semantic relationship if the pair does not appear in the same medical record. Because the pair loss of the field location of the structured data and the corpus does not have the characteristic words that determine the semantic relation. Only a few corpus that meet the above requirements can be found in the traditional medical corpus, and the corresponding semantic relations will exist limitations. So, to find other ways to get clinical knowledge of Chinese medicine is needed.

With the rapid development of the Internet, search engine development and optimization, Web has become an important tool for people to retrieve information and a new way of acquiring knowledge. Typing the words to query in the search box, then the search engine queries the Web page library and return the page that matches the search criteria. Through this can support multi-word search query and we can search a concept pair which means contain two concepts and retrieve statements from pages that contain both concept. However the content obtained through this way is often incomplete and it is hard to guarantee the quality. For how to use Web resources to obtain high-quality clinical concept of knowledge, this paper presents a method based on a variety of encyclopedia complementary. By retrieving the relevant entry of the concepts in the concept pair, the content of the entry is parsed and a regular expression is used to obtain a valid sentence that contains another concept. This sentence that describes the concept pairs of the semantic relations is what we need.

2 Related Work

Information extraction begins with the construction of information from medical data from 20 New York universities in the 1960s, and so far the field of medicine has formed a lot of information extraction system. Such as clinical texts in the medical event Lancet system [7] and the GENIA corpus that has completed the biomedical literature has been compiled and annotated in the GENIA project completed in 2012 [8].

At present, the corpus used in the semantic relations of Chinese medicine domain is mainly composed of clinical record and Chinese classical medical books.

The electronic medical record text has semi-structured features and distinct sub-language features [9] which means have specific word classes and statement types in the clinical field. Yang [10] and Qu [5] based on the characteristics of electronic medical records, put forward a detailed and clear labeling program, and establish a certain size of the Chinese electronic medical record name entity annotation corpus including 992 detailed annotated medical records which provides reliable data sup-port for entity identification. In the construction of the corpus, the labeling process requires the guidance and participation of the doctor and has not yet been public. Researchers are currently still working on unlabeled corpus. Such as Yang's [11] extraction of explicit semantic relations by analyzing part of speech in 3000 unlabeled medical records.

The studies on using Chinese classical medicine books as corpus have a lot. Liu [1] and Bai [12] put forward the design ideas and labeling methods of Chinese medicine books library but they do not form a well-defined corpus. Zhu [13] chooses a repre-sentative of the Chinese medicine books "medical program", and realizes the automatic discovery based on the key verbs in the absence of marked labels. Wang [14] based on the ancient Chinese literature research, chooses a Ming and Qing Dynasties of the classical medical books as a corpus for the name of the entity mining, and designs a multilevel (network library, medical library, finishing library) medical books corpus. But the concept of traditional Chinese medicine books is fuzzy and ambiguous, and its language representation is sundry and abstract. There is a certain distance between language and semantics, such as "wood fire penalty". These features are the barriers to computer processing, so the size of the finishing corpus is small, and requires expert participation when marked.

Outside the domain of Chinese medicine, Web has become a new way for researchers to acquire knowledge. There are corpus using microblogging [15] text and its content is mostly short text with incomplete grammatical structure. The content searched from Web pages [16] is difficult to verity its authority. Use the search engine to build efficient query content [17] needs to be customized according to the specific need to build a query string. In contrast, the use of encyclopedia [18] has more advantages. First, encyclopedia's content is maintained by the many users together which means the correctness of knowledge is guaranteed. Second, the contents of the entry mostly semi-structured text, easy to locate the demand content. Finally, the contents of the sentence statement is complete and have clear composition which are easy to carry out semantic analysis and processing. Therefore, the method of using the Web to acquire knowledge is suitable for apply to the domain of traditional Chinese medicine. Without manual labeling, we can obtain a corpus with a complete sentence structure and a modern language is suitable for analyzing semantic relations.

3   Corpus Construction Method

A sentence is valid if some kind of semantic relation between two concepts can be recognized based on the sentence. We can use search engine to retrieval concepts or terms directly but the search results may not meet our need due to the following reasons:

(1) The reliability of the content. The search result may be an advertisement, a medical consultation or questions from Baidu Know. Even through these search results

contain concept pairs, they are not valid because semantic relationship between two concepts can be recognized based on the search results. (2) The integrity of sentence grammar. The result is not complete that may be a question in the Q & A document or a document directory.

We need to manually select the optimal result from a search results directly retrieved by search engine, which will spend high human costs with low efficiency. Based on the analysis of several texts, most high-quality statements usually come from the encyclopedia platform. So we select encyclopedia as the search platform.

3.1   The Framework

The proposed framework is shown in Fig. 1. The framework includes the following steps: (1) Choose an encyclopedia as search engine from encyclopedia collection; (2) Acquire search results pages of concept e_i and e_j, denoted by $Page_{e_i}$ and $Page_{e_j}$, for a concept pair (e_i, e_j) from the concepts collection C_m not be searched; (3) Analyze the content of $Page_{e_i}$ and $Page_{e_j}$, and get valid sentences collection S after regular expression matching; (4) Add valid sentences S to the corpus if S is not null and add concept pair to concepts pairs set C_{m+1} for next round if S is null; (5) Repeat (2)–(4) step for concept pair in C_{m+1} based on other search engines in encyclopedia collection.

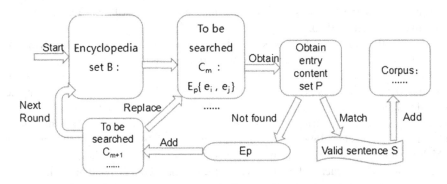

Fig. 1. The proposed framework

3.2   The Method

Automatically Build Query URL. It has been found that search engine use the Get method to submit a search request to the server and write the parameters to URL with which HTTP send request message request. We can automatically build query URL based on the character of search engine. For example, search term "madness" by Medical Encyclopedia, and the search URL is http://www.wiki8.com/search?q=%E7% 8B%82%E7%97%85&d=4&ie=utf-8. "http://www.wiki8.com" represents the search engine and "of %E7%8B%82%E7%97%85" is the term's UTF8 encode which is denoted by the key word "search?q=". We can construct new queries for other concepts based on different Get methods of different search engines.

Choose the Best Search Results. Different search engines have different search results for the same search content. For Baidu Encyclopedia, the search results contains two parts: *Term Direct* and *Approximate Term*. *Term Direct* will link to the term page. The *Approximate Term* lists some similar terms with the search term. Therefore the link of *Term Direct* is a priority to be selected. If there is no *Term Direct*, check whether the term list by *Approximate Term* matches the query word and return matched link.

Parse the Term Page. The contents are extracted from the link of *Term Direct* selected by step2. We locate text by using html language's tag to avoid the catalog or advertisement content and get plain text after removing html tags and useless punctuation.

Obtain Valid Sentence. The other concept in concept pair is searched from the plain text acquired by step3. If the other concept exits, the whole sentence will be extracted from the plain text through regular expression. For the above example, we acquire text matching regular expression pattern "[^。！<>.\" =)]*? schizophrenia[^\" <。;!]* " and remove numeric symbols to get valid sentence "madness is equivalent to modern medicine schizophrenia, mania and so on". The valid sentence has a complete grammatical structure and can express a semantic relation between two concepts, which is the best return result.

Search Based on Other Encyclopedia. We continually other encyclopedia search engine such as Interactive Encyclopedia, Sogou Encyclopedia and 360 Encyclopedia to increase recall in further.

4 Experiments

4.1 Dataset

There are 12 kinds of typical sematic relations in the Clinical Terminology of Traditional Chinese Medicine. We select some concept pairs expressing different semantic relationship. The detail is showed in Table 1.

4.2 Experiment Comparisons

We use the Baidu search engine as a baseline. We search a concept pair and get sentences from search results that contain both concepts. However, the sentence is often incomplete and the quality is hard to guarantee.

In this paper, we take Medical Encyclopedia, Baidu Encyclopedia, Interactive Encyclopedia, Sogou Encyclopedia and 360 Encyclopedia as search engine. In order to compare experiment results, we set up three control groups: (1) Baidu search and Baidu Encyclopedia (short for B); (2) Baidu Encyclopedia and Medical Encyclopedia (short for M); (3) The combination of M and B and five Encyclopedia (denoted by Multi-platform). The experiment results are shown in Table 2.

Table 1. The number of selected concept pairs for different relations.

Relations	Concept pairs' number
Similar concept	100
In the case of	100
Cure	89
Concurrent	71
Have an influence on	100
Bring...cause	53
Prevention	18
The result of	43
Cause	49
Hypernym	157
Simultaneously with	100
Conceptual correspondence	117

Table 2. The experimental results.

Search engine	Precision	Recall	F-measure
Baidu	53.5%	43.6%	48.05%
Baidu Encyclopedia	92.6%	41.9%	57.69%
Medical Encyclopedia	91.0%	51.1%	69.4%
M and B	91.3%	59.1%	71.75%
Multi-platform	90.9%	69.0%	78.51%

4.3   Result Analysis

The results of control group1 show that encyclopedia is more suitable than general search engine. The recall of Baidu search and Baidu Encyclopedia is close while the precision of Baidu search is half of Baidu Encyclopedia. Baidu search obtain more search results but those results are difficult to filter that leads to the low precision. The most sentences obtained from encyclopedia are complete and contain the characteristic words that can clearly explain the semantic relations. Those advantages provide a reliable basis for semantic analysis.

The control group 2 indicates that the knowledge coverage of Medical Encyclopedia is higher than Baidu Encyclopedia and the precision is similar. It's better to choose Medical Encyclopedia as knowledge base.

The control group 3 shows a way to improve the method's recall. Actually some knowledge exists in Baidu Encyclopedia does not appear in Medical Encyclopedic, so we can improve the recall of valid sentences by expanding knowledge base. The combination of two or more encyclopedia means the expansion of knowledge base. The recall is the highest based on a combination of multiple encyclopedias.

However, the precision is only about 90% and some results are still not valid which means that the sentences cannot express a semantic relation between two concepts in spite of containing both concepts. For example concept pair (provoked goiter, goitre), the most search result of concept "provoked goiter" may be not valid because the concept "goiter" is the part of concept "provoked goiter".

In the remaining 439 pairs not acquired search results, both concepts are not retrieved in 133 pairs and the other concept cannot be found from the search result of a concept in 306 pairs. The reason of the former is that the search platform is not comprehensive or the concept is too colloquial to find based on search engine. There are mainly two reasons for the latter: (1) The description of a concept does not contain the other concept; (2) The hypernym of the other concept appears in the result of a concept instead of the other concept.

5   Conclusion

It has own advantages and disadvantages that take Medical records and Chinese classical medical books as the common corpus. In recent years, the Web has become a new way for researchers to acquire knowledge. Through the combination of a variety of encyclopedias and according to the known TCM concept pairs, we extract valid sentences that describe semantic relations provide a reliable corpus for further semantic analysis. In the next step, we will focus on the reasons why we cannot get valid sentence and improve the precision and recall of valid sentences by constructing the synonyms and fuzzy matching methods.

Acknowledgments. This work was supported by National Key R&D Program of China (2016YFF0202806), National Natural Science Foundation of China (81403281), project of China National Institute of Standardization (712016Y-4941, 522016Y-4681).

References

1. Liu, Y., Duan, H., Wang, H., Zhou, Y., Wang, Z., Li, H.: Research on corpus creation and development of Chinese traditional medicine. J. Chin. Inf. Process. **22**(4), 24–30 (2008). http://doi.org/10.3969/j.issn.1003-0077.2008.04.004. (in Chinese)
2. Roberts, A., Gaizauskas, R., Hepple, M., et al.: Building a semantically annotated corpus of clinical texts. J. Biomed. Inform. **42**(5), 950–966 (2009). http://doi.org/10.1016/j.jbi.2008.12.013
3. Chapman, W.W., Savova, G.K., Zheng, J., et al.: Anaphoric reference in clinical reports: characteristics of an annotated corpus. J. Biomed. Inform. **45**(3), 507–521 (2012). http://doi.org/10.1016/j.jbi.2012.01.010
4. Yu, Q., Cui, M., Liu, L., Liu, J., Liu, H.: Current status of research on database of TCM medical records. China Digit. Med. **8**(3), 71–74 (2013). http://doi.org/10.3969/j.issn.1673-7571.2013.03.023. (in Chinese)
5. Qu, C., Guan, Y., Yang, J., Zhao, Y., Liu, X.: The construction of annotated corpora of named entities for Chinese electronic medical records. Chin. High Technol. Lett. **02**, 143–150 (2015). http://doi.org/10.3772/j.issn.1002-0470.2015.02.005. (in Chinese)
6. Feng, L.: Automatic Approaches to Develop Large-scale TCM Electronic Medical Record Corpus for Named Entity Recognition Tasks. BeiJing JiaoTong University (2015). (in Chinese)

7. Li, Z., Liu, F., Antieau, L., Cao, Y., Yu, H.: Lancet: a high precision medication event extraction system for clinical text. J. Am. Med. Inform. Assoc. **17**(5), 563 (2010). http://doi.org/10.1136/jamia.2010.004077

8. Collier, N., Mima, H., Ohta, T., Tateisi, Y., Yakushiji, A.: The GENIA project: knowledge acquisition from biology texts. Genome Inform. **11**, 448–449 (2001). http://doi.org/10.11234/gi1990.11.448

9. Friedman, C., Kra, P., Rzhetsky, A.: Two biomedical sublanguages: a description based on the theories of Zellig Harris. J. Biomed. Inform. **35**(4), 222 (2002). http://doi.org/10.1016/S1532-0464(03)00012-1

10. Yang, J.F., Guan, Y., He, B., Qu, C.Y., Yu, Q.B., Liu, Y.X., Zhao, Y.J.: Corpus construction for named entities and entity relations on Chinese electronic medical records. J. Softw. **27**(11), 2725–2746 (2016). (in Chinese)

11. Yang, Y.: Demonstrative study of semantic relation in comprehensive clinical terminologies of traditional Chinese Medicine. Chinese Academy of traditional Chinese Medicine (2007). (in Chinese)

12. Bai, L., Zhou, Y., Yue, X.: Thoughts and methods of digital informationization of ancient chinese medicine. J. Tradit. Chin. Med. **05**, 12 (2009). (in Chinese)

13. Zhu, L., Yu, T., Yang, F.: Study on semantic relations discovery based on key verbs in chinese classical medical books. China Digit. Med. **05**, 73–75 (2016). http://doi.org/10.3969/j.issn.1673-7571.2016.05.023. (in Chinese)

14. Wang, S.: Study on Pathogenesis of Traditional Chinese Medicine Symptoms and Its Relationship Mining. Xiamen University (2009). (in Chinese)

15. Yao, Y., Wang, S., Xu, R., Liu, G., Gui, L., Lu, Q., Wang, X.: The construction of an emotion annotated corpus on microblog text. J. Chin. Inf. Process. **05**, 83–91 (2014). http://doi.org/10.3969/j.issn.1003-0077.2014.05.011. (in Chinese)

16. Han, Z.: Construction of dynamic corpus based on web - a case study of Chinese political news corpus. China Educ. Technol. Equip. **23**, 66–68 (2013). http://doi.org/10.3969/j.issn.1671-489X.2013.23.066. (in Chinese)

17. Cao, X., Cao, C.: A method for acquiring corpus rich in part-whole relation from the web. J. Chin. Inf. Process. **05**, 17–23 (2011). http://doi.org/10.3969/j.issn.1003-0077.2011.05.003. (in Chinese)

18. Hu, H., Yao, T.: Sentence alignment of bilingual verbs based on Wikipedia. J. Chin. Inf. Process. **01**, 198–203 (2016). (in Chinese)

Author Index

Adams, Saira-Banu 213
Aigbavboa, Clinton 252, 260, 269, 278
Akinlabi, Esther 180
Álvarez, M. 170, 234
Andaluz, V. 170, 234

Cao, Xinyu 557
Cerna, Miloslava 304
Chan, Wai Hong 495
Chang, Chi-Cheng 58, 420
Chang, J.-J. 355
Chang, Jui-Hung 9
Chang, Lei 382
Chang, Shu-Hsuan 433
Chao, Chih Wei 382
Chao, Han-Chieh 223
Chen, Boyu 507, 548
Chen, Dyi-Cheng 154
Chen, H.-R. 355
Chen, Jing 557
Chen, Judy F. 45
Chen, Shih-Yeh 425
Chen, Xiaoxiao 477
Chen, Xieling 507
Chen, Yau-Jane 189
Chen, Yu-Kai 420
Chiang, Hung-Hsi 9
Cho, Hsin-Hung 223
Chou, Pan-Nan 409
Cilliers, Liezel 38, 64, 203
Clinton, Aigbavboa 284
Clotet, G. 170
Cong, Hao 539

De Marsico, Maria 336
Ding, Ting-Jou 3

Eguabor, Eghosa 260, 269
Eybers, S. 106

Fang, J.-F. 355
Fu, Sihui 518

Ge, Shili 477
Glakpe, Emmanuel 180
Gnaur, Dorina 297
Goosen, Leila 19
Granizo, R. 170
Gybas, Vojtech 314

Hansen, Preben 433
Hao, Tianyong 485, 507, 518, 539
Hashim, Shaiful Jahari b. 245
Hattingh, M.J. 106
Hsieh, Yi-Zeng 469
Hsiung, Pao-Ann 189
Huang, Po-Sen 400
Huang, Sheng-Bo 438
Huang, Tien-Chi 433
Huang, Ying-Chia 154
Huang, Yong-Ming 413
Huang, Yueh-Min 400, 446
Huberts, Robert 116
Huerta, M. 170, 234
Hunag, C.-H. 355
Hüttel, Hans 297
Hwang, Jan-Pan 456
Hwang, Ren-Hung 9, 189, 425

Ifije, Ohiomah 278

Jeng, Yu-Lin 438, 469
Jiang, Shengyi 518
Jin, Nana 500
John, Aliu 284
Jordaan, Joyce 75

Klimova, Blanka 326
Klubal, Libor 314
Kostolanyova, Katerina 314

Kriel, Dennis   161
Kritzinger, Elmarie   95, 144
Kwan, Reggie   495

Lai, Chin-Feng   189, 223, 425
Latiff, Nurul Adilah bt. Abdul   245
Latypova, Liliia Agzamovna   400
Lee, Sung-Lin   433
Li, Qiong   446
Li, Ting-Mei   223
Li, Ying-Jian   446
Lin, Hao-Chiang-Koong   363, 372
Lin, Hsiu Ju   45
Lin, Jim-Min   382, 391
Lin, Yangqing   548
Lin, Yi-wen   137
Liu, Chien-Hung   413
Liu, Liangliang   557
Liu, YiChun   463
Loock, Marianne   144
Lu, Yi-Chen   349
Luna, V.   234

Ma, Yu Chun   363
Majd, Saleh   29
Makhetha, Palesa   38
Marie-Hélène, Abel   29
Matthee, Machdel   161
Mbogho, Audrey J.W.   320
Millard, Solly   75
Mohelska, Hana   125, 195
Morales, V.   170
Mukasa-Lwanga, Toppie N.   19
Murire, Obrain   203

Navas, M.   234
Ntlabathi, Siyanda   38

Ohiomah, Ifije   252

Phang, Tan Chee   245
Pretorius, Jan-Harm   252, 260, 269
Prinsloo, Tania   49

Qu, Yingying   528, 539
Quevedo, W.   234

Rivas, D.   170
Rivas-Lalaleo, D.   234
Rokhani, Fakhrul Zaman   245

Santana, A.   234
Sciarrone, Filippo   336
Shabe, Tsosane   144
Shen, Wei-Wei   391
Shih, Timothy K.   223
Shu, Kuen-Ming   58
Shu, Vera Yu   433
Shu, Yu   438
Sokolova, Marcela   125
Starcic, Andreja Istenic   400
Sterbini, Andrea   336
Steyn, Riana   75
Su, Chiu-Nan   3
Su, Mu-Chun   469
Su, Yen-Ning   409
Su, Yu-Sheng   3
Sun, Ai   446
Sung, Tien-Wen   349

Tamayo, W.   170
Tan, Qing   438
Temperini, Marco   336
Thaphelo, Godfey Shai   278
Tsai, Meng-Chun   372
Tsai, Ming-Hsiu Michelle   391
Tseng, P.-H.   355
Tucker, William D.   213
Turpin, Marita   161

Valeeva, Roza Alexeyevna   400
Van Deventer, J.P.   49
van Niekerk, Elzette   64
Vayas, G.   170, 234
Venter, Isabella M.   213

Wang, Fu Lee   495
Wang, Haitao   557
Wang, Ming-Shi   425

Wang, Tzone-I   137
Wang, Xiaowen   485
Warden, Clyde A.   45
Wong, Tak-Lam   495
Wu, Po-Han   3
Wu, Ting-Ting   349, 382

Xie, Haoran   495
Xie, Wenxiu   518

Yan, Yih-Her   58
Yang, Chu-Sing   425

You, Ci-Syong   154
Yu, Xue   477
Yu, Zhiwen   539

Zhang, Chunxia   507
Zhang, Fan   557
Zhang, Xiaoru   557
Zhao, Jing   557
Zhou, Jianfeng   548
Zou, Di   495
Zubr, Vaclav   195

Printed in the United States
By Bookmasters